BAR REVIEW

Professional Responsibility

Richard C. Wydick

Professor of Law

University of California, Davis

THOMSON

BAR/BRI

celebrating over

35 YEARS

of preparing law students for the bar exam

TABLE OF CONTENTS

Test yourself through the Internet

You can now prepare for your exam by using StudySmart® MPRE Software.

Registered BAR/BRI students with Internet access can download the StudySmart® MPRE software from the BAR/BRI website at ***www.barbri.com*** by logging in to the Enrolled Student Center.

Once the download is complete, the program can be installed by going to the directory where the file was saved and double-clicking on the file to begin the installation process.

For StudySmart® technical support call
1-877-385-6238

Get it from the BAR/BRI website at
www.barbri.com

BAR REVIEW

HOW TO USE THIS BOOK

As you start to prepare for the Multistate Professional Responsibility Examination (''MPRE''), be aware that the exam is designed to test your ability to apply a set of detailed legal rules—similar to the legal rules you have learned in other courses in law school. You cannot pass the examination simply by having good morals and good manners. You must know the rules, and you must know how to apply them.

This book contains everything you need to know to pass the MPRE. But before you plunge in, reading cover to cover, we suggest that you use the following approach:

1. Read the **Comprehensive Outline of the Law** starting on page 1. This outline not only summarizes all the essential law, but it also contains many examples to illustrate less obvious points.

2. Test your understanding of concepts by answering the short-answer **Review Questions**. Check your answers against the answers we have provided, referring back to the pertinent section of the outline if you need more review of a particular topic.

3. Attend the **BAR/BRI course**. It is time well spent. The lecturer will review points of law most likely to be tested and will give you tips on exam-taking technique.

4. Become familiar with the format and content of MPRE questions by taking at least two of the four **Practice Exams**. These practice exams simulate the types of questions and issues tested and approximate the various difficulty levels of questions on the actual exam. You should work at least one of the practice exams under timed conditions so that you get a feel for the time pressures you will face on the exam. You can also do practice questions from the exams using your StudySmart® software.

5. Finally, read through the **Conviser Mini Review** (page I) for a final refresher before you take the exam.

One final note: While the MPRE is not easy, it is fair. You will find that a reasonable effort, using the approach detailed above, will produce great rewards. Good luck.

BAR REVIEW

Conviser Mini Review

celebrating over
35 *YEARS*
of preparing law students for the bar exam

PROFESSIONAL RESPONSIBILITY MINI REVIEW

I. REGULATION OF THE LEGAL PROFESSION

A. SOURCES OF REGULATION

1. The State
States may regulate the practice of law in the exercise of their police powers. State courts, not state legislatures, have the ultimate power to regulate the legal profession.

a. Courts
The ultimate power of regulating the legal profession rests with the highest state court. Additionally, *case law*, *rules of court*, and *state statutes* are used in governing the practice of law.

1) Ethics Rules—ABA Model Rules and Judicial Code
Most states have adopted ethics rules patterned after models drafted by the American Bar Association ("ABA"). The majority of states have rules patterned after the Model Rules of Professional Conduct, while the remainder base their rules on the older Model Code of Professional Responsibility. Similarly, most states have enacted some version of the ABA Model Code of Judicial Conduct.

b. Bar Associations
Each state has a bar association. A majority of states have "integrated" bars, meaning that one must be a member of the bar association to practice law in the state. Administration of bar examinations, provision of continuing legal education programs, and assistance with discipline are functions of state bar associations.

c. Legislature
All state legislatures have enacted statutes governing some aspects of legal practice.

2. The Federal System
Each federal court has its own bar, to which an attorney must belong in order to practice before that court. Federal practice is governed by federal statutes, case law, and court or agency rules. Federal government attorneys are subject to state ethics laws and rules in each state where the attorneys engage in their duties.

3. Regulation by Multiple States
A lawyer is subject to regulation by each state in which she is admitted to practice.

B. ADMISSION TO THE PRACTICE OF LAW

1. The Application

a. False Statements
In connection with an application to the bar or a bar disciplinary matter, an applicant or lawyer must not knowingly make a false statement of material fact.

b. Failure to Disclose Information

In connection with an application to the bar or a bar disciplinary matter, an applicant or lawyer must not: (i) fail to disclose a fact that is necessary to correct a misapprehension known by the applicant or lawyer to have arisen in the matter, or (ii) fail to respond to a lawful demand for information. These obligations do not apply to information protected by the ethical duty of confidentiality.

2. Character and Fitness—"Good Moral Character"

Bar applicants are usually required to demonstrate that they are of good moral character. If a question arises as to an applicant's honesty and integrity, the applicant may be asked to appear at a hearing before the admissions committee, where the applicant will be afforded *procedural due process* rights.

a. Relevant Conduct

All aspects of an applicant's past conduct are subject to review. An applicant's criminal conduct (conviction unnecessary) and other acts constituting *moral turpitude* (*e.g.*, false statements or concealment of past conduct to admissions committee) are grounds for the denial of his application for admission to the bar. However, evidence of the applicant's *rehabilitation* will be considered. Note that an applicant's mere membership in an organization such as the Communist Party (without an indication that he advocated the violent overthrow of the government) is insufficient to show lack of moral character.

3. Citizenship and Residency—Not Valid Requirements

A requirement that an applicant be a United States citizen or a citizen of a state is unconstitutional.

C. REGULATION AFTER ADMISSION

1. Misconduct

A lawyer is subject to discipline not only for violating a disciplinary rule, but also for any of the following types of conduct:

a. *Attempting to violate* a disciplinary rule;

b. *Assisting or inducing another person* to violate a disciplinary rule;

c. *Using the acts of another person* to violate a disciplinary rule;

d. Engaging in *criminal conduct* that shows *dishonesty, untrustworthiness, or unfitness* to practice law;

e. Engaging in *any conduct* involving *dishonesty, fraud, deceit, or misrepresentation*;

f. Engaging in conduct that is *prejudicial to the administration of justice*;

g. *Stating or implying an ability to improperly influence* a government agency or official or to achieve results by means that violate the law or legal ethics rules; or

h. *Knowingly assisting a judge in conduct that is illegal* or that violates the Code of Judicial Conduct.

2. **Duty to Report Professional Misconduct**
A lawyer is subject to discipline for failing to report a disciplinary violation committed by another lawyer. The ABA Model Rules limit that duty to disciplinary violations that raise a *substantial* question as to the other lawyer's honesty, trustworthiness, or fitness as a lawyer. A lawyer's obligation to report disciplinary violations by judges is the same as that concerning violations by lawyers. The duty to report does not, of course, apply to information that is protected by the ethical duty of confidentiality or information gained by a lawyer or judge while serving as a member of an approved lawyers' assistance program designed to help lawyers and judges with substance abuse problems.

3. **Disciplinary Process**
Disciplinary proceedings against a lawyer begin when a complaint is filed with the state disciplinary authority. If the complaint is not dismissed, the lawyer is requested to respond to the charges, and the grievance committee will investigate the charges and may hold a hearing on the matter. At the hearing, the accused lawyer is entitled to procedural due process. If discipline is imposed, the lawyer is entitled to review of the decision by the state's highest court.

4. **Choice of Law in Disciplinary Proceedings**
Generally, if a lawyer's alleged misconduct is related to a proceeding that is pending before a tribunal, the ethics rules of the jurisdiction in which the tribunal sits will be applied, unless the tribunal's rules provide otherwise. For any other conduct, the rules of the jurisdiction in which the conduct occurred will apply, but if the predominant effect of the conduct is in some other jurisdiction, that jurisdiction's rules will apply.

5. **Effect of Sanctions in Other Jurisdictions**
Under the majority view, sister *states* accept disciplinary action by one state as conclusive proof of a lawyer's misconduct, but are free to impose their own sanctions. However, each *federal court* makes an independent evaluation, accepting as competent evidence the lawyer's discipline by a state.

6. **Disability Proceedings**
Most jurisdictions have proceedings for incapacitated lawyers (*e.g.*, those suffering from substance abuse), which result in the lawyers' suspension from the practice of law. Diversion into a rehabilitation program is a common procedure used for possible reinstatement.

D. UNAUTHORIZED PRACTICE AND MULTI-JURISDICTIONAL PRACTICE

1. **Unauthorized Practice by Lawyer**
A lawyer is subject to discipline for practicing in a jurisdiction without being licensed to do so.

2. **Permissible Types of Temporary Multi-Jurisdictional Practice**
If a lawyer is admitted to practice in one state, and is not disbarred or suspended from practice in any state, she may provide legal services in a second state on a *temporary basis* in four situations:

a. **Association with Local Lawyer**
A lawyer may practice on a temporary basis in a state in which she is not admitted if she associates a local lawyer who participates in the matter.

b. Special Permission to Practice in Local Tribunal
If a lawyer wants to handle a matter in a jurisdiction in which she is not admitted, she may request special permission from that tribunal to appear "pro hac vice" (*i.e.*, for purposes of this matter only).

c. Mediation or Arbitration Arising Out of Practice in Home State
A lawyer may engage in alternative dispute resolution (*e.g.*, mediation or arbitration) in a state in which she is not admitted to practice if her services arise out of her practice in the state in which she is admitted.

d. Other Practice Arising Out of Practice in Home State
A lawyer may temporarily practice in a state in which she is not admitted if her out-of-state practice is reasonably related to her home-state practice.

3. Permissible Types of Permanent Multi-Jurisdictional Practice
A lawyer who is admitted in one jurisdiction, and is not disbarred or suspended from practice in any jurisdiction, may open a law office and establish a practice in a different jurisdiction only in two limited situations: (i) if the lawyer is a salaried employee of her only client (*e.g.*, in-house corporate lawyer), she may render legal services to her employer even though not admitted in the state (but to litigate in that state she must seek admission pro hac vice); and (ii) when the legal services are authorized by federal or local law.

4. Consequences of Multi-Jurisdictional Practice
A lawyer who is admitted to practice in one state only, but who practices in another state as provided in 2. or 3., above, will be subject to the disciplinary rules of both states.

5. Unauthorized Practice by Nonlawyers
A person not admitted to practice as a lawyer must not engage in the unauthorized practice of law. A lawyer is subject to discipline for assisting a nonlawyer to engage in the unauthorized practice of law.

a. "Practice of Law"
"Practice of law" includes those activities: (i) involving legal knowledge and skill, (ii) which constitute advice concerning binding legal rights, or (iii) traditionally performed by lawyers (*e.g.*, settlement negotiations, drafting legal documents). It is not unauthorized practice for a nonlawyer to appear before an agency that permits nonlawyer professionals (*e.g.*, accountants) to do so, or for a nonlawyer to fill in the blanks on legal forms (*e.g.*, real estate sales contracts). However, the giving of tax law advice by a nonlawyer would probably constitute the unauthorized practice of law.

b. Consequences of Unauthorized Practice
A nonlawyer engaged in the unauthorized practice of law may be subject to injunction, contempt, and criminal prosecution. A lawyer who assists a nonlawyer in the unauthorized practice of law is subject to discipline.

c. Delegating Work to Nonlawyer Assistants
A lawyer must supervise delegated work carefully and must be ultimately responsible for the results.

d. Training Nonlawyers for Law-Related Work

A lawyer may advise and instruct nonlawyers whose employment requires a knowledge of the law.

e. Helping Persons Appear Pro Se

A lawyer may advise persons who wish to appear on their own behalf in a legal matter.

f. Assisting a Suspended or Disbarred Lawyer

A lawyer who assists (*e.g.*, hires) a suspended or disbarred lawyer to do work that constitutes the practice of law is subject to discipline.

II. THE LAWYER-CLIENT RELATIONSHIP—GENERAL POINTS

A. NATURE OF THE RELATIONSHIP

The relationship between a lawyer and client is contractual, and the terms of such contract are derived from custom and mutual agreement. A lawyer is both the client's fiduciary and agent.

B. CREATING THE LAWYER-CLIENT RELATIONSHIP

A lawyer-client relationship arises when a person indicates an intent that the lawyer provide legal services and the lawyer agrees or fails to clearly inform the person that he does not wish to represent her, resulting in implied assent, or when a tribunal appoints a lawyer to represent a client.

1. Implied Assent and Reasonable Reliance

A lawyer's assent is implied when he fails to clearly decline representation and the prospective client reasonably relies on the representation. Reasonableness is a question of fact.

2. Court Appointments

Lawyers have an ethical obligation to help make legal service available to all who need it by accepting a fair share of unpopular matters and unpopular or indigent clients. A lawyer must not seek to avoid court appointments to represent clients except for good cause. Examples of good cause are: (i) to represent the client would require the lawyer to violate a law or disciplinary rule, (ii) representing the client would impose an unreasonable financial burden on the lawyer, or (iii) the lawyer's personal feelings would prevent her from representing the client effectively.

3. Duty to Reject Certain Cases

A lawyer must refuse employment when:

a. The client's motive is to *harass or maliciously injure* a person;

b. The case presents a *factually or legally frivolous position* (but a good faith argument that the facts are as claimed or that the law should be changed is permissible);

c. The lawyer is *incompetent* (or too busy) to handle the matter;

d. The lawyer's strong *personal feelings* may impair his ability of effective representation; or

e. The lawyer's *mental or physical condition* would materially impair the representation.

4. Duties Owed to Prospective Client
If no lawyer-client relationship ensues from a discussion with a prospective client, the lawyer must: (i) protect the person's confidential information, including declining representation of others in the same or a related matter; (ii) protect the prospective client's property; and (iii) use reasonable care in giving the person any legal advice, *e.g.*, whether the claim has merit.

5. Ethical Obligation to Accept Unpopular Cases
A lawyer can fulfill his obligation to assist in the provision of legal services to those in need by accepting a fair share of unpopular matters or indigent or unpopular clients.

C. ATTORNEYS' FEES
The nature and amount of an attorney's fee are subjects for contractual agreement between the attorney and the client (except when the fee is set by statute or court order).

1. When to Agree on Fee
The ABA Model Rules require a lawyer to reach a clear fee agreement with the client, preferably in writing, early in the relationship.

2. Discipline for Unreasonable Fee
A court will not enforce a contract for an unreasonably high fee or an unreasonably high amount for expenses, and the lawyer is subject to discipline for trying to exact such a fee or expenses.

    a. Factors
    Factors considered in determining reasonableness include: the time and labor required; the novelty and difficulty of the questions involved; the skill required; whether the lawyer is precluded from other work; what other lawyers in the community charge; the amount at stake and the results obtained; time limitations; the experience, reputation, and ability of the lawyer; and whether the fee is fixed or contingent.

    b. Items that May and May Not Be Billed
    The attorney must disclose the basis for charges and may not charge the client for ordinary overhead expenses. The attorney may charge the client the actual cost of special services (*e.g.*, computer research, secretarial overtime). Alternatively, the attorney may charge a reasonable amount agreed to in advance.

3. Collecting and Financing Attorneys' Fees

    a. Payment in Advance
    A lawyer may require her fee to be paid in advance, but she must refund any unearned part of the advance if she is fired or withdraws. A lawyer need not return a true retainer fee (*i.e.,* money paid solely to insure the lawyer's availability).

    b. Property for Services
    A lawyer may accept property in return for services, provided that this does not involve a proprietary interest in the cause of action or subject of litigation, but such an arrangement is subject to scrutiny to make sure the lawyer does not take advantage of the client.

c. **Cutting Off Services**
A lawyer must not make a fee agreement that could cut off services in the middle of the relationship and thus put the client at a disadvantage.

d. **Credit Arrangements and Security**
An attorney may permit the client to pay a fee by credit card, to finance fees through bank loans, or to pay by an interest-bearing promissory note. If local law permits, an attorney may use an attorney's lien to secure payment of a fee.

4. **Contingent Fees**
United States law tolerates contingent fees, in which the lawyer receives his fee only upon favorable resolution for his client. Often a contingent fee is a percentage of the client's recovery in the case.

a. **Generally Prohibited in Criminal and Domestic Relations Cases**
A lawyer is subject to discipline for using contingent fees in criminal cases and in domestic relations cases when the contingency is based on the securing of a divorce, the amount of alimony or support, or the amount of a property settlement.

b. **Contingent Fee Must Be Reasonable**
A contingent fee must be reasonable in amount and must not be used if the facts of the case make it unreasonable to do so.

c. **Written Fee Agreement Required**
A contingent fee agreement is required to be in a writing signed by the client. The writing must spell out how the fee is to be calculated, what litigation and other expenses are to be deducted from the recovery, whether deductions for expenses will be made before or after the fee is calculated, and what expenses the client must pay.

5. **Fee Disputes**
A lawyer may not use illegal collection methods, improperly use confidential information, or harass a client to obtain compensation.

a. **Remedies**
In addition to filing suit to recover a fee, a lawyer can generally use a common law or statutory charging lien. Many states also permit the lawyer to exercise a retaining lien under which she can retain documents, funds, and property of the client until her fee is paid—but there is a strong minority view contra. Also, if the lawyer receives funds out of which his fee is to be paid, and the client disputes the fee, the lawyer may retain the disputed amount in a client trust account until resolution of the dispute. Moreover, many jurisdictions have arbitration or mediation services to resolve fee disputes.

6. **Fee Splitting with Other Lawyers**
Generally, a lawyer must not split fees with another lawyer, except as provided below.

a. **Lawyers Within a Firm**
A firm's partners and associates may pool and split legal fees. A law firm may also make payments under a *separation or retirement* agreement to a former partner or associate.

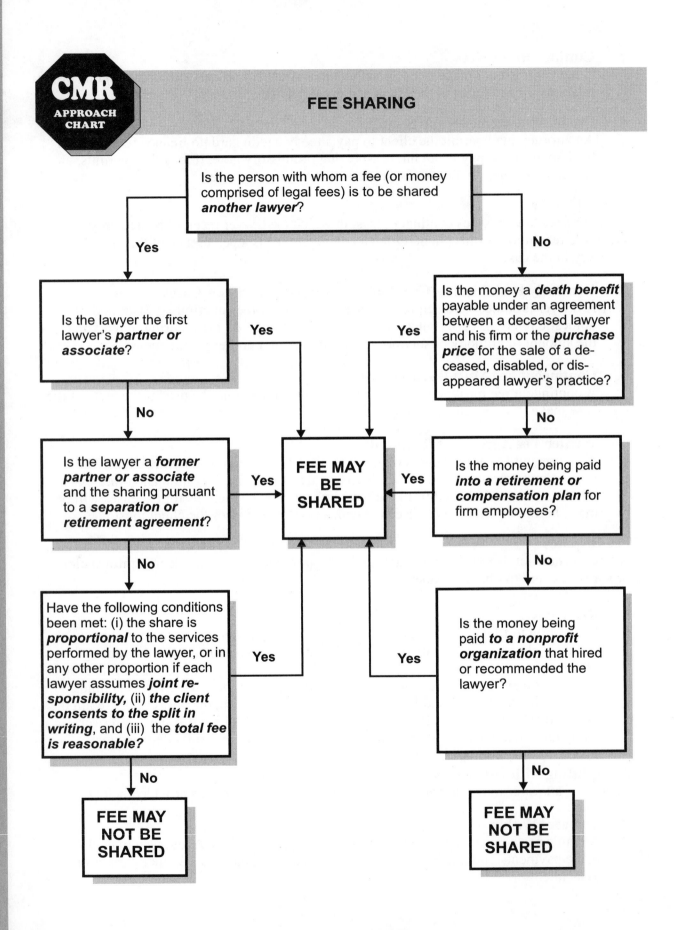

b. **Certain Splits with Lawyers Outside Firm**
A lawyer may split her fee with another lawyer who is not in her firm if:

1) The total fee is *reasonable*;

2) The split is *in proportion to the services performed by each lawyer*, or some different proportion if *each lawyer assumes joint responsibility* for the matter; and

3) The client agrees to the split *in writing*.

7. **Forwarding or Referral Fees**
When one lawyer simply refers a case to a second lawyer and the first lawyer neither works on the case nor assumes responsibility for the case, the second lawyer must not pay the first lawyer a forwarding or referral fee. A lawyer may, however, set up a *reciprocal referral arrangement* in which the lawyer agrees to refer clients to another lawyer or nonlawyer, provided the clients referred are informed of the arrangement.

D. **SCOPE OF REPRESENTATION**
The scope and objectives of representation may be defined by agreement between the lawyer and client and, absent a contrary agreement, the lawyer is obligated to pursue a client's objectives in all reasonably available legal ways. However, a lawyer must not advise or assist a client to commit a crime or fraud, but the lawyer may discuss the legal consequences of a proposed course of action with the client.

1. **Decisions to Be Made by Client**
A lawyer must abide by a client's decisions affecting the client's substantial legal rights, including:

a. Whether to accept a *settlement offer*;

b. What *plea* to enter in a criminal case;

c. Whether to *waive a jury trial* in a criminal case;

d. Whether the client will *testify* in a criminal case; and

e. Whether to *appeal*.

2. **Limits on Lawyer's Responsibility and Authority**
A lawyer may limit the scope of the representation provided the limitation is reasonable under the circumstances and the client gives informed consent. Reasonable circumstances include: (i) when disagreements exist between the lawyer and client about the means to be used to reach the client's objectives, (ii) when the client insists on the lawyer's assistance in violating a law or legal ethics rule, and (iii) when a lawyer discovers that a client has begun an illegal course of action and the conduct is continuing.

3. **Client with Diminished Capacity**

a. Lawyer's Duties
If a client is a minor or has diminished mental capacity, the lawyer has a duty, so far as reasonably possible, to maintain a normal lawyer-client relationship with the client. Even if the client has a guardian or other representative, the lawyer should, so far as possible, treat the client as a client, particularly in communicating with the client about significant developments.

b. Protective Action and Appointment of Guardian
When the client has diminished capacity and faces a substantial risk of physical, financial, or other harm, the lawyer may take reasonable actions to protect the client, including seeking the appointment of a guardian. Under these circumstances, the lawyer has implied authority to reveal the client's confidential information, to the extent necessary to protect the client.

4. Emergency Legal Assistance to Nonclient with Seriously Diminished Capacity
When a person with seriously diminished capacity facing *imminent and irreparable harm* to her health, safety, or financial interest consults a lawyer, that lawyer may take legal action on behalf of the person even if a lawyer-client relationship has not been established if the lawyer reasonably believes the person has no other representative. Any action taken should be limited to that necessary to avoid the harm.

a. Lawyer's Duties
A lawyer has the same duties to an "emergency" nonclient as he would with respect to a client. Normally, the lawyer would not seek compensation for emergency actions taken on behalf of the nonclient.

E. COMMUNICATING WITH THE CLIENT
A lawyer must: (i) promptly inform the client of any decision that requires the client's informed consent, (ii) keep the client reasonably informed about the status of the matter and the means to be used to accomplish the client's objectives, (iii) respond promptly when a client makes a reasonable request for information, and (iv) consult with the client if the client expects the lawyer to do something illegal or unethical.

1. Special Circumstances
The amount and kind of information the lawyer should give to the client depend on the client's situation; *e.g.*, a client with diminished capacity may require extra explanation and assistance. If a lawyer regularly represents a client, the two may work out a convenient arrangement for occasional reporting of routine developments.

2. Withholding Information from Client
A lawyer may delay the transmission of information to a client if the client would be likely to react imprudently to an immediate communication. Moreover, if a court rule or order forbids a lawyer from sharing information with a client, the lawyer must comply.

F. TERMINATING THE LAWYER-CLIENT RELATIONSHIP
The lawyer-client relationship normally continues until the end of the matter, but it can terminate prematurely in three ways: (i) the client can *fire* the lawyer; (ii) in some situations, the lawyer *must* withdraw; and (iii) in some situations, the lawyer *may* withdraw.

1. **Client Fires Attorney**
The client can fire the attorney at any time, with or without cause. The client is then liable to the attorney in *quantum meruit* for the reasonable value of the work done. If the attorney and client had a contract for a flat fee or maximum fee, the attorney cannot recover more than the amount contracted for. If the attorney and client had a contingent fee agreement, the attorney's quantum meruit claim does not arise until the contingency comes to pass (typically until the client gets a favorable judgment or settlement).

2. **Court Permission to Substitute Attorneys**
In a litigation matter, local court rules typically require court permission for a client to fire her attorney, and the court may deny permission if a substitution of attorneys would cause undue delay or disruption. For the same reasons, the court may deny an attorney's request to withdraw, even if there is good cause for withdrawal.

3. **Mandatory Withdrawal**
An attorney *must* withdraw from representation in two situations: (i) the attorney's mental or physical condition would make it unreasonable for him to continue representing the client; or (ii) continued representation would require the attorney to violate a law or disciplinary rule.

4. **Permissive Withdrawal**
An attorney *may* withdraw from representation *for any reason* if withdrawal does not have a material adverse effect on the client's interest or the client consents. An attorney may withdraw despite an adverse impact when the circumstances are so severe as to justify harm to the client's interests and:

   a.   The client persists in *criminal or fraudulent conduct* (if the conduct requires the attorney's assistance, the attorney *must* withdraw).

   b.   The client has used the attorney's services to commit a *past crime or fraud*.

   c.   The client's *objective is repugnant* or against the lawyer's beliefs.

   d.   The client *breaks his promise* to the attorney.

   e.   The representation imposes an *unreasonable financial burden* on the attorney.

   f.   The client *will not cooperate* in the representation.

   g.   Other *good cause* for withdrawal exists.

5. **Attorney's Duties Upon Termination of Representation**
Before withdrawing, an attorney must give the client reasonable notice of his withdrawal and a chance to get another attorney. When an attorney withdraws or is fired, the attorney must refund any advance on fees not yet earned and expenses not yet spent, and must turn over all papers and property to which the client is entitled.

III. LAWYER'S DUTIES OF COMPETENCE AND DILIGENCE

A. COMPETENCE
In representing a client, a lawyer must act competently and with the legal knowledge, skill, thoroughness, and preparation that are reasonably necessary for the representation.

1. Legal Knowledge and Skill

In determining whether a lawyer has the necessary skill to handle a matter, factors to be considered include the complexity and specialized nature of the matter; the lawyer's general experience and his training and experience in the field in question; the amount of preparation and study the lawyer will give to the matter; and whether it is possible for the lawyer to refer the matter to, or consult with, another competent lawyer.

a. Becoming Competent Through Preparation

A lawyer may accept representation if the requisite competence can be achieved by reasonable preparation.

b. Emergency Situations

A lawyer who is not competent in the field may assist a client in an emergency, but the assistance should not exceed what is reasonably necessary to meet the emergency.

2. Thoroughness and Preparation

A lawyer must inquire into and analyze the facts and legal elements in order to adequately prepare a matter.

3. Maintaining Competence—Continuing Legal Education

Lawyers should take reasonable steps to keep abreast of new developments in the fields in which they practice. Moreover, a lawyer must comply with all applicable continuing legal education requirements.

B. DILIGENCE
Once a lawyer takes on a client's matter, the lawyer must:

(i) Act on the client's behalf with *reasonable diligence and promptness;*

(ii) Act with dedication and *zeal*, taking whatever lawful and ethical steps are available to vindicate the client's cause;

(iii) Pursue the matter to *completion* (unless the lawyer is fired, or is required or permitted to withdraw); and

(iv) Either terminate the relationship or act with the required diligence if there is any doubt as to whether a *lawyer-client relationship exists*.

In addition to the above, a solo practitioner has a duty to plan for his untimely death or disability by designating another competent lawyer to review the clients' files and determine whether protective action is required.

C. SINGLE VIOLATION SUFFICIENT TO IMPOSE DISCIPLINE

A single incident of misconduct subjects a lawyer to professional discipline. Special circumstances are considered regarding sanctions, but not as to whether there is a violation. To avoid discipline, a lawyer must act reasonably to put his cases on temporary hold if necessary due to personal circumstances.

D. MALPRACTICE LIABILITY

1. Relationship Between Disciplinary Matters and Malpractice Actions

A malpractice action differs from a disciplinary matter in three ways: (i) the forum in a malpractice action is a civil court, not a disciplinary tribunal; (ii) in a malpractice action, the lawyer's adversary is an injured plaintiff, not the state bar; and (iii) the purpose of a malpractice action is to compensate the injured plaintiff, not to punish the lawyer or to protect the public from future wrongs.

2. Ethics Violation as Evidence of Malpractice

The violation of an ethics rule does not automatically mean that the lawyer has committed malpractice, nor does it create a presumption of malpractice, but courts do treat it as *relevant evidence* of malpractice.

3. Theories of Malpractice Liability

The plaintiff in a legal malpractice action has a choice of legal theories, including: (i) *intentional tort* (such as fraud, misrepresentation, malicious prosecution, abuse of process, or misuse of funds); (ii) *breach of fiduciary duties* (these duties include loyalty, confidentiality, and honest dealing); (iii) *breach of contract* (either an express contract or an implied promise by the lawyer to use ordinary skill and care); and (iv) simple *negligence*, the most common theory in legal malpractice actions.

a. Elements of Negligence

Simple negligence requires the plaintiff to prove four elements: a duty of due care, a breach of that duty, legal causation, and damages.

1) Duty of Due Care

An attorney owes a duty of due care not only to her *client*, but also to *any third party* who is intended to benefit from the legal services she renders to her client. The standard of care for an attorney is the competence and diligence normally exercised by attorneys in similar circumstances. If an attorney represents to a client that she has greater competence or will exercise greater diligence than that normally demonstrated by attorneys undertaking similar matters, she is held to that higher standard.

2) Breach of Duty of Due Care

An attorney is not liable for "mere errors of judgment" as long as the judgment was well-informed and reasonably made. An attorney is expected to do reasonably competent legal research; if the answer to a legal question could have been found by using standard research techniques, the attorney's failure to find it is a breach of the duty of due care. Furthermore, if a reasonably prudent attorney would have referred a difficult matter to a legal specialist, a general practitioner's failure to do so can be a breach of the duty of due care.

3) Legal Causation

A malpractice plaintiff must prove that the injury would not have happened *but for* the defendant's negligence, and that it is fair under the circumstances to hold the defendant liable for unexpected injuries or for expected injuries that happen in unexpected ways.

4) Damages

A malpractice plaintiff must prove damages. The plaintiff can recover for direct losses and indirect but foreseeable losses.

4. Liability for Negligence of Others

An attorney can be held liable for injuries caused by a negligent legal secretary, law clerk, or other person acting within the scope of his employment (*respondeat superior*). Each partner in a law firm is liable for the negligence of other partners committed in the ordinary course of partnership business.

5. Malpractice Insurance

The ABA Model Rules do not require lawyers to carry malpractice insurance, but prudent lawyers carry ample coverage.

6. Contracting with Client to Limit Malpractice Liability

A lawyer is prohibited from contracting with a client to prospectively limit her malpractice liability, unless the client is independently represented in making the contract.

7. Settling Malpractice Claims

A lawyer must not settle a pending or potential malpractice claim with an unrepresented client or former client without first advising that person, in writing, to seek independent advice about the settlement and giving that person time to seek that advice.

CMR **Exam Tip** A lawyer who has breached a duty to his client cannot escape discipline by reimbursing the client for any loss.

IV. DUTY OF CONFIDENTIALITY

As a general rule, a lawyer must not reveal any information relating to the representation of a client. A lawyer may, however, reveal such information if the client gives informed consent or any of the other exceptions discussed in C., *infra*, applies.

A. RELATIONSHIP BETWEEN ETHICAL DUTY AND ATTORNEY-CLIENT PRIVILEGE

1. Compulsion vs. Gossip

The *attorney-client privilege* is an exclusionary rule of evidence law that prevents the *government from compelling* the revelation of privileged communications. In contrast, the *ethical duty* of confidentiality prevents the *attorney from voluntarily disclosing* or misusing confidential information, and it applies in every context where the attorney-client privilege does not apply.

2. **Kinds of Information Covered**

The attorney-client privilege protects only confidential communications between an attorney and client or their respective agents. In contrast, the ethical duty covers communications that are protected by the privilege *plus any other information* the attorney obtains relating to the representation, no matter what the source.

3. **Disclosure vs. Use**

The attorney-client privilege prevents the government from compelling the disclosure of privileged communications. In contrast, the ethical duty of confidentiality prohibits the lawyer from either disclosing confidential information without the client's informed consent or using confidential information to the disadvantage of a client, former client, or prospective client without the affected client's informed, written consent.

B. SUMMARY OF ATTORNEY-CLIENT PRIVILEGE

The attorney-client privilege prohibits a court or other governmental tribunal from compelling disclosure of confidential communications between an attorney and a client, or their respective agents, if the communication concerns the professional relationship.

1. **Client**

A "client" is a person or entity that seeks legal services from an attorney. The privilege covers preliminary communications leading up to an attorney-client relationship, even if no such relationship ultimately develops.

   a. **Corporate Clients**

   When the client is a corporation, the privilege covers communications between the lawyer and a high-ranking corporate official. It also covers communications between the lawyer and another corporate employee if three conditions are met: (i) the employee communicates with the lawyer at the direction of the employee's supervisor; (ii) the employee knows that the purpose of the communication is to obtain legal advice for the corporation; and (iii) the communication concerns a subject within the scope of the employee's duties to act for the corporation.

2. **Attorney**

An "attorney" means a person who is authorized (or whom the client reasonably believes to be authorized) to practice law in any state or nation.

3. **Communication**

"Communication" means information transmitted orally or in writing in either direction between the attorney and the client or their respective agents.

   a. **Mechanics of Relationship**

   The privilege generally does not cover the client's identity or the fee arrangement between the client and attorney, unless disclosing those facts is tantamount to disclosing a privileged communication.

   b. **Preexisting Documents and Things**

   A preexisting document or thing does not become privileged simply by turning it over to an attorney; if it would be discoverable in the client's hands, it is equally discoverable in the attorney's hands. If an attorney comes into possession of the fruits of a crime, or an instrument used to commit a crime, the attorney may keep it long enough to obtain information needed to represent the client, but the attorney must then turn it over to the proper authorities.

4.   "Confidential" Defined
To be a protected "confidential" communication, the communication must have been made by a means not intended to disclose the communicated information to outsiders. Confidentiality is not destroyed by the presence of a third party who is present to aid the attorney-client relationship, and an eavesdropper can be prevented from testifying about a privileged communication. However, the presence of a third party who is not present to further the attorney-client relationship destroys the privilege.

5.   Client Holds Privilege
The client (not the attorney) is the one who can claim or waive the privilege. Waiver will occur when there is a failure to claim the privilege when there is a chance to do so or when there is an intentional revelation of a significant part of the privileged communication. If the client has not waived the privilege, and if someone tries to obtain privileged information when the client is not present, the attorney must claim the privilege on the client's behalf.

6.   Duration of Privilege
The attorney-client privilege continues indefinitely, surviving termination of the relationship and even the death of the client.

7.   Exceptions to Privilege
The privilege does not apply in situations where:

a.   The client seeks the attorney's services to engage in or assist a *future crime or fraud*.

b.   The communication is relevant to an issue of *breach of the duties arising out of the attorney-client relationship*.

c.   Civil litigation arises between two persons who were *formerly joint clients* of the attorney.

d.   The attorney is asked for evidence about the *competency or intent of a client* who has attempted to dispose of property by will or inter vivos transfer.

8.   Related Doctrine of Work Product Immunity
Generally, material prepared by a lawyer for litigation or in anticipation thereof is immune from discovery or other disclosure unless the opposition shows a substantial need for, and an inability to gather, the material without undue hardship. A lawyer's mental impressions or opinions are always immune from discovery unless immunity is waived.

C.   ETHICAL DUTY OF CONFIDENTIALITY AND ITS EXCEPTIONS
The ethical duty of confidentiality applies in every context in which the attorney-client privilege does not apply, and the ethical duty covers a broader range of information. The *exceptions* to the ethical duty are as follows:

1.   Client's Informed Consent
The attorney may disclose or use confidential information if the client gives informed consent or the attorney has implied authority from the client.

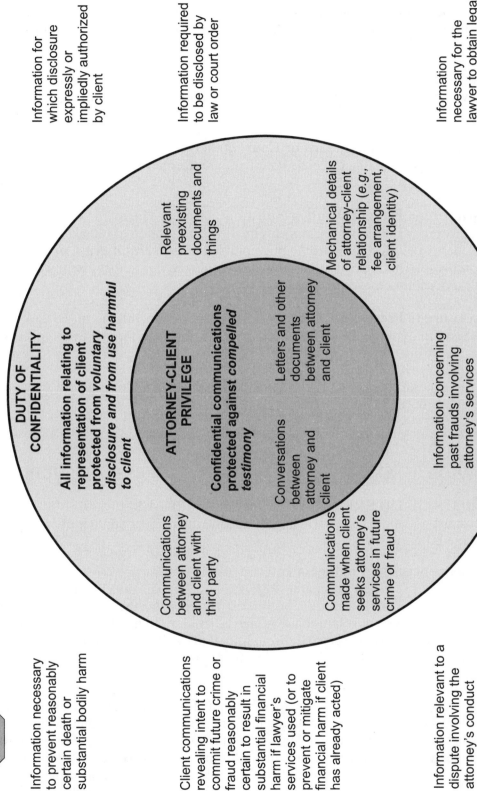

INFORMATION RELATING TO REPRESENTATION: SCOPE OF PROTECTION

Information for which disclosure expressly or impliedly authorized by client

Information required to be disclosed by law or court order

Information necessary for the lawyer to obtain legal ethics advice

DUTY OF CONFIDENTIALITY

All information relating to representation of client protected from *voluntary disclosure and from use harmful to client*

Relevant preexisting documents and things

Mechanical details of attorney-client relationship (*e.g.,* fee arrangement, client identity)

ATTORNEY-CLIENT PRIVILEGE

Confidential communications protected against compelled *testimony*

Letters and other documents between attorney and client

Conversations between attorney and client

Communications between attorney and client with third party

Communications made when client seeks attorney's services in future crime or fraud

Information concerning past frauds involving attorney's services

Information necessary to prevent reasonably certain death or substantial bodily harm

Client communications revealing intent to commit future crime or fraud reasonably certain to result in substantial financial harm if lawyer's services used (or to prevent or mitigate financial harm if client has already acted)

Information relevant to a dispute involving the attorney's conduct (*e.g.,* fee dispute, malpractice case, misconduct charges)

2. Dispute Concerning Attorney's Conduct
The attorney may reveal confidential information to the extent necessary to protect herself against a claim of malpractice, disciplinary violation, complicity with the client in illegal acts, or the like.

3. Disclosure to Obtain Legal Ethics Advice
A lawyer may disclose enough of the client's confidential information as is necessary to obtain legal ethics advice for the lawyer.

4. Disclosure Required by Law or Court Order
A lawyer may reveal her client's confidential information to the extent that she is required to do so by law or court order.

5. Disclosure to Prevent Death or Substantial Bodily Harm
A lawyer may reveal her client's confidential information to the extent that the lawyer reasonably believes necessary to prevent *reasonably certain death or substantial bodily harm*. *Note:* This exception gives the lawyer *discretion* to disclose the confidential information; it does *not require* disclosure.

6. Disclosure to Prevent or Mitigate Substantial Financial Harm
A lawyer may reveal the client's confidential information to the extent necessary to prevent the client from committing a crime or fraud that is reasonably certain to result in *substantial financial harm* to someone, if the client is using or has used the lawyer's services in the matter. The same is true if the client has already acted and the lawyer's disclosure can prevent or mitigate the consequent financial harm.

V. DUTY TO EXERCISE INDEPENDENT PROFESSIONAL JUDGMENT

A. CONFLICTS OF INTEREST—THE GENERAL RULES
A lawyer must not allow her personal interests, the interests of another client, or the interests of a third person to interfere with her loyalty to the client.

1. Consequences of a Conflict of Interest
If a conflict of interest is apparent *before* a lawyer takes on a client's matter, the lawyer must not take it on. If a conflict becomes apparent *after* the lawyer has taken on the client's matter, the lawyer must withdraw. A lawyer's failure to handle a conflict properly can have the following consequences: (i) disqualification as counsel in a litigated matter, (ii) professional discipline, and (iii) civil liability for legal malpractice.

2. Imputed Conflicts of Interest
Generally, lawyers who practice together in a "firm" are treated as a single unit for conflict of interest purposes—*i.e.*, when one lawyer cannot handle a matter because of a conflict, the conflict is said to be "imputed" from the first lawyer to the other lawyers in the "firm." Whether a group of lawyers constitutes a "firm" depends on many factors, including whether: (i) they have a formal agreement, (ii) they hold themselves out as if they practice as a firm, (iii) they share their revenues and responsibilities, (iv) they have physical access to each other's client files, (v) they routinely talk among themselves about the matters they are

LAWYER'S REPRESENTATION OF CURRENT CLIENTS WITH CONFLICTING INTERESTS

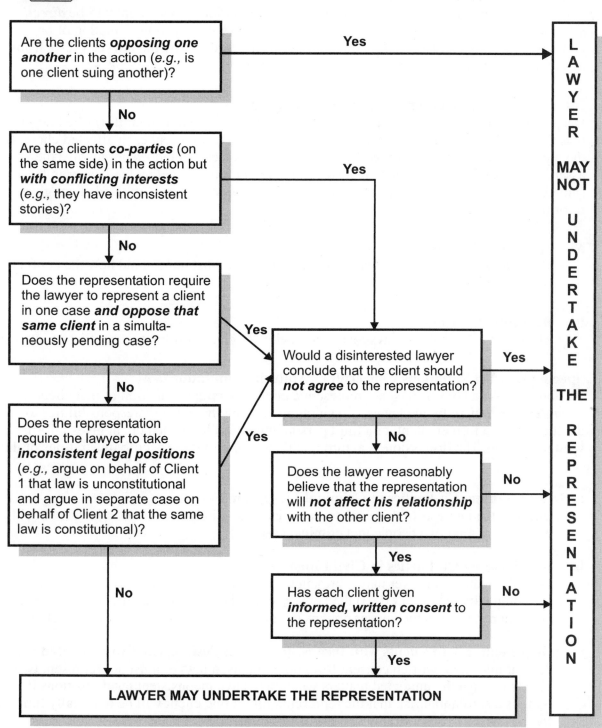

Are the clients **opposing one another** in the action (*e.g.,* is one client suing another)?

Yes → LAWYER MAY NOT UNDERTAKE THE REPRESENTATION

No ↓

Are the clients **co-parties** (on the same side) in the action but **with conflicting interests** (*e.g.,* they have inconsistent stories)?

Yes →

No ↓

Does the representation require the lawyer to represent a client in one case **and oppose that same client** in a simultaneously pending case?

Yes →

No ↓

Does the representation require the lawyer to take **inconsistent legal positions** (*e.g.,* argue on behalf of Client 1 that law is unconstitutional and argue in separate case on behalf of Client 2 that the same law is constitutional)?

Yes →

No ↓

Would a disinterested lawyer conclude that the client should **not agree** to the representation?

Yes → LAWYER MAY NOT UNDERTAKE THE REPRESENTATION

No ↓

Does the lawyer reasonably believe that the representation will **not affect his relationship** with the other client?

No → LAWYER MAY NOT UNDERTAKE THE REPRESENTATION

Yes ↓

Has each client given **informed, written consent** to the representation?

No → LAWYER MAY NOT UNDERTAKE THE REPRESENTATION

Yes ↓

LAWYER MAY UNDERTAKE THE REPRESENTATION

handling, and (vi) the purpose of the particular conflict rule would be served by imputing one lawyer's conflict to other lawyers in the group.

B. CONFLICTS OF INTEREST—CURRENT CLIENTS

1. Concurrent Conflicts of Interest
A lawyer must not represent a client if: (i) the representation of one client will be ***directly adverse*** to another client; or (ii) there is a ***significant risk*** that the representation of one client will be ***materially limited*** by the lawyer's own interest or by the lawyer's responsibilities to another client, a former client, or a third person.

2. Informed, Written Consent Can Solve Some Conflicts
Despite a concurrent conflict of interest, a lawyer ***may*** represent a client if: (i) the lawyer reasonably believes that he can competently and diligently represent each affected client; (ii) the representation is not prohibited by law; (iii) the representation does not involve the assertion of a claim by one client against another client represented by the lawyer in the same litigation (or other proceeding before a tribunal); ***and*** (iv) each affected client gives informed, written consent.

a. "Informed" Consent
"Informed" consent means that each affected client must understand how the conflict can harm him.

b. Revocation of Consent
The client can almost always revoke a previously given consent to a conflict of interest.

3. Specific Conflict Situations Concerning "Material Limitation"
As noted above, a lawyer must not represent a client if the representation of that client may be ***materially limited*** by the lawyer's own interests or by the lawyer's responsibilities to another client, a former client, or a third person, unless each affected client gives informed, written consent. The discussion in a. through h., below, provides specific illustrations of this rule.

a. Representing Co-Parties in Criminal Litigation
Because the interests of criminal co-defendants are likely to diverge, a lawyer should not try to defend two people in a criminal case.

b. Representing Co-Parties in Civil Litigation
In civil litigation, a lawyer may represent two plaintiffs or two defendants whose interests are potentially in conflict if: (i) the lawyer concludes that she can effectively represent both clients, and (ii) the lawyer obtains the informed, written consent of both clients.

c. Representing Two Clients with Inconsistent Legal Positions in Two Unrelated Cases
Absent informed, written consent from both clients, a lawyer must not represent two clients in separate, unrelated matters when they have inconsistent legal positions if there is a substantial risk that the representation of one client will be materially limited by the lawyer's responsibilities to the other client.

d. Unnamed Members of a Class Do Not Count as Clients
In class action litigation, the unnamed members of a class ordinarily are *not* regarded as clients for conflict of interest purposes.

e. Representing Multiple Clients in Nonlitigation Matters
In a nonlitigation context, conflicts of interest are often hard to assess. In determining whether a conflict exists, relevant factors to consider include the length and intimacy of the lawyer's relationship with one or more of the clients, the functions the lawyer will perform, and the likelihood and possible effect of an actual conflict between the clients' interests.

f. Handling Conflicts in Nonlitigation Matters
In nonlitigation matters, a lawyer *may* represent two clients whose interests are potentially in conflict if: (i) the lawyer concludes that she can effectively represent both clients, and (ii) the lawyer obtains the informed, written consent of both clients.

g. Confidentiality and Privilege Problems
In litigation between two former joint clients of a single lawyer, neither client can claim the attorney-client privilege; therefore, before undertaking multiple representation, the lawyer should explain that whatever one client discloses will be shared with the other client.

h. Conflicts Caused by Lawyer's Own Interests
A conflict of interest may be created by a lawyer's own financial interest or by his relationship with another lawyer or client. If a lawyer's own interests are likely to materially limit his ability to represent a client effectively, he must not take on the matter unless he obtains the client's informed, written consent.

C. CONFLICTS OF INTEREST—SPECIFIC RULES FOR CURRENT CLIENTS

1. Business Transactions with Client and Money or Property Interests Adverse to Client
A lawyer must not enter into a business transaction with a client or knowingly acquire an ownership, possessory, security, or money interest that is adverse to a client unless all of the following conditions are satisfied:

(i) The terms of the business transaction (or the terms on which the interest is acquired) are *fair to the client*;

(ii) The terms are *fully disclosed* to the client *in writing*, expressed in a manner that the client can reasonably understand;

(iii) The client is advised *in writing* that he should get the *advice of an independent lawyer* about the arrangement before entering into it; and

(iv) The client gives *informed consent, in writing that the client signs*.

This rule does not apply to an ordinary fee agreement between the lawyer and client or to ordinary commercial transactions in which the lawyer buys goods or services that the client routinely markets to the public.

2. Misuse of Client's Confidential Information

A lawyer must not use a client's confidential information to the client's disadvantage or to benefit the lawyer or someone else, unless the client gives informed consent or some other exception to the duty of confidentiality applies. The same rule applies to misuse of a former client's or a prospective client's confidential information. A lawyer who uses the confidential information for his own pecuniary gain (other than in the practice of law) may be subject to civil liability—*i.e.*, he may have to account to the client, former client, or prospective client for his profits.

3. Gifts to Lawyer from Client Who Is Not a Relative

    a. Soliciting Substantial Gift

    A lawyer is prohibited from *soliciting* a substantial gift from a client who is not the lawyer's relative. A lawyer may, however, accept a small gift from a client, such as a token of appreciation or an appropriate holiday gift. A lawyer also may accept a substantial gift from a client, although the gift may be voidable for undue influence.

    b. Preparing Legal Instrument that Creates Substantial Gift

    A lawyer must not prepare a legal instrument in which the client gives the lawyer or his relatives a substantial gift, except when the client is a relative.

    c. Lucrative Appointments

    A lawyer is not prohibited from seeking to have himself or his law partner or associate named as executor of an estate or counsel to the executor or to some other fee-paying position. However, the general conflict of interest principles do prohibit such efforts if the lawyer's advice is tainted by the lawyer's self-interest.

4. Acquiring Literary or Media Rights Concerning a Client's Case

A lawyer must not acquire literary or media rights to a story based in substantial part on the lawyer's representation of a client. However, a lawyer may acquire such rights *after* the client's legal matter is entirely completed, including appeals.

5. Financial Assistance to Client in Litigation

A lawyer must not financially assist a client whose litigation is pending or contemplated.

    a. Advancing Litigation Expenses

    A lawyer may advance court costs and other litigation expenses on the client's behalf, and repayment may be contingent on the outcome of the case.

    b. Paying Costs and Expenses for Indigent Client

    A lawyer may pay the court costs and litigation expenses for an indigent client, without any provision for repayment.

    c. Other Financial Help Is Prohibited

    A lawyer is subject to discipline for giving a client other financial help in the context of pending or contemplated litigation.

6. Aggregate Settlement Agreements

A lawyer who represents several co-parties in a matter must not participate in the making of an aggregate settlement agreement unless: (i) the clients come to an agreement about how the aggregate sum will be shared; (ii) the lawyer discloses all terms of the sharing agreement to each client and discloses the existence and nature of all claims that will be settled; and (iii) each client gives informed, written consent.

a. Class Action Settlements
In a class action, the lawyer who represents the class ordinarily does not have a complete lawyer-client relationship with the unnamed members of the class. Even so, at settlement time, the class's lawyer must follow all of the class action rules concerning notice and other procedural requirements that protect the unnamed class members.

b. Aggregate Settlement of Criminal Case
The same rules that apply to an aggregate settlement in a civil case also apply to a joint plea bargain in a criminal case.

7. Waiving Malpractice Liability and Settling Malpractice Claims

a. Prospective Waiver or Limit of Malpractice Liability
A lawyer must not make an agreement with a client that prospectively waives or limits the lawyer's liability for legal malpractice unless the client is independently represented in making the agreement. A lawyer *may*, however:

1) Practice in a Limited Liability Entity
A lawyer may practice in a limited liability entity, provided that the lawyer remains personally liable for her own malpractice.

2) Reasonably Limit Scope of Representation
A lawyer may enter into an agreement with her client that reasonably limits the scope of the lawyer's representation in accordance with the ABA Model Rules.

3) Arbitrate Legal Malpractice Claims
A lawyer may agree prospectively with a client to arbitrate all legal malpractice claims, provided that such an agreement is proper under local law and the client understands the scope and effect of the agreement.

b. Settling Malpractice Claims
A lawyer may settle a malpractice claim or potential claim made by his client, but only if the lawyer first advises the client in writing to seek the advice of an independent lawyer about the settlement.

8. Proprietary Interest in Subject of Litigation
A lawyer must not acquire a proprietary interest in the client's cause of action or the subject matter of the litigation. Contingent fees and attorney's liens are exceptions to this rule, even though each gives the lawyer a type of interest in the subject of the litigation.

D. CONFLICTS INVOLVING THE INTERESTS OF THIRD PERSONS

1.   Compensation from Third Person
A lawyer must not accept compensation from a third person for representing a client unless: (i) the client gives informed, written consent, (ii) the third person does not interfere with the lawyer's judgment in representing the client, and (iii) the arrangement does not compromise the client's confidential information.

2.   Conflicts Between Client's Interest and Third Person's Interest
When the interest of a third person creates a substantial risk of materially limiting the lawyer's ability to represent the client effectively, the lawyer may represent the client if: (i) the lawyer reasonably believes that the third person's interest will not adversely affect the representation, and (ii) the client gives informed, written consent.

3.   Conflicts Raised by Liability Insurance
Liability insurance policies commonly provide that the insurance company will select and pay for a lawyer to defend the policyholder in suits arising out of events covered by the policy. The policyholder, in turn, promises to cooperate with the defense. Generally, the policyholder wants a claim handled in a way that minimizes his risk of paying money out of his own pocket. The insurance company, however, generally wants to minimize what it must pay. The question then becomes whom does the lawyer represent. The law on this question varies from state to state. No matter whom the defense lawyer represents, the lawyer's ethical obligations are governed by the Rules of Professional Conduct, not by the insurance contract.

E.   DUTIES TO FORMER CLIENTS

1.   Continuing Duty of Confidentiality
An attorney has a continuing duty to preserve information gained in confidence during the representation, even after the representation ends.

2.   Opposing Former Client—Confidential Information
A lawyer who has confidential information from a former client must not oppose that former client in any matter to which the confidential information would be relevant and must not use that information to the former client's disadvantage, unless the former client gives informed, written consent.

3.   Using Confidential Information to Former Client's Disadvantage
A lawyer must not use confidential information to a former client's disadvantage without the informed, written consent of the former client. This rule is inapplicable to commonly known information or information the lawyer would be permitted to reveal under an exception to the duty of confidentiality.

4.   Opposing Former Client in Substantially Related Matter
Absent informed, written consent of the former client, a lawyer must not represent a client whose interests are materially adverse to those of the former client in a matter that is "substantially related" to a matter in which the lawyer represented the former client.

F.   CONFLICTS WHEN PRIVATE LAWYERS CHANGE JOBS
The ABA Model Rules state two principles that apply when a lawyer switches from one firm to another:

1. **Disqualification of Lawyer's New Firm**
   When a lawyer switches from Firm A and joins Firm B, Firm B must not knowingly represent a person in the same or a substantially related matter in which the switching lawyer, or Firm A, had previously represented a client whose interests are materially adverse to that person and about whom the switching lawyer has acquired confidential information material to the matter, unless the former client gives informed, written consent.

2. **Disqualification of Lawyer's Former Firm**
   When a lawyer switches from Firm A and joins Firm B, Firm A is not prohibited thereafter from representing a person with interests materially adverse to those of a client formerly represented by the switching lawyer, unless: (i) the matter is the same or substantially related to that in which the switching lawyer represented the client, and (ii) any lawyer remaining in Firm A has confidential information relating to the matter.

G. **CONFLICT RULES FOR CURRENT AND FORMER GOVERNMENT OFFICERS AND EMPLOYEES**
   The government has a right to expect that its confidential information will not be abused by a lawyer who switches from government to private practice. On the other hand, the government needs good lawyers, and a rigid rule of disqualification would discourage some lawyers from entering government service. Thus, the ABA adopted disqualification rules (*see* below) that are narrow and flexible.

   1. **Federal and State Conflict of Interest Laws**
      Lawyers who move between government and private jobs must comply not only with the legal ethics rules, but also with various state and federal conflict of interest statutes and regulations.

   2. **Private Work Following Government Work on Same Matter**
      A lawyer who leaves government service and enters private practice must not represent a private client in a *matter* in which the lawyer participated *personally and substantially* while in government service, unless the government agency gives informed, written consent. "*Matter*" means a specific dispute involving specific facts and parties. "*Personally and substantially*" means that the lawyer worked on the matter herself and that her work was more than trifling.

      a. **Imputed Disqualification**
         If a lawyer is disqualified by the above rule, the other lawyers in her firm are also disqualified unless:

         1) The former government lawyer is *timely screened off* from the case;

         2) The former government lawyer is *not apportioned a part of the fee* earned in the case; *and*

         3) *Written notice* is given to the government agency to enable it to make sure that the above conditions are met.

   3. **Subsequent Use of Information Gained During Government Service**
      A government lawyer who receives confidential government information about a person

must not later represent a private client whose interests are adverse to that person, when the information could be used to harm that person.

a.   Imputed Disqualification
If a former government lawyer is disqualified by this rule, then the other lawyers in her firm are also disqualified unless the former government lawyer is timely screened off from the case and is not apportioned any part of the fee earned in the case.

4.   Current Government Service After Private Practice

a.   Ordinary Conflict Rules Apply
The ordinary conflict rules regarding current and former clients apply to a lawyer who enters government service after private practice (or other nongovernmental work). (*See* V. B., E., *supra.*)

b.   "Personal and Substantial" Rule Also Applies
If a lawyer worked "personally and substantially" on a "matter" in private practice (or other nongovernmental employment), the lawyer must not work on that same matter when she later enters government service, whether or not the later work would be adverse to a former client. However, informed, written consent can solve the conflict.

c.   Negotiating for Private Employment
When a person in government service is currently working personally and substantially on a matter, she must not negotiate for private employment with any party or lawyer who is involved in that matter. There is an exception to this rule for law clerks (*see* H.3., below).

H.   CONFLICTS INVOLVING FORMER JUDGES, ARBITRATORS, AND THE LIKE

1.   Switching from Judicial Service to Private Law Practice
The conflict issues and the ethics rules about switching from judicial service to private practice are similar to those described above. The general rule is that a lawyer must not represent a private client in a matter in which the lawyer previously participated personally and substantially while serving as a judge or other adjudicative officer (or as a law clerk to such person) or as an arbitrator, mediator, or other third-party neutral, unless all parties to the proceeding give informed, written consent.

2.   Screening Can Avoid Imputed Disqualification
If a lawyer is disqualified under this rule, the other lawyers in her firm are also disqualified unless the following conditions are met: (i) the lawyer is timely screened off from the matter; (ii) the lawyer is not apportioned any part of the fee earned in the matter; and (iii) written notice is given to the parties and the appropriate tribunal so that they can ensure that the above conditions are met.

3.   Law Clerks Negotiating for Private Employment
A law clerk to a judicial officer must notify the officer before negotiating for private employment with a party (or the attorney for a party) in a matter in which the law clerk is participating personally and substantially.

4. Other Adjudicative Officers Negotiating for Private Employment
The lenient rule that applies to law clerks does not apply to judges, arbitrators, mediators, third-party neutrals, or other adjudicative officers. They are forbidden to negotiate for private employment with a party (or attorney for a party) in a matter in which they are participating personally and substantially.

I. CONFLICTS INVOLVING PROSPECTIVE CLIENTS

1. Lawyer's Duty Concerning Confidential Information
The attorney-client privilege protects confidential communications between a lawyer and a prospective client. The ethical duty of confidentiality also applies to discussions between a lawyer and prospective client. Thus, the lawyer must not reveal or use information learned during those discussions, unless an exception to the duty of confidentiality applies.

2. Lawyer's Duty Concerning Conflict of Interest
A lawyer who obtains confidential information during preliminary discussions with a prospective client must not later represent a different person in the same or a substantially related matter if the confidential information could significantly harm the prospective client. This conflict is imputed to others in the lawyer's firm.

3. How to Overcome a Prospective Client Conflict
One way to overcome a prospective client conflict is to obtain informed, written consent from the affected client and the prospective client. A second way to overcome the conflict is to satisfy all of the following conditions:

a. Demonstrate that the lawyer took care to *avoid exposure to any more confidential information than was necessary* to determine whether to represent the prospective client;

b. Demonstrate that the disqualified lawyer is *timely screened from any participation in the matter* and will not share the fee; and

c. Give *written notice* to the prospective client.

J. ORGANIZATION AS CLIENT

1. Duty of Loyalty to Organization
A lawyer owes a duty of loyalty to the organization, not to the people (stockholders, officers, directors, etc.) who are its constituents.

2. Conflicts Between Organization and Its Constituents
When the interests of the organization and one of its constituents are in conflict, the lawyer for the organization should caution the person in question that she represents the organization, not the person.

3. Protecting Organization's Interests
When a person associated with the organization advocates an action that may cause it substantial injury, a lawyer must protect the interests of the organization. The lawyer ordinarily must report the action to a higher authority in the organization, and if necessary to the highest authority. If the highest authority fails to take timely, appropriate action, the lawyer may report the relevant information to appropriate persons outside of the organization. The

lawyer is only authorized to do so to the extent the lawyer reasonably believes is necessary to prevent substantial injury to the organization. However, when a lawyer is hired by the organization to investigate an alleged violation of law or defend the organization or its constituents against an alleged violation of law, the lawyer may not report any information outside of the organization.

4.   Representing Both Organization and an Associated Person
The lawyer for an organization may represent both the organization and one of its constituents if the ordinary conflict of interest rules are satisfied.

5.   Serving as Both Director and Lawyer
A lawyer may serve as both a director and as a lawyer for an organization, but the dual role can create conflicts of interest. For example, when a lawyer participates in a meeting as a director, the attorney-client privilege will not apply to communications at the meeting, but some of the other directors may not realize that. If there is a substantial risk that the dual role will compromise the lawyer's professional judgment, the lawyer should either resign as director or not act as the organization's lawyer.

6.   Securities Lawyer's Duties Under Sarbanes-Oxley Act
Congress passed the Sarbanes-Oxley Act, which instructs the Securities and Exchange Commission ("SEC") to make rules for securities lawyers who discover that their clients are violating federal or state securities laws. The following discussion includes highlights of the rules adopted by the SEC.

a.   Application to "Securities Lawyers"
The rules apply to lawyers who represent an issuer of securities and who practice before the SEC ("securities lawyers"). This includes lawyers who give advice about a document that will be filed with the SEC or advice about whether information must be filed with the SEC.

b.   Reporting Requirement
If a securities lawyer becomes aware of credible evidence that her client is materially violating a federal or state securities law, she ***must*** report the evidence to her client's chief legal officer ("CLO"). The same reporting duty applies to credible evidence that one of her client's personnel has breached a fiduciary duty under federal or state law, or has committed a "similar material violation" of federal or state law.

c.   Investigation by CLO
The CLO must investigate the situation to determine whether a violation occurred.

d.   If Violation Found—"Appropriate Response" Required
If the CLO concludes that a violation occurred, the CLO must take all reasonable steps to get the client to make an "appropriate response." That means that the client must stop or remedy the violation and make sure it does not happen again. The CLO must report those results to the securities lawyer.

e.   When Appropriate Response Not Taken
If the securities lawyer believes that the CLO did not achieve an appropriate response from the client, the securities lawyer ***must*** report the evidence to either the client's

board of directors, the audit committee of the board, or a committee made up of outside directors. Note that the Sarbanes-Oxley reporting rule is ***mandatory***, unlike ABA Model Rule 1.13(b), which gives the lawyer some discretion about how to proceed (*see* 3., *supra*).

f. Revealing Confidential Information

A securities lawyer ***may*** reveal to the SEC any confidential information that is reasonably necessary to: (i) stop the client from committing a violation that will cause substantial financial injury to the client or its investors; (ii) rectify such a financial injury if the lawyer's services were used to further the violation; or (iii) prevent the client from committing or suborning perjury in an SEC matter or lying in any matter within the jurisdiction of any branch of the federal government.

g. Compliance with Rules

A securities lawyer who complies with the Sarbanes-Oxley rules cannot be held civilly liable for doing so and cannot be disciplined under any inconsistent state rule.

h. Action When Securities Lawyer Is Fired

If a securities lawyer is fired for complying with the Sarbanes-Oxley rules, she may report the firing to the client's board of directors (thus setting up the client for an expensive wrongful termination suit).

VI. SAFEGUARDING THE CLIENT'S MONEY AND PROPERTY

A lawyer is subject to discipline for misappropriating or borrowing a client's money or property or for commingling it with her own money or property.

A. CLIENT TRUST FUND ACCOUNT

All money that a lawyer receives on behalf of a client must promptly be placed in a client trust fund account, separate from the lawyer's own personal and business accounts.

1. Type of Account

The client trust fund account must be located in the state where the lawyer practices (or elsewhere with the client's consent). Ordinarily, a lawyer must not put her own money into the client trust account, but she may do so for the sole purpose of paying bank service charges.

a. Large Sum Held for Long Period

If the lawyer is entrusted with a large sum for a long period, it should go into a separate interest-bearing account, and the interest belongs to the client for whom it is held.

b. Small Sums

If the lawyer is entrusted with a small sum to hold for a short period, the lawyer should put it into a pooled client trust account, which is typically a checking account that holds money entrusted by numerous clients. Under Interest On Lawyer Trust Account ("IOLTA") programs, if a client entrusts a lawyer with a sum that is too small to earn any net interest, the lawyer must put it into a pooled checking account that earns interest. After the bank deducts its service charges from the interest, the bank sends the remaining interest to the state bar or to a legal foundation, which uses the interest to fund charitable legal programs. The United States Supreme Court has upheld the constitutionality of IOLTA programs.

2.   Funds that Must Be Placed in Account

a.   Advances
Advances for costs and expenses and legal fees not yet earned must be put into a trust account. The lawyer may make withdrawals as fees are earned if there is no dispute concerning the lawyer's right to do so.

b.   Funds in Which Both Client and Lawyer Have Interest
When a lawyer receives funds that are to be used, in part, to pay the lawyer's fee, they must be put into a trust account until there is an accounting and severance of the respective amounts due the lawyer and the client.

CMR **Exam Tip**   A common exam fact pattern asks whether an attorney who receives a settlement check or other payment to the client from which his fee is to be paid can properly forward the entire sum to the client. For exam purposes, the answer is yes, it is ethically proper. (As a practical matter, however, most attorneys would prefer to control the purse until the fee is paid; *i.e.,* most attorneys would retain the *fee amount in the client trust fund account* pending an accounting.)

c.   Funds in Which a Third Party Has an Interest
A lawyer may refuse to surrender funds to a client until a third party who has an interest in those funds has been paid.

B.   SAFEGUARDING PROPERTY
A lawyer must identify a client's property as belonging to the client and must put it in a safe place.

C.   DUTY TO NOTIFY, KEEP RECORDS, RENDER ACCOUNTINGS, AND PAY OVER PROMPTLY
A lawyer must keep complete, accurate, and up-to-date records of money or property received on behalf of a client, must render periodic accountings to the client, must notify the client promptly when money or property has been received on the client's behalf, and must promptly pay over money or deliver property when it is due to the client or a third party.

VII.   THE LAWYER AS COUNSELOR

A.   LAWYER AS ADVISOR TO THE CLIENT

1.   Duty to Render Candid Advice
A lawyer must exercise independent judgment and render candid advice to the client.

2.   Giving Advice Beyond the Law
A lawyer may give a client not only legal advice, but also moral, economic, social, or political advice when relevant to the client's situation.

3. **Volunteering Advice**
   When appropriate, a lawyer may volunteer advice without being asked.

B. **EVALUATION FOR USE BY THIRD PERSONS**
   A lawyer may evaluate a client's affairs for the use of a third person if the lawyer reasonably believes that making the evaluation is compatible with the lawyer's other responsibilities to the client. If the lawyer knows that the evaluation will materially harm the client, the lawyer must obtain the client's informed, written consent before making the evaluation.

   1. **Confidentiality**
      Except as disclosure is authorized in connection with a report of an evaluation, the ordinary rules of confidentiality apply to information gained during the evaluation.

   2. **Liability to Third Person**
      A lawyer may be liable to a third person for a negligent evaluation of a client's affairs.

C. **LAWYER AS NEGOTIATOR**
   During negotiations, a lawyer must not make a false statement of *material fact*. However, a lawyer need not volunteer facts that would be detrimental to the client's position or correct an opponent's misapprehension regarding the strength of his client's case. The key factor in determining whether a statement contains a material fact is whether the opponent would be reasonable in relying on the statement; *e.g.*, value estimates and what a party would accept as a settlement are not statements of material fact.

D. **LAWYER AS THIRD-PARTY NEUTRAL**
   A lawyer serves as a third-party neutral when she assists two or more nonclients in resolving a dispute between them (*e.g.*, arbitrator, mediator). When a lawyer serves as a third-party neutral, she is subject not only to the ordinary rules of legal ethics, but also to various codes of conduct devised by groups such as the American Arbitration Association.

   1. **Warning to Unrepresented Parties**
      A lawyer who serves as a third-party neutral does not represent any of the parties. Because a party may erroneously believe that the lawyer is protecting his interests, the lawyer must explain the situation to the unrepresented party. The lawyer should explain that the attorney-client privilege does not apply to communications between them.

   2. **Conflicts of Interest**
      A lawyer who serves as a third-party neutral in a matter must not thereafter become the lawyer for anyone involved in the matter, unless all of the parties give their informed, written consent. Such a conflict is also imputed to lawyers in the disqualified lawyer's firm, but may be cured by screening. No conflict arises when a lawyer who served as a partisan arbitrator for a party is later asked to become that party's lawyer.

VIII. THE LAWYER AS ADVOCATE

A. **MERITORIOUS CLAIMS AND CONTENTIONS ONLY**
   A lawyer is subject to discipline for bringing a frivolous proceeding or taking a frivolous position on an issue in a proceeding. A "frivolous" position is one that cannot be supported by a good

faith argument under existing law and cannot be supported by a good faith argument for changing the law. This rule does not prohibit a lawyer for a **criminal defendant** from conducting the defense so that the prosecutor must prove every necessary element of the crime.

B. DUTY TO EXPEDITE LITIGATION

A lawyer has an affirmative duty to expedite litigation. The duty to expedite does not require the lawyer to take actions that would harm the client's interests, but realizing financial or other gain from delay is *not* a legitimate interest.

C. DUTY OF CANDOR TO THE TRIBUNAL

1. Candor About Applicable Law

An attorney is subject to discipline for knowingly making a false statement of law to the court. Furthermore, an attorney must disclose a legal authority in the **controlling jurisdiction** that is **directly adverse** to his client's position and that has not been disclosed by the adversary.

2. Candor About Facts of Case

An attorney is subject to discipline for knowingly making a false statement of material fact to the court. An attorney's *failure to speak* out is, in some contexts, the equivalent of an affirmative misrepresentation.

3. No Obligation to Volunteer Harmful Facts

An attorney generally has no duty to volunteer a fact that is harmful to his client's case, except that a lawyer in an *ex parte* proceeding must inform the tribunal of *all material facts* known to the lawyer that will help the tribunal make an informed decision.

4. Using False Evidence

A lawyer is subject to discipline for offering evidence that the lawyer *knows* is false and may refuse to offer evidence that she *reasonably believes* is false, except for a criminal defendant's testimony on his own behalf. If a lawyer has offered a piece of evidence and later discovers that it is false, she must:

(i) Talk to the client confidentially and *try to persuade* him to rectify the situation;

(ii) If that fails, seek to *withdraw*; and

(iii) If withdrawal is not permitted or will not remedy the situation, the lawyer must make *disclosure* to the court.

Note that this obligation ceases at the conclusion of the proceedings, which include appeals.

 Exam Tip   Beware of an exam question in which the client prevails in a proceeding, the opposing party does not file an appeal, and the client *then* tells the lawyer in confidence that he lied. Remember that the lawyer is under no obligation to reveal the perjury to anyone because the proceeding is over.

a. False Testimony by Criminal Defendant

Under the ABA Model Rules and the Restatement, when the client insists on testifying to something that the lawyer knows is false, the criminal defense lawyer should follow the three steps stated above.

DUTY OF CANDOR TO THE TRIBUNAL

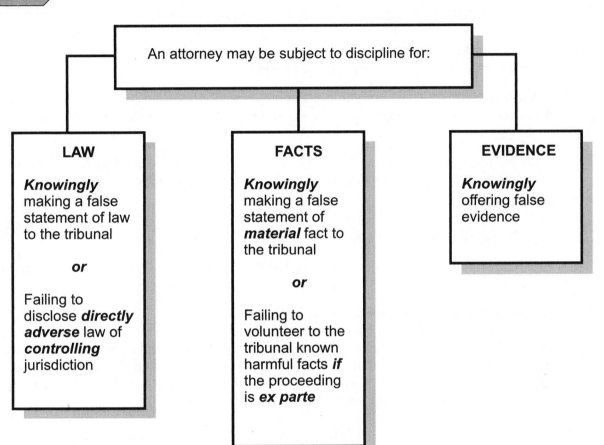

An attorney may be subject to discipline for:

LAW

Knowingly making a false statement of law to the tribunal

or

Failing to disclose ***directly adverse*** law of ***controlling*** jurisdiction

FACTS

Knowingly making a false statement of ***material*** fact to the tribunal

or

Failing to volunteer to the tribunal known harmful facts ***if*** the proceeding is ***ex parte***

EVIDENCE

Knowingly offering false evidence

5. Other Corruption of an Adjudicative Proceeding

A lawyer who represents a client in an adjudicative proceeding must take appropriate measures to prevent any person from committing criminal or fraudulent conduct that will corrupt the proceedings. Examples of such conduct are: (i) hiding or destroying evidence, (ii) bribing a witness, (iii) intimidating a juror, (iv) buying a judge, and (v) failing to obey a law or court order to disclose information.

D. DUTY OF FAIRNESS TO OPPOSING PARTY AND COUNSEL

1. Opponent's Access to Evidence

A lawyer must not suppress or tamper with evidence.

2. Falsifying Evidence and Assisting in Perjury

A lawyer must neither falsify evidence nor counsel or assist a witness to testify falsely.

3. Paying Witnesses

A lawyer must not offer an inducement to a witness that is prohibited by law. Except when local law prohibits, the following payments to witnesses are proper:

a. Travel, meals, and lodging expenses;

b. Compensation for time lost from the witness's job; and

c. Reasonable fees to expert witnesses, but these may not be contingent on the outcome of the case or the content of the expert's testimony.

4. Securing Absence or Noncooperation of Witness

A lawyer must not advise or cause a person to secrete himself or to flee the jurisdiction for the purpose of making him unavailable as a witness. However, a lawyer may advise a person not to voluntarily give information to an opponent or other party if the person is a client or relative, employee, or agent of a client, and the lawyer reasonably believes that the person's interests will not be harmed by not volunteering the information.

5. Violating Court Rules and Orders

A lawyer must not knowingly violate a rule of procedure, a rule of evidence, a rule of court, or an order made by the court, but a lawyer may refuse to obey such a rule or order in making a good faith challenge to its validity.

6. Abusing Discovery Procedures

A lawyer must not make frivolous discovery requests or fail to make reasonable efforts to comply with a legally proper discovery request made by an adversary.

7. Chicanery at Trial

A lawyer is subject to discipline for chicanery at trial, including:

a. Referring to inadmissible material;

b. Asserting personal knowledge of contested facts; and

c. Asserting personal opinions about the justness of a cause, credibility of a witness, culpability of a civil litigant, or guilt or innocence of an accused.

8. **Using Threats to Gain Advantage in Civil Case**

A lawyer may bring, or threaten to bring, criminal charges against her adversary in order to gain an advantage for her client in a civil case if the criminal and civil matters are closely related and the civil case and criminal charges are warranted. However, a lawyer must not threaten to report adversary counsel for a disciplinary violation to gain such an advantage. Disciplinary violations cannot be used as bargaining chips.

9. **Treating Opponents with Courtesy and Respect**

A lawyer should treat all participants in a proceeding with civility, exhibited by a showing of respect and cooperativeness. Conduct involving physical threats, ethnic or gender slurs, etc., is prohibited.

E. **DUTY TO PRESERVE IMPARTIALITY AND DECORUM OF TRIBUNAL**

1. **Improper Influence**

A lawyer must not seek to influence a judge, court official, juror, or prospective juror by improper means.

2. **Improper Ex Parte Communication**

While a proceeding is pending in a tribunal, a lawyer must not have an ex parte communication with a judge, court official, juror, or prospective juror except when authorized by law or court order.

a. **Judges and Court Officials**

A *written* communication to a judicial officer is not ex parte if a copy of the communication is timely sent to the opposing parties. A lawyer, however, must not communicate *orally* on the *merits* of a matter with a judicial officer without giving adequate notice to her adversary.

b. **Jurors and Prospective Jurors**

In general, before and during the trial of a case, a lawyer connected with the case must not communicate on *any subject* with a juror or prospective juror. She may, however, discreetly investigate members of a jury panel for limited reasons, *e.g.*, background, grounds for challenge, etc. After the trial is over and the jury is discharged, a lawyer must not communicate with a former jury member if: (i) local law or a court order prohibits such communication; (ii) the juror has told the lawyer that he does not want to communicate; or (iii) the communication involves misrepresentation, coercion, or harassment.

3. **Disruptive Conduct**

A lawyer must not engage in conduct intended to disrupt a tribunal.

4. **Statements About Judicial and Legal Officials**

a. **False Statements About Judges or Candidates for Public Legal Office**

A lawyer must not make a statement that the lawyer knows is false (or with reckless disregard as to truth or falsity) about the qualifications or integrity of a judge, hearing officer, or public legal official, or about a candidate for judicial or other legal office.

b.   Candidates for Judicial Office
A lawyer who is running for judicial office must comply with the applicable provisions of the Code of Judicial Conduct.

F.   TRIAL PUBLICITY
The litigants' right to a fair trial must be balanced against the rights of the press and the public to disseminate and to receive information. ABA Model Rule 3.6 prohibits a lawyer connected with the case from making out-of-court public statements that the lawyer reasonably should know will have a substantial likelihood of materially prejudicing the case.

1.   Right of Reply
Despite the above rule, a lawyer may make a public statement that a reasonable lawyer would believe is required to protect a client from the substantial undue prejudicial effect of recent publicity not initiated by the lawyer or the lawyer's client.

2.   Additional Constraint on Criminal Prosecutors
A prosecutor must not make extrajudicial comments that have a substantial likelihood of heightening public condemnation of the accused.

3.   Dry Facts About Case Permitted
Despite the general rule against prejudicial statements, a lawyer connected with the case may publicly state certain "dry facts" about the case, including: (i) any information already in the public record, (ii) what claim and defense are involved, (iii) the names of the people involved, (iv) the scheduling or result of any step in litigation, (v) the fact that an investigation is ongoing, (vi) a warning of danger if appropriate, and (vii) routine booking information about a criminal defendant (name, address, arresting officers, etc.).

4.   Rules Apply to Associated Lawyers
The rules on trial publicity apply equally to other lawyers who are associated in a law firm or agency with the lawyers participating in the case.

G.   TRIAL COUNSEL AS WITNESS

1.   Reasons to Avoid Dual Role
Several problems arise when a trial lawyer also testifies as a witness: conflict of interest, confusion of advocacy with evidence, and unfairness to the adversary.

2.   Ethical Limitations Imposed
For the above reasons, a lawyer must not act as an advocate at a trial in which she is likely to be a *necessary* witness.

a.   Exceptions
A lawyer-witness may continue as trial counsel if:

1)   Her testimony will concern only an *uncontested matter* or a *mere formality;*

2)   Her testimony will concern only the nature and value of the *legal services* rendered in the case;

3) Her withdrawal as trial counsel would cause a ***substantial hardship*** on her client; or

4) Another lawyer in her firm is likely to be called as a witness (unless to continue would constitute a conflict of interest).

3. Conflict of Interest Rules Also Apply

In addition to complying with the above rule, a lawyer who is both an advocate and a witness must also comply with the general conflict of interest principles regarding current and former clients. (*See* V.B., E., *supra.*)

H. SPECIAL RESPONSIBILITIES OF A PROSECUTOR

A prosecutor must assure that a defendant is tried by fair procedures and that guilt is decided on proper and sufficient evidence.

1. Must Have Probable Cause

A prosecutor must not proceed with a charge that she knows is not supported by probable cause.

2. Protecting Accused's Right to Counsel

A prosecutor must make reasonable efforts to assure that the accused is advised of the right to counsel, advised of the procedure for obtaining counsel, and given a reasonable opportunity to obtain counsel.

3. Securing Waiver of Pretrial Rights

A prosecutor must not seek to obtain from an unrepresented accused a waiver of important pretrial rights.

4. Disclosing Evidence that May Help Defense

A prosecutor must timely disclose to the defense all evidence and information known to the prosecutor that tends to negate the guilt of the accused or mitigate the degree of the offense.

5. Disclosing Information that May Mitigate Punishment

When a convicted person is to be sentenced, the prosecutor must disclose to the defense and the court all unprivileged mitigating information known to the prosecutor.

6. Public Statements About Pending Matters

Except for statements necessary to inform the public of the nature and extent of the prosecutor's action and that serve a legitimate law enforcement purpose, a prosecutor must not make extrajudicial statements that have a substantial likelihood of heightening public condemnation of the accused. The prosecutor must take reasonable care to prevent investigators, police, employees, and other subordinates from making such statements.

7. Subpoenaing Other Lawyers

A prosecutor must not subpoena a lawyer to give evidence about a client unless the information is not privileged, is essential, and cannot be obtained in any other way.

8. Other Government Lawyers

Many of the above duties also apply to all government lawyers. A government lawyer with discretionary power regarding civil litigation should not institute or continue unfair actions. A government lawyer has a responsibility to develop a full record and must not use her position or power to harass parties or to force unjust settlements or results.

I. ADVOCATE IN LEGISLATIVE AND ADMINISTRATIVE PROCEEDINGS

1. Appearances in a Representative Capacity
When a lawyer appears on behalf of a client before a legislative body or administrative agency, the lawyer must disclose that he is acting in a representative capacity.

2. Duties of Candor and Respect
In such appearances, the lawyer must generally follow the same rules of conduct as though in court.

3. Limits of These Rules
These rules do *not* apply: (i) when a lawyer represents a client in bilateral negotiations with the government, (ii) in an application for a license or other privilege, (iii) when the government is investigating the client's affairs, or (iv) when the government is examining the client's compliance with a regular reporting requirement (such as the filing of tax returns).

IX. TRANSACTIONS WITH THIRD PERSONS

A. TRUTHFULNESS IN STATEMENTS TO THIRD PERSONS

1. Must Not Make False Statements of Material Fact or Law
When dealing on behalf of a client with a third person, a lawyer must not make false statements of law or fact. Conventional puffery, however, is permitted.

2. Must Disclose Material Fact to Avoid Client's Crime or Fraud
A lawyer must disclose material facts to a third person when necessary to avoid assisting the client in a crime or fraud—*unless* the lawyer is forbidden to do so by the *ethical duty of confidentiality*, in which case the ABA Model Rules require the lawyer to withdraw.

B. COMMUNICATION WITH PERSONS REPRESENTED BY COUNSEL

1. When Communication Forbidden
A lawyer must not communicate about a matter with a person the lawyer knows is represented by counsel in that matter, unless that person's counsel consents, or unless the law or a court order authorizes the communication.

2. Application to Organizations
Corporations and other organizations are "persons" for the purpose of this rule. Such entities are comprised of individuals referred to as constituents—*i.e.,* officers, directors, employees, and shareholders of a corporation (or individuals in analogous positions in noncorporate organizations). Thus, a lawyer must get the consent of the organization's counsel before communicating with a *present* organization constituent: (i) who *supervises, directs, or regularly consults with the organization's lawyer* about the matter; (ii) whose conduct may

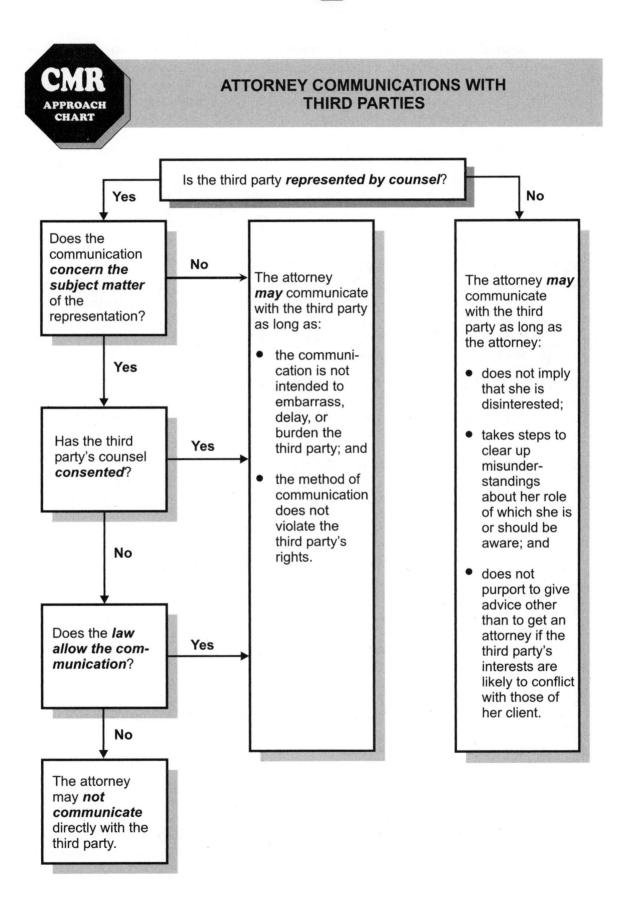

CMR APPROACH CHART

ATTORNEY COMMUNICATIONS WITH THIRD PARTIES

Is the third party **represented by counsel**?

Yes → Does the communication **concern the subject matter** of the representation?

No → The attorney **may** communicate with the third party as long as:

- the communication is not intended to embarrass, delay, or burden the third party; and

- the method of communication does not violate the third party's rights.

Yes → Has the third party's counsel **consented**?

Yes →

No → Does the **law allow the communication**?

Yes →

No → The attorney may **not communicate** directly with the third party.

No → The attorney **may** communicate with the third party as long as the attorney:

- does not imply that she is disinterested;

- takes steps to clear up misunderstandings about her role of which she is or should be aware; and

- does not purport to give advice other than to get an attorney if the third party's interests are likely to conflict with those of her client.

be *imputed* to the organization under civil or criminal law; or (iii) who has ***authority to obligate the organization*** concerning the matter. Consent is ***not*** needed before talking to a ***former*** constituent of the organization. However, when talking with either a present or former constituent, a lawyer must take care not to violate the organization's legal rights, such as the attorney-client privilege.

3. Communications Allowed by Rule
A lawyer may communicate with a represented person when authorized by law or court order or when the communication does not concern the subject of the representation. Also, represented parties are not prohibited from communicating directly with each other. Furthermore, a lawyer is not prohibited from interviewing the intended unrepresented witnesses of the opposing party.

C. DEALING WITH UNREPRESENTED PERSONS
When dealing with an unrepresented person, a lawyer must not state or imply that he is disinterested and must make reasonable efforts to correct any misunderstanding by the unrepresented person as to his role in the matter. Likewise, if the lawyer knows that his client's interests are likely to be in conflict with those of the unrepresented person, he must not give legal advice to that person (other than to get a lawyer).

D. RESPECT FOR RIGHTS OF THIRD PERSONS
In representing a client, a lawyer must not use means that have no substantial purpose other than to embarrass, delay, or burden a third person. A lawyer must not use methods of obtaining evidence that violate the legal rights of a third person.

1. Documents Sent to Lawyer By Mistake
When a lawyer obtains a document by mistake, and knows that it was sent by mistake, she must promptly notify the sender so that the sender can take protective measures.

X. LAW FIRMS AND ASSOCIATIONS

A. TERMS AND DEFINITIONS

1. "Partner"
In a private law firm, "partner" means a person who is a party to the firm's partnership agreement.

2. "Associate"
"Associate" usually means a lawyer employee who is paid by salary.

3. "Of Counsel"
"Of counsel" refers to a lawyer who has a continuing relationship with a law firm other than as a partner or associate.

4. "General Counsel"
"General counsel" often means the person in charge of an in-house law department of a business, but it can also mean a private lawyer who devotes a substantial amount of time to representing a business.

B. RESPONSIBILITIES OF PARTNERS, MANAGERS, AND SUPERVISORY LAWYERS

1. Partners' Duty to Educate and Guide in Ethics Matters
The partners or managing lawyers of a firm, and other supervisory lawyers, must make reasonable efforts to assure that the other lawyers adhere to the Rules of Professional Conduct. A lawyer who directly supervises another lawyer's work must reasonably assure that the other lawyer adheres to the Rules of Professional Conduct.

2. How Duties Are Fulfilled
In a small private law firm, informal supervision may be sufficient. In a larger organization, more elaborate steps may be necessary.

3. Ethical Responsibility for Another Lawyer's Misconduct
A lawyer is subject to discipline for a disciplinary violation committed by a second lawyer if: (i) the first lawyer ordered it or knowingly ratified it, or (ii) the first lawyer is a partner or manager or has direct supervisory responsibility over the second lawyer and learns of the misconduct at a time when it can be remedied but fails to take reasonable remedial action.

C. RESPONSIBILITIES OF A SUBORDINATE LAWYER
If a supervisory lawyer orders a subordinate lawyer to commit a *clear* ethics violation, the subordinate lawyer will be subject to discipline if he carries out the order. A subordinate lawyer will not be subject to discipline, however, for following a supervisory lawyer's reasonable resolution of a *debatable* ethics question.

D. RESPONSIBILITIES CONCERNING NONLAWYER ASSISTANTS

1. Duty to Educate and Guide in Ethics Matters
A lawyer should instruct and guide her nonlawyer assistants concerning legal ethics and should be ultimately responsible for their work.

2. Duty of Partners and Direct Supervisors
Law firm partners and managers and other direct supervisors must make reasonable efforts to assure that their *nonlawyer employees* act ethically.

3. Ethical Responsibility for Nonlawyer's Misconduct
A lawyer is subject to discipline when a nonlawyer does something that would violate a disciplinary rule if: (i) the lawyer ordered the conduct or knew about it and ratified it, or (ii) the lawyer is a partner or manager or has direct supervisory responsibility over the nonlawyer and learns about the misconduct at a time when it can be remedied but fails to take reasonable remedial action.

E. PROFESSIONAL INDEPENDENCE OF A LAWYER

1. Fee Splitting with Nonlawyers
Subject to the exceptions stated below, a lawyer must not share her legal fee with a nonlawyer.

a. Death Benefits Permitted
The lawyers in a firm may agree that when one of them dies, the others will pay a death benefit over a reasonable period of time to the dead lawyer's survivors.

b. Compensation and Retirement Plans for Nonlawyer Employees
The nonlawyer employees of a firm may be included in a compensation or retirement plan even though the plan is based on a profit-sharing arrangement.

c. Sale of a Law Practice
One lawyer's practice can be sold to another lawyer (*see* G., below). One who buys the practice of a dead, disabled, or disappeared lawyer may pay the purchase price to the estate or representatives of the lawyer.

d. Sharing Court-Awarded Fee with Nonprofit Organization
When a court awards attorneys' fees to the winning lawyer in a case, the lawyer may share the fee with a nonprofit organization that hired or recommended him as counsel.

2. Partnership with Nonlawyer to Practice Law Prohibited
A lawyer must not form a partnership with a nonlawyer if *any* part of the partnership activities will constitute the practice of law.

3. Nonlawyer Involvement in Incorporated Firm or Other Association
A lawyer must not practice in an incorporated firm or association if a nonlawyer owns any interest in the firm or association, is a director or officer of the firm or association, or has the right to direct or control the professional judgment of a lawyer.

4. Interference with Lawyer's Professional Judgment
A lawyer must not allow a person who recommends, employs, or pays her for serving a client to direct or regulate the lawyer's professional judgment.

F. RESTRICTIONS ON RIGHT TO PRACTICE PROHIBITED
A lawyer's right to practice after termination of a partnership or employment relationship cannot be restricted except for an agreement concerning benefits upon retirement. Likewise, restrictions on the lawyer's right to practice as part of a settlement agreement are prohibited.

G. SALE OF A LAW PRACTICE

1. When Sale Permitted
A law practice or a field of law practice, including goodwill, may be sold if: (i) the seller ceases to engage in the private practice of law or the sold field of practice in the area in which the practice has been conducted, (ii) the entire practice or field of practice is sold to one or more lawyers or firms, and (iii) written notice is given to the seller's clients.

2. Clients' Fees After Sale
Clients' fees cannot be increased because of the sale. The purchaser must honor existing fee agreements made by the seller.

H. LAW-RELATED (ANCILLARY) SERVICES
Lawyers are permitted to provide law-related services (*e.g.*, financial planning, accounting, lobbying, title insurance) to both clients and nonclients. Even though law-related services are not legal services, a lawyer who provides such services is subject to the Rules of Professional Conduct in two situations:

1. **Nonlegal Services and Legal Services Provided Together**

   If a lawyer provides nonlegal services in circumstances that are not distinct from her provision of legal services to clients, then the Rules of Professional Conduct apply to both the legal and nonlegal services. Additionally, when a client-lawyer relationship exists between the lawyer and the individual receiving the law-related services, the lawyer must comply with Rule 1.8(a), which specifies the conditions a lawyer must satisfy when she enters into a business transaction with her own client. Specifically, the transaction must meet the following requirements: the terms of the transaction must be fair to the client; the terms must be fully disclosed to the client in writing, and such disclosure must cover the essential terms of the transaction and the lawyer's role in the transaction; the client must be advised in writing that he should seek advice from an independent lawyer regarding the arrangement; and the client must give informed consent in a writing signed by the client. (*See also* V.C.1., *supra.*)

2. **Nonlegal Services Provided by Entity that Is Controlled by the Lawyer**

   If a lawyer provides nonlegal services through an entity that is not her law office but that she controls, the lawyer must take reasonable steps to assure that people who receive the nonlegal services understand that those services are not legal services and that the Rules of Professional Conduct do not cover those services. If the lawyer does not take those reasonable steps, then the lawyer is subject to the Rules of Professional Conduct with respect to the nonlegal services.

XI. PUBLIC SERVICE

A. PRO BONO PUBLICO SERVICE

Every lawyer has a professional responsibility to provide legal service to people who cannot afford it. ABA Model Rule 6.1 recommends a minimum of 50 hours per year of uncompensated legal work for poor people or organizations that serve the needs of poor people.

B. MEMBERSHIP IN LEGAL SERVICES ORGANIZATIONS

Lawyers are encouraged to support and work for legal services organizations that provide legal assistance to poor people. But conflicts of interest may arise between people thus served and a lawyer's regular, paying clients.

1. **General Rule—May Serve as Director, Officer, or Member**

   A lawyer may serve as a director, officer, or member of a legal services organization, even though the organization serves persons whose interests are adverse to those of the lawyer's regular clients.

2. **Limitations on Rule**

   A lawyer must not knowingly participate in a decision or action of the organization if doing so: (i) would be incompatible with the lawyer's obligations to a client under the general conflict of interest rules, or (ii) would adversely affect the representation of one of the organization's clients.

C. QUICK-ADVICE PROGRAMS

A lawyer may participate in a quick-advice program sponsored by a court or nonprofit organization, such as a legal-advice hotline, advice-only clinic, or program that shows people how to represent themselves in small claims court. A lawyer-client relationship exists between the lawyer and person who obtains the quick advice, but neither the lawyer nor person expects the relationship to continue past the quick-advice stage.

1.   **Client Consents to Short-Term, Limited Legal Service**
The lawyer must obtain the client's informed consent to the limited scope of the relationship. If the lawyer's quick advice is not enough to set the client on the right track, the lawyer must advise the client to get further legal help.

2.   **Conflict of Interest Rules Are Relaxed**
The conflict of interest rules are relaxed somewhat in a quick-advice situation, but the remainder of the Rules of Professional Conduct fully apply. Because a lawyer who participates in a quick-advice program ordinarily has no time to do an ordinary conflict of interest check, the conflicts principles regarding current and former clients do not apply unless the lawyer **actually knows** that giving the quick advice creates a conflict of interest. (*See* V.B.; E., *supra,* for a discussion of conflict of interest rules)

3.   **Imputed Conflict Rule Is Also Relaxed**
The rule of imputed conflicts of interest is also relaxed in a quick-advice situation. A lawyer may dispense advice in a quick-advice program unless the lawyer **actually knows** that he is disqualified from doing so because of a conflict imputed from another lawyer in his firm. Conversely, a conflict created by advice a lawyer dispenses in a quick-advice program will not be imputed to others in the lawyer's firm.

4.   **Conflicts Rules Apply Fully If Quick Advice Leads to Regular Representation**
If a person who has received quick advice from a lawyer then wants to hire that lawyer to render further service in the matter, the ordinary conflict of interest rules apply to that further service.

D.   LAW REFORM ACTIVITIES AFFECTING CLIENT INTERESTS

1.   **Activities that May Harm Client**
A lawyer may serve as a director, officer, or member of a law reform group, even though a reform advocated by the group may harm one of the lawyer's clients.

2.   **Activities that May Benefit Client**
When a lawyer is working on a law reform project and is asked to participate in a decision that could materially benefit one of the lawyer's clients, the lawyer must disclose that fact— but the lawyer need not identify the client.

E.   POLITICAL CONTRIBUTIONS TO OBTAIN GOVERNMENT EMPLOYMENT
A lawyer or firm must not accept government legal employment or a judicial appointment if the lawyer or firm makes a political contribution *for the purpose of obtaining such employment or appointment*. *Exceptions:* This rule does not apply to employment or appointments: (i) for uncompensated services, (ii) made on the basis of a lawyer's experience and following a process that is free from influence based on political contributions, or (iii) made on a rotating basis from a list compiled without regard to political contributions.

XII. INFORMATION ABOUT LEGAL SERVICES

A. BACKGROUND OF ADVERTISING AND SOLICITATION RULES

"Advertising" is a communication with the public at large. "Solicitation" is a lawyer's individual contact with a layperson designed to entice the layperson into hiring the lawyer. Traditionally, ethics rules banned almost all forms of lawyer advertising and solicitation. Responding to free market and free speech arguments in a series of cases, the Supreme Court recognized lawyer advertising as commercial speech protected by the First and Fourteenth Amendments. States may thus adopt reasonable regulations to ensure that the advertising is not false or misleading, but they may not completely prohibit all lawyer advertising.

1. False and Misleading Ads and In-Person Solicitation May Be Banned
A state may prohibit all lawyer advertising that is false or misleading and may forbid in-person solicitation for profit.

2. Regulation of Truthful, Nondeceptive Advertising
Regulation of commercial speech is subject to intermediate constitutional scrutiny, which means that it may be regulated only if: (i) the government asserts a *substantial interest*, (ii) the government demonstrates that the restriction *directly and materially advances the interest*, and (iii) the regulation is narrowly drawn.

B. ADVERTISING

1. Basic Rule—Communications Must Be True and Not Misleading
ABA Model Rule 7.1 makes a lawyer subject to discipline for any type of statement about the lawyer or his services that is false or misleading. A statement can be false or misleading if it omits material information, creates unjustified expectations, or makes unsubstantiated comparisons.

2. Limits on Advertising
In addition to the basic rule on false or misleading statements, ABA Model Rule 7.2 imposes the following more specific rules:

a. Communications about *fields of law* in which a lawyer practices must comply with ABA Model Rule 7.4 (*see* D., *infra*).

b. Before naming *sample clients* in an ad, a lawyer should obtain their consent.

c. Every ad must include the name and office address of at least one lawyer or law firm that is *responsible for its content*.

3. Payments for Recommending a Lawyer's Services
Except in connection with the sale of a law practice, a lawyer must not pay people for recommending him. But he may pay people for designing and running ads and may pay referral fees to approved lawyer referral services. Also, legal aid offices and group legal service plans may advertise the services they provide.

4. Reciprocal Referral Arrangements

A lawyer may set up a reciprocal referral arrangement with another lawyer or with a nonlawyer professional. A reciprocal arrangement must not be exclusive, the referred client must be told about the arrangement, and the arrangement must not interfere with the lawyer's professional judgment as to making referrals. Reciprocal referral arrangements should not be of indefinite duration and should be reviewed periodically to make sure that they comply with the ABA Model Rules.

C. SOLICITATION

ABA Model Rule 7.3 states the basic rule on solicitation: A lawyer must not seek fee-paying work by initiating personal or live telephone contact, or real-time electronic contact, with a nonlawyer prospect with whom the lawyer has no family, close personal, or prior professional connection.

1. Use of Agents to Solicit

A lawyer must not use agents (runners or cappers) to solicit in a manner that the lawyer could not herself solicit.

2. Offers of Free Legal Service

The solicitation rule applies only when the lawyer's pecuniary gain is a significant motive for the solicitation. Thus, offers of free legal service, made without hope of pecuniary gain, are permitted.

3. Initiating Personal Contacts with Family, Clients, and Former Clients

A lawyer may initiate an otherwise forbidden contact with a family member, close friend, present or past client, or another lawyer.

4. Targeted Direct-Mail Solicitations

Absent actual knowledge that the prospective client does not wish to receive communications from the lawyer, a lawyer is not prohibited from sending truthful, nondeceptive letters to persons known to face a specific legal problem.

5. Harassing Prospective Clients

A lawyer must not coerce or harass prospective clients and must not solicit a prospective client who has indicated that he does not wish to be solicited.

6. Must Label Solicitations as Advertising

Written, electronic, or recorded communications with prospective clients who are known to need specific legal services must be labeled as "Advertising Material." This rule does not apply to a lawyer's communication with relatives, close friends, present and former clients, and other lawyers.

7. Group and Prepaid Legal Service Plan

A lawyer may personally contact a group that proposes to adopt a prepaid or group legal service plan. Furthermore, the plan may itself make personal and live telephone contact with prospective subscribers who are not known to need specific legal services.

D. COMMUNICATION OF FIELDS OF PRACTICE

1. Certified Specialists

Some states and private organizations certify lawyers as specialists in a field of law. A lawyer who has been certified as a specialist in a field may state that fact to the public if the certifying body is identified and if it has been approved by the state or ABA.

2. Statement of Fields of Practice

In public communications, a lawyer may state that he does (or does not) practice in particular fields of law, as long as he does not state or imply that he is a certified specialist.

3. Patent and Admiralty Lawyers

Lawyers who practice admiralty law may call themselves "Proctors in Admiralty," or something similar, and lawyers who have been admitted to practice before the United States Patent and Trademark Office may call themselves "Patent Attorneys," or something similar.

E. FIRM NAMES AND LETTERHEADS

1. Names of Law Firms

Private law partnerships may bear the name(s) of one or more of the partners. When a partner dies or retires, his name may remain on the letterhead of the successor partnership. In addition, the Model Rules permit *trade names* (*e.g.,* "Greater Chicago Legal Clinic") if they are not misleading and do not imply a connection to a charity or governmental agency.

2. Multistate Firms

A law firm having offices in more than one jurisdiction may use the same name, Internet address, or other professional designation in each jurisdiction. However, when the lawyers in a particular office are identified, the identification must indicate the jurisdictional limitations on those lawyers who are not licensed in the jurisdiction where that office is located.

3. Using Names of Lawyers Who Have Entered Public Service

A private law firm must not use the name of a lawyer who holds public office during any substantial period in which the lawyer is not regularly and actively practicing with the firm.

4. False Implications of Partnership

Lawyers must not imply that they are partners or are otherwise associated with each other in a law firm unless they really are.

5. Associated and Affiliated Law Firms

Two firms may hold themselves out as "associated" or "affiliated" if they have a close, regular, and ongoing relationship and if the designation is not misleading.

XIII. JUDICIAL ETHICS

A. SELECTION, TENURE, AND DISCIPLINE OF JUDGES

1. Federal Judges

Federal judges are appointed by the President with the advice and consent of the Senate.

They hold office for life during good behavior. A federal judge can be removed from office by impeachment.

2.   State Judges

In some states, judges are appointed by the governor or the state legislature, while in others they are elected by the voters. In still others, judges are initially appointed and later retained or rejected by the voters.

3.   Code of Judicial Conduct

In 1990, the ABA adopted a new Code of Judicial Conduct ("CJC") to serve as a model for state and federal judiciaries in formulating their own standards of judicial conduct. The CJC is binding on the judges and all persons who perform judicial functions in a jurisdiction when the CJC is adopted by the appropriate authority.

B.   INTEGRITY AND INDEPENDENCE

A judge should participate in establishing, maintaining, and enforcing high standards of conduct, and shall personally observe those standards. This applies to a judge's conduct on and off the bench.

C.   IMPROPRIETY AND THE APPEARANCE OF IMPROPRIETY

A judge must respect and comply with the law, and must act in a way that promotes public confidence in the integrity and impartiality of the judiciary.

1.   Personal Relationships

A judge must not allow family, social, political, or other relationships to interfere with the judge's conduct or judgments.

2.   Misuse of Judicial Prestige

A judge must not lend the prestige of judicial office to advance the private interests of the judge or others. However, as long as the judge is sensitive to abuse of the prestige of the judicial office she may: (i) act as a reference or provide a recommendation for someone; (ii) in response to a formal request, provide information about a person to a sentencing judge, probation officer, or corrections officer; and (iii) testify as a character witness for someone if served with a summons.

CMR **Exam Tip**   The character witness issue is an exam favorite. Often the examiners will give you the opposite rule as a possible choice. Remember: A judge should not *voluntarily* appear as a character witness for someone. A judge may testify as a character witness only if subpoenaed.

3.   Relationships with Discriminatory Organizations

A judge can be disciplined for maintaining a relationship with a discriminatory organization if: (i) the judge is a *member* of an organization that *currently* practices invidious discrimination based on race, sex, religion, or national origin; (ii) the judge, though not a member, *uses* an organization that so discriminates; (iii) the judge belongs to an organization that discriminates on other grounds prohibited by local law; or (iv) the judge publicly manifests a knowing approval of invidious discrimination on any basis. When a judge learns that an organization to which she belongs practices discrimination, the judge must either resign promptly or work to end the discriminatory practice, and not participate in the organization until the situation is remedied.

JUDGE'S USE OF AND MEMBERSHIP IN DISCRIMINATORY ORGANIZATIONS	
Permissible	**Impermissible**
Monday night men-only bridge club consisting of judge and his college chums	Men-only social club with 6,000 members and dining and health club facilities
Women's support group for breastfeeding mothers	Women's bar association that refuses to admit male members
Alumni association of traditionally black college with no nonblack graduates	Community booster group limiting membership to African-Americans
The Bulgarian League, which limits membership to persons of Bulgarian descent and whose purpose is the preservation of Bulgarian traditions	The Irish Business Association, which admits only persons of Irish descent and whose purpose is to promote businesses in the community owned by persons of Irish descent
Talmudic study group that limits membership to members of the judge's temple	Country club that excludes members on the basis of race or religion

D.   DILIGENT, IMPARTIAL PERFORMANCE OF JUDICIAL DUTIES

1.   Judicial Duties
Judicial duties take precedence over all of the judge's other activities.

2.   Hearing and Deciding Adjudicative Matters
A judge must hear and decide all matters assigned to her unless disqualification is required.

3.   Faithfulness to the Law
A judge must be faithful to the law and maintain competence in it.

4.   Order and Decorum in Court
The judge must exercise reasonable direction and control over persons subject to her control.

5.   Patience and Courteousness
A judge must be patient, dignified, and courteous to those with whom she deals in an official capacity, *e.g.*, litigants, lawyers, jurors, and witnesses.

6.   Avoidance of Bias and Prejudice
A judge must avoid bias and prejudice and must require others under her control to do likewise. Even in nonjudicial activities, a judge should avoid making demeaning remarks or jokes that play on prejudices.

7. **Right to Be Heard**

   A judge must give every person who has a legal interest in a proceeding the right to be heard.

8. **Ex Parte Communications**

   A judge must not initiate, permit, or consider communications between the judge and a representative for one side of a matter when no representative from the other side is present, except: (i) when expressly authorized by law; (ii) with the consent of the parties in an attempt to settle or mediate a pending matter; or (iii) as circumstances require in emergency or administrative matters, provided no party will gain an advantage and the other party is properly notified.

9. **Communications from Others**

   Except in the following circumstances, a judge must not initiate, permit, or consider communications to the judge outside the presence of the parties concerning a pending or impending matter.

   a. **Court Personnel**

      A judge may consult other judges and court personnel whose function is to aid the judge in carrying out her responsibilities.

   b. **Disinterested Legal Experts**

      A judge may obtain the advice of a disinterested legal expert, provided the parties' lawyers are notified and given a chance to respond.

   c. **Other Communications**

      A judge may communicate with others (not court personnel or legal experts) about a matter outside the presence of the parties *only* if: (i) the circumstances so require (*e.g.*, parties cannot be reached), (ii) the communication concerns an emergency or administrative matter, (iii) no party will gain an advantage, *and* (iv) the judge notifies the parties of the essence of the communication and gives them an opportunity to respond.

   d. **Communications Between Trial and Appellate Courts**

      Some jurisdictions permit a trial judge to communicate with an appellate court about a proceeding. A copy of any written communication, or the substance of an oral communication, should be given to the parties' lawyers.

10. **Findings of Fact and Conclusions of Law**

    If a judge asks one side to propose findings of fact and conclusions of law, she must tell the other side of the request and give that side a chance to respond.

11. **Independent Investigation of the Facts**

    A judge cannot independently investigate the facts of a case and must consider only the evidence presented.

12. **Promptness, Efficiency, and Fairness**

    A judge must dispose of matters promptly, efficiently, and fairly (*e.g.*, be punctual, monitor cases to avoid delay, devote adequate time to duties).

13. **Public Comments on Cases**
When a case is pending in *any* court, a judge must not make any public comment that might reasonably be expected to affect its outcome or impair its fairness, or make any nonpublic comment that might substantially interfere with a fair trial. The judge must require like abstention from court personnel. This duty continues through appeal, but it does not apply to a judge who is a litigant in a personal capacity.

14. **Promises with Respect to Cases Likely to Come Before Court**
With respect to cases or issues that are likely to come before the court, a judge must not make pledges, promises, or commitments that are inconsistent with the impartial performance of her adjudicative duties.

15. **Commentary on Jury Verdict**
A judge must not commend or criticize jurors for their verdict, but may thank jurors for their service.

16. **Nonpublic Information**
A judge must not disclose or use any nonpublic information acquired in a judicial capacity (*e.g.,* information under seal or obtained in camera).

17. **Administrative Duties**
A judge must discharge her administrative duties diligently and without bias or prejudice, as well as maintain competence in administration and cooperate with others in administrative matters.

18. **Judicial Appointments**
A judge must appoint receivers, referees, guardians, counsel, etc., impartially and on the basis of merit.

19. **Disciplinary Responsibilities**
When a judge *receives information* that a judge or lawyer has violated the applicable rules of ethics, the judge *should* take "appropriate action." What constitutes "appropriate action" depends on the particular situation. If a judge has *actual knowledge* of a violation that raises a substantial question about the judge's fitness for office or the lawyer's fitness to practice, the judge *must* report the violator to the appropriate disciplinary authority. A judge's acts in this regard are privileged and cannot be the basis for a civil suit.

E. **DISQUALIFICATION**

1. **General Rule—Whenever Impartiality Might Be Questioned**
A judge must disqualify himself in a proceeding in which the judge's impartiality might reasonably be questioned.

   a. **Disclosure by Judge**
   A judge should disclose any information the judge believes the parties might consider relevant to the question of disqualification.

   b. **Rule of Necessity**
   In emergency situations, case law has created a rule of necessity that overrides the rules of disqualification and allows a judge to hear a matter even though he would otherwise

be disqualified from doing so but for the necessity. Also, the rules of disqualification do not apply to disqualify a judge from hearing a matter if the disqualifying factor would apply equally to all judges.

2. Bias or Personal Knowledge

A judge must disqualify himself if there is reasonable ground to believe that the judge has: (i) a personal bias concerning a party or lawyer, or (ii) personal knowledge of relevant evidentiary facts.

3. Prior Involvement

A judge who served as a lawyer or material witness in a matter, or was associated in law practice with a person who served as a lawyer in the matter while they practiced together, must disqualify himself.

4. Economic or Other Interest

A judge must disqualify himself if he knows that he or a member of his family (spouse, parent, child, or other member of his household) has: (i) an economic interest in a matter or one of the parties, or (ii) any other interest that could be substantially affected by the proceedings. With certain exceptions (*e.g.*, mutual funds), a person has an "economic interest" if he is an officer, director, advisor, or other active participant in the affairs of a party or owns more than a de minimis legal or equitable interest in a party.

5. Involvement of a Relative

The judge must disqualify himself if a relative of the judge is involved (as a party, lawyer, material witness, or interested third party) in the case. A "relative" is any person (or the spouse of that person) related within the third degree to the judge or the judge's spouse; *i.e.*, anyone related closer than a cousin.

6. Persons Making Contributions to Judge's Election Campaign

A judge who is subject to public election must disqualify himself when he knows or learns that a party or party's lawyer has, within a certain number of years, made contributions to his election campaign that exceed a specified amount.

7. Public Statements of Judicial Commitment

A judge must disqualify himself if, while a judge or judicial candidate, he has made a public statement that commits or appears to commit him regarding an issue or controversy in the proceeding.

8. Remittal of Disqualification

The parties and their lawyers can remit (waive) all of the foregoing grounds for disqualification, except personal bias concerning a party.

F. EXTRAJUDICIAL ACTIVITIES

A judge must conduct extrajudicial activities so that they do not cast doubt on his impartiality, demean the judicial office, or interfere with the judge's duties.

1. Avocational Activities

A judge may speak, write, lecture, teach, and participate in nonjudicial activities involving legal or nonlegal subjects, provided that these activities are consistent with the judge's duties under the Code.

2. **Governmental Hearings and Consultations**

   A judge must not appear at a public hearing before, or otherwise consult with, an executive or legislative body or official except on matters concerning the law, legal system, or administration of justice.

3. **Governmental Committees and Commissions**

   A judge must not accept appointment to a governmental committee or commission or other governmental position concerned with issues that do not relate to the law, legal system, or administration of justice. This includes appointments to the board of any *public* school (other than a law school).

CMR
SUMMARY
CHART

JUDGE'S EXTRAJUDICIAL ACTIVITIES INVOLVING THE GOVERNMENT

Activity	Allowable Only If:		
Appearance at hearing before or consultation with executive or legislative official(s)	***Relates to the law, legal system, or administration of justice***	*Or*	Pro se to protect judge's own interests
Appointment to governmental committee or commission	***Relates to the law, legal system, or administration of justice***	*Or*	Representing governmental unit on purely ceremonial grounds or for a historical, educational, or cultural activity
Act as officer, director, trustee, or nonlegal advisor to public school	***Relates to the law, legal system, or administration of justice***	*And*	Organization not likely to be in proceedings in the judge's court (or court under judge's appellate jurisdiction), and judge not improperly involved in fund-raising or membership solicitation

---

CMR **Exam Tip** Be wary of questions where a judge is appointed to the board of a school. A judge may not accept appointment to the board of a *public school* other than a law school. A judge may, however, accept appointment to the board of any private school. Thus, you must remember that a judge can serve on the board of a public *law* school and *any* private school.

4. **Law-Related Organizations and Nonprofit Organizations**

   A judge must not serve as an officer, director, trustee, or nonlegal advisor of a law-related or nonprofit organization if it is likely that the organization will: (i) be engaged in proceedings that would ordinarily come before the judge, or (ii) frequently be engaged in adversary proceedings in the court on which the judge sits or one under its appellate jurisdiction.

Furthermore, a judge may help plan such an organization's fund-raising, but he must not personally participate in fund-raising activities except to solicit funds from other judges who are not under his authority. A judge may attend an organization's fund-raising event, but may not be the guest of honor or a speaker at the event. A judge also may solicit members for such an organization, provided he does not use the prestige of judicial office or solicit in a manner that may be taken as coercive.

SOLICITATION OF FUNDS BY JUDGES

Permissible	Impermissible
Making recommendations to fund-granting sources concerning law-related projects	Personal participation in fund-raising activity of a law-related or nonprofit organization
Planning a fund-raising drive of a law-related or nonprofit organization	_____
Soliciting funds for a law-related or nonprofit organization from other judges who are not under the judge's supervisory control	_____
Attending a fund-raising event of a law-related or nonprofit organization	Participating as guest of honor or speaker at a fund-raising event of a law-related or nonprofit organization
Signing a general solicitation letter on a law-related or nonprofit organization's letterhead	Sending a solicitation letter for a law-related or nonprofit organization on a judge's judicial letterhead
Establishing campaign committees to solicit public support and reasonable contributions from the public for the judge's election campaign (*see infra*)	Personally soliciting support or accepting campaign contributions for a judge's election campaign (*see infra*)

5. **Investments**

   Unless otherwise improper under the Code, a judge may hold and manage investments for himself or members of his family.

6. **Financial and Business Dealings**

   A judge must not engage in financial or business dealings that might be perceived to exploit the judge's position (*e.g.*, using information gained in judicial capacity for personal gain), or that involve frequent dealings with persons likely to come before the court on which he sits.

7. **Participation in a Business**

   A judge is not permitted to be an officer, director, manager, general partner, advisor, or employee of any business entity. A judge may, however, participate in a business that is closely held by the judge or his family, or a business primarily engaged in investing the judge's or his family's financial resources, unless it is too time-consuming or the business frequently appears before the court on which he sits.

8. **Gifts, Bequests, Favors, and Loans**

Generally, a judge should not accept gifts, bequests, favors, or loans from anyone. Exceptions include: (i) gifts incident to public testimonials; (ii) books, tapes, etc., given by publishers for official use; (iii) invitations to law-related functions; (iv) gifts, awards, or benefits incident to the activities of a member of the judge's household; (v) ordinary social hospitality; (vi) gifts from a relative or friend on a special occasion; (vii) gifts, bequests, favors, or loans from a relative or close friend whose appearance in a case would disqualify the judge in any event; (viii) loans from lending institutions in the ordinary course of their business on the same terms as to nonjudges; (ix) scholarships or fellowships; and (x) any other gift or favor by a person not likely to come before the judge.

9. **Fiduciary Activities**

Generally, a judge must not serve as an executor, administrator, trustee, guardian, or other fiduciary. A judge may serve as a fiduciary for a member of his family, but only if it will not interfere with his judicial duties or involve him in proceedings in the court on which he sits or one under its appellate authority. If the judge's fiduciary duties conflict with his judicial duties, he should resign as fiduciary.

10. **Service as Arbitrator or Mediator**

A *full-time* judge must not act as an arbitrator, mediator, or private judge unless expressly authorized by law.

11. **Practice of Law**

A *full-time* judge must not practice law, but he may, without compensation, advise or draft documents for a member of his family and act pro se.

12. **Outside Compensation and Expenses**

Unless more rigorous requirements apply in a jurisdiction, a judge may receive compensation and reimbursement of expenses for proper outside activities if they do not create the appearance of impropriety and are reasonable. A judge must report activities for which he receives compensation, where and when the activity took place, and the amount of compensation. However, except when required by the reporting or disqualification rules, judges do not have to disclose their financial affairs.

G. JUDGES AND POLITICS

Generally, a judge must avoid politics. However, a judge may participate in those political activities: (i) designed to improve the law, (ii) specifically authorized by law, and (iii) permitted under the Code (*see infra*).

1. **Rules Applicable to All Judges and Judicial Candidates**

   a. **Definition of "Candidate"**

   A person seeking to obtain or retain judicial office or a judge seeking nonjudicial office, either by election or appointment, is a candidate when she: (i) publicly announces her candidacy, (ii) declares or files her candidacy with the appropriate authority, or (iii) authorizes solicitation or acceptance of contributions.

b. General Prohibitions
Except when specifically permitted by the CJC, a judge or candidate must not:

1) Act as a leader or hold office in a political organization;

2) Publicly endorse or oppose another candidate for public office;

3) Make speeches on behalf of a political organization;

4) Attend political gatherings; or

5) Financially support a political organization or candidate.

c. Explanation of General Prohibitions
When false statements are publicly made about a judicial candidate, a judge or judicial candidate who knows the facts may make the facts public without violating the above prohibitions. Furthermore, a judge or candidate does not violate the prohibitions by *privately* expressing her views on candidates for public office. A public official may retain her office while running for judicial office.

d. Judges Who Run for Nonjudicial Office
A judge must resign when she becomes a candidate for a nonjudicial office.

2. Rules Applicable to Candidates for Judicial Office
A candidate must act with the dignity, impartiality, integrity, and independence expected of a judge and take appropriate steps to assure that her subordinates act with the same restraint. A candidate must not make: (i) with respect to cases or issues likely to come before the court, pledges, promises, or commitments that are inconsistent with the impartial performance of her adjudicative duties, or (ii) knowing misrepresentations about the identity, qualifications, present position, or other facts about herself or an opponent. A candidate may, however, respond to attacks on herself or her record.

3. Rules Applicable to Candidates for Appointed Positions
A candidate for a judgeship or other government position filled by appointment must not solicit or accept funds for her candidacy. In addition, the candidate must not engage in political activity to secure the position, except that she may communicate with the appointing authority, seek support from groups regularly offering such support, and provide information about her qualifications to the appointing authority or support groups. Note that *nonjudge candidates* for these offices may retain an office in a political organization and attend political gatherings. Nonjudge candidates can also pay ordinary assessments and make ordinary contributions to these organizations.

4. Rules Applicable to Judges and Candidates Subject to Public Election
Certain exceptions to the prohibitions on political activity apply to judges who are subject to public election, judges seeking nonjudicial elected office, and candidates for elected judicial office.

a. **Party Politics**

These judges and candidates *may at any time*, whether or not they are standing for election, buy tickets and attend political gatherings, identify themselves as members of a party, and contribute to a political organization.

b. **Election Politics**

When standing for election, these people *may* speak at gatherings on their own behalf, appear in advertisements, distribute campaign literature, publicly endorse or oppose other candidates for the same office, and allow their names to be listed on election materials along with the names of candidates for other offices.

c. **Campaign Activities**

These persons may engage in campaign activities, but they must neither personally solicit publicly stated support nor solicit or accept campaign contributions. They may, however, establish campaign committees, which may solicit support and reasonable contributions, as well as put on candidate forums, publish campaign literature, and manage campaign funds. Campaign committees may solicit contributions and support no earlier than one year before an election and no later than 90 days after the last election in which the candidate participates.

CMR COMPARISON CHART

POLITICAL ACTIVITIES OF JUDGES SUBJECT TO PUBLIC ELECTION

Activity	Noncandidate Judge	Candidate Judge
Act as leader or hold office in political organization	Impermissible	Impermissible
Publicly endorse or oppose *another candidate* for *other public office*	Impermissible	Impermissible
Publicly endorse or oppose candidates for *same judicial office*	Impermissible	Permissible
Make speeches on behalf of political organization	Impermissible	Impermissible (but may speak at political gatherings on own behalf)
Purchase tickets for and attend political gatherings	Permissible	Permissible
Solicit funds for a political organization	Impermissible	Impermissible
Make contributions to a political organization	Permissible	Permissible

5. Sanctions for Violating Rules on Political Activity

A successful candidate who violates the rules on political activity is subject to judicial discipline. An unsuccessful candidate who violates the rules and is a lawyer is subject to lawyer discipline.

H. APPLICATION OF THE CODE OF JUDICIAL CONDUCT

In jurisdictions that adopt the CJC, it applies to all persons who perform judicial functions, including magistrates, court commissioners, and referees. Part-time and retired judges are exempt from many, but not all, of the provisions that restrict outside activities and political activities.

BAR REVIEW

Comprehensive Outline

celebrating over **35** **YEARS** *of preparing law students for the bar exam*

TABLE OF CONTENTS

I. REGULATION OF THE LEGAL PROFESSION

A. SOURCES OF REGULATION

1. The State

The practice of law, like other professions and businesses, affects the public interest and is, therefore, subject to regulation by the states in the exercise of their police powers.

a. Courts

Because the practice of law is intimately connected with the administration of justice, the courts have the *inherent* power to regulate the legal profession in and out of court. The ultimate power thus rests with the *highest court* in the state, not with the state legislature. The highest court generally promulgates the ethics rules and oversees the discipline of lawyers.

1) Ethics Rules—The American Bar Association ("ABA") Model Rules and Judicial Code

Every state has professional ethics rules that govern the conduct of lawyers. In most states, the ethics rules are patterned after models created by the ABA. A large majority of states have now adopted some version of the ABA Model Rules of Professional Conduct, with most of the remaining states following some version of its predecessor, the ABA Model Code of Professional Responsibility. Likewise, most of the states have adopted some version of the ABA Model Code of Judicial Conduct.

2) Case Law

Every state has a body of judge-made case law concerning the rights and duties of lawyers. For example, the case law of a state may limit a lawyer's ability to enforce a fee contract after being fired by the client.

3) Rules of Court

State courts typically have rules of court with which lawyers must comply. For example, a rule of court may govern the lawyer's obligation to represent an indigent client at the court's request.

b. Bar Associations

Each state has an association of lawyers, commonly called the state bar association. A majority of states have an "integrated" bar system, meaning that every lawyer who is admitted to practice in the state must be a member of the state bar association. Common functions of a state bar association are to administer the state's bar examination, to provide continuing education programs for practicing lawyers, and to assist the state courts in regulating and imposing professional discipline on lawyers.

c. The Legislature

Every state has a body of statutes that govern some aspects of the practice of law. For example, a state evidence statute may define the scope of the attorney-client privilege.

2. The Federal System

a. Courts
A lawyer who practices in a federal court or agency is also constrained by federal statutes, federal case law, and the rules of that particular court or agency. Each federal court has its own bar, and a lawyer cannot practice before a particular court without first becoming a member of its bar.

b. Government Attorneys
An attorney for the federal government is subject to state laws and rules (as well as local federal court rules) governing attorneys in each state in which the attorney engages in her duties. [28 U.S.C. §530B(a)] Note that federal regulations interpret this statute as pertaining only to rules that prescribe ethical conduct for attorneys and that would subject an attorney to professional discipline (*e.g.*, it does not apply to state rules of evidence or procedure, or state substantive law). [28 C.F.R. §§77.2, .3]

3. Regulation by Multiple States
A lawyer is subject to regulation by *each* state in which the lawyer is *admitted* to practice, regardless of where the lawyer actually practices law. [ABA Model Rule 8.5] If the rules of the states in which the lawyer is admitted are in conflict, choice of law rules apply (*see* C.4., *infra*).

B. ADMISSION TO THE PRACTICE OF LAW
In most states, to be admitted to the practice of law, a person must have successfully completed college and law school, passed a bar examination, and submitted to a bar admission committee an application for admission, which generally includes proof of good moral character. If the committee approves the application, the candidate is sworn in to practice before the highest court of the state. Note that each state has its own "bar" (roster of lawyers who are admitted to practice), and admission to the bar of one state does not, without more, entitle a person to practice law in any other state.

1. The Application
An applicant for admission to the bar must respond truthfully and completely to inquiries made on the application or otherwise by the admissions committee.

a. False Statements
An applicant for admission to the bar, or a lawyer in connection with a bar admission application, must not *knowingly* make a false statement of material fact. [ABA Model Rule 8.1(a)]

Example: When A applied for admission to the bar, he was required to fill out a personal information form that asked whether he had ever been convicted of a crime, received less than an honorable discharge from the military service, or been disciplined for dishonesty by any school. A knowingly failed to reveal that he had been suspended from college for a semester for cheating on an examination. A's failure to reveal the suspension is grounds for denying his bar application. If A's failure to reveal is discovered after A is admitted to the bar, A is subject to discipline. [*See* Carter v. Charos, 536 A.2d 527 (R.I. 1988)]

b.   Failure to Disclose Information

Likewise, an applicant (or a lawyer in connection with an applicant's application for admission to the bar) must not: (i) *fail to disclose* a fact necessary to correct a misapprehension *known* by the person to have arisen in the matter, or (ii) *knowingly fail to respond* to a lawful demand for information from an admissions authority. [ABA Model Rule 8.1(b)] This rule does not, however, require disclosure of information otherwise protected by the confidentiality provisions of the Rules of Professional Conduct. (*See* IV., *infra.*)

Example: Bar applicant B applied for admission using a forged certificate of graduation from the State University School of Law. Attorney A knew about B's forgery, and she knew that the forgery had not been detected by the bar admission officials. A must voluntarily tell the bar admission officials about the forgery.

2.   Character and Fitness—"Good Moral Character"

The state has an interest in insuring that lawyers admitted to practice possess high moral standards and are mentally and emotionally stable.

a.   Investigative Procedure

A bar applicant is usually required to fill out a detailed questionnaire and list a number of references as part of his application. (Some states also require the applicant to submit fingerprints and photographs.) This information is then checked either by letter or personal investigation. If there is a question concerning the applicant's moral fitness, the applicant may be asked to appear at a hearing before the committee.

1)   Burden of Proof and Duties of Applicant

The burden of coming forward and establishing good moral character is on the applicant. In addition, the applicant owes a duty to cooperate in reasonable investigations by the state bar and to make disclosures relevant to his fitness to practice law. [*In re* Anastaplo, 366 U.S. 82 (1961)]

2)   Procedural Rights

A bar applicant has a right to due process in committee proceedings. Thus, he has the right to know the charges filed against him, to explain away derogatory information, and to confront critics. [Willner v. Committee, 373 U.S. 96 (1963)] An applicant who is denied admission on the basis of bad moral character is entitled to judicial review, usually by the state's highest court.

b.   Conduct Relevant to Moral Character

All aspects of an applicant's past conduct that reflect on his honesty and integrity are relevant to an evaluation of moral character. The committee may consider any conduct or charges against the applicant—including those charges of which the applicant was acquitted—and any litigation to which the applicant was a party.

Example: In one case, an applicant was denied admission because of personality traits that were deemed to make him unfit to practice. It was shown that the applicant was overly sensitive, rigid, and suspicious; was excessively self-important; and had a tendency to make false accusations against others and ascribe evil motives to them. [Application of Ronwin, 555 P.2d 315 (Ariz. 1976)]

1) **Criminal Conduct**

Mere conviction of any crime is not sufficient to deny the admission of an applicant to practice law. To cause disqualification of an applicant, the crime in question must involve ***moral turpitude***, such as a crime involving intentional dishonesty for the purpose of personal gain (*e.g.*, forgery, bribery, theft, perjury, robbery, extortion) or a crime involving violence (*e.g.*, murder, rape, mayhem). The nature of the offense and the motivation of the violator are also factors in determining whether moral turpitude exists.

a) **"Adolescent Misbehavior" and Civil Disobedience**

Examples of criminal behavior that do not rise to the level of moral turpitude include an applicant's arrest when he was a youth for a fistfight (adolescent behavior that does not necessarily bear on the applicant's current fitness to practice law) and an applicant's arrest for nonviolent civil disobedience. [*See* Hallinan v. Committee of Bar Examiners, 65 Cal. 2d 447 (1966)]

2) **Rehabilitation**

An applicant may still gain admission to the legal profession despite past conduct involving moral turpitude if he can demonstrate sufficient rehabilitation of his character and a present fitness to practice law. [*See, e.g.,* March v. Committee of Bar Examiners, 67 Cal. 2d 718 (1967)]

3) **Concealment of Past Conduct Constitutes Moral Turpitude**

False statements or concealment of facts in response to an inquiry by the admissions committee is itself evidence of sufficient lack of moral character to deny admission—even if the underlying conduct does not involve moral turpitude. [ABA Model Rule 8.1; *and see* Geoffrey C. Hazard, Jr. and W. William Hodes, The Law of Lawyering (hereafter "Hazard & Hodes") §62.7 (3d ed. 2000 and 2003 Supp.)]

4) **Political Activity**

An applicant who refuses to take the oath to uphold the state and federal Constitutions may be denied admission because there is a rational connection between this requirement and the practice of law. [Law Students Research Council v. Wadmond, 401 U.S. 154 (1971)] However, an applicant's mere membership in the Communist Party (when there is no showing that the applicant engaged in or advocated actions to overthrow the government by force or violence) is not sufficient to show a lack of moral character and deny the applicant admission to practice law. [Schware v. Board of Bar Examiners, 353 U.S. 232 (1957)]

3. **Citizenship and Residency Are Not Valid Requirements**

A state cannot require that a person be a United States citizen to be admitted to the practice of law; such a requirement violates the Equal Protection Clause of the United States Constitution. [*In re* Griffiths, 413 U.S. 717 (1973)] Similarly, a requirement that a bar applicant be a resident of the state in which he is seeking admission to practice law violates the Privileges and Immunities Clause of the Constitution and is, therefore, invalid. [Supreme Court of New Hampshire v. Piper, 470 U.S. 274 (1985)]

C. REGULATION AFTER ADMISSION

Upon admission to the bar, a person becomes a lawyer and is thus subject to the applicable law governing such matters as professional discipline, procedure and evidence, civil remedies, and criminal sanctions.

1. Misconduct

a. Violation of the Rules of Professional Conduct

It is professional misconduct for a lawyer to: (i) violate or *attempt* to violate any of the Rules of Professional Conduct, (ii) knowingly *assist or induce another* person to violate the Rules, or (iii) *use the acts of another person* to commit a violation. [ABA Model Rule 8.4(a)]

Example: Attorney A knows that it is a violation of the Rules to approach an accident victim at the scene of the accident and offer his legal services. A asks his brother-in-law T, a tow truck driver, to give A's business cards to people involved in the accidents that T is called to tow. A is guilty of professional misconduct for using the acts of another to violate a rule.

b. Certain Criminal Acts

A lawyer is subject to discipline for committing a criminal act that reflects adversely on his honesty, trustworthiness, or fitness as a lawyer in other respects. [ABA Model Rule 8.4(b)] To constitute professional misconduct, the crime must involve some characteristic that is relevant to the practice of law. For example, crimes involving dishonesty, breach of trust, substantial interference with the administration of justice, and most crimes involving violence reflect on the lawyer's fitness to practice law. Other crimes (*e.g.,* solicitation of prostitution, single offense of drunk driving, possession of a marijuana cigarette), while punishable by law, do not necessarily trigger professional discipline.

Examples: 1) Attorney A willfully failed to file a personal federal income tax return, knowing that she owed a substantial amount of tax. Even though A's conduct was not connected with her practice of law, A is subject to discipline.

2) Lawyer L is arrested for soliciting sexual acts from an undercover police officer whom L believed to be a prostitute. L is not subject to discipline because his criminal conduct does not show dishonesty, untrustworthiness, or unfitness to practice law.

c. Dishonesty, Fraud, Deceit, or Misrepresentation

Any conduct involving dishonesty, fraud, deceit, or misrepresentation constitutes professional misconduct. [ABA Model Rule 8.4(c)] Examples of this type of misconduct, which need not rise to the level of a crime, include cheating on a bar examination [*see In re* Lamb, 49 Cal. 3d 239 (1989)—lawyer who impersonated her husband for exam was disbarred], plagiarism [*see In re* Lamberis, 443 N.E.2d 549 (Ill. 1982)— plagiarism in preparation of LL.M. thesis resulted in discipline], and defrauding one's own law firm by misusing expense accounts [*see In re* Siegel, 627 A.2d 156 (N.J. 1993); *and see* Hazard & Hodes, §65.5].

d. Conduct Prejudicial to the Administration of Justice

A lawyer is subject to discipline for engaging in conduct that is prejudicial to the administration of justice. [ABA Model Rule 8.4(d)] This rule is rarely invoked because nearly all of the offenses that would arise under it (*e.g.*, falsifying evidence, improper delaying tactics, frivolous claims) are dealt with more specifically in the rules relating to litigation (*see* VIII., *infra*). One situation, however, in which this rule may be invoked is where a lawyer, during representation of a client, *knowingly manifests bias* based on race, sex, religion, national origin, disability, age, sexual orientation, or socioeconomic status, and such action is prejudicial to the administration of justice. [Comment 3 to ABA Model Rule 8.4]

e. Stating or Implying Ability to Improperly Influence Officials

A lawyer must never state or imply that he has the ability to improperly influence a government agency or official or to achieve results by means that violate the law or legal ethics rules. [ABA Model Rule 8.4(e)]

Example: Lawyer L is a member of a very politically prominent family. Both his mother and brother are judges, and his father was once governor of the state. It would be improper for L to mention his prominent relatives in the course of procuring legal employment, as this implies he has some sort of improper influence with the courts or the government. If a client mentions L's relatives, L is obligated to explain that he has no special influence to wield on the client's behalf. [*See* Comment 13 to ABA Model Rule 1.3]

f. Assisting a Judge in Violation of Judicial Code

A lawyer is subject to discipline for *knowingly* assisting a judge or judicial officer in conduct that violates the Code of Judicial Conduct or other law. [ABA Model Rule 8.4(f)]

Example: R graduated from law school and became a member of the bar, but he never practiced law. Instead, he entered politics and was ultimately elected to a high federal office. When a drug charge was brought against R's chief deputy, R met personally with the judge before whom the case was pending and attempted to convince the judge to dismiss the charge. [*See* CJC 3(A)(4)—prohibits ex parte communications about a pending matter] R is subject to discipline.

2. Duty to Report Professional Misconduct

The legal profession prides itself on being self-policing. One element of a self-policing group is that each member of the group must be obligated to report misconduct by the other members. [*See* Comment 1 to ABA Model Rule 8.3] Therefore, a lawyer who *knows* that another lawyer has violated the Rules of Professional Conduct in such a way that it raises a *substantial* question as to that lawyer's honesty, trustworthiness, or fitness as a lawyer must report the violation to the appropriate professional authority. [ABA Model Rule 8.3(a)] Similarly, a lawyer who knows that a judge has violated the Code of Judicial Conduct in a way that raises a substantial question as to the judge's fitness for office must report the violation to the appropriate authority. [ABA Model Rule 8.3(b)]

Examples: 1) Attorney A learned that attorney B and accountant T had formed a tax service partnership in which T would do solely accounting work and B would do solely legal work. B has thus violated the disciplinary rule against partnerships with nonlawyers. (*See* X.E.2., *infra.*) A may report the violation, but she will not be subject to discipline if she fails to do so. A may decline to report B's violation because it concerns an arcane guild rule and does not indicate that B is dishonest, untrustworthy, or unfit to practice law. Other examples of violations that may not raise a substantial question as to a lawyer's fitness to practice include some types of improper solicitation and the improper use of nonlawyer assistants.

2) Lawyer M and lawyer N are good friends and golfing buddies. One day, they were golfing and mutually complaining about the tax laws; N mentioned that he does not worry about tax increases because he just underreports his income when the taxes go up. M must report N to the disciplinary authorities. Despite the fact that N was discussing his conduct in his personal affairs, it is illegal conduct involving dishonesty and must be reported. [*See* Hazard & Hodes, §64.4]

a. **Key Definitions**
"Knowledge" means actual knowledge, but it may be inferred from the circumstances. [ABA Model Rules, Terminology] It has been held to mean more than mere suspicion. Thus, while a lawyer *may* report *suspected* misconduct, she *must* report *known* misconduct. "Substantial" means "a matter of clear and weighty importance." [ABA Model Rules, Terminology]

b. **Sanctions for Failure to Report Misconduct**
A lawyer who fails to report this type of misconduct is herself subject to discipline for violating the rule requiring disclosure. [ABA Model Rule 8.3]

c. **Exception for Confidential Knowledge**
This rule does not require disclosure of information protected by the confidentiality rules. [*See* ABA Model Rule 1.6] Thus, if a lawyer learns about another lawyer's misconduct through a privileged communication with the other lawyer or one of his clients, the lawyer has no duty to report the misconduct. Indeed, the lawyer would be subject to discipline for violating the confidentiality rules if he did report it. Moreover, there is no duty to disclose information gained by a lawyer or judge while serving as a member of an approved lawyers' assistance program that helps lawyers and judges with substance abuse problems. [ABA Model Rule 8.3(c) and Comment 5]

Examples: 1) Lawyer L sought legal advice from his mentor, lawyer M, as to what L should do about offering a certain piece of evidence in court. L made it plain that he was seeking advice from M in M's role as a lawyer. L told M that he knew the evidence was false. M, of course, advised L not to offer the evidence. A few months later, M learned that L had ignored his advice and had offered the evidence. Because M's knowledge of the matter is protected by the ethical duty of confidentiality, M must not report L's disciplinary violation.

2) Attorney X had long been aware that attorney Y, another partner in his firm, had a very serious drinking problem, but X did not have any proof that it was affecting Y's job performance. One day, X ran into Y as Y

was on his way into court. Y was clearly drunk and could barely follow their conversation. X cautioned Y not to appear before the judge, but Y responded that he had tried cases when he was in worse shape than this. X must report Y to the disciplinary authorities. X did not learn of Y's substance abuse in the context of an approved lawyers' assistance program or an attorney-client relationship.

3. Disciplinary Process

"Professional discipline" means punishment imposed on a lawyer for breaking a rule of professional ethics.

a. Complaint

Disciplinary proceedings against a lawyer begin when a complaint is made to the state disciplinary authority (usually the state bar). Complaints are often brought by aggrieved clients, but may also be brought by anyone with knowledge of the misconduct. Filing a complaint against a lawyer is considered privileged, and thus cannot be the basis of an action (*e.g.*, defamation) by the lawyer against the complainant.

b. Screening

If the complaint is without merit, it might be dismissed by the grievance committee without ever involving the lawyer. If the complaint appears to have merit, the lawyer will be asked to respond to the charges. After further investigation, the committee will either dismiss the complaint or schedule a hearing. If the committee dismisses the complaint, the complainant does not have any right to appeal; the decision is final.

c. Hearing

1) Due Process Required

If there is a hearing on the complaint, the accused lawyer is entitled to procedural due process, which means that she has the right to counsel, to proper notice, to be heard and introduce evidence, and to cross-examine adverse witnesses. In addition, the hearing must be limited to the charges made in the complaint. [*In re* Ruffalo, 390 U.S. 544 (1968)]

2) Application of Other Rights

The exclusionary rules of criminal law do not apply to disciplinary proceedings. Thus, evidence obtained through an illegal search, for example, is admissible in a disciplinary proceeding. A lawyer may, however, invoke his Fifth Amendment privilege and refuse to answer questions at the hearing, and *no disciplinary action can be taken* against the lawyer if it is based solely on the claim of Fifth Amendment privilege. [Spevack v. Klein, 385 U.S. 511 (1967)]

3) Burden of Proof

The burden of proof is on the party prosecuting the charge, and most states require proof of the charge beyond a preponderance of the evidence (but less than beyond a reasonable doubt). Most states also require that only evidence admissible under the rules of evidence be considered; thus, inadmissible hearsay would be excluded.

4) Decision and Review

After the hearing, the grievance committee will either dismiss the charges or recommend sanctions. If sanctions are recommended or disciplinary action is actually taken, the lawyer is entitled to review of the decision by the state's highest court. The burden is then on the lawyer to show that the committee's action or recommendation is not supported by the record or is otherwise unlawful.

d. Sanctions

The most common sanctions imposed on a lawyer found to have committed professional misconduct are:

(i) ***Private or public reprimand or censure***, which is an acknowledgment of misconduct that goes on the lawyer's record with the disciplinary authorities;

(ii) ***Suspension*** of the lawyer's license to practice for a definite period of time, at the end of which the right to practice is automatically reinstated; and

(iii) ***Disbarment***, which is the ***permanent*** revocation of the lawyer's license to practice. A disbarred lawyer may, however, apply for readmission upon proof of rehabilitation.

Other sanctions available include probation, restitution, costs of the disciplinary proceedings, and limitations on the lawyer's practice. [*See* ABA Model Rule for Lawyer Disciplinary Enforcement 10] Which sanction is imposed generally depends on the severity of the misconduct and the presence or absence of mitigating or aggravating circumstances.

4. Choice of Law in Disciplinary Proceedings

If the conduct in question occurred in connection with a proceeding that is pending before a tribunal, the ethics rules of the jurisdiction in which the tribunal sits will be applied, unless the tribunal's rules provide otherwise. [ABA Model Rule 8.5(b)(1)] For any other conduct, the rules of the jurisdiction in which the conduct occurred will apply, but if the predominant effect of the conduct is in some other jurisdiction, that jurisdiction's rules will apply. [ABA Model Rule 8.5(b)(2)] A lawyer will ***not*** be subject to discipline if her conduct is proper in the jurisdiction in which she reasonably believes the predominant effect of her conduct will occur. [*Id.*]

Example: The legal ethics rules of East Dakota prohibit a lawyer from paying a "referral fee" to another lawyer as compensation for the referral of a legal matter. The legal ethics rules of West Dakota permit such referral fees if they are reasonable in amount and if the referred client consents. East Dakota lawyer Ed referred an estate planning client to West Dakota lawyer Wes. The client lives in West Dakota and most of her property is located there. With the client's consent, Wes sent Ed a reasonable referral fee. Wes is not subject to discipline in either state.

5. Effect of Sanctions in Other Jurisdictions

A suspension or disbarment in one jurisdiction does not automatically affect a lawyer's ability to practice in another jurisdiction.

a. Other States

Professional discipline imposed by one state is not necessarily binding on another. Most states recognize the determinations of lawyer misconduct by sister states, but they do not agree on the reasons for recognition. The preferred view is that sister states accept disciplinary action by one state as conclusive proof of the misconduct, but not of the sanctions imposed. [*See* Kentucky Bar Association v. Signer, 558 S.W.2d 582 (Ky. 1977); Florida Bar v. Wilkes, 179 So. 2d 193 (Fla. 1965); ABA Model Rule for Lawyer Disciplinary Enforcement 22E] Under this view, sister states are free to impose their own sanctions for the misconduct.

b. Federal Courts

Each federal court in which a lawyer is admitted to practice must make an independent evaluation of the lawyer's conduct. [Theard v. United States, 354 U.S. 278 (1957)] The fact that a lawyer has been disciplined by a state, however, is competent evidence in a federal proceeding and may in itself be sufficient to convince a federal court to impose a similar sanction. [*See In re* Rhodes, 370 F.2d 411 (8th Cir. 1967)]

6. Disability Proceedings

A lawyer who is incapacitated by an impairment such as substance abuse poses a particular risk of harm to clients, the public, and legal institutions. Most jurisdictions have disability proceedings, which result in the disabled lawyer's suspension from practice until she can show that rehabilitation has occurred. The procedures followed are generally the same as those of disciplinary proceedings, but provision may be made for psychiatric evaluation and diversion into a rehabilitation program. [Restatement of the Law (Third) Governing Lawyers (hereinafter "Restatement") ch. 1, topic 2, tit. C, introductory note]

D. UNAUTHORIZED PRACTICE AND MULTI-JURISDICTIONAL PRACTICE

The rule against unauthorized practice of law has two prongs: (i) a lawyer is subject to discipline for practicing in a jurisdiction where she is not admitted to practice, and (ii) a lawyer is subject to discipline for assisting a nonlawyer to engage in the unlicensed practice of law. [ABA Model Rule 5.5(a)]

1. Unauthorized Practice by Lawyer

A lawyer who is admitted to practice law in one jurisdiction is not, without more, authorized to practice in any other jurisdiction. A lawyer is subject to discipline for practicing in a jurisdiction where she is not admitted to practice. [ABA Model Rule 5.5(a)] Except as allowed by that jurisdiction's laws or ethics rules, the unadmitted lawyer must not: (i) represent that she is admitted to practice in that jurisdiction, or (ii) establish an office or other systematic or continuous presence for the practice of law in that jurisdiction. [ABA Model Rule 5.5(b)]

2. Permissible Types of Temporary Multi-Jurisdictional Practice

The nature of modern law and commerce requires many lawyers to practice across state lines. ABA Model Rule 5.5(c) recognizes this fact and provides that if a lawyer is admitted to practice in one state, and is not disbarred or suspended from practice in any state, then she may provide legal services in a second state *on a temporary basis* in four situations:

a. Association with Local Lawyer

A lawyer may practice on a temporary basis in a state in which she is not admitted if she associates a local lawyer who ***actively participates*** in the matter. [ABA Model Rule 5.5(c)(1)]

Example: Attorney A is admitted to practice in State One only, and she works for a law firm that regularly represents a nationwide labor union. The union is trying to organize workers in State Two, and A is sent there to give legal advice to the union's organizers. With the union's consent, A associates local labor lawyer L and rents a temporary office near L's office. L works actively with A in handling legal problems arising from the union's organizing efforts. A's temporary practice in State Two is proper.

b.   Special Permission to Practice in Local Tribunal

An out-of-state lawyer may request special permission from a local court, administrative agency, or other tribunal to handle a matter in that tribunal. [ABA Model Rule 5.5(c)(2)] In a court, such permission is commonly called admission "pro hac vice," which means admission for purposes of this matter only. (The rules of many states require the out-of-state lawyer to associate local counsel as a condition of pro hac vice admission.) An out-of-state lawyer who reasonably expects to be admitted pro hac vice may engage in preliminary activities in the state, such as meeting with clients, reviewing documents, and interviewing witnesses.

Example: Toxic tort lawyer L is admitted to practice in Oklahoma only. He has been retained by three Oklahoma clients to bring a class action on behalf of persons injured by a herbicide manufactured by a California defendant. L plans to file the class action in a California state court, and he reasonably expects to be admitted pro hac vice to handle the case in that court. It would be proper for L to take a two-week trip to California to interview other potential class representatives, even though he has not yet filed the case in California or been admitted pro hac vice.

c.   Mediation or Arbitration Arising Out of Practice in Home State

A lawyer may mediate, arbitrate, or engage in another form of alternative dispute resolution in a state in which she is not admitted to practice if her services arise out of, or are reasonably related to, her practice in the state in which she is admitted. [ABA Model Rule 5.5(c)(3)]

Example: Attorney A is admitted to practice in State One only. She represents a State One client in a contract dispute, and the contract states that all such disputes will be submitted to arbitration in State Two. It is proper for A to represent her client in the State Two arbitration, and the same would be true of a mediation or other form of alternative dispute resolution.

d.   Other Temporary Practice Arising Out of Practice in Home State

ABA Model Rule 5.5(c)(4) is a catch-all category that permits a lawyer to temporarily practice out of state if the lawyer's out-of-state practice is reasonably related to the lawyer's home-state practice.

Example: Lawyer L is admitted to practice in State One only. He represents a State One client that buys up and revitalizes run-down shopping centers. That client asks L to travel to State Two to negotiate with the owner of a State Two shopping center, and to draft a purchase agreement that will satisfy the owner and that will be valid under the law of State Two. It would be proper for L to render those services in State Two.

3. Permissible Types of Permanent Multi-Jurisdictional Practice

A lawyer who is admitted in one jurisdiction, and who is not disbarred or suspended from practice in any jurisdiction, may open a law office and establish a systematic and continuous practice in a different jurisdiction in two narrowly limited situations:

a. Lawyers Employed by Their Only Client

Some lawyers are salaried employees of their only client, *e.g.*, in-house corporate lawyers and lawyers employed by the government. They may set up a permanent office to render legal services to their employer in a state in which they are not admitted to practice, but if they want to *litigate* a matter in that state, they must seek admission pro hac vice. [ABA Model Rule 5.5(d)(1)]

Example: Attorney A is admitted to practice in Maryland and Virginia. She is employed by General Motors ("GM"), which assigns her to be the legal advisor in the GM office in Idaho. A need not be admitted to practice in Idaho, but if she wants to represent GM in a suit pending in an Idaho court, she must seek admission pro hac vice.

b. Legal Services Authorized by Federal or Local Law

In rare instances, federal or local law authorizes a lawyer to practice a restricted branch of law in a state in which he is not otherwise admitted to practice. [ABA Model Rule 5.5(d)(2)]

Example: Lawyer L is admitted to practice law in New York, and he is admitted to prosecute patents in the United States Patent and Trademark Office, which is located in Washington, D.C. When L "retired" and moved to Florida, he did not become a member of the Florida bar; rather, he set up a Florida practice that is limited to patent prosecution in the Patent and Trademark Office. L does not handle other patent matters, such as patent licensing or patent infringement, and he does not practice any other kind of law. L's restricted practice in Florida is proper. [*See* Sperry v. Florida, 373 U.S. 379 (1963)]

4. Consequences of Multi-Jurisdictional Practice

A lawyer who is admitted to practice in one state only, but who practices in another state pursuant to 2. or 3., above, will be subject to the disciplinary rules of both states. [ABA Model Rule 8.5(a); Comment 19 to ABA Model Rule 5.5] Furthermore, an in-house or government lawyer who practices under 3.a., above, may be subject to the second state's client security assessments and continuing legal education requirements. [Comment 1 to ABA Model Rule 5.5]

5. Unauthorized Practice by Nonlawyers

A person not admitted to practice as a lawyer must not engage in the unauthorized practice of law, and a lawyer must not assist such a person to do so. [ABA Model Rule 5.5(a); Restatement §4]

a. **General Considerations in Defining "Practice of Law"**
Important considerations in determining whether the practice of law is involved include: (i) whether the activity involves legal *knowledge and skill* beyond that which the average layperson possesses; (ii) whether the activity constitutes advice or services concerning *binding legal rights* or remedies; and (iii) whether the activity is one *traditionally* performed by lawyers. [ABA, Annotated Model Rule of Professional Conduct 5.5, p. 455 (4th ed. 1999)]

1) **Activities Constituting Law Practice**
Examples of activities that courts have found constitute law practice when done on behalf of another include: appearing in judicial proceedings; engaging in settlement negotiations; and drafting documents that affect substantial legal rights or obligations (*e.g.*, contracts, wills, trusts). Preparing an estate plan is generally considered the province of lawyers, and some courts have also held that nonlawyer clinics on how to obtain a low-cost divorce constitute unauthorized practice.

2) **Activities Not Constituting Law Practice**
There are some activities that a nonlawyer may undertake that do not constitute the practice of law. For example, state and federal agencies often permit nonlawyers, such as accountants, to appear before them representing clients. Also, while nonlawyers may not draft legal documents, they can act as scriveners, filling in the blanks on standard forms. Thus, real estate brokers, title insurance companies, and escrow companies are usually permitted to fill in the blanks on standard documents related to the sale of real property. Nonlawyers can also publish books or pamphlets offering general advice, including most do-it-yourself books and kits.

3) **Tax Advice**
Giving advice on tax *law* would probably constitute the unauthorized practice of law, but an accountant or other layperson may prepare tax returns and answer questions incidental to the preparation of the returns.

b. **Consequences of Unauthorized Practice**
A nonlawyer who engages in the unauthorized practice of law is subject to several sanctions, including injunction, contempt, and criminal conviction. [Restatement §4, comment a] A lawyer who assists in such an endeavor is subject to professional discipline.

c. **Delegating Work to Nonlawyer Assistants**
The rule stated above does not, of course, prohibit a lawyer from delegating tasks to a paralegal, law clerk, student intern, or other such person. But the lawyer must *supervise* the delegated work carefully and must be *ultimately responsible* for the results. [Comment 2 to ABA Model Rule 5.5]

Example: Paralegal P is working under attorney A's supervision on a complex real estate transaction. P may write and sign letters on the law firm letterhead to make routine requests for information from banks, mortgage companies, and governmental agencies, provided that P indicates that she is a paralegal, not a lawyer. But P should not sign letters to clients, adversaries, opposing counsel, or tribunals; she may draft such letters, but they should be approved and signed by A. That helps assure that A is properly supervising P's work. [New Jersey Op. 611 (1988)]

d. Training Nonlawyers for Law-Related Work
A lawyer may advise and instruct nonlawyers whose employment requires a knowledge of the law—*e.g.,* claims adjusters, bank trust officers, social workers, accountants, and government employees. [Comment 3 to ABA Model Rule 5.5]

e. Helping Persons Appear Pro Se
A lawyer may advise persons who wish to appear on their own behalf in a legal matter. [*Id.*]

Example: Client C asked attorney A to represent her in a dispute with her landlord concerning the stopped-up plumbing in her apartment. After hearing C's explanation, A advised C that she would be able to handle the matter herself in small claims court at far less expense. A instructed C on how to obtain the proper forms for small claims court and gave her general advice on what facts to gather and how to prove her case. A's conduct is proper.

f. Assisting a Suspended or Disbarred Lawyer
A lawyer violates ABA Model Rule 5.5(a) if he assists a lawyer whose license has been suspended or revoked in practicing law. It is proper to hire a suspended or disbarred lawyer to do work that a layperson is permitted to do, but the suspended or disbarred lawyer must not be permitted to do any work that constitutes the practice of law.

II. THE LAWYER-CLIENT RELATIONSHIP—GENERAL POINTS

A. NATURE OF THE RELATIONSHIP
The relationship between a lawyer and client is contractual. The terms of that contract are generally implied by custom, but for the most part can be varied by mutual agreement. The lawyer operates as both the client's fiduciary and agent, with the duties and limitations of those designations. For example, because the lawyer is considered a fiduciary, the contract between the lawyer and client will be construed against the lawyer and closely scrutinized for fairness. Similarly, the lawyer is subject to the limitations imposed by the laws of agency.

B. CREATING THE LAWYER-CLIENT RELATIONSHIP
In lore, although perhaps not in fact, an English barrister has an ethical duty to take any case offered upon tender of a proper fee. [Wolfram, Modern Legal Ethics §10.2.2 (1986)] In contrast, lawyers in the United States are generally free to refuse service to any person for any reason. A lawyer-client relationship arises when:

(i)   A person manifests an intent that the lawyer provide legal services and the lawyer *agrees*;

(ii) A person manifests an intent to have the lawyer represent him, the lawyer fails to make clear that he does not want to undertake the representation, and the lawyer knows or should know that the prospective client is *reasonably relying* on the lawyer to provide the services; or

(iii) A tribunal *appoints* a lawyer to represent a client.

[Restatement §14]

1. **Implied Assent and Reasonable Reliance**

The lawyer's assent is implied when he fails to clearly decline representation and the prospective client reasonably relies on the representation. The reasonableness of the reliance is a question of fact.

Examples: 1) Client Carla writes a letter to attorney Aida, asking Aida to represent her in a personal injury case. Aida never responds to the letter. One year later, the statute of limitations expires on Carla's claim, and she sues Aida for malpractice for failing to file the suit. Here, there was no attorney-client relationship. Although Aida did not expressly decline the representation, it was unreasonable for Carla to rely on Aida's representation based on an unanswered letter. [*See* Restatement §14, illus. 3]

2) Client Casey calls lawyer Lisa's office asking that Lisa represent him in a court proceeding relating to his arrest for driving under the influence ("DUI"). Lisa is out of the office. Casey tells Lisa's secretary that he understands that Lisa handles many DUI cases and hopes that she will take the case even though the court date is only 10 days away. The secretary tells Casey to send over all papers relevant to the proceeding. She does not tell him that Lisa will decide whether to take the case only after reviewing the papers. One day before Casey's court date, Lisa phones Casey and declines to represent him. Here, it would likely be found that an attorney-client relationship existed because Casey's reliance was reasonable. Lisa regularly handled DUI cases, her agent responded to his request for help by asking him to send the papers, and the imminence of the hearing made it appropriate for Lisa to decline while there was still time for Casey to get another lawyer. [Restatement §14, illus. 4]

2. **Court Appointments**

Trial and appellate courts often find it necessary to appoint lawyers to represent indigent clients and clients with unpopular causes. ABA Model Rule 6.2 provides that a lawyer must not seek to avoid such an appointment except for good cause. Examples of good cause are stated below.

a. **Violation of Law or Disciplinary Rule**

A lawyer must decline a court appointment if to accept it would require the lawyer to violate a law or disciplinary rule. [ABA Model Rule 6.2(a)]

Example: When attorney A was a deputy public defender, he represented client Q in an aggravated assault case, and he learned a great deal of confidential information about Q's life and criminal background. Later, A entered private practice, and the local court appointed him to defend D, who was charged with the attempted murder of Q. The confidential information A obtained from Q is highly relevant to the defense of D. (*See* V.C., *infra.*) A must therefore decline the appointment to defend D.

b. **Unreasonable Financial Burden**

A lawyer may seek to be excused from an appointment if to accept it would impose an unreasonable financial burden on the lawyer. [ABA Model Rule 6.2(b)]

Example: The Supreme Court of West Dakota appointed lawyer L to represent D in the appeal of D's conviction and death sentence for three murders. The trial of D's case lasted 13 months and resulted in a trial record in excess of 150,000 pages. To handle the appeal properly, L would be required to work at least 600 hours. The West Dakota legislature has set legal fees at a paltry $17 per hour for appellate counsel in death penalty cases. L is a struggling solo practitioner and will not be able to support his family if he is required to take that much time away from his regular clients. L may seek to be excused from the supreme court appointment.

c.   Personal Inability to Represent Client Effectively
A lawyer may seek to be excused from a court appointment if the lawyer finds the client or the cause so repugnant that the lawyer-client relationship would be impaired or the lawyer could not represent the client effectively. [ABA Model Rule 6.2(c)]

Example: The trial court appointed attorney A to defend accused child molester M. As a young boy, A himself was molested by a similar person, and A finds that he cannot even look comfortably at M, much less represent him zealously. A may seek to be excused from the court appointment.

3.   Duty to Reject Certain Cases
A lawyer must refuse employment in the following situations:

a.   Client's Motive Is Harassment
A lawyer is subject to discipline for bringing an action, conducting a defense, asserting a position, or taking other steps if the client's motive is to harass or maliciously injure any person. [ABA Model Rule 4.4(a)] Thus, a lawyer must reject any case where he believes this is the prospective client's motive.

b.   Unsupportable Factual or Legal Position
A lawyer who is serving as an advocate in a legal proceeding must not take a position that is either factually or legally frivolous. [ABA Model Rule 3.1] A position is not frivolous if the lawyer can make a good faith argument that the facts are as claimed or that the present law should be changed. A position also is not frivolous merely because the lawyer does not have all the facts at hand at the outset, but expects to develop them during discovery. Note that in a criminal case, the defense lawyer may defend his client to the extent allowed by constitutional law even if the defense would otherwise violate this rule. [Comments 1 - 3 to ABA Model Rule 3.1; *and see* VIII.A.2., *infra*]

c.   Lawyer Not Competent
A lawyer must reject a case if he is too busy or too inexperienced to handle the matter competently. [ABA Model Rule 1.1]

d.   Strong Personal Feelings
If a lawyer's personal feelings about a case are so strong that they would impair his ability to effectively represent the client, he must refuse the case. [ABA Model Rules 1.16(a)(1), 1.7(a)(2)]

e.   Impaired Mental or Physical Condition
A lawyer must decline a case if his mental or physical condition would materially impair his ability to represent the client. [ABA Model Rule 1.16(a)(2)]

4.   Duties Owed to Prospective Client
When a person discusses with a lawyer the possibility of forming a lawyer-client relationship,

and no such relationship ensues, the lawyer has a duty to: (i) protect the prospective client's confidential information, which includes declining to represent other clients in the same or a related matter if the confidential information would be harmful to the prospective client; (ii) protect any property the prospective client has given to the lawyer; and (iii) use reasonable care in giving the person any legal advice, such as whether the claim has merit, whether conflicts of interest exist, and when the action must be commenced. [Restatement §15]

5. Ethical Obligation to Accept Unpopular Cases
Lawyers have an ethical obligation to help make legal service available to all who need it. A lawyer can fulfill this obligation by accepting a *fair share* of unpopular matters or indigent or unpopular clients. [Comment 1 to ABA Model Rule 6.2]

C.   ATTORNEYS' FEES
The nature and amount of an attorney's fee are subjects for contractual agreement between the attorney and the client (except when the fee is set by statute or court order). In theory, the attorney and client bargain at arm's length over the fee, but in practice many clients are inexperienced with attorneys' fees. Thus, in fee disputes, courts strain to give the benefit of the doubt to the client. [*See, e.g.,* Terzis v. Estate of Whalen, 489 A.2d 608 (N.H. 1985); with respect to fee setting in general, *see* Restatement §§34 - 43]

1. When to Agree on Fee
When a lawyer has not regularly represented the client, the basis or rate of the fee and the expenses for which the client will be responsible must be communicated to the client, preferably in writing, before or within a reasonable time after commencing the representation. [ABA Model Rule 1.5(b)]

Examples: 1) At the close of her first appointment with a new client, attorney A gave the client a simple written memorandum. The memorandum explained that her fee would be calculated at $175 per hour, and that the number of hours could not be predicted with certainty but would probably be about 100. Later, when the matter proved more difficult than A had anticipated, A gave the client a supplemental memorandum that doubled the estimated number of hours. A handled the fee issue properly under the ABA Model Rules.

2) At the end of his third appointment with lawyer L, a new client asked how L planned to charge him for the work. L responded: "In a matter of this nature, it's simply impossible to tell you in advance what the fee will be. But you have my assurance that it will be a fair fee." L's conduct is a disciplinary violation under ABA Model Rule 1.5(b).

2. Discipline for Unreasonable Fee
A court will not enforce a contract for an unreasonably high attorney's fee or an unreasonably high amount for expenses, and the attorney is subject to discipline for trying to exact such a fee or expenses. [ABA Model Rule 1.5(a)]

a. Factors
The factors considered in determining the reasonableness of a fee are:

(i)   The *time and labor* required;

(ii) The *novelty and difficulty* of the questions involved;

(iii) The *skill* needed to perform the legal services properly;

(iv) The likelihood, if apparent to the client, that *the work for this client will preclude the lawyer from doing fee-paying work for others*;

(v) The *fee customarily charged* in the locality for similar legal work;

(vi) The *amount at stake and the results obtained* for the client;

(vii) The *time limitations* imposed by the client or the circumstances;

(viii) The *nature and length of the relationship* between the lawyer and the client;

(ix) The *experience, reputation, and ability of the lawyer* performing the services; and

(x) Whether the fee is *fixed or contingent* (a contingent fee can be higher because it requires the lawyer to take a gamble).

[ABA Model Rule 1.5(a)]

b. **Items that May and May Not Be Billed**
The attorney must disclose the basis on which a client will be charged for legal services and expenses, and the attorney's bill should clearly show how the amount due has been computed. The attorney must not charge the client for ordinary overhead expenses associated with staffing, equipping, and running the attorney's office, but the attorney may charge the client for the *actual cost to the attorney* of special services such as photocopying, long distance calls, computer research, special deliveries, secretarial overtime, and the like. [Restatement §38(3)(a)] Alternatively, the attorney may charge a reasonable amount to which the client has agreed in advance. [Comment 1 to ABA Model Rule 1.5] The attorney must not charge the client more than her actual cost for services provided by third parties, such as court reporters, travel agents, and expert witnesses. Furthermore, the attorney must not "double bill" her time. [*See* ABA Formal Op. 93-379 (1993)]

Example: Attorney spends three hours working on client A's case while flying on an airplane to take depositions in client B's case. Attorney must not bill B for three hours of travel time if she elects to bill A for three hours of work time. She may charge either one or the other for the full three hours, or she may divide the time ratably between the two clients.

3. **Collecting and Financing Attorneys' Fees**

a. **Payment in Advance**
A lawyer may require her fee to be paid in advance, but she must refund any unearned part of the advance if she is fired or withdraws. [ABA Model Rule 1.16(d); Comment 4 to ABA Model Rule 1.5; *and see* F.5., *infra*] Be careful to distinguish a true retainer fee from a payment of a fee in advance. A true retainer fee is money that is paid solely to ensure the availability of the lawyer, and the lawyer who is fired or withdraws generally need not refund the retainer fee.

Examples: 1) XYZ Oil Company pays the A & B environmental defense firm a monthly retainer fee of $1,000 simply to be available to represent XYZ in the case of an oil spill. The retainer fee agreement provides that the $1,000 per month will not be credited against hours spent on XYZ's legal work. This is a true retainer fee. If the A & B firm withdraws or is fired from a particular case, it may keep the retainer payments provided: (i) the retainer amount was reasonable, and (ii) it has not violated the retainer agreement.

2) Lawyer L agreed to represent client C in a divorce case for $100 per hour. L's written fee contract with C provided that C would pay L a $2,500 "nonrefundable retainer" and that the retainer would be "credited against C's charges." C fired L after L did $1,000 worth of work on the case, but L refused to refund any part of the retainer. L must refund $1,500 to C; the fee contract does not clearly explain the meaning of "nonrefundable retainer," and it ought to be construed against L, who drafted it. [*See* Jacobson v. Sassower, 66 N.Y.2d 991 (1985)]

b. Property for Services

A lawyer may accept property in return for services (*e.g.,* an ownership interest in a business), provided that this does not involve a proprietary interest in the cause of action or subject of litigation contrary to ABA Model Rule 1.8(i) (*see* V.C.8., *infra*). Such an arrangement is also subject to scrutiny as a conflict of interest because it may be a business transaction between the lawyer and the client. [Comment 4 to ABA Model Rule 1.5]

c. Cutting Off Services

A lawyer must not make a fee agreement that could curtail services in the middle of the relationship and thus put the client at a bargaining disadvantage. [Comment 5 to ABA Model Rule 1.5]

Example: Attorney A agreed to defend client D in a drug smuggling case. A clause buried in the middle of A's wordy fee agreement provides that all work must be paid for in advance. D paid A $2,000 in advance. In the middle of preparation for trial, A told D that the original advance was used up and that if D did not advance more money, the work would stop. A's conduct is not proper. [*Id.*; *and see* State v. Mayes, 531 P.2d 102 (Kan. 1975)]

d. Credit Arrangements and Security

A lawyer may permit the client to pay a legal fee by credit card [ABA Formal Op. 00-419 (2000)], and a lawyer may participate in a bar association program that enables clients to finance fees through bank loans. A lawyer may also take an interest-bearing promissory note from a client to secure the payment of fees. [*See* Hulland v. State Bar, 8 Cal. 3d 440 (1972)] When permitted by local law, a lawyer may use a statutory, common law, or contractual attorney's lien to secure the payment of a fee. [ABA Model Rule 1.8(i)(1)]

4. Contingent Fees

Under a contingent fee agreement, the lawyer collects a fee only if the matter is resolved in the client's favor. Often, the fee is expressed as a percentage of the client's eventual recovery in the case. However, a contingent fee need not be a percentage of the amount recovered; an otherwise proper contingent fee may still be proper even if there is no *res*, or pool of money, from which the fee can be paid. Contingent fees are regarded as unethical in some common law countries, but they are tolerated in the United States. Critics contend that they stir up litigation, encourage excessive fees, and give the lawyer an unprofessional stake in the outcome of the case. Proponents reply that only through a contingent fee arrangement can a client of modest means afford to litigate a claim. Some states have set statutory limits on the contingent fee percentages a lawyer can exact in personal injury, medical malpractice, and similar types of cases.

a. When Contingent Fee Prohibited

1) Criminal Cases
A lawyer is subject to discipline for using a contingent fee arrangement when defending a person in a criminal case. [ABA Model Rule 1.5(d)(2)]

2) Domestic Relations Cases
A lawyer is also subject to discipline for using a contingent fee in a domestic relations case when the contingency is based on the securing of a divorce, the amount of alimony or support, or the amount of a property settlement. [ABA Model Rule 1.5(d)(1); *see also* Restatement §35, comment g] However, a lawyer may use a contingent fee in a suit to recover money that is *past due* under an alimony or support decree. [Comment 6 to ABA Model Rule 1.5]

Example: Lawyer L agreed to represent W in a marital dissolution case in exchange for 10% of the amount to be received by W as a property settlement. The arrangement would subject L to discipline.

b. Contingent Fee Must Be Reasonable
A contingent fee must be reasonable in amount; moreover, a lawyer must not use a contingent fee when the facts of the case make it unreasonable to do so. [Comment 3 to ABA Model Rule 1.5]

Example: Client C asked lawyer L to represent her as plaintiff in a medical malpractice case. Liability was clear, the damages were large, and the defendants were affluent. The case was a clear winner, and L knew that he could settle it with only a few hours of work. Nonetheless, L signed C up to a 33⅓% contingent fee agreement. After two hours of work, L arranged a lucrative settlement that C accepted. It was unreasonable for L to use a contingent fee agreement in the first place, and it would be unreasonable for L to collect one-third of the settlement proceeds. [*See* Comment 3 to ABA Model Rule 1.5]

c. Writing Requirement for Contingent Fee Agreements
A contingent fee agreement must be in a writing signed by the client, and the writing must state:

(i)   How the fee is to be *calculated,* including the percentage that the lawyer will get if the case is settled before trial, won after trial, or won after appeal;

(ii) What *litigation and other expenses* are to be *deducted* from the recovery;

(iii) Whether *deductions for expenses* will be made *before or after* the contingent fee is calculated; and

(iv) What *expenses the client must pay*, whether or not she wins the case.

At the *end* of a contingent fee case, the lawyer must give the client a written statement showing the outcome of the case, the remittance to the client, and how the remittance was calculated. [ABA Model Rule 1.5(c)]

5. Fee Disputes

a. In General
In seeking compensation from a client, a lawyer may not employ collection methods forbidden by law, improperly use confidential information, or harass a client. [Restatement §41]

b. Remedies

1) Liens
In addition to filing a lawsuit to recover their fees, lawyers have several remedies if a client refuses to pay all or a portion of a fee. Most states recognize a common law or statutory charging lien, under which any recovery obtained for the client serves as security for the lawyer's fees. Even states that do not recognize a charging lien usually recognize such a lien if created by the lawyer and client's express agreement. [3 A.L.R.2d 148 (1949)] Many states also permit the lawyer to exercise a retaining lien, under which he can retain documents, funds, and property of the client until his fee is paid, but there is a strong minority view contra.

2) Retention of Funds in Trust Account
If a lawyer receives funds on behalf of a client from which his fee is to be paid (*e.g.,* a settlement check), and the client disputes the amount of his fee, the lawyer may retain the *disputed* amount in a client trust account (VI.B.2.c., *infra*) until the dispute is resolved. [ABA Model Rule 1.15(e)]

3) Arbitration or Mediation
Bar associations in many jurisdictions have established arbitration or mediation services to help lawyers resolve fee disputes with their clients. Comment 9 to ABA Model Rule 1.5 urges lawyers to use these services when they are available.
Example: Lawyer L's standard retainer agreement includes a provision that requires arbitration of both fee disputes and legal malpractice claims. The agreement is proper, provided that it is clear and that L's clients truly understand its ramifications. [District of Columbia Bar Op. 190 (1988)]

6. Fee Splitting with Other Lawyers
As a general rule, a lawyer must not split a legal fee with another lawyer. The rule is designed to prevent lawyers from becoming "client brokers" and to discourage excessive fees. The general rule is subject to three exceptions.

a. Lawyers Within a Firm

The partners and associates within a law firm may, of course, pool and split legal fees—that is the essence of practice in a law firm.

b. Separation and Retirement Agreements

A law firm may make payments to a former partner or associate under a separation or retirement agreement.

Example: The partnership agreement of the P, D & Q law firm provides that when partner Q retires, the firm will pay her monthly benefits equal to 30% of Q's average monthly billings during the year prior to her retirement. The arrangement is proper.

c. Certain Splits with Lawyers Outside Firm

Sometimes two or more lawyers from different firms work together on a case. ABA Model Rule 1.5(e) permits them to submit a single bill to the client, and then to split the fee, *if* the following conditions are met:

(i) The total fee is *reasonable*;

(ii) The split is *in proportion to the services performed by each lawyer*, or some different proportion if *each lawyer assumes joint responsibility* for the matter; and

(iii) The *client agrees to the split in a writing that discloses the share each lawyer will receive*.

Example: In a complex corporate tender offer matter that involves both antitrust and securities law issues, lawyers from three firms join forces to represent Grundy, Inc. Lawyers from firm A will do whatever courtroom work needs to be done. Lawyers from firm B will do the out-of-court work on the antitrust issues, and lawyers from firm C will do the out-of-court work on the securities law issues. The three firms do not agree to assume joint responsibility for the matter, but they agree to send Grundy, Inc. a single bill and to divide the proceeds in proportion to the work done by each firm. Grundy, Inc. is advised of the arrangement and consents to it in writing. Assuming that the total fee is reasonable, the arrangement is proper.

7. Forwarding or Referral Fees

Referral of cases between lawyers is common, for instance, when the referring lawyer is too busy to handle a case or does not feel competent to handle a case. ABA Model Rule 7.2(b) prohibits a lawyer from paying anyone—including another lawyer—for recommending him or referring a matter to him. Furthermore, ABA Model Rule 1.5(e) does not permit fee splitting with a referring lawyer who neither assumes responsibility for a matter nor does work on the matter (*see* 6.c., above). A lawyer may, however, set up a "reciprocal referral" arrangement with another lawyer or with a nonlawyer professional in which each person agrees to refer clients or customers to the other. The arrangement must not be exclusive, and the lawyer's client must be informed of the existence and nature of the arrangement. [ABA

Model Rule 7.2 and Comment 8] These reciprocal referral arrangements are discussed further in XII.B.3.e., *infra*.

D. SCOPE OF REPRESENTATION

The scope and objectives of a lawyer's representation of a client may be defined and limited by agreement between the lawyer and client. In the absence of an agreement to the contrary, a lawyer should pursue a client's objectives in all reasonably available legal ways. However, a lawyer must not advise or assist a client to commit a crime or fraud, but a lawyer may discuss the legal consequences of a proposed course of action with the client. [ABA Model Rule 1.2(d)] Furthermore, a lawyer may help the client determine the validity, scope, and meaning of a law. [*Id.*] A lawyer also may take actions that are ***impliedly authorized*** to carry out the representation. [ABA Model Rule 1.2(a)]

1. Decisions to Be Made by Client

When a client brings a legal problem to a lawyer, it is the client who must decide what shall be the objectives of the lawyer's work. Thus, it is the client who must make the key decisions that affect the client's substantial legal rights. A lawyer must therefore abide by the client's decision regarding the following matters:

(i)   Whether to accept a ***settlement offer***;

(ii)   What ***plea*** to enter in a criminal case;

(iii) Whether to ***waive a jury trial*** in a criminal case;

(iv)   Whether the client will ***testify*** in a criminal case; and

(v)   Whether to ***appeal***.

[ABA Model Rule 1.2(a); Restatement §22(1)]

Examples: 1) Lawyer L agrees to represent C on a contingent fee basis in C's suit against D for slander. L's fee agreement provides that the suit cannot be settled before trial without L's consent. L is subject to discipline. The decision to settle a suit is made by the client, not the lawyer—even in a contingent fee case. [*See* ABA Model Rule 1.2(a)]

2) Attorney A is defending B in a burglary case. A has carefully advised B about the legal and practical consequences of pleading not guilty, waiving a jury trial, and testifying on his own behalf. Having done that, A must now allow B to make the final decision on those three vital issues. [*Id.*]

2. Limits on Lawyer's Responsibility and Authority

A lawyer may limit the scope of the representation if the limitation is reasonable under the circumstances, and if the client gives informed consent. For example, a lawyer might agree to counsel her client about a dispute with the client's landlord, but stipulate that if the dispute has to be arbitrated or litigated, the client will hire another lawyer for that purpose. [ABA Model Rule 1.2(c) and Comment 7]

a. Disagreements Between Lawyer and Client

Lawyers and clients sometimes disagree about the means to be used to reach the client's objectives. Clients normally defer to their lawyers about issues of law, tactics, and strategy. Conversely, lawyers normally defer to their clients about questions of expense and concern for third persons who might be affected by a legal tactic. A lawyer and client should try to resolve their disagreements, but if they cannot, the lawyer may withdraw or the client may fire the lawyer. [*See* ABA Model Rule 1.16(a)(3), (b)(4)]

b. Telling the Client "No"
When a lawyer discovers that her client expects assistance that violates a law or legal ethics rule, the lawyer must explain why she cannot do what the client expects. If the client insists on the lawyer's assistance in violating the law or ethics rule, the lawyer *must* withdraw. [ABA Model Rule 1.16(a)(1)]

c. Discovering a Client's Illegal Conduct
When a lawyer discovers that a client has begun an illegal course of action and the action is continuing, the lawyer must not assist in the wrongdoing, *e.g.,* by drafting fraudulent documents or suggesting how the wrongdoing can be concealed. [ABA Model Rule 1.2(d) and Comment 10] In this situation, the lawyer *must* withdraw. [ABA Model Rule 1.16(a)(1)] Sometimes withdrawal alone is not enough—the lawyer may have to make a "noisy withdrawal" in which she gives outsiders notice of her withdrawal and disaffirms any of her prior opinions, documents, affirmations, or the like that the client is using to carry out the wrongdoing. [Comment 10 to ABA Model Rule 1.2] The lawyer's noisy withdrawal may put the client's victim on guard, but that is permissible (and probably praiseworthy). [*See also* ABA Model Rule 4.1(b) and Comment 3—concerning disclosure of confidential information]

3. Client with Diminished Capacity

a. Lawyer's Duties
Normally, it is assumed that a client can make decisions about important matters, but if the client is a minor or has diminished mental capacity, that may not be true. Nevertheless, such a client may be able to make some kinds of decisions that affect her own well-being. For example, even very young children can have valuable opinions about who should have custody of them. Similarly, even very old clients can handle routine financial matters, although they may need legal protection concerning major transactions. The lawyer has a duty, so far as reasonably possible, to maintain a normal lawyer-client relationship with the client. [ABA Model Rule 1.14(a) and Comment 1] The lawyer must treat the client with attention and respect. Even if the client has a guardian or other representative, the lawyer should, so far as possible, treat the client as a client, particularly in communicating with the client about significant developments. [Comment 2 to ABA Model Rule 1.14]

b. Protective Action and Appointment of Guardian
When the client has diminished capacity and faces a substantial risk of physical, financial, or other harm, the lawyer may take reasonable actions to protect the client. These actions include consulting with people or entities that can protect the client, and, when appropriate, seeking the appointment of a guardian or similar surrogate. [ABA Model Rule 1.14(b)] When taking protective action, the lawyer has implied authority to

reveal the client's confidential information, but only to the extent necessary to protect the client. [ABA Model Rule 1.14(c)]

> *Example:* For many years, lawyer L has represented widower W in personal and business matters. Now W's physical and mental condition make it unsafe for him to continue living alone in the old family home, and he has no close relatives or friends to assist him. L may search out suitable living quarters for W, where eating facilities and medical help are close at hand. To the extent possible, L should involve W in making the decision to move. If L reasonably believes that W needs a conservator, she may seek to have one appointed; in the appointment process, she may, if necessary, disclose confidential information about W's condition. After a conservator is appointed, L should still treat W as her client, consulting with him, keeping him advised of developments, and allowing him to make all decisions of which he is capable.

4. Emergency Legal Assistance to Nonclient with Seriously Diminished Capacity

When a person with seriously diminished capacity faces *imminent and irreparable harm* to her health, safety, or financial interest, a lawyer may take legal action on her behalf, despite her inability to establish a lawyer-client relationship or to make or express considered judgments about the matter. However, the lawyer cannot act until the person (or someone acting on her behalf) has consulted the lawyer, and the lawyer should not act unless he reasonably believes the person has no other representative available. Any action undertaken should be limited to that which is reasonably necessary to avoid imminent and irreparable harm. [Comment 9 to ABA Model Rule 1.14]

a. Lawyer's Duties

A lawyer who represents a person in such emergency circumstances has the same duties as he would with respect to a client. [*Id.*] In an emergency situation, confidences may be disclosed only to the extent necessary to accomplish the intended protective action. The lawyer should disclose the nature of his relationship with the person to any tribunal or counsel involved in the matter. Furthermore, steps should be taken to regularize the relationship as soon as possible. [Comment 10 to ABA Model Rule 1.14]

b. No Compensation for Lawyer

Normally, a lawyer would not seek compensation for emergency actions taken on behalf of a nonclient. [*Id.*]

E. COMMUNICATING WITH THE CLIENT

1. Matters that Require Informed Consent

The lawyer must promptly inform the client of any decision or circumstance that requires the client's *informed consent*. [ABA Model Rule 1.4(a)] "Informed consent" means that the client agrees to a proposed course of conduct after the lawyer has sufficiently explained the material risks and reasonable alternatives. [ABA Model Rule 1.0(e)]

> *Examples:* 1) ABA Model Rule 1.7(b) permits a lawyer, in defined circumstances, to represent two clients who have a concurrent conflict of interests. One prerequisite is that both clients give informed consent in writing. The lawyer must sufficiently explain the material risks and reasonable alternatives to both clients before they can give valid consent.

2) If an adversary offers to settle a civil case, or offers a plea bargain in a criminal case, the lawyer must promptly convey the offer to her client unless the client has previously instructed the lawyer that an offer on those terms is acceptable or unacceptable or has authorized the lawyer to accept or reject such an offer. [Comment 2 to ABA Model Rule 1.4]

2. Information About Status of the Matter and Means to Be Used

The lawyer must keep the client reasonably informed about the status of the matter [ABA Model Rule 1.4(a)(3)] and about the means by which the lawyer plans to accomplish the client's objectives [ABA Model Rule 1.4(a)(2)]. If the lawyer must make an immediate decision (such as whether to object to a line of questioning during a trial), the lawyer need not consult with the client before acting. [Comment 3 to ABA Model Rule 1.4] However, in less urgent situations, the lawyer should consult with the client before acting.

Example: Client C hired lawyer L to negotiate on C's behalf in a real estate dispute. C told L: "You have complete authority—just get the best deal you can." Despite the grant of broad authority, L should keep C advised of the progress of the negotiations. When there is time to do so, L should review the material issues with C before taking final action.

3. Request for Information

If the lawyer keeps the client properly informed of developments in the matter, the client will not often need to ask the lawyer for information. When a client does make a reasonable request for information, the lawyer must respond promptly. [ABA Model Rule 1.4(a)(4)] If that is impossible, then the lawyer or a member of her staff should acknowledge the client's request and tell the client when the information will be available. In particular, the client's telephone calls should be promptly returned or acknowledged because few things make clients more irate than having their telephone calls ignored.

4. Consultation About Illegal or Unethical Conduct

If the client expects the lawyer to do something that is either illegal or unethical, the lawyer must consult with the client and explain why he cannot do what the client wants. [ABA Model Rule 1.4(a)(5)]

Example: Attorney A is representing defendant D at a criminal trial. They expected to use an alibi defense based on the testimony of witness W, but the prosecution's case-in-chief proves beyond doubt that W's proposed testimony would be perjurious. In a recess before the defense's case-in-chief, D tells A to call W according to plan. A must explain to D why he cannot use W's testimony and must consult with D about an alternative defense strategy.

5. Special Circumstances

The amount and kind of information and explanations the lawyer should give to the client depend on the client's situation. If the client is young or has diminished capacity, the lawyer may have to do more explaining and assisting than if the client is an ordinary adult. [*See* ABA Model Rule 1.14; Comment 6 to ABA Model Rule 1.4] If the client is an organization or group, the lawyer should ordinarily communicate with the appropriate officer. [Comment 6 to ABA Model Rule 1.4] If the client and the lawyer have a regular, established relationship concerning many routine matters, the two of them may agree on a convenient arrangement for only limited or occasional reporting. [*Id.*]

Example: For many years, attorney A has done the routine collection work for a major bank. In a normal week, the bank sends A 20 to 30 new collection cases. Over the years, A and the bank have settled on a standard procedure for handling these cases. It would be proper for A and the bank to agree that A must report only major or unusual occurrences.

6. Withholding Information from Client

A lawyer may delay the transmission of information to a client if the client would be likely to react imprudently to an immediate communication. [Comment 7 to ABA Model Rule 1.4] The lawyer must not, however, withhold information to serve the lawyer's or a third person's interest or convenience. [*Id.*]

Example: Defendants D and E were charged with the felony murder of X, and they were granted separate trials. In the depths of despondency, D vowed to take his own life if E was convicted. That same day, E was convicted. D's lawyer may withhold that information from D until D is able to react to it more rationally.

a. Court Rule or Order

A court rule or order may forbid a lawyer from sharing certain information with a client, and the lawyer must comply with such a rule or order. [ABA Model Rule 3.4(c); Comment 7 to ABA Model Rule 1.4]

Example: In a patent infringement case, the patentee's lawyer demanded production of all of the defendant's laboratory operating manuals. The defendant complied with the demand and gave the patentee's lawyer the manuals. Subsequently, however, the defendant convinced the judge that the manuals contained valuable trade secrets, and the judge therefore issued a protective order forbidding the patentee's lawyer from sharing the information in the manuals with her client. Patentee's lawyer must either obey the order or use appropriate legal means to challenge its validity.

F. TERMINATING THE LAWYER-CLIENT RELATIONSHIP

Once established, the lawyer-client relationship ordinarily continues until the completion of the work for which the lawyer was hired. However, the relationship can end prematurely in any of three ways: (i) the client can *fire* the lawyer; (ii) in some situations, the lawyer *must* withdraw; and (iii) in some situations, the lawyer *may* withdraw. [*See* Restatement §32]

1. Client Fires Attorney

The client's complete trust is an essential part of any attorney-client relationship. The law thus allows the client to fire the attorney at any time, with or without just cause. [*See, e.g., Fracasse v. Brent,* 6 Cal. 3d 784 (1972)] Even if the client fires the attorney for no good reason, the client will not be held liable for breach of contract; for policy reasons, courts construe all attorney employment contracts as being terminable at will by the client. [*Id.*]

a. Client's Liability for Fees

When the client fires the attorney, the client is liable to the attorney in quantum meruit (an equitable action to avoid unjust enrichment) for the reasonable value of the work the attorney did before being fired. If the contract between the attorney and client provides for a flat fee or a maximum fee, that constitutes a ceiling on the quantum meruit recovery. [*See* Rosenberg v. Levin, 409 So. 2d 1016 (Fla. 1982)] That is, the attorney cannot recover *more* than was provided for by express contract.

b. Contingent Fee Cases

When a client hires a lawyer on a contingent fee basis, and then fires the lawyer before the case is over, the lawyer is still entitled to quantum meruit recovery for the reasonable value of the work done before the firing. However, the lawyer's claim does not arise until the contingency comes to pass. [*Id.*]

Example: Lawyer L agreed to represent plaintiff P in a personal injury case. L agreed to do the work for 40% of P's recovery, but not more than $10,000. After L spent hundreds of hours preparing the case for trial, P fired L for no apparent reason. Then P settled the case for $40,000. Before the settlement, L had no claim against P because the contingency had not come to pass. After the settlement, L is entitled to the reasonable value of his services, but not more than $10,000 (the maximum set in the contract).

2. Court Permission to Substitute Attorneys

After a lawsuit has been filed, the rules of most courts require the court's permission for a substitution of attorneys. When a party wants to fire her attorney, courts almost always grant the necessary permission, but permission may be denied if a substitution of attorneys would cause undue delay or disruption. [*See, e.g.,* Ruskin v. Rodgers, 399 N.E.2d 623 (Ill. 1979)— permission denied when client tried to fire attorney without cause two days before date set for trial] On the other hand, when an attorney seeks to withdraw from a case, the court may deny the necessary permission; in that event, the attorney must continue the representation, even if there is good cause for withdrawal. [ABA Model Rule 1.16(c)]

3. Mandatory Withdrawal

a. Disability

An attorney *must* withdraw if the attorney's mental or physical condition materially impairs the attorney's ability to continue representing the client. [ABA Model Rule 1.16(a)(2)]

b. Illegality or Ethical Violation

If to continue with the representation will require the attorney to violate a law or a disciplinary rule, the attorney *must* withdraw. [ABA Model Rule 1.16(a)(1)]

Example: Attorney A agreed to represent client C in a slander suit against D. At the outset, A believed in good faith that C had a sound claim against D. Discovery later showed not a shred of evidence to support C's contentions. C finally confessed to A that she was maintaining the suit simply to harass and injure D. A must withdraw because to continue would require him to violate the disciplinary rule against frivolous litigation. [ABA Model Rule 3.1]

4. Permissive Withdrawal

An attorney *may* withdraw from representing a client *for any reason* if it can be done without material adverse effect on the client's interests or if the client consents. [ABA Model Rule 1.16(b)(1)] In addition, the attorney may withdraw despite an adverse impact on the client's interests in the situations listed below, provided the circumstances are severe enough to justify harming the client's interests. [*See* Restatement §32]

a. **Client Persists in Criminal or Fraudulent Conduct**
A lawyer *may* withdraw from representing a client if the client persists in a course of action that involves the lawyer's services and that the lawyer *reasonably believes* is criminal or fraudulent. [ABA Model Rule 1.16(b)(2)] Note that if the client's criminal or fraudulent conduct involves some assistance by the lawyer, then the lawyer *must* withdraw. [ABA Model Rules 1.16(a)(1), 1.2(d)]

b. **Client Has Used Attorney's Services to Commit Past Crime or Fraud**
An attorney *may* withdraw from representing a client if the client has used the attorney's services to commit a past crime or fraud. [ABA Model Rule 1.16(b)(3)]

c. **Client's Objective Is Repugnant or Against Lawyer's Beliefs**
An attorney *may* withdraw from representing a client if the client insists on taking action that the attorney considers to be repugnant or with which the lawyer has a fundamental disagreement. [ABA Model Rule 1.16(b)(4)]

d. **Client Breaks Promise to Attorney**
An attorney *may* withdraw from representing a client if the client substantially fails to fulfill an obligation to the attorney and has been warned that the attorney will withdraw unless it is fulfilled (for instance, client refuses to pay attorney's fee, or refuses to appear for scheduled hearings despite promises to attorney). [ABA Model Rule 1.16(b)(5)]

e. **Financial Hardship for Attorney**
An attorney *may* withdraw from representing a client if to continue the representation will impose an unreasonable financial burden on the attorney. [ABA Model Rule 1.16(b)(6)]

f. **Client Will Not Cooperate**
An attorney *may* withdraw from representing a client if the client has made the attorney's work unreasonably difficult (*e.g.*, where the client refuses to cooperate with the attorney in discovery proceedings). [*Id.*]

g. **Other Good Cause**
An attorney *may* withdraw if there is other good cause for withdrawal. [ABA Model Rule 1.16(b)(7)]

5. **Attorney's Duties Upon Termination of Representation**
An attorney who withdraws from a matter must comply with local laws that require notice to or permission of the tribunal before withdrawal. [ABA Model Rule 1.16(c)] Moreover, upon termination of the representation, the attorney must take reasonable steps to protect the client's interests, including:

(i) Providing the client with *reasonable notice* of the withdrawal;

(ii) Providing the client with *time* to obtain another attorney;

(iii) *Refunding attorneys' fees* paid in advance and not yet earned and expense advances not yet spent; and

(iv) *Returning all papers and property* to which the client is entitled.

[ABA Model Rule 1.16(d)]

Examples: 1) Lawyer L decided to withdraw from representing client C in a workers' compensation case because C repeatedly failed to comply with the adversary's legitimate discovery requests, repeatedly failed to show up to have his deposition taken, and deliberately refused to make the monthly fee payments that he had promised to L. C asked L to turn the case files over to C's new lawyer, but L refused to do so until his past due fees had been paid. The law of L's state (following the better view) does not allow a lawyer to hold case files hostage to compel payment of legal fees. [*See* Academy of California Optometrists, Inc. v. Superior Court, 51 Cal. App. 3d 999 (1975)] L is subject to discipline.

2) Attorney A was retained to represent client C in a divorce case. With C's consent, C's parents paid A $1,000 as an advance on attorneys' fees not yet earned. The parents understood that they could not attempt to influence A's judgment about how to handle C's case. (*See* V.D.1., *infra.*) C then departed for parts unknown, making it impossible for A to pursue the divorce case. The parents would now like to have their $1,000 back, and A would like to withdraw from the matter. In these circumstances, it is proper for A to withdraw and to refund the fee advance to C's parents. [New York City Bar Op. 83-62 (1983)]

III. LAWYER'S DUTIES OF COMPETENCE AND DILIGENCE

A. COMPETENCE

When representing a client, a lawyer must act competently, *i.e.*, with the legal knowledge, skill, thoroughness, and preparation reasonably necessary for the representation. [ABA Model Rule 1.1]

1. Legal Knowledge and Skill

a. Factors in Determining Requisite Skill

In deciding whether a lawyer has the knowledge and skill required to handle a particular matter, the following factors should be considered:

(i) The complexity and specialized nature of the matter;

(ii) The lawyer's general experience;

    (iii) The lawyer's training and experience in the field in question;

    (iv) The preparation and study the lawyer is able to give the matter; and

    (v) Whether it is feasible to refer the matter to, or associate or consult with, a lawyer of established competence in the field.

[Comment 1 to ABA Model Rule 1.1] Note that most matters do not require specialized skill and that every lawyer is capable of competence either through necessary study or association of another lawyer. Thus, a lack of legal knowledge or skill really means a failure to seek it. [Hazard & Hodes, §3.2]

b. **Becoming Competent Through Preparation**
It follows from the above that a lawyer may accept representation despite lacking competence in the field involved if the requisite competence can be achieved by reasonable preparation. This often comes into play when a lawyer is appointed as counsel for an unrepresented person. [Comment 4 to ABA Model Rule 1.1]

c. **Emergency Situations**
In an emergency, a lawyer may assist a client, even if the lawyer does not have the skill ordinarily required in the field in question if referral to or consultation with another lawyer would be impractical. However, the assistance should not exceed what is reasonably necessary to meet the emergency. [Comment 3 to ABA Model Rule 1.1]

    Example: In the middle of the night, attorney A's neighbor calls him and asks what to do about her estranged husband who is drunkenly trying to get into her house, in violation of a court order. The neighbor's regular lawyer is unavailable, and A knows little or nothing about family law. In this emergency situation, A may advise the neighbor, but his advice should be limited to the emergency at hand.

2. **Thoroughness and Preparation**
To handle a matter competently, a lawyer must inquire into and analyze the facts and legal elements of the problem, applying the methods and procedures used by competent practitioners. Competence, of course, requires adequate preparation. [Comment 5 to ABA Model Rule 1.1]

3. **Maintaining Competence—Continuing Legal Education**
Lawyers should take reasonable steps to keep abreast of current literature and developments in the fields of law in which they practice. One way to do that is by taking advantage of continuing legal education programs sponsored by the organized bar. In addition, a lawyer must comply with all applicable continuing legal education requirements. [Comment 6 to ABA Model Rule 1.1]

B. **DILIGENCE**
A lawyer must act with ***reasonable diligence and promptness*** in representing a client. [ABA Model Rule 1.3]

1. **Diligence Defined**
A lawyer should pursue a matter on the client's behalf despite opposition, obstacles, and

personal inconvenience, and may take whatever lawful and ethical measures are required to vindicate the client's cause. The lawyer should act with dedication and commitment to the client's interests and with *zeal in advocacy* on the client's behalf. [Comment 1 to ABA Model Rule 1.3]

a. Diligence Does Not Require Incivility
A lawyer should use good judgment in determining the means by which a matter is pursued, and the lawyer is not bound by Rule 1.3 to press every conceivable advantage. Moreover, the duty of diligence does not require the lawyer to be offensive or uncivil toward the adversary or other persons. [*Id.*]

b. Workload
A lawyer must control his workload so that each matter can be adequately handled. [Comment 2 to ABA Model Rule 1.3]

2. Promptness
Procrastination is perhaps the professional shortcoming most widely resented. [Comment 3 to ABA Model Rule 1.3] Procrastination often has severe or devastating consequences to the client's interests, as when a court-ordered deadline is missed or the statute of limitations is permitted to run. Even when procrastination does not harm the client's substantive interests, it can cause the client needless anxiety and can undermine confidence in the lawyer's trustworthiness. A lawyer may, of course, agree to a reasonable postponement if it will not prejudice her client. [*Id.*]

3. Completion of the Matter
Once a lawyer agrees to handle a matter for a client, the lawyer must see the matter through to completion (unless, of course, the lawyer is fired or is required or permitted to withdraw). If there is doubt about whether the lawyer-client relationship has come to an end, the lawyer should clarify it, preferably in writing. [Comment 4 to ABA Model Rule 1.3]

Examples: 1) Over the past 15 years, attorney A has served as trademark counsel for Webb Corp., but in recent months the relationship has become somewhat strained. A is uncertain whether Webb Corp. wishes to continue to use her services. Today A read in a trademark newsletter that one of Webb's competitors is attempting to register a trademark that will seriously interfere with Webb's business. A should promptly call the matter to Webb's attention and ask Webb whether it wishes her to act on its behalf in this matter.

2) Client C hired lawyer L to defend her in a drunk driving case. At trial, C was convicted and her driver's license was suspended. L is uncertain whether C expects him to do anything about an appeal. L must consult with C about the possibility of an appeal before relinquishing responsibility for the matter.

4. Existence of Lawyer-Client Relationship
A lawyer's obligation under the duties stated above, as with most of the lawyer's ethical duties, depends on whether there is a lawyer-client relationship. If there is any doubt, however, as to whether the lawyer-client relationship was either formed or terminated, the lawyer must either take affirmative steps to terminate the relationship or act with the required diligence. [Hazard & Hodes, §6.5]

5. Solo Practitioner's Duty to Plan for Death or Disability

The untimely death or disability of a solo practitioner can create havoc for her clients. To prevent that, every solo practitioner should designate another competent lawyer to review the clients' files, notify the clients of the circumstances, and determine whether protective action is needed. [Comment 5 to ABA Model Rule 1.3]

C. SINGLE VIOLATION SUFFICIENT TO IMPOSE DISCIPLINE

Neither Rule 1.1 (competence) nor Rule 1.3 (diligence) requires a pattern of misconduct; a single incident is sufficient to impose professional discipline. Special circumstances should be considered when imposing the sanction, but not when determining whether there has been a violation. Even when the lawyer is in the midst of a personal crisis, he must take reasonable steps to put his cases on temporary hold, until he can give them his full attention. [Hazard & Hodes, §6.4, illus. 6-4]

Example: Client Cathy came to lawyer Larry with a medical malpractice claim, the statute of limitations on which was due to run out within the week. Larry agreed to take the case and began drafting the complaint. Two days later, Larry's son was hit by a car. For several days, during which time the doctors performed several surgeries, they did not know whether the child would live or die. Larry did not leave his son's side during this critical time, and thus did not file Cathy's case within the statutory period. Cathy filed both a malpractice case and a disciplinary complaint against Larry. Larry is subject to discipline for lack of diligence in handling Cathy's case. The disciplinary authority will likely consider the circumstances in assessing a sanction, but they are irrelevant to the question of whether Larry breached his duty to Cathy. [*See* Hazard & Hodes, §6.4, illus. 6-4]

D. MALPRACTICE LIABILITY

1. Relationship Between Disciplinary Matters and Malpractice Actions

Professional discipline is only one of the possible consequences of incompetent or neglected legal work. Another possible consequence is civil liability for legal malpractice. A malpractice action differs from a disciplinary matter in three ways: (i) in a malpractice action, the forum is a *civil court*, not a disciplinary tribunal; (ii) in a malpractice action, the attorney's adversary is an *injured plaintiff*, not the state bar; and (iii) the purpose of a malpractice action is to *compensate* the injured plaintiff, not to punish the attorney, and not to protect the public from future wrongs.

2. Ethics Violation as Evidence of Legal Malpractice

If a lawyer violates a legal ethics rule, does that automatically mean that she has also committed legal malpractice? If not, does it create a presumption that she has committed malpractice? The "Scope" section of the ABA Model Rules answers "no" to both questions: the legal ethics rules are for disciplinary purposes. They are not designed to be a basis for civil liability, and a lawyer's breach of an ethics rule does not automatically or presumptively mean that the lawyer has committed malpractice. Courts do, however, regard an ethics violation as *relevant evidence* that the lawyer's conduct was below the appropriate standard of care. [*See* Fishman v. Brooks, 487 N.E.2d 1377 (Mass. 1986); *and see generally* Hazard & Hodes, §4.1]

3. Theories of Malpractice Liability

The plaintiff in a legal malpractice case can invoke a variety of legal theories. The choice of theories can be important because of differences in the statutes of limitation and measures of damages.

a. Intentional Tort

One theory is intentional tort. An attorney is liable (just as any nonprofessional would be) for fraud, misrepresentation, malicious prosecution, abuse of process, or misuse of funds.

b. Breach of Fiduciary Duties

A second theory is breach of fiduciary duties. An attorney acting as a fiduciary for the client owes the client all of the customary duties of a fiduciary, including loyalty, confidentiality, and honest dealing.

c. Breach of Contract

A third theory is breach of contract. For instance, an attorney may have breached a term of an express oral agreement with the client. If there is no express contract, a court may be willing to find an implied promise by the attorney to use ordinary skill and care to protect the client's interests.

d. Negligence

A fourth theory, by far the most common, is unintentional tort—*i.e.,* simple negligence. [*See generally* Restatement §§48 - 54] Using this theory, the plaintiff must establish the routine elements of any negligence case: a duty of due care, a breach of that duty, legal causation, and damages. These elements are discussed separately in the paragraphs that follow.

1) Duty of Due Care

a) To Clients

An attorney owes a duty of due care to a client, but it is not always clear when a person becomes a client. [*Id.* §50] Courts are quick to find that an attorney-client relationship has been established if the attorney's neglect has misled the alleged client. [*See* Restatement §14]

Example: C asked attorney A to represent him as plaintiff in a products liability case. A said she would have to check with her partners to make sure the case posed no conflict of interest, and A said that she would "get back to C one way or the other." A never checked with her partners, and she totally forgot C's case. The statute of limitations ran. A court could conclude that an attorney-client relationship had been established between A and C.

b) To Third Parties

An attorney also owes a duty of due care to any third party who was ***intended to benefit*** by the attorney's rendition of legal services and to other nonclients in certain circumstances. [*See* Restatement §51]

Examples: 1) C hired attorney A to draft a trust agreement naming B as beneficiary. A drafted the trust agreement negligently, making it subject to an unnecessary tax; the tax reduced the amount that B could receive from the trust. Because B was intended to benefit from A's services, and because the potential for harm to B should have been obvious, B has a good malpractice claim against A.

2) M hired lawyer L to bring a civil suit against D. As it turned out, M's claim against D had no sound factual basis, and L would have recognized that from the outset had L not been negligent. D incurred trouble and expense in defending the suit. D has no negligence claim against L because D was not intended to benefit from L's services and D was not any other type of protected nonclient.

c) Standard of Care

The standard of care for an attorney is the competence and diligence normally exercised by attorneys in similar circumstances. [*Id.* §52] If an attorney represents to a client that he has greater competence (*e.g.,* is a specialist) or will exercise greater diligence than that normally demonstrated by attorneys undertaking similar matters, he is held to that higher standard. [*Id.* §52, comment d]

2) Breach of Duty of Due Care

a) Errors of Judgment

An attorney is liable for negligence, but not everything that causes harm is negligence. An attorney is not liable for "mere errors in judgment" if the judgment was ***well-informed and reasonably made***.

Examples: 1) Attorney A decided not to take the pretrial deposition of witness X. A's motive was to save litigation expenses for her client; further, it appeared that X's testimony would be peripheral and unimportant. At trial, X turned out to be a critical witness for the adversary. Even if A's failure to take X's deposition caused A's client to lose the case, A has not committed malpractice if her judgment was well-informed and reasonably exercised.

2) In a surgical malpractice case, lawyer L failed to interview the operating room nurse, an obvious witness who might have knowledge of key facts. L's client lost the case because of the failure to prove a fact that the nurse's testimony could have supplied. When the client sued L for legal malpractice, L responded that he had made a "tactical judgment" not to interview the nurse. Holding L liable, the court noted that "there is nothing tactical about ignorance."

b) Knowledge of Law

An attorney is expected to know the ordinary, settled rules of law known to practitioners of ordinary competence and diligence. Furthermore, an attorney has a duty to go to the library to look up rules of law that he does not know. If the answer is there to be found through standard research techniques and sources, and if the attorney does not find it, he has breached the duty of due care. [*See, e.g.,* Aloy v. Mash, 38 Cal. 3d 413 (1985)] Obviously, some issues of law are unsettled and debatable; if the attorney has done reasonable legal research, then he has fulfilled the duty of due care—even if he makes the wrong guess about how an unsettled issue will ultimately be resolved by the courts.

c) Calling in a Specialist

Some legal problems are uniquely within the competence of a legal specialist. It is a breach of the duty of due care for a general practitioner to attempt to handle such a problem if a reasonably prudent lawyer would have sent the client to a specialist.

Example: Client C asked attorney A to help him obtain legal protection for a new manufacturing process that C had invented. A realized that he was totally ignorant about the law of patents and trade secrets, but he nevertheless tried to advise C. As a result, C lost his opportunity to apply for a United States patent on his invention. A breached the duty of due care by failing to send C to a patent attorney.

3) Legal Causation

As in any tort case, the plaintiff in a professional negligence case must prove that the defendant's conduct was the legal cause of the plaintiff's injury. That is, the injury would not have happened ***but for*** the defendant's negligence, and furthermore, that it is fair to hold the defendant liable for unexpected injuries or for expected injuries that happen in unexpected ways. [*See* Restatement §53]

Examples: 1) P hired lawyer L to represent her in a suit against the federal government. L neglected P's case, and the statute of limitations ran. P then sued L for legal malpractice. In the malpractice case, P must prove that she had a good claim against the federal government. If P did not have a good claim in the first place, then L's negligence was not the legal cause of injury to P.

2) History professor H hired attorney A to defend her in a plagiarism case. H lost the case because of A's failure to prepare adequately. The loss broke H's mind and spirit; she became a hopeless alcoholic and was fired from her university position. If H files a legal malpractice suit against A, a court would probably conclude that H's loss of earning power was not legally caused by A's negligence.

4) Damages

The plaintiff in a professional negligence case must prove damages—*e.g.,* the money paid out to discharge an adverse judgment, or the value of a lost cause of action. The plaintiff can recover for direct losses and also for losses that are indirect but foreseeable. [*Id.* §53]

Example: Attorney A did the legal work for the acquiring corporation in a large merger transaction. A bungled the merger agreement; in consequence, the merger fell through, and A's client suffered large legal expenses in defending against suits brought by aggrieved shareholders. In a malpractice action, A's client can recover both the legal expenses and the profits lost due to the aborted merger, provided that it can prove its losses with reasonable certainty.

4.   Liability for Negligence of Others

The ordinary principles of *respondeat superior* apply in suits for professional negligence. Thus, an attorney can be held liable for injuries caused by a negligent legal secretary, law clerk, paralegal, or employee associate when acting within the scope of employment. Furthermore, under general principles of partnership law, each partner in a law firm is liable for the negligence of another partner committed in the ordinary course of the partnership business. The law varies widely from state to state concerning vicarious liability among shareholders in an incorporated law firm.

5.   Malpractice Insurance

Because legal malpractice actions are now commonplace, malpractice insurance has become an expensive but necessary part of law practice. The ABA Model Rules do not require lawyers to carry malpractice insurance, but prudent lawyers carry ample coverage, both to protect their personal assets and to promote their public image as reliable professionals.

6.   Contracting with Client to Limit Malpractice Liability

A lawyer must not make an agreement prospectively limiting the lawyer's liability to a client for malpractice unless the client is independently represented in making the agreement. [ABA Model Rule 1.8(h)]

Example: Lawyer L requires his clients to sign a standard, preprinted retainer agreement that provides, in part, that the client cannot sue L for malpractice. L's clients are not independently represented in signing his retainer agreement. L is subject to discipline.

7.   Settling Malpractice Claims

A lawyer must not settle a pending or potential malpractice claim with an unrepresented client or former client without first advising that person, in writing, to seek advice from an independent lawyer about the settlement and giving that person time to seek that advice. [*Id.*]

Example: Defendant D hired attorney A to defend him in a criminal case, and D gave A $5,000 as an advance against attorneys' fees yet to be earned. Shortly before trial, D became dissatisfied with A's work, fired her, and threatened to sue her for malpractice. A returned the unearned portion of the fee advance to D by a check that had an endorsement on the back purporting to release A from all liability for malpractice. A did not advise D to seek advice from an independent lawyer. A is subject to discipline. [*See, e.g.,* New York State Bar Op. 591 (1988)]

8.   Reimbursement of Client

A lawyer who has breached a duty to his client with monetary effect *cannot escape discipline* by reimbursing the client for any loss. [*See* Hazard & Hodes, §3.2] Thus, even if the lawyer pays the client back for any damage he caused, he is still subject to discipline.

IV. DUTY OF CONFIDENTIALITY

A. GENERAL RULE

As a general rule, a lawyer must not reveal any information relating to the representation of the client. [ABA Model Rule 1.6] A lawyer may, however, reveal such information if the client gives *informed consent*, or if the disclosure is *impliedly authorized* to carry out the representation. [*Id.*] The ethical duty is subject to some additional exceptions, discussed in D., *infra*. The rationale of the ethical duty is that it encourages candor between the lawyer and the client, encourages the client to seek early legal advice, and helps the lawyer discover all of the information relevant to the client's legal problem. [*See* Comment 2 to ABA Model Rule 1.6; with respect to the ethical duty of confidentiality, *see generally* Restatement §§59 - 67]

B. RELATIONSHIP BETWEEN ETHICAL DUTY OF CONFIDENTIALITY AND ATTORNEY-CLIENT PRIVILEGE

The ethical duty of confidentiality is closely related to the attorney-client privilege, but the two doctrines differ in three important ways.

1. Compulsion vs. Gossip

The *attorney-client privilege* is an exclusionary rule of evidence law. It prevents a court, or other governmental tribunal, from using the twin powers of subpoena and contempt to compel the revelation of confidential communications between an attorney and a client. In contrast, the *ethical duty of confidentiality* prohibits an attorney from *voluntarily* revealing information relating to the representation of a client—it applies in every context where the attorney-client privilege does not apply. [*See* Comment 3 to ABA Model Rule 1.6]

Examples: 1) During the course of a civil trial, lawyer L's adversary called her to the witness stand and posed questions about her confidential communications with her client. In this context, the rights and duties of L and her client are governed by the attorney-client privilege, not by the ethical duty of confidentiality.

2) When lawyer L was chatting with a friend at a cocktail party, the friend asked L for some information that L had gained in the course of representing one of her clients. In this context, the attorney-client privilege is irrelevant—the privilege does not apply at cocktail parties. Here, L is governed by the ethical duty of confidentiality.

2. Kinds of Information Covered

The ethical duty of confidentiality covers *more* kinds of information than the attorney-client privilege. The attorney-client privilege protects only *confidential communications* between the attorney and client (or the agents of either of them). The ethical duty, in contrast, covers not only confidential communications, but also *any other information* that the attorney obtains relating to the representation of the client, no matter what the source of that information. The ethical duty thus applies to *all* information that relates to the representation of the client, regardless of whether it is privileged, whether the client asked for it to be kept in confidence, and whether revealing it might harm or embarrass the client. For purposes of this outline, the term "confidential information" means all information protected by the duty of confidentiality expressed in ABA Model Rule 1.6.

Example: Attorney A is representing client C in proceedings to challenge the will left by C's mother. While conducting her own investigation of the facts of the case, A learns from a third party that C is the illegitimate son of an itinerant book salesman. This information is not protected by the attorney-client privilege because A did not gain it through a confidential communication with C. Nevertheless, under ABA Model Rule 1.6, the information is covered by the ethical duty of confidentiality.

3. Disclosure vs. Use

The attorney-client privilege concerns only the disclosure of information. In contrast, the ethical duty of confidentiality concerns both the disclosure and use of information. An attorney can be disciplined for *disclosing* a client's confidential information without the client's informed consent (unless one of the exceptions to the ethical duty is applicable) [ABA Model Rule 1.6(a)], or for *using* confidential information to the disadvantage of a client, former client, or prospective client, without the affected client's informed, written consent. [ABA Model Rules 1.8(b), 1.9(c), 1.18(b)]

C. SUMMARY OF ATTORNEY-CLIENT PRIVILEGE

Because the ethical duty of confidentiality is so closely related to the attorney-client privilege, the following is a brief summary of the main features of the privilege. [*See* Restatement §§68 - 86—restates the law of attorney-client privilege]

1. Basic Rule

The attorney-client privilege prohibits a court or other governmental tribunal from compelling the revelation of confidential communications between an attorney (or an attorney's agent) and a client (or a client's agent) if the subject of the communication concerns the professional relationship between the attorney and the client.

2. Client

A "client" means a person or entity that seeks legal services from an attorney. The privilege covers preliminary communications leading up to an attorney-client relationship, even if no such relationship develops. [*See also* ABA Model Rule 1.18—duty of confidentiality to a prospective client]

Example: H wants to hire a lawyer to obtain a dissolution of his marriage. After speaking in confidence with lawyer L about his marital problems, H decides not to hire L as his lawyer. Even though no attorney-client relationship ultimately develops between H and L, the attorney-client privilege protects what H told L in confidence.

a. Corporate Clients

When the client is a corporation, the privilege covers communications between the lawyer and a high-ranking corporate official. It also covers communications between the lawyer and another corporate employee if the following conditions are met:

(i)   The employee communicates with the lawyer *at the direction of the employee's superior*;

(ii) The employee knows that the *purpose of the communication is to obtain legal advice for the corporation*; and

(iii) The communication concerns a *subject within the scope of the employee's duties to act* for the corporation.

[*See* Upjohn Co. v. United States, 449 U.S. 383 (1981)]

3. Attorney

An "attorney" means a person who is authorized (or whom the client reasonably believes to be authorized) to practice law in any state or nation. However, for the privilege to apply, the attorney must be acting as an attorney—not in some other capacity, such as a friend, business advisor, or member of the family.

4. Communication

The term "communication" covers information passed from the client to the attorney and from the attorney to the client. It also covers information passed to or from the agents of either the attorney or the client.

Example: Whitney Corp. hires attorney A to represent it in a dispute over the construction of a nuclear power plant. A hires structural engineer E to assist her on the technical aspects of the case. At A's direction, E talks with F, the chief engineer of Whitney Corp., to find out certain facts about the case. E's discussion with F is covered by the attorney-client privilege.

a. Mechanical Details of Relationship

Usually the attorney-client privilege does not cover the mechanical details of the attorney-client relationship, such as the identity of the client, the fee arrangement between the attorney and client, and the bare fact that the attorney is acting for the client. But these mechanical details can be protected by the privilege if revealing them is tantamount to revealing a privileged communication. [*See* Christopher Mueller & Laird Kirkpatrick, Evidence §5.19 (3d ed. 2003)]

Example: X came to lawyer L's office and asked to employ L in a confidential matter. X then said that he was the hit and run driver in the car wreck reported on the front page of today's newspaper. X asked L to negotiate with the authorities for him, but not to reveal his identity without first getting X's specific permission. Later, the parents of the victim in the hit and run brought a wrongful death action against a John Doe defendant. They subpoenaed L and asked her to reveal the identity of the person who had consulted her about the hit and run. A court cannot compel L to disclose X's identity; the attorney-client privilege protects it because to reveal it would be tantamount to revealing X's statement that he was the hit and run driver. [*See* Baltes v. Doe I, 4 ABA/BNA Lawyer's Manual on Professional Conduct 356]

b. Preexisting Documents and Things

The attorney-client privilege covers both oral and written communications. However, the client cannot protect a preexisting document or thing from discovery simply by turning it over to the attorney. If the document or thing would be discoverable in the client's hands, it is equally discoverable in the attorney's hands.

Examples: 1) Client C hires attorney A to defend her in a breach of contract case. C turns over to A her entire file of records relating to the contract. If the records would be discoverable when in the possession of C, they are equally discoverable when in the possession of A.

2) D tells his lawyer, L: "I just shot X, and I threw the revolver in the trashcan behind my apartment." The revolver itself is not privileged, but D's communication with L about the revolver is privileged. [California v. Meredith, 29 Cal. 3d 682 (1981)] L's knowledge of the whereabouts of the revolver is privileged. If L simply looks in the trashcan to confirm D's story, D can invoke the privilege and prevent L from testifying about what he saw. [*Id.*] L has no legal or ethical duty to retrieve the revolver from the trashcan. Furthermore, absent D's informed consent, L must not tell anyone where the revolver is. [ABA Model Rule 1.6] If L retrieves the revolver from the trashcan, he may keep it long enough to obtain from it any information that may be useful in D's defense. Then L must turn it over to the proper authorities. [California v. Meredith, *supra*; State v. Olwell, 394 P.2d 681 (Wash. 1964)] By removing the revolver from the trashcan, L has destroyed a valuable piece of evidence—the incriminating **location** of the revolver. L's action requires a compromise between the need to protect privileged communications and the need for relevant evidence. The compromise reached in *Meredith* and *Olwell* is as follows: The trier of fact will be told where the revolver was found, but the trier of fact will not be told that L was the source of that information. For example, L and the prosecutor can simply stipulate that the jury at D's trial will be informed of the location of the revolver, without telling them the source of that information. However, if L retrieves the revolver from the trashcan and hides or destroys it, L may face criminal liability for tampering with evidence, and L is also subject to professional discipline. [*In re* Ryder, 263 F. Supp. 360 (E.D. Va. 1967)]

5. **"Confidential" Defined**

To be covered by the attorney-client privilege, a communication must be "confidential"; it must have been made by a means not intended to disclose the communicated information to outsiders, and the communicating person must reasonably believe that no outsider will hear the contents of the statement.

a. **Presence of Third Party**

The presence of a third party will not destroy the confidentiality *if* the third party was present to help further the attorney-client relationship. However, the third party need not play a direct role in the communication and may be present because of the client's psychological needs (*e.g.,* a family member accompanying the client). [Restatement §70, comment f]

Example: Five persons were present during an office conference between Client and Attorney. In addition to Client and Attorney, the persons present were Client's accountant (who was there to help explain Client's books of account), Attorney's law clerk (who was there to assist Attorney in drafting some interrogatory answers), and Attorney's legal secretary (who was there to take dictation). The presence of the accountant, the law clerk, and the secretary does not destroy the confidentiality.

Compare: During a recess in trial, Attorney and Client discussed Client's intended testimony in a crowded courthouse corridor where bystanders could obviously overhear. This conversation is not confidential for purposes of the attorney-client privilege. Thus, the privilege does not bar examination of either Client or Attorney regarding the conversation.

b. Eavesdroppers
In days gone by, the presence of an unsuspected eavesdropper was sometimes held to destroy the confidentiality of a communication. Under modern evidence law, that is no longer true; an eavesdropper can be prohibited from testifying about a confidential communication.

6. Client Is Holder of Privilege
The attorney-client privilege exists for the benefit of the client, not for the benefit of the attorney. Therefore, the client is the "holder" of the privilege—*i.e.,* the client is the one who can claim or waive the privilege.

a. Waiver of Privilege
A waiver consists of a failure to claim the privilege when there is an opportunity to do so, or the intentional revelation of a significant portion of the privileged communication.

Example: Client C shows his next-door neighbor the first two pages of a three-page privileged letter. In a later civil case, C's adversary can compel production of the entire letter. C has waived the privilege.

b. Lawyer's Duty to Invoke Privilege
If the client has not waived the privilege, and if someone tries to obtain privileged information when the client is not present, the lawyer must claim the privilege on the client's behalf.

Example: Lawyer L represents client C in a civil case. On a day when C is not present in court, C's adversary calls L to the witness stand and poses questions about confidential communications between C and L. L must claim the privilege on C's behalf.

7. Duration of Privilege
The attorney-client privilege continues indefinitely. Termination of the relationship, even for cause, does not terminate the privilege. The privilege even survives the death of the client. [Swidler & Berlin v. United States, 524 U.S. 399 (1998)] Thus, a lawyer has a continuing obligation to assert the privilege on behalf of a client who has died, subject to exceptions relating to the deceased's disposition of property. [Restatement §77, comment c]

8. **Exceptions to Privilege**
Modern evidence law provides several *exceptions* to the attorney-client privilege.

    a.   The privilege does not apply if the client seeks the attorney's services *to engage in or assist a future crime or fraud*. [*See* Restatement §82]

    b.   The privilege does not apply to a communication that is *relevant to an issue of breach* (by either the attorney or the client) *of the duties arising out of the attorney-client relationship*. [*Id.* §83]

    c.   The privilege does not apply *in civil litigation between two persons who were formerly the joint clients of the attorney*. [*Id.* §75(2)]

    d.   The privilege does not apply in a variety of situations in which the attorney can furnish evidence about the *competency or intention of a client who has attempted to dispose of property by will or inter vivos transfer*.

9. **Related Doctrine of Work Product Immunity**
Generally, material prepared by a lawyer for litigation or in anticipation of litigation is immune from discovery or other compelled disclosure unless the opposition shows a substantial need for the material and an inability to gather the material without undue hardship. A lawyer's mental impressions or opinions are immune from discovery or compelled disclosure regardless of the opposition's need unless the immunity has been waived. [*See* Restatement §§87 - 93]

D. ETHICAL DUTY OF CONFIDENTIALITY AND ITS EXCEPTIONS
As explained previously (*see* B.1., *supra*), the ethical duty of confidentiality applies in every context in which the attorney-client privilege does not apply. The ethical duty also covers a broader range of information than the privilege. Finally, the ethical duty concerns not only the disclosure of information, but also the use of information to the disadvantage of a client, a prospective client, or a former client.

1. **Duty Not Destroyed by Presence of Third Party**
Unlike the attorney-client privilege, the presence of a nonprivileged third person does not necessarily destroy an attorney's duty of confidentiality. Confidential information remains confidential even if it is known to others, *unless the information becomes generally known*. Whether information is generally known depends on all the surrounding circumstances, but information is *not generally known* when it can be obtained only by means of *special knowledge or substantial difficulty or expense*.

2. **Exceptions to the Duty of Confidentiality**
The *exceptions* to the ethical duty are discussed separately in the following paragraphs.

    a.   **Client's Informed Consent**
An attorney may reveal or use confidential information if the client gives informed consent. [ABA Model Rule 1.6(a)] Remember that "informed consent" means that the client agrees to a proposed course of action after the lawyer has adequately explained the risks and reasonable alternatives. [ABA Model Rule 1.0(e)]

Example: Attorney A is representing defendant D in an armed robbery case. D reluctantly tells A that at the time of the alleged robbery, D was 10 miles away visiting a house of prostitution, and that at least five witnesses can vouch for his presence there. A may disclose and use this embarrassing information in the defense of the armed robbery case if D gives informed consent.

b. Implied Authority

An attorney has implied authority from the client to use or disclose confidential information when appropriate to carry out the representation—unless, of course, the client gives specific instructions to the contrary. [ABA Model Rule 1.6(a)]

Examples: 1) Lawyer L represents client A in negotiating a construction contract. Unless A instructs L to the contrary, L has implied authority to disclose confidential information about A's business if that will serve A's interests in the negotiation. [Comment 5 to ABA Model Rule 1.6]

2) Lawyer M represents client B in litigation. Unless B instructs M to the contrary, M has implied authority to disclose confidential information in a fact stipulation if that will serve B's interests in the litigation. [*Id.*]

3) Lawyer N is drawing up a will and a trust agreement for client C. Unless C instructs N to the contrary, N has implied authority to discuss C's confidential information with other lawyers in N's firm if that will serve C's interests. [*Id.*]

4) Lawyer O is representing client D in a bankruptcy case. Unless D instructs O to the contrary, O has implied authority to allow her paralegal, her law clerk, her legal secretary, and the law firm's copy-machine operator to have access to D's confidential business papers. However, O must take reasonable steps to assure that those employees preserve the confidentiality of the information. [ABA Model Rule 5.3; ABA Formal Op. 95-398 (1995)]

5) Lawyer Q is representing X Corp. in secret merger negotiations with Y Corp. Secrecy is vital because if word leaks out, the stock prices of the two companies will move apart, making the merger impossible. On one knotty issue, Q seeks the informal, uncompensated advice of his friend, lawyer R, a merger expert in a different law firm. Q poses the issue to R in the form of a hypothetical that does not identify either X Corp. or Y Corp. by name. Unfortunately, Q is careless in posing the hypothetical, which allows R to deduce the identities of X Corp. and Y Corp. Q is subject to discipline for breaching the duty of confidentiality. A lawyer may use a hypothetical to obtain advice from a fellow lawyer for the benefit of the client, but the hypothetical must be discreet enough to preclude any reasonable chance that the fellow lawyer will be able to deduce the identity of the client or the situation at hand. [Comment 4 to ABA Model Rule 1.6; ABA Formal Op. 98-411]

c.   **Dispute Concerning Attorney's Conduct**

An attorney may reveal a client's confidential information to the extent necessary to protect the attorney's interests in a dispute that involves the conduct of the attorney. [ABA Model Rule 1.6(b)(5)] In using this exception, the attorney should: (i) reveal only what is necessary, (ii) attempt to limit the disclosure to those who need to know it, and (iii) obtain protective orders or take other steps to minimize the risk of unnecessary harm to the client. [Comment 14 to ABA Model Rule 1.6]

Examples: 1) Attorney A represented client C in a child custody case. C told A in confidence about C's emotional difficulties, alcoholism, and inability to hold steady employment. These confidential disclosures made the task of representing C vastly more difficult and time-consuming than A had originally anticipated. C ultimately lost the child custody case. C then refused to pay A's legal fee, claiming that it was unreasonably high. If A is unable to settle the fee dispute amicably and has to sue C to collect the fee, A may reveal C's confidential disclosures to the extent necessary to prove why A's fee is reasonable under the circumstances. [ABA Model Rule 1.6(b)(5)]

2) Lawyer L defended client D in an arson case. D told L in confidence that he did burn the building, hoping to collect the fire insurance. After careful consideration, D followed L's advice and did not testify on his own behalf at the trial. Furthermore, L refused to call two alibi witnesses whose testimony L knew would be false. D was convicted. D then sued L for legal malpractice. In defending against D's malpractice claim, L may reveal as much of D's confidential disclosures as is necessary to prove why L did not present the testimony of D and the two alibi witnesses. [*Id.*]

3) In the arson example described above, instead of suing L for malpractice, D filed a complaint with the state bar, accusing L of incompetence in the conduct of the trial. At the disciplinary hearing, L may reveal as much of D's confidential disclosures as is necessary to prove why L did not present the testimony of D and the two alibi witnesses. [*Id.*]

4) Client T hired attorney Y to help him form a limited partnership venture for real estate investments. T furnished Y with confidential data for Y to use in preparing financial statements and other documents needed in connection with the sale of the partnership shares. Unbeknownst to Y, some of the confidential data was fraudulent, and T's partners lost their investments as a consequence. Two of the partners confronted Y and accused him of being knowingly involved in the fraud. Y *may* reveal enough of T's confidential information to convince the partners that Y did not know that the data was fraudulent, even though Y has not yet been formally charged with a criminal or civil wrong or a disciplinary violation. [*See* Comment 10 to ABA Model Rule 1.6] This illustrates the doctrine called "preemptive self-defense." [*See* Hazard & Hodes, §9.23]

d. Disclosure to Obtain Legal Ethics Advice

A lawyer may disclose enough of the client's confidential information as is necessary to obtain legal ethics advice for the lawyer. [ABA Model Rule 1.6(b)(4)]

Example: Client C came to attorney A's office carrying a mysterious package about the size of a shoebox. C explained that federal narcotics agents were looking for C in connection with the illegal importation of a significant quantity of uncut heroin; C told A that he had no connection with any heroin or any other drug trade. A agreed to represent C, and he asked C for a $5,000 advance on attorneys' fees. C replied that he had no ready cash, but that he would entrust A with the mysterious package, assuring A that its contents were worth much more than $5,000. A was uncertain about his ethical obligations in this situation so he excused himself, went to another room, and telephoned T, his old legal ethics professor. After disclosing enough facts to give T the essence of the problem—but not enough to disclose C's identity or the precise circumstances—A asked T for legal ethics advice. A's disclosure was proper. [*Id.*]

e. Disclosure Required by Law or Court Order

ABA Model Rule 1.6(b)(6) permits a lawyer to reveal her client's confidential information to the extent that she is required to do so by law or court order.

Examples: 1) Suppose that a federal anti-terrorism statute arguably requires lawyer L to reveal the whereabouts of client C, who is suspected of illegal entry into the United States. If L knows of C's whereabouts only because of a confidential communication from C, the information is protected by both the attorney-client privilege and the ethical duty of confidentiality. L must first determine whether the anti-terrorism statute purports to supercede the privilege and ethical duty. [*See* Comment 12 to ABA Model Rule 1.6] If L concludes that it does, she must next disclose the situation to C because this is the kind of vital information that a lawyer must communicate to a client. [*See* ABA Model Rule 1.4(a)(3)] If L cannot find a nonfrivolous ground for challenging the validity or applicability of the statute, ABA Model Rule 1.6(b)(6) permits her to reveal the information about C's whereabouts. [*See* Comments 12 and 13 to ABA Model Rule 1.6]

2) In the situation described in 1), above, suppose that a federal district judge is considering whether to order L to disclose C's whereabouts. Absent C's informed consent to the disclosure, L should assert all nonfrivolous grounds for not disclosing the information. If the court orders disclosure, L should consult with C about an appeal. If no appeal is taken, or if the order is upheld on appeal, then ABA Model Rule 1.6(b)(6) permits L to reveal the information about C's whereabouts. [*Id.*]

f. Disclosure to Prevent Death or Substantial Bodily Harm

ABA Model Rule 1.6(b)(1) permits a lawyer to reveal the client's confidential information to the extent that the lawyer reasonably believes necessary to prevent ***reasonably***

certain death or substantial bodily harm. [*Accord* Restatement §66] Note that the exception applies to death or bodily harm whatever the cause; it need not be caused by the client, and the cause need not be a criminal act. Notice also that the death or bodily harm need not be imminent—it need only be reasonably certain. Finally, notice that the exception gives the lawyer ***discretion*** to disclose the confidential information; it does ***not require*** disclosure. Some states, however, do require disclosure.

Examples: 1) Kidnapper K is in custody pending trial, and he hires attorney A to defend him against a charge that he kidnapped and murdered victim V. K tells A in confidence where he buried V's body. This is a completed crime—disclosure of K's secret could not prevent death or substantial bodily harm to anyone. If A reveals K's secret, A will be subject to discipline.

2) Kidnapper J telephones attorney B and asks for B's legal advice. J tells B in confidence that he has kidnapped victim U, that he has her bound and gagged in the back of his van, and that he is on the road to Lonesome Pine, where he plans to hold U for ransom. The legal advice J seeks from B is whether the penalty for murder is more serious than the penalty for kidnapping for ransom. B promises to call J back in a few minutes. B then telephones the police, tells them the situation, and tells them that J is on the road to Lonesome Pine. B's conduct is proper in light of the reasonably certain risk of death or substantial bodily injury to U.

g.   **Disclosure to Prevent or Mitigate Substantial Financial Harm**
The Restatement, about 90% of the states, and now the ABA Model Rules permit a lawyer to reveal the client's confidential information to the extent necessary to prevent the client from committing a crime or fraud that is reasonably certain to result in ***substantial financial harm*** to someone, if the client is using or has used the lawyer's services in the matter. The same is true if the client has already acted, and the lawyer's disclosure can prevent or mitigate the consequent financial harm. [*See* Restatement §67; ABA Model Rule 1.6(b)(2), (3), as amended in August 2003]

V.   DUTY TO EXERCISE INDEPENDENT PROFESSIONAL JUDGMENT

A.   THE GENERAL RULES CONCERNING CONFLICTS OF INTEREST
Loyalty is an essential element in the relationship between a lawyer and client. The lawyer's professional judgment must be exercised solely for the benefit of the client, free of compromising influences and loyalties. [*See* Restatement §§121 - 135—restates the law of conflicts of interest; *and see* Comment 1 to ABA Model Rule 1.7] Thus, absent the necessary informed consent, a lawyer must not represent a client if a conflict of interest exists. A conflict of interest arises when there is a substantial risk that the lawyer's representation of the client will be materially and adversely affected by the lawyer's own interests or the lawyer's duties to another current client, a former client, or a third person. [Restatement §121; ABA Model Rule 1.7(a)]

1.   Consequences of a Conflict of Interest
If a conflict of interest is apparent ***before*** a lawyer takes on a client's matter, then the lawyer

must not take it on. [ABA Model Rule 1.7(a)] If a conflict becomes apparent only *after* the lawyer has taken on the client's matter, and if informed consent of the affected client(s) will not solve the problem, then the lawyer must withdraw. [ABA Model Rule 1.16(a)(1); Comment 4 to ABA Model Rule 1.7] A lawyer's failure to handle a conflict properly can have three unpleasant consequences: (i) disqualification as counsel in a litigated matter, (ii) professional discipline, and (iii) civil liability for legal malpractice.

2. Imputed Conflicts of Interest

Generally, lawyers who practice together in a "firm" are treated as a single unit for conflict of interest purposes. That is, when one of the lawyers cannot take on a matter because of a conflict of interest, the other lawyers in the "firm" are also barred from taking on that matter. [ABA Model Rule 1.10(a)] The conflict is said to be "imputed" from the first lawyer to the other lawyers.

a. Meaning of "Firm"

The term "firm" includes not only an ordinary private law firm, but also other groups of lawyers who practice closely together, such as lawyers in a corporate law department, legal aid office, or prosecutors' or public defenders' office. [*See* ABA Model Rule 1.0(c) and Comments 2 - 4] Whether a group of lawyers should be regarded as a "firm" for conflict of interest purposes depends on many factors, including: (i) do the lawyers have a formal agreement among themselves, (ii) do they hold themselves out in a way that would make the public think they practice together as a firm, (iii) do they share their revenues and responsibilities, (iv) do they have physical access to each other's client files, (v) do they routinely talk among themselves about the matters they are handling, and (vi) would the purpose of the particular conflict rule be served by imputing one lawyer's conflict to other lawyers in the group.

b. Exceptions to Imputed Disqualification

As will be seen in the paragraphs below, some kinds of conflicts are *not* imputed to other lawyers in the firm. Generally, these conflicts are uniquely personal to the lawyer in question, which makes it unlikely that other lawyers in the firm would have divided loyalties. [ABA Model Rule 1.10(a) and Comment 3]

Example: Client C hires attorney A to defend her in a copyright infringement action. After A takes on C's case, C commences a sexual relationship with lawyer L, who is one of A's law partners. ABA Model Rule 1.8(j) prohibits a lawyer from starting a sexual relationship with a client (*see* B.4.h.3), *infra*); therefore, L would be subject to discipline if he himself were defending C in the copyright case. However, L's conflict is uniquely personal to L and is not likely to affect the way L's partner A handles C's case. Thus, L's conflict is not imputed to partner A.

B. CONFLICTS OF INTEREST—CURRENT CLIENTS

1. Concurrent Conflicts of Interest

Except on the conditions stated in 2., below, a lawyer must not represent a client if the representation creates a concurrent conflict of interest. A concurrent conflict exists in two situations:

(i) The representation of one client will be ***directly adverse*** to another client; or

(ii) There is a ***significant risk*** that the representation of one client will be ***materially limited*** by the lawyer's own interest or by the lawyer's responsibilities to another client, a former client, or a third person.

[ABA Model Rule 1.7(a)]

Example: Client C asked attorney A to defend her in a vehicular manslaughter case in which C is charged with killing victim V while driving drunk. Unbeknownst to C, V was A's college roommate, and they remained best friends until V's death. There is a significant risk that A's efforts on C's behalf would be materially limited by A's personal grief at the loss of his best friend. Therefore, A must not take on C's case.

2. Informed, Written Consent Can Solve Some Conflicts

Despite a concurrent conflict of interest, a lawyer ***may*** represent a client if all four of the following conditions are satisfied: (i) the lawyer reasonably believes that he can competently and diligently represent each affected client, despite the conflict of interest; (ii) the representation is not prohibited by law; (iii) the representation does not involve asserting a claim by one client against another client represented by that lawyer in the same litigation (or other proceeding before a tribunal); and (iv) each affected client gives informed, written consent. [ABA Model Rule 1.7(b)]

a. Consent Must Meet Reasonable Lawyer Standard

Notice that the consent rule creates a ***reasonable lawyer standard***. That is, if a reasonable lawyer looking at the facts would conclude that the client's interests would not be adequately protected in light of the conflict, then the conflict is ***unconsentable***, meaning that the client's consent will not solve the conflict. [*See* Comments 14 and 15 to ABA Model Rule 1.7]

Example: General practitioner G represents husband H in legal matters arising out of the investment of H's inherited fortune. G has represented H for many years, and he knows all of H's innermost secrets, both financial and personal. Now wife W has asked G to represent her in obtaining a divorce from H. In light of all of the confidential information G has learned about H over the years, a reasonable lawyer would have to advise H ***not*** to consent to the conflict of interest. Thus, even if H did consent, the consent would not solve the conflict.

b. Consent Must Be Informed

Only ***informed*** consent will solve a conflict. That means that the affected client is aware of all of the relevant circumstances, reasonable alternatives, and foreseeable ways the conflict might harm her. [*See* ABA Model Rule 1.0(e); Comment 18 to ABA Model Rule 1.7] Sometimes a lawyer cannot obtain informed consent from one client without revealing a fact that she learned in confidence from another client; if the second client will not permit the lawyer to reveal that confidence, then the lawyer cannot represent the first client; consent will not solve the conflict.

c. Consent Must Be in Writing

A consent that is merely oral will not solve a conflict. The consent must be "confirmed in writing." Usually that means either of two things: (i) there is a **_tangible or electronic record_** that is physically or electronically **_signed_** by the client; or (ii) there is an **_oral_** consent that is **_promptly memorialized_** in a tangible or electronic record that is promptly sent to the client. [*See* ABA Model Rule 1.0(b), (n); Comment 20 to ABA Model Rule 1.7] *But note*: The client's consent to an aggregate settlement or a business transaction with the lawyer must be **_signed by the client_** (*see* C.1.a. and C.6., *infra*). [ABA Model Rule 1.8(a), (g)]

1) Rationale

The writing requirement has two purposes: (i) it helps impress on the client that consent to a conflict is a serious matter, and (ii) it helps avoid later disputes that might arise if there were no writing.

d. Revocation of Consent

Just as a client can almost always fire a lawyer, the client can almost always revoke a previously given consent to a conflict. [Comment 21 to ABA Model Rule 1.7] The revocation may or may not mean that the lawyer can continue representing other clients in the matter, depending on the particular facts. [*Id.*]

e. Consent to Future Conflicts

A lawyer may properly ask a client to consent to conflicts that may arise in the future, but only if it is **_reasonable_** to do so, and only if the client truly understands the particular kinds of conflicts that may arise and the consequences of consenting. [Comment 22 to ABA Model Rule 1.7]

Example: The standard contract that a firm of class action lawyers uses when signing up class representatives provides that: "Client hereby consents to and waives any and all conflicts of interest, both present and future." The contract does not explain the possible present or future conflicts, nor do the lawyers offer any explanation when they sign up the class representatives. The consent provision is invalid.

3. Specific Conflict Situations Concerning "Direct Adversity" Between Clients' Interests

ABA Model Rule 1.7(a) prohibits a lawyer from representing one client whose interests are **_directly adverse_** to those of another client, unless both of the affected clients give their informed, written consent. The following examples show the bounds of "direct adversity."

Examples: 1) Lawyer L represents patent owner O in connection with the licensing of O's patent. Manufacturer M is one of O's licensees, but M does not realize that L represents O. M asks L's law partner P to sue O for a declaratory judgment that O's patent is invalid and that O's license agreements are void. Obviously, L herself could not represent M because M's interests are directly adverse to O's interests. L's conflict is imputed to her law partner P. A reasonable lawyer would advise O and M not to consent to this conflict. Moreover, consent will not solve the conflict when one client sues another client represented by the lawyer in the same litigation. [*See* ABA Model Rule 1.7(b)(3)] Therefore, P must not represent M.

2) Attorney A represents GenCorp, a genetic engineering company that is working on a cure for melanoma. A's law partner P represents BioTek, another genetic engineering company that is working on an entirely different

way to cure melanoma. BioTek and GenCorp are head-to-head adversaries in an economic sense, but their interests are not adverse in any legal sense. If A and her partner P can disclose the situation to their respective clients without revealing confidential information, they may do so for the sake of client goodwill, but they would not be subject to discipline for failing to do so. [*See* Comment 6 to ABA Model Rule 1.7]

3) Lawyer L is defending D, who is accused of the armed robbery of a liquor store. L is stunned when he sees the prosecutor's witness list because it includes Z, a purported eyewitness to the armed robbery. L knows Z very well because he is defending Z in a drunk driving case. From confidential information L gathered in the drunk driving case, L knows that Z is an alcoholic who sometimes sees things that are not there and sometimes remembers things that did not happen. In defending D, L will have to cross-examine Z about his capacity to perceive, remember, and relate events accurately. If L cross-examines Z vigorously, he might seem to be using information about Z that he learned in confidence, or at least Z might think so. On the other hand, if L soft-peddles the cross-examination of Z, D might think he is not getting the effective assistance of counsel. A reasonable lawyer would have to advise D and Z not to consent to this conflict of interest. L must seek the court's permission to withdraw from one case or the other, preferably the case in which his withdrawal will be least harmful to the client. [*See* Comment 6 to ABA Model Rule 1.7]

4) Attorney A represents client C as plaintiff in an employment discrimination case against Mack's Grill. While that matter is pending, one of A's regular clients, Grinch Rentals, Inc., asks A to represent it in unlawful detainer proceedings to have C thrown out of her apartment for failure to pay rent. Even if the two cases are completely unrelated, A faces a conflict of interest. If A agrees to represent Grinch, C could feel betrayed by her own lawyer, and that could destroy A's ability to represent C effectively in the employment discrimination case. [*See* Comment 6 to ABA Model Rule 1.7] Would the conflict be solved by getting the informed, written consent of both C and Grinch? Comment 6 suggests that it could. (Do you agree?)

5) Lawyer L represents buyer B in negotiations for the purchase of a run-down shopping center from seller S. While those negotiations are in progress, S seeks to hire L to represent it in negotiations with the Planning Commission of a different city concerning an urban renewal project S wants to pursue. The shopping center sale is totally unrelated to the urban renewal project. Nevertheless, L must not represent S without first getting the informed, written consent of both B and S. [*See* Comment 7 to ABA Model Rule 1.7]

4. Specific Conflict Situations Concerning "Material Limitation"

The discussion in 3., above, concerned conflicts caused by "direct adversity" between the interests of two clients. ABA Model Rule 1.7 also covers a second kind of conflict—situations in which there is a *significant risk* that the lawyer's representation of a client will be *materially limited* by the lawyer's own personal interests or by the lawyer's responsibilities to: (i) a different client, (ii) a former client, or (iii) a third person. [ABA Model Rule 1.7(a)(2)] When there is such a risk, the lawyer must not take on the matter (or must withdraw), unless each affected client gives informed, written consent. Illustrations of these "material limitation" conflicts are discussed in a. through h., below.

a. Representing Co-Parties in Litigation

Suppose that two plaintiffs or two defendants ask a single lawyer to represent both of them in a litigated matter. The advantages of having a single lawyer are obvious: the cost will probably be lower than having two lawyers, and the single lawyer can present a united front for both clients. The disadvantages are also obvious: the interests of the two clients may be mostly harmonious but partly or potentially in conflict (*e.g.*, one personal injury plaintiff may need money badly and may therefore be anxious to accept a joint settlement offer that the other plaintiff thinks is too low).

1) Criminal Litigation

The Sixth Amendment guarantees every criminal defendant the right to effective assistance of counsel. Because the interests of criminal co-defendants are very likely to diverge, ordinarily a lawyer should not try to defend two people in a criminal case. [Comment 23 to ABA Model Rule 1.7] If a trial judge requires two criminal defendants with divergent interests to share a single lawyer, and if they are prejudiced as a result, their Sixth Amendment rights have been violated. [*See* Strickland v. Washington, 466 U.S. 668 (1984); Cuyler v. Sullivan, 446 U.S. 335 (1980)] Here are four examples of divergent interests:

a) One defendant seeks to put the blame on the other;

b) The story told by one defendant is inconsistent with the story told by the other;

c) One defendant has a strong defense that is compromised to protect the other; and

d) The trial tactics that would help one would harm the other.

2) Civil Litigation

In civil litigation, one lawyer *may* represent two plaintiffs or two defendants whose interests are potentially in conflict, but *only if* the two clients give informed, written consent. [*See* Comment 23 to ABA Model Rule 1.7] There is a four-step guide for handling this situation:

a) First, the lawyer should *analyze the facts* of the case and the applicable law. If she concludes that she can *effectively represent both clients*, despite their potentially conflicting interests, then she can move to the second step. [*See* Comment 15 to ABA Model Rule 1.7]

b) Second, the lawyer should *disclose the potential conflict* to each client and explain how it can harm each client, the reasonably available alternatives, and the disadvantages of having only one lawyer for the two of them. [*See* Comment 18 to ABA Model Rule 1.7]

c)   Third, when the clients fully understand the situation, the lawyer may invite their *informed, written consent* to the joint representation. [*Id.*]

d)   Fourth, *if the potential conflict eventually ripens into a present conflict*, the lawyer must repeat steps a), b), and c), above. The lawyer must withdraw from the joint representation if a reasonable lawyer would have to advise either of the two clients not to consent. [*See* Comments 4, 14, and 15 to ABA Model Rule 1.7] The lawyer may continue to represent one consenting client, but only if the client who is dropped gives informed, written consent to the continuation. [*See* ABA Model Rule 1.9(a)]

Example: Attorney A agreed to defend Ace Corp. and Bay Corp. in a negligence case. At the outset, A believed that neither Ace nor Bay caused the harm to the plaintiff. A went through steps a), b), and c), above, and obtained Ace's and Bay's informed, written consent to the joint representation. Discovery revealed that Ace had a credible defense, but that Bay was very likely negligent, and that its negligence probably harmed the plaintiff. A repeated steps a), b), and c), at which point Ace insisted on obtaining a separate lawyer. A *may* continue representing Bay, but *only if* Ace gives informed, written consent under ABA Model Rule 1.9(a), and Bay gives informed, written consent under ABA Model Rule 1.7(b).

b.   **Representing Two Clients with Inconsistent Legal Positions in Two Unrelated Cases**

Suppose a lawyer represents two clients in different cases that are pending in different tribunals. On behalf of Client One, the lawyer needs to argue that a certain statute is unconstitutional. On behalf of Client Two, the lawyer needs to argue that the same statute is constitutional. Aside from that legal issue, the cases are unrelated. On those bare facts, there is no conflict of interest between Client One and Client Two. [Comment 24 to ABA Model Rule 1.7] Suppose, however, that Client One's case will be heard next week in the intermediate appellate court that hears cases from Judicial District Six. Client Two's case will be tried seven months from now in a trial court in Judicial District Six. Thus, the appellate court's decision in Client One's case is likely to become the controlling precedent in Client Two's case. That presents a substantial risk that the lawyer's representation of one client will be materially limited by her responsibilities to the other client. [*Id.*] Therefore, the lawyer must fully disclose the situation to both clients and seek their informed, written consent. If either or both clients will not consent, the lawyer must seek the court's permission to withdraw from one or both cases. [*Id.*]

c.   **Unnamed Members of a Class Do Not Count as Clients**

In class action litigation, the unnamed members of a class ordinarily are *not* regarded as clients for conflict of interest purposes. [Comment 25 to ABA Model Rule 1.7]

Example: Lawyer L is presently representing victim V in a medical malpractice case against Dr. D. Today, United Motors Corp. asked L to defend it in a class action case that is unrelated to the malpractice case. V is not a named plaintiff in the class action, but she will be a member of the class if the court eventually certifies the case as a class action. L does not need to obtain V's consent before agreeing to defend United Motors. [*Id.*]

d. **Representing Multiple Clients in Nonlitigation Matters**
Lawyers are often asked to represent more than one client in nonlitigation matters. Whether that creates a conflict of interest depends on many factors, including the length and intimacy of the lawyer's relationship with one or more of the clients, the kind of work the lawyer is asked to do, the chances of disagreement between the clients, and the consequences to the clients if the joint representation breaks down. [*See* Comment 26 to ABA Model Rule 1.7]

Examples: 1) Clients X, Y, and Z ask lawyer L to represent the three of them in forming a new business venture. X will supply the capital, Y will supply a valuable trade secret, and Z will supply the managerial skill. Although their interests are mostly harmonious, there are potential conflicts. For instance, if the venture folds, who will own the trade secret? L *may* represent all three clients if she follows the four steps outlined in e., below.

2) Estate planning attorney E is asked to prepare estate plans and wills for four members of a family—G (the wealthy grandmother), H and W (the irresponsible parents), and D (the talented daughter). All four have the same basic goals: to maximize the family's wealth and to allocate it rationally. However, their interests are potentially in conflict. For instance, H and W may want to get their hands on money that G wants to preserve for D. E *may* represent all of the family members if she follows the four steps outlined in e., below.

e. **Handling Conflicts in Nonlitigation Matters**
The same four-step process discussed in a.2), *supra*, is suitable for handling conflicts in nonlitigation matters:

1) The lawyer should *analyze the facts* and law to see if she can *effectively represent* the various clients, despite their potentially conflicting interests.

2) Next, the lawyer should *disclose the potential conflicts* to each client and explain how they can harm each client, the reasonable alternatives, and the disadvantages of having only one lawyer.

3) When the clients fully understand the situation, the lawyer may invite their *informed, written consent* to the joint representation.

4) If a *potential conflict ripens into a present conflict*, the lawyer must repeat steps 1), 2), and 3), above. The lawyer must withdraw from the joint representation if a reasonable lawyer would have to advise any of the clients not to consent. [*See* Comments 4, 14, and 15 to ABA Model Rule 1.7] The lawyer may continue to represent one or more consenting clients, but only if the clients who are dropped give their informed, written consent to the continuation. [See ABA Model Rule 1.9(a)]

f. **Special Problems of Representing More than One Client**
A lawyer is often able to create or adjust a relationship between two or more clients by

identifying and building on the interests that the clients have in common. [Comment 28 to ABA Model Rule 1.7] When doing this, the lawyer must be impartial in dealing with the several clients. [Comment 29 to ABA Model Rule 1.7] If the relationships among the clients are already antagonistic, or if contentious negotiations or litigation is on the horizon, a single lawyer ordinarily should not try to represent all of the clients. [*Id.*]

g. Confidentiality and Privilege Problems

In litigation between two people who were formerly joint clients of a single lawyer, neither of them can claim the attorney-client privilege for their communications with that lawyer. [*See* 1 McCormick on Evidence 365-366 (Practitioner's 5th ed. 1999)] That is one disadvantage of having one lawyer for multiple clients, and the lawyer should warn the clients about it before undertaking multiple representation. Moreover, a multiple representation is unlikely to work if one client wants to disclose material to the lawyer in confidence and wants to keep it confidential from the other clients. [Comment 31 to ABA Model Rule 1.7] Therefore, the lawyer should ordinarily make clear to all clients at the outset that whatever one client discloses will be shared with all of the other clients. [*Id.*] In special situations, however, the clients may agree that one of them may disclose a given item of information to the lawyer but not to the other clients.

Example: Clients X, Y, and Z hire attorney A to represent all of them in forming a new business venture. Z's contribution to the business will be a valuable invention. Z has applied for a patent, but until a patent issues, the specifics of the invention are protected as Z's trade secret. X, Y, and Z may agree that Z may disclose the specifics of the invention to A in confidence and that A will not share that information with X or Y.

h. Conflicts Caused by Lawyer's Own Interests

If a lawyer's own interests are likely to materially limit her ability to represent a client effectively, then she must not take on the matter (or she must withdraw) unless she obtains the client's informed, written consent. [*See* ABA Model Rule 1.7(a)(2)] The following paragraphs illustrate some of the lawyer's interests that may create a conflict.

1) Lawyer's Financial Interest

A conflict of interest may be created by a lawyer's own financial interest. Suppose that attorney A is representing client C in a gender discrimination action against Magnum Corp. After one of the pretrial hearings, the general counsel of Magnum spoke quietly to A in the courthouse hallway, saying: "Your courtroom skills are first-rate. When you want to start playing in the big leagues, please come to see me—our law department could really use a person like you, and we pay top money." If the employment overture creates a substantial risk that A will curry favor with Magnum at C's expense, A must fully disclose the situation to C and obtain C's informed, written consent before continuing as C's counsel.

2) Lawyers Who Are Close Relatives

A conflict of interest also may be created by a lawyer's relationship to another lawyer. Suppose that lawyer L is a partner in the J, K, & L firm. L lives with her parents, and her mother M is the senior litigation partner of the M, N, & O firm. M regularly serves as trial counsel for the Kansas Central Railway Co. in railway accident cases. L's regular client C was badly injured when his car was struck at a crossing by one of Kansas Central's trains, and C asked L to represent him in a suit against Kansas Central. If L serves as C's lawyer, and M serves as Kansas Central's lawyer, there is a risk that client confidences may be compromised (*e.g.*, if M takes a telephone message at home for L, M may inadvertently learn something confidential about C). [*See* Comment 11 to ABA Model Rule 1.7] Moreover, the family relationship may interfere with the loyalty or independent judgment of the two lawyers. [*Id.*] Thus, L and M must each disclose the situation to their respective clients and must not proceed without their respective client's informed, written consent. The same is true of other lawyers who are closely related by blood or marriage (*e.g.*, parent, child, spouse, or sibling). This kind of conflict is personal in nature and is ordinarily *not* imputed to other lawyers in a firm. [*Id.*]

3) Sexual Relationship Between Lawyer and Client

A sexual relationship between a lawyer and client may create a conflict of interest. Suppose that client C hired lawyer L to represent him in divorce proceedings commenced by his wife. Perhaps because he was at a vulnerable time in his life, C made sexual overtures to L, and she responded with enthusiasm. Because a sexual relationship between a lawyer and client is likely to distort the lawyer's professional judgment and endanger confidentiality and the attorney-client privilege, such a relationship makes the lawyer *subject to discipline*, whether or not the client consents and whether or not the client is harmed. [*See* ABA Model Rule 1.8(j); Comment 12 to ABA Model Rule 1.7; Comments 17, 18, and 19 to ABA Model Rule 1.8] The prohibition also applies to a lawyer who represents an organization and who has a sexual relationship with the organization's liaison person. Note that the prohibition does not apply when the sexual relationship began before the lawyer-client relationship began, but even then the lawyer should stop to consider whether the sexual relationship will impair the lawyer-client relationship. [Comment 18 to ABA Model Rule 1.8] The conflict created by a sexual relationship is personal and is *not* imputed to other lawyers in the lawyer's firm. [*See* ABA Model Rule 1.8(k)]

C. CONFLICTS OF INTEREST—SPECIFIC RULES FOR CURRENT CLIENTS

The discussion in B., *supra*, covered the general principles concerning conflicts of interests that involve one or more current clients, which is the subject matter of ABA Model Rule 1.7. However, some kinds of conflicts arise time and time again in law practice. They are so common that the drafters of the ABA Model Rules devised specific rules to deal with them. These rules are the subject matter of ABA Model Rule 1.8, discussed below.

1. Business Transactions with Client and Money or Property Interests Adverse to Client

a. Statement of the Rule

A lawyer's professional training, together with the bond of trust and confidence between a lawyer and client, create a risk that the lawyer can overreach the client in a business, property, or financial transaction. Therefore, a lawyer must not enter into a business transaction with a client or knowingly acquire an ownership, possessory, security, or money interest that is adverse to a client, unless all of the following conditions are satisfied:

(i) The terms of the business transaction (or the terms on which the interest is acquired) are *fair to the client*;

(ii) The terms are *fully disclosed* to the client *in writing*, expressed in a manner that the client can reasonably understand (not legal gobbledygook). The lawyer's disclosure to the client must cover the *essential terms* of the transaction and the *lawyer's role* in the transaction (including whether the lawyer is acting as the client's lawyer in the transaction);

(iii) The client is advised *in writing* that he should get the *advice of an independent lawyer* about the arrangement before entering into it (and the client must be given a reasonable chance to obtain that advice); and

(iv) The client gives *informed consent, in a writing that the client signs*.

[ABA Model Rule 1.8(a)]

b. Outer Limits of the Rule
The lawyer need not advise the client to consult independent counsel if the client already has independent counsel in the matter. Moreover, if the client has independent counsel, the disclosure of conflict can be made by the independent counsel. Finally, the rule about business transactions and adverse interests does not apply to an ordinary fee agreement between a lawyer and client or to ordinary commercial transactions in which the lawyer buys goods or services that the client routinely markets to the public (*e.g.*, the lawyer who buys a car from his car dealer client or the lawyer who uses a client as her stockbroker). [*See* Comments 1 - 4 to ABA Model Rule 1.8]

2. Misuse of Client's Confidential Information
As was discussed previously in IV.A., *supra*, a lawyer has a duty not to disclose information relating to the representation of a client, except when an exception to the duty of confidentiality applies. In addition, a lawyer must not use such information to the *client's disadvantage*, unless the client gives informed consent or some other exception to the duty of confidentiality applies. [*See* ABA Model Rule 1.8(b)] The same rule applies to misuse of a *former or prospective* client's confidential information. [*See* ABA Model Rules 1.9(c)(1), 1.18(b)]

Example: Prospective client P came to patent attorney A's office, seeking to hire A to file a patent application on P's behalf. In the course of their preliminary discussions, P told A what chemical compound he uses to make his invention work. P ultimately decided not to hire A. A then told one of his other inventor clients about the chemical compound, and that client used the information in a way that prevented P from obtaining a patent. A is subject to discipline. [*See* ABA Model Rule 1.18(b)]

a. Use to Benefit Lawyer or Someone Else
The rule applies not only when the lawyer uses the information for the lawyer's own benefit, but also when the lawyer uses it to benefit someone else, such as another client or a third party.

Example: While representing client Chez Nous Catering Co., lawyer L learned that Chez Nous was teetering on the edge of insolvency. L knew that his good friend F had contracted with Chez Nous to cater F's daughter's big wedding reception. L advised F to cancel the contract and hire a different caterer. L is subject to discipline for using the information to the disadvantage of Chez Nous.

b.   Possible Civil Liability Even When Client Is Not Disadvantaged
Note that the rule applies only when the lawyer's misuse of confidential information disadvantages the client, former client, or prospective client. However, a lawyer who uses the confidential information for his own pecuniary gain (other than in the practice of law) may be subject to *civil liability*—*i.e.*, he may have to account to the client, former client, or prospective client for his profits. [Restatement §60(2)]

Example: Attorney A's client C told A in confidence that she was about to build a large new medical complex on the corner of 5th and Main Streets. Without telling C, A quietly bought land at 4th and Main and built a four-story parking garage to serve the new medical complex. The garage did not harm C; in fact it was a benefit to her. Nevertheless, A must disgorge the garage profits to C because A used C's confidential information to enrich himself other than in the practice of law.

3.   Gifts to Lawyer from Client Who Is Not a Relative
The following rules limit a lawyer's freedom to solicit or accept a substantial gift from a client who is not the lawyer's relative. The same rules apply to a substantial gift from a client to the lawyer's relative. In this rule, "relative" includes a spouse, child, parent, grandparent, grandchild, and other persons with whom the lawyer maintains a close, familial relationship. [ABA Model Rule 1.8(c)] "Gift" includes a testamentary gift. [*Id.*]

a.   Soliciting Substantial Gift
A lawyer must not *solicit* a *substantial* gift from a client who is not the lawyer's relative. However, a lawyer may accept a small gift from a client, such as a token of appreciation or an appropriate holiday gift. [Comment 6 to ABA Model Rule 1.8] Indeed, the rule does not prohibit a lawyer from accepting even a substantial gift, although the gift may be voidable for undue influence.

Example: Lawyer L is a loyal alumnus of Port Arthur School of Law. The school asked L to serve as a pro bono legal advisor to a committee that was drafting a new affirmative action policy for the school. L gladly agreed and worked many hours on the project for no fee. When the work was done, L told the school's dean that his daughter would love to attend the school, but that she could not afford the high tuition. The dean then arranged for L's daughter to be admitted on a full scholarship. L is subject to discipline for soliciting a substantial gift from the school to his daughter.

b.   Preparing Legal Instrument that Creates Substantial Gift
ABA Model Rule 1.8(c) also prohibits a lawyer from preparing a legal instrument (such as a will or a deed of gift) that creates a substantial gift to the lawyer (or the lawyer's relative), except when the donor is one of the lawyer's relatives.

Example: Attorney A's aged father asks her to draft a new will for him. The father tells A that he wants to set up a testamentary trust that will provide college funds for A's children. A may draft the will and related documents, but only because the client is her father.

c. **Lucrative Appointments**

ABA Model Rule 1.8(c) does not prohibit a lawyer from seeking to have himself or his law partner or associate named as executor of an estate or counsel to the executor or to some other fee-paying position. However, the general conflict of interest principles expressed in ABA Model Rule 1.7 do prohibit such efforts if the lawyer's advice is tainted by the lawyer's self-interest. [Comment 8 to ABA Model Rule 1.8] Moreover, lawyers with long experience in probate and estate planning law know that clients tend to rebel when they discover the lawyer trying to feather his own nest in this manner.

4. **Acquiring Literary or Media Rights Concerning Client's Case**

A lawyer must not acquire literary or media rights to a story based in substantial part on information relating to the lawyer's representation of a client. However, a lawyer may acquire such rights *after* the client's legal matter is entirely completed, appeals and all. [ABA Model Rule 1.8(d)] The reason behind the rule is that the client's interest in effective representation may conflict with the lawyer's interest in maximizing the value of the literary or media rights. For instance, the lawyer might conduct the client's criminal trial in a sensational manner, simply to pump up public interest in the client's story. The rule does not apply to literary or media rights that are not substantially based on information relating to the representation. [Comment 9 to ABA Model Rule 1.8]

Example: Legendary rock star Deep River wrote an autobiography that tells the story of his rise from a poverty-stricken childhood to a beloved musical icon. Attorney A agreed to represent River in negotiating a book contract and a motion picture contract. In lieu of money, A agreed to do the legal work in return for 5% of the book and movie royalties. The literary rights rule does not apply to this arrangement because River's manuscript is about his life and not about negotiation of the book and movie contracts. [*Id.*] However, the arrangement must comply with ABA Model Rule 1.5 (prohibits unreasonably high fee) and ABA Model Rule 1.8(a) (business transactions with a client).

5. **Financial Assistance to Client in Litigation**

ABA Model Rule 1.8(e) prohibits a lawyer from financially assisting a client in connection with pending or contemplated litigation. The prohibition harkens back to ancient English common law, which forbade lawyers from stirring up litigation or supporting it out of their own purse. More to the point, a lawyer who has too great a financial stake in a case may be unable to give the client objective legal advice.

a. **Advancing Litigation Expenses**

A lawyer may advance court costs and other litigation expenses on the client's behalf, and repayment may be contingent on the outcome of the case. [ABA Model Rule 1.8(e)(1)]

Example: Lawyer L's fee agreement with personal injury victim V provides that L will advance the court costs and litigation expenses in V's suit against the person who injured him. The agreement also states that if V wins the case, L will be repaid out of the judgment or settlement proceeds, but that if V loses, L will not be repaid. The fee agreement is proper.

b. **Paying Costs and Expenses for Indigent Client**

A lawyer may simply pay the court costs and litigation expenses for an indigent client, without any provision for repayment. [ABA Model Rule 1.8(e)(2)]

c. **Other Financial Help Is Prohibited**
A lawyer is subject to discipline for giving a client other financial help in the context of pending or contemplated litigation. [ABA Model Rule 1.8(e)]

Example: Chem Corp.'s chemical plant blew up, spreading toxic fumes across pasture land belonging to dozens of dairy farmers. The grass shriveled, the cows died, and the farmers became destitute. The law offices of E.Z. Bucks took out newspaper ads offering to represent the farmers on contingency, to advance the costs and expenses of litigation, and to lend them money to restore their pastures and dairy herds. The last feature of that offer makes the lawyers subject to discipline.

6. **Aggregate Settlement Agreements**
When a lawyer represents several co-parties in a matter (*e.g.*, several plaintiffs or several defendants), the adversary sometimes makes an "aggregate settlement offer," for example, an offer to settle all claims for a lump sum of $1 million. That creates a potential conflict of interest among the lawyer's several clients. Some of them may want to settle for that amount, but others may want to hold out for a better offer. Moreover, the several clients may disagree about how the lump sum is to be allocated—who pays how much or who receives how much. Because of the potential conflict, the lawyer must not participate in the making of an aggregate settlement agreement unless all of the following conditions are met:

(i) The lawyer must assure that the ***clients have come to an agreement*** among themselves about how the aggregate sum will be shared (who will pay how much or receive how much);

(ii) The lawyer must ***disclose all of the terms*** of the sharing agreement to each client and must ***disclose the existence and nature of all of the claims*** that will be settled; and

(iii) Each client must give informed consent to the aggregate settlement agreement in a ***writing signed by the client***.

[ABA Model Rule 1.8(g)]

a. **Class Action Settlements**
In a class action, the lawyer who represents the class ordinarily does not have a complete lawyer-client relationship with the unnamed members of the class. Even so, at settlement time, the class's lawyer must follow all of the class action rules concerning notice and other procedural requirements that protect the unnamed class members. [Comment 13 to ABA Model Rule 1.8]

b. **Aggregate Settlement of Criminal Case**
The same rules that apply to an aggregate settlement in a civil case also apply to a joint plea bargain in a criminal case [ABA Model Rule 1.8(g)], although ordinarily one lawyer will not be representing more than one defendant in a criminal case [*see* Restatement §129(1)].

7. **Waiving Malpractice Liability and Settling Malpractice Claims**

a. **Prospective Waiver or Limit of Malpractice Liability**
A lawyer must not make an agreement with a client that prospectively waives or limits

the lawyer's liability for legal malpractice (except in the unlikely event that the client is independently represented in making the agreement). [ABA Model Rule 1.8(h)(1)] A lawyer *may*, however, do the following:

1) **Practice in a Limited Liability Entity**

   A lawyer may practice in a limited liability entity, provided that the lawyer remains personally liable to the client for her own malpractice, and the entity complies with legal requirements for notice, insurance coverage, and the like. [Comment 14 to ABA Model Rule 1.8]

2) **Reasonably Limit Scope of Representation**

   A lawyer may enter into an agreement with his client that reasonably limits the scope of the lawyer's representation in accordance with ABA Model Rule 1.2. [*Id.*]

   Example: Client C is thinking of purchasing the worldwide distribution rights to a strain of pest-resistant rice. C asks lawyer L to find out whether any nation imposes trade restrictions on that kind of rice. L tells C that to research the laws of every nation could take as much as 300 hours and cost $60,000, but C said he could not afford that much enlightenment. C and L agreed that L would research as many nations as he could in 100 hours, starting with C's most likely markets. The agreement is proper.

3) **Arbitrate Legal Malpractice Claims**

   A lawyer may agree prospectively with a client to arbitrate all legal malpractice claims, provided that such an agreement is proper under local law and the client understands the scope and effect of the agreement. [*Id.*]

b. **Settling Malpractice Claims**

   The law always favors the amicable settlement of claims. Thus, a lawyer *may* settle a malpractice claim or potential claim made by his client, but *only if* the lawyer first advises the client *in writing* to seek the advice of an independent lawyer about the settlement, and the lawyer gives the client a reasonable chance to obtain such advice. [ABA Model Rule 1.8(h)(2)]

8. **Proprietary Interest in Subject of Litigation**

   Except as permitted below, a lawyer must not acquire a proprietary interest in the cause of action or the subject matter of litigation that the lawyer is conducting for the client. [ABA Model Rule 1.8(i); Restatement §36(1)]

   Examples: 1) Lawyer L regularly does consumer loan collection work for American Consumer Finance Company. When one of American's debtors defaults, American assigns the debt and cause of action to L; in return, L immediately pays American 50% of the face value of the debt. If L ultimately collects more than the 50%, she pays half of the excess to American and keeps the other half. L is subject to discipline.

   2) F owns a United States patent on a process for manufacturing fertilizer. R brings a declaratory judgment action against F, alleging that F's patent is invalid. Attorney A agrees to represent F in the declaratory judgment action in exchange for an assignment of a one-half ownership interest in F's patent. A is subject to discipline.

a. Contingent Fee Exception

Despite the rule stated above, a lawyer may enter into a contingent fee arrangement with a client in a civil case. A contingent fee arrangement gives the lawyer a personal stake in the outcome of the case and may thus affect the lawyer's objectivity. This arrangement is thus clearly at odds with the spirit of the rule. Nevertheless, because contingent fees have been so long tolerated in the United States, they are excepted from the rule. [*See* ABA Model Rule 1.8(i)(2)]

Example: In both the American Consumer Finance example and the patent case example (above), the lawyers can escape the general rule by using a contingent fee arrangement rather than an assignment of the cause of action or assignment of one-half ownership of the patent. In both examples, a contingent fee arrangement would be proper.

b. Attorney's Lien Exception

In some states, an attorney is allowed to secure payment of her fee and repayment of advanced litigation expenses by taking a lien on the proceeds of a client's case. Some states authorize attorney's liens by statute or case law. In other states, they must be created by contract between the attorney and the client. [*See generally* Pennsylvania Bar Op. 94-35 (1994)] An attorney's lien gives the attorney a personal stake in the outcome of the client's case, but this situation is tolerated as an exception to the general rule. [ABA Model Rule 1.8(i)(1)]

Example: The law of East Carolina permits an attorney to contract with a client for a lien to secure the attorney's fee and advanced litigation expenses. Attorney A's fee agreement with client C provides that A shall have a lien on whatever C recovers in her case against X to secure payment of A's fee and to secure repayment of litigation expenses that A advances on C's behalf. This provision of A's fee agreement is proper.

D. CONFLICTS INVOLVING THE INTERESTS OF THIRD PERSONS

1. Compensation from Third Person

A lawyer must not accept compensation from a third person for representing a client, *unless* three conditions are met:

(i)   The client *gives informed, written consent*;

(ii)   The third person *does not interfere with the lawyer's independence* or the representation of the client; and

(iii) The arrangement *does not compromise the client's confidential information*.

[ABA Model Rules 1.8(f), 1.7(b), 5.4(c)]

Examples: 1) T, a pimp, seeks to employ attorney A to defend C, who is charged with prostitution. T demands to be present whenever A talks with C, and T directs C to plead not guilty, promising to pay the fine if C is found guilty after trial. If A agrees to represent C under these conditions, A is subject to discipline.

2) Midwest Highway Construction Corp. and its executive vice president C are both indicted for conspiring with other highway contractors to rig the

bids on government highway contracts. Midwest seeks to employ lawyer L to serve as C's separate defense counsel. Midwest will pay L's fee, but will not interfere with L's handling of the case or with the confidentiality of the relationship between L and C. Under these conditions, L may agree to represent C.

3) Trimmers and Fitters Union Local #876 established a group legal service program for the benefit of its members. Using money from union dues, the Local hired the law firm of R, S, and T to provide the necessary legal services to members. Union member C asked the firm to represent her in a sexual harassment case against her fellow worker D, a loyal member of the union. When the president of the Local heard about C's case, he called the law firm, demanding to know what C said about D and demanding that the firm dismiss the case. The law firm must not allow the union or its officials to interfere with the handling of C's case.

2. Conflict Between Client's Interest and Third Person's Interest

Sometimes the interest of a third person may create a substantial risk of materially limiting the lawyer's ability to represent the client effectively. [ABA Model Rule 1.7(a)(2)] When that is true, the lawyer may represent the client, provided that: (i) the lawyer reasonably believes that the third person's interest will not adversely affect the representation; and (ii) the client gives informed, written consent. [ABA Model Rule 1.7(b)]

Examples: 1) Carter Corp. and its executive vice president K were indicted for mail fraud in connection with the interstate sale of certain investment properties. The bylaws of Carter Corp. provide that the corporation will pay for separate legal representation of any officer accused of wrongdoing in the course of the corporation's business; however, there is no provision for indemnifying officers who are found guilty of wrongdoing. Carter Corp. asks lawyer L to provide the necessary separate representation for K. L's fee will be paid by Carter Corp. L may represent K if: (i) the arrangement between Carter Corp. and L assures L's independence, (ii) L reasonably believes that he can represent K effectively, and (iii) K gives informed, written consent.

2) The United Coastal Charities Fund offers to pay attorney A's fee for drafting the will of any person who leaves a bequest of $2,000 or more to the Fund. If A agrees to the arrangement, he will be subject to discipline. [New York City Bar Op. 81-69 (1981)]

3) Lawyer L is a staff attorney for the County Legal Aid Society. Her salary is set by the board of directors of the society, but her clients are those who come to the society for legal assistance and are assigned to L. The board of directors may set general operating policies, but L must not allow the board of directors to influence her independent legal judgment about how to handle a particular client's legal matter. [ABA Model Rule 5.4(c); ABA Formal Op. 334 (1974)]

3. Conflicts Raised by Liability Insurance

a. Policyholder's Interests

Liability insurance policies commonly provide that the insurance company will select and pay for a lawyer to defend the policyholder in suits arising out of events covered by the policy. The policyholder, in turn, promises to cooperate with the defense. Generally, the policyholder wants a claim handled in a way that minimizes his risk of paying money out of his own pocket (*e.g.*, if the policy limit is $50,000, but the claimant wins a judgment for $60,000, the policyholder would have to pay the $10,000 difference from his own pocket).

b.   Insurance Company's Interests
The insurance company generally wants a claim handled in a way that minimizes what it must pay, whether in litigation costs or payments to a claimant. To minimize litigation costs (and thus to keep insurance premiums affordable), some insurance companies adopt spending limits and audit procedures that limit the defense lawyer's fees and expenses for various steps in the litigation process. Insurance defense lawyers have complained that these limits sometimes undercut their ability to represent policyholders effectively.

c.   Whom Does the Defense Lawyer Represent?
Does an insurance defense lawyer represent the policyholder (a person he is likely to encounter only once) or the insurance company (which pays his fees and can send him repeat business)? Curiously, the law on this question varies from state to state. [*See* ABA Formal Op. 01-421, nn. 6, 7 (2001)] Some states say that the client is the policyholder only, but others say that the policyholder and the insurance company are joint clients. [*See* Restatement §134, comments a and f—insurance law and contract law determine who is the client] No matter whether the defense lawyer represents the policyholder only or both the policyholder and the insurance company, the defense lawyer's ethical obligations are governed by the Rules of Professional Conduct and not by the insurance contract. [ABA Formal Op. 01-421]

d.   Conflicts Between Insurance Company and Policyholder
Most of the time, the insurance company's interests are in harmony with those of the policyholder. Both of them want to see the claim defeated or settled at the least possible expense. Their respective interests can, however, come into conflict, as in the following examples.

1)   Is the Event Covered by the Policy?
Suppose that G drove her car over her boyfriend B in circumstances that make it unclear whether G acted intentionally or only negligently. B sued G, alternatively alleging negligence and intentional conduct. G's auto liability policy covers negligence, but not intentional conduct. G's insurance company hired lawyer L to defend the case, but it sent G a "reservation of rights" letter, informing her that it might ultimately contend that G acted intentionally, thus freeing the company from liability. During pretrial preparation, G told L in confidence that she ran over B intentionally. L must not disclose that confidential information to the insurance company. [*See* Parsons v. Continental National American Group, 550 P.2d 94 (Ariz. 1976)] If G's confidential statement means that L cannot defend G effectively, L must withdraw. [Restatement §134, comment f]

2)   Settlement Within the Policy Limits
Suppose that Insco Insurance Co. hires attorney A to defend policyholder D in a

slip-and-fall case brought by P. The liability limit in D's policy is $100,000, and P offers to settle for $90,000. D wants to settle because that would free him from paying P anything from his own pocket. Insco, on the other hand, might rather go to trial because its exposure is only $10,000 more than the settlement offer. The settlement offer creates a conflict of interest that has the following consequences: (i) A and Insco must disclose the conflict to D and invite D to obtain independent counsel (at Insco's expense) to advise D on the settlement issue; (ii) if A fails to do that and negligently or in bad faith advises D to reject the settlement offer, A is subject to discipline and perhaps civil liability to D for malpractice; and (iii) if Insco negligently or in bad faith rejects the settlement offer, Insco will be liable for the entire judgment P obtains against D, even the amount over the policy limits. [Easley v. State Farm Mutual Insurance Co., 528 F.2d 558 (5th Cir. 1976)]

3) Settlement Controlled by Insurance Company

Although the policyholder is usually glad to have the insurance company settle a claim within the policy limits, that is not always true. For example, a physician might not want her malpractice insurance company to settle for fear that the settlement will tarnish her medical reputation. Some insurance policies authorize the insurance company to control the defense and to settle within the policy limits at the company's sole discretion. In that situation, a lawyer hired by the insurance company must inform the policyholder, as early in the case as possible, about the constraints on the representation. Having done that, the lawyer may then follow the insurance company's instructions about settlement. If the lawyer knows that the policyholder objects to a settlement, the lawyer must not proceed without first giving the policyholder a chance to reject the insurance company's defense and to assume responsibility for her own defense at her own expense. [ABA Formal Op. 96-403]

4) Unreasonable Limits on Defense Fees and Expenses

Seeking to control litigation costs, some insurance companies insist on detailed audits of a defense lawyer's time records and litigation files. Some companies also limit the amount a defense lawyer can spend in preparing the case for trial. Some companies use "litigation managers" who look over the lawyer's shoulder and sometimes try to micromanage the defense. A defense lawyer must not disclose a policyholder's confidential information to an outside auditor without the policy-holder's informed consent, but he may disclose bills and time records containing confidential information to the insurance company itself if doing so will aid, not harm, the policyholder. [ABA Formal Op. 01-421] Furthermore, a defense lawyer must refuse to follow insurance company litigation management guidelines that interfere with the lawyer's professional judgment or prevent the lawyer from representing the policyholder competently. If the insurance company will not relent, the lawyer must withdraw. [*Id.*]

E. DUTIES TO FORMER CLIENTS

1. Continuing Duty of Confidentiality

An attorney's duty to preserve a client's confidential information does not cease when the representation ends. The attorney has a continuing obligation to preserve information gained in confidence during the representation. [ABA Model Rule 1.9(c)]

Examples: 1) When A retired from his solo law practice, he sold his practice to another lawyer. The purchaser received not only books, furniture, and an office lease, but also all of A's files relating to past and pending legal matters. Many of the files contained confidential information, and A made no effort to obtain the consent of his clients and former clients before transferring the files. A is subject to discipline. [*See* ABA Model Rules 1.17(c), 1.6, 1.9(c)]

2) Lawyer L, a solo practitioner, left instructions for the winding up of his law practice in the event of his unexpected death. L directed his personal representative to contact each client to find out whether that client's files should be delivered directly to the client, to another lawyer of the client's choice, or to a young lawyer designated by L. L's instructions are proper.

2. Opposing Former Client—Confidential Information

When a former client has imparted confidential information to a lawyer, the lawyer must not then oppose the former client in any matter in which the confidential information would be relevant, unless the former client gives informed, written consent. [ABA Model Rule 1.9(a), (c); *and see* Trone v. Smith, 621 F.2d 994 (9th Cir. 1980)]

Example: For many years, lawyer L represented client H in matters relating to H's business and personal finances. Then L and H had a sharp disagreement and came to a parting of the ways. Later, X asked L to represent her in a civil case against H. If any information that L obtained in confidence about H's business and personal finances would be relevant in X's suit against H, then L must not represent X unless H gives informed, written consent. [*See* Comment 3 to ABA Model Rule 1.9]

3. Using Confidential Information to Former Client's Disadvantage

When a lawyer has obtained confidential information from a former client, the lawyer must not thereafter use the confidential information to the former client's disadvantage, unless the former client gives informed, written consent. This rule does not apply to information that has become commonly known. Furthermore, it does not apply to any information that the lawyer would be allowed to reveal or use under an exception to the general ethical duty of confidentiality. [ABA Model Rule 1.9(c)]

Example: Three years ago, attorney A represented C, the son of a movie star, in a drug possession case. In that connection, C told A in confidence that he had abused drugs for several years and had become a hard drug addict. Based on information from other sources, several tabloid newspapers and gossip magazines published stories about C's drug problems; within a few weeks, the public knew all there was to know about C. Now A represents C's ex-wife in a dispute with C over the custody of their infant daughter. In the custody dispute, A may use publicly known information about C's history of drug abuse.

4. Opposing Former Client in Substantially Related Matter

A lawyer must not represent one client whose interests are materially adverse to those of a former client in a matter that is "substantially related" to a matter in which the lawyer represented the former client (unless the former client gives informed, written consent). [ABA Model Rule 1.9(a); *and see, e.g.,* Carlson v. Langdon, 751 P.2d 344 (Wyo. 1988)] One purpose of this rule is to protect confidential information that the lawyer may have received from the former client, but the rule applies even when the former client cannot demonstrate that the lawyer received any confidential information.

a. **Meaning of "Substantially Related" Matter**

Whether a matter is "substantially related" depends on the facts of the particular situation. [Comment 3 to ABA Model Rule 1.9] When a lawyer has been directly involved in a specific transaction, the lawyer cannot later oppose the former client in a dispute concerning that same transaction absent informed, written consent. On the other hand, if a lawyer routinely handled a type of problem for a former client, the lawyer may later oppose that former client in a wholly different problem of the same general type. [*Id.*]

Examples: 1) Summitville Hospital employed lawyer L to draft a consent form to be signed by all patients scheduled for elective surgery at the hospital. L drafted the form and thereafter did no further legal work for the hospital. Three years later, client C asked L to represent her in a suit against the hospital; in that suit, C will contend that the consent form violates public policy and is therefore void. L must not represent C unless the hospital gives informed, written consent.

2) When attorney A was an associate in the M, N, O & P firm, she regularly represented the Magnum Oil Company in suits to eject service station dealers for failure to comply with the terms of their service station leases. Two years ago, A left the firm to enter solo practice. Now S, a Magnum service station dealer, has asked her to defend him in an ejectment suit brought by Magnum. A may represent S without getting Magnum's consent.

F. CONFLICTS WHEN PRIVATE LAWYERS CHANGE JOBS

In modern law practice, it is common for a lawyer to change jobs, perhaps several times over the span of a career. This can create conflict of interest problems for both the lawyer's former firm and the lawyer's new firm. Clients should be able to count on continuing loyalty and on continuing protection of their confidential information. A broad, rigid rule of imputed disqualification would serve those two interests, but it would also have two drawbacks: (i) lawyers would be hindered in changing jobs and taking on new clients; and (ii) clients would face a reduced choice of legal counsel. [Comment 4 to ABA Model Rule 1.9; *and see* Restatement §124—concerning screening when a lawyer switches between private firms] ABA Model Rules 1.9(b) and 1.10(b) provide two specific rules concerning lawyers who switch between private law firms. (ABA Model Rule 1.11 applies to lawyers who switch to or from a government law office; *see* G., *infra*.)

1. **Disqualification of Lawyer's New Firm**

ABA Model Rule 1.9(b) states the ethical obligations of the new firm—the firm that hires the switching lawyer: "A lawyer shall not knowingly represent a person in the same or a substantially related matter in which a firm with which the lawyer formerly was associated had previously represented a client (1) whose interests are materially adverse to that person; and (2) about whom the lawyer had acquired information protected by Rules 1.6 and 1.9(c) that is material to the matter; unless the former client gives informed consent, confirmed in writing."

Example: Lawyer L is an associate at Firm One. Firm One represents client A in the case of *A v. B.* L works on the *A v. B* case, and he receives reams of confidential information about the case from A. L then quits Firm One and becomes an associate at Firm Two.

L may not now represent B in the *A v. B* case.

No other lawyer at Firm Two may represent B in the *A v. B* case.

Furthermore, neither L nor any other lawyer at Firm Two may represent C in the case of *C v. A* if the *C v. A* case is substantially related to the *A v. B* case and if the confidential information L obtained from A is material to the *C v. A* case.

The disqualification can be waived if A gives informed, written consent. Thus, if A consents, the results of the foregoing hypotheticals would be the opposite.

2. Disqualification of Lawyer's Former Firm

ABA Model Rule 1.10(b) states the ethical obligations of the former firm—the firm with which a lawyer terminated association: "When a lawyer has terminated an association with a firm, the firm is not prohibited from thereafter representing a person with interests materially adverse to those of a client represented by the formerly associated lawyer and not currently represented by the firm, unless: (1) the matter is the same or substantially related to that in which the formerly associated lawyer represented the client; and (2) any lawyer remaining in the firm has information protected by Rules 1.6 and 1.9(c) that is material to the matter."

Example: Lawyer L is a partner at Firm One. L and three associates of Firm One represent client A in the *A v. B* case. L and the three associates obtain reams of confidential information from A about the case. Then L leaves Firm One to form Firm Two. The three associates stay at Firm One. Now L and Firm Two represent client A in the *A v. B* case.

No lawyer at Firm One may represent B in the *A v. B* case because the three associates who obtained confidential information from A are still at Firm One.

No lawyer at Firm One may represent C in the case of *C v. A* if that case is substantially related to the *A v. B* case, and if the confidential information the three associates obtained from A is material to the *C v. A* case.

If the three associates had also left Firm One, and if no other lawyer in Firm One had been privy to the confidential information received from A, then any lawyer at Firm One may represent B in the *A v. B* case or C in the *C v. A* case.

The disqualification can be waived if A gives informed, written consent. Thus, if A consents, the results of the foregoing hypotheticals would be the opposite.

G. CONFLICT RULES FOR CURRENT AND FORMER GOVERNMENT OFFICERS AND EMPLOYEES

When a lawyer serves as an officer or employee of the government for a period and then leaves to enter private law practice, the government has a right to expect that its confidential information will not be abused. [*See* Comments 3 and 4 to ABA Model Rule 1.11] Furthermore, private clients should not be allowed to gain an unfair advantage from information known to a lawyer only because of prior government service, and lawyers should not be in a position to benefit private clients because of prior government service. Finally, possible future benefit to private clients should not distort a lawyer's professional judgment while working for the government. [*Id.*] All of the foregoing would suggest that there should be a broad, rigid rule of disqualification for lawyers who move from the government to private practice. However, such a rule would have a serious drawback—the government would be hindered in recruiting good lawyers for short-term government service. Thus, the ABA Model Rules establish disqualification rules that are relatively narrow and flexible. [*See also* Restatement §133]

1. Federal and State Conflict of Interest Laws

Lawyers who move between government and private jobs must comply not only with the ethics rules but also with various state and federal statutes and regulations. [*See, e.g.,* Federal Ethics in Government Act, 18 U.S.C. §§207-208] Those are not covered in this outline, but they must be considered in solving an actual problem of successive government and private employment.

2. Private Work Following Government Work on Same Matter

Except when expressly permitted by law, a lawyer who leaves government service and enters private practice must not represent a private client in a ***matter*** in which the lawyer participated ***personally and substantially*** while in government service, unless the government agency gives informed, written consent. [ABA Model Rule 1.11(a)]

a. Meaning of the Term "Matter"

As used in this rule, "matter" has a narrow, technical meaning. It does ***not*** mean "general topic" or "broad subject area." It means a specific set of facts involving some specific parties. [ABA Formal Op. 342 (1975)] ABA Model Rule 1.11(e) defines it more fully as, "any judicial or other proceeding, application, request for a ruling or other determination, contract, claim, controversy, investigation, charge, accusation, arrest, or other particular matter involving a specific party or parties" (plus anything else that is covered under the conflict of interest rules of the government agency in question).

Examples: 1) When lawyer L worked for the State Consumer Protection Agency, she was assigned to draft some regulations to govern the conduct of door-to-door salespeople. The regulations that she drafted were ultimately adopted, almost verbatim, by the agency. A year later, L left government service and entered private practice. She was asked to represent American Encyclopedia Company (a door-to-door sales company) in a dispute with the State Consumer Protection Agency. The essence of the dispute is the proper application of the regulations that L herself drafted. L may represent American because the drafting of regulations is not a "matter"; it does not involve specific facts and specific parties.

2) When serving as Oakville City Attorney, lawyer L drafted a city ordinance for the rezoning of a particular tract of land owned by developer R. The drafting of the ordinance is a "matter" because it involved

one narrow, specific situation. Thus, when L later enters private law practice, she may not work on a case that involves that ordinance. [*See* Restatement §133]

b. Meaning of "Personally and Substantially"

The term "personally and substantially" means just what it says—the disqualification rule applies only when the lawyer's work on a matter was both personal and substantial. The term does not include work that is trifling, and it does not include mere supervisory responsibility. [*See* ABA Formal Op. 342 (1975)]

Example: Attorney A is the District Attorney of Colma County. She is in charge of 16 deputies working out of five different offices spread through the county. A's rubber-stamped signature appears on every paper that goes out of the five offices. In theory, she is personally responsible for every detail of every case; in fact, most of A's day is consumed in supervision and administration. The disqualification rule would cover only the few, exceptional cases in which A does become personally and substantially involved. [*Id.*]

c. Imputed Disqualification

If a lawyer is disqualified by the rule stated above, then everyone in that lawyer's firm is also disqualified *unless* the following three conditions are met:

(i)   The lawyer ***must be timely screened off from the case***. That is, the lawyer must not work on the case, discuss it with those who do, or have access to the case files.

(ii)   The lawyer ***must not be apportioned a part of the fee earned in the case***. That does not prevent the lawyer from receiving a regular salary or partnership share set by prior independent agreement. It means only that the lawyer's compensation must not be "directly related . . . to the fee in the matter in which the lawyer is disqualified." [Comment 6 to ABA Model Rule 1.11]

(iii)   ***Written notice must promptly be given to the governmental agency*** to enable it to make sure that the above conditions are being met.

Example: When lawyer L worked for the State Environmental Safety Bureau, he participated personally and substantially in an investigation of Noxatox Corp. concerning the dumping of radioactive industrial waste in Evergreen Slough. Later, L quit the Bureau and became a partner in the T, S & U firm. One of L's law partners is now asked to defend Noxatox in private litigation arising out of the Evergreen Slough matter. L will not work on the case, will have no access to the case files, and will not discuss the case with others in the office. L will receive his ordinary share of the proceeds of the partnership, set by prior independent agreement. Finally, the Bureau will be promptly informed of the foregoing facts in writing. Under these conditions, the partner may represent Noxatox.

3. Subsequent Use of Information Gained During Government Service

ABA Model Rule 1.11(c) provides that (except when expressly permitted by law) a government lawyer who receives confidential government information about a person must not later represent a private client whose interests are adverse to that person, when the information could be used to the material disadvantage of that person. The rule covers only information *actually received* by the government lawyer, not information that could be fictionally imputed to the lawyer. [Comment 8 to ABA Model Rule 1.11] "Confidential government information" means information that is gained under government authority and which the government is prohibited from revealing, or has a privilege not to reveal, and which is not otherwise available to the public. [ABA Model Rule 1.11(c)]

Example: When attorney A worked on the legal staff of the State Parole Board, he received confidential information about the personal life, character, and criminal proclivities of X, a parolee. Later, A entered private practice as a criminal defense lawyer. He was assigned to defend D in a case in which it appeared quite likely that X, not D, was the perpetrator. The proper defense of D would require a thorough investigation of the very facts that A learned about X in confidence. A must request the court to relieve him of the assignment to defend D.

a. Imputed Disqualification

If a former government lawyer is disqualified by this rule, then everyone in that lawyer's firm is also disqualified unless:

(i) The lawyer is timely screened off from the matter; and

(ii) The lawyer is not apportioned any part of the fee earned in the matter.

[ABA Model Rule 1.11(c)]

Example: In the State Parole Board example above, attorney A's law partner P may defend D if A is screened off from the case and is not apportioned any part of the fee earned in the case.

4. Current Government Service After Private Practice

ABA Model Rule 1.11(d) states the rules that apply to a person who becomes a government officer or employee after private practice or other nongovernmental work.

a. Ordinary Conflict Rules Apply

The ordinary conflict rules stated in ABA Model Rules 1.7 (current clients) and 1.9 (former clients) apply to a lawyer who enters government service after private practice or other nongovernmental work. [ABA Model Rule 1.11(d)(1)]

Example: For the past five years, lawyer L worked for the M & N law firm. In that job, L worked on a few matters for Cosmoplex, a diversified communications company, and he gained considerable confidential information about the company's finances. Now, L has quit M & N and has gone to work for the United States Department of Labor, which is about to sue Cosmoplex for fraud in connection with the purchase of overvalued company stock for its employee pension plan. ABA Model Rule 1.9 prohibits L from working on that suit (unless Cosmoplex gives informed, written consent). However, if L is timely screened off from the suit, other labor department lawyers may work on it—L's conflict will not be imputed to them. [*See* Hazard & Hodes, §15.9—screening procedure is implied, although not expressed]

b. **"Personal and Substantial" Rule Also Applies**
If a lawyer worked "personally and substantially" on a "matter" in private practice or other nongovernmental employment, the lawyer must not work on that same matter when she later enters government service, whether or not the later work would be adverse to a former client. However, informed, written consent can solve the conflict.

Example: In private practice, attorney A represented Electro Corp. in trying to obtain a license from the State Energy Commission to build a geothermal electric generating plant. While Electro's application was still pending, A quit private practice to become a lawyer for the Commission. A must not work on the Electro application unless she obtains the informed, written consent of both the Commission [ABA Model Rule 1.11(d)(2)(ii)] and Electro [ABA Model Rule 1.9(a)].

c. **Negotiating for Private Employment**
When a person in government service is currently working personally and substantially on a matter, she must not negotiate for private employment with any party or lawyer who is involved in that matter. [ABA Model Rule 1.11(d)(2)(ii)] There is a special exception for judges' and adjudicative officers' law clerks who are seeking work after their clerkships (*see* H.3., *infra*) end.

Example: Lawyer L currently serves on the State Agriculture and Fisheries Commission. L's work for the Commission is strictly nonlegal; he does not function as a lawyer for the Commission. Currently, L and the other Commissioners are working personally and substantially on a matter involving the Shady Bay Salmon Farm. Now, Shady Bay approaches L, asking if he would like to become Shady Bay's in-house general counsel. If L negotiates for employment with Shady Bay, he will be subject to discipline. Notice that the rule applies to L, even though his work for the Commission is nonlegal.

H. CONFLICTS INVOLVING FORMER JUDGES, ARBITRATORS, AND THE LIKE

The conflict of interest problems posed when a lawyer switches between government and private practice are also present when a judge leaves the bench and enters private practice. Thus, the rules discussed here are similar to those discussed above.

1. **Switching from Judicial Service to Private Law Practice**
A lawyer must not represent a private client in a matter in which the lawyer has earlier participated personally and substantially while serving as a judge or other adjudicative officer (*e.g.*, a referee or special master) or as a law clerk to such person, or as an arbitrator, mediator, or other third-party neutral, unless all parties to the proceedings give informed, written consent. [ABA Model Rule 1.12(a)] The same rule applies to a lawyer who has earlier served as an arbitrator, mediator, or other third-party neutral. However, an arbitrator who is selected as a partisan of a party in a multi-member arbitration panel may subsequently represent that party. [ABA Model Rule 1.12(d)]

Examples: 1) Lawyer L was selected as the partisan of union U on a three-member arbitration panel. L may serve as U's lawyer in later proceedings relating to the dispute that was arbitrated.

2) Law clerk C worked on the case of *P v. D* and made recommendations to Judge J about some discovery motions and a motion for default judgment. When C completes her clerkship and enters private practice, she cannot work on the case of *P v. D*. [*See* Maryland State Bar Op. 85-23 (1985)]

3) J was one of 15 judges on the County Superior Court (a trial court) while the case of *State v. Able* was pending in that court. However, the *Able* case was assigned to a different judge, and Judge J never had anything to do with it. Later, Judge J resigned from the bench and entered private practice. Able asked J to represent her on the appeal of her case. J may represent Able because J did not personally work on the *Able* case. [*See* ABA Model Rule 1.12(a)]

4) S was the Senior Presiding Judge of the Circuit Court of Appeal (an intermediate appellate court). In that capacity, Judge S was responsible for all court administration and for assigning judges to hear various cases. During that period, the case of *Commonwealth v. Beale* was heard and decided by the court, but Judge S had nothing to do with that case except to assign it to three other judges. Later, Judge S left the bench and entered private practice. S may represent Beale in a subsequent stage of Beale's case. [*Id.*]

2. Screening Can Avoid Imputed Disqualification

If a lawyer is disqualified under Rule 1.12(a), everyone else in the lawyer's firm is also disqualified unless the following conditions are met:

(i)   The lawyer is timely screened off from the matter;

(ii) The lawyer is not apportioned any part of the fee earned in the matter; and

(iii) Written notice is given to the parties and the appropriate tribunal so that they can ensure that the foregoing conditions are met.

[ABA Model Rule 1.12(c); ABA Formal Op. 342 (1975)]

3. Law Clerks Negotiating for Private Employment

A law clerk to a judge or other adjudicative officer must ***notify*** that person before negotiating for private employment with a party (or the attorney for a party) in a matter in which the law clerk is participating personally and substantially. [ABA Model Rule 1.12(b)] Law clerks are specially treated because they are usually newly admitted lawyers for whom a clerkship is only a temporary first step in a legal career.

Example: After graduating from law school, S became a law clerk for Judge J. In that capacity, S wrote the bench brief and drafted an opinion in the case of *Arner v. Bosch*. While that case was still pending before the court, the attorney for Bosch invited S to visit her law firm and interview for a job. S must notify Judge J before discussing future employment with the attorney.

4. Other Adjudicative Officers Negotiating for Private Employment
The lenient rule that applies to law clerks does not apply to judges, arbitrators, mediators, third-party neutrals, and other adjudicative officers. They are forbidden to negotiate for private employment with a party (or the attorney for a party) in a matter in which they are participating personally and substantially. [ABA Model Rule 1.12(b)]

I. CONFLICTS INVOLVING PROSPECTIVE CLIENTS

1. Lawyer's Duty Concerning Confidential Information
A prospective client is someone who discusses with a lawyer the possibility of forming a lawyer-client relationship. [ABA Model Rule 1.18(a)] The attorney-client privilege protects confidential communications between a lawyer and a prospective client. The ethical duty of confidentiality also applies to discussions between a lawyer and prospective client. Thus, the lawyer must not reveal or use information learned during those discussions, unless an exception to the duty of confidentiality applies.

Examples: 1) Prospective client PC came to lawyer L's office seeking L's legal advice about a plan to murder PC's sister-in-law without getting caught. The attorney-client privilege would not protect PC's communication because he was seeking L's aid to commit a future crime. Furthermore, the ethical duty of confidentiality would not prohibit L from warning the sister-in-law and telling the police if L reasonably believes that PC really will carry out the plan. [ABA Model Rules 1.18(b), 1.6(b)(1)]

2) Senator S telephoned attorney A, asking A to visit him in the county jail. When A arrived, S explained in confidence that he was picked up for felony drunk driving, that he was very drunk at the time, and that he wanted A to represent him. A was overburdened with other work and could not do so. Several weeks later, the entire story of Senator S's drunken escapade became common knowledge after S talked about it on Oprah Winfry's television show. Not long afterward, in an unrelated matter, A had occasion to cross-examine S, who had testified on behalf of A's adversary. A asked S: "Sir, shortly before witnessing the events about which you testified on direct, had you drunk any alcohol?" S was outraged and accused A of violating the duty of confidence owed to a potential client. A's conduct was proper. The question on cross-examination was designed to test S's ability to perceive correctly. Furthermore, the information about S's drinking, although originally confidential, lost its protection when S himself made it public on television. [*See* ABA Model Rules 1.18(b), 1.9(c)(1)]

2. Lawyer's Duty Concerning Conflict of Interest
Subject to the exceptions stated in 3., below, a lawyer who obtains confidential information during preliminary discussions with a prospective client must not later represent a different person in the same or a substantially related matter if the confidential information could significantly harm the prospective client. [ABA Model Rule 1.18(c)] This conflict is imputed to others in the lawyer's firm, but the imputation can be overcome by screening, as stated in 3., below.

3. How to Overcome a Prospective Client Conflict
One way to overcome the conflict described in 2., above, is to obtain informed, written

consent from both the affected client and the prospective client. [ABA Model Rule 1.18(d)(1)] A second way to overcome the conflict is to satisfy all of the following conditions:

(i) Demonstrate that the lawyer who held discussions with the prospective client took care to **avoid exposure to any more confidential information than was necessary** to determine whether to represent the prospective client;

(ii) Demonstrate that the disqualified lawyer is **timely screened from any participation in the matter** and will not share the fee (but he may take his ordinary salary or partnership share); and

(iii) Give **written notice** to the prospective client.

[ABA Model Rule 1.18(d)(2)]

J. ORGANIZATION AS CLIENT

1. Duty of Loyalty to Organization

A corporation, governmental agency, unincorporated association, or similar organization is a legal entity, but it must act through the people who make up the organization—the directors, officers, agency employees, shareholders, owners, or the like. A lawyer who represents an organization obviously must work through those people. However, when the organization is the lawyer's client, the lawyer owes the duty of loyalty to the **organization**—not to the people who are its constituents. [ABA Model Rule 1.13(a); Restatement §96]

2. Conflicts Between the Organization and Its Constituents

Ordinarily, there is no conflict between the interests of the organization and the interests of the people who make up the organization. Sometimes, however, their interests do come into conflict. When they do, the lawyer for the organization should caution the person in question that the attorney represents the organization, not the person. [Comment 10 to ABA Model Rule 1.13] For instance, the lawyer should warn the person that communications between them may not be protected by the attorney-client privilege. [*Id.*] Furthermore, when appropriate, the lawyer should advise the person to obtain independent legal counsel. [*Id.*]

Example: The board of directors of Growers' Export Corp. instructed the corporation's general counsel to give classes for all management personnel concerning the laws and corporate rules against using bribery and kick-backs when negotiating business contracts in foreign nations. After such a class, one of the foreign office managers told the general counsel that he had frequently used bribes to secure business for the corporation. The general counsel should remind the manager that she represents the corporation, not the manager, that bribery is both illegal and against the rules of the corporation, and, if appropriate, that the manager should seek independent legal counsel. [*See* ABA Model Rule 1.13(f); Comment 10 to ABA Model Rule 1.13]

3. Protecting the Organization's Interests

If the lawyer for an organization learns that a person associated with the organization has acted, or is about to act, in a way that violates a duty to the organization or a law in a way that might be imputed to the organization, and if the violation is likely to cause substantial injury to the organization, the lawyer must proceed as is reasonably necessary to protect the interests of the organization. [ABA Model Rule 1.13(b)]

a. **Duty to Report to Higher Authority in Organization**
In the situation described above, the lawyer must ordinarily report the violation to a higher authority in the organization (*e.g.*, to a corporation's president). If necessary, the lawyer must report it to the organization's highest authority (*e.g.*, a corporation's outside directors). ABA Model Rule 1.13(b) does, however, give the lawyer a narrow range of discretion—she need not report the violation if she reasonably believes that the organization's best interests do not require the violation to be reported. [*Id.*]

b. **Duty to Report Outside the Organization**
If the lawyer reports the violation to the organization's highest authority, but the highest authority fails to take timely, appropriate action, the lawyer *may* report the relevant information to appropriate persons outside of the organization. This is true even if the information would otherwise be protected by the duty of confidentiality expressed in ABA Model Rule 1.6. [ABA Model Rule 1.13(c)] However, the lawyer's authority to report to outsiders applies only if, and to the extent that, the lawyer *reasonably believes* that reporting is necessary to *prevent substantial injury* to the organization. The authority to report to outsiders does not apply to a lawyer who is hired by the organization to investigate an alleged violation of law or to defend the organization or its constituents against a claimed violation of law. [ABA Model Rule 1.13(d)]

Example: Attorney A's corporate client produces frozen chicken pies. C's production process creates large quantities of liquid waste, which C is supposed to pump into recycling tanks. C's manufacturing vice president sometimes orders his workers to dump the waste into a ditch that drains into some neighboring wetlands; the dumping is cheaper and quicker, but it gradually destroys the wetlands in violation of state and federal environmental laws. When A learns about the dumping, she reports it to C's president and warns him that C will be fined millions of dollars if it gets caught. C's president ignored A's warning, so A reported the matter to the highest authority in the company—the audit committee of the board of directors. The audit committee did nothing. If A reasonably believes that the company will be seriously injured if the dumping continues, A *may* report the relevant information to the appropriate environmental enforcement authority, even if some of that information would otherwise be protected by the duty of confidentiality.

c. **Whistle Blower Protection**
A lawyer who reasonably believes that she has been fired because she acted pursuant to Model Rule 1.13(b) or (c) (*see* a. and b. above), or who withdraws under circumstances that require or permit her to act pursuant to either of those paragraphs, must proceed as she reasonably believes necessary to assure that the organization's highest authority is informed of the firing or withdrawal. [ABA Model Rule 1.13(e)]

4. **Representing Both the Organization and an Associated Person**
The lawyer for an organization may represent both the organization and one or more directors, officers, employees, or other persons associated with the organization, provided that the ordinary conflict of interest rules are satisfied. [ABA Model Rule 1.13(g); Restatement §§96, comment h, 131, comment e] When dual representation requires the consent of the organization, the consent must be given by an appropriate person other than the person to be represented. [ABA Model Rule 1.13(g)]

Example: The Anti-Nuclear Coalition sued Consolidated Light and Power Co. and the president of Consolidated under federal, state, and common law to prevent Consolidated from starting up a nuclear generating plant that it had constructed. The firm of W, X & Y was retained to represent both Consolidated and its president. After careful examination, the firm concluded that it could represent both clients effectively, even though their interests potentially conflict on one or two points. After the firm explained the potential conflicts, the president gave informed, written consent on his own behalf, and the chairman of the board of directors gave informed, written consent on behalf of the company. The dual representation is proper.

5. Serving as Both Director and Lawyer

The ABA Model Rules do not forbid a lawyer from serving as both a director of an organization and as a lawyer for the organization, but the Model Rules point out that the dual role can create conflicts of interest. [*See* Comment 35 to ABA Model Rule 1.7] For instance, when the lawyer participates in a meeting as a director (rather than as the organization's lawyer), the attorney-client privilege will not apply to communications at the meeting, but some of the other directors may not realize that. If there is a substantial risk that the dual role will compromise the lawyer's professional judgment, the lawyer should either resign as director or not act as the organization's lawyer when a conflict arises. [*Id.*]

6. Securities Lawyer's Duties Under Sarbanes-Oxley Act

In response to the collapse of several high-flying corporations in 2002, Congress passed the Sarbanes-Oxley Act. Among other things, the Act instructs the Securities and Exchange Commission ("SEC") to make rules for securities lawyers who discover their clients violating the federal or state securities laws or similar laws. The SEC did make rules, which are now part of the "law of lawyering" that is covered on the MPRE. [*See* 17 C.F.R. §205] The following discussion includes highlights of the Sarbanes-Oxley rules.

a. Application to "Securities Lawyers"

The rules apply to lawyers who represent an issuer of securities and who practice before the SEC ("securities lawyers"). This includes not only lawyers who transact business with the SEC, communicate with it, or represent a securities issuer before it, but also lawyers who give advice about a document that will be filed with the SEC or advice about whether information must be filed with the SEC.

b. Reporting Requirement

If a securities lawyer becomes aware of credible evidence that her client is materially violating a federal or state securities law, she ***must*** report the evidence to her client's chief legal officer ("CLO") or chief executive officer. The same reporting duty applies to credible evidence that one of her client's personnel has breached a fiduciary duty under federal or state law or has committed a "similar material violation" of federal or state law.

c. Investigation by CLO

The CLO must investigate the situation to determine whether a violation occurred. Alternatively, the CLO can turn the matter over to a legal compliance committee, but for purposes of this discussion, that complication will be ignored.

d. If Violation Found—"Appropriate Response" Required
If the CLO concludes that no violation occurred, he must report that conclusion back to the securities lawyer. If the CLO concludes that a violation did occur, is occurring, or is about to occur, the CLO must take all reasonable steps to get the client to make an "appropriate response." Roughly stated, that means that the client must stop or remedy the violation and make sure that it does not happen again. The CLO must report those results to the securities lawyer.

e. When Appropriate Response Not Taken
If the securities lawyer believes that the CLO did not achieve an appropriate response from the client, the securities lawyer *must* report the evidence to one of the following: (i) the client's whole board of directors, (ii) the audit committee of the board, or (iii) a committee made up of outside directors (directors who are not beholden to the client). Notice that the Sarbanes-Oxley reporting rule is *mandatory*, unlike ABA Model Rule 1.13(b), which gives the lawyer some discretion about how to proceed (*see* 3., *supra*).

f. Revealing Confidential Information
The securities lawyer *may* reveal to the SEC, without the client's consent, any confidential information that is reasonably necessary to: (i) stop the client from committing a violation that will cause substantial financial injury to the client or its investors; (ii) rectify such a financial injury if the lawyer's services were used to further the violation; or (iii) prevent the client from committing or suborning perjury in an SEC matter or lying in any matter within the jurisdiction of any branch of the federal government.

g. Compliance with Rules
A securities lawyer who violates the Sarbanes-Oxley rules can be disciplined by the SEC, but a securities lawyer who complies with the Sarbanes-Oxley rules cannot be held civilly liable for doing so and cannot be disciplined under any inconsistent state rule.

h. Action When Securities Lawyer Is Fired
If a securities lawyer is fired for complying with the Sarbanes-Oxley rules, she may report the firing to the client's board of directors (thus setting up the client for an expensive wrongful termination suit).

VI. SAFEGUARDING THE CLIENT'S MONEY AND PROPERTY

A. GENERAL DUTY
When money or property belonging to a client comes into the lawyer's hands, the lawyer must not steal it, borrow it, or put it to the lawyer's own use. Furthermore, the lawyer must keep it separated from the lawyer's own money and property. A lawyer is subject to discipline for commingling the client's money or property with the lawyer's own personal or business funds or property. [ABA Model Rule 1.15; *and see* Restatement §44—lawyer safeguarding client's property acts as a fiduciary and is subject to civil liability for failure to safeguard such property]

B. CLIENT TRUST FUND ACCOUNT
All money that a lawyer receives on behalf of a client (whether from the client or a third party)

must promptly be placed in a client trust fund account, separate from the lawyer's own personal and business accounts. [*Id.*]

1. Type of Account

The client trust fund account must be located in the state where the lawyer practices. [ABA Model Rule 1.15(a)—however, the account may be elsewhere if the client consents] Ordinarily, a lawyer must never put her own money or her firm's money into the client trust account, but she may put some of her own money into that account for the sole purpose of paying bank service charges. [ABA Model Rule 1.15(b)]

a. Large Sum Held for Long Period

If a lawyer is entrusted with a large sum to hold for a long period, the lawyer should put it into a separate, interest-bearing account, and the interest it earns will belong to the client. [*See* Restatement §44, comment d] A separate account is recommended when the lawyer is administering estate funds or the like. [Comment 1 to ABA Model Rule 1.15]

b. Small Sums

Usually, lawyers are entrusted with only relatively small sums to hold for relatively short periods of time. The lawyer should put these sums into a pooled client trust account; the account is pooled in the sense that it holds funds entrusted to the lawyer by a variety of different clients. The pooled client trust account is typically a checking account that earns interest. If each client's small sum were put in an individual account, the amount of interest it could earn would be less than the bank's service charge for maintaining the individual account. The 50 states devised Interest On Lawyer Trust Account ("IOLTA") programs. If a client entrusts a lawyer with a sum that is too small to earn any net interest, the lawyer must put it into a pooled checking account that earns interest. After the bank deducts its service charges from the interest, the bank sends the remaining interest to the state bar or to a legal foundation, which uses the interest to fund charitable legal programs. In short, an IOLTA program creates an asset that would otherwise not exist, and it then puts that asset to a public use. In *Brown v. Legal Foundation of Washington,* 538 U.S. 216 (2003), a sharply divided Supreme Court upheld the constitutionality of IOLTA programs, holding that the individual clients whose interest was "taken" for "public use" were not entitled to "just compensation" because they did not lose anything they would otherwise have had.

2. Funds that Must Be Placed in Account

a. Money Advanced by Client to Cover Costs and Expenses

When the client entrusts the lawyer with money to pay costs and expenses not yet incurred, the advance *must* be put into the lawyer's client trust fund account. [ABA Model Rule 1.15] The lawyer can then pay the expenses with checks drawn on the account.

b. Legal Fees Advanced by Client

Sometimes a client entrusts the lawyer with an advance against legal fees that the lawyer has not yet earned. Such an advance must be put into the client trust account. That is because a lawyer must refund to the client any unearned, prepaid legal fees at the close of the representation, and an irresponsible lawyer could harm a client by frittering away a fee advance. When a lawyer holds a fee advance in her client trust account, she may make withdrawals as fees are earned if there is no existing dispute about the lawyer's right to do so. [*See* Restatement §44, comment f] To make sure there is no dispute, cautious lawyers send the client an itemized bill before withdrawing legal fees from the trust account. [*See* Restatement §44, comment f]

c. **Funds in Which Both Client and Lawyer Have an Interest**
A lawyer sometimes receives funds from a third party that are to be used, in part, to pay the lawyer's fee. The lawyer must place such funds in a client trust account until there is an accounting and severance of the respective interests of the client and the lawyer. [ABA Model Rule 1.15(e)] If the client disputes the amount that is due to the lawyer, then the disputed portion must be kept in the client trust account until the dispute is resolved. [*Id.*]

Example: Attorney A agreed to represent P as plaintiff in a products liability case. P agreed to pay A $75 per hour for her work, and P agreed that the fee could be deducted from the proceeds of the suit before remittance to P. After expending 100 hours on the case, A arranged a settlement of $50,000, and the defendant sent A a check in that amount. A deposited the check in her client trust fund account and notified P that it had arrived. The same day, A sent P a statement for services showing 100 hours of work and a total fee of $7,500. P protested the fee, saying that she would pay $5,000, but not a cent more. Furthermore, P demanded immediate payment of the entire $50,000. A then sent P $42,500, transferred $5,000 to her personal bank account, and kept the remaining $2,500 in her client trust fund account. P and A ultimately submitted their fee dispute to arbitration; when the arbitrator ruled in A's favor, she transferred the $2,500 to her personal bank account. A handled the matter properly. [*See* Restatement §44, comment f]

d. **Funds in Which a Third Party Has an Interest**
Sometimes a third party has an interest in funds that come into the lawyer's possession on behalf of a client. [Comment 4 to ABA Model Rule 1.15] Statute, common law, or contract may require the lawyer to protect the third party's interest against interference by the client; accordingly, when the third party's claim is not frivolous, the lawyer must refuse to surrender the funds to the client until the third party has been paid. [*Id.*] However, a lawyer should not unilaterally presume to arbitrate a dispute between the client and the third party. [*Id.*] If there are substantial grounds for the dispute, the lawyer may file an interpleader action to have a court resolve the dispute. [*Id.*] The lawyer must promptly distribute any sums that are not in dispute. [ABA Model Rule 1.15(e)]

Example: When attorney A agreed to represent client C in a personal injury case, A and C made a three-way agreement with C's physician that A would pay C's medical bills out of the proceeds of C's suit. When C won a $10,000 judgment, he demanded that the entire sum be immediately paid over to him because of a dispute between C and the physician over the medical bills. A's legal and ethical obligation is to hold the amount of money necessary to pay C's medical bills until the dispute between C and the physician is resolved.

C. SAFEGUARDING PROPERTY

When the lawyer comes into possession of property (other than money) to be held on a client's behalf, the lawyer must identify it as belonging to the client and must put it in a safe place. [ABA Model Rule 1.15(a)] For small items, most lawyers use a bank safe deposit box.

Example: Lawyer L represented horse breeder B in negotiating a contract whereby B exchanged two valuable horses for a lakeside cottage. While the transfer was pending, B turned the two horses over to L for safekeeping. L arranged for them to be boarded at a certified and bonded stable. L's conduct was proper.

D. DUTY TO NOTIFY, KEEP RECORDS, RENDER ACCOUNTINGS, AND PAY OVER PROMPTLY

A lawyer has the following additional duties respecting a client's money or property:

(i) The lawyer must **notify the client promptly** when a third party turns over money or property to the lawyer to hold on the client's behalf;

(ii) The lawyer must **keep complete, accurate, and up-to-date records** of all money and property held on behalf of the client. These records must be kept in accordance with generally accepted accounting practice, and they must be preserved for five years after the termination of the representation;

(iii) The lawyer must **render appropriate accountings** of all money and property held on behalf of the client; and

(iv) When the time comes to **pay over money or deliver property** to which the client or a third party is entitled, the lawyer must do so **promptly**.

[ABA Model Rule 1.15(a), (d)]

VII. THE LAWYER AS COUNSELOR

A. LAWYER AS ADVISOR TO THE CLIENT

1. Duty to Render Candid Advice

When acting as advisor to a client, a lawyer must exercise independent judgment and render candid advice. [ABA Model Rule 2.1] Candid advice is sometimes hard to take—the facts may be harsh and the choices unattractive. The lawyer should attempt to keep the client's morale up but should neither sugarcoat the advice nor delude the client. [*See* Comment 1 to ABA Model Rule 2.1]

2. Giving Advice Beyond the Law

A lawyer may give a client not only legal advice, but also moral, economic, social, or political advice when relevant to the client's situation. [ABA Model Rule 2.1] When appropriate, a lawyer may also urge a client to seek advice from persons in related professions—*e.g.*, advice from an accountant, psychiatrist, physician, or family counselor. [*See* Comment 4 to ABA Model Rule 2.1]

3. Volunteering Advice

A lawyer ordinarily has no duty to give advice until asked. However, if the lawyer knows that the client is planning a course of action that will have substantial adverse legal consequences for the client, the lawyer may volunteer advice without being asked. [*See* Comment 5 to ABA Model Rule 2.1]

Example: Client C hired lawyer L to do some tax work. In the course of that work, L learned that C was regularly putting large amounts of money into a trust established for her grandchildren. If L reasonably believes that C is endangering her ability to provide for her own needs in old age, L may call that fact to C's attention, and L may assist C in working out a safer plan for investment and disposition of her assets.

B. EVALUATION FOR USE BY THIRD PERSONS

ABA Model Rule 2.3 concerns the lawyer who is asked, expressly or impliedly, to evaluate the affairs of a client and to supply the evaluation for use by third persons.

Examples: 1) Client X asks her lawyer to evaluate her legal title to 40 acres of ranch land and to furnish the evaluation to a proposed purchaser of the land.

2) Client Y Corp. wants to borrow a large sum from a bank and asks its lawyer to evaluate its legal and business affairs and to furnish a report to the bank.

3) Client Z, a school district, proposes to issue some school bonds and asks its lawyer to examine its situation and its proposed bond issue and to render a legal opinion for use by election officials, voters, and potential investors.

Note that in each of the foregoing examples, the client is the person or entity whose affairs are to be evaluated by the lawyer. ABA Model Rule 2.3 does not apply when a client asks a lawyer to evaluate the affairs of a third party and then to make a report to the client.

Example: Bank proposes to lend a large sum of money to Y. Bank therefore asks its own lawyer to evaluate Y's business and legal affairs and to report back to Bank. ABA Model Rule 2.3 does *not* apply to this situation. [Comment 2 to ABA Model Rule 2.3]

1. Requirements of the Rule

A lawyer may evaluate a client's affairs for the use of a third person if the lawyer reasonably believes that making the evaluation is compatible with the lawyer's other responsibilities to the client. [ABA Model Rule 2.3(a)]

Example: Lawyer L is defending client D Company in a suit for infringement of three United States patents. If D loses the infringement suit, its business will be virtually wiped out. D seeks to borrow a substantial sum of money from trust company T, and D asks L to evaluate its business and its pending litigation and to render a report to T. L should decline to perform the evaluation. L's responsibilities to D as an advocate in the patent infringement case are not compatible with rendering a candid evaluation for use by T. [*See* Comment 3 to ABA Model Rule 2.3]

2. Harmful Evaluation

If the lawyer knows or should know that the evaluation will materially harm the client, the lawyer must obtain the client's informed, written consent before making the evaluation.

3. Confidentiality

Except as disclosure is authorized in connection with a report of an evaluation, the ordinary rules of confidentiality apply to information gained during the evaluation. [ABA Model Rule 2.3(b)] The client may limit the scope of the evaluation or the sources of information available to the lawyer, but the lawyer should describe any material limitations in the report furnished to the third person. The lawyer may have other legal duties to the third person in connection with the report—that depends on the applicable law and is not covered in ABA Model Rule 2.3. [Comment 3 to ABA Model Rule 2.3]

4. Lawyer's Liability to Third Person

A lawyer who is hired to evaluate a client's affairs for a third person may be liable to the third person for negligence in rendering the evaluation.

Example: Client C hired attorney A to evaluate C's financial condition for bank B in the hope that B would lend money to C. A's opinion letter to B negligently misrepresented C's financial condition, as a direct result of which B suffered a large loss. A is liable to B for the negligent misrepresentation. [*See* Vereins-Und Westbank, AG v. Carter, 691 F. Supp. 704 (S.D.N.Y. 1988)]

5. Cases in Which Opinion Is to Be Widely Disseminated

When a lawyer agrees to certify facts to a large number of persons who can be expected to rely on the lawyer, the lawyer has a special obligation to be complete, accurate, and candid.

a. Securities Cases

This special obligation most often arises when a lawyer has prepared an opinion letter to be used in disclosure documents for securities investors. The lawyer may be held liable for both misstatements and omissions of material facts. [SEC v. National Student Marketing Corp., 457 F. Supp. 682 (D.D.C. 1978)]

1) Due Diligence Required

A lawyer is not a guarantor of every fact in the disclosure materials about the company or transaction. However, if the disclosures are inconsistent, or the lawyer has any reason to doubt their accuracy, the lawyer has a *duty to inquire* to determine the correct facts. [ABA Formal Op. 335 (1974)]

b. Tax Shelter Opinions

When a lawyer gives a widely disseminated legal opinion about the tax treatment likely to be afforded an investment, the lawyer must candidly disclose and estimate the degree of risk that the IRS will not allow the tax treatment being sought, even if such disclosure will be contrary to the interest of the client in selling the investment. [ABA Formal Op. 346 (1982)]

C. LAWYER AS NEGOTIATOR

Lawyers must negotiate in both litigation (*e.g.,* settlement negotiations) and nonlitigation contexts (*e.g.,* real estate transaction, business merger negotiation). Issues of honest and affirmative disclosure often arise in connection with such negotiations. Thus, the Rules prohibit a lawyer from making a false statement of *material fact*. [ABA Model Rule 4.1(a)] However, the lawyer is under no duty to do the other side's fact research or volunteer any facts that would undermine the client's position.

1. Puffing and Subjective Statements

Because it is the essence of negotiation that the lawyer attempt to magnify the strength of the client's position, there are some statements that the ABA Model Rules will allow even though they may constitute "puffing" of the client's position—*i.e.*, they are not considered statements of material fact. The key factor to examine when determining if a statement contains a material fact is whether the opposing party would be reasonable in relying on the statement made. Certain types of subjective statements, such as those relating to the relative merits of the case, estimates of price and value, and a party's intentions as to an acceptable settlement are not considered statements of material fact in this context. [Comment 2 to ABA Model Rule 4.1]

2. Misapprehension

A lawyer who believes an opponent is underestimating the strength of his client's position has no duty to correct that misapprehension unless the lawyer or the client caused it. [Brown v. County of Genessee, 872 F.2d 169 (6th Cir. 1989)—opponent miscalculated amount of lost pay] However, in certain instances, the opponent's lack of knowledge of pertinent facts may be so important that disclosure is required.

Examples: 1) Plaintiff's lawyer failed to disclose to the defendant that, during the settlement negotiations, the plaintiff, who was considered to be a strong witness, died. The settlement of the case was set aside. [Virzi v. Grand Trunk Warehouse, 571 F. Supp. 507 (E.D. Mich. 1983)]

2) Prosecutor had a duty to disclose to a criminal defendant that, prior to the acceptance of his guilty plea, physical evidence of the defendant's guilt was accidentally destroyed. [Fambo v. Smith, 433 F. Supp. 590 (W.D.N.Y. 1977)]

D. LAWYER AS THIRD-PARTY NEUTRAL

1. General Principles

A lawyer serves as a third-party neutral when she assists two or more nonclients in resolving a dispute or other matter that has arisen between them. [ABA Model Rule 2.4(a)] Examples of a third-party neutral are an arbitrator, mediator, conciliator, or evaluator. [Comment 1 to ABA Model Rule 2.4] Nonlawyers can serve as third-party neutrals, but some court rules require lawyers for some types of cases. When a lawyer serves as a third-party neutral, she is subject not only to the ordinary rules of legal ethics, but also to various codes of conduct devised by groups such as the American Arbitration Association. [Comment 2 to ABA Model Rule 2.4]

2. Warning to Unrepresented Parties

A lawyer who serves as a third-party neutral does not represent any of the parties. A party who is not familiar with arbitration, mediation, or the like, and who is not represented by counsel, may erroneously believe that the lawyer third-party neutral is protecting his interests, but that is not so. The lawyer must therefore clearly explain the situation to the unrepresented party; *e.g.*, the lawyer should explain that the attorney-client privilege does not apply to communications between them. [Comment 3 to ABA Model Rule 2.4]

3. Conflicts of Interest

A lawyer who serves as a third-party neutral in a matter must not thereafter become the lawyer for anyone involved in the matter, unless all of the parties give their informed, written consent. [ABA Model Rule 1.12(a)] This conflict is imputed to other lawyers in the lawyer's firm, but it can be solved by screening the lawyer from the matter, assuring that he does not share the fee, and notifying the parties about the screening arrangement. [ABA Model Rule 1.12(c)] No conflict arises when a lawyer who served as a *partisan* arbitrator for a party is later asked to become that party's lawyer. [ABA Model Rule 1.12(d)]

VIII. THE LAWYER AS ADVOCATE

A. MERITORIOUS CLAIMS AND CONTENTIONS ONLY

1. Discipline for Asserting Frivolous Position

A lawyer is subject to discipline for bringing a frivolous proceeding, or for asserting a frivolous position in the defense of a proceeding. Likewise, a lawyer is subject to discipline for taking a frivolous position on an *issue* in a proceeding. [ABA Model Rule 3.1; Restatement §110; *and see* Fed. R. Civ. P. 11—litigation sanctions for frivolous pleadings and motions] A "frivolous" position is one that cannot be supported by a good faith argument under existing law *and* that cannot be supported by a good faith argument for changing the existing law. [*Id.*] Note the following:

(i)   It is *not* frivolous to assert a position without first fully substantiating all the facts. [Comment 2 to ABA Model Rule 3.1]

(ii) It is *not* frivolous to assert a position knowing that vital evidence can be uncovered only through discovery proceedings. [*Id.*]

(iii) It is *not* frivolous to assert a position even though the lawyer believes that the position will not ultimately prevail. [*Id.*]

Examples: 1) C purchased land bordering a government forest, hoping to obtain the necessary government approval to build a ski resort. When the government refused to grant the necessary approval, C hired lawyer L to sue the government for taking C's property without just compensation. L advised C that her legal position was contrary to the existing law, but L developed two tenable arguments for distinguishing C's case from the existing law. Even though L believed that his arguments were sound, he did not believe that they would ultimately prevail in the United States Supreme Court. L is not subject to discipline.

2) An attorney may advise a client to take a tax position if the attorney believes that the position has a "realistic possibility of success if the matter is litigated." The attorney need not be convinced that the position will ultimately prevail. But when advising a client about a debatable tax position, the attorney must warn the client about possible penalties and other adverse legal consequences. [ABA Formal Op. 85-352 (1985)]

2. Defending in Criminal Proceedings

Despite the general rule against taking frivolous positions, the lawyer for the defendant in a criminal case (or for the respondent in a proceeding that could result in incarceration) may conduct the defense so that the prosecutor must prove every necessary element of the crime. [ABA Model Rule 3.1; Restatement §110(2)]

Example: Attorney A agrees to defend D in a kidnapping case. From the facts related in confidence by D, A concludes that D is clearly guilty as charged. If D nevertheless wishes to plead not guilty, A will not be subject to discipline for putting the prosecution to its proofs and requiring every element of the case to be proven beyond a reasonable doubt.

B. DUTY TO EXPEDITE LITIGATION

1. Reasonable Efforts to Expedite Litigation

A lawyer must make reasonable efforts to expedite litigation, consistent with the interests of the client. [ABA Model Rule 3.2] A lawyer may occasionally ask for a postponement for personal reasons, but he should not make a habit of it. [*See* Comment 1 to ABA Model Rule 3.2]

2. Interests of the Client

The duty to expedite does not require the lawyer to take actions that would harm the client's legitimate interests. [*See* ABA Model Rule 3.2] However, realizing financial or other benefit from otherwise improper delay is *not* a legitimate interest. [*Id.*]

Example: Client C lost her case at trial, and a judgment for $500,000 was entered against her. C's obligation to pay the judgment was stayed pending appeal. C instructed her lawyer to appeal the case and to drag out the appeal as long as possible, pointing out that she could earn an 11% return on the $500,000 while the appeal was pending. C's lawyer obtained every possible extension of time and delayed the appeal as long as he could. Ultimately, the appellate court affirmed the judgment below. C's lawyer is subject to discipline for causing delay.

C. DUTY OF CANDOR TO THE TRIBUNAL

1. Candor About Applicable Law

An attorney must be candid with the court about the *law* that applies to the case.

a. False Statements of Law

An attorney is subject to discipline for knowingly making a false statement of law to the court. [ABA Model Rule 3.3(a)(1)]

Examples: 1) During oral argument, attorney A cited the court to an intermediate appeals court opinion, knowing that the opinion had later been reversed by the state's highest court. A is subject to discipline.

2) In a memorandum of points and authorities, attorney B cited an obscure case for a proposition, knowing that the case held precisely the opposite. B is subject to discipline.

b. Failing to Disclose Controlling Authority

An attorney is subject to discipline for knowingly failing to disclose to the court a legal authority in the *controlling jurisdiction* that is *directly adverse* to the client's position and that has not been disclosed by the opposing counsel. [ABA Model Rule 3.3(a)(2);

Restatement §111(2); *and see* Jorgenson v. Volusia County, 846 F.2d 1350 (11th Cir. 1988)—Rule 11 sanctions imposed for failure to cite adverse authority] The attorney is, of course, free to argue that the cited authority is not sound or should not be followed.

Examples: 1) Lawyer L is representing client C in a diversity of citizenship case pending in the United States District Court for the District of Nevada. Under the *Erie* doctrine, Nevada law (including Nevada's choice of law rules) governs on issues of substance. In the case at hand, Nevada's choice of law rules make the controlling law that of the state of New York. L's adversary fails to call the court's attention to a New York Court of Appeals case that is directly contrary to the position taken by L's client. L must cite the case to the court.

2) Under the facts given in the example above, L would have no duty to cite the court to a directly adverse Utah case or to a directly adverse case decided by the United States Court of Appeals for the Fifth Circuit. Nor would L have a duty to cite the court to a New York Court of Appeals case that was against L's position only by analogy. (Note, however, that many lawyers would cite these cases to the court as a matter of sound tactics.)

2. Candor About Facts of Case

An attorney is subject to discipline for knowingly making a false statement of material fact to the court. [ABA Model Rule 3.3(a)(1)] Ordinarily, an attorney is not required to have personal knowledge of the facts stated in pleadings and other litigation documents—those contain assertions made by the client or by other persons, not by the attorney. [Comment 3 to ABA Model Rule 3.3] But when an attorney does make an assertion of fact to the court (*e.g.,* in an affidavit or when asserting facts in oral argument), the attorney is expected either to **know** that the assertion is true or to **believe** it to be true based on reasonably diligent inquiry. Furthermore, an attorney's **failure to speak out** is, in some contexts, the equivalent of an affirmative misrepresentation (*e.g.,* when the attorney or the client has caused a mistake or misunderstanding). [*Id.*]

Examples: 1) When the court was pondering whether to release attorney A's client on his own recognizance, the court asked A: "Does your client have a steady job here in the city, counsel?" A answered: "Oh, yes, Your Honor." If A knew that his client was unemployed, A is subject to discipline. Furthermore, if A had never inquired about his client's employment status and had no reasonable basis for the assertion, A is subject to discipline.

2) When the court was deciding what sentence to impose on attorney B's client, the court said: "I assume that this is your client's first drunk driving offense, counsel, so I am ordering him to attend drunk driving school and to pay a fine of $100." B knew that his client had two prior drunk driving offenses and that the mandatory sentence for the third such offense is revocation of license and 90 days in the county jail. Because neither B nor his client caused the court's mistake, B may keep quiet. *But note:* If B or his client had caused the mistake, B would have to speak up and correct it.

3. No Obligation to Volunteer Harmful Facts

An attorney generally has no obligation to volunteer a fact that is harmful to his client's case. The adversary system assumes that opposing sides can use discovery proceedings and their own investigations to find out the facts. [*See* Comment 14 to ABA Model Rule 3.4] If an attorney's adversary fails to uncover a harmful fact, an injustice may result, but that is simply the way the adversary system works.

Example: Lawyer L is defending D at the trial of a private treble damages antitrust case. Plaintiff's case-in-chief is defective. L knows that the defect could be cured if plaintiff were aware of a certain meeting between D and D's competitors. Throughout the long discovery proceedings, plaintiff never inquired about this meeting, although he had ample opportunity to do so. L has no duty to volunteer information about the meeting; L's ethical obligation is to move for a directed verdict at the close of plaintiff's case-in-chief.

a.   Exception—Ex Parte Proceedings

In an ex parte proceeding, only one side is present. Because the other side has no opportunity to offer its version of the facts, the model of the adversary system does not apply in the ex parte context. Therefore, a lawyer in an ex parte proceeding *must inform* the tribunal of *all material facts* known to the lawyer that will help the tribunal make an informed decision. [ABA Model Rule 3.3(d); Restatement §112(2)]

Example: The same day that W filed for divorce from H, W's lawyer petitioned for a temporary restraining order to prevent H from entering the family home and from bothering the children. Because H could not be found, the court agreed to hear the petition ex parte. At the hearing, W's lawyer must inform the court of *all the material facts*, both helpful and harmful, that bear on the issue before the court.

4.   Using False Evidence

In a matter pending before a tribunal, a lawyer is subject to discipline for offering evidence that the lawyer *knows* is false. [ABA Model Rule 3.3(a)(3)] "Knows" means actual knowledge, but actual knowledge can be inferred from the circumstances. [ABA Model Rule 1.0(f)] A lawyer should resolve doubts about veracity in favor of her client, but a lawyer cannot ignore an obvious falsehood. [Comment 8 to ABA Model Rule 3.3] Furthermore, a lawyer *may* refuse to offer evidence that she *reasonably believes* is false, except for a criminal defendant's testimony on his own behalf. [ABA Model Rule 3.3(a)(3)] These principles apply, not just in court, but also in an ancillary proceeding, such as a deposition.

a.   Discovery of Falsity After Evidence Has Been Offered

If a lawyer has offered a piece of evidence and later discovers that it is false, she must take reasonable remedial measures. First, the lawyer must speak confidentially with her client, urging the client's cooperation in withdrawing or correcting the false evidence. [Comment 10 to ABA Model Rule 3.3] Second, if the client will not cooperate, the lawyer should consider asking the court's permission to withdraw. Ordinarily, withdrawal is not mandatory, but it becomes mandatory if the lawyer's discovery of the false evidence creates such a rift between the lawyer and client that the lawyer can no longer represent the client effectively. [Comment 15 to ABA Model Rule 3.3] Withdrawal alone is not a sufficient remedial step if it leaves the false evidence before the tribunal. The lawyer should also move to strike the false evidence or take other steps to cancel out its effect. [*See* Restatement §120, comment h] Third, if withdrawal is not permitted or will not solve the problem, the lawyer *must* disclose the situation to the judge, even if that means disclosing the client's information that would otherwise be protected under the duty of confidentiality. [Comment 10 to ABA Model Rule 3.3]

Note that the duty to rectify false evidence continues until the end of the proceedings, which means when a final judgment has been affirmed on appeal or the time for appeal has expired. [Comment 13 to ABA Model Rule 3.3]

b.   False Testimony by Criminal Defendant

One of the thorniest problems in legal ethics arises when a criminal defense lawyer learns that her client has testified falsely, or is about to testify falsely, in his own defense. A criminal defendant has a Sixth Amendment right to the effective assistance of counsel. A criminal defendant also has a constitutional right to testify on his own behalf. [Rock v. Arkansas, 483 U.S. 44 (1987)] On the other hand, a criminal defense lawyer must not present evidence that he knows is false, and ordinarily he must not reveal the client's confidential information. What is the criminal defense lawyer to do when the client insists on testifying to something that the lawyer knows (because of the client's confidential disclosures) is false?

1)   ABA Model Rules and Restatement Solution

When you take the MPRE, apply the solution adopted by the ABA Model Rules and the Restatement. [*See* ABA Model Rule 3.3(a)(3); Restatement §120, comment i] That is, the criminal defense lawyer should follow the same three steps stated in a., above. First, the lawyer must try to convince the defendant not to testify falsely. Second, if the defendant insists on testifying falsely, the lawyer should consider withdrawal, if that will solve the problem. Usually it will not solve the problem, either because the court will not permit withdrawal or because withdrawal will not erase or prevent the false testimony. Third, if all else fails, the lawyer must reveal the situation to the judge, even if that means disclosing the client's confidential information. The judge must then decide what to do, perhaps declare a mistrial, make some kind of statement to the jury, or perhaps nothing. The duty to rectify false evidence continues until the end of the proceedings, which means when a final judgment has been affirmed on appeal or the time for appeal has expired. [Comment 13 to ABA Model Rule 3.3] This solution to the problem does not violate a criminal defendant's constitutional right to effective assistance of counsel. [Nix v. Whiteside, 475 U.S. 157 (1986)]

2)   Minority View

Several jurisdictions (including New York and California) handle the problem by allowing the criminal defendant to testify in "narrative fashion." That means that the defense lawyer questions the defendant in the ordinary way up to the point of the false testimony. At that point, the defense lawyer asks a question that calls for a narrative answer (such as "What else happened?"). The defendant then tells his story. The defense lawyer is not permitted to rely on the false parts of the story when arguing the case to the trier of fact. ABA Model Rule 3.3 defers to the local law in jurisdictions that follow the minority view. [Comment 7 to ABA Model Rule 3.3]

5.   Other Corruption of an Adjudicative Proceeding

A lawyer who represents a client in an adjudicative proceeding must take appropriate measures to prevent any person (a client or anyone else) from committing criminal or fraudulent conduct that will corrupt the proceedings. [*See* ABA Model Rule 3.3(b)] Examples of such conduct are: (i) hiding or destroying evidence, (ii) bribing a witness, (iii) intimidating a juror, (iv) buying a judge, and (v) failing to obey a law or court order to disclose information. [Comment 12 to ABA Model Rule 3.3] Appropriate measures include disclosure to the court, if that becomes necessary.

Example: Attorney A is defending surgeon S in a medical malpractice case. Student nurse N observed the operation in question, including the act that allegedly constitutes the malpractice. Two days before plaintiff took N's deposition, S's father told N: "If you testify at your deposition that you saw S do the act in question, I'll make sure you never get a nursing job in this state." At her deposition, N testified that she was not in the operating room at the time of the alleged act. Two days after the deposition, A learned what S's father did. A must set the record straight; if all else fails, A must tell the tribunal what happened.

D. DUTY OF FAIRNESS TO OPPOSING PARTY AND COUNSEL

1. Opponent's Access to Evidence

A lawyer must not unlawfully obstruct another party's access to evidence. Furthermore, a lawyer must not unlawfully alter, destroy, or conceal a document or other item having evidentiary value. In addition, a lawyer must not counsel or assist another person to do any of these things. [ABA Model Rule 3.4(a); Restatement §118] Suppressing or tampering with evidence may also constitute a crime. [*See, e.g.,* Cal. Penal Code §135]

Example: A special prosecutor was appointed to investigate certain allegations against a government official. The official told his lawyer about some highly incriminating documents in a file in his office. The lawyer suggested that the official "deep six" the file in the nearest river. The lawyer is subject to discipline.

2. Falsifying Evidence and Assisting in Perjury

A lawyer must not falsify evidence. [ABA Model Rule 3.4(b); Restatement §118] Furthermore, a lawyer must not counsel or assist a witness to testify falsely. [*Id.*] Well-prepared lawyers seldom pass up an opportunity to talk to a witness before the witness testifies. The lawyer may probe the witness's memory, explore the basis of the witness's knowledge, point out holes and fallacies in the witness's story, and seek to refresh the witness's recollection by proper means. [Restatement §116] However, the lawyer must not try to "bend" the testimony or put words in the witness's mouth. New York's Judge Finch put the matter this way in an 1880 disciplinary case: "[The lawyer's] duty is to extract the facts from the witness, not to put them into him; to learn what the witness does know, not to teach him what he ought to know." [*In re* Eldridge, 82 N.Y. 161 (1880)]

3. Paying Witnesses

A lawyer must not offer an inducement to a witness that is prohibited by law. [ABA Model Rule 3.4(b); Restatement §117] However, except when prohibited by local law, the following payments to witnesses are proper.

a. Travel, Meals, and Lodging

An attorney may pay expenses reasonably incurred by the witness in attending and testifying (*e.g.,* travel, hotel, meals, and incidental expenses). [Comment 3 to ABA Model Rule 3.4]

b. Loss of Time

An attorney may pay reasonable compensation for the witness's loss of time in attending and testifying (*e.g.,* the amount the witness would have earned at her job had she not had to come to testify). [Restatement §117, comment b]

c. Experts' Fees

An attorney may pay a reasonable fee to an *expert* witness for preparing to testify and for testifying. The fee must not be contingent on either the content of the testimony or the outcome of the case. [Comment 3 to ABA Model Rule 3.4]

Example: In a complex securities case, client C needed the testimony of an expert on securities brokerage. C's lawyer L agreed to advance the expenses for expert E and promised to pay E's travel, hotel, meal, and incidental expenses. L also promised E a witness fee of $1,000 or 2% of C's eventual recovery, whichever was greater. The arrangement for expenses was proper, but the witness fee arrangement makes L subject to discipline.

4. Securing Absence or Noncooperation of Witness

A lawyer must not advise or cause a person to secrete himself or to flee the jurisdiction for the purpose of making him unavailable as a witness. [ABA Model Rule 3.4(a); Restatement §116] A lawyer may, however, advise a person not to voluntarily give information to an opponent or other party if the following conditions are met:

(i) The person is a client, or a relative, employee, or agent of a client; and

(ii) The lawyer reasonably believes that the person's interests will not be harmed by not volunteering the information.

[ABA Model Rule 3.4(f)]

Example: Attorney A represents W in a child custody dispute with W's former husband, H. A believes that H's lawyer will probably try to interview W's sister to find out information about W's fitness as a parent. Absent some kind of harm to the sister, A may advise the sister that she need not speak voluntarily with H's lawyer about the matter. However, if A learns that H's lawyer is trying to serve a deposition subpoena on the sister, A must not advise the sister to leave town or hide from the process server.

5. Violating Court Rules and Orders

A lawyer must not knowingly violate a rule of procedure, a rule of evidence, a rule of court, or an order made by the court—but a lawyer may openly refuse to obey such a rule or order for the purpose of making a good faith challenge to the validity of the rule or order. [ABA Model Rule 3.4(c); Restatement §105]

Examples: 1) At the jury trial of D for automobile theft, the trial judge ordered prosecutor P to make no mention whatsoever of D's former misdemeanor convictions. In cross-examining one of D's witnesses, P asked: "When you and D were cellmates in the county jail back in 1998, did D invite you to join a car theft operation after your release?" If P was intentionally trying to evade the trial judge's order, P is subject to discipline.

2) In the civil suit of *P v. D,* P demanded production of some documents that D claimed were protected by the attorney-client privilege. The trial judge ordered the documents to be produced *in camera* so that he could determine whether the documents were privileged. D's lawyer asserted that the state law of attorney-client privilege did not authorize the judge to require an *in camera* examination. The trial judge refused to stay the order long enough to allow D to pursue an interlocutory appeal. D's lawyer may refuse to produce the documents while she seeks a writ of mandamus or prohibition to test the validity of the trial judge's order. [*See also In re* Tamblyn, 695 P.2d 902 (Or. 1985)—attorney may advise client not to obey void court order]

6. Abusing Discovery Procedures

A lawyer must not make a frivolous discovery request, or fail to make reasonable efforts to comply with a legally proper discovery request made by the adversary. [ABA Model Rule 3.4(d)] Abuse of discovery proceedings can also subject both the lawyer and the client to fines and other sanctions. [*See, e.g.,* Fed. R. Civ. P. 37(b); Roadway Express, Inc. v. Piper, 447 U.S. 752 (1980)—federal court has inherent authority to hold counsel personally responsible for expenses and attorneys' fees incurred because of counsel's bad faith in discovery]

Example: Lawyer L intentionally failed to produce a certain set of handwritten notes that were clearly called for by a court order. L's conduct caused L's adversary to spend several hundred hours in developing alternative evidence of the facts stated in the notes. L is subject to discipline and is subject to such other sanctions as the court may see fit to impose.

7. Chicanery at Trial

A lawyer is subject to discipline for engaging in the following types of chicanery during the trial of a case.

a. Referring to Inadmissible Material

During the trial of a case, a lawyer must not refer to material that the lawyer does not reasonably believe is relevant or that will not be supported by admissible evidence. [ABA Model Rule 3.4(e); Restatement §107]

Examples: 1) At the trial of a railway accident case, plaintiff's lawyer made repeated reference to the great size and wealth of the railway company. The comments were irrelevant to any issue in the case and were made solely to inflame the jury. The lawyer is subject to discipline. [*See also* Simmons v. Southern Pacific Transportation Co., 62 Cal. App. 3d 341 (1976)—verdict for plaintiff reversed because of counsel's misconduct]

2) During her opening statement to the jury, the defense lawyer pointed out that plaintiff had offered to settle his claim for a small sum. The defense lawyer knew that evidence of the settlement offer would not be admissible. The lawyer is subject to discipline.

b. Asserting Personal Knowledge of Contested Facts

During the trial of a case, a lawyer must not assert personal knowledge of facts in issue (except when testifying as a witness). [ABA Model Rule 3.4(e)]

Example: Lawyer L represented the plaintiff in a dog bite case. The defendant contended that he was not the owner of the offending dog. In his closing argument to the jury, L said: "The defendant has solemnly told you that he does not own the dog. As it happens, I live down the street from the defendant, and every night about 10, I see the defendant taking that very same dog for a walk." L is subject to discipline.

c. Asserting Personal Opinions

During the trial of a case, a lawyer must not state a personal opinion about:

(i) The justness of a cause;

(ii) The credibility of a witness;

(iii) The culpability of a civil litigant; or

(iv) The guilt or innocence of an accused.

[ABA Model Rule 3.4(e); Restatement §107] A lawyer may, of course, make an argument based on the *evidence* concerning any of these matters.

Examples: 1) During his closing argument in a routine traffic accident case, attorney A said: "D has told you that the light was green. I was appalled to hear the man say that from the witness stand, under oath! I don't believe him for a minute, and I ask you not to believe him either." A's argument is not proper.

2) In the example above, it would have been proper for A to make his point by referring to the evidence rather than expressing personal opinion. For instance: "D has told you that the light was green. D stands to lose a great deal of money in this case. Two eyewitnesses, who have nothing to lose, testified that the light was red. It is up to you jurors to decide whom to believe."

8. Using Threats to Gain Advantage in Civil Case

Under the ABA Model Rules, a lawyer may bring, or threaten to bring, criminal charges against her adversary in order to gain an advantage in a civil case, provided that the criminal and civil matters are closely related and that both the civil case and criminal charges are warranted by the law and the facts. [ABA Formal Op. 92-363 (1992)] However, a lawyer must not threaten to report adversary counsel for a disciplinary violation in order to gain an advantage for her client in a civil case. If the adversary counsel's disciplinary violation is the kind that must be reported, the lawyer should simply report it—she should not use it as a bargaining chip in the civil case. [ABA Formal Op. 94-383 (1994)]

Example: Lawyer L has personal knowledge that adversary counsel lied to the judge about a certain document that L had requested in discovery. Lying to a judge is the kind of conduct that raises a substantial question about a person's fitness to practice, and L therefore must report it. L told adversary counsel: "If you accept my client's settlement proposal, then I will not report you for lying to the judge about that document." L's conduct is improper; she should simply have reported adversary counsel, not used the misconduct as a bargaining chip in the civil case.

9. Treating Opponents with Courtesy and Respect

The professional ideal is that advocates relate to each other with a respectful and cooperative attitude marked by civility consistent with their responsibility to their clients. Lawyers also should treat all participants in a proceeding with such respect and cooperativeness. Certain conduct toward other participants is prohibited and includes: physical force or threat; ethnic, racial, or gender-based slurs; and reckless charges of wrongdoing. [Restatement §106, comment d]

Example: Witness W repeatedly lied during her deposition. Lawyer L finally lost her temper and slapped W hard across the face. L is subject to criminal and civil liability for assaulting and battering W. L is also subject to discipline for conduct that is prejudicial to the administration of justice and conduct that shows unfitness to practice law. [ABA Model Rule 8.4(b), (d); *see also* Restatement §106, comment d; ABA Model Rule 3.5(d) and Comment 5— prohibits conduct intended to disrupt a tribunal, including a deposition]

E. DUTY TO PRESERVE IMPARTIALITY AND DECORUM OF TRIBUNAL

1. Improper Influence

A lawyer must not seek to influence a judge, court official, juror, or prospective juror by improper means. [*See* ABA Model Rule 3.5(a)] For example, a lawyer must not offer a gift to a judge unless the judge would be allowed to accept it under the ABA Code of Judicial Conduct.

Example: Attorneys A and B frequently appear as counsel in the Superior Court. C is the chief clerk of that court. All three of them are avid fishermen. A and B invite C to join them, at their expense, for a week of salmon fishing at B's lodge in Alaska. It would not be proper under ABA Code of Judicial Conduct 5(C)(4) for C to accept such a gift, and it is not proper for A and B to offer it to C.

2. Improper Ex Parte Communication

While a proceeding is pending in a tribunal, a lawyer must not have an ex parte communication with a judge, court official, juror, or prospective juror except when authorized by law or court order. [*See* ABA Model Rule 3.5(b)] An "ex parte communication" is a communication that concerns the matter at issue and occurs outside the presence and without the consent of the other parties to the litigation or their representatives. [Restatement §113, comment c]

a. Judges and Court Officials

As ABA Model Rule 3.5(b) recognizes, local law and court orders may vary concerning ex parte communications with judges and court officials. Generally, a ***written*** communication to a judicial officer is not ex parte if a copy of the communication is timely sent to the opposing parties. [Restatement §113, comment c] A lawyer must not, however, communicate ***orally*** on the ***merits*** of a matter with the judge or other official before whom the matter is pending without giving ***adequate notice*** to the adversary. If the local rules of court allow lawyers to appear ex parte, without notice to the adversary, to obtain extensions of time to plead or respond to discovery, a lawyer may do so—but the lawyer must not discuss the ***merits*** of the case when requesting the extension of time. [*See* Restatement §113(1)]

b. Jurors and Prospective Jurors

ABA Model Rule 3.5(b) recognizes that local law may vary concerning contact between lawyers and jurors or prospective jurors. In general, however, before and during the trial of a case, a lawyer who is connected with the case must not communicate (outside of official proceedings) with a juror or member of the panel from which the jurors will be chosen. This rule forbids communication on *any subject*—even the weather. It does not matter who initiates the communication. If a juror or prospective juror attempts to communicate with a lawyer, the lawyer must refuse. [Restatement §115]

1) **Investigation of Prospective Jurors**
It is not improper for a lawyer to investigate members of a jury panel to determine their backgrounds and the existence of any factors that would be grounds for a challenge (*e.g.*, bias, relationship to a party). Such an investigation must be done discreetly and must not involve contact with the prospective juror or, in most cases, her family.

2) **Post-Trial Communications with Jurors**
After the trial is over and the jury is discharged, a lawyer must not communicate with a former jury member (or even a person who was a prospective juror) if any of the following conditions is met: (i) local law or a court order prohibits such communication; (ii) the juror has told the lawyer that he does not want to communicate; or (iii) the communication involves misrepresentation, coercion, or harassment. [ABA Model Rule 3.5(c)]

3. **Disruptive Conduct**
A lawyer must not engage in conduct intended to disrupt a tribunal. [ABA Model Rule 3.5(d)] This rule applies in depositions as well as in the courtroom. [Comment 5 to ABA Model Rule 3.5]
Example: Despite repeated warnings by the trial judge, attorney A persisted in banging on the counsel table, interrupting the judge in mid-sentence, making sour faces while witnesses were examined, and leaning over the jury rail in an intimidating manner. A is subject to discipline (and, at the court's discretion, to punishment for contempt of court).

4. **Statements About Judicial and Legal Officials**

a. **False Statements About Judges or Candidates for Public Legal Office**
A lawyer must not make a statement that the lawyer knows is false about the qualifications or integrity of a judge, hearing officer, or public legal official, or about a candidate for a judicial or legal office. The same rule applies to statements made with reckless disregard as to truth or falsity. [ABA Model Rule 8.2(a); Restatement §114]
Example: Lawyer L was representing D in a widely publicized fraud trial pending in Judge J's court. After Judge J denied L's motion for a directed verdict, L held an impromptu press conference at a tavern near the courthouse. L told the reporters: "The reason Judge J knows less law than a Duroc hog is that he got his degree through a mail order correspondence course." L knows that Judge J is a graduate of the Harvard Law School. L is subject to discipline.

b. **Candidates for Judicial Office**
A lawyer who is running for judicial office must comply with the applicable provisions of the Code of Judicial Conduct. [ABA Model Rule 8.2(b)]

Example: Attorney A was one of two candidates for a vacant superior court judgeship. She personally solicited and accepted campaign contributions from other members of her law firm, a violation of ABA Code of Judicial Conduct 7(B)(2). A is subject to discipline.

F. TRIAL PUBLICITY

The litigants in a trial have a Fifth Amendment right to have their dispute resolved on admissible evidence, by fair procedures, in a tribunal that is not influenced by public sentiment or outcry. Protection of that right requires some limits on the kinds of information that can be disseminated to the public before trial—particularly where the trial is to be by jury. On the other hand, the public and the press have countervailing rights under the First Amendment. The public has a right to know about threats to its safety, and it has an interest in knowing about the conduct of judicial proceedings. Moreover, the subjects of litigation are often significant in debate over questions of public policy.

1. General Rule

A lawyer who is connected with a case must not make a public statement outside the courtroom that the lawyer reasonably should know would have a "substantial likelihood of materially prejudicing" the case (*e.g.,* discussing the character or credibility of a party or witness, performance or results of an examination, possibility of a guilty plea, or existence or contents of a confession). [ABA Model Rule 3.6(a); Restatement §109]

2. Right of Reply

A lawyer may, however, make a public statement that "a reasonable lawyer would believe is required to protect a client from the substantial undue prejudicial effect of recent publicity not initiated by the lawyer or the lawyer's client." [ABA Model Rule 3.6(c)]

Example: Professional tennis star Jacques LaMont was arrested for sexually assaulting an employee in the hotel where he was staying. Dozens of media reporters descended on the inexperienced prosecutor assigned to LaMont's case. The reporters demanded to know what evidence there was against LaMont, who was reputed to be a clean-living family man. The prosecutor said he could not disclose any details, but that there was "some incriminating physical evidence," plus a "helpful signed statement that LaMont gave to the police voluntarily." The prosecutor's comments got wide coverage in the press and on television. LaMont's counsel feared that the prosecutor's characterization of LaMont's signed statement as "helpful" would make people think that LaMont had incriminated himself. Seeking to dispel that false impression, LaMont's counsel told reporters, quite accurately, that the most "incriminating" parts of LaMont's statement were that he was a paying guest of the hotel on the night in question and that at the time in question LaMont was asleep in his own hotel room, alone. The prosecutor is subject to discipline, but the defense lawyer's statement was proper. [*See* ABA Model Rule 3.6(c) and Comment 5; *see also* ABA Model Rule 3.8(f)]

3. Additional Constraint on Criminal Prosecutors

There is an additional constraint on the prosecutor in a criminal case. The prosecutor must not make extrajudicial comments that have a "substantial likelihood of heightening public condemnation of the accused." [ABA Model Rule 3.8(f)]

4.   Dry Facts About Case Permitted

Notwithstanding the general rule against prejudicial statements, a lawyer who is connected with the case may publicly state the following "dry facts" about the case:

a.   The claim, charge, or defense involved (provided there is an accompanying statement that the charge is only an accusation and that the party is deemed innocent until proven guilty);

b.   The names of persons involved (unless the law prohibits it);

c.   Any information that is already in the public record;

d.   The scheduling or result of any step in litigation;

e.   The fact that an investigation is ongoing, a request for help in getting information, and a warning of danger (if appropriate); and

f.   Routine booking information about a criminal defendant, such as his name, address, occupation, family status, the time and place of arrest, the names of arresting officers, and the names of investigating officers or agencies.

5.   Rules Also Apply to Associated Lawyers

The rules stated above apply equally to other lawyers who are associated in a law firm or agency with the lawyers participating in the case.

G.   TRIAL COUNSEL AS WITNESS

1.   Reasons to Avoid Dual Role

Several problems are posed when a client's trial counsel also testifies as a witness at the trial.

a.   Conflict of Interest

The dual role may create a conflict of interest between the client and the trial counsel. For example, the trial counsel's testimony may contradict the client's testimony, or the trial counsel's obvious bias may make her an ineffective witness on behalf of the client. [Comment 6 to ABA Model Rule 3.7]

b.   Differing Functions

The functions of trial counsel and witness are different. A witness must state facts objectively, but a trial counsel is supposed to present facts as a partisan advocate. When the two roles are combined, it may be unclear whether a particular statement is to be taken as evidence or as advocacy. The tribunal itself can object when the dual role may confuse or mislead the trier of fact. [Comment 2 to ABA Model Rule 3.7]

c.   Effect on Adversary

The adversary may be handicapped in challenging the credibility of one who serves as both trial counsel and witness. Courtesy and sound tactics may force the adversary to tread softly on cross-examination. Furthermore, a favorable impression created as trial counsel may lend unjustified believability to the trial counsel's words as witness.

2. **Ethical Limitations Imposed**
   For the foregoing reasons, the ABA Model Rules place limits on serving as both trial counsel and witness. [*See also* Restatement §108] Except in the situations discussed below, a lawyer must not act as an advocate at a trial in which the lawyer is likely to be a ***necessary*** witness. [ABA Model Rule 3.7(a)]

   a. **Uncontested Matter or Mere Formality**
      A lawyer may serve as trial counsel if her testimony as a witness will relate solely to an uncontested matter or to a mere formality. [*See* ABA Model Rule 3.7(a)(1)]
      Example: Attorney A's testimony will be limited to the authentication of a letter, and there is no reason to doubt the letter's authenticity. Either A or another lawyer in her firm may serve as trial counsel.

   b. **Testimony About Legal Services Rendered in the Case**
      A lawyer may serve as trial counsel if his testimony will relate solely to the nature and value of legal services he has rendered in the case. [ABA Model Rule 3.7(a)(2)]
      Example: State law allows attorneys' fees to be awarded to the victor in environmental suits brought under the public trust doctrine. Attorney B's client won such a case. At the fee setting hearing, B may continue as trial counsel and may also testify about the number of hours he spent on the case, the nature of the services, and the amount of his ordinary hourly fee.

   c. **Substantial Hardship on Client**
      A lawyer may serve as trial counsel and also testify about any matter if withdrawal as trial counsel would cause "***substantial***" hardship. [ABA Model Rule 3.7(a)(3)] Courts tend to be narrow-minded in applying this exception. Mere duplication of legal fees or the loss of a long working relationship with counsel are sometimes held not to constitute substantial hardship.
      Example: For the past five years, attorney C has worked full time on the discovery and pretrial preparation of a major tax fraud case. Just before trial, C discovered that she would have to testify on a contested issue concerning some entries in her client's books of account. If C withdraws as trial counsel, it will cost her client many thousands of dollars in extra legal fees, and it will delay the trial by 18 months. The substantial hardship exception ***ought to*** apply here, but there is some authority to the contrary.

   d. **Other Lawyers in Firm May Be Witnesses**
      A lawyer is permitted to act as an advocate at a trial in which another lawyer in the lawyer's firm is likely to be called as a witness unless precluded from doing so by the conflict of interest rules. [ABA Model Rule 3.7(b)]

3. **Conflict of Interest Rules Also Apply**
   A lawyer who is asked to be both an advocate and a witness must comply not only with ABA Model Rule 3.7, but also with the general conflict of interest principles stated in ABA Model Rules 1.7 (current clients) and 1.9 (former clients). For instance, the dual role can create a conflict between the current client's interest in winning the case and the lawyer's interest in earning a fee as trial counsel.

Example: Rock climbers A, B, C, and L (a lawyer) went on a rock climbing venture guided by professional climber Bea Lai Long. C was badly injured on the climb, allegedly by Bea's foolhardy decision to take an exposed route when a storm was approaching. A, B, and L were the only people who saw what happened to C, and their testimony will be vital to C's claim against Bea. C has asked L to be her trial counsel. L would like to earn the fee, but he also knows that his testimony about the accident will be open to attack for bias; C might be better off having another trial counsel and using L only as an eyewitness. L must not represent C unless he fully explains the conflict to C and obtains her informed, written consent.

H. SPECIAL RESPONSIBILITIES OF A PROSECUTOR

The prosecutor in a criminal case is not simply an advocate but also a minister of justice; the prosecutor's primary goal is to *seek justice*, not to convict. [Comment 1 to ABA Model Rule 3.8] Thus, the prosecutor must assure that the defendant is tried by fair procedures and that guilt is decided on proper and sufficient evidence. Local laws may impose additional duties on a prosecutor, and failure to comply with such laws is grounds for professional discipline. [*Id.*]

1. Prosecuting Without Probable Cause

A prosecutor must not prosecute a charge that she knows is not supported by probable cause. [ABA Model Rule 3.8(a)]

2. Protecting Accused's Right to Counsel

A prosecutor must make reasonable efforts to assure that the accused is:

(i)   Advised of the right to counsel;

(ii) Advised of the procedure for obtaining counsel; and

(iii) Given a reasonable opportunity to obtain counsel.

[ABA Model Rule 3.8(b)]

Example: Sheriff S is in charge of the county jail. S has established jail regulations that frequently result in an accused being held incommunicado for a long period before being given a chance to use the telephone. County District Attorney A must make reasonable efforts to have the jail regulations changed. [*See* ABA Model Rule 3.8(b)]

3. Securing Waiver of Pretrial Rights

A prosecutor must not seek to obtain from an unrepresented accused a waiver of important pretrial rights, such as the right to a preliminary hearing. [ABA Model Rule 3.8(c)]

Example: Indigent accused, A, was advised of his right to remain silent and of his right to have counsel appointed to defend him. A asked for the services of a public defender, and A said that he did not want to make any statement. Before the public defender arrived, A was brought to a small room and allowed to relax over a cup of coffee. At that time, prosecutor P urged him to "assist us voluntarily in finding out what happened so we can clear this up and get you out of here without getting into legal technicalities." P is subject to discipline.

4. Disclosing Evidence that May Help Defense

A prosecutor must timely disclose to the defense all evidence and information known to the prosecutor that tends to negate the guilt of the accused or mitigate the degree of the offense. [ABA Model Rule 3.8(d)] Failure to disclose material information may deprive the defendant of due process. [*See* Brady v. Maryland, 373 U.S. 83 (1963), *explained in* United States v. Bagley, 473 U.S. 667 (1985)]

Example: D was accused of second degree murder. Prosecutor P asked the county coroner to pay special attention to the size, shape, and location of the stab wound that killed the victim. The coroner reported that the wound was probably inflicted by a person who was being held down on the ground by the victim. Since this information tends to suggest self-defense, P must promptly report it to D's lawyer.

5. Disclosing Information that May Mitigate Punishment

When a convicted person is to be sentenced, the prosecutor must disclose to the defense and to the court all unprivileged mitigating information known to the prosecutor (except when a protective order of the court relieves the prosecutor of this obligation). [ABA Model Rule 3.8(d)]

6. Public Statements About Pending Matters

Except for statements that are necessary to inform the public of the nature and extent of the prosecutor's action and that serve a legitimate law enforcement purpose, a prosecutor must not make extrajudicial statements that have a "substantial likelihood of heightening public condemnation of the accused." A prosecutor must take reasonable care to prevent investigators, police, employees, and other subordinates from making such statements. [ABA Model Rule 3.8(f)]

7. Subpoenaing Other Lawyers

A prosecutor must not subpoena another lawyer to give evidence about a client or former client unless the evidence is not privileged, is essential, and cannot be obtained in another way. [ABA Model Rule 3.8(e)]

8. Other Government Lawyers

Many of the above duties are incumbent on all government lawyers, not merely public prosecutors.

a. Terminating Actions

A government lawyer with discretionary power relative to civil litigation should not institute or continue actions that are obviously unfair. [Freeport-McMoRan Oil & Gas Co. v. F.E.R.C., 962 F.2d 45 (D.C. Cir. 1992)]

b. Developing Full Record

Even if litigation appears warranted, a government lawyer has a responsibility to develop a full and fair record. The lawyer must not use her position or the economic power of the government to harass parties or to force unjust settlements or results.

I.   ADVOCATE IN LEGISLATIVE AND ADMINISTRATIVE PROCEEDINGS

1. **Appearances in a Representative Capacity**
   Lawyers sometimes appear before legislatures, city councils, executive agencies, regulatory boards, and other groups that act in a rule-making or policy-making capacity. [*See* Comment to ABA Model Rule 3.9] When a lawyer appears on behalf of a client before a legislative body or administrative agency, the lawyer must disclose that she is acting in a representative capacity (not on her own behalf). [ABA Model Rule 3.9; Restatement §104]

   Example: The Columbia Association of Manufacturers and Retailers hired lawyer L to assist it in opposing a proposed new inventory tax. In that capacity, L testified in hearings before the Finance Committee of the Columbia Municipal Council. In her testimony, L presented both legal and economic arguments against the proposed tax. L must disclose to the Finance Committee that she is acting in a representative capacity.

2. **Duties of Candor and Respect**
   When a lawyer represents a client before a legislative body or administrative agency in an official hearing or meeting at which the lawyer or client presents evidence or argument, the lawyer must, generally speaking, follow the same rules as though in court. [*Id.*] For example, the lawyer must not make false statements of fact or law, offer evidence known to be false, obstruct access to evidence, knowingly violate the rules and orders of the legislative or administrative body, seek to use undue influence, or engage in disruptive conduct. [ABA Model Rules 3.9, 3.3(a) - (c), 3.4(a) - (c), 3.5] A lawyer should comply with these rules even though the rules do not bind nonlawyers who do similar work. [Comment 2 to ABA Model Rule 3.9]

3. **Limits of These Rules**
   The rules stated in 1. and 2., above, do *not* apply: (i) when a lawyer represents a client in bilateral negotiations with the government, (ii) in an application for a license or other privilege, (iii) when the government is investigating the client's affairs, or (iv) when the government is examining the client's compliance with a regular reporting requirement (such as the filing of tax returns).

IX.   TRANSACTIONS WITH THIRD PERSONS

A.   TRUTHFULNESS IN STATEMENTS TO THIRD PERSONS

1. **Must Not Make False Statements of Material Fact or Law**
   When dealing on behalf of a client with a third person, a lawyer must not knowingly make a false statement of law or material fact. [ABA Model Rule 4.1(a); Restatement §98] Generally, a lawyer has no duty to inform a third person of relevant facts. [Comment 1 to ABA Model Rule 4.1] However, a lawyer must not misrepresent the facts.

   a. **Types of Misrepresentation**
      A misrepresentation can occur when the lawyer makes a statement knowing that it is false, when the lawyer affirms or incorporates a statement knowing that it is false, when the lawyer states something that is partly true but misleading, or in some contexts when the lawyer fails to speak or act. [*Id.*]

Examples: 1) Lawyer L represented seller S in negotiating a sale of S's farm to buyer B. L and S accompanied B on a walking tour of the farmlands, and it soon became apparent to them that B knew little or nothing about farming. When B looked over the north 40 acres, he said: "I assume that the soil and water here would be good for a nice walnut orchard." L and S both knew that the soil was far too wet and heavy to grow walnuts. S replied: "Oh, you'd be surprised what can grow here." L said nothing. L's failure to speak out in this context is equivalent to an affirmative misrepresentation. L is subject to discipline.

2) Attorney A represented plaintiff P in a personal injury case. P died while settlement negotiation was going on with the defendant. A must not pursue the settlement negotiation without notifying the defense lawyer of P's death. [ABA Formal Op. 95-397 (1995)]

b. Distinguish Conventional Puffery

Under generally accepted conventions in negotiation, certain types of statements ordinarily are not taken as statements of material fact. [Comment 2 to ABA Model Rule 4.1] Estimates of price or value placed on the subject of a transaction are ordinarily regarded as mere puffery, and so is a statement of a party's intentions as to settlement of a claim. [*Id.*]

Example: Attorney A was employed by Consolidated Liability Insurance Company to defend its insured, D, in an automobile accident case. After careful investigation, A concluded that D was clearly at fault. A advised Consolidated to settle, and Consolidated authorized A to settle the case for any sum under $10,000. A few days later, plaintiff's lawyer telephoned A and suggested that they meet to discuss a settlement. A responded: "I will be glad to listen to whatever you have to propose, but I sincerely doubt that Consolidated will be interested in settling—I think we can win this one at trial." Under generally accepted conventions, A's statements would be regarded as mere puffery, not as false statements of material fact.

2. Failure to Disclose Material Facts—Client's Crime or Fraud

A lawyer must disclose material facts to a third person when necessary to avoid assisting the client in a crime or fraud—unless the lawyer is forbidden to do so by the ethical duty of confidentiality. [ABA Model Rule 4.1(b)] Under the ABA Model Rules view, where the duty of confidentiality prevents the lawyer from disclosing material facts, and where continued representation would require the lawyer to assist in the client's crime or fraud, the lawyer must withdraw. [*See* ABA Model Rules 1.16(a)(1), 1.2(d); ABA Formal Op. 92-366 (1992)] The lawyer may notify the affected third person of the withdrawal and may withdraw or disaffirm any opinion, document, or affirmation previously furnished in connection with the matter. [*See* Comment to ABA Model Rule 1.6; ABA Formal Op. 92-366 (1992)]

Example: Client C hired attorney A to obtain import licenses to sell C's chemical fertilizer in Australia and New Zealand. While the license applications were pending, C and A negotiated a contract to sell C's entire fertilizer business to X. At C's request, A prepared a "Statement of Operations, Assets, and Liabilities" for X. In the statement A represented that the Australian and New

Zealand import licenses were pending and that in A's opinion they would be granted. Before the sale was closed, both Australia and New Zealand notified C that they would not issue the import licenses, and C conveyed this information to A in confidence. A advised C that X must be informed of this material fact, but C responded: "To hell with X—your job is to get the sale completed. Now get busy." Under the ABA Model Rules view, the duty of confidentiality forbids A from revealing the license denial to X, but if A continues with the representation, he will be assisting C in defrauding X. A must withdraw. A may advise X of his withdrawal, and he may disaffirm his prior opinion as respects the Australian and New Zealand import licenses. The Restatement takes a simpler, more forthright position. The news of the license denial is not protected by the duty of confidentiality because the law of fraud requires A to disclose it to X. [*See* Restatement §§63, 98, comment d]

B.   COMMUNICATION WITH PERSONS REPRESENTED BY COUNSEL

1.   When Communication Forbidden

A lawyer must not communicate about a matter with a person the lawyer knows is represented by counsel, unless that person's counsel consents, or unless the law or a court order authorizes the communication. [ABA Model Rule 4.2; Restatement §99]

Examples: 1) In the case of *P v. D*, the lawyer for D had excellent reason to believe that P's lawyer had failed to convey D's settlement offer to P. D's lawyer therefore telephoned P and made the settlement offer directly. D's lawyer is subject to discipline for communicating with a represented person without consent of that person's counsel. [ABA Formal Op. 92-362 (1992)] P's lawyer is also subject to discipline if he failed to convey D's settlement offer to P.

2) Defendant D was in jail awaiting trial for murder. D was represented by appointed counsel. Without the consent of the appointed counsel, the prosecutor visited D at the jail and discussed the possibility of a plea bargain with D. The prosecutor is subject to discipline. [Comment 5 to ABA Model Rule 4.2; ABA Formal Op. 95-396 (1995); Restatement §99, comment h]

2.   Application to Organizations

Corporations and other organizations are "persons" for purposes of this rule. Thus, a lawyer must get the consent of the organization's counsel before communicating with the following constituents of the organization:

(i)   A person who *supervises, directs, or regularly consults with the organization's lawyer* about the matter at hand;

(ii)   A person whose conduct may be *imputed* to the organization for purposes of criminal or civil liability; or

(iii) A person who has *authority to obligate the organization* concerning the matter.

[Comment 7 to ABA Model Rule 4.2] Consent is *not* needed before talking to a *former* constituent of the organization. [*Id.*] However, when talking with either a present or former constituent, a lawyer must take care not to violate the organization's legal rights, such as the attorney-client privilege.

Example: Lawyer L represents the plaintiff in a defamation action against the Herald Newspaper Corp. Without getting the permission of the Herald's counsel, L interviewed the newspaper's former editor-in-chief and convinced him to disclose some privileged communications he had with the newspaper's lawyer about the case. L acted improperly in prying into the privileged communications. [*Id.*; *and see* Comment 1 to ABA Model Rule 4.4]

3. Communications Allowed by the Rule

The rule does not prohibit: (i) a lawyer from communicating with a represented person when the communication is authorized by law or court order or when the communication does not concern the subject of the representation; (ii) represented persons from communicating directly with each other; and (iii) a lawyer from interviewing an unrepresented person who will be called as a witness by some other party. [Comment 4 to ABA Model Rule 4.2; *and see* Lewis v. S.S. Baune, 534 F.2d 1115 (5th Cir. 1976)]

Example: In a complex contract suit between P and D, both parties were represented by counsel. For several months, the respective sets of lawyers tried to work out a satisfactory settlement, but without success. P concluded that the lawyers had become befogged by petty detail and bickering. P therefore invited D out to lunch, and the two of them worked out a settlement within the space of an hour. Direct communication between represented persons is not prohibited by the rule.

C. DEALING WITH UNREPRESENTED PERSONS

When dealing with an unrepresented person, a lawyer must not state or imply that the lawyer is disinterested. [ABA Model Rule 4.3; Restatement §103] When the lawyer knows, or reasonably should know, that the unrepresented person misunderstands the lawyer's role in the matter, the lawyer must make reasonable efforts to correct the misunderstanding. [*Id.*] Likewise, if the lawyer knows or should know that her client's interests are likely to be in conflict with those of the unrepresented person, she must not give legal advice to that person (other than to get a lawyer). [*Id.*] The rule does not, however, prevent a lawyer from negotiating a transaction or settling a client's dispute with an unrepresented person. [Comment 2 to ABA Model Rule 4.3]

Example: Property owner O wants to lease his empty retail store to merchant M, who wants to use it for a shoe store. M does not have a lawyer, but O is represented by attorney A. In negotiating the terms of the lease, A may communicate directly with M, but A should make clear to M that A represents O and is not looking out for M's interests. During the lease negotiations, A may tell M what terms will be acceptable to O. A may also draft a proposed lease agreement and may explain to M what A believes the legal effect of the lease will be. [*Id.*]

D. RESPECT FOR RIGHTS OF THIRD PERSONS

1. Heavy-Handed Tactics

In representing a client, a lawyer must not use means that have no substantial purpose other than to embarrass, delay, or burden a third person. [ABA Model Rule 4.4(a)] Furthermore, a lawyer must not use methods of obtaining evidence that violate the legal rights of a third person.

Examples: 1) When preparing to cross-examine witness W, attorney A discovered that W had six misdemeanor convictions for prostitution. A knew that under the applicable evidence law, he would not be allowed to use those misdemeanor convictions for impeachment, and A knew that they were not otherwise relevant to the proceeding. Nonetheless, on cross-examination, A asked: "How old were you when you decided to devote your life to prostitution, Miss W?" A is subject to discipline.

2) Lawyer L represented P in a complicated trade secrets case against D Corporation. During discovery, L used a subpoena duces tecum to require E Corporation (a nonparty) to produce thousands of documents in connection with the depositions of some employees of E Corporation. The lawyer for E Corporation allowed L to personally go through E Corporation's files to pick out and photocopy documents responsive to the subpoena. While doing that, L made copies of many other documents that were not covered by the subpoena, and L did not tell the lawyer for E Corporation what he had done. L is subject to discipline.

3) Deputy District Attorney A was assigned to prosecute a bank robbery case against D. A suspected that heroin addict X could probably furnish valuable evidence against D but that X would doubtless refuse to do so. Therefore, A told the police: "Go pick up X on suspicion of drug peddling, and we'll find out what he knows about D and the bank robbery." A is subject to discipline.

2. Documents Sent to Lawyer by Mistake

Lawyers sometimes receive documents that were sent to them by mistake. That happens with e-mail, fax transmission, postal service, and even personal messenger service. It can also happen when documents are produced pursuant to a discovery request. When a lawyer obtains such a document, and when she knows or reasonably should know that it was sent by mistake, she must promptly notify the sender so that the sender can take protective measures. [ABA Model Rule 4.4(b) and Comment 2] The Model Rule does not address some related questions on which state law is split: *e.g.*, whether the recipient must return the document to the sender, and whether the inadvertent disclosure of the document waives a privilege that would otherwise protect it.

X.   LAW FIRMS AND ASSOCIATIONS

A.   TERMS AND DEFINITIONS

1.   "Partner"

In the context of a private law firm, the term "partner" means a person who is a party to the firm's partnership agreement. [*See* ABA Formal Op. 310 (1963)] In an incorporated law firm, the shareholders are the equivalent of partners. The term "member of the firm" usually means the same as "partner." [*Id.*] The rules explained in B., *infra*, apply not only to private law firms, but also to the law departments of governmental agencies, law departments of businesses, and similar groups of lawyers. For purposes of those rules, a lawyer who has supervisory or managerial responsibility over other lawyers in a governmental agency, business, or other group of lawyers is the equivalent of a partner.

2. "Associate"
In the context of a private law firm, the term "associate" means a lawyer who has a regular relationship with the firm other than as a partner. Usually an associate is an employee who is paid by salary, but the term is also sometimes used to refer to a regularly retained independent contractor. Two lawyers who merely share office space should not refer to themselves as "associates." [*Id.*] Furthermore, two lawyers must not falsely hold themselves out as a partnership or similar entity. [ABA Model Rule 7.5(d)]

3. "Of Counsel"
The term "of counsel" refers to a lawyer who has a continuing relationship with a law firm other than as partner or associate. The term is commonly used to designate a retired partner who remains active in the firm. It is also sometimes used to refer to an independent contractor who is regularly retained by the firm to do certain kinds of work. In the context of a lawsuit, "of counsel" is sometimes used to designate a firm or lawyer who has been called in to assist the counsel of record on a specific task—for instance, writing an appellate brief or advising on a special field of law.

4. "General Counsel"
The term "general counsel" is often used to designate the person in charge of the in-house law department of a business. It may also be used to designate a private firm or lawyer who devotes a "substantial amount of professional time" to the representation of the business or organization in question.

B. RESPONSIBILITIES OF PARTNERS, MANAGERS, AND SUPERVISORY LAWYERS

1. Partners' Duty to Educate and Guide in Ethics Matters
The partners or managing lawyers of a law firm (and the supervisory lawyers in a governmental agency, business, or other group of lawyers) must make reasonable efforts to assure that the other lawyers adhere to the Rules of Professional Conduct. [ABA Model Rule 5.1(a); Restatement §11]

2. Duties of Direct Supervisor
A lawyer who directly supervises the work of another lawyer must make reasonable efforts to assure that the other lawyer adheres to the Rules of Professional Conduct. [ABA Model Rule 5.1(b)]

3. How Duties Are Fulfilled
The steps necessary to fulfill these two duties depend on the kind and size of the firm or other group. In a small private law firm, informal supervision and occasional admonition may be sufficient. [Comment 3 to ABA Model Rule 5.1] In a larger organization, more elaborate steps may be necessary. Some firms provide continuing legal education programs in professional ethics, and some firms have designated a partner or committee to whom a junior lawyer may turn in confidence for assistance on an ethics issue. [*Id.*]

4. Ethical Responsibility for Another Lawyer's Misconduct
A lawyer is subject to discipline for a disciplinary violation committed by a second lawyer if:

(i)   The first lawyer *ordered* the second lawyer's misconduct or *knew about it and ratified it* [ABA Model Rule 5.1(c); Restatement §11]; or

(ii)   The first lawyer is a partner or manager or has direct supervisory responsibility over the second lawyer, *and* she knows about the misconduct at a time when its consequences can be avoided or mitigated and *fails to take reasonable remedial action* [*Id.*].

Examples: 1) Attorney A is not a partner in the M, N & O firm, but she is a senior associate and has been assigned direct supervisory responsibility for the work of junior associate J in the case of *Cox v. Fox*. A told J to interview Ms. Cox and to prepare her to have her deposition taken. In a fit of misdirected zeal, J advised Ms. Cox to testify to a patent falsehood. After the Cox deposition was taken, but while Ms. Cox was still available as a witness, A discovered what had happened. A made no effort to reopen the Cox deposition or otherwise remedy J's misconduct. A is subject to discipline.

2) In the *Cox v. Fox* example, above, suppose that M, a partner in the firm, is not J's supervisor and has no connection whatever with the *Cox v. Fox* case. In a casual lunchtime conversation with J, M learned that J had advised Ms. Cox to testify falsely at her deposition. M made no effort to rectify the consequences of J's misconduct. M is subject to discipline.

C.   RESPONSIBILITIES OF A SUBORDINATE LAWYER

1.   Duties Concerning Clear Ethics Violation

Orders from a supervisory lawyer are *no excuse* for clearly unethical conduct—a lawyer must follow the ethics rules even when acting under the directions of another person. [ABA Model Rule 5.2; Restatement §12] However, the fact that a subordinate lawyer was acting on directions from a supervisor may be relevant in determining whether the subordinate had the *knowledge* that is required for some ethics violations. [Comment 1 to ABA Model Rule 5.2]

Example: Partner P gave associate A a memorandum of fact and asked A to draft a complaint for fraud based on the information in the memorandum. A had no way to know whether the information in the memorandum was complete and truthful. A's lack of opportunity to gather the facts personally is relevant in deciding whether to discipline A for participating in the filing of a frivolous complaint.

2.   Duties Concerning Debatable Ethics Questions

A subordinate lawyer does *not* violate the rules of professional conduct by acting in accordance with a supervisor's reasonable resolution of an *arguable question* of professional duty. [ABA Model Rule 5.2(b); Restatement §12] When a debatable ethics question arises, someone must decide on a course of action, and that responsibility must rest with the supervisory lawyer. If the supervisor's judgment turns out to have been wrong, the subordinate lawyer should not be disciplined for doing what the supervisor directed. [Comment 2 to ABA Model Rule 5.2]

Example: Subordinate lawyer L was assisting supervisor S on a summary judgment motion in a products disparagement case. When drafting the reply memorandum on the motion, L stumbled across a new appellate decision in the controlling jurisdiction concerning libel and slander of persons. The new decision had not been cited by S and L's adversary. S and L's duty to call the new decision to the attention of the trial judge depends on whether it is "directly adverse" to their position. L argues that the law of products disparagement and the law of personal libel and slander are so closely related that the new decision must be considered "directly adverse." S, on the other hand, argues that the two bodies of law are similar only by crude analogy. On this debatable point of ethics, the responsibility for making the final decision rests with S, and L should not be disciplined for following S's instructions not to mention the new decision in the reply memorandum.

D. RESPONSIBILITIES CONCERNING NONLAWYER ASSISTANTS

1. Duty to Educate and Guide in Ethics Matters
Law firms, governmental and business law departments, and other groups of lawyers employ many kinds of nonlawyers—secretaries, investigators, paralegals, law clerks, messengers, and law student interns. Lawyers who work with such employees must instruct them concerning the ethics of the profession and should be ultimately responsible for their work. [Comment 1 to ABA Model Rule 5.3]

2. Duty of Partners Respecting Nonlawyer Employees
The partners and managers in a law firm (and the supervisory lawyers in a governmental agency, business, or other group of lawyers) must make reasonable efforts to assure that the conduct of the nonlawyers is compatible with the obligations of the profession. [ABA Model Rule 5.3(a)]

Example: Lawyer L hired secretary S without carefully checking her background. L put S in charge of his client trust fund account, but did not carefully supervise her bookkeeping procedures. S stole a substantial sum from the account. L failed to fire S even after he discovered her theft. L is subject to discipline for gross negligence. [*See In re* Scanlan, 697 P.2d 1084 (Ariz. 1985)]

3. Duties of Direct Supervisor Respecting Nonlawyer Employees
A lawyer who directly supervises the work of a nonlawyer employee must make reasonable efforts to assure that the conduct of the nonlawyer is compatible with the obligations of the profession. [ABA Model Rule 5.3(b); Restatement §11(4)]

Example: Deputy Public Defender D directly supervises the work of her secretary, S, and her investigator, I. D must instruct S and I about the need to keep clients' information in confidence, and D must make reasonable efforts to assure that they do so.

4. Ethical Responsibility for Nonlawyer's Misconduct
A lawyer is subject to discipline in two situations when a nonlawyer does something that, if done by a lawyer, would violate a disciplinary rule. The lawyer is subject to discipline if:

a. The lawyer *ordered* the conduct *or knew* about it and ratified it [ABA Model Rule 5.3(c)(1)]; or

b. The lawyer is a partner or manager or has direct supervisory responsibility over the nonlawyer, *and* the lawyer knows about the misconduct at a time when its consequences can be avoided or mitigated and fails to take reasonable remedial action [ABA Model Rule 5.3(c)(2)].

E. PROFESSIONAL INDEPENDENCE OF A LAWYER

1. Fee Splitting with Nonlawyers and Temporary Lawyers

Except as provided below, a lawyer must not share her legal fee with a nonlawyer. [ABA Model Rule 5.4(a); Restatement §10] The purpose of this rule is ill-defined, but it is said to help "protect the lawyer's professional independence of judgment." [Comment 1 to ABA Model Rule 5.4] Obviously, the salaries of nonlawyer employees of a firm are paid with money earned as legal fees, but that is not regarded as "sharing" a fee. Furthermore, a firm can employ temporary lawyers through a placement agency without violating the fee-splitting rule.

Example: Lawyer L wants to practice law part-time, doing work for law firms that need extra temporary help. L gives copies of her resume to LawTemp, Inc., a placement agency that is owned by nonlawyers. When law firms need extra help, they call LawTemp, which sends them resumes of several available lawyers. By this route, L obtains temporary work at a firm that agrees to pay her $100 per hour for her work and to pay LawTemp a "placement fee" equal to 5% of the total amount it pays to L. The law firm's bill to its client includes the amount the firm pays to L and the "placement fee" paid to LawTemp. This arrangement is ***proper.*** [ABA Formal Op. 88-356 (1988)]

a. Death Benefits Permitted

The lawyers in a firm may agree that, when one of them dies, the others will pay a death benefit over a reasonable period of time to the dead lawyer's estate or to designated persons. [ABA Model Rule 5.4(a); Restatement §10]

Example: The R, S & T firm set up a death benefit program. After a partner or associate dies, the firm will make monthly payments to her estate for three years after the death, each payment to equal 40% of her average monthly income during the year before death. The death benefit program is proper.

b. Compensation and Retirement Plans for Nonlawyer Employees

The nonlawyer employees of a firm may be included in a compensation or retirement plan even though the plan is based on a profit-sharing arrangement. [*Id.*]

Example: The U, R & S firm sets aside 10% of all legal fees in a fund to be used for year-end bonuses to the partners, associates, and nonlawyer employees. The year-end bonus program is proper, even though it is a profit-sharing arrangement with nonlawyers.

c. Sale of a Law Practice

One lawyer's practice can be sold to another lawyer pursuant to rules that are discussed in G., *infra.* One who buys the practice of a dead, disabled, or disappeared lawyer may pay the purchase price to the estate or representatives of the lawyer. [*Id.*]

d. Sharing Court-Awarded Fee with Nonprofit Organization

When a court awards attorneys' fees to the winning lawyer in a case, the lawyer may share the fee with a nonprofit organization that hired or recommended him as counsel.

Example: Justice International, a nonprofit organization, hired lawyer L to represent a class of persons who were imprisoned after 9/11 in violation of their civil rights. L won the case, and the court awarded her attorney fees to be paid by the defendants. L may share the fees with Justice International. [*Id.*]

2. Partnership with Nonlawyer to Practice Law Prohibited

A lawyer must not form a partnership with a nonlawyer if ***any*** part of the partnership activities will constitute the practice of law. [ABA Model Rule 5.4(b)] Distinguish this from ancillary services provided by a separate entity (*see* H., *infra*).

Example: Family lawyer F formed a partnership with marital psychologist P; their purpose was to offer a full range of counseling and legal services to family clients. All of the legal work was done by F, and all of the other counseling was done by P—neither transgressed into the domain of the other. Nevertheless, F is subject to discipline because part of the partnership activity constitutes the practice of law.

3. Nonlawyer Involvement in Incorporated Firm or Other Association

A lawyer must not practice in an incorporated law firm or association authorized to practice law for profit if:

(i)   A nonlawyer owns any interest in the firm or association (but, when a lawyer dies, her estate may hold an interest during the administration of the estate);

(ii)   A nonlawyer is a corporate director or officer or the equivalent thereof; or

(iii) A nonlawyer has the right to direct or control the professional judgment of a lawyer.

[ABA Model Rule 5.4(d)]

Example: M is a nonlawyer. She is the business manager of W, Y & U Ltd., an incorporated law firm. As business manager, she keeps the firm's calendar, does the firm's accounting, hires, fires, and supervises all of the firm's nonlawyer employees, procures all of the firm's supplies and equipment, and runs the firm's library. Despite M's central role in the firm's operations, M cannot become a stockholder in the firm.

4. Interference with Lawyer's Professional Judgment

A lawyer must not allow a person who recommends, employs, or pays her for serving a client to direct or regulate the lawyer's professional judgment. [ABA Model Rule 5.4(c)]

Example: Federated Life Insurance Company employs lawyer L to prepare estate plans for potential life insurance customers. The potential customer pays nothing for the estate planning service; L works on a flat salary paid by Federated. L, realizing who provides his daily bread, makes sure that every estate plan includes a careful explanation of the "benefits of balanced protection through Federated's term and whole life policies." L is subject to discipline.

F.   RESTRICTIONS ON RIGHT TO PRACTICE

1. Restrictive Partnership and Employment Agreements

A lawyer must neither make nor offer a partnership or employment or similar agreement that restricts a lawyer's right to practice after termination of the relationship, except for an agreement concerning benefits upon retirement. [ABA Model Rule 5.6(a); Restatement §13] Such agreements not only limit a lawyer's autonomy but also limit the freedom of clients to choose a lawyer.

Examples: 1) Oakville practitioner A employed young lawyer L by an agreement that purported to prohibit L from practicing in Oakville after leaving A's employment. Both A and L are subject to discipline.

2) Sixty-four-year-old solo practitioner S took young lawyer Y in as a partner. Their partnership agreement provided that after S retired, the firm would pay S a retirement benefit of $5,000 per month so long as S did not re-enter the practice of law. The agreement is proper.

2.   Restrictive Settlement Agreements

A lawyer must neither make nor offer an agreement in which a restriction on the lawyer's right to practice is part of the settlement of a client controversy. [ABA Model Rule 5.6(b); *and see* ABA Formal Op. 93-371 (1993)]

Example: Over a period of several years, attorney A represented a series of federal employees in personal injury suits against the federal government concerning cancers allegedly caused by working in the Dos Arboles Radiation Laboratory. The government settled each suit as it came along, but the more suits the government settled, the more new plaintiffs A was able to find. Ultimately, the government offered to settle all then-pending suits for generous sums, provided that A would never again represent a claimant in a Dos Arboles Radiation case. If A agrees to settle on those terms, A will be subject to discipline. [*See* ABA Formal Op. 95-394 (1995)]

G.   SALE OF A LAW PRACTICE

1.   When Sale Permitted

ABA Model Rule 1.17 permits the sale of a law practice or a field of law practice, including goodwill, under certain circumstances. Pursuant to this rule: (i) the seller must *cease to engage in the private practice of law* or in the sold field of practice in the area where the practice has been conducted; (ii) the entire practice, or the entire field of practice, must be sold to one or more lawyers or firms; and (iii) *written notice* must be given to the seller's clients regarding the sale, proposed changes in fee arrangements, the clients' right to retain other counsel or to take possession of their files, and the fact that consent to the transfer of the clients' files will be presumed if a client takes no action within 90 days of receipt of the notice. If notice cannot be given to a client, a court order is required to authorize the transfer of the representation of that client to the purchaser.

a.   Selling Lawyer May Practice in Limited Circumstances

After the sale of his practice, a lawyer may still be employed as a lawyer on the staff of a public agency or legal services entity that provides legal services to the poor, or as in-house counsel to a business. Additionally, a lawyer's return to private practice because of an unanticipated change in circumstances does not necessarily violate the Rules.

2.   Clients' Fees After Sale

Clients' fees must not be increased because of the sale. [ABA Model Rule 1.7(d)] The purchaser must honor existing fee agreements made by the seller. [Comment 10 to ABA Model Rule 1.7]

H. LAW-RELATED (ANCILLARY) SERVICES

Lawyers are permitted to provide law-related services. Law-related services (often referred to as ancillary services) are services that might reasonably be performed in conjunction with (and are related to) the provision of legal services and that are not prohibited as unauthorized practice of law when provided by a nonlawyer. Examples of law-related services include financial planning, accounting, lobbying, trust services, real estate counseling, providing title insurance, and preparing tax returns. Even though law-related services are not legal services, a lawyer who provides such services is subject to the Rules of Professional Conduct in two situations:

1. **Nonlegal Services and Legal Services Provided Together**

   If a lawyer provides nonlegal services in circumstances that are not distinct from her provision of legal services, then the Rules of Professional Conduct apply to both the legal and nonlegal services. [ABA Model Rule 5.7(a)(1)]

   Example: Attorney A is an expert in setting up new business ventures. He also knows many wealthy people who invest money in untried business ventures—so-called venture capitalists. When A draws up the articles of incorporation for client C's new business venture and also finds some willing investors for C, A is subject to the Rules of Professional Conduct in both activities.

2. **Nonlegal Services Provided by Entity that Is Controlled by the Lawyer**

   If a lawyer provides nonlegal services through an entity that is not her law office but that she controls (either alone or with other lawyers), that lawyer must take reasonable steps to assure that people who receive the nonlegal services understand that those services are not legal services and that the Rules of Professional Conduct do not cover those services. For instance, the attorney-client privilege does not apply to the nonlegal services. If the lawyer does not take those reasonable steps, then the lawyer is subject to the Rules of Professional Conduct with respect to the nonlegal services.

   Example: Lawyer L is a certified specialist in family law. Many of her clients are women who want to divorce their husbands and also want to find work outside the home. L and one of her nonlawyer friends own and manage Jobs-4-U, a job placement service. When one of her law clients needs a job, L usually refers the client to Jobs-4-U. L is always careful to tell the client that she has a personal financial stake in Jobs-4-U, but L does not explain that the Rules of Professional Conduct do not apply to services rendered by Jobs-4-U. L is therefore bound by the Rules of Professional Conduct in her job placement work.

3. **Providing Nonlegal Services to Clients**

   When a *client-lawyer relationship* exists between the lawyer and the individual receiving the law-related services, the lawyer must comply with Rule 1.8(a), which specifies the conditions a lawyer must satisfy when she enters into a business transaction with her own client. [Comment 5 to ABA Model Rule 5.7] Specifically, the transaction must meet the following requirements: the terms of the transaction must be fair to the client; the terms must be fully disclosed to the client in writing, and such disclosure must cover the essential terms of the transaction and the lawyer's role in the transaction; the client must be advised in writing that he should seek advice from an independent lawyer regarding the arrangement; and the client must give informed consent in a writing signed by the client. (*See also* V.C.1.a., *supra*.)

XI. PUBLIC SERVICE

A. PRO BONO PUBLICO SERVICE

Every lawyer has a professional responsibility to provide legal service to people who cannot pay for it. [ABA Model Rule 6.1] ABA Model Rule 6.1 states an ethical obligation; violating it is not grounds for professional discipline. However, Model Rule 6.1 recommends that every lawyer *should* spend 50 hours per year on pro bono work; a "substantial majority" of those hours should be spent doing unpaid legal service for poor people or organizations that address the needs of poor people.

B. MEMBERSHIP IN LEGAL SERVICES ORGANIZATIONS

1. Statement of the Problem

Lawyers are encouraged to support and participate in legal services organizations—*e.g.*, local legal aid societies that provide free legal assistance to underprivileged persons in civil matters. [*See* Comment 1 to ABA Model Rule 6.3] An officer or member of such an organization does not have a lawyer-client relationship with persons served by the organization, but there can be potential conflicts between the interests of those persons and the interests of the lawyer's regular, paying clients. [*Id.; and see* South Dakota Op. 88-6 (1988)]

2. General Rule

A lawyer may serve as a director, officer, or member of a legal services organization (apart from the lawyer's regular employment) even though the organization serves persons whose interests are adverse to the lawyer's regular clients. [ABA Model Rule 6.3] This general rule is, however, subject to the limitations stated below.

(i) The lawyer must not knowingly participate in a decision or action of the organization if doing so would be incompatible with the lawyer's obligations to a client under the general conflict of interest rules. [*See* ABA Model Rules 1.7, 6.3(a)]

(ii) The lawyer must not knowingly participate in a decision or action of the organization if doing so would adversely affect the representation of one of the organization's clients whose interests are adverse to those of a client of the lawyer. [*See* ABA Model Rule 6.3(b)]

Example: Lawyer L is a member of the board of directors of the Cuttler County Legal Aid Society. The board sets guidelines for the kinds of cases the society will and will not handle. The society's budget has recently been cut, and the board is forced to revise the guidelines to eliminate some kinds of service. L is also a partner in the R, S & T firm, and that firm is outside general counsel to the Cuttler County Apartment Owners Association, a trade association for landlords. One proposal pending before the Legal Aid Society Board is to eliminate free legal service in landlord-tenant cases. L must not participate in this decision.

C. QUICK-ADVICE PROGRAMS

Some courts and nonprofit organizations have established programs in which lawyers offer quick advice to people who can then handle their own legal problem without further assistance. Examples are programs that show people how to fill out their own EZ tax forms, legal-advice hotlines, advice-only legal clinics, and programs that show people how to represent themselves in small claims court. A lawyer-client relationship exists between the lawyer and the person who obtains the quick advice, but neither person expects the relationship to continue past the quick-advice stage. [Comment 1 to ABA Model Rule 6.5] A lawyer may participate in a quick-advice program sponsored by a court or nonprofit organization, subject to the following rules.

1. Client Consents to Short-Term, Limited Legal Service

The lawyer must obtain the client's informed consent to the limited scope of the relationship. [Comment 2 to ABA Model Rule 6.5] If the lawyer's quick advice is not enough to set the client on the right track, the lawyer must advise the client to obtain further legal help. [*Id.*]

2. Applicability of Ethics Rules

In a quick-advice situation, the conflict of interest rules are relaxed somewhat, as explained in 3., below. However, the remainder of the Rules of Professional Conduct apply to a quick-advice situation.

Example: When attorney A was answering telephone calls on the bar association hotline, she took a call from a farmer who explained that six months ago he hired a farmhand to help him. The farmhand insisted on being paid in cash and insisted that the farmer not withhold any income taxes or pay any Social Security contributions on his behalf. Based on the farmer's answers to A's questions, A concluded that the farmhand was an employee, not an independent contractor. A then advised the farmer about his potential tax liability. The farmer's statements to A are protected by the attorney-client privilege and the ethical duty of confidentiality; therefore, A must not disclose the farmer's confidential information or use it to the farmer's disadvantage. [*See* ABA Model Rules 1.6, 1.9(c)]

3. Conflict of Interest Rules Are Relaxed

A lawyer who participates in a quick-advice program ordinarily has no time to conduct an ordinary conflict of interest check. Therefore, the general conflicts principles expressed in Rule 1.7 (current clients) and 1.9 (former clients) do not apply unless the lawyer actually knows that giving the quick advice creates a conflict of interest. [ABA Model Rule 6.5(a)(1)] As in other contexts, actual knowledge can be inferred from the circumstances. [ABA Model Rule 1.0(f)]

4. Imputed Conflict Rule Is Also Relaxed

The rule of imputed conflicts of interest [ABA Model Rule 1.10] is also relaxed in a quick-advice situation. Therefore, a lawyer may dispense advice in a quick-advice program unless the lawyer **actually knows** that he is disqualified from doing so because of a conflict imputed from another lawyer in his firm. [ABA Model Rule 6.5(a)(2)] Conversely, a conflict created by advice a lawyer dispenses in a quick-advice program will not be imputed to others in the lawyer's firm. [ABA Model Rule 6.5(b)]

Examples: 1) Lawyer L and partner P are partners in the 300-lawyer firm of R & Q. L participates in a quick-advice program sponsored by a local court. In that context, L advised apartment tenant T that she could withhold rent from her landlord Z to pay for repairing a leaking roof that made the apartment uninhabitable. L did not realize that Z had recently hired L's partner P to deal with legal issues arising out of the apartment house in question.

2) In the example above, if L advised T about withholding rent on May 1, and landlord Z did not hire partner P until July 30, L's conflict is not imputed to P.

5. Conflicts Rules Apply Fully If Quick Advice Leads to Regular Representation

If a person who has received quick advice from a lawyer then wants to hire that lawyer to render further service in the matter, the ordinary conflict of interest rules apply to that further service. [Comment 5 to ABA Model Rule 6.5]

Example: After attorney A dispensed advice to client C in a quick-advice program, C asked to hire A as his trial counsel in the matter. Before agreeing to render the further service to C, A should check for conflicts of interest to make sure that neither she nor other lawyers in her office have a conflict that would disqualify her.

D. LAW REFORM ACTIVITIES AFFECTING CLIENT INTERESTS

1. Activities that May Harm Client

A lawyer may serve as a director, officer, or member of a law reform group, even though a reform advocated by the group may harm one of the lawyer's clients. [*See* ABA Model Rule 6.4]

Example: Attorney A is a member of the West Carolina Law Revision Commission, a private organization that drafts and recommends new legislation to the West Carolina Legislature. The commission is now working on new statutes that will revise the West Carolina law respecting administration of trusts. One of A's clients is the First Carolina Bank. The bank's trust operations will become less profitable if the legislature passes the statutes recommended by the commission. A may work on the trust law project for the commission, unless doing so would violate the general conflict of interest rules. [*See* ABA Model Rule 1.7; Comment to ABA Model Rule 6.4]

2. Activities that May Benefit Client

When a lawyer is working on a law reform project and is asked to participate in a decision that could materially benefit one of the lawyer's clients, the lawyer must disclose that fact—but the lawyer need not identify the client. [ABA Model Rule 6.4]

Example: In the Law Revision Commission example above, suppose that one of the statutes proposed by the commission will substantially increase trustee fees paid to commercial banks. Before participating in a decision about that statute, A must disclose to the other commissioners that she represents a major commercial bank, but she need not identify which bank.

E. POLITICAL CONTRIBUTIONS TO OBTAIN GOVERNMENT EMPLOYMENT

A lawyer or firm must not accept a government legal engagement (*i.e.*, employment that a public official has the power to award) or an appointment by a judge if the lawyer or firm makes or solicits a political contribution *for the purpose of obtaining such employment or appointment* ("pay to play" contributions). [ABA Model Rule 7.6 and Comment 1]

1.   Prohibited Contributions

This rule does not prohibit all political contributions by lawyers or firms—only those that would not have been made *but for the desire to be considered for the employment or appointment*. The circumstances of the contribution may indicate its purpose. Contributions that are substantial compared to contributions made by other lawyers or firms, are made for the benefit of an official who can award such work, and are followed by an award to the lawyer or firm support an inference that the contributions were for the purpose of obtaining the work. Other factors, such as a family or professional relationship with the judge or a desire to further a political, social, or economic interest, weigh against inferring a prohibited purpose. [Comment 5 to ABA Model Rule 7.6]

2.   Excluded Employment

Excluded from the ambit of the rule are: (i) uncompensated services; (ii) engagements or appointments made on the basis of experience, expertise, qualifications, and cost, following a process that is free from influence based on political contributions; and (iii) engagements or appointments made on a rotating basis from a list compiled without regard to political contributions. [Comment 3 to ABA Model Rule 7.6]

XII.   INFORMATION ABOUT LEGAL SERVICES

A.   BACKGROUND OF ADVERTISING AND SOLICITATION RULES

"Advertising" generally refers to a lawyer's communication with the public at large or a segment of the public. In contrast, "solicitation" generally refers to individual contact with a layperson, initiated by a lawyer (or lawyer's agent), that is designed to entice the layperson to hire the lawyer. A blatant form of solicitation is "ambulance chasing," in which a lawyer (or lawyer's agent) seeks out injured people and urges them to hire the lawyer to represent them.

1.   The Attack on Tradition

From 1908 until the late 1970s, professional ethics rules banned lawyer advertising and solicitation. In the 1970s, public interest groups and some groups of lawyers began to question the wisdom and validity of the traditional ban on advertising and solicitation. They based their arguments on the free speech principles embodied in the First and Fourteenth Amendments and on free market principles that are commonplace in antitrust doctrine. They argued that laypersons cannot select lawyers intelligently without easy access to information about what is available in the legal marketplace. Furthermore, they argued that the advertising ban restricts price and quality competition among lawyers, thus harming the public. Finally, they argued that the solicitation ban sometimes prevents laypeople from recognizing and pursuing worthy claims.

2.   The Supreme Court's Response

In 1977, the Supreme Court recognized lawyer advertising as commercial speech protected by the First and Fourteenth Amendments, holding that a state may adopt reasonable regulations to insure that lawyer advertising is not false or misleading, but may not flatly prohibit all lawyer advertising. [Bates v. State Bar of Arizona, 433 U.S. 350 (1977)]

a. False and Misleading Ads and In-Person Solicitation May Be Banned
A state may flatly prohibit lawyer advertising that is false or misleading. [*In re* RMJ, 455 U.S. 191 (1982)] Similarly, a state may adopt prophylactic rules to forbid in-person solicitation for profit in circumstances that are likely to result in overreaching or misleading a layperson. [Ohralik v. Ohio State Bar Association, 436 U.S. 447 (1978)]

b. When Regulation of Truthful, Nondeceptive Advertising Permitted
Since attorney advertising is commercial speech, regulation of it is subject to only intermediate, rather than strict, scrutiny. [Florida Bar v. Went For It, Inc., 515 U.S. 618 (1995)] Thus, this type of commercial speech may be regulated if the government satisfies a three-prong test:

(i) The government must assert a *substantial interest* in support of its regulation;

(ii) The government must demonstrate that the restriction on commercial speech *directly and materially advances the interest*; and

(iii) The regulation must be *narrowly drawn*.

[Florida Bar v. Went For It, Inc., *supra—citing* Central Hudson Gas & Electric Corp. v. Public Service Commission of New York, 447 U.S. 557 (1980)]

Example: After conducting a two-year study on the effect of lawyer advertising on public opinion, which included surveys and hearings, Florida adopted a rule prohibiting lawyers from sending *any* targeted direct-mail solicitations to victims and their relatives for 30 days following an accident or disaster. The United States Supreme Court upheld the regulation, finding that it met the three-prong test above. The Court found that: (i) the state has a substantial interest in protecting the privacy and tranquility of its citizens as well as in protecting the reputation of the legal profession; (ii) the studies show that the public was offended by these solicitations and that the 30-day ban directly advances the state's interests; and (iii) the regulation is narrowly tailored to achieve the desired results. [Florida Bar v. Went For It, Inc., *supra*]

B. ADVERTISING

1. Basic Rule—Communications Must Be True and Not Misleading
A lawyer is subject to discipline for *any type* of communication about the lawyer or the lawyer's services that is *false or misleading*. [ABA Model Rule 7.1] This rule applies to all kinds of communications, including advertisements, personal communications, office signs, professional cards, professional announcements, letterheads, brochures, letters sent by post or e-mail, and recorded telephone messages. [*See* Comment 1 to ABA Model Rule 7.1]

2. Types of False or Misleading Communications

a. Outright Falsehoods
Obviously, a lawyer must not use a communication that is simply false.
Example: Attorney A's office letterhead lists him as "Trial Counsel—ExxonMobil

Corporation." Indeed, A used to do trial work in the in-house law department of ExxonMobil, but no member of that department carries the title "Trial Counsel"; moreover, A left ExxonMobil 18 months ago. The listing is an outright falsehood.

b. True Communications that Mislead

A communication can be true but misleading if it omits a fact that is necessary to make the communication as a whole not materially misleading. [Comment 2 to ABA Model Rule 7.1]

Example: Lawyer L's display advertisement in the telephone book Yellow Pages includes the phrase "Yale Law School—1987." Indeed, L did attend a two-week summer program at Yale Law School in 1987, but he earned his law degree at a school of considerably less distinction. The statement is misleading.

c. Communications that Create Unjustified Expectations

A true communication about a lawyer's accomplishments in past cases is misleading if it could make a reasonable person think that the lawyer could do as well in a similar case, without regard to the facts and law in that case. [Comment 3 to ABA Model Rule 7.1]

Example: Attorney A won jury verdicts in excess of $500,000 in the last three asbestos cases she took to trial. Her television advertisement includes that truthful statement without explaining that the recovery in asbestos cases varies dramatically, depending on the precise facts surrounding the plaintiff's exposure to asbestos. A's statement is misleading.

d. Unsubstantiated Comparisons

An unsubstantiated comparison of a lawyer's services or fees with those of other lawyers is misleading if it could make a reasonable person think that it can be substantiated. [*Id.*]

Example: Lawyer L advertises that her fees for estate planning service are "15% lower than the prevailing rate in Fairmont County." If L cannot substantiate that statement with hard data, she is subject to discipline.

3. Limits on Advertising

ABA Model Rule 7.2(a) gives lawyers broad latitude in advertising their services in a true and nonmisleading manner. They may advertise in written, recorded, and electronic media, including public media. But even true, nonmisleading advertisements are subject to the following limits:

a. Fields of Practice

Statements about the fields of law in which the lawyer practices must comply with ABA Model Rule 7.4 (*see* D., *infra*).

b. Consent of Named Clients

If a lawyer wishes to identify some regular clients in an advertisement, the lawyer should first obtain the clients' consent. [Comment 2 to ABA Model Rule 7.2]

c.   Identification of Advertiser

Every advertisement must include the name and office address of at least one lawyer or law firm that is responsible for its content. [ABA Model Rule 7.2(d)]

d.   Payments for Recommending a Lawyer's Services

Except in connection with the sale of a law practice, a lawyer must not give anything of value to a person for recommending the lawyer's services. [ABA Model Rule 7.2(b)] This rule does not prohibit a lawyer from paying the reasonable cost of advertising, nor does it prohibit a lawyer from paying people to prepare and disseminate the advertising. Furthermore, it does not prohibit an organization (such as a legal aid office or a group legal service plan) from advertising the services offered by the organization. Finally, it does not prevent a lawyer from paying the usual charges of a legal service plan or a nonprofit or qualified lawyer referral service. [*Id.*] "Qualified" means that the lawyer referral service has been approved by the appropriate regulatory authority. [Comment 6 to ABA Model Rule 7.2]

Example: The A, B & C firm seeks to increase its client base. The firm may hire and pay a media consultant to design some newspaper advertisements, and it may pay the newspaper for the advertising space. The firm may also participate in a prepaid legal service plan that advertises to obtain new members. Furthermore, some of the lawyers in the firm are listed with the nonprofit lawyer referral service run by the local county bar association; when those lawyers obtain clients through the referral service, they may pay the referral fees charged by the service.

e.   Reciprocal Referral Arrangements

Despite the general rule that a lawyer must not pay anyone for the referral of a case, the ABA Model Rules permit a lawyer to set up a reciprocal referral arrangement with another lawyer or with a nonlawyer professional—*i.e.,* "I will refer potential clients, patients, or customers to you if you will do likewise for me." [ABA Model Rule 7.2(b)(4)] Such a reciprocal arrangement is subject to the following restrictions:

1)   The arrangement must *not be exclusive* (*i.e.,* the lawyer must not promise to refer *all* potential estate planning clients to his friend F and to no one else). [ABA Model Rule 7.2(b)(4)]

2)   The referred client *must be told about the arrangement.* [*Id.*] If the arrangement creates a conflict of interest for either the referring or the receiving lawyer, then that lawyer must obtain the client's informed, written consent under ABA Model Rule 1.7. [*See* Comment 8 to ABA Model Rule 7.2] (*Comment:* One wonders whether a reciprocal referral arrangement invariably creates a conflict because it gives the referring lawyer a personal financial interest in sending the case to his referral counterpart rather than to some other lawyer.)

3)   The reciprocal arrangement must *not interfere with the lawyer's professional judgment as to making referrals.* [*Id.*] (*Comment:* One wonders whether a reciprocal referral arrangement would work if it had no influence on the referring lawyer's judgment about whom to send the case.)

4)   Reciprocal referral arrangements should *not be of indefinite duration* and should *be reviewed periodically* to make sure they comply with the ABA Model Rules. [*Id.*]

C. SOLICITATION

The basic rule is this: A lawyer must not seek fee-paying work by initiating personal or live telephone contact, or real-time electronic contact, with a nonlawyer prospect with whom the lawyer has no family, close personal, or prior professional relationship. [*See* ABA Model Rule 7.3(a)] Thus, an attorney who hangs around in the hallway of the courthouse, offering legal services for a fee to criminal defendants who are not represented by counsel, is subject to discipline. [*See* Attorney Grievance Commission of Maryland v. Gregory, 536 A.2d 646 (Md. 1988)] Likewise, a lawyer who hears on the radio that a person was badly injured in an accident and promptly telephones that person's spouse offering legal services for a fee is subject to discipline. [*See also* 49 U.S.C. §1136(g)(2)—federal law prohibits lawyers from communicating with victims of airplane accidents, or their families, until 45 days after the accident]

1. Use of Agents to Solicit

ABA Model Rule 8.4(a) prohibits a lawyer from using an agent to do that which the lawyer must not do, *e.g.,* violate a law or disciplinary rule. Thus, a lawyer must not use an agent (sometimes called a "runner" or "capper") to contact prospective clients in a manner that would violate ABA Model Rule 7.3.

Examples: 1) Lawyer L hired R to be a "claims investigator." R's work involved checking accident and crime reports at the local police station and then personally contacting those involved to "advise them of their legal rights." L furnishes R with copies of her standard form retainer agreement and instructs R to sign up clients when possible. L is subject to discipline.

2) Attorney A has a reciprocal referral arrangement with a "debt consolidation" company. Employees of the company initiate personal, face-to-face conversations with debtors and advise them about loans and ways to get out of debt. If it appears that a debtor needs legal assistance, the company employee refers the debtor to A. In return, when one of A's clients needs help getting a loan or managing debts, A refers the client to the company. A is subject to discipline because he is using the debt consolidation company to initiate personal, face-to-face communications with potential clients.

2. Offers of Free Legal Service

The basic rule expressed in ABA Model Rule 7.3(a) applies only "when a significant motive" for the lawyer's solicitation "is the lawyer's pecuniary gain." [*See also In re* Primus, 436 U.S. 412 (1978)—lawyer could not be disciplined for offering free legal services of the ACLU] Thus, a lawyer who volunteers to represent someone without a fee, and without other hope of pecuniary gain, is not subject to discipline for solicitation.

Example: When lawyer L learned that the police arrested 65 persons in an animal rights protest, she went to the police station, spoke with the leader of the group, and volunteered to represent the arrested persons without a fee. L realized that the case might receive wide press coverage, and that the publicity might lure fee-paying clients in other matters, but this was not a substantial motive for her offer. L is not subject to discipline for solicitation.

3. Initiating Personal Contacts with Family Members, Clients, and Former Clients

The basic rule expressed in ABA Model Rule 7.3(a) does not prohibit a lawyer from initiating an otherwise forbidden contact with a family member, close friend, present or past client, or another lawyer.

Example: Attorney A prepared an estate plan for client C. A did no further work for C. Two years later, the state repealed its inheritance tax, thus creating a much more advantageous way for C to dispose of her assets on death. A may telephone or write a letter to C, advising C to have her estate plan revised, and A may do the necessary work if C asks her to do so.

4. Targeted Direct-Mail Solicitations

Absent actual knowledge that the prospective client does not wish to receive communications from the lawyer, a lawyer is not prohibited from sending truthful, nondeceptive letters to persons known to face a specific legal problem. [ABA Model Rule 7.3]

5. Harassing Prospective Clients

A lawyer must not use "coercion, duress, or harassment" when making contact with a prospective client. [ABA Model Rule 7.3(b)] Furthermore, the rule prohibits a lawyer from making contact with prospective clients who have "made known to the lawyer a desire not to be solicited by the lawyer."

Example: Lawyer L obtained a mailing list of all persons who used a certain prescription drug that allegedly caused grave side effects. L sent personal letters to each person, offering to represent them for a fee in litigation against the drug manufacturer. C, one of the recipients of L's letters, telephoned L's office and told her that she did not want to sue anybody and did not want to hear further from L. L failed to remove C from the mailing list so C received a series of follow-up letters, each urging C to join in litigation against the drug manufacturer. L is subject to discipline.

6. Labeling Solicitations as Advertising

All written, electronic, or recorded communications with prospective clients who are known to need specific legal services must include the words "Advertising Material." For written communications, this must appear on the outside of the envelope and on the first page of the communication. Recorded and electronic communications must begin and end with such an announcement. [ABA Model Rule 7.3(c)] Communications with relatives, close friends, clients, former clients, and other lawyers are exempt from the labeling requirement. Furthermore, the requirement does not apply to a lawyer's professional announcements or responses to inquiries made by potential clients. [Comments 4 and 7 to ABA Model Rule 7.3]

Example: Attorney A uses TeleMarket, Inc. to solicit fee-paying legal work from persons who have been named as defendants in debt collection cases. TeleMarket employees obtain lists of prospective clients from current court filings. Then TeleMarket uses computerized phone equipment to call each prospective client and play a recorded message from A. A's recorded message must begin and end with an announcement that identifies it as advertising material.

7. Group and Prepaid Legal Service Plans

A lawyer is permitted to participate in a group or prepaid legal service plan, even though the plan uses personal contacts and live telephone contacts to offer the plan to persons who are not known to need specific legal services. [ABA Model Rule 7.3(d)] Furthermore, a lawyer may personally contact a group that might wish to adopt a legal service plan for its members. [Comment 6 to ABA Model Rule 7.3]

Example: The X, Y & Z law firm learns that the Lincoln Teachers' Association wants to form a group legal service program for school teachers. In such a program, the association would contract with a local law firm to provide a specified yearly amount of legal service to each teacher subscriber. The X, Y & Z firm may initiate personal contact with the association to present a proposed plan. [*Id.*] Furthermore, if the association ends up hiring the X, Y & Z firm, it is proper for the association to make personal contact and live telephone contact with school teachers to urge them to subscribe to the plan. [ABA Model Rule 7.3(d)]

D. COMMUNICATION OF FIELDS OF PRACTICE

Unlike the medical profession, the legal profession was slow to officially recognize specialization. For decades, the bar clung to the quaint notion that every lawyer is a generalist and can handle almost any kind of legal problem. Most lawyers do, in fact, limit their practice to one or a few fields, but the bar would not let them tell that to the public. The restrictions have been loosened in recent years, as explained below.

1. Certified Specialists

Some states and private organizations certify lawyers as specialists in a field of law. A lawyer who has been certified as a specialist in a field may state that fact to the public if the certifying body is identified and if it has been approved by the state or the ABA. [ABA Model Rule 7.4(d)]

2. Statement of Fields of Practice

In public communications, a lawyer may state that he does (or does not) practice in particular fields of law, but must not state or imply that he is a certified specialist except as provided above. [ABA Model Rule 7.4(a)]

3. Patent and Admiralty Lawyers

Patent and admiralty lawyers have traditionally been accorded special treatment. A lawyer who is admitted to practice before the United States Patent and Trademark Office may use the designation "Patent Attorney," or something similar. [ABA Model Rule 7.4(a)] A lawyer who is engaged in admiralty practice may use the designation "Proctor in Admiralty," or something similar. [ABA Model Rule 7.4(b)]

E. FIRM NAMES AND LETTERHEADS

1. Names of Law Firms

A private law partnership may be designated by the names of one or more of the partners. When partners die or retire, their names may be carried over to successor partnerships. For example, a law partnership may properly continue to practice under the name "the X partnership," even though lawyer X is now retired. The firm's letterhead may list X's name as a retired partner. [Comment 1 to ABA Model Rule 7.5; ABA Informal Op. 85-1511 (1985)]

a. Trade Names

Trade names (*e.g.,* "Greater Chicago Legal Clinic"; "The Smith Firm")—even ones that do not include the names of one or more partners—are *permitted*, provided the name is not misleading and does not imply a connection with a governmental agency or with a public or charitable legal services organization. [ABA Model Rule 7.5(a)]

2.   Multistate Firms

A law firm that has offices in more than one jurisdiction may use the same name, Internet address, or other professional designation in each jurisdiction. [ABA Model Rule 7.5(b)] However, when the lawyers in a particular office are identified (*e.g.,* on the office letterhead), the identification must indicate the jurisdictional limitations on those lawyers not licensed in the jurisdiction where the office is located. [*Id.*]

Example: The firm of Diaz and Farnsworth has offices in New York City, Washington, D.C., and Houston, Texas. The letterhead used in the Houston office lists all of the firm's partners, not just those who practice in Houston. The letterhead must indicate which partners are not licensed in Texas. For example: "Ruben Diaz (admitted in New York only)."

3.   Using Names of Lawyers Who Have Entered Public Service

A private law firm must not use the name of a lawyer who holds public office (either as part of the firm name or in communications on the firm's behalf) during any *substantial* period in which the lawyer is not regularly and actively practicing with the firm. [ABA Model Rule 7.5(c)]

Example: Attorney Tzao took an indefinite leave of absence from the Tzao, Dean & Goldberg firm to serve as a commissioner on the Federal Communications Commission. The firm must remove Tzao's name from the firm name until he returns to regular, active practice.

4.   False Indications of Partnership

Lawyers must not imply that they are partners or are otherwise associated with each other in a law firm unless they really are. [ABA Model Rule 7.5(d)]

Example: Attorneys A and B share office space, secretarial services, and a common law library. They frequently refer cases to one another, and they continually consult each other on difficult legal questions. The sign on their office door says: "Offices of A and B, Attorneys at Law." The sign is not proper; it implies that they are in partnership when they are not. [Comment 2 to ABA Model Rule 7.5]

5.   Associated and Affiliated Law Firms

Two law firms may hold themselves out to the public as being "associated" or "affiliated" if they have a close, regular, ongoing relationship and if the designation is not misleading. But using such a designation has a significant drawback—ordinarily the two firms would be treated as a single unit for conflict of interest purposes. [ABA Formal Op. 85-351 (1985)]

Example: The ABC firm practices business law in Denver. For many years it has worked regularly and closely with the XYZ firm, which practices patent law in Washington, D.C. If the ABC firm letterhead lists the XYZ firm as its Washington, D.C., affiliate in patent matters, then any conflict of interest that would disqualify the XYZ firm will ordinarily also disqualify the ABC firm.

XIII.   JUDICIAL ETHICS

A.   SELECTION, TENURE, AND DISCIPLINE OF JUDGES

1. **Federal Judges**
   Justices of the United States Supreme Court and judges of other Article III federal courts are appointed by the President with the advice and consent of the Senate. They hold office for life during good behavior. [U.S. Const. art. III, §1] A federal judge can be removed from office by impeachment and can be disciplined in less drastic ways by a committee of federal judges. [U.S. Const. art. II, §4; 28 U.S.C. §§332, 372(c)(1) - (17); *and see In re* Complaints, 783 F.2d 1488 (11th Cir. 1986)] The ABA Code of Judicial Conduct is the official standard of conduct for all federal judges.

2. **State Judges**
   The constitutions of most states specify how judges are to be selected. In some states, judges are appointed by the governor or the state legislature, while in others they are elected by the voters. In still other states, judges are initially appointed and later retained or rejected by the voters. State judges can be removed from office or otherwise disciplined in accordance with state constitutional and statutory provisions.

3. **Code of Judicial Conduct**
   As with lawyer conduct, the ABA has provided standards for judicial conduct. In 1924, the ABA adopted the Canons of Judicial Ethics, which were superseded in 1972 by the Code of Judicial Conduct. In 1990, the ABA adopted a new Code of Judicial Conduct, which is intended as a model that the states and the federal judiciary can follow in formulating their own standards of judicial conduct. The following sections discuss the 1990 ABA Code of Judicial Conduct ("CJC").

   a. **Adoption of the CJC**
      The CJC becomes binding on the judges in a jurisdiction when it is adopted (sometimes with significant amendments) by the appropriate authority in that jurisdiction. [*See, e.g.,* California Code of Judicial Ethics]

   b. **Who Is Subject to the CJC?**
      Where adopted, the CJC applies to all persons who perform judicial functions, including magistrates, court commissioners, referees, and special masters. [CJC, Application] Retired judges, part-time judges, and pro tempore part-time judges are exempted from some provisions of the CJC, as explained in H., below.

B. INTEGRITY AND INDEPENDENCE
To preserve the public's confidence in an honest, independent judiciary, a judge should participate in establishing, maintaining, and enforcing high standards of conduct, and shall personally observe those standards. [CJC 1]

1. **Conduct On the Bench**
   The general standard of integrity and independence obviously applies to a judge's conduct on the bench in a judicial capacity. Although judges must be independent, they must also comply with the law. [CJC 1, Commentary]
   Example: Judge H was an outspoken opponent of laws against prostitution and gun control, and he routinely dismissed prostitution and gun control cases, despite contrary instructions from reviewing courts. Judge H is subject to discipline for repeatedly refusing to follow the law. [*See In re* Hague, 315 N.W.2d 524 (Mich. 1982)]

2. Conduct Off the Bench

The duty of integrity and independence also applies to a judge's behavior in his personal life. [*See* CJC 1, 2]

Examples: 1) Judge R discovered his estranged wife in an automobile with another man. The judge broke the car window (causing the other man to be cut with broken glass) and slapped his estranged wife. Judge R is subject to discipline, even though his conduct was unconnected with his judicial duties. [*See In re* Roth, 645 P.2d 1064 (Or. 1982)]

2) While driving under the influence of alcohol, Judge L ran a traffic signal and violated other traffic laws. Judge L is subject to discipline. [*See* Matter of Lawson, 590 A.2d 1132 (N.J. 1991)]

C. IMPROPRIETY AND THE APPEARANCE OF IMPROPRIETY

A judge must respect and comply with the law and must act in a way that promotes public confidence in the integrity and impartiality of the judiciary. [CJC 2A] Like CJC 1, this duty applies to conduct both on and off the bench. A judge is subject to constant public scrutiny and must therefore accept constraints that would be burdensome to the ordinary citizen. [CJC 2A, Commentary]

1. Personal Relationships

A judge must not allow family, social, political, or other relationships to interfere with the judge's conduct or judgments. [CJC 2B]

Example: Judge A was assigned to hear a case in which a well-known legislator was charged with a RICO violation. Judge A and the accused legislator are members of the same charitable organization and the same political party. Judge A must not allow these relationships to influence her decisions in the case.

2. Misuse of Judicial Prestige

A judge must not lend the prestige of judicial office to advance the private interests of the judge or others. [CJC 2B]

Examples: 1) When Judge B was stopped for a routine traffic violation, he imperiously informed the traffic officer: "I am a judge in this town, young man, and I don't take kindly to being stopped for petty reasons!" Judge B is subject to discipline.

2) Judge C used her official court stationery when writing to a building contractor with whom she was having a personal contract dispute. Judge C is subject to discipline. [*See* CJC 2B, Commentary]

3) When Judge D's teenage daughter was charged with shoplifting, Judge D called Judge E, to whom the daughter's case was assigned. D said: "E, as a fellow judge, I want to tell you that my little girl is a good kid who deserves a break." Judge D is subject to discipline. [*See* CJC 2B, Commentary]

4) Judge F writes materials and gives lectures for a proprietary continuing legal education company. Judge F should retain control over the company's advertisements of his materials and lectures to avoid exploitation of his judicial office.

a. **Permissible Acts**

The Commentary to CJC 2B indicates that the following acts are permissible, as long as the judge is sensitive to abuse of the prestige of the judicial office:

1) **References and Recommendations**

Based on personal knowledge, a judge may act as a reference or provide a recommendation for someone.

2) **Sentencing and Probation Information**

In response to a *formal request* from a sentencing judge, probation officer, or corrections officer, a judge may provide relevant information about a person. A judge *must not initiate* the communication of such information.

3) **Character Witness**

Judges *must not appear voluntarily* as character witnesses, and (except when the demands of justice require) they should discourage people from requiring them to serve as character witnesses. If served with a summons, however, a judge may testify as a character witness.

3. **Relationships with Discriminatory Organizations**

A judge can be disciplined for membership in or use of a discriminatory organization or for publicly manifesting a knowing approval of an invidious discrimination.

a. **Discrimination Based on Race, Sex, Religion, or National Origin**

CJC 2C prohibits a judge from being a member of an organization that currently practices "invidious discrimination" based on four specified grounds: race, sex, religion, or national origin. This category does not include an "intimate, purely private organization" whose membership limitations could not be constitutionally prohibited. Furthermore, this category does not include an organization that is "dedicated to the preservation of religious, ethnic, or cultural values of legitimate common interest to its members." [CJC 2C, Commentary]

Examples: 1) Judge G belongs to the Slovenian League, which limits its membership to all descendants (regardless of sex or race) of persons from Slovenia, a former republic of Yugoslavia. The object of the organization is to preserve the culture and traditions of the Slovenian people. The organization does not stigmatize as inferior those who do not fall within its membership requirements. Judge G may belong to the Slovenian League because it does not practice "invidious discrimination." [*See* Moser, The 1990 ABA Code of Judicial Conduct: A Model for the Future, 4 Geo. J. Legal Ethics 731, 739-44 (1991)]

2) Judge H belongs to the Wednesday Morning Prayer Club, which limits its membership to 12 persons who are members of the Oakdale Evangelical Church. The object of the club is to meet every Wednesday morning for prayer and study of religious writings. Judge H may belong to the club because it is an intimate, purely private organization whose membership limitations could not be constitutionally prohibited. [*Id.*]

3) Judge J belongs to Maplehurst College Alumnae Society. Maplehurst is a women's college, and membership in the Alumnae Society is limited

to graduates of the college. The object of the organization is to raise money for the college and to put on college-related social events for its members. Because the organization has a rational basis for its single-sex limitation, and because it does not stigmatize nonmembers as inferior, Judge J may belong to the Alumnae Society. [*Id.*]

4) Judge K belongs to the Ashmount Golf and Tennis Club, which limits its membership to 1,200 white male Protestants. The object of the organization is to provide golf, tennis, and social facilities for its members. Conversations in the clubhouse frequently concern business and professional matters, and membership in the club offers significant business and professional advantages. Judge K is subject to discipline. [*See* CJC 2C, Commentary]

b. Use of Organization that Invidiously Discriminates

Even if a judge is *not a member* of an organization that invidiously discriminates based on race, sex, religion, or national origin, the judge can be disciplined under CJC 2A for using such an organization. [CJC 2C, Commentary]

Examples: 1) Judge L does not belong to the Ashmount Golf and Tennis Club (described in Example 4), above), but once or twice a week he eats lunch at the club as a guest of various members. Judge L is subject to discipline under CJC 2A for regularly using the club. [CJC 2C, Commentary]

2) Judge M does not belong to the Ashmount Golf and Tennis Club (described in Example 4), above), but he rents one of the club rooms to hold a meeting of the Bench and Bar Society. Judge M is subject to discipline under CJC 2A for arranging the meeting at the club. [CJC 2C, Commentary]

c. Organizations that Discriminate in Violation of Local Law

The proscription in CJC 2C covers only organizations that invidiously discriminate based on race, sex, religion, or national origin. The laws of some jurisdictions proscribe discrimination on other grounds (*e.g.,* sexual orientation). A judge in such a jurisdiction is subject to discipline under CJC 2A for belonging to an organization that violates that jurisdiction's anti-discrimination laws.

Example: Judge N belongs to the Elmdale Auto and Cycle Club, which excludes gay males and lesbian women in violation of state statute. Judge N is subject to discipline under CJC 2A. [*Id.*]

d. Public Approval of Invidious Discrimination

The Commentary to CJC 2C states that a judge can be disciplined under CJC 2A for publicly manifesting a knowing approval of "invidious discrimination on any basis." The scope of this phrase is unclear. [*But see* Moser, a., *supra*] Read in context, it appears to cover more than race, sex, religion, and national origin. Perhaps it can be read to include grounds of discrimination that have been condemned in various state and federal statutes, such as sexual orientation, age, disability, and socioeconomic status. [*See* CJC 3B(5), 4A, Commentary] In any event, to warrant discipline the judge must: (i) know of the discrimination, and (ii) publicly manifest approval of it.

Example: The Pinecrest Union is an association of young business and professional men and women. Its bylaws exclude persons over age 55. Membership in the Pinecrest Union offers significant business and professional advantages, and the membership limitation has become a topic of heated public controversy. Judge O is not a member of the Pinecrest Union, but he publicly endorses its age limitation. If this age limitation constitutes "invidious discrimination," Judge O is subject to discipline under CJC 2A.

e. Judicial Efforts to End Discrimination
The Commentary to CJC 2C states that when a judge learns that an organization to which she belongs practices discrimination that would bar the judge's membership under CJC 2A or 2C, the judge must either:

1) *Resign* promptly; or

2) *Work to end the discriminatory practice*, and not participate in other activities of the organization in the meantime. If the organization does not end the discrimination within a year, then the judge must resign.

D. DILIGENT, IMPARTIAL PERFORMANCE OF JUDICIAL DUTIES

1. Judicial Duties—In General
Judicial duties include all the duties of the judge's office that are prescribed by law. Judicial duties take precedence over all of the judge's other activities. [CJC 3A]
Example: Judge P's elderly, infirm sister needs a custodian to look after her personal and financial affairs. Judge P should not undertake this responsibility if it will interfere with the proper performance of her judicial duties. [*See* CJC 3A, 5D]

2. Hearing and Deciding Adjudicative Matters
A judge must hear and decide all matters assigned to her, except those in which disqualification is required. [CJC 3B(1)]

3. Faithfulness to the Law
A judge must be faithful to the law and maintain professional competence in it. A judge must not be swayed by partisan interests, public clamor, or fear of criticism. [CJC 3B(2)]
Example: Judge Q frequently hears criminal cases, but she has not kept up on changes in the law of search and seizure. She routinely decides search and seizure issues on a combination of intuition and what she learned in law school many years ago. Judge Q is subject to discipline for failing to maintain her professional competence.

4. Order and Decorum in Court
A judge must require order and decorum in court proceedings. [CJC 3B(3)] "Require" means that the judge must exercise reasonable direction and control over persons who are subject to the judge's direction and control. [CJC, Terminology]

5. Patience, Dignity, and Courteousness
A judge must be patient, dignified, and courteous to those with whom the judge deals in an

official capacity, including litigants, lawyers, jurors, and witnesses. A judge must require like behavior of lawyers, court officers and staff, and others who are under the judge's direction and control. [CJC 3B(4)]

Example: Judge R routinely permits the lawyers in her courtroom to browbeat witnesses, and she occasionally does some browbeating herself. Judge R is subject to discipline.

6. Avoidance of Bias and Prejudice

A judge must avoid bias and prejudice and must require others (including lawyers) who are under the judge's direction and control to do likewise. [CJC 3B(5), (6)] Prejudice in this context includes, but is not limited to, prejudice based on race, sex, religion, national origin, disability, age, sexual orientation, or socioeconomic status. Even in nonjudicial activities, a judge should avoid making demeaning remarks or jokes that play on these prejudices. [*See* CJC 4A, Commentary] A judge's duty to control lawyers does not preclude legitimate advocacy by lawyers when issues of prejudice arise in a case. [CJC 3B(6)] A judge should be aware that facial expression and body language can convey prejudice as easily as words. [CJC 3B(5), Commentary]

Example: Whenever an old person testifies in Judge S's court, Judge S speaks extra loud and in a patronizing manner. Whenever Judge S conducts the voir dire of a jury panel member who is poor, Judge S scowls and adopts a tone of voice normally reserved for slow learners and errant pets. Judge S is subject to discipline.

7. Right to Be Heard

A judge must give every person who has a legal interest in a proceeding (or that person's lawyer) the right to be heard in accordance with the law.

8. Ex Parte Communications

"Ex parte" means one side only. An ex parte communication means a communication between a judge and representative from one side of a matter when no representative from the other side is present. A judge must not initiate, permit, or consider ex parte communications except in these three situations:

a. Expressly Authorized by Law

A judge may have ex parte communications when expressly authorized by law [CJC 3B(7)(e)], which is defined to include court rules and decisional law, as well as constitutional and statutory law. [CJC, Terminology]

b. Mediation or Settlement

With the consent of the parties, the judge may confer separately with the parties and their lawyers in an effort to settle or mediate a pending matter. [CJC 3B(7)(d)]

c. Emergencies or Administrative Matters

In other situations, the judge may have an ex parte communication, only if ***all four*** of the following conditions are met:

(i) The ***circumstances*** require the judge to communicate with one side only (if the other side cannot be reached);

     (ii)   The communication concerns an ***emergency or a scheduling or administrative matter*** as distinct from a substantive matter or matter affecting the merits;

     (iii)   The judge believes that ***no party will gain a procedural or tactical advantage*** from the communication; and

     (iv)   The judge ***notifies*** the lawyers for the other parties of the essence of the communication and gives them an opportunity to respond.

[CJC 3B(7)(a)]

9. Communications from Others

A judge must not initiate, permit, or consider communications from others made to the judge outside the presence of the parties' lawyers concerning a pending or impending matter, except in these four situations:

a. Court Personnel

A judge may consult about a matter with other judges and with other court personnel whose function is to aid the judge in carrying out adjudicative responsibilities (*e.g.,* the judge's law clerk). [CJC 3B(7)(c)]

b. Disinterested Legal Experts

A judge may obtain the advice of a disinterested expert on the applicable law, provided that the judge tells the parties' lawyers what expert was consulted, what the expert said, and gives the parties' lawyers a chance to respond. [CJC 3B(7)(b)] A common and often desirable way to get the advice of a legal expert is to invite the expert to file a brief amicus curiae. [CJC 3B(7), Commentary]

c. Other Communications

A judge must not have communications about a matter outside the presence of the parties' lawyers with any person not mentioned above, unless the four conditions stated in 8.c., *supra*, are satisfied. [CJC 3B(7)(a)]

Example: In the middle of a trial, juror A telephoned Judge T at home and blurted out that she had accidentally overheard a graphic radio report about the trial and felt unable to continue as a juror. Judge T calmed A and instructed her to come to court the next morning and report the incident in the presence of the lawyers for the parties. Judge T handled the matter properly.

d. Communications Between Trial and Appellate Courts

Some jurisdictions permit a trial judge to communicate with an appellate court about a proceeding. A copy of any written communication, or the substance of any oral communication, should be provided to the parties' lawyers. [CJC 3B(7), Commentary]

10. Findings of Fact and Conclusions of Law

If a judge asks the lawyers for one side to propose findings of fact and conclusions of law, the lawyers for the other parties must be told of the request and given a chance to respond to the proposed findings and conclusions. [CJC 3B(7), Commentary]

11. Independent Investigation of Facts

A judge must not independently investigate the facts in a case and must consider only the evidence presented. [CJC 3B(7), Commentary]

Example: Judge U took a case under submission. While reading the transcript and pondering her decision, she became puzzled about the testimony of witness W. To save time and effort, Judge U simply telephoned W and asked him to clarify the point that puzzled her. Judge U's conduct is improper.

12. Promptness, Efficiency, and Fairness

A judge must dispose of judicial matters promptly, efficiently, and fairly. This duty requires the judge to:

(i)   Respect the rights of the parties, but resolve issues without unnecessary expense or delay;

(ii) Monitor cases closely to eliminate dilatory practices, avoidable delays, and unnecessary costs;

(iii) Encourage settlements, but without forcing the parties to give up their right to adjudication;

(iv) Devote adequate time to judicial duties;

(v)   Be punctual in attending court;

(vi) Be expeditious in deciding matters under submission; and

(vii) Insist that the parties, lawyers, and court personnel cooperate in achieving the objectives stated above.

[CJC 3B(8)]

13. Public Comments on Cases

When a case is pending or impending in *any* court, a judge must not make any *public* comment that might reasonably be expected to affect its outcome or impair its fairness, or make any *nonpublic* comment that might substantially interfere with a fair trial. This duty continues through appeal and until the case is finally disposed of. The judge must require like abstention from court personnel under her control.

a. Official Duties Excepted

The duty to abstain from comment does not prohibit judges from making public statements in the course of their official duties, or from publicly explaining court procedures.

b. Judge as a Party

The duty to abstain from comment does not apply if the judge is a litigant in a personal capacity. The duty does apply, however, if the judge is a litigant in an official capacity, as in writ of mandamus proceedings.

Example: During the trial of a state criminal case, Judge V ordered the State Governor to appear as a witness and to bring certain documents that the

Governor claimed were protected as government secrets. The State Attorney General sought a writ of prohibition from the appellate court to block Judge V's order. At that point, Judge V made a public statement that "the Governor apparently has a lot to hide." If Judge V's statement might reasonably be expected to impair the fairness of the proceedings, Judge V is subject to discipline.

14. Promises with Respect to Cases Likely to Come Before Court

With respect to cases or issues that are likely to come before the court, a judge must not make pledges, promises, or commitments that are inconsistent with the impartial performance of the adjudicative duties of the office. [CJC 3B(10)]

15. Commentary on Jury Verdict

A judge must not commend or criticize jurors for their verdict, but a judge may thank jurors for their service. This duty does not apply to judicial commentary on a verdict in a court order or judicial opinion. [CJC 3B(11)]

Example: After the jury came in with a multimillion-dollar verdict for the plaintiff, Judge X told the jurors: "Apparently you people just didn't understand what was going on in this case." Judge X then issued a court order setting aside the jury verdict and ordering a new trial. Judge X's order was proper, but her comment to the jury was not.

16. Nonpublic Information

A judge must not disclose or use, for nonjudicial purposes, any nonpublic information acquired in a judicial capacity. [CJC 3B(12)] Nonpublic information includes, without limitation, information that is under seal, impounded, or obtained in camera, and information obtained in grand jury proceedings, presentencing reports, dependency cases, and psychiatric reports. [CJC, Terminology]

17. Administrative Duties

Judges must discharge their administrative duties diligently without bias or prejudice, maintain their competence in judicial administration, and cooperate with others in administrative matters. [CJC 3C(1)] Judges must require those under their direction and control to do likewise. [CJC 3C(2)] Supervising judges must take reasonable steps to insure the prompt disposition of matters in their courts. [CJC 3C(3)]

18. Judicial Appointments

A judge must exercise the power of appointment *impartially and on the basis of merit* (*e.g.,* when appointing referees, special masters, receivers, guardians, assigned counsel, and court personnel). A judge must not make unnecessary appointments, must avoid nepotism and favoritism, and must not approve compensation for appointees beyond the fair value of their services. [CJC 3C(4)]

a.   Appointments of Lawyers Making Contributions to Judge's Election Campaign

A judge who is subject to public election must not appoint a lawyer to a position if the judge either knows that the lawyer has contributed to the judge's election campaign more than the jurisdiction's specified dollar amount within a designated number of years prior to the judge's campaign, or learns of such contribution through a timely motion by a party or other interested person. [CJC 3C(5)] This provision does not apply if the appointed position is substantially uncompensated, the lawyer is selected in a rotation from a list of qualified and available attorneys compiled without regard to their having made political contributions, or the judge finds that no other lawyer is willing, competent, and able to accept the position.

19. Disciplinary Responsibilities
Judges have the following duties respecting misconduct by lawyers and other judges:

a. Judicial Misconduct
If Judge A *receives information* indicating a substantial likelihood that Judge B has committed a violation of the CJC, Judge A *should* take appropriate action. [CJC 3D(1)] What constitutes "appropriate action" depends on the situation; it could range from simply speaking directly with Judge B about the matter to reporting Judge B to the relevant disciplinary authority. [CJC 3D(1), Commentary] If Judge A has actual *knowledge* that Judge B has committed a violation of the CJC that raises a substantial question as to Judge B's *fitness* for office, Judge A *must* inform the appropriate disciplinary authority.

b. Lawyer Misconduct
If a judge *receives information* indicating a substantial likelihood that a lawyer has violated the Rules of Professional Conduct, the judge *should* take appropriate action. If a judge has actual *knowledge* that a lawyer has committed a violation of the Rules of Professional Conduct that raises a substantial question about the lawyer's honesty, trustworthiness, or fitness to practice, then the judge *must* report the lawyer to the relevant disciplinary authority. [CJC 3D(2)]

c. Privilege
A judge's acts in dealing with misconduct by a lawyer or other judge are privileged and cannot be the basis for civil suit. [CJC 3D(3)]

E. DISQUALIFICATION

1. General Rule—Whenever Impartiality Might Reasonably Be Questioned
CJC 3E(1) states the broad, general rule on disqualification of a judge: A judge must disqualify himself in a proceeding in which the judge's impartiality might reasonably be questioned. (Disqualification of federal judges is governed by 28 U.S.C. section 455.) Note that the rule uses the objective standard of reasonableness; a far-fetched argument or litigant's whim is not sufficient to disqualify a judge. [*See In re* Drexel Burnham Lambert Inc., 861 F.2d 1307 (2d Cir. 1988), *cert. denied*, 490 U.S. 1102 (1989)]

a. Disclosure by Judge
The judge should disclose on the record any information the judge believes that the parties or their lawyers might consider relevant to the question of disqualification, even if the judge believes there is no reasonable basis for disqualification. [CJC 3E(1), Commentary]

Example: Judge Y plans to retire from the bench at the end of the year and return to private law practice. Judge Y has held tentative discussions with the private firm of A, B & C about joining that firm. Now Judge Y is assigned to hear a case in which the defendant is represented by the A, B

& C law firm. Judge Y should disclose the facts and let the parties decide whether to waive disqualification.

b. Rule of Necessity

Case law has created a rule of necessity that overrides the rules of disqualification. [CJC 3E(1), Commentary] For example, suppose that Judge Z is the only judge available to rule on an emergency motion for a temporary restraining order. Judge Z may rule on the motion even though she might be disqualified were it not an emergency. Even in such a situation, Judge Z should disclose the ground for disqualification on the record and should use reasonable efforts to transfer the matter to a different judge as soon as possible. Furthermore, a judge should not be disqualified for a reason that would apply equally to all other judges to whom the matter might be assigned.

Examples: 1) State trial judge A is assigned to hear a case concerning the constitutionality of a statute that will raise the salary of all trial judges in the state. Judge A may hear the case because the reason for disqualification applies equally to all other judges to whom the case might be assigned.

2) Judge B was assigned to hear a sex discrimination case, and the defendant moved to disqualify her on the sole ground that she is a woman. Since all judges are of one sex or the other, Judge B is not disqualified.

2. Bias or Personal Knowledge

A judge must disqualify himself if there is reasonable ground to believe that the judge has: (i) a personal bias concerning a party or a party's lawyer; or (ii) personal knowledge of relevant evidentiary facts. [CJC 3E(1)(a)] To be disqualifying, a bias must be personal and must stem from an extrajudicial source; adverse attitudes toward a party formed on the basis of evidence presented in the case are not disqualifying. [*See, e.g., In re* Cooper, 821 F.2d 833 (1st Cir. 1987)]

3. Prior Involvement

A judge must disqualify himself if the judge previously:

(i)   Served as a *material witness* in the matter;

(ii) Served as a *lawyer* in the matter; or

(iii) Was *associated in law practice* with a person who served as a lawyer in the matter at the time they practiced together.

[CJC 3E(1)(b)]

Examples: 1) Before her appointment as a state supreme court justice, Justice C practiced law with lawyer L. At the time C and L were in practice together, L represented X in the trial of *X v. Y.* After the trial, L withdrew as X's lawyer. Now the case is on appeal to the state supreme court. Justice C is disqualified.

2) In the preceding example, suppose that L did not begin representing X until C had left the practice and become a supreme court justice. Justice C

need not recuse herself unless her prior association with L creates a reasonable question about her impartiality under the general rule of disqualification (*see* 1., *supra*).

3) Before taking the bench, Judge D was a lawyer for the United States Justice Department. At that time, attorney A was also a lawyer for the Justice Department. Now Judge D is assigned to hear a case in which A represents the Justice Department. Ordinarily, a lawyer in a government agency is not "associated" with the other lawyers in the agency for purposes of the Code. Thus, Judge D is not disqualified unless his prior work with A creates a reasonable question about his impartiality under the general rule of disqualification stated in 1., above. [CJC 3E(1)(b)]

4. Economic or Other Interest

A judge must disqualify himself if the judge knows that he, either as an individual or as a fiduciary: (i) has an *economic* interest in the matter or in one of the parties; or (ii) has *any other interest* that is more than de minimis and that could be substantially affected by the proceedings. [CJC 3E(1)(c)] Disqualification is also required if the interest is held by the judge's spouse, parent, or child (wherever residing) or by any other member of the judge's family who resides in the judge's household. [*Id.*] A judge must keep informed about his economic interests, and must make a reasonable effort to keep informed about those of the judge's spouse and minor children residing in the judge's household. [CJC 3E(2)]

a. Definition of "Economic Interest"

For the purpose of this rule, the term "economic interest" has a very technical definition; it means that the judge (or judge's spouse, parent, child, or family member residing in the judge's household):

(i) Is an officer, director, advisor, or other active participant in the affairs of a party; or

(ii) Owns more than a de minimis legal or equitable interest in a party.

[CJC, Terminology]

b. Exceptions to the Definition

The definition of "economic interest" contains the following exceptions:

1) Mutual Funds

Ownership of an interest in a mutual fund or common investment fund that holds securities is not an economic interest in those securities unless: (i) the judge participates in the management of the fund; or (ii) the proceeding could substantially affect the value of the interest.

Example: Judge D's son owns 100 shares of Universal Diversified Fund, a mutual fund that owns common stocks of many different companies, including Ohio Chemicals, Inc. Judge D is assigned to hear a case in which Ohio Chemicals is the defendant. The outcome of the case will not significantly affect the value of the mutual fund shares, and Judge D does not participate in the management of the fund. Judge D is not disqualified.

2) Securities Held by Organization

Suppose that a judge is an officer, director, advisor, or other active participant in an educational, religious, charitable, fraternal, or civic organization. Suppose, further, that the organization owns securities of the XYZ Corporation, which is a party to a case that the judge is assigned to hear. The judge's involvement with the organization does ***not*** give the judge an economic interest in the XYZ Corporation. The same is true of ***any type*** of organization in which a judge's spouse, parent, child, or family member residing in the judge's household is an officer, director, advisor, or other active participant.

Example: Judge E's wife is a vice president of the National Life Insurance Company. Among its many investments, National Life owns 1,000 shares of common stock in Delta Coal & Steel Inc. Judge E is assigned to hear a case in which Delta is a party. Judge E is not disqualified.

3) Bank Deposits, Mutual Insurance Policies, and the Like

Suppose that a judge, or member of the judge's family, owns a deposit in the First Federal Bank. That does not disqualify the judge from hearing a case in which First Federal is a party, unless the proceedings could substantially affect the value of the deposit. The same rule applies to a deposit in a mutual savings association or credit union, and also to the proprietary interest of a policy holder in a mutual insurance company.

Example: Judge F's mother owns a disability insurance policy issued by the Toledo Mutual Insurance Company. This does not disqualify Judge F from hearing a case in which Toledo is a party.

4) Government Securities

Ownership of government securities is not a disqualifying economic interest, unless the value of the securities could be substantially affected by the proceedings.

Example: Judge G has invested a substantial part of her retirement nest egg in municipal bonds issued by the city of Springfield. Springfield is on the brink of fiscal collapse, and Judge G is assigned to hear a case in which the outcome could substantially affect the value of her bonds. Judge G is disqualified.

5. Involvement of a Relative

A judge must disqualify himself if the judge has a relative involved in the case. [*See* CJC 3E(1)(d)] The terms "relative" and "involved" have technical definitions:

a. Meaning of "Relative"

For the purpose of this rule, the term "relative" means a person (or the spouse of a person) who is related within the third degree to the judge or to the judge's spouse. The third degree of relationship means: great-grandparents, grandparents, parents, uncles, aunts, brothers, sisters, children, grandchildren, and great-grandchildren—in short, anyone related closer than cousin. [CJC, Terminology] Remember that spouses are included on both ends of the calculation.

Example: Judge H is married to Mable. The third husband of Mable's aunt Lulu is the plaintiff in a case assigned to Judge H. Judge H is disqualified.

b.   **Meaning of "Involved"**
The term "involved" means that the relative is:

(i)   A party, or an officer, director, or trustee of a party;

(ii)   A lawyer in the proceedings;

(iii)   Known by the judge to have more than a de minimis interest that could be substantially affected by the proceedings; or

(iv)   Known by the judge to be a likely material witness in the proceedings.

> *Example:*   Judge J is assigned to hear a case in which the state Attorney General seeks suspension of the license of the Shady Acres Nursing Home until Shady Acres provides more humane living conditions for its residents. Judge J's husband's great-grandmother is a Shady Acres resident. Because the great-grandmother's interests could be substantially affected, Judge J is disqualified.

6.   **Persons Making Contributions to Judge's Election Campaign**
A judge who is subject to public election must disqualify himself if he knows, or learns through a timely motion, that a party or a party's lawyer has, within a designated number of prior years, made contributions to the judge's election campaign that exceed the jurisdiction's specified amount. [CJC 3E(1)(e)]

7.   **Public Statements of Judicial Commitment**
A judge must disqualify himself if he, while a judge or a candidate for judicial office, has made a public statement that commits or appears to commit him with respect to an issue in the proceeding or the controversy in the proceeding. [CJC 3E(1)(f)]

8.   **Remittal of Disqualification**
The parties and their lawyers can remit (waive) all of the foregoing grounds of disqualification, except personal bias concerning a party. [CJC 3F] The procedure for remittal is as follows:

(i)   The judge discloses on the record the ground for disqualification. The judge may then ask whether the parties and their lawyers wish to discuss waiver.

(ii)   The lawyers consult privately with their respective clients.

(iii)   All the parties and their lawyers meet, outside the presence of the judge, and agree that the judge should not be disqualified. As a practical matter, the judge may wish to have all the parties and their lawyers sign a remittal agreement.

(iv)   If the judge is willing to do so, she may then proceed with the case.

[*See* CJC 3F, Commentary]

F.   EXTRAJUDICIAL ACTIVITIES
A judge must conduct all extrajudicial activities so that they do not:

(i)   Cast doubt on the judge's impartiality;

(ii) Demean the judicial office; or

(iii) Interfere with the judge's judicial duties.

[CJC 4A]

1. **Avocational Activities**

A judge may speak, write, lecture, teach, and participate in nonjudicial activities that involve either legal or nonlegal subjects, provided that these activities are consistent with the duties stated elsewhere in the Code of Judicial Conduct. [CJC 4B] Because judges are in a unique position to help improve the law, they are encouraged to do so through bar associations, judicial conferences, and the like. [CJC 4B, Commentary]

2. **Governmental Hearings and Consultations**

A judge must not appear at a public hearing before, or otherwise consult with, an executive or legislative body or official, except on matters concerning the law, the legal system, or the administration of justice. This duty does not apply when the judge is acting pro se in a matter that involves the judge or his interests. [CJC 4C(1)]

Examples: 1) Judge M is invited to testify before the State Assembly Committee on Criminal Justice concerning a proposed revision of the state's mandatory sentencing statute. Judge M may testify.

2) Judge N met privately with the Mayor of the city of Glenview to protest the city's plan to open a city dump adjacent to Judge N's property. The meeting was proper because it concerned Judge N's own interests.

3. **Governmental Committees and Commissions**

A judge must not accept appointment to a governmental committee or commission or other governmental position that is concerned with fact or policy issues that do not relate to the law, the legal system, or the administration of justice. [CJC 4C(2)] Such appointments are likely to be very time-consuming, can involve the judge in controversial matters, and can interfere with the independence of the judiciary. [*See* CJC 4C(2), Commentary] A judge may, however, represent a governmental unit on a ceremonial occasion, or in connection with a historical, educational, or cultural activity.

4. **Law-Related Organizations and Nonprofit Organizations**

A judge may serve as an officer, director, trustee, or nonlegal advisor of: (i) a government agency or private organization devoted to the improvement of the law, the legal system, or the administration of justice; and (ii) a nonprofit educational, religious, charitable, fraternal, or civic organization. Note that service on the board of a public educational institution other than a law school is prohibited [CJC 4C(2)], but service on the board of a public law school or any private educational institution would generally be permitted [CJC 4C(3)]. [*See* CJC 4C(2), Commentary]

Examples: 1) The Governor appointed Judge O to serve on the State University Board of Directors. Judge O must decline the appointment because State University is a public school. That fact makes this a governmental appointment, and the position is not related to the law, the legal system, or the administration of justice. (*See* 3., *supra*.)

2) The Governor appointed Judge P to serve on the board of directors of the State University School of Law. Judge P may accept the appointment, even though it is a governmental appointment, because it involves the law.

3) Judge Q was appointed to serve on the board of directors of Butterfield University, a private school. Judge Q may accept the office because Butterfield University is not a governmental institution.

a. Exception If Litigation Likely

A judge must *not* serve as an officer, director, trustee, or nonlegal advisor of an organization if it is likely that the organization:

(i) Will be engaged in proceedings that would ordinarily come before the judge; or

(ii) Will frequently be engaged in adversary proceedings in the court on which the judge sits or one under its appellate jurisdiction.

[CJC 4C(3)(a)]

Examples: 1) State supreme court justice R is invited to be a director of the Forest Protection League, a nonprofit organization that frequently brings lawsuits to block the logging of old-growth forest areas. Justice R must decline the invitation.

2) Judge S is the only trial judge who sits in Oceanside County. She is invited to be a trustee of the Oceanside Memorial Hospital, which is frequently named as a defendant in medical malpractice cases filed in Oceanside County. Judge S must decline the invitation.

b. Fund and Membership Solicitation

A judge must not use the prestige of the judicial office for fund-raising or membership solicitation for an organization. [CJC 4C(3)(b)(iv)] A judge must not solicit members for an organization in a manner that might be taken as coercive. [CJC 4C(3)(b)(iii)] A judge may, however, make recommendations to fund-granting sources concerning law-related projects. [CJC 4C(3)(b)(ii)] Furthermore, a judge may help plan fund-raising for an organization, and may help manage and invest the organization's funds. [CJC 4C(3)(b)(i)] However, a judge must not *personally* participate in fund-raising activities, except for soliciting funds from other judges who are not under his supervisory or appellate authority. The same rules apply to membership solicitations that are essentially used to raise funds. A judge may attend an organization's fund-raising event, but may not be a guest of honor or a speaker at the event. [CJC 4C(3)(b), Commentary]

Examples: 1) Judge T is the treasurer of International House, a nonprofit organization that serves foreign students at the local college. Each year International House puts on a "membership drive," which is essentially a fund-raising device. Judge T may help plan the annual drive, may help manage the funds thus raised, and may solicit memberships from co-equal judges, but not from other people.

2) In the previous example, Judge T may sign a general membership solicitation letter on the International House letterhead. The letterhead may list Judge T as the treasurer of International House, and it may identify him as a judge if others on the letterhead are comparably identified. [CJC 4C(3)(b), Commentary]

3) In the previous example, Judge T may attend the International House annual membership solicitation dinner, but not as a speaker or guest of honor.

5. Investments

Unless otherwise improper under the Code of Judicial Conduct, a judge may hold and manage investments (including real estate) for himself or members of his family. [CJC 4D(2)] In managing his own investments, a judge must seek to minimize the number of cases in which he will be disqualified. As soon as it can be done without serious loss, a judge must eliminate investments that might require frequent disqualification. [CJC 4D(4)]

6. Financial and Business Dealings

A judge must not engage in financial or business dealings that might be perceived to exploit the judge's position, or that involve frequent dealings with lawyers or others who are likely to come before the court on which the judge sits. [CJC 4D(1)] A judge who acquires information in a judicial capacity must not use it for private gain. A judge should discourage members of his family from engaging in dealings that might be perceived to exploit the judge's position. [CJC 4D(1), Commentary]

Example: Judge U's son sells life insurance and is on the lookout for prospective customers. He introduces himself as "Judge U's son" when soliciting members of the local bar. Judge U should discourage this practice.

7. Participation in a Business

A judge must not be an officer, director, manager, general partner, advisor, or employee of any business entity. A judge may, however, manage or participate in a business that is closely held by the judge or members of his family, or a business that is primarily engaged in investing the judge's or the family's financial resources. [CJC 4D(3)] A judge should not participate in even a closely held family business if it will take too much time, or if the business frequently appears before the court on which the judge sits. [CJC 4D(3), Commentary]

8. Gifts, Bequests, Favors, and Loans

As a general rule, a judge should not accept gifts, bequests, favors, or loans from anyone. A judge should urge family members who reside in the judge's household not to accept such items either. The exceptions to the general rule are as follows:

(i)   A gift incident to a public testimonial, except when the donor frequently appears on the same side in litigation (*e.g.*, an organization of criminal prosecutors);

(ii)   Books, tapes, and the like, given by publishers for official use;

(iii)   An invitation to the judge and his spouse to a law-related function;

(iv) A gift, award, or benefit incident to the activities of the judge's spouse or a family member living in the judge's household, unless it could be perceived as intended to influence the judge;

(v) Ordinary social hospitality (*e.g.,* a dinner invitation);

(vi) A gift from a relative or friend on a special occasion (*e.g.,* a birthday or wedding gift), if it is commensurate in value to the relationship and the occasion (not an expensive gift from a distant friend);

(vii) A gift, bequest, favor, or loan from a relative or close personal friend whose appearance in a case would disqualify the judge in any event (*e.g.,* a new car from the judge's parents);

(viii)A loan from a lending institution, made in the regular course of its business and on the same terms available to nonjudges;

(ix) A scholarship or fellowship given on the same terms as to other people; and

(x) Any other gift, bequest, favor, or loan by a person who has not, and is not likely to, come before the judge as a litigant or lawyer (if the value exceeds $150, the judge must report it in the manner described in 12.b., below).

[CJC 4D(5)]

9. **Fiduciary Activities**
Generally, a judge must not serve as an executor, administrator, trustee, guardian, or other fiduciary. However, a judge may serve in such a capacity for a member of the judge's family, but only if the service will not:

(i) Interfere with the judge's judicial duties;

(ii) Involve the judge in proceedings that would ordinarily come before him; or

(iii) Involve the judge in adversary proceedings in the court on which the judge sits or one under its appellate jurisdiction.

[CJC 4E]

a. **Financial Dealings as Fiduciary**
The restrictions on financial dealings that apply to a judge personally also apply when the judge acts as a fiduciary. [CJC 4E(3)]

b. **Conflicting Duties**
When the duties of a fiduciary conflict with the judge's duties under the Code of Judicial Conduct, the judge should resign as fiduciary.
Example: Judge V is appointed as trustee of a fund for the use and benefit of his invalid brother. The trust fund includes common stock of several companies that frequently appear as litigants before Judge V. CJC 4D(4)

requires a judge to manage her investments in a way that minimizes disqualifications. If the trust fund would be harmed by divestiture of those stocks, Judge V should not serve as trustee. [CJC 4E(3), Commentary]

10. Service as Arbitrator or Mediator
A *full-time* judge must not act as an arbitrator, mediator, or private judge unless expressly authorized by law. [CJC 4F] This does not, of course, prevent the judge from participating in arbitration, mediation, or settlement conferences in a judicial capacity. [CJC 4F, Commentary]

11. Practice of Law
A *full-time* judge must not practice law. However, a judge may act pro se and may, without compensation, give legal advice to, and draft or review documents for, a member of her family. [CJC 4G] A judge must not, however, act as an advocate or negotiator for a family member in a legal matter. [CJC 4G, Commentary]

12. Outside Compensation and Expenses
The federal government and many other jurisdictions have adopted rigorous requirements concerning receipt and reporting of judges' outside compensation and expense reimbursement. The following rules apply only where not supplanted by more rigorous requirements.

   a.   General Requirements
   A judge may receive compensation and reimbursement of expenses for proper outside activities if:

     1)   The compensation or expense reimbursement does not create an appearance of impropriety or of influencing the judge's performance of judicial duties;

     2)   The compensation is reasonable for the work done and does not exceed what would be given to a nonjudge; and

     3)   The reimbursement of expenses does not exceed actual expenses reasonably incurred by the judge and, when appropriate to the occasion, the judge's spouse or guest.

   b.   Reports of Compensation
   A judge who receives compensation for outside activities must report: the activity, when and where it took place, the payor, and the amount. A judge must make such reports annually in a public court document. In a community property state, compensation received by the judge's spouse is not attributed to the judge for this purpose. [CJC 4H(2)]

   c.   Judge's Financial Privacy
   Like other citizens, judges are entitled to reasonable privacy concerning their income, debts, investments, and other assets. Except when required by reporting rules, or by the rules concerning disqualification, judges are not required to disclose their financial affairs. [CJC 4I, Commentary]

G. JUDGES AND POLITICS

The general rule is simple: Judges must stay out of politics. The general rule has three exceptions:

(i) A judge may participate in political activities *designed to improve the law*, the legal system, or the administration of justice;

(ii) A judge may participate in political activities where *specifically authorized* by law; and

(iii) A judge may participate in political activities that are *permitted under the Code* of Judicial Conduct, as explained below.

[CJC 5D]

1. Rules Applicable to All Judges and Judicial Candidates

The following rules apply to all judges and candidates for judicial office. [CJC 5A] As you read all of the provisions on political activity, be aware that various federal and state laws may restrict such activities more than the Code of Judicial Conduct does. Where that is true, judges and candidates must, of course, obey the applicable law.

a. Definition of "Candidate"

A "candidate" is a person who seeks to obtain or retain a judicial office either by election or appointment. The same definition applies to a judge who seeks an elected or appointed nonjudicial office. A person becomes a candidate when she does any one of the following things:

(i) Makes a *public announcement* of candidacy;

(ii) *Declares or files* as a candidate with the election or appointment authority; or

(iii) *Authorizes solicitation* or acceptance of contributions or support.

Example: Seeking new challenges and a higher salary, Municipal Court Judge A filed with the Governor's Appointments Committee for appointment as a Commissioner on the State Transport and Communications Commission. With that act, Judge A became a candidate for a nonjudicial office.

b. General Prohibitions

Except where specifically permitted by the CJC, a judge or candidate for judicial office must not:

(i) Act as a leader or hold office in a political organization;

(ii) Publicly endorse or oppose another candidate for public office;

(iii) Make speeches on behalf of a political organization;

(iv) Attend political gatherings; or

(v) Financially support a political organization or candidate, which includes soliciting funds, making contributions, paying assessments, and buying tickets for political dinners or other functions.

[CJC 5A(1)] These general prohibitions have some exceptions that are discussed in 3. and 4., *infra*.

c. **Explanation of General Prohibitions**
When false statements are publicly made about a judicial candidate, a judge or judicial candidate who knows the facts may make the facts public. A public officer, such as a prosecutor, may retain that office while running for an elective judicial office. A judge or judicial candidate may privately express her views on candidates for public office. A candidate does not "endorse" another candidate simply by running on the same political ticket. [CJC 5A(1), Commentary]

Example: In State X, a supreme court justice is subject to a retention vote by the public every seventh year. When Chief Justice B was up for her retention vote, her opponents publicly maligned her skills as a judicial administrator. Her fellow justices, who have firsthand knowledge of her skills, may publicly respond with the facts.

d. **Judges Who Run for Nonjudicial Office**
A judge must resign from judicial office when she becomes a candidate for a nonjudicial office. (However, a judge need not resign when seeking to become a delegate to a state constitutional convention.) [CJC 5A(2)]

2. **Rules Applicable to Candidates for Judicial Office**
The following rules apply to all candidates for judicial office. (Remember that that includes an incumbent judge who seeks retention, *see* 1.a., *supra*.)

a. **Dignity, Impartiality, Integrity, and Independence**
A candidate must act with the dignity, impartiality, integrity, and independence expected of a judge. [CJC 5A(3)(a)] A candidate must encourage members of her family to adhere to the same standards expected of the candidate when they act in support of the candidate. [CJC 5A(3)(a)]

b. **Control of Subordinates and Agents**
A candidate must take appropriate steps to assure that her subordinates and agents act with the same restraint expected of the candidate. [*See* CJC 5A(3)(b), (c)]

c. **Response to Attacks**
Subject to the rules stated in d., below, candidates may respond to attacks on themselves or their records.

d. **Statements, Promises, and Pledges**
When seeking judicial office, a candidate must ***not***:

(i) With respect to cases, controversies, or issues that are likely to come before the court, ***make pledges, promises, or commitments*** that are inconsistent with the impartial performance of the adjudicative duties of the office; or

(ii) ***Knowingly misrepresent*** the identity, qualifications, present position, or other fact concerning the candidate or an opponent.

[CJC 5A(3)(d)] A candidate may make pledges or promises to improve judicial administration, and an incumbent judge may speak privately with other judges and court personnel in the performance of judicial duties. The duties stated in this section apply to any statements made in the process of securing judicial office, including statements to selection, tenure, and confirmation authorities. [CJC 5A(3)(d), Commentary]

Examples: 1) The United States Senate Judiciary Committee is holding a hearing to determine whether to recommend lawyer L to the Senate for confirmation as a Supreme Court Justice. A committee member asked L, "Tell us whether you believe the Blotz Anti-Conspiracy Act is constitutional." If the constitutionality of the Act is likely to come before the Court, L should decline to commit herself.

2) In the situation posed in Example 1), suppose a committee member asked, "Tell us your views on the role of stare decisis in interpreting the Bill of Rights." L should answer the question candidly, but without indicating how she would rule on any specific issue that is likely to come before the Court.

1) But Note—"Announce Clause" Is Unconstitutional

The United States Supreme Court has held that an "announce clause"—*i.e.*, a clause prohibiting candidates for judgeships from announcing their views on disputed legal or political issues—is unconstitutional because it violates the First Amendment. [Republican Party of Minnesota v. White, 536 U.S. 765 (2002)] The Court examined the announce clause in the Minnesota Code of Judicial Conduct and stated that the clause prohibited speech on the basis of content and burdened the speech of political candidates.

3. Rules Applicable to Candidates for Appointed Positions

Where a judgeship or other government position is filled by appointment, a candidate is subject to the following rules:

a. Ban on Fund Solicitation

A candidate must not solicit or accept funds (even through a campaign committee) to support her candidacy. [CJC 5B(1)]

b. Limits on Politicking

A candidate must not engage in political activity to secure the appointed position, except that she *may:*

(i) Communicate with the appointing authority and screening groups;

(ii) Seek support from groups that regularly offer such support (or from individuals, where requested by the appointing authority); and

(iii) Provide information about her qualifications to the appointing authority and to support groups.

[CJC 5B(2)(a)]

Example: State Superior Court Judge B would like to be appointed by the Governor to the State Court of Intermediate Appeals. To that end, Judge B may inform the Governor's Appointments Committee of her interest, be interviewed by the committee, solicit support from the State Bar Committee on Judicial Appointments, and provide information about her qualifications to the above entities.

c. **Nonjudge Candidates for Appointed Judicial Positions**
In addition to the acts permitted in b., above, a nonjudge candidate for an appointed judicial position may:

(i) Retain an office in a political organization;

(ii) Attend political gatherings; and

(iii) Pay ordinary assessments and make ordinary contributions to a political organization or candidate and purchase tickets for political party dinners and other functions.

[CJC 5B(2)(b)]
Example: District Attorney C is seeking appointment to the local State Superior Court. C may retain her position as District Attorney, retain her position as treasurer of the local Democratic Party, and buy tickets to and attend the annual $100 a plate Democratic Party fund-raising dinner. [CJC 5B(2)(b)]

4. **Rules Applicable to Judges and Candidates Subject to Public Election**
In G. and G.1.b., above, you read some general rules that are designed to insulate judges and candidates for judicial office from routine politics. Those general rules have some exceptions that apply to positions filled by public election. The exceptions recognize the practicalities of elective politics in a democratic system—if the system is to work, the participants must be allowed some freedom to engage in politicking and campaigning. The exceptions cover three classes of persons:

(i) Judges who are subject to public election;

(ii) Candidates for a judicial position filled by public election; and

(iii) Judges who seek a nonjudicial position filled by public election.

[*See* CJC 5C(1); CJC, Terminology (definition of candidate)] These three classes of persons *may* do the following things:

a. **Party Politics**
They *may* at *any time* (whether or not they are then standing for election):

(i) Buy tickets for and attend political gatherings;

(ii) Identify themselves as members of a political party; and

(iii) Contribute to a political organization.

[CJC 5C(1)(a)]

b. **Election Politics**
When standing for election, they *may*:

(i) Speak at gatherings on their own behalf;

(ii) Appear in advertisements supporting their candidacy;

(iii) Distribute campaign literature supporting their candidacy;

(iv) Publicly endorse or oppose other candidates for the same judicial office; and

(v) Allow their names to be listed on election materials along with the names of candidates for other elective offices, and appear in promotions of the political ticket.

[CJC 5C(1)(b), (3)]

c. **Campaign Activities**
These parties may engage in campaign activities, subject to the following rules:

1) **Ban on Personal Solicitation**
These parties must neither personally solicit publicly stated support nor solicit or accept campaign contributions. [CJC 5C(2)]

2) **Campaign Committees**
These parties *may,* however, establish campaign committees, which may: (i) put on candidate forums and publish campaign literature; (ii) manage campaign funds; and (iii) solicit public support and *reasonable* contributions from members of the public, including lawyers. Note that if a judge knows the identity of contributing lawyers or litigants, that fact may require the judge to disqualify himself under CJC 3E (*see* E., *supra*). [CJC 5C(2), Commentary]

   a) **Solicitation Time Limits**
   Campaign committees may solicit contributions and public support no earlier than one year before an election and no later than 90 days after the last election in which the candidate participates during the election year.
   Example: Lawyer L hopes to be elected County Court Judge in 2005. The primary election will be held on June 15, 2005, and the general election will be held on November 5, 2005. L's campaign committee may start gathering contributions and public support on June 15, 2004, and must cease such activity by February 5, 2006.

   b) **Excessive Campaign Contributions**
   A candidate must instruct her campaign committee not to accept contributions in excess of the jurisdiction's specified limits. Also, the campaign

committee must file with the designated state office a report stating the name, address, occupation, and employer of each person who has made such excessive contributions. [CJC 5C(3), (4)]

5. Sanctions for Violating Rules on Political Activity
A successful candidate who violates the foregoing rules on political activity is subject to *judicial discipline*. An unsuccessful candidate who is a lawyer and who violates the rules is subject to *lawyer discipline*. [CJC 5E]

H. APPLICATION OF THE CODE OF JUDICIAL CONDUCT
In jurisdictions that adopt the Code of Judicial Conduct, it applies to all persons who perform judicial functions, including magistrates, court commissioners, and special masters and referees. The Application section at the end of the CJC contains a group of highly detailed exceptions that make various parts of the CJC inapplicable to several categories of retired and part-time judges. If your purpose in reading this book is to answer a specific question about the conduct of such a person, you should examine the Application section of the CJC with care. On the other hand, if your purpose is to prepare for the Multistate Professional Responsibility Examination, we suggest that mastering the detailed exceptions is not the best use of your time, and that you be content with the following broad generalizations:

1. A *retired judge* subject to recall is allowed to serve as an arbitrator or mediator, and (except when acting as a judge) to serve as a fiduciary.

2. *Continuing part-time judges, periodic part-time judges*, and *pro tempore part-time judges* are exempt from many, but not all, of the CJC provisions that restrict outside activities and political activities.

REVIEW QUESTIONS

**FILL IN
ANSWER**

Answer each of the following review questions "Yes" or "No."

1. While lawyer Limpet was a law student, he took a job interview trip to a distant city. He requested and received reimbursement from two different law firms for the full expenses of his trip—thus receiving double what the trip cost him. Limpet's conduct came to light only *after* he was admitted to the bar of State A. State A has a statute that specifies under what circumstances a lawyer can be disciplined for misconduct, and the statute says nothing about discipline for conduct committed *before* being admitted to the bar. Is Limpet **subject to discipline** by the supreme court of State A for his dishonest conduct?

    ———————

2. Lawyer Lupus is a member of the bar of State A, and one of his clients was sued in the United States District Court that sits in State A. Would it be **proper** for Lupus to serve as counsel of record in the case without being separately admitted to practice in that United States District Court?

    ———————

3. Oster is a member of the bar of West Carolina, but he never practiced law in that state. After 27 years in politics, he was appointed to the United States Supreme Court. A few years later, he resigned from the Court under the threat of a bribery investigation. Would Oster be **subject to discipline** in West Carolina?

    ———————

4. Attorney Abydos is a member of the bar of State A, but not of State B. Some of Abydos's clients live across the river in State B. When one of her State B clients becomes a party to litigation pending in State B, **may** Abydos serve as counsel of record, without being admitted pro hac vice in State B and without associating with a State B lawyer?

    ———————

5. To apply for admission to the state bar of East Dakota, one must fill out a long, complicated information form. One of the questions on the form asks for the address of every place the applicant has lived for longer than one month, from birth onward. Bar applicant Appleby had lived in a great many places and could not remember the addresses of most of them; furthermore, she concluded that the state bar had no business knowing such information in any event. Therefore, she listed only her current address and the address of the house in which she spent most of her childhood years. Was this **proper?**

    ———————

6. Client Cronin asked lawyer Lavelle to take over as her counsel in a civil case. Cronin explained in confidence that she had fired Aspner, her former counsel, because he had used threats of violence to force her to have sexual relations with him. Cronin instructed Lavelle not to tell anyone what Aspner had done to her. **Should** Lavelle nevertheless report Aspner's conduct to the appropriate disciplinary authorities?

    ———————

7. Mertin, a nonlawyer, worked as a messenger for lawyer Lefkowitch's law firm. Mertin asked Lefkowitch to refer him to a good form book so that Mertin could

prepare the legal papers that his sister needed to adopt a baby. **Should** Lefkowitch comply with Mertin's request?

_____

8. Shelby is employed by a cosmetics company, where she serves as in-house counsel. Shelby is licensed in the state of Oberon and has been working for the company in that state for 10 years; however, the company wants to relocate Shelby to the state of Tiberon. Shelby is not licensed in Tiberon. Would it be **proper** for Shelby to set up an office and conduct a continuous practice in Tiberon without being admitted to practice there?

_____

9. Client Cardwell asked her neighbor's friend, lawyer Lubner, to represent her in a paternity suit against the suspected father of her first child. Without mentioning the matter of legal fees, Lubner did the work promptly and effectively. Then, when the matter was completed, Lubner sent Cardwell a bill for a reasonable fee. Was Lubner's conduct **proper?**

_____

10. After a night of heavy drinking, Duphus and his friend Pugman got into a fight with each other. Pugman got the worst of it. The next day he sued Duphus for civil assault and battery. Duphus retained lawyer Laud, who agreed to defend Duphus for a $5,000 flat fee, payable in advance. Duphus paid Laud the fee. Two days later, Duphus and Pugman became friends again, and Pugman dismissed his suit. Duphus conveyed his good news to Laud and asked for his money back, but Laud would not return any of it. Was Laud's conduct **proper?**

_____

11. Attorney Alarcon is one of the three best municipal bond attorneys in the state. He has done all of the bond work for the city of Denton for the past 28 years. Now, the city of Denton has asked him to write an opinion letter concerning a new paving and sewer bond issue. Alarcon consulted a similar letter he had written for Denton eight months earlier, checked to confirm the accuracy of the facts supplied to him, reread a recent appellate decision on municipal bonds, and completed the new opinion letter—all in less than six hours. For this work, Alarcon charged the city of Denton $10,000. Is Alarcon **subject to discipline?**

_____

12. Is it true that a lawyer **may** allow clients to pay for legal fees by credit card?

_____

13. Client Coro hired lawyer Low to defend him in a cocaine smuggling case. Coro agreed to pay Low $3,000 in advance and another $30,000 if Coro is acquitted. If $33,000 would be a reasonable fee in light of the nature of the case and the amount of work required, is Low's conduct **proper?**

_____

14. One of the clauses in attorney Altman's standard employment contract provides that in the event that Altman and the client disagree over Altman's fee, the two of them will submit the matter to arbitration before a mutually agreeable arbitrator. Is Altman **subject to discipline?**

_____

15. Client Culpa asked his neighbor, lawyer Ledbetter, for her advice about bringing suit against his employer for age discrimination. Ledbetter advised Culpa to retain attorney Arneson, an expert in employment discrimination matters. Culpa did so,

and Arneson agreed to handle the case on a one-third contingent fee basis. When Culpa won a large judgment, Arneson sent Ledbetter 5% of the contingent fee. Was this **proper?**

16. Private criminal defense attorney Axelrodd was hired to defend Dervish in a mayhem case. After Dervish described the facts to Axelrodd in confidence, Axelrodd concluded that Dervish was guilty as charged. Dervish, however, insisted on pleading not guilty and going to trial. **May** Axelrodd continue as Dervish's counsel if Dervish persists in his desire to plead not guilty?

17. Lawyer Leonard represented the plaintiff in a products liability suit. The defense lawyer telephoned Leonard and made a settlement offer that was unreasonably low. Leonard rejected it instantly and said: "Don't call again unless you have something to say, meatball." Is Leonard **subject to discipline?**

18. Lawyer Lispley is defending Toxatec, Inc., in an air pollution case. At the close of discovery, Toxatec instructed Lispley to move for summary judgment. Lispley explained that there were a host of disputed fact issues and that a motion for summary judgment would be frivolous. Toxatec persisted in its instruction. **Must** Lispley do as his client has instructed?

19. Is it true that when representing a mentally disabled person, a lawyer **should** herself make the decisions that would ordinarily be made by the client?

20. Client Coleman obtained the services of legal aid attorney Adler in a dispute with the State Handicapped Assistance Commission over Coleman's eligibility for special medical assistance. The Commission Hearing Officer ruled that Coleman was not eligible for assistance. Such rulings can be appealed to the full Commission. Adler believed that an appeal would probably not be successful, and she therefore did not advise Coleman of the possibility of an appeal. Was Adler's conduct **proper?**

21. Client Croaque asked his friend and neighbor, lawyer Lugash, for legal advice about a problem that Croaque was having with attorney Ahman. Croaque had hired Ahman to do some legal work. One of the clauses in Ahman's standard form employment contract provided that Croaque could "terminate this contract at any time upon five days' notice and payment of a $10,000 severance fee." Before Ahman had spent any substantial amount of time on Croaque's matter, Croaque had lost confidence in Ahman's ability to do the work properly. Croaque asked Lugash whether he could fire Ahman without having to pay the so-called severance fee. Without telling Croaque that he and Ahman were good friends, Lugash advised Croaque that he would have to pay the severance fee if he fired Ahman. Is Lugash **subject to discipline?**

22. Is it true that a lawyer **may** withdraw from representing a client simply because the lawyer believes that the client's objectives are imprudent?

23. Solo practitioner Plebert agreed to represent client Cisco in a real property dispute. The dispute became more and more complex as time wore on, and Cisco became

unable to pay Plebert's fees. Ultimately, the matter became a serious threat to Plebert's financial well-being. **May** she withdraw from the matter? _____

24. Lawyer Lerner was representing client Caufman in negotiations for the sale of Caufman's business. Despite Lerner's earnest admonitions, Caufman insisted that certain contingent liabilities not be disclosed to the prospective buyer. Finally, Lerner had no choice but to withdraw. In these circumstances, **must** Lerner give Caufman advance notice and time to get another lawyer? _____

25. Lawyer Legree is the in-house general counsel of TransCoastal Corporation, a company that employs 500 people and sells its products in interstate commerce. As general counsel, Legree has overall responsibility for the company's legal affairs. Does Legree have any duty to keep abreast of current literature and current developments in the field of labor law? _____

26. The state bar of State A brought disciplinary proceedings against attorney Admetus for incompetence in defending Dorner in a criminal case. Ultimately, the state bar decided not to impose discipline on Admetus. Thereafter, Dorner sued Admetus for legal malpractice; Dorner's claim was based on the same facts as the disciplinary proceedings. Can Admetus invoke the doctrine of res judicata and have Dorner's suit dismissed? _____

27. Lawyer Lemur represented D in the civil case of *A v. D*. Later, Lemur represented B in a substantially related civil suit against D. D sued Lemur for legal malpractice. Lemur's state has adopted the ABA Model Rules of Professional Conduct. At the trial of the malpractice case, D offered evidence that Lemur's conduct was in violation of ABA Model Rules 1.7 and 1.9. Lemur objected that the evidence should be excluded as irrelevant. **Should** the trial judge sustain Lemur's objection? _____

28. One of the terms of attorney Adoula's retainer agreement with client Cruz provided that Adoula would "exercise ordinary care in performing the aforementioned legal services." Two and a half years after Cruz learned that Adoula had been negligent in performing the legal services, Cruz sued Adoula for legal malpractice. Cruz's complaint alleged both tort and contract claims. The state law provides a two-year statute of limitations for negligence claims and a four-year statute of limitations for actions based on written contracts. Is Adoula entitled to have Cruz's entire complaint dismissed as untimely? _____

29. Lawyer Lingam is a certified specialist in taxation law in State A. Lingam muddled a tax transaction for client Chang, and Chang sued Lingam for legal malpractice. In that suit, Chang asserted that the relevant standard of care is that of certified specialists in taxation, not that of ordinary lawyers. Is Chang correct? _____

30. Attorney Aisha lost her client's case because she placed her total reliance on an appellate court case that had later been overruled. Had Aisha bothered to Shepardize the case, or to use WESTLAW or LEXIS, she would have discovered that the case had been overruled. If her client sues her, is Aisha **subject to civil liability?** _____

31. When the local newspaper printed a patently false story about Crullner, he hired Arnott (who is engaged in general civil and criminal practice) to sue the paper for libel. The newspaper won the case on summary judgment. Is Arnott **subject to civil liability** for failing to refer the case to a specialist in the law of libel and slander?

_____

32. When young attorney Amax was training his new legal secretary, Stacey, he told her always to send a copy of litigation papers to opposing counsel. Amax was assigned to assist senior partner Pough in pretrial phases of a civil case. After careful study, Pough and Amax concluded that their client would probably lose if the case went to trial. Pough told Amax to write a confidential letter to their client to explain the weaknesses in the case and to recommend settling it for whatever sum the adversary would offer. Amax wrote the letter, and Stacey dutifully sent a copy of the letter to opposing counsel. If the client is able to prove that this blunder resulted in a lower settlement than he otherwise would have received, is senior partner Pough **subject to civil liability?**

_____

33. Is it true that a lawyer **must** carry a "reasonably adequate" amount of malpractice insurance?

_____

34. When lawyer Langur was fired by client Conorf, Langur declined to send Conorf's litigation files to Conorf's new lawyer until Conorf signed a release discharging Langur from liability for malpractice. Was Langur's conduct **proper?**

_____

35. Deputy Public Defender Fox was assigned to defend Dix on a charge of selling heroin. In confidential communications with Fox, Dix insisted that he was not guilty and had been framed by the police. Fox then sought out and found an ex-convict whom she knew to be a heroin user; the ex-convict told her that Dix was widely known throughout the city as a steady source for heroin. Is the information that Fox got from the ex-convict protected by the attorney-client privilege?

_____

36. Robul showed up unannounced in the offices of attorney Astorian, told Astorian that he had robbed a bank and was being pursued by the police, and asked Astorian to give him legal assistance. Astorian told Robul that he was an estate planning specialist, never practiced criminal law, and did not wish to represent Robul. Robul thereupon left as quickly as he had come. The police arrested Robul a block down the street, and they then asked Astorian what Robul had said to him. **May** Astorian respond to the police inquiry?

_____

37. The president of Dorsett Corporation suspected that some of the corporation's sales personnel were engaging in price-fixing with their counterparts from other corporations. She therefore hired an outside lawyer, Longfellow, to investigate the matter and to prepare a full report for her use. She instructed each of the corporation's regional sales representatives to cooperate completely with Longfellow's investigation. Longfellow interviewed each sales representative and wrote a report to the president in which he concluded that some of the sales representatives had indeed engaged in unlawful price-fixing. Longfellow was later subpoenaed to testify before a grand jury about the communications he previously had with the regional sales representatives. **May** he do so?

_____

38. Angus and Bane jointly consulted an attorney on a problem that concerned both of them. The attorney was unable to help them resolve their problem amicably, and Angus ultimately sued Bane. Is it true that in this litigation neither Angus nor Bane can claim the attorney-client privilege regarding communications they had with the attorney? _____

39. Client Custer told attorney Ames in confidence that he had figured out a way to tap a local bank's computer records and to transfer funds from other accounts to his own. Custer asked for Ames's legal services in devising a money laundering operation for the funds thus transferred. Ames refused to assist Custer. Ames's state has adopted the ABA Model Rules. **May** Ames warn the bank of Custer's scheme? _____

40. Dornan and Demming were charged with acting jointly to defraud the United States Postal Service. They asked the firm of Apelt & Aluss to defend them at their joint trial. The testimony of witness Woeler will implicate Dornan but will exculpate Demming. Would it be **proper** for partner Apelt to defend Dornan and for partner Aluss to defend Demming? _____

41. Attorney Argus has her office in a small town where there are only two other lawyers. She represents Cox in a suit for partition of some real property. While that suit is pending, Cramer asks Argus to represent her in a personal injury suit against Cox. Is Argus **subject to disqualification** if she represents Cramer without obtaining Cox's consent? _____

42. Attorney Acosta represents Poponovich in a suit against Detroit Investors Corporation. While that suit is pending, another client offered Acosta a 10% ownership interest in Detroit Investors in lieu of a fee the other client owed Acosta. If Acosta accepts the 10% ownership interest without obtaining the written consent of Poponovich, will Acosta be **subject to discipline?** _____

43. Lawyer Lundstrum represented Dreggs at his trial for the murder of 10 schoolboys. After the trial and all possible appeals, Lundstrum acquired the right to publish a book about the case. Is Lundstrum's conduct **proper?** _____

44. Client Courbert was severely injured when he was struck by a golf ball while watching a celebrity golf tournament. Attorney Addison agreed to represent him in a personal injury suit, to do the work for a contingent fee, to pay Courbert's medical bills, and to advance the costs of the litigation. Is Addison **subject to discipline?** _____

45. Lawyer Lutza represented four physicians in a medical malpractice case. The plaintiff offered to settle the case for a lump sum of $1.1 million. Because the liability seemed clear and the injuries were very serious, the insurance carrier for the four defendants agreed to contribute $1 million toward settlement. Three of the physician defendants agreed to contribute the other $100,000. Lutza did not consult the fourth physician about the settlement until after it was accomplished because Lutza knew that the fourth physician would contribute nothing and would insist on taking the case to trial. Was Lutza's conduct **proper?** _____

46. The city of Pautuckette brought a lawsuit to close down and dismantle the Inglewood Rendering and Glue Works on the grounds that it was a public nuisance and a source of noxious odors. Practitioner Pugh agreed to defend the Inglewood corporation in the case in return for 12% of Inglewood's common stock. Assuming that the value of the stock is less than a reasonable fee would be, is Pugh's conduct **proper?**

47. Lawyer Lim was employed on the in-house legal staff of Marketway Stores, Inc., for five years. He was assigned to handle all of Marketway's labor law matters. Later Lim entered private practice in partnership with lawyer Lee. Lee was asked to represent the plaintiff in an employment discrimination action against Marketway. The alleged discriminatory acts took place while Lim was still working for Marketway. If Marketway consents in writing after consultation, **may** Lee take the case?

48. Lawyer LaRosa was one of three attorneys who defended Pakilite Fabrics Corp. in a series of suits concerning flammable pajama fabric sold by Pakilite. Several years later, LaRosa left her former law firm and entered solo practice. She was asked to represent client Cantrell in a suit against Pakilite concerning flammable raincoat fabric. Pakilite used the same chemicals to treat both the pajama fabric and the raincoat fabric. **May** LaRosa represent Cantrell without Pakilite's consent?

49. For three years following her graduation from law school, attorney Alcock worked for the State Internal Revenue Department. One of the cases that occupied a substantial amount of her time was *State v. Devereaux Industries,* a complex inventory tax matter. Later, Alcock quit government service and entered private practice with the Cerle & Meros firm. Devereaux Industries asked senior partner Meros to represent it in an appeal of the inventory tax case to the United States Supreme Court. **May** Meros represent Devereaux, provided that Alcock does not work on the appeal?

50. Attorney Aikawa was the in-house general counsel of MacroComp, Inc., and was gathering information to be included in an SEC disclosure statement. In doing so, Aikawa discovered that one of MacroComp's vital manufacturing steps was clearly infringing two patents held by one of the company's competitors. Aikawa informed MacroComp's president of this new development, and she advised the president that the securities laws require such information to be disclosed. After checking to make sure no one else knew of the infringement, the president told Aikawa: "For the good of the company, and for my sake, and for your own sake, I am instructing you simply to forget what you have learned. May I have your promise to do that?" Under the ABA Model Rules, **must** Aikawa do as the president has asked?

51. Is it true that a lawyer is **subject to discipline** for depositing clients' funds in an interest-bearing time-deposit account?

52. When lawyer Stillwater agreed to represent the Minnequa Tribe in a fishing rights dispute, the tribe gave him a $5,000 advance to cover future litigation expenses.

Would it be **proper** for Stillwater to deposit the advance in his client trust fund account?

_____

53. When attorney Ayala settled a personal injury case on behalf of his client, Cooper, the defendant sent Ayala a check for $12,000. At the outset, Ayala and Cooper had agreed that Ayala's fee would be one-third of the eventual recovery in the case. When Ayala received the check, he cashed it, deposited $4,000 in his personal checking account, and deposited the other $8,000 in his client trust fund account. Did Ayala handle the matter **properly?**

_____

54. Solo practitioner Pendergast told her legal secretary, Brett, to manage her client trust account and to keep the appropriate records in an office ledger book. When Pendergast suddenly learned that the account was overdrawn, she found that, over a period of 18 months, Brett had been keeping the records by the "shoebox" method—a shoebox filled with a tangle of deposit receipts, cancelled checks, unverified bank statements, and mysterious notes written on scraps of waste paper. Is Pendergast **subject to discipline?**

_____

55. Client Coddlemeyer asked lawyer Lutza to draft him a new will in which Coddlemeyer's daughter would receive nothing. Lutza was aware that Coddlemeyer, a truculent old scoundrel, had convinced the daughter to give up her job in the big city to return home to care for Coddlemeyer in his old age. Would it be **proper** for Lutza to point out the moral, as well as the legal, implications of disinheriting his daughter?

_____

56. In the case described above, suppose that Lutza is unable to convince Coddlemeyer to change his mind. Would it be **proper** for Lutza to refuse to draft the new will for Coddlemeyer?

_____

57. In the case described above, suppose that Lutza is unable to convince Coddlemeyer to change his mind. Would it be **proper** for Lutza to tell the daughter of her father's plan in an effort to remedy whatever has come between the two of them?

_____

58. Professors Herch, Loomis, and Jantrell jointly wrote a treatise on the aboriginal cultures of North America. The three authors were unable to come to an agreement on who should receive primary credit for the work and on how the publication royalties should be divided among them. Therefore, the three asked attorney Abberman to help them work out a mutually acceptable compromise. **May** Abberman serve in this role?

_____

59. Client Cullen asked lawyer Langtree to represent her as plaintiff in a medical malpractice action against a physician and others who helped deliver her first child. Based solely on the physical condition of the mother and child immediately after the birth, it appeared that some malpractice had been committed—aside from that, Langtree could obtain no other information about what had happened in the delivery room. Would it be **proper** for Langtree to file a malpractice action?

_____

60. Attorney Atherton represents the plaintiff shareholders in a shareholder derivative action. After 18 months of intensive discovery, Atherton's clients instructed him to

prepare and file a massive fifth set of interrogatories. When he protested that a fifth set of interrogatories would be a patent waste of time and money for everyone concerned, they responded: "Our adversaries can't hold out much longer; if we make it expensive enough, they will come begging to settle." Is Atherton **subject to litigation sanction** if he prepares and files a fifth set of interrogatories?

61. Is it true that a lawyer is **subject to discipline** for citing a case to the court knowing that the case does not stand for the proposition for which it is cited?

62. Under West Dakota law, a defendant cannot appeal from an adverse money judgment in a civil case without first posting an appeal bond in a sum equal to the judgment. Trial courts, however, routinely waive the appeal bond if it appears that the defendant is solvent and can pay the judgment if the appeal is unsuccessful. Lawyer Loutson requested such a waiver based on his client's affidavit. The affidavit incorporated a statement of net worth that materially understated the client's liabilities. Loutson knew of this inaccuracy and knew that his client was in a precarious financial condition. Is Loutson **subject to discipline?**

63. Is it true under the ABA Model Rules that a lawyer **must** allow his criminal defendant client to testify even if the lawyer knows that the client will testify falsely?

64. Lawyer Lucinda represents defendant Dodgeville Motor Company in a products liability action brought by plaintiff Paul. Paul had purchased the new model Z manufactured by Dodgeville. Two weeks after his purchase, Paul was injured when his car crashed into a stoplight because the brakes had failed. Paul has requested all documents and reports pertaining to the design and manufacture of the model Z. Dodgeville's president, Dufus, gives Lucinda a report that indicates that the brakes on the model Z failed in half of the model Z's test drives (Dufus ignored the report and released the model Z for sale without redesigning the brakes). Lucinda tears up the report and tells Dufus: "Forget that this report ever existed or you won't stand a chance at trial!" Is Lucinda **subject to criminal liability?**

65. Attorney Ahern was preparing a summary judgment motion on behalf of her client. She needed an affidavit of her client to establish certain facts, but the client had just left the state for a five-week vacation. Ahern, therefore, prepared the affidavit and signed her client's name to it. Ahern had her secretary notarize the affidavit, and Ahern filed it with the court along with the other summary judgment papers. Everything stated in the affidavit was true, and the client would happily have signed it had he been there to do so. Was Ahern's conduct **proper?**

66. Lawyer Lew represents the plaintiff in an automobile case pending in Hawaii. Plaintiff's key witness is Werner. Werner lives in Iowa, and she saw the accident while vacationing in Hawaii. **May** Lew have his client pay Werner's airfare, hotel, meal, and other expenses incurred in coming back to Hawaii to testify at the trial?

67. The State Air Quality Control Board has brought a civil action against Elmore Electric & Power Company for polluting the air with the discharge from its generating plant smokestacks. Attorney Ackroid is defending Elmore. Ackroid asks Elmore to advise all of its employees that they need not talk about the case with

anyone representing the Air Quality Control Board, and that if any such person attempts to interview them, they should contact Ackroid. Is this **proper?**

_____

68. At the jury trial of a civil action against Donato Linen Supply Corp., one of the defense witnesses was old Mr. Donato, the founder and majority shareholder of the company. Everyone in town knows that 25 years ago, Mr. Donato served time in jail for tax fraud, and common gossip has it that he was also once connected with organized crime. At the final pretrial conference, the trial judge ordered plaintiff's lawyer, Lippert, not to refer to either of these matters at the trial, holding that they were too far distant in the past to be used fairly for impeachment. In his closing argument to the jury, Lippert said: "You jurors are probably all aware of Mr. Donato's unsavory background—but you should not consider that in deciding whether to believe what he told you on the witness stand. Who knows, he may have changed in his old age." Is Lippert **subject to discipline?**

_____

69. Lawyer Langdon defended Dostert Manufacturing Company in a Robinson-Patman Act price discrimination case. The plaintiff requested production of Dostert's copies of the invoices for all of Dostert's sales over the relevant four-year period—more than 35,000 individual pieces of paper. Langdon agreed to furnish plaintiff's counsel with xerographic copies of the invoices (made at plaintiff's expense), and Langdon agreed further to keep the original invoices available at Dostert's offices, should plaintiff need to examine them. At Dostert's offices the invoices were filed in chronological order in labeled file drawers. Before Langdon turned the xerographic copies over to plaintiff, he instructed his assistant to thoroughly shuffle the copies so as to put them in a purely random order. Langdon's object was to make it difficult and expensive for plaintiff to find out anything useful from the invoices. Is Langdon **subject to litigation sanction?**

_____

70. Is it true that, in arguing a case to the jury, a lawyer **may** state personal opinions, as long as they are supported by evidence in the record?

_____

71. During the recess between the morning and afternoon sessions of a jury trial, lawyer Luban went to a local delicatessen for lunch. The delicatessen was crowded, and Luban found himself seated at a table with two jurors in the case he was trying. To avoid embarrassment, Luban greeted them in an ordinary way, and the three of them chatted over lunch about the local baseball team's chances of ending up in the World Series. Is Luban **subject to discipline?**

_____

72. Judge Jordach was assigned to preside at the trial of a notorious police brutality case that had received a vast amount of coverage in the national media. Prosecutor Prunella held a press conference at which she discussed the evidence that the prosecution would offer at the trial and expressed her personal opinion that the "defendants have lied about this matter repeatedly; they are guilty as sin, and the jury will soon find that out." Is Prunella **subject to discipline?**

_____

73. Lawyer Lindner is plaintiff Papman's trial counsel in a civil rights action where there is a fee-shifting statute that makes the loser pay the winner's attorneys' fees. The jury awarded Papman a large sum, and the judge then called for evidence on

attorneys' fees. **May** Lindner take the witness stand and testify about the number of hours she spent on the case and the rates she ordinarily charges for similar work?

_____

74. Midway through the trial of a criminal case, defense lawyer Lucero overheard the prosecutor tell a witness: "Listen, buddy, if you don't stick to the story we rehearsed, you will spend the rest of this century in a prison cell." Lucero was the only person who overheard the prosecutor's threat. **May** Lucero testify about what he heard and still continue to serve as trial counsel for the defense?

_____

75. Does a prosecutor have a duty to assure that criminal suspects are told how to secure legal representation?

_____

76. When a member of the bar is acting as a lobbyist, and not as an attorney, is she **subject to discipline** for conduct that violates the rules of legal ethics?

_____

77. Client Cejay hired attorney Arbor to represent her in connection with the sale of a controlling block of stock in Ceamus Corporation. Cejay authorized Arbor to sell the stock for $30 per share, or more if possible. When the lawyer for a prospective buyer telephoned Arbor and offered $28 per share, Arbor responded: "I'm sorry, but you are not even in the ballpark. This is a controlling block of stock, and it's worth at least $45 per share." Is Arbor **subject to discipline** for misrepresentation?

_____

78. Carl and Cora hired separate counsel to represent their respective interests in their divorce proceedings. One Saturday afternoon, Carl was unable to reach his own lawyer, so he telephoned Cora's lawyer to ask a simple question about a proposed division of the marital assets. Cora's lawyer refused to discuss the matter with Carl and told him to call his own lawyer on Monday morning. **Should** Cora's lawyer have responded differently?

_____

79. Lawyer Lutenberger agreed to represent Price for a one-third contingent fee in a personal injury action against Dolen. Lutenberger told Price that his claim against Dolen was worth at least $100,000 if settled before trial. The case dragged on for several years, despite several settlement efforts by the lawyers for the respective parties. Finally, Price became impatient, got in touch with Dolen directly, and agreed with Dolen to settle for $50,000. When Price told Lutenberger about the settlement and asked Lutenberger to prepare the settlement papers, Lutenberger was outraged. He refused to draw up the settlement papers, and he promptly sent Price a bill for $33,333. Was Lutenberger's conduct **proper?**

_____

80. Attorney Arundale was representing two engineers, Enman and Erwin, in seeking venture capital for their new medical equipment company. Potential investor Ibbersole (who was not represented by a lawyer in the matter) asked Arundale what risks she would be taking if she invested in the company. Would it be **proper** for Arundale to advise Ibbersole in this matter?

_____

81. Young lawyer Lacy was assisting senior partner Parner in a civil case. Parner assigned Lacy to take the deposition of a nonparty witness, Woeford. Because it was

Lacy's first deposition, Parner accompanied her to provide advice and assistance. Counsel for the adversary party was present at the deposition, but witness Woeford was not represented by counsel. During a recess in the deposition, Parner instructed Lacy to ask Woeford to reveal what Woeford had told his wife about a certain matter. Lacy protested, pointing out that Woeford's communications with his wife are protected by the marital communications privilege and that they could not lead to relevant evidence in any event. Parner responded: "Do as I say. Woeford probably doesn't know about the privilege. Even if he does, your questions will get him rattled and upset, and he may blurt out something that could be useful to us." **Should** Lacy follow Parner's instructions?

82. With reference to private law firms, is it true that the term "member of the firm" usually means the same as "associate"?

83. Is it true that a nonlawyer employee of an incorporated law firm **may** be a shareholder in the firm?

84. Is it true that a lawyer is **subject to discipline** for failing to do 50 hours per year of pro bono work?

85. Attorney Adelano opened her own law office in a neighborhood shopping center. She announced the opening of the office by distributing circulars door-to-door at every house in the neighborhood. The circulars invited everyone in the neighborhood to attend an "office warming party" to meet Adelano and to celebrate the opening of her office. Is Adelano's conduct **proper?**

86. Shortly after attorney Andrews opened his solo law practice in Bakersburg, 1,250 students from Bakersburg City College were arrested during a demonstration to protest the use of United States military personnel in Central America. Andrews visited one of the demonstration leaders in the city jail and offered to defend all of them without charging any fee. Is Andrews **subject to discipline?**

87. Lawyer partners Layton and Letonen have both been certified as specialists in criminal defense work by the American Institute of Criminal Defense Counsel, a private organization that has rigorous, carefully enforced standards for certifying specialists. The state in which Layton and Letonen practice has no program for approving private certification agents, and the organization has not been approved by the ABA. In their law firm advertising material, **may** Layton and Letonen state that they are "Certified Specialists in Criminal Defense"?

88. Is it true that, because federal judges hold office for life during good behavior, the only way a federal judge can be disciplined for misconduct is through impeachment proceedings?

89. Judge Jarmon's staff includes an attractive young woman, attorney Lightner. When Lightner is present in chambers during the judge's conferences with male attorneys, the judge invariably makes lecherous comments about her. He does not make such comments in open court or in other public places. **May** Lightner report Judge Jarmon to the appropriate authorities?

90. Attorney Allright is a trustee of Welborne College. Allright frequently appears as counsel in Judge Jerginson's court. When Allright learned that Judge Jerginson's daughter had applied to Welborne, he visited the judge in his chambers and offered to drive the judge and his daughter up to the campus for a weekend visit and to do all that he could to make sure that her application was accepted. **May** Judge Jerginson accept Allright's offer?

91. A judge **should not** comply with a subpoena to serve as a character witness, but a judge **may** appear voluntarily as a character witness. Is this a true statement?

92. Judge Jones regularly eats lunch at a local restaurant that refuses to comply with a state law requiring eating establishments to provide access facilities and restrooms for persons in wheelchairs. When the issue became a topic of heated public debate, Judge Jones publicly stated: "Why should the restaurant have to spend thousands changing its facilities; people in wheelchairs have plenty of other places they can eat." Is Judge Jones's comment **proper?**

93. Justice Juarez is a member of the board of directors of the American Institute for Mental Health, a nonprofit organization that funds scientific research in the field of mental health. The Institute's endowment fund holds 10,000 shares of the common stock of Carnegie Steel Corporation. Carnegie Steel is the appellant in a case now pending before Justice Juarez's court. The appellee in the case is represented by Justice Juarez's best friend, lawyer Lee. **Should** Justice Juarez hear the appeal?

94. When she was appointed to the bench, Judge Jimerson was an active member of the Cascades Club, a conservation group that is heavily involved in environmental protection litigation. The club is a party litigant in hundreds of cases pending around the state, but none of the cases is presently pending in Judge Jimerson's court. Would it be **proper** for Judge Jimerson to serve as treasurer of the organization and to engage in public fund-raising activities on its behalf?

95. Judge Joiner serves full-time as a United States District Court Judge. When his Aunt Agnes died, he discovered that she had designated him to serve as attorney for the executor of her estate. Would it be **proper** for Judge Joiner to serve in that capacity?

96. Justice Jessup and her husband were invited to attend the State Bar Convention in a distant state; Justice Jessup was scheduled to be the keynote speaker at the convention. **May** she accept an honorarium for giving the speech, and may she accept reimbursement of the expenses that she and her husband incur in attending the convention?

97. Lawyer Lenox would like to be appointed by the Governor to a municipal court judgeship. Lenox is the vice-chair of the local Republican Party. Would it be **proper** for Lenox to retain his vice-chair position and to make his ordinary contributions to the Republican Party after communicating his interest in the judicial appointment to the Governor's Appointments Committee?

98. Attorney Anton is running for a publicly elected judicial office against incumbent Judge Jordache. The election will be held on March 14, 2005. **May** Anton begin to personally solicit funds for his campaign in January 2004?

ANSWERS TO REVIEW QUESTIONS

1. **YES**   The highest court of a state, not the state legislature, has inherent final author-ity to regulate the legal profession. [Page 1, I.A.1.a.; Stratmore v. State Bar of California, 14 Cal. 3d 887 (1975); *see also In re* Nellelson, 390 N.E.2d 857 (Ill. 1979)]

2. **NO**   Each federal court has its own bar, and a lawyer must become a member of that bar before appearing for a client in that court. [Page 2, I.A.2.a.]

3. **YES**   West Carolina has jurisdiction to discipline Oster, even though his conduct may have taken place elsewhere. [Page 2, I.A.3.; Page 10, I.C.5.a.] If Oster did in fact take a bribe, then he is **subject to discipline** because bribery is a crime that involves dishonesty and demonstrates his unfitness to practice law. [Page 5, I.C.1.b.]

4. **NO**   The right to practice in one state does not, without more, entitle an attorney to practice in another state. A lawyer **may** temporarily practice in a state in which she is not admitted if: (i) she associates with a local lawyer, (ii) she is admitted pro hac vice, (iii) she is mediating or arbitrating a dispute arising out of her home-state practice, or (iv) her out-of-state practice is reasonably related to her home-state practice. [Page 2, I.B.; Pages 10-12, I.D.1.-2.] Here, Abydos is not associating with a State B lawyer or seeking admission pro hac vice. More-over, her State B practice is not reasonably related to her State A practice; neither does it involve mediation or arbitration arising out of her State A prac-tice. Thus, Abydos may not serve as counsel of record in State B.

5. **NO**   A bar applicant **must** provide all of the information requested, to the best of her ability. [Page 2, I.B.1.] In most states, the state bar conducts a routine character investigation of some or all candidates; the purpose of asking for the addresses where the applicant has lived is to facilitate this investigation. If Appleby could not remember all of the addresses and could not obtain them from others in her family, she should simply have explained that on the application form.

6. **NO**   Aspner's conduct is a disciplinary violation because it is criminal and demon-strates his unfitness to practice law. [Page 5, I.C.1.b.] Ordinarily, another law-yer who learns of such conduct **must** report it to the appropriate professional authority. [Page 6, I.C.2.] Here, however, Lavelle knows of Aspner's conduct only through a privileged communication from Cronin, and he **must** respect Cronin's instructions to keep the information in confidence. [Page 7, I.C.2.c.; Page 38, IV.A.] (Common sense, however, suggests that Lavelle should ex-plain to Cronin why it is important to have such information reported; that may cause her to change her instructions.)

7. **NO**   A lawyer **must not** assist a nonlawyer in the unlicensed practice of law. [Page 10, I.D.; Page 12, I.D.5.]

8. **YES**   A lawyer **may** open a law office and establish a systematic and continuous practice in a jurisdiction in which she is not admitted if the lawyer is a salaried employee of her only client. Note though that Shelby may not litigate a matter in Tiberon without being admitted pro hac vice. [Page 12, I.D.3.a.]

9. **NO**   A lawyer **must** reach an early, clear agreement with the client about the lawyer's fee unless the lawyer has regularly represented the client in the past. [Page 17, II.C.1.]

10. **NO**   A lawyer is **subject to discipline** for charging an unreasonable fee. [Page 17, II.C.2.] Five thousand dollars seems clearly unreasonable for little or no work in a common assault and battery case. [*See In re* Kutner, 399 N.E.2d 963 (Ill. 1979)—attorney censured for charging $5,000 in similar circumstances]

11. **NO**   If the number of hours spent were the only relevant factor in setting a reasonable fee, then Alarcon's fee would seem exorbitant, but many other factors are relevant. [Pages 17-18, II.C.2.a.] No doubt Alarcon's many years of experience enabled him to do the work in much less time than other lawyers would have taken. Furthermore, the issuer of municipal bonds commonly wants an opinion letter from a recognized expert. Alarcon's reputation, built over many years of work, justifies a higher fee than would be charged by an unknown novice.

12. **YES**   A lawyer may permit a client to pay her fee by credit card. [ABA Formal Op. 00-419 (2000)] [Page 19, II.C.3.d.]

13. **NO**   A lawyer is **subject to discipline** for using a contingent fee arrangement in a criminal case. [Page 20, II.C.4.a.1)]

14. **NO**   One **proper** way to resolve a fee dispute with a client is to submit it to arbitration, and the client and lawyer may agree in advance to do that. [Page 21, II.C.5.b.3)]

15. **NO**   A lawyer is **subject to discipline** for splitting fees with another lawyer unless: (i) the total fee is reasonable; (ii) the split is in proportion to the services performed by each lawyer or some other proportion if each lawyer assumes joint responsibility for the matter; and (iii) the client agrees to the split in a writing that discloses the share each lawyer will receive. The arrangement described here does not meet all of the above requirements and, thus, is an impermissible forwarding or referral fee. [Pages 22-23, II.C.6.c. and 7.]

16. **YES**   The decision to plead either guilty or not guilty to a criminal charge is for the client, not the lawyer, to make. [Page 23, II.D.1.] Furthermore, Axelrodd **may** conduct the defense so as to require the prosecutor to prove every element of the crime, even though Axelrodd may personally believe that Dervish is guilty. [Page 85, VIII.A.2.]

17. **YES**   Leonard is **subject to discipline** for failing to convey the settlement offer to his client before rejecting it—settlement is for the client, not the lawyer, to

decide. [Page 23, II.D.1.; Pages 25-26, II.E.1.] Incidentally, Leonard also breached his duty of courtesy to the opposing lawyer. [Page 94, VIII.D.9.]

18. **NO**   The decision to move for summary judgment is a tactical decision, and clients normally defer to their lawyers regarding tactical decisions. If there is a dispute between the lawyer and client regarding a tactical decision that cannot be resolved, the lawyer may withdraw as counsel or the client may fire the lawyer. [Pages 23-24, II.D.2.a.] Moreover, if Lispley files a summary judgment motion that he knows is frivolous, he is **subject to discipline.** [Pages 84-85, VIII.A.1.]

19. **NO**   The lawyer's obligations depend on the particular facts and the extent of the client's disability. A client with diminished mental capacity may be able to make some kinds of decisions on her own behalf. In addition, the lawyer has a duty to maintain a normal lawyer-client relationship with the client so far as possible—treating the client as a client. Under some circumstances, the lawyer may be required to seek the appointment of a guardian for the client. [Pages 24-25, II.D.3.]

20. **NO**   An attorney must promptly inform the client of any decision or circumstance that requires the client's informed consent. [Pages 25-26, II.E.1.] Also, the attorney should act with zeal on the client's behalf; once the attorney has taken on a matter, she should see it through to completion. [Pages 31-32, III.B.1; Page 32, III.B.3.] Adler **should** have advised Coleman of the possibility of an appeal, although she might also advise that an appeal would probably not succeed.

21. **YES**   The law allows a client to fire a lawyer at any time, with or without cause, subject only to liability for the fair value of the work the lawyer has already done. [Pages 27-28, II.F.1.] Lugash is **subject to discipline** for incompetence (if his erroneous advice resulted from ignorance of the law) or for disloyalty (if his erroneous advice resulted from a desire to protect his friend Ahman).

22. **YES**   An attorney **may** withdraw from representing a client if the attorney considers the client's objective to be repugnant or against the attorney's beliefs. [Page 29, II.F.4.c.]

23. **YES**   ABA Model Rule 1.16(b)(6) permits an attorney to withdraw from representing a client when the continuation of the representation would impose an unreasonable financial burden on the attorney. [Page 29, II.F.4.e.]

24. **YES**   Even when the withdrawal results from the client's reprehensible conduct, the attorney must take reasonable steps to protect the client's interests. [Pages 29-30, II.F.5.]

25. **YES**   Labor law is of obvious importance to TransCoastal, and a lawyer should keep abreast of current literature and current developments in the fields of law in which the lawyer practices. [Page 31, III.A.3.]

26. **NO**   The purposes and issues in a malpractice case are different from those in a disciplinary proceeding. [Page 33, III.D.1.] (In any event, Admetus could not

invoke the collateral estoppel branch of the res judicata doctrine against Dorner because Dorner was not a party to the prior proceeding.)

27. **NO**   According to the Scope section of the ABA Model Rules, a disciplinary violation does not itself give rise to civil liability and does not create a presumption that a legal duty has been breached. However, Lemur's violation of ABA Model Rules 1.7 and 1.9 is at least **relevant** to the issue of whether his conduct falls below the applicable standard of care. [Page 33, III.D.2.]

28. **NO**   An action for legal malpractice can be based on many different theories, including negligence and breach of contract. Cruz's contract claim is timely, even though his negligence claim is barred by the two-year statute of limitations. [Pages 33-34, III.D.3.]

29. **YES**   A lawyer who purports to be a specialist is held to a higher standard of care than ordinary lawyers—it is the degree of care, skill, and prudence possessed by other lawyers who specialize in the field in question. [Page 35, III.D.3.d.1)c)]

30. **YES**   If Aisha's failure to do standard legal research is the legal and proximate cause of injury to her client, she has committed malpractice and is **subject to civil liability**. [Pages 35-36, III.D.3.d.2)b)] Every first-year law student is taught never to rely on a case without checking its history through one of the standard research sources.

31. **NO**   In some instances, an attorney's failure to refer a case to a specialist can constitute malpractice, thereby subjecting the attorney to civil liability. [Page 36, III.D.3.d.2)c)] Libel, however, is a routine part of tort law, well within the capacity of a general civil and criminal practitioner. As long as Arnott's work met the standard of care of general practitioners, he should not be held liable for malpractice. [Page 35, III.D.3.d.1)c)]

32. **YES**   Under general partnership principles, as well as the doctrine of respondeat superior, partner Pough is civilly liable for the negligence of other lawyers in the firm and of nonlawyer employees. [Page 37, III.D.4.]

33. **NO**   The ABA Model Rules do not impose such a duty, but prudent lawyers carry adequate malpractice insurance in their own self-interest. [Page 37, III.D.5.]

34. **NO**   Langur is **subject to discipline** for attempting to free himself from potential malpractice liability in this manner. [Page 37, III.D.6. and 7.] A lawyer who is fired **must** promptly return all papers to which the client is entitled, and that includes litigation files. [Pages 29-30, II.F.5.] (A lawyer may, however, make and retain *copies* of the files.)

35. **NO**   The information is not protected by the attorney-client privilege because it is not a confidential communication. Fox obtained the information from a third party, not from her client or an agent of her client. The information is, however, covered by Fox's ethical duty of confidentiality. [Pages 38-39, IV.B.]

36. **NO**   The attorney-client privilege and the ethical duty of confidentiality apply here, even though no attorney-client relationship ultimately developed. Robul was *seeking* legal assistance from Astorian, even though he did not get it. [Page 39, IV.C.1. and 2.]

37. **NO**   Longfellow's communications with the regional sales representatives are covered by the attorney-client privilege. [Pages 39-40, IV.C.2.a.] In the grand jury proceeding, Longfellow **must** claim the attorney-client privilege on Dorsett's behalf. [Page 42, IV.C.6.b.]

38. **YES**   The attorney-client privilege cannot be claimed by either of two joint clients in later litigation between them concerning the subject of the joint consultation. [Page 43, IV.C.8.c.]

39. **NO**   Under the ABA Model Rules, a lawyer may reveal a client's confidential information to the extent necessary to prevent the client from committing a crime or fraud that is reasonably certain to result in substantial financial harm to someone, *if the client is using or has used the lawyer's services in the matter.* [Page 46, IV.D.7.] Here, Custer did not use Ames's services in transferring the funds, and Ames refused to assist in the money laundering; thus, Ames may not warn the bank of Custer's scheme.

40. **NO**   A lawyer must not represent a client if the representation creates a concurrent conflict of interest. A concurrent conflict exists if there is a significant risk that the representation of one client will be materially limited by the lawyer's responsibility to another client. [Page 48, V.B.1.] This conflict is imputed to other lawyers in the lawyer's firm. [Pages 47-48, V.A.2.]

41. **YES**   Even assuming that the two suits are totally unrelated, an attorney must not represent one client if the representation of that client will be directly adverse to another client, without the informed, written consent of each affected client. [Pages 48-49, V.B.2.]

42. **YES**   Acosta would be acquiring a pecuniary interest adverse to Poponovich. [Page 56, V.C.1.a.]

43. **YES**   After a matter is entirely completed, a lawyer **may** acquire such publication rights. [Page 58, V.C.4.]

44. **YES**   The contingent fee and advance of litigation costs are **proper**, but the agreement to pay the client's medical bills is not. [Pages 58-59, V.C.5.]

45. **NO**   An attorney representing co-parties in litigation may not agree to an aggregate settlement without the informed, written consent of each client after disclosure of the settlement terms. Therefore, Lutza is **subject to discipline** for failing to consult the fourth physician about the settlement. [Pages 59-60, V.C.6.]

46. **NO**   If the suit is lost, Inglewood will be closed down and dismantled. By acquiring 12% of the stock, Pugh has, in essence, acquired an ownership interest in the

subject of the litigation, which is impermissible under ABA Model Rule 1.8. [Page 61, V.C.8.]

47. **YES**   Ordinarily, Lee could not handle a matter that was substantially related to work Lim did for Marketway, but he may do so with Marketway's informed, written consent. [Page 66, V.E.4.]

48. **NO**   An attorney must not oppose a former client in a matter that is "substantially related" to a matter in which the attorney represented the former client without the former client's informed, written consent. Here, the two matters are "substantially related" because of the chemicals used to treat both types of fabric. [Page 66, V.E.4.] Thus, LaRosa cannot represent Cantrell without Pakilite's consent.

49. **NO**   Three other conditions must be met as well. Alcock must be screened off from the case, and she must not be apportioned any part of the fee in the case. Furthermore, the State Internal Revenue Department must be notified in writing so that it can make sure these conditions are met. [Pages 69-70, V.G.2.c.]

50. **NO**   Under the ABA Model Rules, when a lawyer for an organization learns that a person associated with the organization has acted in a way that violates a duty to the organization, the lawyer must ordinarily report the violation to a higher authority in the organization, or if necessary, to the highest authority in the organization. [Pages 75-76, V.J.3.] Aikawa's client is the company, not the president. She must not allow the president to interfere with her legal judgment about how best to protect the company's interests. If necessary, she should go over the president's head to the highest authority in the corporation, the board of directors. [Pages 75-76, V.J.3.] Notice that under the Sarbanes-Oxley Act, Aikawa would be required to report the violation to the organization's board of directors, and she may reveal confidential information concerning the violation to the SEC. [Page 78, V.J.6.e. and f.]

51. **NO**   Lawyers' client trust fund accounts are usually ordinary checking accounts, but if a lawyer is asked to hold a large sum of money for a long period, an interest-bearing time-deposit account would be appropriate. [Pages 78-79, VI.B.1.]

52. **YES**   ABA Model Rule 1.15 *requires* such advances to be put into the client trust fund account. [Page 79, VI.B.2.a.]

53. **NO**   The **proper** procedure would have been to deposit the entire $12,000 in the client trust fund account. Ayala was not entitled to withdraw his portion until he rendered an accounting to Cooper and obtained Cooper's agreement to the amount due. [Page 79, VI.B.2.c.]

54. **YES**   Pendergast's failure to supervise her secretary's recordkeeping is grounds for discipline. [Page 80, VI.D.; Pages 107-108, X.D.; *see* Gassman v. State Bar of California, 18 Cal. 3d 125 (1976)—attorney disciplined for failing to oversee secretary's records of client trust account]

55.	**YES**	A lawyer **may** dispense moral advice as well as legal advice. The client need not accept it, but the lawyer is entitled to offer it. [Page 81, VII.A.2.]
56.	**YES**	Lutza is not required to render legal services to Coddlemeyer. [Page 14, II.B.] If Lutza has already entered into an attorney-client relationship with Coddlemeyer, he **may** withdraw if he finds Coddlemeyer's objectives repugnant. [Page 29, II.F.4.c.]
57.	**NO**	Lutza would be **subject to discipline** for breach of the ethical duty of confidentiality if he revealed the plan to the daughter without Coddlemeyer's consent. [Page 43, IV.D.]
58.	**YES**	Abberman **may** serve as a third-party neutral. A third-party neutral assists two or more nonclients to resolve a dispute between them. Note that the third-party neutral must inform all unrepresented parties that he does not represent any of the parties and is not protecting their interests. [Page 83, VII.D.]
59.	**YES**	As long as Langtree is acting in good faith, it is *not* frivolous for him to file a malpractice complaint, even though he knows that the evidence needed to back up the complaint can be obtained only through discovery proceedings. [Pages 84-85, VIII.A.1.]
60.	**YES**	To file a frivolous discovery request solely to harass the adversary is grounds for litigation sanction. [Page 84, VIII.A.1.; Page 91, VIII.D.6.]
61.	**YES**	Intentionally trying to mislead the court about the applicable law is grounds for discipline. [Page 86, VIII.C.1.]
62.	**YES**	Loutson has knowingly used false evidence. [Pages 87-88, VIII.C.4.] Also, because an attorney is subject to discipline if he knowingly makes a false statement of material fact to the court, Loutson is also subject to discipline for violating this duty of candor to the tribunal. [Pages 86-87, VIII.C.2.]
63.	**NO**	Under the ABA Model Rules, a lawyer must first try to persuade his client to testify truthfully. If that fails, the lawyer may seek to withdraw if that will remedy the situation, but if withdrawal will not remedy the situation, the lawyer must disclose the situation to the court. [Page 88, VIII.C.4.b.]
64.	**YES**	It is a crime to suppress or tamper with evidence. Here, Lucinda knowingly destroyed a report requested by the plaintiff. Lucinda also would be **subject to discipline** for unlawfully destroying a document having evidentiary value. [Page 89, VIII.D.1.]
65.	**NO**	Ahern is **subject to discipline** for using false evidence. [Page 90, VIII.D.2.] An affidavit is supposed to be made under oath and signed by the affiant. Ahern has also corrupted her secretary, the notary public, by having her attest to the forged signature. [*See* Garlow v. State Bar of California, 180 Cal. Rptr. 831 (1982)—attorney disciplined for, among other things, signing client's name to declaration under oath]
66.	**YES**	Except when prohibited by local law, it is **proper** to pay such expenses incurred by a lay witness. [Page 90, VIII.D.3.]

67. **YES**   This is **proper**, as long as Ackroid reasonably believes that the employees' interests will not be harmed by declining to be interviewed. [Pages 90-91, VIII.D.4.; *and see* Page 103, IX.B.2.—concerning impropriety of interviewing employees of represented adversary]

68. **YES**   Lippert is **subject to discipline**, both for violating the judge's order given at the final pretrial conference and for referring in closing argument to material not in the record. [Page 92, VIII.D.5.; Page 92, VIII.D.7.a.]

69. **YES**   Even if Langdon has not technically obstructed plaintiff's access to evidence, he has abused the discovery process by destroying the meaningful order of the documents. [Page 91, VIII.D.6.] Here, at the very least, the trial judge would be justified in ordering Langdon to furnish plaintiff with a new set of copies, properly arranged, at no cost to plaintiff. Landon also would be **subject to discipline** for abusing the discovery process.

70. **NO**   A lawyer is **subject to discipline** for stating personal opinions when arguing a case to the jury. The proper technique is to point out the relevant evidence in the record and to let the jurors form their own opinions and conclusions. [Pages 92-93, VIII.D.7.c.]

71. **YES**   During the trial of a case, a lawyer who is connected with the case **must not** communicate with a juror on *any* subject. [Page 94, VIII.E.2.b.; *and see* Florida Bar v. Peterson, 418 So. 2d 246 (Fla. 1982)—lawyer disciplined in similar circumstances]

72. **YES**   Prunella is **subject to discipline** for violating Rule 3.6, which states that a lawyer connected with a case must not make a public statement outside the courtroom that the lawyer reasonably should know would have a substantial likelihood of materially prejudicing a case. [Page 95, VIII.F.1.] Furthermore, as a prosecutor, Prunella is **subject to discipline** for violating Rule 3.8, which provides that a prosecutor must not make extrajudicial statements that have a substantial likelihood of heightening public condemnation of the accused. [Page 96, VIII.F.3.; Pages 99-100, VIII.H.6.]

73. **YES**   Trial counsel may testify as a witness if her testimony is limited to the nature and value of the services she rendered in the case. [Pages 97-98, VIII.G.2.b.]

74. **YES**   On the facts given, it is fair to assume that the defendant would suffer substantial hardship if he were forced to obtain a new lawyer in the middle of the trial. Thus, it would be **proper** for Lucero to testify and to continue as trial counsel. [Page 98, VIII.G.2.c.]

75. **YES**   A prosecutor **must** make reasonable efforts to assure that the accused is advised of the procedure for obtaining counsel. [Page 99, VIII.H.2.]

76. **YES**   Attorneys are subject to the rules of legal ethics in whatever capacity they act. Further, when an attorney is acting for a client in the legislative arena, the attorney must follow the same rules of candor and forthrightness as though in court. [Pages 100-101, VIII.I.2.]

77. **NO**   A statement like this one is regarded as mere puffery, a conventional bargaining ploy. [Page 101, IX.A.1.b.]

78. **NO**   A lawyer **must not** communicate about a matter with a represented adversary, absent the consent of the adversary's counsel. [Pages 102-103, IX.B.1.]

79. **NO**   Whether to settle a case is a decision to be made by the client, not by the lawyer. [Page 23, II.D.1.] The rule that prohibits a lawyer from communicating directly with a represented adversary does not prohibit the parties themselves from communicating directly with each other. [Page 103, IX.B.3.] Thus, Lutenberger **should** have drawn up the settlement papers as Price requested because a lawyer is normally required to see a matter through to completion. [Page 32, III.B.3.] Furthermore, Lutenberger is entitled to only $16,666 (one-third of $50,000) as his fee. [Pages 19-20, II.C.4.]

80. **NO**   When dealing with an unrepresented person on behalf of a client, a lawyer **must not** give legal advice to the unrepresented person if the client's interests are likely to conflict with those of the unrepresented person. [Page 104, IX.C.]

81. **NO**   Parner is asking Lacy to abuse the rights of an unrepresented third person. [Pages 104-105, IX.D.] When an ethics question is *reasonably debatable*, a junior lawyer **may** abide by a senior supervising lawyer's resolution, but query whether Parner's position is reasonably debatable. [Page 108, X.C.2.] As a practical matter, Lacy would be prudent to ask Parner to explain his position more fully before she decides whether to ignore his instructions.

82. **NO**   "Member of the firm" usually means the same as "partner" in a law partnership or "shareholder" in an incorporated law firm. [Page 106, X.A.1.]

83. **NO**   A nonlawyer must not own any interest in an incorporated law firm. [Pages 109-110, X.E.3.]

84. **NO**   A lawyer **should** do such work, but the ABA Model Rules do not impose discipline for failing to do so. [Page 112, XI.A.]

85. **YES**   If the information in the circulars is true and not misleading, her conduct is **proper**. [Page 116, XII.B.1.]

86. **NO**   ABA Model Rule 7.3 prohibits solicitation only when a "significant motive" is the "lawyer's pecuniary gain." [Pages 119-120, XII.C.2.] (One might argue that Andrews volunteered his free legal services in this case with the ulterior motive of seeking publicity and thus luring fee-paying clients in other cases. Query whether such conduct could constitutionally be prohibited.)

87. **NO**   An attorney may state to the public that he is a certified specialist only if the certifying body has been approved by the state or the ABA. [Page 121, XII.D.1.] Here, the state has no program for approving private certification, and the ABA has not approved the certifying body; thus, Layton and Letonen may not state

in their firm advertising material that they are certified specialists in criminal defense.

88. **NO** Federal law authorizes federal judges to be disciplined (by sanctions less drastic than removal from office) upon recommendation by a specially constituted group of other federal judges. [Page 123, XIII.A.1.]

89. **YES** A judge must maintain high standards of personal conduct, both in and out of the courtroom. [Pages 123-124, XIII.B.; *and see* Geiler v. Commission on Judicial Qualifications, 10 Cal. 3d 270 (1973)—judge removed from the bench for similar conduct] If the judge's conduct raises a substantial question about his fitness for office, a lawyer who learns of the conduct must report it to the appropriate authorities. [Pages 6-7, I.C.2.]

90. **NO** A judge must not allow family or social relationships to interfere with the judge's conduct or judgments. [Page 124, XIII.C.1.] Furthermore, a judge generally should not accept favors from someone who is likely to appear before the judge. [Pages 139-140, XIII.F.8.]

91. **NO** The statement is backwards. A judge **must not** appear voluntarily as a character witness, but **may** comply with a subpoena to serve as a character witness. [Page 125, XIII.C.2.a.3)]

92. **NO** Assuming the restaurant has engaged in invidious discrimination, Judge Jones is **subject to discipline** for publicly manifesting her approval of it. [Pages 126-127, XIII.C.3.d.]

93. **NO** The Institute's ownership of the Carnegie stock does not disqualify Justice Juarez because a judge may be a director of a nonprofit organization and that organization may own securities of a party appearing in a case before the judge. [Page 135, XIII.E.4.b.2)] However, a judge **must** disqualify himself in a case in which his impartiality might reasonably be questioned. A judge should disclose any information the judge believes the parties or their lawyers might consider relevant to the question of disqualification, even if the judge believes there is no reasonable basis for disqualification. [Page 132, XIII.E.1.] In this case, the judge's impartiality can reasonably be questioned by Carnegie, the appellant, because the appellee's lawyer, Lee, is the judge's best friend. Thus, the judge should disclose his friendship with Lee, and if the parties believe that the judge can be impartial, they can always waive the judge's disqualification. [Page 136, XIII.E.8.]

94. **NO** A judge shall not serve as an officer of an organization that frequently is engaged in adversary proceedings in the court on which the judge sits. Assuming that the Cascades Club's cases often are brought in Judge Jimerson's court, she should not serve as treasurer. [Page 138, XIII.F.4.a.] Also, a judge must not personally participate in fund-raising activities for an organization, except for soliciting funds from other judges who are not under her supervisory or appellate authority. [Page 138, XIII.F.4.b.]

95. **NO**   A full-time judge **must not** practice law. [Page 141, XIII.F.11.] Acting as attorney for the executor of Aunt Agnes's estate probably does not fall within the limited exception that allows a full-time judge to render some kinds of uncompensated legal service for family members.

96. **YES**   She **may** accept the honorarium if it is reasonable and does not exceed the amount that would be paid to a nonjudge, and she **may** accept reimbursement of reasonable expenses incurred by herself and her husband. [Page 141, XIII.F.12.a.]

97. **YES**   Because Lenox is not now a judge, and because he is seeking an appointed rather than elective judicial position, he **may** retain his position and make his ordinary contributions. [Page 145, XIII.G.3.c.]

98. **NO**   Indeed, Anton must not personally solicit campaign funds at any time. [Page 146, XIII.G.4.c.1)] He **may** have a campaign committee do that on his behalf, but the campaign committee cannot begin soliciting funds before March 14, 2004. [Page 146, XIII.G.4.c.2)]

INSTRUCTIONS FOR PRACTICE EXAMS

Four full practice exams follow. You have *two hours and five minutes* to answer the questions in an exam. An answer sheet is provided after each set of practice exam questions. Approximately 6 - 10% of the questions contained in each practice exam will measure aspects of the ABA Code of Judicial Conduct. The remaining questions are designed so that disciplinary questions can be answered solely under the ABA Model Rules of Professional Conduct, including the Preamble to and the Comments accompanying the Model Rules. All other questions should be answered under the general law governing lawyering, including statutory and common law.

When a question refers to discipline by the "bar" or "state bar," it refers to whatever agency in the jurisdiction has the authority to administer the standards for admission to practice and for maintenance of professional competence and integrity.

Each of the questions in the exams contains four suggested answers. You are to choose the *best* of the four stated choices.

The exams each contain 60 questions, as does the actual MPRE. On the actual exam, 50 questions are scored and 10 are nonscored "pretest" questions. Because you will not know which are the nonscored questions, you must answer all questions.

Your score will be based on the number of questions you answer correctly. It is therefore to your advantage to answer as many questions as you can. Use your time effectively. If a question seems too difficult, go on to the next one. Nevertheless, you should try to answer *all* questions because wrong answers are not deducted from the right answers.

PRACTICE EXAM 1

Question 1

Judge Jackman is a full-time judge in State A. Her father lives in a retirement home in State B. Judge Jackman's father told her on the telephone that several of his friends in the retirement home had employed attorney Abbott to write wills for them, that in each will attorney Abbott had included a bequest to himself, and that each bequest was approximately 50% of the estimated total value of the person's probable estate. The friends told Judge Jackman's father that they did not really want to leave Abbott anything; they had assumed it was merely a matter of routine, a part of the attorney's compensation for drafting the will. Abbott is admitted to practice in State B, but not in State A. Judge Jackman did not talk personally with any of her father's friends, but she believes that her father's rendition of the story is entirely accurate.

Would it be **proper** for Judge Jackman to communicate directly with attorney Abbott about the matter, and if that does not satisfy her, to communicate with the attorney disciplinary authority in State B about the matter?

(A) Yes, because she has received information indicating a substantial likelihood that Abbott has violated a legal ethics rule.

(B) Yes, because she has personal knowledge that Abbott has violated a legal ethics rule.

(C) No, because legal ethics violations that take place outside State A are not her concern.

(D) No, because she is not allowed to communicate directly with Abbott about the supposed legal ethics violation.

Question 2

Lawyer Long, three years out of law school, had never set foot in a courtroom. Long was on the board of directors of the Community Nursery School ("CNS"), a nonprofit preschool for underprivileged children. One of the CNS teachers was charged with felony child abuse for allegedly molesting three of the CNS pupils. After conducting its own careful investigation, the CNS board of directors concluded that the criminal charge was totally unfounded, and the board resolved to provide defense counsel for the teacher. Long volunteered to do the work without a fee. A few days before the trial was to begin, Long got cold feet and became convinced that he was incompetent to serve as the teacher's trial counsel. He asked the trial judge for permission to withdraw. After thoroughly questioning Long about his preparation for trial, the judge said:

> Mr. Long, I understand your anxiety, but you are perfectly competent to handle this case. Your motion to withdraw is denied; I will postpone the trial for seven days to allow you to complete your preparation. Now go do your job.

Instead of doing what the judge ordered, Long advised the teacher that he would not defend her. He handed her all of the files in the case and advised her to retain another lawyer.

Is Long **subject to discipline**?

(A) Yes, because he abandoned his client in direct violation of the trial judge's order.

(B) No, because he believed that he was not competent to represent his client at trial.

(C) Yes, because he undertook a case that he was not competent to handle.

(D) No, because he was working pro bono, not for a fee.

GO ON TO THE NEXT PAGE

Question 3

During a brief recess in jury deliberations in a criminal case, juror Jimmerson telephoned a friend of hers, attorney Aulet, and asked for help in understanding a legal concept that was puzzling the jury—the meaning of "beyond a reasonable doubt." Aulet explained the term as best he could, given the circumstances and shortness of time.

Is Aulet *subject to discipline*?

(A) Yes, because he communicated with a juror about a pending case.

(B) Yes, because given the circumstances and shortness of time, his explanation may have been misleading.

(C) No, unless he was not competent in the field of criminal law.

(D) No, unless he was in some manner connected with the case.

Question 4

Duffy graduated from law school, but he never took the bar examination and was never admitted to practice. He works as an investigator and paralegal for the law firm of Schnell & Gao, a professional corporation.

Which of the following statements are true?

I. On Duffy's recommendation, one of Duffy's friends retained lawyer Gao to represent her as plaintiff in a personal injury case. It would be *proper* for Schnell & Gao to pay Duffy 10% of its fee in the case as compensation for the referral.

II. Lawyer Schnell frequently assigns Duffy to draft wills for Schnell's estate planning clients. Schnell supervises Duffy's work, revises Duffy's drafts, and is ultimately responsible for the final product. Schnell is *subject to discipline* for assisting a nonlawyer to engage in the unauthorized practice of law.

III. Schnell & Gao established a retirement plan that is funded partly by legal fees earned by the firm's lawyers. The firm *may* include Duffy as a beneficiary of the retirement plan.

IV. Schnell & Gao established a stock option plan to compensate its personnel for hard work. The options allow recipients to purchase shares of stock in the law firm at a reduced price. It would be *proper* for Duffy to acquire stock in the firm through the stock option plan.

(A) I., II., III., and IV.

(B) III. and IV. only.

(C) III. only.

(D) None of the above.

Question 5

Pringle consulted lawyer Louder, hoping to hire Louder to represent him as plaintiff in a medical malpractice action against Dr. Dooley. Without mentioning Dr. Dooley's name, Pringle described the alleged acts of malpractice and said that they happened more than two years ago. Only at that point did Pringle mention Dr. Dooley's name. Louder immediately stopped Pringle and said: "I am sorry, but I cannot represent you in this matter. I am presently representing Dr. Dooley in an entirely unrelated lawsuit, but that means that I cannot represent you. You will need to consult another lawyer." That was the end of the conversation. Pringle did nothing further for 15 months, at which point he consulted another lawyer. By that time, the statute of limitations had run on Pringle's claim against Dr. Dooley. Pringle then sued Louder for legal malpractice, alleging that Louder was negligent in not warning him about the statute of limitations.

Is Louder *subject to civil liability* in Pringle's malpractice case?

(A) No, because Louder did what a reasonably prudent lawyer would do in the circumstances—decline to represent Pringle and suggest that he consult other counsel.

(B) No, because Pringle never became Louder's client and is therefore not a proper plaintiff in a malpractice action against Louder.

(C) Yes, because Louder had no legal or ethical reason to reject Pringle as a client and therefore had a duty to warn Pringle about the statute of limitations.

(D) Yes, because a reasonably prudent lawyer would have foreseen that Pringle might delay in consulting another lawyer.

Question 6

Client Chason hired lawyer Lucero to do the legal work in connection with a complex public securities offering. Lucero agreed to do the work for $160 per hour. Lucero did a great deal of legal research, prepared numerous memoranda of fact and law, and drafted most of the documents needed for the public offering. At that point, Chason became angry with Lucero for no apparent reason and fired him. Chason paid Lucero at the agreed rate for the work Lucero had done, and Chason demanded that Lucero turn over to him the papers that Lucero had prepared, including the legal and fact memoranda and the document drafts.

What papers *must* Lucero turn over to Chason?

(A) Only the document drafts, but not the legal and fact memoranda.

(B) Only the legal and fact memoranda, but not the document drafts.

(C) None of the papers, because Chason fired Lucero.

(D) All of the papers, even though Chason fired Lucero.

GO ON TO THE NEXT PAGE

Question 7

Judge Jeffery serves on a State A trial court that has nine other judges. Her husband, Horace, is a life insurance salesman for the Amalgamated Life Insurance Company. Amalgamated is occasionally a litigant in the court on which Judge Jeffery sits. Every year Amalgamated runs a national sales contest in which the person who sells the most life insurance during the year receives a valuable prize. Horace has just learned that he is the winner this year. The prize is an all-expense-paid vacation in Europe for two people.

May Judge Jeffery urge Horace to accept the prize and take her on the European vacation?

(A) Yes, but only if Judge Jeffery makes a public report of that portion of the prize that exceeds $150 in value.

(B) Yes, unless giving Horace the prize could reasonably be perceived as an attempt to influence Judge Jeffery in the performance of her judicial duties.

(C) Yes, because the prize was won by Horace, not by Judge Jeffery.

(D) No, because Amalgamated may later appear as a litigant in the court on which Judge Jeffery sits.

Question 8

Seymour is applying for admission to the State A Bar. When Seymour was in high school, he and his parents lived in State B, next door to attorney Azevedo. Azevedo is admitted to practice in State B, but not in State A. Seymour seemed to be a promising lad, and Azevedo was disappointed to learn that during Seymour's senior year in high school, he was convicted of burglarizing a liquor store. After serving his sentence, Seymour went to college and later to law school. Azevedo has had no contact with Seymour since his high school years, but so far as Azevedo knows, Seymour has not done anything since high school that would reflect badly on his character. The Bar of State A sent Azevedo a routine questionnaire, asking a series of questions about Seymour's character. Azevedo does not know whether Seymour disclosed the burglary conviction on his bar application, and she does not know where to contact him to find out.

Which of the following would be a *proper* response to the questionnaire?

(A) She should not respond at all because she has no relevant information to provide.

(B) She should not respond at all because as a State B lawyer she is not obligated to provide information to the Bar of State A.

(C) She should not mention Seymour's burglary conviction in her response unless she first contacts him and obtains his permission to do so.

(D) She should state what she knows about Seymour, including mention of his burglary conviction.

GO ON TO THE NEXT PAGE

Question 9

Attorney Anderson received her law degree two years ago from Flatland College of Law and Technical Sciences. Last summer she attended a three-day trial practice seminar at the Harvard Law School. During her brief career, she has tried five cases—two jury trials and three bench trials. She won both of the jury trials and two of the three bench trials.

Anderson placed an ad under the subject heading "Trial Lawyers" in the classified pages of the local phone book. Her ad states in relevant part:

Arlene Anderson, Trial Attorney
Harvard Trained
Never Lost a Jury Trial

Which of the following make Anderson *subject to discipline*?

I.   Placing her ad under the heading "Trial Lawyers" in the phone book classified pages.

II. Describing herself as a "Trial Attorney" in her ad.

III. Describing herself as "Harvard Trained" in her ad.

IV. Stating "Never Lost a Jury Trial" in her ad.

(A) None of the above.

(B) I., II., III., and IV.

(C) IV. only.

(D) III. and IV. only.

Question 10

Two years ago, Weaver obtained a divorce from her husband, Hubbard, in State A. The court awarded Weaver custody of the three children and ordered Hubbard to pay Weaver $3,000 per month in child support and alimony payments. The attorney who represented Weaver in the divorce proceedings died. Hubbard failed to make the $3,000 payments for 17 months in a row. Weaver ran out of money, and in desperation, hired attorney Avilla to represent her in a proceeding to collect the past due payments from Hubbard. State A has no law or court rule that requires the loser to pay the winner's attorneys' fees in domestic relations matters. Because Weaver had no money to pay Avilla a regular fee, Avilla agreed to do the work on a contingent fee basis for 10% of whatever amount Weaver was ultimately able to recover. Avilla won an award for Weaver of the entire amount due ($51,000), and by tracking down and attaching Hubbard's secret bank account, he got the full amount paid to Weaver. He then sent Weaver a bill for his share, $5,100.

Is Avilla *subject to discipline*?

(A) No, unless $5,100 is an unreasonably high fee for the work Avilla did.

(B) No, because Weaver had no money to pay a regular fee.

(C) Yes, because Avilla used a contingent fee in a domestic relations matter.

(D) Yes, because Avilla took a portion of the money that was intended for support of Weaver and the children.

GO ON TO THE NEXT PAGE

Question 11

Lawyer Lohman (age 34) regularly represented client Cruikshank (age 78) in matters relating to the investment of Cruikshank's considerable wealth. Cruikshank told Lohman that he wanted to put $500,000 into a sound, income-producing investment. Lohman suggested that the two of them pool their money and talent and buy an attractive new apartment house. Lohman would put up $75,000 and do the legal work, and Cruikshank would put up $500,000 and serve as the live-in manager of the apartment house. Cruikshank enthusiastically agreed to the arrangement and told Lohman to draw up the papers.

Lohman drafted an agreement between himself and Cruikshank, negotiated the purchase of the apartment house, and drafted a deed from the seller to himself and Cruikshank as joint tenants with right of survivorship. Lohman gave Cruikshank a carefully written explanation of the terms of the transaction, but he forgot to explain the significance of the joint tenancy, *i.e.*, that upon the death of one joint tenant, the property would pass automatically to the other joint tenant. Lohman advised Cruikshank in the writing explaining the terms of the transaction to have an outside lawyer look over the transaction, and he also urged him orally to do so. However, Cruikshank said that he trusted Lohman and signed all of the papers without further ado. Lohman and Cruikshank operated the apartment house successfully for several years, until Cruikshank died at age 83. The executor of Cruikshank's estate sued Lohman to have the apartment house declared part of Cruikshank's estate, but the court concluded that the joint tenancy created a gift to Lohman, effective on Cruikshank's death.

Were Lohman's actions *proper*?

(A) Yes, because the court concluded that the joint tenancy created a gift from Cruikshank to Lohman.

(B) Yes, because Lohman might have died first, thus bestowing a gift on Cruikshank.

(C) No, because Lohman entered into a business transaction with Cruikshank.

(D) No, because Lohman drafted the deed that bestowed a substantial gift on himself.

GO ON TO THE NEXT PAGE

Question 12

For the past five years, attorney Arles has represented art dealer Corot in the sale of many valuable paintings. One of the major transactions occurred three years ago, when the American Museum of Art paid Corot $23 million for a Post-Impressionist landscape purportedly painted by Vincent Van Gogh in 1890. The American Museum of Art subsequently resold the painting to the Amsterdam Fine Arts Museum for $35 million.

Today, Corot asked Arles to do the legal work in connection with the sale of a smaller, less valuable landscape, also a purported Van Gogh. The proposed purchase price is $12 million, and the prospective purchaser is Lavita Lavish, a wealthy television personality who knows noth-ing about art. During a confidential conversation in Arles's office, Arles said to Corot: "I assume you have appraisal letters certifying the painting as a genuine Van Gogh?" Corot replied: "Of course I have letters! I forged them myself, just as I did for that bogus Van Gogh you helped me sell to the American Museum of Art three years ago!" When Arles inquired further, Corot told him in confidence that both of the purported Van Gogh paintings were in fact counterfeits created by a clever art student.

Which of the following *must* Arles do at this point?

I. Report Corot to the law enforcement authorities.

II. Warn Lavita Lavish about the proposed sale.

III. Inform the American Museum of Art of the truth about the first painting.

IV. Refuse to represent Corot in the present transaction.

(A) None of the above.

(B) I., II., III., and IV.

(C) II., III., and IV. only.

(D) IV. only.

Question 13

Two years ago, attorney Azari represented client Claubert in the sale of Blackacre to buyer Boyer. Unbeknownst to Azari, Claubert made some fraudulent statements to Boyer about the value of some mineral deposits on Blackacre. Boyer recently discovered the fraud and is now in Azari's office threatening to immediately file a civil fraud suit against both Claubert and Azari. Boyer accuses Azari of engineering the fraud and helping Claubert carry it out. The only way that Azari can convince Boyer that he had no part in the fraud is to tell Boyer a fact that Claubert disclosed to him in the deepest confi-dence when he was working on the Blackacre transaction.

May Azari disclose the fact without the consent of Claubert?

(A) No, if doing so will harm Claubert.

(B) No, because doing so would breach his duty of confidentiality to Claubert.

(C) Yes, but only after Boyer files the civil fraud suit against him.

(D) Yes, even if doing so will subject his client to civil or criminal liability.

Question 14

Attorney Adams is defending defendant Dutcher at his trial for armed robbery of a liquor store. Dutcher tells Adams in confidence that at the time in question, he was sitting at home watching television with his aged mother, and that his mother can confirm his alibi. Adams interviews the mother, who solemnly confirms Dutcher's story. After talking with her, Adams strongly suspects that she is lying to protect Dutcher. Adams does not know for sure that Dutcher and his mother are lying, but every instinct tells him that they are. Adams has warned both of them about the dangers of perjury, but both have insisted that they want to testify to the alibi at trial.

May Adams call Dutcher, or his mother, or both, as trial witnesses?

(A) Yes, as to both Dutcher and his mother.

(B) Yes, as to Dutcher, but no, as to his mother.

(C) No, as to both Dutcher and his mother.

(D) No, as to Dutcher, but yes, as to his mother.

Question 15

The Bar of State Alpha has established an Interest on Lawyers' Trust Accounts ("IOLTA") program, whereby lawyers deposit client trust funds into special client trust accounts that pay interest to the Bar of State Alpha, which then uses the money to help fund legal services for poor people. The State Alpha IOLTA program requires lawyers to deposit a particular client's funds in an IOLTA account unless the funds would earn more than $50 in interest during the time they are entrusted to the lawyer. If the client's funds would earn more than $50 in interest during that time, the lawyer must deposit them in a separate interest-bearing trust account and pay the interest to the client. State Alpha lawyer Longfisher settled a personal injury case brought by her client Choy. The defendant sent Longfisher a check for $9,000. Because she was leaving that day for a one-month vacation in Fiji, Longfisher instructed her assistant to deposit the check in Longfisher's IOLTA account. The assistant is authorized to make deposits to and withdrawals from the account. Longfisher did not tell her assistant to notify Choy that the check had arrived. When Longfisher returned a month later, she notified Choy that the check had been received, and Choy came to Longfisher's office that same day to collect the $9,000. At the prevailing rate of interest, the $9,000 would have earned $40 during the month that Longfisher was gone.

Was Longfisher's handling of the matter *proper*?

(A) No, because she should have instructed her assistant to deposit the check in a separate trust account that would earn interest for Choy.

(B) No, because she should have instructed her assistant to notify Choy promptly that the check had arrived.

(C) Yes, because she handled the matter in accordance with the State Alpha IOLTA program.

(D) Yes, because Choy was not harmed.

GO ON TO THE NEXT PAGE

Question 16

After lawyer Laben graduated from law school, she joined the congressional staff of United States Senator Senders. In that role, she personally drafted a bill that was ultimately enacted as the Educational Rights of Disabled Americans Act ("ERDAA"), a far-reaching statute that requires colleges and universities to make many changes in the facilities they supply to blind, deaf, and physically impaired students. Shortly thereafter, Laben moved to State A, where she became an associate in the private law firm of Dillard & Dornish. Seeking legal advice on how to comply with the ERDAA, the University of State A hired partner Dillard and specifically asked Dillard to assign Laben to assist him in doing the work.

In light of Laben's earlier role as the drafter of the ERDAA, which of the two lawyers *may* work on the matter?

(A) Neither Dillard nor Laben.

(B) Dillard only, and only if Laben is properly screened off from the matter.

(C) Both Dillard and Laben.

(D) Dillard only, and only if the University consents after full disclosure.

Question 17

Consolidated Insurance Corporation offers a legal services insurance policy. In return for a yearly premium, an insured person will be reimbursed by Consolidated for a specified amount of legal services during the year. The insured selects a lawyer from a list of "Authorized Providers" supplied by Consolidated. Any lawyer who agrees to follow a maximum fee schedule set by Consolidated can become an "Authorized Provider." Consolidated solicits insurance sales by in-person and live telephone contact with potential insurance buyers.

Will attorney Alvarado be *subject to discipline* if he becomes an "Authorized Provider" and receives clients through Consolidated's insurance plan?

(A) No, unless Consolidated solicits persons whom it knows are in need of legal services in a particular matter covered by its insurance plan.

(B) No, because Consolidated's insureds are allowed to select whatever lawyer they wish from among the "Authorized Providers."

(C) Yes, unless Consolidated's fee schedule provides for legal fees that are reasonable in light of the nature and amount of legal services performed.

(D) Yes, because Consolidated uses in-person and live telephone solicitation to get business.

GO ON TO THE NEXT PAGE

Question 18

State Alpha lawyer LaFrank represents Inventex Corp., a State Alpha corporation that owns a valuable United States patent. State Beta lawyer Levin represents Demonics, Inc., a State Beta corporation. Inventex believes that Demonics is infringing the Inventex patent, and for the past three months LaFrank has been negotiating with Levin, seeking an amicable resolution of the dispute. The negotiations have broken down, and Inventex has decided to sue Demonics for infringement.

Venue in an action for patent infringement is proper in any United States judicial district where the defendant or its agent resides or can constitutionally be served with process. For tactical reasons, LaFrank wants venue in State Alpha. She believes, but is not certain, that Demonics has a branch sales office somewhere in State Alpha. To find out for sure, LaFrank telephones Demonics's headquarters in State Beta and asks to speak with the president of the company. Without identifying herself, she asks the president where in State Alpha she can find a sales office for Demonics's products. The president politely tells her the address of the office and the name of Demonics's head sales agent in State Alpha.

Is LaFrank *subject to discipline*?

(A) No, because at the time she talked with the president, Inventex had not yet sued Demonics.

(B) No, because her conversation with the president did not concern the substance of the dispute between the parties.

(C) Yes, because when she talked with the president, she did not identify herself as counsel for Inventex.

(D) Yes, because she talked with the president about the matter without getting Levin's consent.

Question 19

Building contractor Carter and his lawyer Lewis met with landowner Owens to negotiate a contract whereby Carter would construct an office building on land owned by Owens. Carter, Lewis, and Owens were the only persons present at the meeting. Ultimately, the three of them worked out a written agreement, and Carter commenced work on the building. It soon became apparent that the building site required far more preparation work than Carter had contemplated when he agreed to the contract price. Carter and Owens got into a dispute about who had to pay for the additional site preparation. One important issue is whether Owens made certain oral representations to Carter during the contract negotiating session that Lewis attended. Carter contends that Owens did make the representations, and Owens contends that he did not. Lewis was present during the entire negotiating session, and she is virtually certain that Owens did not make the representations.

Carter stopped work on the building and refused to proceed until Owens paid for the extra site preparation. Owens then sued Carter for specific performance of the construction contract. Carter asked Lewis to represent him as trial counsel.

Lewis *should*:

(A) Agree to serve as trial counsel for Carter because Carter is entitled to the counsel of his choice.

(B) Agree to serve as trial counsel for Carter because she can refuse to testify if she is called as a witness by Owens.

(C) Decline to serve as trial counsel for Carter because a lawyer is not allowed to testify in a manner that is prejudicial to her client.

(D) Decline to serve as trial counsel for Carter because she can foresee that she will be called as a witness.

GO ON TO THE NEXT PAGE

Question 20

Author Arthur wrote a best-selling novel based on the life and crimes of John Dillinger, the famous bank robber. Arthur sold the movie rights to film producer Prosser, who promised to pay Arthur a lump-sum royalty of $5 million upon the release of the movie. After Prosser hired actor Clint Nickleman to play the lead role and made other expensive preparations for filming, Arthur repudiated the contract. Prosser hired lawyer Laine to sue Arthur for a declaratory judgment that the contract was valid and enforceable. At Prosser's request, Laine agreed to do the legal work on a contingent fee basis: If Prosser wins, Laine will be paid 1.75% of the gross receipts from the movie, but if Prosser loses, Laine will be paid nothing. Prosser and Laine entered into a written fee agreement that contains all the details required by the rules of legal ethics.

Which of the following statements is true?

(A) Laine is *subject to discipline* for entering into a publication rights contract with his client.

(B) Laine is *subject to discipline* for acquiring a personal interest in the subject of the litigation.

(C) Laine's fee agreement is *proper*, but only if Arthur gives informed consent.

(D) Laine's fee agreement is *proper*, even though it gives Laine a personal interest in the subject of the litigation.

Question 21

For many years lawyer Lacy has done business transactions work for wealthy client Chung. Chung was recently injured in an automobile crash, and she has asked Lacy to represent her as plaintiff in an action against the driver who injured her. Lacy has taken some business cases to trial, but has never handled a personal injury case.

Lacy would like to earn a profit from Chung's case. Which of the following would be *proper* ways for him to do so?

I.   Take the case and, with Chung's consent, associate a co-counsel who is competent in the field of personal injury law.

II. Refer Chung to a competent personal injury lawyer and charge that lawyer a $1,000 forwarding fee.

III. Take the case and do the study and research needed to handle it competently.

IV. Refer Chung to a competent personal injury lawyer and charge Chung a reasonable sum for the time spent in making the referral.

(A) I. and III. only.

(B) I., II., and III. only.

(C) I. and IV. only.

(D) I., III., and IV. only.

GO ON TO THE NEXT PAGE

Question 22

Attorney Adams is a voting member of the legislation committee of Citizens for Safer Food ("CSF"), a consumer-based law reform group that drafts and advocates the passage of proposed statutes on food safety. CSF is currently debating a draft statute that sets quality and safety standards for growth hormones administered to chickens, turkeys, and other poultry. Adams is also engaged in the private practice of patent law. She regularly represents Genetico, Inc., a biotechnology firm. Using the techniques of genetic engineering, Genetico invents, develops, and sells a variety of patented growth hormones. Adams herself has obtained patents on some of these hormones for Genetico. If enacted into law, CSF's proposed statute on poultry hormones could materially increase Genetico's hormone sales because it is the only firm whose hormones would meet the statute's quality and safety requirements.

Would it be *proper* for Adams, as a member of the CSF legislation committee, to participate in the debate on, and to cast her vote on, the proposed statute?

(A) No, because the statute could materially benefit Genetico.

(B) No, because Adams may not serve as a member of CSF while representing Genetico.

(C) Yes, provided that she informs the legislation committee that she represents an unnamed client whose interests could be materially benefited by the statute.

(D) Yes, provided that she informs the legislation committee that she represents Genetico, whose interests could be materially benefited by the statute.

Question 23

Judge Jettelson sits on a United States Court of Appeals. He and two other Court of Appeals judges heard a diversity of citizenship case in which they were required to interpret a statute of State A concerning the marital communications privilege. Judge Jettelson's two colleagues wrote the majority opinion, in which they concluded that the statute gives only the witness-spouse the right to claim the privilege. Judge Jettelson wrote a vigorous and scholarly dissent, arguing that the statute gives both spouses the right to claim the privilege.

Later, a State A senator legislator introduced a bill to amend the statute to reflect Judge Jettelson's position. The State Senate Justice Committee invited Judge Jettelson to testify about the public policy reasons for giving both spouses the right to claim the privilege.

May Judge Jettelson testify?

(A) Yes, but only if the two judges who wrote the majority opinion are also allowed to testify.

(B) Yes, because a judge may engage in activities designed to improve the law.

(C) No, because a judge must not become involved in politics, subject to certain exceptions that do not apply here.

(D) No, because a judge is not allowed to make public statements about disputed propositions of law, except when acting in his judicial capacity.

GO ON TO THE NEXT PAGE

Question 24

Attorney Anthony Altamirez has organized his law practice as a professional corporation. Altamirez is the sole shareholder. The sign on the office door states:

Anthony Altamirez, P.C.— Attorney at Law
Corporate and Business Law
Torts and Domestic Relations

Altamirez has only one lawyer-employee, Leola Lipkis, who was admitted to practice two years ago. Altamirez pays Lipkis a modest monthly salary plus 60% of the fees collected in cases that Lipkis handles by herself. Altamirez has a general business practice, and when a client needs representation in a tort or domestic relations matter, Altamirez turns the case over to Lipkis. When Altamirez turns a case over to Lipkis, he provides general guidance and is available to answer any questions she may have, but he does not supervise every step she takes.

Is Altamirez **subject to discipline**?

(A) Yes, because he splits fees with Lipkis in matters she handles by herself.

(B) Yes, because he does not closely supervise the work done by Lipkis.

(C) No, unless he is not certified as a specialist in the areas noted on his office sign.

(D) No, because Lipkis is a lawyer-employee of Altamirez.

Question 25

Attorney Atley was representing plaintiff Putkis at the bench trial of a civil action pending before Judge Joiner. Midway through Putkis's case-in-chief, the judge called Atley into his chambers and said: "You've known me a long time, and I've always been honest with you. I'm going to be honest with you now, I don't think you have much of a case here. I may be mistaken though—my mind is distracted by money troubles. If only I could get a loan of $50,000 somewhere, it would free my mind considerably." Atley responded: "Your Honor, a loan of $50,000 is not a problem, and I'd be glad to help you out as a friend." Later that afternoon, a messenger delivered an envelope containing $50,000 in cash to Judge Joiner's chambers. No mention was made of a promissory note, a repayment date, or an interest rate. Two days later, Putkis settled his lawsuit so Judge Joiner never had to decide the case. Three months later, Judge Joiner repaid the $50,000 to Atley, together with interest at the market rate.

Is Atley **subject to criminal liability** for lending the money to the judge?

(A) Yes, if it is proven that Judge Joiner intended to induce Atley to make the loan in return for a decision in favor of Putkis.

(B) Yes, if it is proven that, in making the loan, Atley intended to induce Judge Joiner to decide the case in favor of Putkis.

(C) No, because as the matter turned out, Judge Joiner never had to decide Putkis's case.

(D) No, because Judge Joiner repaid the loan with interest.

GO ON TO THE NEXT PAGE

Question 26

Universal Steel, Inc. merged with Delta Iron Corp. The Attorney General of State A sued Universal and Delta in federal court to enjoin the merger, alleging that it was in violation of the federal antitrust laws. The federal district judge enjoined the merger, and Universal appealed the judge's decision to the United States Court of Appeals for the Fourth Circuit. Universal's lawyer on the appeal is attorney Alvarez.

In doing the legal research for the appeal, Alvarez found a recent merger decision rendered by the Federal Trade Commission ("FTC") that is directly adverse to Universal's position. FTC decisions do not control in the United States Courts of Appeal, but they are persuasive. The Attorney General for State A failed to cite the FTC decision.

Must Alvarez disclose it to the court?

(A) Yes, because it is persuasive authority.

(B) Yes, because the FTC decision is directly adverse to Universal's position.

(C) No, because an attorney has no obligation to volunteer facts harmful to his client's case.

(D) No, because the Court of Appeals is not obliged to follow the FTC ruling.

Question 27

Solo practitioner Proctor is one of only three lawyers in the small town of Sandy Gulch. Proctor is presently defending client Cridley in a criminal action for assault and battery. This morning one of Proctor's regular clients, the Sandy Gulch Gas & Grocery, asked Proctor to sue Cridley to recover $638.64 that is past due on Cridley's gasoline and grocery charge account.

Would it be *proper* for Proctor to represent the Sandy Gulch Gas & Grocery in the charge account case?

(A) Yes, unless Proctor has gotten confidential information from Cridley that would be relevant to the charge account case.

(B) Yes, unless there is a substantial relationship between the charge account case and the assault and battery case.

(C) No, unless both Cridley and the Sandy Gulch Gas & Grocery consent in writing after full disclosure of the conflict.

(D) No, unless the other two lawyers in town are disqualified from representing the Sandy Gulch Gas & Grocery.

GO ON TO THE NEXT PAGE

Question 28

Lawyer Lorenz agreed to represent wife Withers on an hourly fee basis in securing a divorce from her husband Hullar. Hullar is represented in the matter by attorney Atwell. Despite repeated warnings by Lorenz, Withers kept pestering Lorenz with telephone calls and office visits concerning inconsequential details and trifling personal complaints. When Withers was unable to contact Lorenz on the phone or in person, she would telephone Atwell, her husband's attorney, and try to put her questions and complaints to him. Atwell always refused to talk to Withers. Lorenz repeatedly told Withers not to contact Atwell, but to no avail. Finally, Lorenz told Withers that she would withdraw unless Withers changed her ways, but Withers did not do so. Lorenz withdrew and sent Withers a fee bill for the total number of hours she had spent on the case. Withers refused to pay the bill, and after futile efforts to settle the matter, Lorenz sued her to collect the fee.

Which of the following propositions are true?

I. It was *proper* for Lorenz to withdraw.

II. It was *proper* for Atwell to refuse to talk with Withers on the phone.

III. It was *proper* for Lorenz to bill Withers for the total amount of time she spent on the case.

IV. It was *proper* for Lorenz to sue Withers to collect the unpaid fee.

(A) I., II., III., and IV.

(B) None of the above.

(C) I. and III. only.

(D) II. only.

Question 29

Lawyer Lars is defending Castco, Inc. in a suit brought in federal district court in the Second Circuit. One of the issues in the case is whether Castco violated a workplace rule promulgated by the Federal Employment Commission ("FEC"). Castco denies having done the act that allegedly violated the FEC rule. As a fallback position, Castco argues that even if it did the act, the rule should be interpreted to exclude acts of that kind.

For which of the following actions is Lars *subject to discipline*?

I. Failing to turn over incriminating documents that Castco gave him in confidence upon his employment, and which were requested during discovery.

II. Failing to cite a case directly on point decided last month by the Ninth Circuit Court of Appeals.

III. Failing to notify the opposing side of a witness who can testify that the president of Castco specifically instructed one of her deputies to commit the act in question.

IV. Failing to cite a three-week-old FEC decision that Lars found in a computer search and that interprets the FEC rule to include precisely the kind of act Castco allegedly committed.

(A) II. and IV., but not I. and III.

(B) I. and III., but not II. and IV.

(C) I., III., and IV., but not II.

(D) I. and IV., but not II. and III.

GO ON TO THE NEXT PAGE

Question 30

The Bar of State A has established a peer counseling program whereby lawyers who are addicted to alcohol or other drugs can receive confidential counseling from other lawyers. The Bar of State A's ethics rule on confidential information provides that communications between the counselor lawyer and the counseled lawyer are to be treated just like confidential communications between an attorney and client. Lawyer Loomis is addicted to alcohol and is receiving peer counseling under the program from lawyer Lin. Loomis is a large, strong man, and his addiction has made him subject to periodic fits of physical violence. This afternoon, during their peer counseling session, Loomis told Lin: "My client Crothers has refused to pay the fees he owes me; the next time I get drunk enough, I'm going to smash the little creep's face in." From working with Loomis over an extended period, Lin believes that he may really do it.

May Lin disclose Loomis's statement to Crothers and the police?

(A) No, unless Loomis consents.

(B) No, unless Lin is certain that Loomis will carry out his threat.

(C) Yes, even if Loomis objects.

(D) Yes, because Lin is serving as a peer counselor, not a lawyer.

Question 31

Wilma is the only living child of widower Warner, age 83. Warner's main asset is a 51% partnership interest in Mobiland, Ltd., a wealthy real estate syndicate that owns and operates mobile home parks throughout the state. Wilma is married to attorney Atwater. One of Atwater's regular clients, Christopher, asks Atwater to represent him in negotiating the sale of 3,000 acres of roadside property to Mobiland. Mobiland is represented by its own lawyer in the matter.

May Atwater represent Christopher?

(A) No, even if Christopher gives informed, written consent.

(B) Yes, because Atwater has no significant personal interest in Mobiland.

(C) No, because to do so would create an appearance of impropriety.

(D) Yes, but only if Christopher gives informed, written consent.

GO ON TO THE NEXT PAGE

Question 32

Swimming coach Larry was charged with assaulting the coach of the opposing team. Larry hired criminal attorney Bailey to conduct his defense. Subsequently, Larry pleaded not guilty and was released on his own recognizance. At his first trial, a jury was empaneled, and prosecutor Portman was almost finished presenting the testimony of her first witness when a signal from her electronic pager interrupted her. Trial Judge Judy granted her request for a short recess, at the end of which Portman told Judge Judy: "My office has instructed me not to proceed with this case at this time, your Honor. I am sorry for this inconvenience." Judge Judy responded: "If you stop now, counsel, this man will go free—is that what you want?" Portman replied: "Do what you have to do, your Honor." With that, Judge Judy entered a judgment of acquittal and set Larry free.

Twenty days later, Portman recharged Larry with the same offense. Larry again hired Bailey to defend him. Judge Judy presided over the second trial. Bailey made no pretrial motions. This time Portman did not falter, and in due course the jury at the second trial found Larry guilty as charged. Judge Judy sentenced him to prison for the period required by law, but she stayed the sentence and released him on his own recognizance pending appeal. Larry reluctantly paid Bailey's bill for the second trial—$5,000. However, Larry hired new lawyer Cochran for the appeal, and in due course the appellate court reversed the conviction and set aside the prison sentence, stating in the appellate opinion: "We have never seen a clearer double jeopardy violation, nor a worse error by a criminal defense attorney."

Will Bailey be *subject to civil liability* in a legal malpractice action brought by Larry for having missed the double jeopardy issue?

(A) No, because Larry never served jail time as a result of Bailey's error.

(B) No, even if Larry proves by a preponderance of evidence that he did not commit the assault on the coach.

(C) Yes, provided that Larry proves by a preponderance of evidence that he did not commit the assault on the coach.

(D) Yes, but Larry can recover only nominal damages.

Question 33

Lawyer London and her nonlawyer friend Ferguson created a partnership to serve people who want to invest in commercial real estate. Ferguson, a licensed real estate developer, finds promising commercial real estate projects, brings together groups of investors, and works with local planning authorities to gain approval for the projects. London drafts the legal documents for the projects, assists the investors with the legal technicalities, advises the investors on their tax liabilities, and does whatever legal work the investors need in connection with management and operation of the projects. London and Ferguson charge the investors a single fee for their work, and they divide the partnership profits 50%-50%.

Is London *subject to discipline*?

(A) No, provided the investors give informed, written consent to the potential conflicts of interest.

(B) No, because Ferguson does only development work, and London does only legal work.

(C) Yes, because Ferguson and London are partners in the business.

(D) Yes, because she is aiding Ferguson in the unauthorized practice of law.

GO ON TO THE NEXT PAGE

Question 34

Union Bank and Trust Company maintains a list of Approved Estate and Trust Lawyers as a service to Union customers who seek Union's advice on estate planning matters. When lawyer Lieu opened her trust and estate practice in town, she asked other lawyers how she could get on Union's approved list. They explained that Union lists lawyers who always name Union in wills and trust agreements they draft for clients who need an institutional executor or trustee. Union is one of the most stable and reputable banks in the state, and its fees for executor and trustee services are competitive with those of similar institutions.

In light of what she has been told by the other lawyers, *may* Lieu seek to have her name included on Union's list?

(A) No, because a tacit condition of being on the list is always to name Union as executor or trustee.

(B) No, because a lawyer must not solicit business through an intermediary.

(C) Yes, because naming Union causes no harm to clients who need an institutional executor or trustee.

(D) Yes, because those who use Union's list are already Union customers.

Question 35

Carla alleges that she was assaulted by Devlin, a very wealthy businessman. Carla contacted lawyer Lazar about representing her in a civil action against Devlin. After several lengthy discussions with Lazar about the merits of the case, Carla decided to employ attorney Arnold instead. Devlin was later charged with criminal assault in connection with this incident, and his trial was televised. Lazar watched the trial and was astonished when Carla testified to facts that Lazar knew from their previous discussions to be false.

Lazar sent a letter with a messenger over to the court to notify the court that Carla had perjured herself.

Were Lazar's actions *proper*?

(A) Yes, because his actions were necessary to prevent Carla from perpetrating a fraud on the court.

(B) Yes, because Carla committed a criminal act by testifying falsely.

(C) No, unless he sent copies of the letter to the prosecution and defense attorneys and they are given an opportunity to respond.

(D) No, because Lazar's information was gained during his discussions with Carla.

GO ON TO THE NEXT PAGE

Question 36

Lawyer Laden regularly represents Electratec, Inc., a manufacturer of electric kitchen appliances. One morning the president of Electratec called Laden and said excitedly:

> Did you read in this morning's paper about the woman who got electrocuted when she opened the door of her dishwasher? The paper said that the washer was three years old, and I'm pretty sure that it was one of ours. I found our quality control records from that period, and some of our washers left the plant without proper testing. Those records should have been shredded after two years, but somehow this batch was overlooked. I'm going to send them to the shredder now, unless you tell me that I can't.

Must Laden advise the president to keep the records?

(A) Yes, unless the company has a clearly established policy of shredding quality control records after two years.

(B) Yes, because the records have potential evidentiary value if the company gets sued.

(C) No, because at this point there is no litigation pending against the company respecting this matter.

(D) No, unless it was certain that the company was the manufacturer of the dishwasher in question.

Question 37

Lawyer Leavitt practices environmental law. He also happens to be one of the nation's leading experts on the environmental effects of filling wetlands. The legislature of State A has scheduled hearings on a bill to prohibit the filling of wetlands surrounding Clearwater Bay. One of Leavitt's regular clients is Bay View Development Company, which owns development rights to some of the wetlands in question. Bay View wants to fill its wetlands so that it can build low-cost housing for underprivileged families. Bay View hired Leavitt to appear as a witness at the legislative hearings and to testify in opposition to the ban on wetland filling. Leavitt appeared as a witness, identified himself as an expert on wetlands, and testified vigorously against the proposed legislation.

Was Leavitt's conduct *proper*?

(A) Yes, unless his testimony was contrary to his own beliefs about the environmental effects of filling wetlands.

(B) No, unless he informed the legislators that he was appearing in a representative capacity.

(C) Yes, because he is a leading expert on the environmental effects of filling wetlands.

(D) No, because a lawyer must not be a witness for his client on a contested matter.

GO ON TO THE NEXT PAGE

Question 38

Lawyer Ladner represents defendant Dewey in a criminal case. Dewey is charged with vehicular homicide, a felony. Under the criminal statute in question, a defendant is guilty if he caused the victim's death by driving a motor vehicle either intentionally or recklessly in disregard of the safety of others. In Dewey's case, the critical issue is whether the traffic light facing Dewey's traffic lane was green at a specified moment. If the light was green, then Dewey is not guilty, but if it was red, then Dewey is guilty.

Dewey himself has blocked the entire event from memory and has no idea whether the light was green or red. Five bystanders were in a position to see the light at the time in question. Ladner interviewed four of them. With varying degrees of uncertainty, all four of them told Ladner that they believe the light was red but that they are not positive. Based on their recollections, as well as certain physical evidence in the case, Ladner herself believes that the light was probably red, but of course she was not present at the scene and cannot be certain. Then Ladner interviewed the fifth bystander, Battista, who said that he simply could not remember what color the traffic light was. Ladner replied: "My client is facing 20 years in jail, and the whole case against him turns on the color of that light. My client and I would both be eternally grateful to you if you could testify that the light was green. Would you help us out?" After thinking it over, Battista said he would be glad to help by testifying that the light was green. At the trial, Ladner presented Battista's testimony that he saw the light, that he remembers what color it was, and that it was green. The jury believed Battista, and Dewey was acquitted.

Is Ladner *subject to criminal liability* for inducing Battista to testify falsely?

(A) Yes, because both Battista and Ladner knew that Battista did not remember what color the light was.

(B) Yes, because neither Battista nor Ladner was certain that the light was green.

(C) No, because neither Battista nor Ladner was certain what color the light was.

(D) No, because the defense lawyer in a criminal case must resolve all doubtful facts in her client's favor when she presents evidence on her client's behalf.

GO ON TO THE NEXT PAGE

Question 39

Law professor Pompman was selected as the neutral arbitrator of a boundary line dispute between land owners Owens and Osborne. Pompman decided the matter in favor of Owens. Shortly thereafter, Pompman quit his teaching position and entered private law practice. Osborne brought suit to have the arbitration award set aside. Owens asked Pompman to represent him in the suit.

If Pompman takes the case, will he be *subject to discipline*?

(A) No, because serving as Owens's lawyer is consistent with his decision as arbitrator in favor of Owens.

(B) No, because by seeking to hire Pompman, Owens is deemed to have consented to the conflict of interest.

(C) Yes, because his earlier service as neutral arbitrator creates a conflict of interest.

(D) Yes, because there is reasonable ground to doubt his impartiality in the case.

Question 40

Paul Poller brought a civil action to recover damages for personal injuries he suffered as the victim of alleged police brutality inflicted by defendant police officers Able, Baker, and Carter. The trial was widely reported by the media. The jury returned a verdict in favor of Poller and against the three police officers for $500 million. When Trial Judge Johnston received the verdict, he was shocked by the size of the award. Before dismissing the jurors, Judge Johnston directed the following statements to the jury:

When you people were sworn in as jurors in this case, you promised that you would deliver a verdict based on the evidence, and that you would not be swayed by passion or prejudice.

You have failed in those duties and made a mockery of justice. You should be ashamed of yourselves.

He then dismissed the jury, and the defense lawyers renewed their motion for judgment as a matter of law and, alternatively, moved for a new trial. Judge Johnston announced that he would rule on the motions the following Monday at 10 a.m. in open court. The press reports of the verdict and the judge's comments to the jury created a great public tumult in the city where the case was tried.

On the following Monday, the courtroom was jammed with reporters. Primarily for the purpose of educating the reporters, Judge Johnston first gave a detailed explanation of the legal requirements for granting a renewed motion for judgment as a matter of law and for granting a new trial motion. He then granted the renewed motion for judgment as a matter of law and, alternatively, the motion for a new trial.

Were Judge Johnston's actions *proper*?

(A) Both the statements to the jury and the communication with the reporters were proper.

(B) Neither the communication with the reporters nor the statements to the jury were proper.

(C) The statements to the jury were proper, but the communication with the reporters was not.

(D) The communication with the reporters was proper, but the statements to the jury were not.

GO ON TO THE NEXT PAGE

Question 41

Client Corrales lives in State A and is a regular client of attorney Amundson, who is admitted to practice only in State A. When Corrales was on vacation in distant State B, she was injured in a car accident caused by a resident of State B. Corrales hired Amundson to represent her in a civil action against the State B driver. For reasons of jurisdiction and venue, the case had to be filed and tried in State B. The written fee agreement between Corrales and Amundson provided that:

(1) Amundson would assume full responsibility for the case as lead lawyer;

(2) Corrales would pay Amundson 40% of the net recovery after deduction of litigation expenses;

(3) Amundson would associate State B lawyer Linz to serve as trial counsel in State B;

(4) Linz would assume responsibility only for his work as trial counsel; and

(5) Amundson would pay Linz an appropriate portion of the 40% contingent fee.

Would it be *proper* for Amundson to split his fee with Linz under the circumstances described above?

(A) No, because Amundson is not admitted in State B.

(B) No, because the share that each lawyer will receive was not disclosed in the written fee agreement.

(C) Yes, because Linz was assuming responsibility for his work as trial counsel.

(D) Yes, because there was a written fee agreement.

Question 42

Lawyer Lawrence is a partner in the firm of Lawrence & Loeb. That firm regularly provides legal services to three major banks and two other important lending institutions in the community of Farmdale. Lawrence has been invited to become a member of the board of directors of the Farmdale Legal Aid Society, the group that sets overall governing policies for the local legal aid office. One of the major issues that will soon face the board of directors is whether to amend the Case Intake Guidelines to allow the legal aid office to represent clients in disputes with banks and other lending agencies.

Which of the following statements is most nearly correct?

(A) Lawrence *may* join the board of directors, but she *must* refrain from participating in the decision about the Case Intake Guidelines.

(B) Lawrence will be *subject to discipline* if she joins the board of directors because service on the board is in conflict with the interests of her firm's bank and lending institution clients.

(C) It would be *proper* for Lawrence to join the board of directors, and it would be *proper* for her to participate in the decision about the Case Intake Guidelines.

(D) Lawrence *may* join the board of directors to help discharge her pro bono obligation, and she *may* vote in favor of amending the Case Intake Guidelines in order to make it easier for low income persons to sue banks and other lending institutions.

GO ON TO THE NEXT PAGE

Question 43

Twelve-year-old Jimmy was badly injured when he was struck by a dump truck owned by Damassa Construction Corp. and driven by Damassa's employee Edmonds. Jimmy and his parents sued Damassa and Edmonds. The first count of their complaint alleges that Edmonds drove negligently while acting within the scope of his duties for Damassa, and that Damassa is therefore liable for Jimmy's injuries. The second count alleges that Edmonds drove negligently while on a frolic of his own, and that Edmonds is therefore liable for Jimmy's injuries.

Damassa hired lawyer Lazarro to defend both Damassa and Edmonds. Lazarro conducted a careful investigation of the facts and concluded that Edmonds was in no way negligent; he was driving slowly and carefully when Jimmy suddenly ran out into traffic from between two parked cars. Lazarro further concluded that Edmonds was acting within the scope of his duties when the accident happened. Lazarro concluded that he could win the case because of the lack of negligence, and that he could effectively represent both Edmonds and Damassa. He then carefully explained the potential conflicts of interest to both of them and obtained their informed, written consent to the joint representation. After exhaustive discovery proceedings, Lazarro remained convinced that Edmonds was not negligent, but he nonetheless explained the potential conflicts to Edmonds and Damassa a second time and again obtained their informed, written consent to the joint representation. Three weeks before the case was scheduled for trial, counsel for the plaintiffs moved to disqualify Lazarro due to a conflict of interest between Edmonds and Damassa.

Must the trial judge disqualify Lazarro?

(A) No, because there is no actual or potential conflict between Edmonds and Damassa.

(B) No, because Edmonds and Damassa gave informed, written consent to the joint representation.

(C) Yes, because the potential conflict creates an appearance of impropriety.

(D) Yes, even though Edmonds and Damassa gave informed, written consent to the joint representation.

Question 44

Client Carlin hired attorney Adler to put together a complex real estate syndicate. In connection with that work, Carlin disclosed to Adler a great deal of confidential information about Carlin's financial affairs. When the task was about half completed, Adler's wife was killed in a car accident, and his family's house burned down, all in the same week. Adler was so emotionally and physically drained that he felt he could not competently continue with the work for Carlin. Carlin refused to allow Adler to withdraw, stating: "Listen, Adler, you are the only person I trust to handle this matter. I know you are distraught, but hard work may help take your mind off the disasters that have befallen you." Adler begged Carlin to allow him to turn the files over to Adler's law partner, Parner, an excellent real estate lawyer who was completely trustworthy and perfectly competent to handle the matter. Carlin refused to allow his files to be turned over to any other lawyer and insisted that Adler himself promptly complete the work.

What *should* Adler do?

(A) Turn the files over to Parner, and remain available to assist Parner to the extent possible.

(B) Withdraw and turn Carlin's files over to Carlin.

(C) Set Carlin's work aside until he recovers from the ills that have befallen him.

(D) Continue with the matter and do the best that he can under the circumstances.

Question 45

Lawyer Lubner is defending client Marine Supply, Inc. in a civil action brought by the State Attorney General under the State Corrupt Practices Act of 1931. That statute makes it a civil offense for any person or business entity to bribe or give a kickback to a state official. The statute authorizes fines of up to $100,000 per transaction for any violation. Marine Supply has a strict corporate policy that prohibits its employees from bribing or giving kickbacks to anyone. Employees who violate the policy are subject to immediate discharge and are required to indemnify Marine Supply for any loss it suffers as a consequence of the violation.

The Attorney General has noticed the depositions of dozens of Marine Supply employees, including one Dan Dowling. Prior to his recent retirement, Dowling was the sales manager of Marine Supply. Lubner met with Dowling to prepare him for his deposition. At the outset of the interview, Lubner agreed to represent Dowling without charge, and Lubner told Dowling that anything said between them would be confidential. During the interview, Lubner asked Dowling whether he had ever bribed any State A officials. Dowling responded: "Certainly. All our competitors were doing it too, and I had to do it to sell anything to the state."

What course of action *may* Lubner pursue at this point?

(A) Withdraw from the case and inform the Attorney General what Dowling said.

(B) Withdraw from the case and keep Dowling's statement in confidence.

(C) Withdraw from representing Dowling and inform Marine Supply what Dowling said.

(D) Continue in the case, inform Marine Supply what Dowling said, and advise Marine Supply to seek prompt settlement.

Question 46

Criminal defendant DeVries exercised his Fifth Amendment privilege against self-incrimination and elected not to testify on his own behalf at his trial. Prosecutor Prichard presented compelling evidence of DeVries's guilt. In her closing argument to the jury, Prichard made the following statements:

I.   DeVries knows where he was on that fatal night. I have presented the testimony of three witnesses that he was with the victim. Did DeVries deny it? No! He sat there saying nothing.

II. What are you to make of defense witness Fergus Grutz? You heard evidence that Grutz has twice been convicted of perjury. Could there be better proof that Grutz is a liar?

III. You may wonder why I cross-examined defense witness Emma Schlarp so vigorously. When you've been a prosecutor as long as I have, you can tell who is truthful and who is not. Was Emma Schlarp telling you the truth? I don't think so. Do you?

IV. Is DeVries guilty? That's what you have to decide, but I hope you will conclude that the evidence points only one way: guilt beyond a reasonable doubt.

Which of Prichard's statements were *proper*?

(A) None of the above.

(B) I., II., and III. only.

(C) II. and IV. only.

(D) I., II., and IV. only.

Question 47

Casper, a Hollywood movie producer who was charged under a criminal statute for unfair trade practices, now faces a civil claim under the same statute. Casper retains attorney Adams to represent him in both suits. Adams is a nationally known defense attorney who has represented many famous people. Most recently, he defended a celebrity in a notorious murder case that held the country rapt for several weeks. Adams explains to Casper that the representation is very complex and would take a majority of his time for several months. Given Adams's steep hourly rate, Casper's legal fees would likely be around $1 million. Casper is short on cash and makes the following proposal: If Adams will represent him in both the civil and criminal suits, Casper will produce a movie based on Adams's most famous past cases, told from the lawyer's viewpoint. Adams would have complete creative control and would be entitled to all of the movie's profits, which could be anything from $0 to $100 million. Casper had his personal attorney draw up a proposal to this effect, and Casper submitted it to Adams.

Assuming that Adams receives any consent necessary from his former clients who might be portrayed in the movie, is this proposed arrangement *proper*?

(A) Yes, but only if the payment from the movie profits is for the civil suit only.

(B) Yes, but only if the ultimate amount paid to Adams is not excessive in light of the work done.

(C) No, because any amount over $1 million is clearly excessive, and this arrangement could be worth $100 million.

(D) No, because a lawyer must not acquire media rights to a story concerning the lawyer's representation of a client.

Question 48

Patent attorney Amari focuses her practice on patents that involve genetically engineered medicines. Representatives of Biogenco had a preliminary conversation with Amari about representing Biogenco in a patent infringement action against Turner-Kline Pharmaceuticals, Inc. Amari had never represented either company previously. Biogenco's representatives talked to Amari for more than an hour about Biogenco's patent and about Turner-Kline's supposedly infringing product. This conversation covered only public information, nothing confidential. Biogenco's representatives detected a distinct lack of enthusiasm from Amari, and they ended the conversation cordially but without hiring her. In due course, Biogenco hired a different patent attorney and sued Turner-Kline for patent infringement. Turner-Kline hired Amari as defense counsel in the infringement case. Biogenco's attorney promptly made a motion in the trial court to disqualify Amari because of her earlier conversation with Biogenco's representatives.

Is Amari *subject to disqualification*?

(A) Yes, because Biogenco had previously consulted Amari on the same matter.

(B) Yes, because the infringement suit is substantially related to the earlier conversation between Amari and Biogenco's representatives.

(C) No, because Biogenco was never Amari's client.

(D) No, because the prior conversation between Amari and Biogenco's representatives did not involve confidential information.

GO ON TO THE NEXT PAGE

Question 49

Plaintiff Prentice, represented by lawyer Leer, brought suit in federal district court against Exterminate, Inc., a pest control company, and nine chemical companies for "grave physical and emotional injuries" Prentice suffered after accidentally inhaling cockroach spray emanating from an apartment that had recently been fumigated by Exterminate. Leer's theory for suing the nine chemical companies was that Exterminate had probably purchased its cockroach spray from at least one of the nine chemical companies. The law firm of Alvarez & Aarons represented one of the nine chemical company defendants, Calloway Chemicals Corp. By using depositions and document demands early in the discovery phase of the case, the Alvarez firm established that Calloway had never at any time sold any type of chemical to Exterminate. The Alvarez firm then moved for summary judgment as to Calloway. Leer offered no substantive response to that motion, but rather filed a countermotion to disqualify the Alvarez firm on the ground that the firm was "seeking on behalf of its client to evade the jurisdiction of this court," that the firm was "biased against the plaintiff" and was seeking to "deprive plaintiff of a judgment on the merits," and that the firm was "guilty of gross conflicts of interest," the specifics of which were not stated.

The trial judge denied the motion to disqualify the Alvarez firm and granted Calloway's summary judgment motion, whereupon Leer immediately moved for a rehearing, moved to stay the trial judge's two orders, and moved to disqualify the trial judge for "demonstrated gross bias and prejudice against the plaintiff and in favor of the defendant Calloway," the nature of the bias and prejudice being unspecified. The disposition of these motions consumed an entire year, due to Leer's obstreperousness and his repeated requests for postponements and extensions of time. Meanwhile, the Alvarez firm had to stay actively involved in the case to protect Calloway's position. This year-long ordeal ended up costing Calloway $14,500 in attorneys' fees and $6,750 in litigation costs.

Is Leer *subject to litigation sanction* in the form of an order against Leer personally to pay the $14,500 in attorneys' fees and the $6,750 in litigation costs?

(A) No, because Leer was representing his client zealously within the bounds of the law as he was required to do by the rules of legal ethics.

(B) No, because litigation sanctions can be imposed only on parties to the litigation, not on their lawyers personally.

(C) Yes, even if Leer was acting in good faith, mistakenly but genuinely believing in the validity of the legal positions he took.

(D) Yes, provided that Calloway can show that Leer either intentionally or recklessly took frivolous legal positions in order to harass Calloway.

GO ON TO THE NEXT PAGE

Question 50

Police officer Owens was charged with murder. He is alleged to have savagely beaten and ultimately killed a teenage gang member in the course of an arrest. Neither the police department nor officer Owens's union was willing to provide legal counsel for his defense, and Owens himself lacked funds to hire private counsel. The public defender's office could not represent him due to a conflict of interest from a related case. The trial court therefore appointed lawyer Lee to defend Owens. Lee is only three years out of law school. Lee practices criminal defense, but he has never handled a murder case before.

For which of the following reasons *may* Lee decline the court appointment?

I.   Based on what he has read in the newspapers, he sincerely believes that Owens is guilty.

II. He has no experience in the defense of a murder case.

III. He is of the same race as the teenage victim, and he is in sympathy with the plight of young gang members.

IV. Many of his clients are of the same race as the teenage victim, and they will be irate if he defends Owens.

(A) None of the above.

(B) III. and IV. only.

(C) II. only.

(D) I. and II. only.

Question 51

Sigmund and Fritz are partners in a bakery that makes Austrian pastry. Their partnership agreement says that they will share the work and the profits equally. They are the best of friends, but they constantly bicker—each claims that the other is taking an unfair share of the profits and shirking on the work. Six months ago, they hired lawyer Ludwig to act as a third-party neutral, to help them resolve their differences once and for all. At the outset, Ludwig explained that he would be strictly neutral between them; he would not be representing either one, and neither of them would be entitled to the protections afforded by an attorney-client relationship. After a long series of meetings with them (sometimes separately, sometimes jointly), Ludwig proposed a solution. Sigmund and Fritz liked his solution, reduced it to writing, and signed it, vowing to end their bickering forever. Six months later, the feud erupted again, worse than ever. Fritz asked Ludwig's law firm to represent him in a lawsuit against Sigmund, seeking to declare the partnership at an end and to bar Sigmund from entering the bakery premises.

Which of the following is most nearly correct?

(A) Ludwig is *subject to discipline* for his failed effort to serve both Sigmund and Fritz when their interests were patently in conflict.

(B) It would be *proper* for Ludwig to represent Fritz in the lawsuit, even without the informed, written consent of Sigmund.

(C) Ludwig's law partner Leonora *may* represent Fritz in the lawsuit, but only if Sigmund is notified in writing, and only if Ludwig is timely screened and does not share in the fee earned in the lawsuit.

(D) Ludwig's law partner Leonora would be *subject to discipline* for representing Fritz in the lawsuit, even if Ludwig is timely screened and does not share in the fee earned in the lawsuit.

GO ON TO THE NEXT PAGE

Question 52

After graduating from law school, attorney Ayala was admitted to practice in State One, and not in any other jurisdiction. She joined the United States Army Judge Advocate General's ("JAG") Corps—the corps of lawyer-soldiers who provide legal services to the Army throughout the world. After completing her officer training and her training in military law, she was assigned to the JAG office at Fort MacArthur in State Two. Even though she was not admitted to practice in State Two, she was assigned to the legal assistance desk. According to Army regulations, her job is to provide legal services to military personnel and their dependents concerning a wide range of personal legal problems, including civil, domestic, and financial matters. Corporal and Mrs. Smithers ask Ayala for legal advice about financing a mobile home, which they plan to put in a mobile home park located in the town closest to Fort MacArthur. Ayala knows absolutely nothing about the business and legal issues involved in financing a mobile home.

Would it be **proper** for Ayala to give the requested advice to the Smitherses?

(A) Yes, but only if she does the research necessary to give competent advice on mobile home financing.

(B) Yes, but only if she gets admitted pro hac vice to practice in State Two.

(C) No, because she is not admitted to practice general civil law in State Two.

(D) No, because mobile home financing is not directly related to the Army's mission.

Question 53

Personal injury lawyer Lingenfelter and orthopedic surgeon Sturgeon are good friends, and they have a high mutual regard for each other's professional abilities. One day on the golf course, they made a reciprocal referral agreement: whenever Lingenfelter has a personal injury client with need for an orthopedic surgeon, Lingenfelter promised to refer the client to Sturgeon. Similarly, whenever Sturgeon has an injured patient with a need for a personal injury lawyer, Sturgeon promised to refer the patient to Lingenfelter. The agreement was oral, not written, and there was no mention of an expiration date; both women simply assumed that the agreement would continue indefinitely until one or the other wanted to end it. Likewise, they did not discuss whether the agreement would be exclusive; both women simply assumed that neither of them would refer someone to a competitor of the other.

Was it **proper** for Lingenfelter to make this agreement with Sturgeon?

(A) No, because the agreement was not reduced to writing.

(B) No, because the agreement was of an indefinite duration.

(C) No, because a lawyer must not give anything of value to a person for recommending her services.

(D) No, because a lawyer must not enter into a reciprocal referral agreement with a non-lawyer.

GO ON TO THE NEXT PAGE

Question 54

The Attorney General's Office of State One does not include any lawyers who are skilled in the field of condemnation law (the law of eminent domain). Consequently, whenever State One wants to use its power of eminent domain to condemn some private property for a public use, the Attorney General must hire a private law firm to represent the state in the condemnation proceedings. In contrast to the paltry fees that State One pays to appointed defense counsel in criminal cases, the Attorney General pays quite handsomely for condemnation work. In State One, the Attorney General is a partisan political position that is filled by a contested election every four years. The law firm of Feldspar & Flynt limits its practice to condemnation law. The founding partner, Reginald "Rocky" Feldspar, is an 87-year-old multimillionaire who remains active on the firm's management committee. When it is time to elect a new Attorney General, Feldspar makes large donations from his personal wealth to each candidate who has any reasonable chance of becoming the next Attorney General. The other members of the firm's management committee know about Feldspar's contributions, and they have formally and informally expressed the firm's thanks for helping the firm obtain future appointments by the Attorney General.

May the firm accept an appointment from the new Attorney General to represent State One in a condemnation case?

(A) Yes, because Feldspar makes his contributions from his personal wealth, and he has a constitutional right to participate personally in the political process.

(B) Yes, because Feldspar's personal political contributions cannot be imputed to the law firm.

(C) No, because a lawyer or law firm must not accept appointed legal work from a governmental official after making a political contribution for the purpose of obtaining such work.

(D) No, because to accept such an appointment would create an appearance of impropriety in light of Feldspar's political contributions.

Question 55

Retired lawyer Regeria practiced admiralty and maritime law for 45 years in Maine. He stopped paying his bar dues in Maine when he retired, and he is no longer licensed to practice there. He and his wife moved to a retirement village in New Mexico, but he did not seek to become licensed to practice law in New Mexico. After a few months of playing golf and puttering in the garden, Regeria got bored and started missing the challenges of law practice. He therefore joined the unpaid staff of volunteer lawyers at the Rio Grande Walk-In Legal Advice Clinic, which is run by a nonprofit organization. The clinic's purpose is to offer free, quick, accurate, compassionate legal advice to walk-in clients who cannot afford ordinary legal service and who have legal problems that can be solved quickly, without litigation or other time-consuming procedures. Before they ever see one of the clinic's lawyers, all of the clients must give informed consent to the limited nature of the legal services they will receive. Regeria works at the clinic three days a week, and he dispenses legal advice on all sorts of matters—although he has yet to find a client who needed admiralty or maritime advice. Regeria enjoys the work because it makes him feel useful again, and because it gives him a cornucopia of interesting stories to tell his wife about his clients' various legal troubles.

Which of the following statements are correct?

I. Regeria is **subject to discipline** for practicing law without a license.

II. Regeria is **subject to discipline** for telling his wife about his clients' legal troubles.

III. Regeria's volunteer work is **proper** because one does not need to be licensed to dispense legal advice at a quick-service clinic like this one.

IV. Regeria's conversations with his wife are **proper** because no confidential lawyer-client relationship is formed at a quick-service clinic like this one.

(A) III. and IV. only.

(B) II. and III. only.

(C) I. and IV. only.

(D) I. and II. only.

GO ON TO THE NEXT PAGE

Question 56

Lawyer Lim practices real estate law in State One, an old-fashioned jurisdiction in which almost every real estate transaction requires the services of one or more lawyers. Lim is also licensed by State One as a real estate broker. Lim conducts her law practice and her real estate brokerage business in a single office, using one secretary and one paralegal as her support staff. Lim specializes in small, relatively old apartment buildings (from 4-12 units) that are not in peak condition. They make good investments because they can be bought cheap, fixed up, and leased at favorable rates. Lim generates most of her business by discovering who owns a likely looking building and then making a face-to-face pitch to the owners, trying to interest them in selling and using her to find a buyer. After the owners sign her up as their real estate broker, Lim lets them know that she can also do the necessary legal work—the title search, the financing documents, the land transfer documents, and the like.

Is Lim *subject to discipline*?

(A) Yes, because a person who is engaged in full-time law practice must not conduct a related business from a single office.

(B) Yes, because a person who offers legal services along with real estate brokerage services must not initiate face-to-face contact with prospective clients to drum up business.

(C) No, because Lim's real estate brokerage services are ancillary to her law practice, and the two operations are conducted from a single office.

(D) No, so long as her face-to-face pitch to the owners of apartment buildings is truthful and not misleading.

Question 57

Lawyer Langdell was a widely admired, highly compensated, trial lawyer in solo practice. He represented clients in all types of civil and criminal litigation, mostly in high-profile cases that draw a lot of media attention. The governor of the state where Langdell practiced had been harshly criticized for appointing appellate judges who lack significant experience as trial counsel. Hoping to silence his critics, the governor appointed Langdell to serve out the remaining seven years of recently deceased Supreme Court Justice Korptz's 12-year term. After the seven years, Langdell can run for election to a new 12-year term. Before taking the oath as judge, Langdell sold his entire law practice—books, client files, office lease, furniture, and goodwill—to attorney Altamont. Langdell gave appropriate advance notice to the clients, and Altamont covenanted that he would not raise their legal fees. A few years later, one of the cases that Langdell transferred to Altamont came before the State Supreme Court on appeal.

Which of the following propositions are true?

I.   Langdell's sale of his law practice to Altamont was *proper*.

II. Altamont's covenant not to increase the fees paid by Langdell's clients was *proper*.

III. A practicing lawyer who is appointed to a judgeship *may* sell his law practice.

IV. Langdell *must* disqualify himself from the case involving his former client.

V.   Langdell *may* participate in the decision of the case involving his former client, provided that all of the other supreme court justices give their informed consent.

(A) I., II., and V. only.

(B) I., II., III., and IV. only.

(C) II. and V. only.

(D) III. and IV. only.

GO ON TO THE NEXT PAGE

Question 58

Client Cox hired lawyer Lerner to draft a will for him. Cox willed his entire estate to Ruby Riddle, the 43-year-old widow of Ralph Riddle. Cox told Lerner in confidence that he was neither a relative nor a friend of the Riddles. Cox explained that he felt a moral obligation to Ruby because he had killed her husband, Ralph, and he had never become a suspect or confessed his sin to anyone. One day after signing the will, Cox committed suicide. In due course, all of Cox's assets were distributed to Ruby Riddle, and the probate court closed his estate and discharged his executor. Lerner never told Ruby or anyone else that Cox had confessed to killing Ralph. Now, a few years later, an enthusiastic young prosecutor is charging Harry Hapless with murdering Ralph in the first degree with aggravating circumstances, and the prosecutor is seeking the death penalty.

May lawyer Lerner voluntarily tell Hapless's defense counsel what Cox told him in confidence about killing Ralph?

(A) Yes, Lerner not only *may*, but he *must*, tell the defense counsel what Cox told him.

(B) Yes, Lerner *may* tell, but he would not be *subject to discipline* if he decides not to do so.

(C) No, Lerner would be *subject to discipline* if he told defense counsel because the attorney-client privilege survives the death of the client.

(D) No, because Cox's confidential confession to Lerner would be inadmissible hearsay if offered against the prosecution in Hapless's case.

Question 59

The University of West Dakota ("UWD") receives 45% of its annual budget from the state of West Dakota. The other 55% of the budget comes from private sources. UWD is chartered by the Constitution of West Dakota, and it is regarded for all purposes as a unit of West Dakota's government. The governing body of UWD is its Board of Overseers, a group of 17 West Dakota citizens. The chief executive officer of UWD is the Chancellor, and the chief legal officer is the General Counsel. UWD has always strived for a student body and faculty that are diverse in age, politics, wealth, race, nationality, religion, sex, and sexual orientation. One year ago, the voters of West Dakota passed a ballot initiative that prohibits all units of the West Dakota government, including UWD, from considering a person's race when offering employment or admission to school. The initiative prohibits giving any state funds to a governmental unit that violates the initiative. With reluctance, the UWD Board of Overseers adopted a new university-wide regulation that requires all admissions officers and hiring committees to obey the initiative. The West Dakota Supreme Court sustained the constitutionality of the initiative, and the United States Supreme Court denied certiorari. Lawyer LaRue is one of 15 lawyers in the UWD General Counsel's in-house law office. The General Counsel assigned LaRue to work with UWD's School of Engineering to develop new admissions criteria that will comply with the initiative. At the outset, LaRue reminded Engineering's Admissions Director that she was not his lawyer, but rather the university's lawyer. The Admissions Director told LaRue: "The engineering profession in this state has long been dominated by white males. You can draft whatever new admissions criteria you wish, but in practice, I will continue to consider race when I admit students because I believe that's the right thing to do." Deep in her heart, LaRue agrees with the Admissions Director.

Which of the following *may* LaRue do in responding to this situation?

I.   Keep the Admissions Director's statement in confidence, even if she reasonably believes that UWD is likely to lose its state funding as a consequence.

II. Promptly disclose the Admissions Director's statement to the Attorney General of West Dakota, who is the official in charge of enforcing the voter initiative.

III. Attempt to convince the Admissions Director to obey the voter initiative, and if he refuses, then disclose the situation to UWD's General Counsel.

IV. Anonymously leak the Admissions Director's statement to the UWD Board of Overseers.

(A) III. only.

(B) II. or IV. only.

(C) III. and IV. only.

(D) I. only.

Question 60

Prospective client Corbin comes to the law offices of Lewis & Smith seeking a lawyer to defend him in a civil action for aggravated assault and battery. Lawyer Lewis agrees to talk preliminarily with Corbin, just to obtain enough background information to decide whether she can defend him. Corbin explains that he has an alcohol problem; indeed, he gets roaring drunk about three nights a week. On the night in question, Corbin said that a loud-mouthed stranger in his neighborhood tavern made a derogatory comment about Corbin's favorite basketball team. Corbin responded by "tapping" the stranger over the head with a pool cue, not once but four times. At that point, Lewis suddenly realizes that Corbin must be the rotten husband in the hotly disputed divorce and child custody case in which her law partner, Smith, is representing the aggrieved wife. Lewis stops Corbin and tells him that she cannot defend him in the assault and battery case because of Smith's work for Corbin's wife. Corbin responds: "Oh, man, I didn't know that your Smith is her Smith!" With that, Corbin leaves the law office.

Which of the following is most nearly true?

(A) Smith *must* withdraw from representing the wife because Lewis has received confidential information from Corbin that would be harmful to Corbin if used in the divorce and child custody case.

(B) It would be *proper* for Smith to represent the wife and for Lewis to represent Corbin in the assault and battery case because the two matters are not substantially related.

(C) Smith *may* continue representing the wife, but only if the wife gives informed, written consent.

(D) Smith *may* continue representing the wife if Lewis is screened off from participation in the case and obtains no part of the fee in the case, and if the firm promptly sends Corbin written notice of the situation.

STOP

ANSWER SHEET

1 Ⓐ Ⓑ Ⓒ Ⓓ		31 Ⓐ Ⓑ Ⓒ Ⓓ	
2 Ⓐ Ⓑ Ⓒ Ⓓ		32 Ⓐ Ⓑ Ⓒ Ⓓ	
3 Ⓐ Ⓑ Ⓒ Ⓓ		33 Ⓐ Ⓑ Ⓒ Ⓓ	
4 Ⓐ Ⓑ Ⓒ Ⓓ		34 Ⓐ Ⓑ Ⓒ Ⓓ	
5 Ⓐ Ⓑ Ⓒ Ⓓ		35 Ⓐ Ⓑ Ⓒ Ⓓ	
6 Ⓐ Ⓑ Ⓒ Ⓓ		36 Ⓐ Ⓑ Ⓒ Ⓓ	
7 Ⓐ Ⓑ Ⓒ Ⓓ		37 Ⓐ Ⓑ Ⓒ Ⓓ	
8 Ⓐ Ⓑ Ⓒ Ⓓ		38 Ⓐ Ⓑ Ⓒ Ⓓ	
9 Ⓐ Ⓑ Ⓒ Ⓓ		39 Ⓐ Ⓑ Ⓒ Ⓓ	
10 Ⓐ Ⓑ Ⓒ Ⓓ		40 Ⓐ Ⓑ Ⓒ Ⓓ	
11 Ⓐ Ⓑ Ⓒ Ⓓ		41 Ⓐ Ⓑ Ⓒ Ⓓ	
12 Ⓐ Ⓑ Ⓒ Ⓓ		42 Ⓐ Ⓑ Ⓒ Ⓓ	
13 Ⓐ Ⓑ Ⓒ Ⓓ		43 Ⓐ Ⓑ Ⓒ Ⓓ	
14 Ⓐ Ⓑ Ⓒ Ⓓ		44 Ⓐ Ⓑ Ⓒ Ⓓ	
15 Ⓐ Ⓑ Ⓒ Ⓓ		45 Ⓐ Ⓑ Ⓒ Ⓓ	
16 Ⓐ Ⓑ Ⓒ Ⓓ		46 Ⓐ Ⓑ Ⓒ Ⓓ	
17 Ⓐ Ⓑ Ⓒ Ⓓ		47 Ⓐ Ⓑ Ⓒ Ⓓ	
18 Ⓐ Ⓑ Ⓒ Ⓓ		48 Ⓐ Ⓑ Ⓒ Ⓓ	
19 Ⓐ Ⓑ Ⓒ Ⓓ		49 Ⓐ Ⓑ Ⓒ Ⓓ	
20 Ⓐ Ⓑ Ⓒ Ⓓ		50 Ⓐ Ⓑ Ⓒ Ⓓ	
21 Ⓐ Ⓑ Ⓒ Ⓓ		51 Ⓐ Ⓑ Ⓒ Ⓓ	
22 Ⓐ Ⓑ Ⓒ Ⓓ		52 Ⓐ Ⓑ Ⓒ Ⓓ	
23 Ⓐ Ⓑ Ⓒ Ⓓ		53 Ⓐ Ⓑ Ⓒ Ⓓ	
24 Ⓐ Ⓑ Ⓒ Ⓓ		54 Ⓐ Ⓑ Ⓒ Ⓓ	
25 Ⓐ Ⓑ Ⓒ Ⓓ		55 Ⓐ Ⓑ Ⓒ Ⓓ	
26 Ⓐ Ⓑ Ⓒ Ⓓ		56 Ⓐ Ⓑ Ⓒ Ⓓ	
27 Ⓐ Ⓑ Ⓒ Ⓓ		57 Ⓐ Ⓑ Ⓒ Ⓓ	
28 Ⓐ Ⓑ Ⓒ Ⓓ		58 Ⓐ Ⓑ Ⓒ Ⓓ	
29 Ⓐ Ⓑ Ⓒ Ⓓ		59 Ⓐ Ⓑ Ⓒ Ⓓ	
30 Ⓐ Ⓑ Ⓒ Ⓓ		60 Ⓐ Ⓑ Ⓒ Ⓓ	

Answer to Question 1

(A) Yes, it would be proper for Judge Jackman to take the steps mentioned because she has received information indicating a substantial likelihood that Abbott has violated a legal ethics rule. Abbott has apparently violated ABA Model Rule 1.8(c), which generally prohibits a lawyer from drafting a will under which he will receive a substantial gift. A judge who receives "information indicating a substantial likelihood" that a lawyer has violated a legal ethics rule *should* take "appropriate action," which may include direct communication with the lawyer, direct action, and reporting the violation to the appropriate authority. If a judge *knows* that a lawyer has committed an ethics violation that raises a substantial question about the lawyer's honesty, trustworthiness, or fitness to practice law, then the judge *must* inform the appropriate authority. [CJC 3D(2)] (B) is wrong because Judge Jackman does not have "personal knowledge" as that term is used in evidence law. [*See* CJC, Terminology] (C) is wrong because the duties imposed by CJC 3D(2) are not confined to lawyers in the judge's own jurisdiction. (D) is wrong because "appropriate action" may include direct communication with the lawyer who violated the legal ethics rule. [CJC 3D(2), Commentary]

Answer to Question 2

(A) When ordered to do so by a tribunal, a lawyer must continue representation notwithstanding good cause for terminating the representation. [ABA Model Rule 1.16(c)] Even if Long was absolutely convinced of his own incompetence, he is subject to discipline for abandoning the teacher in violation of the trial judge's order. (B) is wrong for the reason stated above. (C) is wrong because a lawyer is not subject to discipline for taking on a case that he is not competent to handle if he puts in the time and study needed to make

himself competent to handle it. [*See* Comment 4 to ABA Model Rule 1.1] Having volunteered to take on the case, Long's duty was to put in the requisite time and study. (D) is wrong because a lawyer's duties of competence, diligence, and loyalty are no lower in a pro bono matter than in a fee-paying matter.

Answer to Question 3

(A) Aulet is subject to discipline because he communicated with a juror about a pending case. During the trial of a case, *no lawyer*, whether or not connected with the case, is allowed to communicate with a juror *about the case*. [ABA Model Rule 3.5(b)—referring the matter to local law, which generally prohibits communication with a juror during the trial of the case or jury deliberations; *see also* ABA Model Rule 8.4(d)—proscribing conduct that is prejudicial to the administration of justice] (B) is wrong because Aulet should not have communicated with Jimmerson about the case at all, whatever the quality of his advice. (C) is wrong because Aulet is subject to discipline for communicating with a juror, regardless of whether he was or was not competent in the field of criminal law. (D) is wrong because the prohibition against a lawyer communicating with a juror while a trial is pending applies to all lawyers, not just to those connected with the case.

Answer to Question 4

(C) Only item III. is true. Item I. is improper because it involves fee splitting with a nonlawyer. [ABA Model Rule 5.4(a)] Item II. is not grounds for discipline. When Duffy's work is properly supervised by Schnell, Schnell is not assisting a nonlawyer to engage in unauthorized practice. [*See* ABA Model Rule 5.5(a) and Comment 2] Item III. is proper because a nonlawyer employee of a law firm may participate in a retirement plan that is funded by legal fees.

[ABA Model Rule 5.4(a)(3)] Item IV. is not proper because a nonlawyer must not hold stock in an incorporated law firm. [ABA Model Rule 5.4(d)(1)]

Answer to Question 5

(A) Generally speaking, a lawyer must not represent a client in a presently pending piece of litigation and simultaneously oppose that client in a different piece of litigation, without each client's informed, written consent. [*See* Comment 6 to ABA Model Rule 1.7] Here, Louder may have believed that the conflict of interest that would have been created by his undertaking representation of Pringle was unconsentable. Thus, he acted properly in declining to represent Pringle, even though Pringle's case was unrelated to the one in which Louder was representing Dr. Dooley. However, a lawyer does owe a duty of reasonable care to a prospective client, even though no attorney-client relationship ever comes about. [*See* Restatement of the Law Governing Lawyers (hereinafter "Restatement") §15] Ordinarily, that duty would include cautioning the prospective client about an impending statute of limitations deadline. [*Id.*] Here, however, a cautionary word to Pringle would constitute disloyalty to the existing client, Dr. Dooley. [*See, e.g.,* Flatt v. Superior Court, 9 Cal. 4th 275 (1994)—warning prospective client about statute of limitations was not required when it would be disloyal to present client] Louder therefore acted properly in simply suggesting that Pringle consult other counsel. (B) is incorrect because a lawyer does owe a duty of reasonable care to a prospective client. (C) is incorrect because Louder did have a legal and ethical reason to reject Pringle as a client: the simultaneous representation of Dr. Dooley in the unrelated matter. (D) is incorrect because the foreseeability of the harm is not the whole of the analysis. Even if Louder could foresee that Pringle would dawdle and let the statute of limitations run, Louder's duty of loyalty to Dr. Dooley required him not to warn Pringle about the statute of limitations.

Answer to Question 6

(D) Lucero must turn over all of the papers to Chason. When a lawyer is fired, he must return all "papers and property to which the client is entitled." [ABA Model Rule 1.16(d)] In this case, Chason is entitled to all the papers Lucero has prepared. Under the law of many states, an attorney can assert a lien on client papers in her possession to secure the payment of her fee, but here Chason has paid Lucero for all the work Lucero did. (A) is wrong because Lucero must turn over the memoranda as well as the other documents. (B) is wrong because Lucero must give Chason the document drafts as well as the memoranda. (C) is wrong because the fact that Lucero was fired, even without cause, does not in any way change Lucero's duty to give Chason all of the papers.

Answer to Question 7

(B) Judge Jeffery may urge Horace to accept the prize unless giving Horace the prize could reasonably be perceived as an attempt to influence Judge Jeffery in the performance of her judicial duties. A judge must urge members of her family who live in her household not to accept a gift, bequest, favor, or loan from anyone, subject to eight exceptions. [CJC 4D(5)] One exception provides that it is permissible to accept a "gift, award, or benefit" that is incident to the business of the judge's spouse, unless it could reasonably be perceived as an effort to influence the judge in her judicial duties. [CJC 4D(5)(b)] (A) is wrong because the exception stated in it [CJC 4D(5)(h)] applies only if the donor is not likely to appear before the judge, and the facts state that Amalgamated is occasionally a litigant in Judge Jeffery's court. (C) is wrong because it ignores the general rule on family members' accepting gifts and other benefits. (D) is wrong because if the prize is proper under CJC 4D(5)(b), it does not become improper simply because Amalgamated may later appear as a litigant in Judge Jeffery's court. (Judge Jeffery may, of course, have to disqualify herself in such a case pursuant to CJC 3E(1).)

Answer to Question 8

(D) Azevedo should state what she knows about Seymour, including mentioning his burglary conviction. An attorney who is properly asked for information about a bar applicant's character has a duty to respond and to do so accurately. [ABA Model Rule 8.1] (A) is wrong because Azevedo does have relevant information—she knows about Seymour's burglary conviction, and that is relevant to (but certainly not conclusive of) the inquiry about his character. (B) is wrong because an attorney's duty to provide bar applicant information is not confined to the state in which the attorney practices. (C) is wrong because the burglary conviction is relevant to the character inquiry, and nothing indicates that Azevedo learned about it in confidence.

Answer to Question 9

(D) Anderson is subject to discipline for the last two statements in her advertisement. She is subject to discipline for item III. because it is misleading for her to state that she is "Harvard Trained." Reasonable readers could interpret that to mean that she received her law degree from that school. [*See* ABA Model Rule 7.1 and Comment 2] Anderson is also subject to discipline for item IV. because the statement "Never Lost a Jury Trial," although literally true, could create unjustified expectations and is therefore misleading. [*See* ABA Model

Rule 7.1 and Comment 3] Items I. and II. would not make Anderson subject to discipline. Given her brief time in law practice, she has had significant experience as a trial lawyer. A lawyer is allowed to state the fields of law in which she does or does not practice. [ABA Model Rule 7.4(a)]

Answer to Question 10

(A) Avilla is not subject to discipline for this fee arrangement unless $5,100 is an unreasonably high fee. The ABA Model Rules flatly prohibit a lawyer from using a contingent fee arrangement when the payment of the fee is contingent on the securing of a divorce or an amount of alimony or support (or property settlement in lieu thereof). The Rules do not, however, prohibit a lawyer from using a contingent fee to recover money that is past due under a child support order. [ABA Model Rule 1.5(d)(1) and Comment 6] In Weaver's case, she had already obtained her divorce, and the amount of alimony and child support payment had already been set. The only problem was extracting the money from Hubbard; thus, Avilla's use of the contingent fee arrangement in this case was proper. The contingent fee arrangement is particularly appropriate in light of Weaver's lack of money to pay a regular fee and State A's failure to provide for fee shifting in domestic relations matters. [*See* Restatement §35, comment b] (B) is wrong because it ignores the possibility that $5,100 may be unreasonably high for the work Avilla did. Also, Avilla would not necessarily be subject to discipline for using this fee arrangement even if Weaver had money to pay a regular fee. (C) is wrong because the collection of past due amounts of child support on a contingency fee basis is not considered a prohibited contingent fee in a domestic relations case under the Rules. (D) is wrong because it invokes a nonexistent policy. Contingent fees are generally allowed, even though they typically involve taking a share of money awarded for the support or compensation of the client (as in the ordinary personal injury case).

Answer to Question 11

(D) Lohman's actions were not proper because a lawyer may not draft a legal instrument for a client that gives a substantial gift to the lawyer, unless the client is a relative of the lawyer. [ABA Model Rule 1.8(c)] The deed creating the joint tenancy bestows a substantial gift on Lohman, particularly in light of the high likelihood that Cruikshank would die first. The transaction is also particularly suspect in light of Lohman's failure to explain the joint tenancy to Cruikshank. [*See* ABA Model Rule 1.8(a)—business transaction with client requires full disclosure of interest granted lawyer] (A) is wrong because the court's determination does not free Lohman from discipline for drafting the deed that bestowed the gift on him. (B) is wrong because the right of survivorship is a substantial gift regardless of who actually dies first; thus, it was not proper for Lohman to draft the document. (C) is wrong because it is overbroad. A lawyer may enter into a business transaction with a client, provided he follows certain safeguards. Here, for example, had Lohman met all of the requirements of ABA Model Rule 1.8(a), the transaction would have been a proper business transaction. However, the transaction still would have been improper because Lohman drafted the deed.

Answer to Question 12

(D) Arles must refuse to represent Corot in the present transaction. Note that the call of the question asks what Arles *must* do, not what he would be *allowed* to do. ABA Model Rule 1.2 states that a lawyer must not counsel or assist a client in conduct that the lawyer knows is criminal or fraudulent. Here, Arles must refuse to represent Corot

in the sale of the painting to Lavish because the sale would be fraudulent—Arles knows that the painting is not a Van Gogh as Corot represented to Lavish. ABA Model Rule 1.6(b) permits a lawyer to reveal a client's confidential information to the extent necessary to prevent the client from committing a crime or fraud that would result in substantial financial harm to a person, if the client is using or has used the lawyer's services to further the crime or fraud. A lawyer also may reveal confidential information if the client has already acted and the disclosure will mitigate the consequent financial harm. Thus, Arles is permitted to disclose information to law enforcement authorities in order to prevent harm to Lavish and possibly mitigate subsequent financial harm caused by the first transaction to the American Museum of Art; however, Arles is *not* required to do so. The same holds true regarding Arles's warning Lavish about the proposed sale. Consequently, I. and II. are wrong. III. is also wrong because even if it can be argued that Arles's revealing information about the fraudulent sale to American would mitigate subsequent financial harm, Arles is not required to reveal Corot's confidential information.

Answer to Question 13

(D) Azari may reveal the confidence even if doing so will subject his client to civil or criminal liability. A lawyer may disclose a client's confidence "to establish a defense to a criminal charge or civil claim against the lawyer based upon conduct in which the client was involved . . . ." [ABA Model Rule 1.6(b)(5)] Although the lawyer must wait until the assertion of misconduct arises, he need not await the filing of a formal charge or complaint. The lawyer may defend himself by responding directly to a third party who has made such an assertion. [*See* Restatement §64, comment c] (A) is wrong because the lawyer may disclose the fact even if doing so harms the client. (C) is wrong because the lawyer need not wait for the complaint to be filed, as explained above. (B) is wrong because it ignores the self-protection exception to the general rule of confidentiality.

Answer to Question 14

(A) A lawyer has a general duty of loyalty to the client and a general duty to represent the client with dedication and commitment to the client's interest and with zeal in advocacy on the client's behalf. When acting as an advocate for a client, as Adams is doing here, a lawyer must resolve reasonable doubts in favor of his client. There are certain situations under which the lawyer must act in a way that is adverse to his client, but each of the situations requires that the lawyer have *actual knowledge* of adverse facts, not just doubt or suspicion. [*See* ABA Model Rule 3.3(a)] Here, Adams does not have actual knowledge that Dutcher and his mother are lying or even any knowledge of circumstantial facts that indicate that they are lying; at best, he has a strong suspicion based on his instincts. This falls well short of actual knowledge. Note that a lawyer *may refuse* to offer evidence if he *reasonably believes* that it is false, other than the testimony of a criminal defendant. [ABA Model Rule 3.3(a)(3)] This rule does not apply to Dutcher's testimony because Dutcher is a criminal defendant; it also does not apply to Dutcher's mother's testimony for two reasons: First, the question asks whether Adams *may offer* the testimony, not whether he may *refuse* to offer it. Second, there is nothing in the facts to indicate that Adams's belief that the testimony is false is reasonable. Thus, Adams may call Dutcher and his mother as trial witnesses.

Answer to Question 15

(B) Longfisher's handling of the matter was not proper because she should have made sure that Choy was promptly notified that the check had arrived. When someone delivers money to a lawyer to hold for the lawyer's client, the lawyer must promptly notify the client that the money has arrived. [ABA Model Rule 1.15(d)] Had Choy known that the money had arrived, she could have promptly collected it and put it to her own use. (A) is wrong because the State Alpha IOLTA program required the funds to be deposited in an IOLTA account. (C) is wrong because although Longfisher did comply with the IOLTA requirement, she failed to take appropriate steps to have Choy promptly notified that the money had arrived. (D) is wrong because Choy was harmed; she was deprived of the use of the money during the month that Longfisher was on vacation in Fiji.

Answer to Question 16

(C) Both Dillard and Laben may work on the matter, assuming Laben complies with the applicable federal statutes and regulations concerning former government employees. Drafting a piece of legislation is not regarded as a "matter" for purposes of the legal ethics rules on former government employees. [ABA Model Rule 1.11(e); ABA Formal Op. 342 (1975)] Therefore, Laben may advise the University. Because Laben is not disqualified, neither is her firm. Thus, Dillard may also work on this project. (A) is wrong because, as discussed above, Laben's congressional work disqualifies neither Laben nor Dillard. (B) is wrong because it states one of the requirements for Dillard's representation had Laben been disqualified. As discussed above, Laben is not disqualified and thus need not be screened off. (D) is wrong for the reasons stated above. Moreover, it is not the University that would need protection if this were a "matter" for the purpose of disqualification under the conflict of interest rules. In that case, Laben would have been screened off, Laben would not be apportioned any part of the fee, and written notice would be promptly given to the *government agency*.

Answer to Question 17

(A) Alvarado will not be subject to discipline if he becomes an authorized provider under Consolidated's plan. Consolidated has set up a prepaid legal services plan of the kind referred to in the ABA Model Rules. A lawyer may receive legal business through such a plan, unless the operator of the plan uses in-person or live telephone contact to solicit people who it knows are in need of legal services in a particular matter covered by the plan. [ABA Model Rule 7.3(d)] (B) is wrong because there is no rule concerning the selection of counsel in a legal services insurance plan. (C) is also wrong because it would be an antitrust violation (and also an ethics violation) for a group of lawyers to conspire to follow a minimum or maximum fee schedule [*see* Arizona v. Maricopa County Medical Society, 457 U.S. 332 (1982)], but it is neither illegal nor unethical for a lawyer to agree to follow an insurance company's maximum fee schedule for work done for that company's insureds. (D) is wrong because it is too broad. ABA Model Rule 7.3(d) permits in-person and live telephone solicitation by the operator of an insurance plan, except of persons who are known "to need legal services in a particular matter covered by the plan."

Answer to Question 18

(D) LaFrank is subject to discipline because she talked with the president about the matter without obtaining Levin's consent. A lawyer must obtain the consent of adversary counsel before she speaks "about the subject of the representation" with a person who supervises, directs, or regularly consults with the organization's lawyer about the matter at hand. [Comment 7 to ABA Model Rule 4.2] The president of the company is clearly a person who supervises, directs, or consults with the organization's lawyer about legal matters. "Subject of the representation" is not limited to the substantive legal and factual issues concerning the alleged patent infringement; it also includes significant procedural matters, such as the factual predicate for laying venue in State Alpha. [*See* Hazard & Hodes, The Law of Lawyering (hereinafter "Hazard & Hodes") §38.5 (3d ed. 2000 & Supp. 2004)—"anything that could have an impact on the contested matter"] (A) is wrong because the rule against direct communication applies to all manner of disputes, whether or not suit has been filed. In this case, the claim of infringement had clearly been made—negotiations had been ongoing for three months. (B) is wrong because the conversation concerned a significant procedural matter, as explained above. (C) is wrong because, without Levin's consent, the conversation would have been unethical even had she properly identified herself.

Answer to Question 19

(D) Lewis should decline to serve as trial counsel because she can foresee that she will be called as a witness. A lawyer must not act as an advocate at a trial at which the lawyer is likely to be a *necessary* witness. [ABA Model Rule 3.7(a)] Lewis was the only person other than the parties present at the negotiating session. Owens will almost certainly call Lewis as a witness. Because Lewis can foresee at the outset that she will likely be called as a witness, she should decline to serve as trial lawyer for Carter, even if Carter is willing to consent to the conflict of interest. [ABA Model Rule 1.7(a); Comment 6 to ABA Model Rule 3.7] (A) is wrong because a person's choice of counsel is limited by the restraints imposed by the ethics rules. The client may choose Lewis, but Lewis cannot ethically accept the employment. (B) is wrong because Lewis cannot refuse to testify if Owens calls her to the witness stand. (C) is wrong because if a lawyer is called to the witness stand and sworn to tell the truth, she must do so, even if it is prejudicial to her client.

Answer to Question 20

(D) Laine's fee agreement is proper even though it gives Laine a personal interest in the subject of the litigation. Laine has acquired a personal interest in the movie, which is in one sense the real subject of the litigation. However, the rule against acquiring a personal interest in the subject of litigation has an exception that allows a lawyer to represent a client for a contingent fee. [ABA Model Rule 1.8(i)(2)] (A) is wrong because the rule on literary rights contracts covers only literary works based in substantial part on information relating to the representation. Here, the movie concerns John Dillinger, not producer Prosser. [*See* ABA Model Rule 1.8(d)] (B) is wrong because, as discussed above, a lawyer may acquire an interest in the subject matter of the litigation in the form of a contingent fee. (C) is wrong because the fee agreement between Prosser and Laine does not require Arthur's informed consent. Arthur is not a current or former client of Laine's, and Arthur has no apparent interest that would cause Laine a conflict and force him to disclose and explain the material risks and available alternatives and obtain Arthur's consent.

Answer to Question 21

(D) Items I. and III. are proper because a lawyer may take on a case that he is not competent to handle if he either: (i) puts in the time and study needed to become competent to handle it, or (ii) obtains his client's consent to associate a lawyer who is competent to handle it. [Comment 2 to ABA Model Rule 1.1] Item IV. is proper because a lawyer may refer her client to another lawyer who is competent to handle the case. Making a sound referral can take a significant amount of time, especially if the referring lawyer needs to research the backgrounds of several lawyers with whom she is not personally familiar. It is appropriate for the referring lawyer to charge her client for the time spent making the referral, subject of course to the general rule on reasonableness. [ABA Model Rule 1.5] (As a practical matter, however, many lawyers would not charge a regular client for making such a referral.) Item II. is not proper because a "forwarding fee" is another term for a "referral fee," and payments for referrals are prohibited. [ABA Model Rule 7.2(b)]

Answer to Question 22

(C) It would be proper for Adams to participate in the debate and cast her vote on the proposed legislation, provided that she informs the committee that she represents a client whose interests could be materially benefited by the statute. A lawyer may participate in a law reform activity that will affect the interests of the lawyer's client. [ABA Model Rule 6.4] When a lawyer knows that a client will be materially benefited by the activity, the lawyer must disclose that fact, but she need not name the client. (A) is wrong because a lawyer is not prohibited from engaging in a law reform activity that might benefit her client. (B) is wrong because a lawyer is not prohibited from participating in a law reform activity, unless the participation would create an impermissible conflict of interest. [ABA Model Rule 1.7(a)] That is not the case here. A client who hires a lawyer does not thereby purchase the right to control the lawyer's views and activities in all contexts. [*See* ABA Model Rule

1.2(b)] Adams may even advocate new legislation that she thinks is sound that would harm Genetico's sales. [*See* ABA Model Rule 6.4] (D) is wrong because Adams need not disclose the name of her client; simply disclosing the fact of representation will inform the CSF legislation committee of her possible bias.

Answer to Question 23

(B) Judge Jettelson may testify because a judge may engage in activities designed to improve the law. Under the CJC, judges are permitted to engage in nonjudicial activities that concern the law. [CJC 4B] Judges are in a unique position to help improve the law, including the revision of substantive and procedural law. Moreover, a judge may appear at a public hearing before a legislative body on a matter that concerns the law, the legal system, or the administration of justice. [CJC 4C] (A) is wrong because there is no rule requiring "equal time." (C) is wrong because it is overbroad. The general rule on judicial involvement in politics limits only *some* types of political activities, not including legislative testimony. [CJC 5A] (D) is wrong because, with respect to issues that are likely to come before the court, a judge is prohibited from making pledges, promises, or commitments that are inconsistent with the impartial performance of his duties. [CJC 3B(10)] That rule does not apply here because Judge Jettelson's testimony, which would be designed to improve the law, would not constitute a promise that is inconsistent with the performance of his adjudicative duties.

Answer to Question 24

(D) Altamirez is not subject to discipline. Because Lipkis is a lawyer-employee of Altamirez, she is regarded as being "in the same firm." She and Altamirez are thus allowed to split fees without complying with the rules that govern fee splits between lawyers who are not in the same firm. [ABA Model Rule 1.5(e)] (A) is

wrong for the reason just stated. (B) is wrong because no rule requires Altamirez to supervise Lipkis at every turn, so long as he takes reasonable steps to assure that she performs her work competently and otherwise within the bounds of legal ethics. [*See* ABA Model Rule 5.1—supervisory duties of lawyers within a firm] (C) is wrong because a lawyer may state that he does (or does not) practice in particular fields of law. [ABA Model Rule 7.4(a)] Altamirez has not held himself out as a specialist in these areas; thus, no certification is required. [*See* ABA Model Rule 7.4(d)]

Answer to Question 25

(B) Atley is subject to criminal liability if he intended to induce Judge Joiner to decide the case in Putkis's favor. The common law crime of bribery consists of the corrupt payment or receipt of anything of value in return for official action. The $50,000 loan was obviously a thing of value. Thus, if Atley intended the loan as an inducement to Judge Joiner to decide the case in favor of Putkis, then Atley is guilty of bribery. (A) is wrong because in deciding whether Atley is subject to criminal liability, it is Atley's intent that counts, not Judge Joiner's intent. (C) is wrong because Atley's crime was complete when he gave the loan, even though Judge Joiner never had to decide the case. (D) is wrong because bribery does not require an outright gift; a $50,000 loan is a thing of value, especially a loan with no repayment date, no promissory note, and no interest specified.

Answer to Question 26

(D) Alvarez need not disclose the FTC ruling because the court need not follow the decision. An attorney can be disciplined for failing to cite the court to legal authority that is "directly adverse" to the client's position and is from the "controlling jurisdiction." [ABA Model Rule 3.3(a)(2)] Although the decision is directly adverse to Universal's position, the facts state that

FTC decisions do not control in the United States Courts of Appeal. Thus, the decision is not from the "controlling jurisdiction." (A) is wrong because in order to invoke the disclosure rule, the decision must be from a controlling jurisdiction, not merely persuasive. (B) is wrong because it states only one portion of the test that triggers the disclosure rule. While true that the decision is adverse, it is not from a controlling jurisdiction, and thus need not be revealed. (C) is wrong because although the rule as stated is true, in this case we are not concerned with harmful *facts*. The issue is whether Alvarez must reveal harmful *law*.

Answer to Question 27

(C)   It would not be proper for Proctor to represent the Grocery unless both Cridley and the Grocery give informed, written consent to the representation. A lawyer who is presently representing a client in one litigation matter should not simultaneously oppose that client in a different litigation matter, even if the two matters are unrelated. [ABA Model Rule 1.7(a) and Comment 6] The purpose of the rule is to avoid putting the client into the difficult position of treating the lawyer simultaneously as friend and foe. The conflict can be solved only by the informed, written consent of both Cridley and Sandy Gulch Gas & Grocery. (A) is wrong because the rule prohibiting the representation applies regardless of whether Proctor has obtained relevant confidential information. (B) is wrong because the rule applies even if the two cases are unrelated. (D) is wrong because the conflict is not obviated by the shortage of legal talent in Sandy Gulch.

Answer to Question 28

(A)   Item I. is true because one of the grounds for permissible withdrawal is that the client has made the lawyer's task unreasonably difficult (*e.g.,* the client will not cooperate with the lawyer). [ABA Model Rule

1.16(b)(6)] Item II. is true because a lawyer must not communicate about a matter with a person who is represented by another lawyer in the matter, unless that other lawyer consents. [ABA Model Rule 4.2] Item III. is true because there is no reason in this case for Lorenz to charge Withers less than the full amount (assuming, of course, that the fee is reasonable in the circumstances). Item IV. is true because a lawyer may sue to collect her fee. Comment 3 to ABA Model Rule 1.5 urges lawyers to take advantage of arbitration schemes to avoid fee suits. Lorenz has tried to settle with Withers, but to no avail; in this situation, a suit may be her only way to get the money.

Answer to Question 29

(D)   Lars is subject to discipline for failing to turn over evidence given to him by his client and for failing to cite authority directly adverse to his case from a controlling authority. [*See* ABA Model Rules 3.3(a)(2), 3.4(a)] Item I. is correct because a client cannot protect a preexisting document or thing from discovery simply by turning it over to the attorney. The privilege does not apply; if the thing is discoverable in the client's hands, it is equally discoverable in the attorney's hands. Furthermore, an attorney must not unlawfully obstruct another party's access to evidence, which is the result here if Lars fails to turn over the documents. Item II. is incorrect because the case is not from a controlling authority. This case is in the Second Circuit and the case to be cited is from the Ninth Circuit; as such, it does not control the courts in the Second Circuit. Item III. is incorrect because an attorney has no obligation to notify the other side of adverse factual evidence, unless of course, the opponent has made a proper discovery request for the information. Item IV. is correct because the FEC would be the controlling authority on the interpretation of an FEC rule; thus, Lars was obligated to cite it.

Answer to Question 30

(C) Lin may disclose the statement even if Loomis objects. State A's ethics rule on confidentiality treats communications between Loomis and Lin just like communications between an attorney and a client. If Lin had heard one of her clients make this threat, she could have warned the police and the intended victim. An attorney may reveal confidential information to the extent she reasonably believes necessary to prevent reasonably certain death or substantial bodily harm. [ABA Model Rule 1.6(b)(1)] Thus, Lin may warn Crothers and the police. (A) is wrong because Lin may act to prevent Loomis from causing substantial bodily harm. Loomis's consent is not necessary. [ABA Model Rule 1.6(b)(1)] (B) is wrong because if an attorney reasonably believes that her client (or anyone else) is about to inflict substantial bodily harm on someone, she may take steps to prevent it, even if she is not certain that the client (or other person) will do it. (D) is wrong because the State A ethics rule on confidentiality equates the peer counselor relationship with the relationship between an attorney and client; thus, the ability to disclose is the same.

Answer to Question 31

(D) Atwater may represent Christopher if Christopher gives informed, written consent to the representation. Atwater's wife, Wilma, is likely to inherit Warner's interest in Mobiland. That gives Atwater a personal interest in Mobiland, albeit an attenuated interest. If Atwater is to represent Christopher in selling land to Mobiland, he must first disclose his personal interest to Christopher. If Christopher gives informed consent, confirmed in writing, then Atwater may represent Christopher. [ABA Model Rule 1.7(b)] (A) is wrong because informed,

written consent will solve the potential conflict of interest. (B) is wrong because Atwater's personal interest is significant, even though it is remote. (C) is wrong because informed, written consent will solve the conflict problem and avoid the appearance of impropriety.

Answer to Question 32

(C) Bailey will be subject to civil liability in a legal malpractice action brought by Larry for failing to object to the second trial on double jeopardy grounds. A reasonably competent criminal defense attorney would know that a defendant is put in jeopardy when a jury is empaneled and sworn, not to mention that Portman started presenting her case-in-chief. Larry was obviously a proper plaintiff, and he was injured by Bailey's error; he should be able to recover at least part of the $5,000 attorneys' fee, plus damages for his anguish and for the reputational injury caused by the conviction at the second trial. Note that (C) provides that in the malpractice action Larry must prove by a preponderance of the evidence that he was innocent of the underlying criminal offense. That is required by the law of most states that have ruled on the issue. [*See* Restatement §53, comment d] Observe that in this particular case, a good argument can be made for allowing Larry to recover even without proof of innocence. Here, the malpractice was Bailey's failure to object to the second trial. If Bailey had acted competently, the second trial would never have taken place, and Larry would have lawfully gone free, even if he were unquestionably guilty of the assault. [*See* Levine v. Kling, 123 F.3d 580 (7th Cir. 1997)—Judge Posner's dictum] (A) and (D) are incorrect because they overlook the $5,000 fee and other less tangible injuries Larry suffered. (B) is incorrect for the reasons stated above with respect to (C).

Answer to Question 33

(C) London is subject to discipline because she and Ferguson are partners in the above-described business. A lawyer is prohibited from entering into a partnership with a nonlawyer if any of the partnership activities constitutes the practice of law. [ABA Model Rule 5.4(b)] The rationale and social policy behind this rule have been sharply questioned, but the ABA has not abandoned its traditional distrust of partnerships with nonlawyers. [*See* Hazard & Hodes, §45.7] (A) is wrong because although there are potential conflicts here in that London appears to work partly for the investors and partly for Ferguson and herself in putting the real estate projects together, informed, written consent by the investors will solve these conflict issues. In any event, London is still subject to discipline for entering into the partnership with a nonlawyer. (B) is wrong because the division of responsibility does not solve the partnership with a nonlawyer problem. (D) is wrong because Ferguson is not engaging in activities that could be construed as practicing law. All of the legal work (*i.e.*, work calling for the professional judgment of a lawyer) is done by London.

Answer to Question 34

(A) Lieu may not seek to have her name included on the list because naming Union as executor or trustee in wills and trusts is a tacit condition of being on the list. A lawyer may not give anything of value to a person for recommending the lawyer's services. [ABA Model Rule 7.2(b)] When a lawyer names a bank as institutional executor or trustee for a client, the lawyer confers a monetary benefit on the bank in the form of the fees the bank will earn from the client's trust or estate. Here, Union apparently lists only those lawyers who are willing to compensate it in this manner. That makes the arrangement "exclusive" and prevents the arrangement from being a reciprocal referral agreement of the kind permitted by ABA Model Rule 7.2(b)(4). Moreover, Union's scheme creates a conflict of interest between the lawyer and the client who needs an institutional executor or trustee. The lawyer has a personal interest in staying on Union's referral list, and that interest may skew the lawyer's judgment in advising a client whether to name Union or a different institution. [*See* ABA Model Rule 1.7(a)] (B) is wrong because it is overbroad and does not hit on the specific problem with Union's scheme. In proper circumstances, a lawyer may solicit business through an intermediary, *e.g.*, through a prepaid legal service program or an approved lawyer referral service. (C) is wrong because a client is entitled to the unbiased advice of a lawyer in deciding what institutional trustee or executor to name. Even if Union is just as good and its fees are as reasonable as other institutional fiduciaries, Union's scheme deprives clients of unbiased advice. (D) is wrong because clients who use Union for their routine banking needs might nevertheless desire to name some other institution as their executor or trustee; in any event, they are entitled to unbiased legal advice on that subject.

Answer to Question 35

(D) Lazar's actions were not proper because his information was gained from a confidential lawyer-client communication. [*See* ABA Model Rule 1.6] It was both privileged and confidential, and could be disclosed only if one of the exceptions to the duty of confidentiality applies. None of the exceptions applies here. The fact that Carla did not hire Lazar to represent her does not affect his duty of confidentiality; she was seeking legal advice and representation when she spoke to him. [*See* ABA Model Rule 1.18(b)] (A) is wrong because there is no exception to the duty of confidentiality to prevent a fraud on the court when the lawyer is not appearing before the court. (B) is wrong because this too does not fit within any exception to the duty of nondisclosure. A lawyer may reveal confidential information to the extent he reasonably believes necessary to prevent, mitigate, or rectify substantial injury to the financial interests of another that is reasonably certain to result or has resulted from the client's commission of a crime or fraud, if the client has used the lawyer's services in furtherance of such crime or fraud. [ABA Model Rule 1.6(b)(3)] Here, the facts do not indicate that Carla used Lazar's services in furtherance of her perjurious testimony. Thus, although the perjury could result in substantial injury to Devlin's financial interests, Lazar is not permitted to reveal the confidential information. (C) is wrong because it states the rule for an ex parte communication to the judge by one of the parties. Here, Lazar does not represent one of the parties. Furthermore, the information is confidential and cannot be disclosed to the disadvantage of the client regardless of whether Lazar sends copies to all parties.

Answer to Question 36

(B) Laden must advise the president to keep the records because the records have potential evidentiary value if the company is sued. A lawyer must not counsel or assist a person to destroy material that has "potential evidentiary value." [ABA Model Rule 3.4(a)] Although it is not certain that the company manufactured the dishwasher in question, the president said he was "pretty sure that it was one of ours." Furthermore, it is not certain that the company will be sued if it was one of their washers, but the chances are good that it will be. If commencement of proceedings can be foreseen, the documents have potential evidentiary value and cannot be destroyed. [Comment 2 to ABA Model Rule 3.4] (A) is wrong because even if the company's

records retention program called for the routine shredding of these records long ago, they were not shredded then, and they have potential evidentiary value now. (C) is wrong because commencement of proceedings is foreseeable. (D) is wrong because the standard is backward. The records should be preserved until the company is certain that the dishwasher in question was *not* manufactured by Electratec.

Answer to Question 37

(B) Leavitt's conduct was not proper unless he informed the legislators that he was appearing in a representative capacity. When a lawyer appears before a nonadjudicative body on behalf of a client, he must disclose that he is acting in a representative capacity. [ABA Model Rule 3.9] One important purpose of the rule is to enable the members of the nonadjudicative body to assess the biases that may influence the lawyer's testimony. In this case, the legislators might well think that Leavitt was speaking in his capacity as a wetlands expert, rather than as a developer's spokesman. (A) is wrong because Leavitt should have told the legislators that he was acting in a representative capacity, whether or not his testimony was consistent with his own views. (C) is wrong; indeed, the fact that he is an expert in his own right makes his appearance particularly misleading. (D) is wrong because it invokes a nonexistent rule. There are limits on when a client's trial counsel may testify in a court proceeding, but no such limits apply in nonadjudicatory proceedings.

Answer to Question 38

(A) Ladner is subject to criminal liability because he knew that Battista did not remember the color of the light. The crime of subornation of perjury is the corrupt procurement of perjured testimony. [*See* R. Perkins & R. Boyce, Criminal Law (hereinafter "Perkins & Boyce") 524-26 (3d ed. 1982)] Perjured testimony means a false oath in a judicial proceeding in regard to a material matter. [*Id.*] A false oath means a willful and corrupt sworn statement made without sincere belief in its truthfulness. [*Id.*] In this case, the falsehood was not about the color of the traffic light, but rather about Battista's *memory* of the color of the traffic light. Battista testified that he saw the light and remembered what color it was—but in truth, he did not remember. Ladner knew that Battista did not remember, and Ladner knew that Battista knew that he did not remember. Therefore, Ladner is guilty of subornation of perjury. (B) and (C) are both incorrect because they focus on the wrong thing—the color of the light, rather than the witness's memory. (D) is a generally correct statement, but it does not apply here. A criminal defense lawyer must indeed resolve doubtful facts in her client's favor, but the state of Battista's memory was not a doubtful fact—Battista told Ladner at the outset that he "simply could not remember what color the traffic light was."

Answer to Question 39

(C) Pompman would be subject to discipline for representing Owens because his earlier service as neutral arbitrator creates a conflict of interest. A lawyer must not represent a private client in a matter in which the lawyer has earlier participated personally and substantially while serving as an arbitrator. [ABA Model Rule 1.12(a)] (A) is wrong because the consistency of his position does not solve the conflict of interest. (B) is wrong because it does not go far enough. Informed, written consent by both Owens and Osborne would solve the conflict, but consent by Owens alone will not suffice (and Owens did not consent in writing). (D) is wrong because it invokes a nonexistent rule; unlike judges, lawyers are not expected to be impartial. Here, Pompman would be acting as an advocate, not as a judge or arbitrator; thus, he should be partial to his client. The issue here is not partiality but conflict of interest.

Answer to Question 40

(D) The communication with the reporters was proper, but the statements made to the jury were not. A judge should not "commend or criticize jurors for their verdict other than in a court order or opinion in a proceeding." A judge's commendation or criticism may impair a juror's ability to be impartial in a subsequent case. [CJC 3B(10)] Judge Johnston's statements to the jury clearly violate this rule; thus, (A) and (C) are incorrect. Although judges should not comment on pending cases in a manner that might interfere with justice, judges are not prohibited "from making public statements in the course of their official duties or from explaining for public information the procedures of the court." [CJC 3B(9)] Judge Johnston's explanation of the motions to the reporters was an appropriate way to inform the public of the meaning and significance of Judge Johnston's decision to reject the $500 million verdict; thus, (B) and (C) are incorrect.

Answer to Question 41

(B) It would not be proper for Amundson to split his fee with Linz because the written fee agreement with Corrales does not comply with the ABA Model Rules. ABA Model Rule 1.5(e) allows a lawyer to split a fee with a lawyer who is not in his firm if: (i) the total fee is reasonable; (ii) the split is in proportion to the services rendered by each lawyer, or in some other proportion if each lawyer assumes joint responsibility for the matter; and (iii) the client agrees to the split in a writing that discloses the share that each lawyer will receive. Here, the written fee agreement did not specify the share that each lawyer will receive; thus, a fee split between Amundson and Linz would be improper. (A) is wrong because there is no requirement that a lawyer be licensed in the same state as the attorney with whom he is splitting a fee. (C) is wrong because the written fee agreement with Corrales did not indicate the share that each lawyer will receive, and thus the agreement was improper regardless of whether Linz was assuming responsibility for his work. (D) is wrong because even though there was a fee agreement, it did not comply with the ABA Model Rules.

Answer to Question 42

(A) Lawrence may join the board of directors, but she must refrain from participating in the decision about the Case Intake Guidelines. A lawyer may not participate in a legal service board decision that may adversely affect one of the lawyer's clients. [ABA Model Rule 6.3(b)] (B) is wrong because ABA Model Rule 6.3 encourages work with a legal services organization, even if the organization serves people whose interests conflict with the interests of the lawyer's clients. (C) and (D) are wrong because ABA Model Rule 6.3(b) prohibits a lawyer from taking part in a legal services organization decision if the decision will adversely affect one of the lawyer's clients.

Answer to Question 43

(B) The judge must not disqualify Lazarro because Edmonds and Damassa gave informed, written consent to the joint representation. The interests of Edmonds and Damassa are in potential conflict as respects the agency issue: If Edmonds were on a frolic of his own, Damassa will not be liable, but if he were acting within the scope of his duties, Damassa will be liable. A lawyer may represent two clients in civil litigation if their interests are potentially in conflict, provided that the lawyer: (i) reasonably believes he can represent both clients effectively, (ii) discloses the potential conflict and explains how it can harm each client, and (iii) obtains the informed, written consent of each client. Because it

appears that Edmonds was not negligent, the conflict between Edmonds and Damassa is only potential. Lazarro apparently believes that he can represent both parties effectively and took all of the right steps to deal with this potential conflict. Because Edmonds and Damassa gave informed consent in writing, the trial judge should refuse to disqualify Lazarro. [ABA Model Rule 1.7(b); Restatement §122] The judge should also consider that it is the plaintiffs who seek the disqualification; one may reasonably conclude that they were trying to harass the defendants rather than serve the interests of justice. (A) is wrong because, as discussed above, there is a potential conflict between Edmonds and Damassa. (C) is wrong because the potential conflict has been handled properly and does not create an appearance of impropriety. (D) is wrong because informed, written consent is sufficient in this situation. A client cannot be asked to consent when a disinterested lawyer would conclude that the client's interests would not be adequately protected in light of the conflict. Here, the conflict is merely *potential*; thus, a disinterested lawyer could conclude that the clients can agree to the representation. Consequently, Edmonds's and Damassa's informed, written consent are sufficient to solve the potential conflict of interest.

Answer to Question 44

(B) A lawyer must withdraw if the lawyer's physical or mental condition will materially impair his ability to represent the client. [ABA Model Rule 1.16(a)(2)] Carlin may be right in thinking that hard work will be good for Adler, but Adler has to be the ultimate judge of his own physical and mental capacity to carry on. If Adler believes that his condition prevents him from serving Carlin competently, he must withdraw regardless of what Carlin wants. (A) is wrong because the files include confidential information about Carlin's financial affairs, and Adler cannot turn them over to Parner against Carlin's express wishes. [ABA Model Rule 1.6] (C) is wrong because Carlin has asked Adler to complete the work promptly. Adler's recovery may take months or years. Adler must not continue representing Carlin unless he can complete the work with reasonable diligence and promptness. [ABA Model Rule 1.3] (D) is wrong because, as discussed above, if Adler believes his mental and physical conditions prevent him from serving Carlin competently, he must withdraw.

Answer to Question 45

(B) Lubner may withdraw from the case and keep Dowling's statement in confidence. When an organization is the lawyer's client, the lawyer owes a duty of loyalty to the organization. When the interests of the organization and its constituents conflict, the lawyer should remind the person that the lawyer represents the organization and not the person. It would be appropriate for the lawyer to remind the person that communications between them may not be protected by the attorney-client privilege, and that the person may want to obtain independent counsel. [ABA Model Rule 1.13] Here, Lubner should not have asked the question unless he was prepared for an affirmative answer. He should have known before asking that if the answer was yes, Dowling's interests and Marine Supply's interests would conflict; thus, Lubner should not have offered to represent Dowling, and certainly should not have promised to keep Dowling's statements in confidence. (Note that Lubner could be subject to discipline for this conduct.) The issue here, however, is what course of action Lubner may now take. Now that Lubner has agreed to represent Dowling, and Dowling has confessed in confidence, the only thing Lubner can do is withdraw from the matter entirely and keep Dowling's

confession in confidence. [*See* ABA Model Rule 1.9] (A) is wrong because he would violate Dowling's confidence by disclosing the confession to the Attorney General. (C) and (D) are wrong because revealing Dowling's confession to Marine Supply would also violate Dowling's confidence.

Answer to Question 46

(C) Items II. and IV. are proper; items I. and III. are not. Item I. is improper because a lawyer may not state or allude to any matter that the lawyer does not reasonably believe will be supported by admissible evidence. A prosecutor is prohibited from commenting on a defendant's failure to testify; any such reference violates the defendant's Fifth Amendment privilege against self-incrimination. [Griffin v. California, 380 U.S. 609 (1965)] Thus, Prichard's allusion in closing arguments to the defendant's failure to testify is reference to inadmissible evidence, and is improper. [ABA Model Rule 3.4(e)] In addition, a lawyer, especially a prosecutor, must not intentionally violate established rules of evidence or procedure. [ABA Model Rule 3.4(c)] Item II. is proper because Prichard was inviting the jury to draw its own conclusion about Grutz's credibility, not stating her own opinion about his credibility. [*See* ABA Model Rule 3.4(e)] Item III. is improper because Prichard was stating her own opinion about Schlarp's truthfulness. A lawyer must not state a personal opinion as to the credibility of a witness. [ABA Model Rule 3.4(e)] Item IV. is proper because Prichard's statement did not contain her own opinion about DeVries's guilt; rather, she was inviting the jury to reach the conclusion that she desired.

Answer to Question 47

(B) This arrangement is proper if the fee is reasonable under the circumstances. As long as the fee paid does not turn out to be excessive, taking into account Adams's risk of not being paid, the delay in payment, etc., this arrangement is acceptable. A lawyer may enter into a business relationship with a client, provided certain safeguards, such as an opportunity to consult with independent counsel, are used. [ABA Model Rule 1.8(a)] (A) is wrong because although it is improper to use a contingent fee in a criminal case, this fee is not a contingent fee. Whether Adams gets paid does not depend on the outcome of the case; it depends on how well the movie does. (C) is wrong because it is not clear that any amount over $1 million is excessive, given that Adams is risking that he will be paid nothing and is delaying payment by a substantial period of time. (D) is wrong because it misstates or incompletely states the rule. The rule is that *prior to the conclusion of the representation of the client*, a lawyer cannot acquire media rights to a story based substantially on information relating to the representation. In this case, the movie does not relate to the current representation, rather it involves past representations in Adams's career. While Adams could not disclose any information related to those representations without the clients' consents, the acquisition of such media rights is not improper.

Answer to Question 48

(D) ABA Model Rule 1.18 provides that a lawyer must not use or reveal confidential information of a prospective client. [*See also* ABA Model Rule 1.6] Here, the information communicated to Amari was not confidential; thus, Amari's undertaking representation of Turner-Kline did not create a concurrent conflict of interest—there is no significant risk that the representation of Turner-Kline would be materially limited by Amari's responsibilities to Biogenco. Consequently, Amari may continue to represent Turner-Kline. (A) is wrong because it does not matter that

Biogenco previously consulted Amari on the same matter if Amari did not obtain any confidential information that would limit her representation of Turner-Kline, and she does not breach any duty owed to Biogenco. (B) is wrong for the same reason as (A)—even if the infringement suit is substantially related to Amari's conversation with Biogenco's representatives, unless Amari obtained confidential information from Biogenco, she may represent Turner-Kline. (C) is not as good as (D) because (C) is general, while (D) is specifically on point. Here, Amari did not get any material confidential information from Biogenco's representatives during the preliminary conversation, but if she had, she would be subject to disqualification as defense counsel, even though Biogenco never became Amari's actual client.

Answer to Question 49

(D) Leer is subject to litigation sanction because Federal Rule of Civil Procedure 11 provides that sanctions can be imposed on a lawyer, firm, or party for filing a pleading, motion, or other paper merely to harass, delay, or multiply expense for the opponent. [*See also* Hudson Motors Partnership v. Crest Leasing Enterprises, Inc., 845 F. Supp. 969 (E.D.N.Y. 1994)—federal courts have inherent power to sanction lawyers for frivolous legal positions to harass or delay; *and see* 28 U.S.C. §1927—court can impose sanctions on lawyers who knowingly or recklessly multiply proceedings unreasonably and vexatiously] (A) is incorrect because it is beyond the bounds of the law to harass an opponent with a legal position that the proponent knows is frivolous. (B) is incorrect because Rule 11 allows the court to sanction both the lawyers and the parties they represent. (C) is incorrect because lawyers are not subject to litigation sanction for taking legal positions that they, in good faith, believe to be meritorious.

Answer to Question 50

(A) None of the reasons given would allow Lee to decline the appointment. A lawyer is subject to discipline for trying to avoid a court appointment without good cause. [ABA Model Rule 6.2] None of the four items listed would constitute good cause. Item I. is not good cause because a lawyer's belief that the defendant is guilty is not a sufficient reason to turn down a court appointment. Competent defense of a murder case certainly does not require a defense lawyer to believe in the client's innocence. Item II. is not good cause because the facts state that Lee is three years out of law school and practices criminal defense law. That indicates that his training in criminal law and procedure is recent, and that he knows how to defend a criminal case, even though he has not handled a murder case before. Thus, Lee cannot claim lack of competence as an excuse for turning down the appointment. [*See* Hazard & Hodes, §51.3] ABA Model Rule 6.2(c) recognizes that a lawyer may turn down an appointment if the client or cause is so repugnant to him as to interfere in the lawyer-client relationship. Neither Lee's race nor his sympathy for young people who get involved with gangs should be regarded, without more, as likely to interfere with Lee's ability to represent Owens competently. Thus, item III. is not good cause. Finally, item IV. is not good cause because Lee must not allow his other clients to control his work in matters that do not affect them. [ABA Model Rule 1.2(b)] Even if some of those other clients might take their work elsewhere in the future, that would not create the kind of immediate unreasonable financial burden that would justify Lee in rejecting the court appointment. [*See* ABA Model Rule 6.2(b)]

Answer to Question 51

(C) Ludwig was not representing either Sigmund or Fritz; rather, he was acting as a third-party neutral to help them resolve their differences. ABA Model Rule 2.4 permits a lawyer to serve in that role. Therefore, (A) is incorrect. (B) is incorrect because, when a lawyer has served as a third-party neutral between two conflicted parties, he cannot later represent one of the parties in that matter, unless both parties give informed, written consent. [ABA Model Rule 1.12(a)] (C) is correct because ABA Model Rule 1.12(c) permits screening to avoid a conflict in this situation. (D) is incorrect for the same reason.

Answer to Question 52

(A) Ayala does not need to be admitted to practice in State Two because the JAG Corps is an organ of the federal government, and army regulations authorize JAG officers to provide legal services to Army personnel and their dependents on a wide range of personal legal problems. [*See* ABA Model Rule 5.5(d)(2)] But before she advises the Smitherses, Ayala must do enough research to become competent on the legal aspects of mobile home financing. [*See* Comment 2 to ABA Model Rule 1.1] (B) is wrong for two reasons. First, as stated above, federal law authorizes Ayala to dispense this kind of advice in State Two. Second, the pro hac vice procedure does not entitle a person to practice law throughout a state—it only permits a person to handle a particular case before a particular tribunal [*See* ABA Model Rule 5.5(c)(2) and Comment 9] (C) is wrong for the reason stated in the first sentence, above. (D) is wrong because the problem specifies that army regulations authorize a legal assistance officer to give legal advice on a wide range of personal legal problems that affect military personnel and their dependents. These regulations reflect the Army's strong interest in keeping its people out of legal troubles no matter what the source.

Answer to Question 53

(B) ABA Model Rule 7.2(b)(4) permits a lawyer to make a reciprocal referral agreement with another lawyer, or with a non-lawyer professional, if the agreement is not exclusive and the referred person is told about the agreement. However, Comment 8 to ABA Model Rule 7.2 cautions lawyers that such an agreement should not be indefinite in duration. (A) is wrong because ABA Model Rule 7.2(b)(4) does not require a reciprocal referral agreement to be in writing. (C) is wrong because reciprocal referral agreements are one of four exceptions to the general rule that a lawyer must not give something of value for a referral. [*See* ABA Model Rule 7.2(b)] (D) is wrong because ABA Model Rule 7.2(b)(4) expressly permits reciprocal referral agreements with nonlawyer professionals.

Answer to Question 54

(C) ABA Model Rule 7.6 prohibits "a lawyer or law firm" from accepting an appointed legal engagement if "the lawyer or law firm" makes a political contribution "for the purpose of obtaining or being considered for" that kind of legal engagement. The tricky part of this question is whether a political contribution by one of the firm's lawyers ought to bar the entire firm from taking subsequent appointments. Neither the rule nor its comments speak directly to that point, but the purpose of the rule would be served by imputing one lawyer's contribution to the entire firm, just as a conflict of interest would be imputed under ABA Model Rule 1.10(a). To adopt the opposite position would make ABA Model Rule 7.6 too easy to evade—the firm could simply ask its lawyers to make "pay to play" contributions from their own pockets. Using a different theory, at least Feldspar's colleagues on the management committee should be barred from accepting appointments from the Attorney General because they knew about Feldspar's political contributions and thanked him rather than stopped him. [*See* ABA Model Rule 5.1(c)—ratification or acquiescence by managing lawyers] (B) is wrong for the reasons stated above. (A) is wrong because Feldspar's practice of contributing generously to all candidates who have a reasonable chance to win the Attorney Generalship demonstrates that his purpose is to secure business for the firm, not to participate legitimately in the political process. (D) is not as good as (C) because (D) relies on the outdated "appearance of impropriety" rubric of the old ABA Model Code, Canon 9. That rubric was cast aside in the ABA Model Rules—seeking to avoid even the "appearance of impropriety" is useful in a person's own moral creed, but it is too amorphous to be useful in a professional code of conduct.

Answer to Question 55

(D) Item I. is correct because Regeria's dispensation of legal advice constitutes the "practice of law," and he is doing it in a jurisdiction where he is not licensed. [*See* ABA Model Rule 5.5(a)] Item II. is correct because there is a lawyer-client relationship between Regeria and his walk-in clients. [Comment 1 to ABA Model Rule 6.5] One element of that relationship is the lawyer's duty of confidentiality [ABA Model Rule 1.6], and Regeria breaches that duty when he tells his wife about his clients' legal troubles. Item III. is incorrect because one does need to be licensed in order to dispense legal advice at a walk-in legal clinic. [*See* ABA Model Rule 6.5, which loosens the conflict of interest rules for clinic lawyers but does not authorize them to practice without a license] A law student or similar unlicensed person can work at such a clinic under the close supervision of a lawyer, but the question makes no mention of Regeria's work being supervised. [*See* Comment 1 to ABA Model Rule 5.3] Item IV. is incorrect for the reason stated above concerning item II.

Answer to Question 56

(B) Lim's real estate brokerage business is a "law-related service" within the meaning of ABA Model Rule 5.7, and Lim offers her real estate brokerage services "in circumstances that are not distinct from" her provision of legal services. [*See* ABA Model Rule 5.7(a)(1)] That means that she must follow the rules of legal ethics in her real estate brokerage work as well as her law work. [*Id.*] One of the legal ethics rules forbids a lawyer from initiating in-person contact with a prospective client when a significant motive for doing so is the lawyer's pecuniary gain. [*See* ABA Model Rule 7.3(a)] Therefore, Lim must not initiate face-to-face contact with potential real estate clients to interest them in using her brokerage services. [*See* Comment 10 to ABA Model Rule 7.3] (A) is wrong because it overstates the rule expressed in ABA Model Rule 5.7. (C) is wrong because it turns ABA Model Rule 5.7 on its head—because Lim is offering her ancillary service in circumstances that are not distinct from her legal service, she must follow the legal ethics rule for both kinds of service. (D) is wrong because Lim's face-to-face pitches violate the no-solicitation rule even if her statements are truthful and not misleading. [*Compare* ABA Model Rule 7.1 *with* ABA Model Rule 7.3(a)]

Answer to Question 57

(B) Item I. is true. ABA Model Rule 1.17 permits the sale of an entire law practice, or an area of practice, subject to some conditions, all of which are met here. Item II. is true. ABA Model Rule 1.17(d) provides that when a practice is sold, the fees charged to the clients cannot be increased by reason of the sale. Item III. is true. The sale of a solo practice by a newly appointed judge is a good example of where ABA Model Rule 1.17 can be beneficial. [*See* Comment 2 to ABA Model Rule 1.17]

Item IV. is true. CJC 3E(1)(b) says that a judge must disqualify himself if he previously served as a lawyer in the matter. Item V. is false. CJC 3F explains remittal of a judge's disqualification, and remittal requires the agreement of all of the parties and their lawyers, not the other justices.

Answer to Question 58

(B) The controlling doctrine in this case is the lawyer's ethical duty of confidentiality, not the attorney-client privilege. Lerner needs to know whether he can *voluntarily* reveal Cox's confession, not whether he would be forced to do so if he were put on the witness stand in a court. ABA Model Rule 1.6(b)(1) states the applicable exception to the ethical duty of confidentiality: A lawyer *may* reveal confidential information if the lawyer reasonably believes that doing so is necessary to prevent reasonably certain death or substantial bodily harm. One might quibble whether Hapless's death is "reasonably certain" when his trial has not even started, but surely the ethics rule should not be read to require Hapless to order his last meal before being loosed from the executioner's grip. (A) is wrong because ABA Model Rule 1.6(b)(1) gives Lerner *discretion* to reveal Cox's confession; the rule does not force him to do so. [*See* Comment 15 to ABA Model Rule 1.6] (A few states go farther and *require* disclosure to prevent death or substantial bodily harm, but they are a small minority.) (C) is wrong for two reasons. First, the applicable doctrine is the ethical duty of confidentiality, not the attorney-client privilege. Second, even if the privilege were the applicable doctrine, who could claim it in this situation? Cox cannot because he is dead. Cox's executor cannot because Cox's estate was closed and the executor was discharged. Lawyer Lerner cannot claim it because a lawyer's right to claim the privilege is only derivative from the client. (D) is wrong for two reasons. First, the admissibility of this hearsay is irrelevant to the ethics issue. Second, Cox's confession would likely be admissible if offered by Hapless against the prosecution because it is a declaration against penal interest by an unavailable declarant, and Cox's will and suicide are independent evidence of the confession's trustworthiness. [*See* Fed. R. Evid. 804(b)(3); *see also* Chambers v. Mississippi, 410 U.S. 284 (1973)—due process violation where another man's confession was excluded in a murder trial].

Answer to Question 59

(A) ABA Model Rule 1.13 governs this question. LaRue has been informed about the stated intent of a university Admissions Director to violate the voter initiative in a manner that imperils 45% of the university's funding. LaRue began her conversation with the Admissions Director in a proper manner by reminding him that she is the university's lawyer, not his lawyer. However, LaRue may not allow her personal views about the use of race in university admissions to affect how she responds to the Director's stated intent. Here, the voters have spoken by passing the initiative, the university's Board of Overseers has acquiesced in the initiative, and the constitutional challenge to the initiative has failed. If LaRue feels strongly enough about the issue to resign her position, she may do so [*see* ABA Model Rule 1.16(b)(4)], but she cannot remain in the General Counsel's office while subverting the voter initiative. Thus, item I. is wrong. Item III. is correct; if LaRue cannot convince the Admissions Director to obey the voter initiative, she **must** "refer the matter to higher authority in the organization." [ABA Model Rule 1.13(b) and Comment 4] In this instance, LaRue's immediate boss, the General Counsel, is the obvious first choice. ABA Model Rule 1.13 requires LaRue to report up the chain of command, not leap immediately to the top rung. [*Id.*] Only if her report to the General Counsel proves

futile should she take the matter to the Board of Overseers, and if she needs to report it to the Board of Overseers, she should do so forthrightly, not by an "anonymous leak" that the Board would be likely to ignore. Therefore, item IV. is wrong. Item II. is wrong because it appears to allow LaRue to report first to the West Dakota Attorney General, who should be regarded as outside the structure of the university for this purpose. [*See* ABA Model Rule 1.13(c)] True, the university is part of the state, and the Attorney General is the state's highest law enforcement official, but ABA Model Rule 1.13 seeks to have legal issues resolved at the lowest possible command level, not the highest possible level. [*Compare* Rule 1.13(b) *with* 1.13(c) and Comment 6]

Answer to Question 60

(D) This question is governed by ABA Model Rule 1.18, which concerns duties to a prospective client—a person like Corbin. The information that Lewis obtained about Corbin's alcohol abuse and his violent response to the stranger's comment could be harmful to Corbin if the wife uses it to help prove that the couple should be divorced and that Corbin should not be given custody of their children. Therefore, Lewis herself could not represent the wife in the divorce and child custody case. [*See* ABA Model Rule 1.18(c)] Lewis's disqualification is imputed to her law partner Smith. [*Id.*] However, if the conditions mentioned in (D) are satisfied, then Smith may continue representing the wife. [*See* ABA Model Rule 1.18(d)(2)] (C) is wrong because it calls for informed, written consent by the wife only. ABA Model Rule 1.18(d)(1) would require informed, written consent by both Corbin and the wife. (B) is wrong because the two matters are "substantially related" [ABA Model Rule 1.18(c)] in that use of the information that Corbin disclosed to Lewis could be harmful to Corbin if used in the divorce and child custody case. (A) is wrong because it ignores the two possible ways that would allow Smith to continue representing the wife. [ABA Model Rule 1.18(d)(1), (2)]

PRACTICE EXAM 2

Question 1

For the past 40 years, solo practitioner Febell has practiced municipal bond law in State A. Because he is nearing retirement age, Febell takes in young attorney Spryte as a partner. Their partnership agreement provides that Febell will train Spryte in municipal bond law, that Febell will receive 75% of the partnership's net earnings during the first three years, and that Spryte will receive the remaining 25%. The agreement further provides that if Spryte leaves the partnership before the end of the first three years, he will remit to Febell 75% of all fees he earns thereafter from municipal bond work he does in State A. Finally, the agreement provides that if Febell and Spryte are still partners when Febell retires, Spryte will pay Febell retirement benefits of $3,000 per month until Febell's death; in return, upon his retirement, Febell will turn over to Spryte all of the partnership assets (including goodwill) and will not thereafter practice municipal bond law in State A.

Are Febell and Spryte *subject to discipline* for entering into this partnership agreement?

(A) No, because the agreement gives Febell retirement payments in return for the restriction on his right to practice.

(B) No, because the agreement enables Febell to sell the partnership assets in return for the restriction on his right to practice.

(C) Yes, because of the restriction on both Febell's and Spryte's right to practice.

(D) Yes, because of the restriction on Spryte's right to practice if he leaves the partnership within the first three years.

Question 2

Justice Jacobs was on the supreme court of State Beta. State Beta's Supreme Court Rules provide that in capital punishment cases, any one justice of the supreme court is empowered to grant a stay of execution pending appeal to the supreme court. Justice Jacobs granted such a stay in the case of *People of State Beta v. Dillon*, on the ground that Dillon had been denied the effective assistance of counsel at his trial. A few months later, Justice Jacobs retired from the supreme court and went back to private law practice.

In due course, the supreme court heard the appeal in the *Dillon* case, rejected Dillon's effective assistance of counsel contention, and affirmed the death penalty. Acting as an indigent in propria persona, Dillon then commenced a federal habeas corpus proceeding in the United States District Court for the Eastern District of State Beta and asked that court to appoint a private lawyer to represent him in the habeas corpus proceeding. The district court appointed Jacobs to represent Dillon. A key issue in the habeas corpus proceeding is whether Dillon was deprived of the effective assistance of counsel at his trial.

May Jacobs represent Dillon without getting the informed, written consent of all parties to the habeas corpus proceeding?

(A) No, because there is reasonable ground to doubt Jacobs's impartiality in the matter.

(B) No, because when Jacobs was a supreme court justice he granted a stay of execution to Dillon.

(C) Yes, because Jacobs was appointed by the district court, and his prior involvement in the matter is not sufficient grounds for refusing the appointment.

(D) Yes, because the respondent in the habeas corpus case is the prison warden, not the People of State Beta.

Question 3

Farmer Farner asked attorney Anderson to represent him in an eminent domain proceeding in which the state sought to obtain a right-of-way across Farner's farm. Anderson had not handled an eminent domain case before, but she planned to make herself competent through diligent research and study. As it turned out, Anderson did not have enough time to do what she had planned, so she associated an eminent domain specialist, lawyer Ling, as her co-counsel in the case. Anderson did not consult Farner about associating Ling. Ling did about 90% of the work in the case, and Anderson did the other 10%. Together they secured a very favorable result for Farner, and Anderson sent Farner a fee bill for a reasonable amount. Farner paid the bill, and Anderson remitted 90% of the proceeds to Ling.

Is Anderson *subject to discipline*?

(A) Yes, because she took on a case she was not competent to handle.

(B) Yes, because she did not consult Farner about associating Ling.

(C) No, because the fee split was in proportion to the work done by the two lawyers.

(D) No, because she associated a co-counsel who was competent to handle the case.

Question 4

Attorney Aoki is defending client Childs in a civil fraud case in which it is relevant to know what advice Childs received in confidence from an independent certified public accountant, Ben Counter. This jurisdiction has no evidentiary privilege for confidential communications between accountants and their clients. Counter telephoned Aoki and asked how he should respond to the plaintiff's lawyer's request to speak with him privately about the case. Reasonably believing that Counter would not be harmed by refusing to talk informally with the plaintiff's lawyer, Aoki responded: "If the plaintiff's lawyer subpoenas you to testify, then you must do so, but I encourage you not to talk to him about the case unless you are under subpoena."

Was her advice to Counter *proper*?

(A) No, because the advice Counter gave Childs was not protected by an evidentiary privilege.

(B) No, because Aoki interfered with the plaintiff's access to evidence.

(C) Yes, because Counter acted as Childs's agent in rendering accounting advice to Childs.

(D) Yes, because it was improper for the plaintiff's lawyer to seek a private discussion with Counter about the case.

GO ON TO THE NEXT PAGE

Question 5

Solo practitioners Arias and Armer share office space. Each of them has organized her practice as a professional corporation. The sign on their office door reads:

Arlene Arias, P.C.
Personal Injury Law

Alice Armer, P.C.
General Practice

Arias and Armer frequently consult with each other about their respective cases, and they often refer clients to one another. Sometimes they work on cases together under a fee-sharing arrangement. When one of them is out of the office, the other responds to client inquiries to the extent that she is able; to facilitate that practice, each attorney has physical access to the other's client files. Plaintiff Puente hired Arias to sue McDougal's Bakery for personal injuries he sustained when he bit into a piece of glass in a dinner roll baked by McDougal's. McDougal's liability insurance carrier, American Assurance Associates, asked Armer to serve as defense counsel in the case.

May Armer take the case?

(A) Yes, but only if Arias and Armer believe that they can effectively represent their respective clients, and only if Puente, McDougal's, and American give informed, written consent.

(B) Yes, because the rule of imputed disqualification does not apply to Arias and Armer.

(C) No, even if Arias and Armer believe that they can effectively represent their respective clients, and even if Puente, McDougal's, and American give informed, written consent.

(D) No, unless Arias and Armer believe that they can effectively represent their respective clients.

Question 6

Client Crowell made a preliminary contact with lawyer Lear to see if she wanted to hire Lear to defend her in a tort case that had been assigned to Judge Johnson. Lear told her that the initial consultation was free of charge. After listening to Crowell's brief outline of the case, Lear told her:

> I know how to get a favorable decision from Judge Johnson. He will be running for reelection 18 months from now, and he will need money for his campaign. You should send him a $2,000 campaign contribution now, with a nice note wishing him well in his bid for reelection. Judge Johnson's opponent in the election will be a local lawyer, Willard Wampler. Wampler is an honest fellow, but I know that his two brothers are associated with organized crime. I can write a guest editorial for the local paper, praising Judge Johnson's judicial record and implying that Wampler is a crook. With your contribution and my letter, I think we can count on Judge Johnson to reach a wise decision in your case.

Crowell hired Lear and sent Judge Johnson the $2,000. Lear wrote the guest editorial, and it was published in the local paper.

For which of the following is Lear *subject to discipline*?

I. Saying that he knew how to get a favorable ruling from Judge Johnson.

II. Advising Crowell to send Judge Johnson a campaign contribution.

III. Writing the guest editorial.

IV. Accepting the case following free legal advice.

(A) I., II., and III. only.

(B) I., II., III., and IV.

(C) II. only.

(D) I., II., and IV. only.

GO ON TO THE NEXT PAGE

Question 7

A series of brutal daylight muggings in downtown Sedatia brought fear to the citizens of that normally placid city. The police captured one Diablo, who was charged with the muggings and, in due course, was ordered to stand trial in Sedatia. Two days before the jury selection began, a local newspaper reporter cornered the prosecutor, District Attorney Axelrod, in the Sedatia Cafe and got her to make the following statement:

> I'm certain Diablo is the right man; among other things, we have discovered that he was previously convicted three times for brutal muggings in other states.

Is Axelrod *subject to discipline* for making the statement to the reporter?

(A) No, because prior criminal convictions are a matter of public record.

(B) No, because a lawyer has a First Amendment right to inform the public about pending cases.

(C) Yes, because she should have known that the statement would be quite likely to prejudice the trial.

(D) Yes, because a prosecutor must not make public comment on a pending case.

Question 8

Lawyer Lederlee was assigned by the court to defend an indigent person, former college English teacher Deniew, at her trial for the murder of her husband. The jury convicted Deniew, and she was sentenced to 40 years in prison. Lederlee's court appointment expired at the end of the trial, but he promised Deniew that he would represent her without cost in taking an appeal from her conviction. Lederlee advanced $350 on Deniew's behalf to cover the expenses of the appeal, knowing that Deniew would probably not be able to pay him back. While the appeal was pending, Deniew wrote the manuscript for a book about life in a women's prison. She hired Lederlee to negotiate a contract with a publisher to have the book published, and in return for the contract work, she promised to pay Lederlee 30% of the royalties from her book.

Is Lederlee *subject to discipline*?

(A) Yes, because he entered into a literary rights contract with his client while her appeal was still pending.

(B) Yes, because he advanced appeal expenses for his client, knowing that she probably could not pay him back.

(C) No, unless 30% of the book royalties is unreasonably high for the contract negotiation work.

(D) No, even if 30% of the book royalties is unreasonably high for the contract negotiation work.

GO ON TO THE NEXT PAGE

Question 9

Probate attorney Adamson was representing the executor of decedent Denman's estate. The executor removed the contents of Denman's safe deposit box and brought them to Adamson to be inventoried and appraised. The items included Denman's collection of valuable antique gold coins. Adamson put the coin collection into a heavy brown envelope and labeled it as part of the Denman estate. Because he intended to start preparing the inventory immediately after lunch, Adamson put the brown envelope and Denman's other belongings into the file drawer of his desk; he then left for lunch without locking the file drawer. Adamson's secretary saw the coins and saw what Adamson did with them. During the lunch hour, the secretary took the envelope of coins and disappeared, never to be seen again.

Is Adamson *subject to discipline*?

(A) Yes, because he did not put the coins in a safe place.

(B) Yes, because he is responsible for his employee's dishonest act.

(C) No, because the loss was proximately caused by the secretary's dishonesty, not by his conduct.

(D) No, because he took reasonable precautions to safeguard the coins in the circumstances.

Question 10

Paralegal Platten works for the law firm of Dahlers & Sentz. Her direct supervisor is partner Dahlers, whose practice is limited to international trade law. Partner Sentz is the firm's leading trial lawyer, both in commercial and personal injury cases. On her way to work one morning, Platten saw a pedestrian run down in a crosswalk by a speeding car. Platten rendered first aid, and while she was waiting with the pedestrian for the ambulance, Platten said: "Here, call the number on this card and talk to attorney Seymour Sentz; he's really good, and he can help you recover money for the injury you have suffered." When she got to work, she told partner Dahlers what she had done. Dahlers admonished Platten not to hand out the firm's cards in such situations, but he did not discuss the matter with partner Sentz.

Is Dahlers *subject to discipline*?

(A) Yes, because he failed to warn Sentz not to take the pedestrian's case.

(B) Yes, because as Platten's supervisor, he is responsible for any unethical act she commits.

(C) No, because as a nonlawyer, Platten is free to recommend a lawyer to someone if she wishes.

(D) No, because Platten may not have been aware at the time that she did anything wrong.

GO ON TO THE NEXT PAGE

Question 11

For several years, attorney Aston worked at the United States Department of Labor as part of a small group of attorneys whose responsibilities included compiling certain corporate safety records and monitoring compliance with federal regulations. Under a federal statute, factories of a certain type and size must report all work-related accidents to Aston's office. Aston's duties included compiling an annual report containing the accident statistics of all of the reporting companies. The report is used internally and in discussions with companies, but it is not distributed to the general public. A person may obtain a copy of the report, but must file a formal request under the Freedom of Information Act procedures adopted by the Labor Department. During the last three years, Chemco has had more accidents than any of the other reporting companies. Six months ago, Aston left the Labor Department and took a job with a private law firm. Charles comes to Aston seeking representation in a suit against Chemco for injuries he sustained last month while working at one of Chemco's factories. Although unsure as to whether he should take the case, Aston, who is just starting out in private practice and cannot afford to turn clients away, agrees to represent Charles.

Is Aston *subject to discipline*?

(A) Yes, because he obtained relevant information on Chemco while working as a government attorney.

(B) Yes, unless Aston obtains the consent of the Department of Labor.

(C) No, because the information is available by formal request under the Freedom of Information Act.

(D) No, if Aston does not use the information obtained while employed as a government attorney to the material disadvantage of Chemco.

Question 12

Attorney Alexander and her client Cardone endured a stormy attorney-client relationship until Alexander finally withdrew due to Cardone's repeated refusals to pay Alexander's fee bills. At the end of the relationship, Cardone owed Alexander more than $10,000. Cardone said he would not pay because Alexander's legal services were "defective." In a final effort to avoid having to sue Cardone for the unpaid fees, Alexander proposed a settlement agreement to Cardone. Under the proposed agreement, Alexander would accept $4,000 as full payment, reserving the right to sue Cardone for the other $6,000 if Cardone filed a State Bar disciplinary complaint against Alexander or filed a legal malpractice action against Alexander. Cardone signed the settlement agreement without consulting outside counsel, and Alexander did not suggest that he should consult outside counsel before signing it.

Is Alexander *subject to discipline* for entering into the settlement agreement with Cardone?

(A) No, because Alexander brought about an amicable settlement of the fee dispute with Cardone.

(B) No, provided that there was a good faith dispute between Alexander and Cardone about the quality of Alexander's services and the amount of fees due.

(C) Yes, because Alexander did not advise Cardone to seek outside counsel before entering into the settlement agreement.

(D) Yes, because Alexander compromised a potential malpractice claim by contract with her client.

GO ON TO THE NEXT PAGE

Question 13

Worker Workman sued his employer, Drexel Moving and Storage Co., claiming that he was permanently and totally disabled due to a back injury he suffered on the job. Lawyer Lenhart represented Drexel in the case. Lenhart strongly suspected, but had no proof, that Workman continued his hobby of skydiving after the alleged back injury. In due course, Lenhart met with Workman's lawyer for a settlement discussion. Lenhart told Workman's lawyer: "We won't give you a dime on this claim; we've got movies of your guy jumping out of an airplane two weeks after his phoney injury." Workman's lawyer excused herself to make a telephone call to Workman. When she asked Workman whether he had been skydiving after the accident, he admitted that he had. With the consent of their respective clients, the two lawyers then settled the case for $400.

Is Lenhart *subject to discipline*?

(A) No, because bluffing is an accepted tactic in settlement negotiations between lawyers.

(B) No, because Lenhart's bluff successfully unmasked a fraudulent claim.

(C) Yes, because it was improper to pay $400 to settle a fraudulent claim.

(D) Yes, because Lenhart lied about having movies.

Question 14

Bar applicant Lingenfelter is applying to become a member of the Bar of State A. The application questionnaire asks whether she has ever used any narcotic in violation of State A law. When she was a high school student in State A, Lingenfelter occasionally smoked marijuana, which is a minor misdemeanor under State A law. The statute of limitations has long since run on those offenses. Lingenfelter is convinced that she could not validly be kept out of the State A Bar for those offenses. She therefore believes that the question is irrelevant and an invasion of her privacy in violation of State A's Constitution. She fears, however, that challenging the question could brand her as a troublemaker and delay her admission to the bar.

Which of the following would be *proper*?

I.   Answer the question in the negative, without saying more.

II. Answer the question in the affirmative, but explain the circumstances.

III. Decline to answer the question, citing the invasion of privacy provision of the State A Constitution.

IV. Decline to answer the question, citing the federal constitutional privilege against self-incrimination.

(A) I., II., III., and IV.

(B) None of the above.

(C) II. and III. only.

(D) II., III., and IV. only.

GO ON TO THE NEXT PAGE

Question 15

Judge Jamagian sits on a State A trial court. Every six years, State A trial judges must stand as candidates in a public election to determine whether they will retain their positions. Judge Jamagian will be a retention candidate in the election to be held nine months from now. In that same election, her husband, attorney Ali, will be a candidate for Lieutenant Governor of State A.

Which of the following *may* Judge Jamagian do?

I. Establish a campaign committee that will immediately begin soliciting reasonable contributions for Judge Jamagian's campaign.

II. Allow her name to be listed on Republican Party election materials, along with the name of her husband and other Republican candidates for elective offices.

III. Publicly endorse her husband as a candidate for Lieutenant Governor.

IV. Attend political gatherings in the company of her husband, and speak on behalf of both herself and him.

V. Personally solicit contributions to her own campaign.

VI. Personally solicit contributions to her husband's campaign.

(A) I., II., and IV. only.

(B) I., II., and III. only.

(C) II., IV., V., and VI. only.

(D) I. and II. only.

Question 16

Continuously since 1910, the law firm of Hardwicke & Chandler has practiced under that name in State A. The founders of the firm, Horace Hardwicke and Carlisle Chandler, are long dead. No partner named Chandler now practices with the firm. Horace Hardwicke IV (the great-grandson of the founder) is presently the managing partner of the firm. Five years ago, Hanna Hardwicke, the daughter of Horace Hardwicke IV, became a partner in the firm. Hanna recently left law practice to take a life tenure appointment on the State A Supreme Court.

May the firm continue to use the name Hardwicke & Chandler?

(A) No, because no partner named Chandler now practices with the firm.

(B) No, because Hanna ceased private practice to enter public service.

(C) Yes, unless the firm name would be misleading.

(D) Yes, even if the firm name will mislead some prospective clients.

GO ON TO THE NEXT PAGE

Question 17

From 2000 through 2003, attorney Arnett was a partner in the firm of Able & Aman. During that period, Arnett represented client Cobb in obtaining a business loan from a bank. Cobb disclosed to Arnett a great deal of confidential information about his business and his personal assets. No other lawyer in Able & Aman gained access to that confidential information. In late 2003, Arnett died. In 2004, Carlton asked attorney Able (the senior partner of Able & Aman) to represent him in a civil suit for serious personal injuries Carlton suffered when he was run over by a delivery truck driven by one of Cobb's employees.

Would it be *proper* for Able to represent Carlton?

(A) Yes, because the information obtained by Arnett about Cobb's assets has no effect on liability in a personal injury suit.

(B) Yes, because neither Able nor any other lawyer in Able & Aman gained access to Cobb's confidential information.

(C) No, because the conflict created by Arnett's work for Cobb is imputed to Able.

(D) No, unless Able gets Cobb's informed, written consent.

Question 18

Young associate Aster was assisting senior partner Parker in writing the reply brief in an appeal for one of Parker's clients. In doing the legal research, Aster discovered a recent case from the controlling jurisdiction that had not been cited in the adversary's brief. In Aster's opinion, the case was directly opposed to the position of Parker's client. Aster asked Parker about citing it in the reply brief, but Parker explained that, in his view, the case was not directly on point and did not have to be cited. Aster and Parker argued back and forth at some length and finally decided to submit the question to one of the other senior partners in the firm for a fresh view. That partner sided with Parker, and the reply brief was filed without mentioning the case.

May Aster write a short letter to the appellate court and the adversary lawyer, explaining his position and enclosing a copy of the case?

(A) Yes, because Aster had a duty to call the case to the court's attention.

(B) Yes, because Aster must not allow another person to interfere with his professional judgment.

(C) No, because Aster must not communicate with a court ex parte about the merits of a pending case.

(D) No, because Aster should abide by Parker's resolution of the matter.

GO ON TO THE NEXT PAGE

Question 19

L'Etoille Women's Wear, Inc. is incorporated in and has its principal place of business in State A, and it is represented by a lawyer who is licensed to practice in State A. L'Etoille owns the valuable, federally registered trademark *L'Etoille*® for use on various items of women's wearing apparel, and it licenses the trademark to garment makers in various states for use on items of apparel that are manufactured in accordance with style and quality specifications set by L'Etoille. Lawyer Londrell is licensed to practice only in State B. She represents DonnaDell Clothing Co., which is incorporated in and has its sole place of business in State B. Londrell and the president of DonnaDell traveled to State A, where they negotiated with L'Etoille's lawyer for a license to use its trademark on apparel to be manufactured at DonnaDell's plant in State B.

Londrell is not licensed to practice before the United States Patent and Trademark Office. The license agreement between L'Etoille and DonnaDell provides that the agreement is to be construed in accordance with the law of State A, and that any disputes arising under the license will be arbitrated in State A.

Is Londrell *subject to discipline*?

(A) No, because admission to practice in State A was not necessary to negotiate the trademark license there.

(B) No, unless the licensing agreement was actually drafted by Londrell in State A.

(C) Yes, because she was not admitted to practice in State A.

(D) Yes, because she was not admitted to practice before the United States Patent and Trademark Office.

Question 20

Attorney Abrahamson recently opened his solo law practice in Crystal Springs. His practice is fairly evenly divided between civil litigation and criminal defense. The Crystal Springs Superior Court has just appointed him to represent defendants Denton and Drews, who will be tried jointly for their alleged kidnapping and brutal murder of nine Crystal Springs school children.

For which of the following reasons *may* Abrahamson decline the appointment?

I.   He believes that to represent Denton and Drews will take so much time away from his newly opened practice as to impose an unreasonable financial burden on him.

II. He believes that Denton coerced Drews into helping kidnap and kill the children.

III. He believes many of his potential clients in Crystal Springs will be outraged if he defends Denton and Drews.

IV. He believes that confidential information he received when representing one of the prosecution's key witnesses will be useful in impeaching that witness's credibility.

(A) I., II., III., and IV.

(B) II. and IV. only.

(C) I., II., and IV. only.

(D) II. only.

GO ON TO THE NEXT PAGE

Question 21

Federal prosecutor Fedman is stationed in Maryland; he is gathering evidence to support federal racketeering charges against a swindler named Phatseaux. Fedman believes in good faith that a wealthy Florida banker, Bucks, has personal knowledge about three federal felonies committed by Phatseaux, but Bucks will not disclose what he knows about Phatseaux. However, Fedman has recently learned from a secret informant that Bucks illegally drained off $4.7 million from a failing Florida savings and loan institution—a state felony punishable by 10 years in prison. Fedman therefore mailed a letter from his office in Maryland to Bucks in Florida, stating in relevant part: "I am coming to Florida next week. If you don't give me what I need concerning Phatseaux, I am going to tell the Florida prosecutors what you did to that savings and loan. Do you know what those old boys in state prison do with fellows like you?"

Is Fedman *subject to criminal liability* because of his evidence-gathering technique?

(A) No, because Fedman had a legal right to tell the Florida prosecutors about Bucks, and he simply warned Bucks what he intended to do if Bucks did not cooperate.

(B) No, because Fedman was acting in good faith, believing that Bucks had relevant, unprivileged information that was material to an ongoing federal criminal investigation.

(C) Yes, because Fedman made an interstate threat to accuse Bucks of a crime for the purpose of extracting valuable information that he could use against Phatseaux.

(D) Yes, because Fedman acted under color of law to deprive Bucks of his federally protected civil rights.

Question 22

Lawyer Loomis is the head of the in-house law department of Darlington KiddieWear Corp., which has its principal place of business in State A. Under the law of State A, it is a felony to manufacture or sell children's sleepwear that is not fire retardant. The president of Darlington informed Loomis in confidence that Darlington is stuck with a whole warehouse full of children's pajama fabric that does not meet State A's fire standards, and that to avoid financial disaster, Darlington will use the fabric to make children's sleepwear and take its chances on legal liability. Loomis was unable to convince the president to change his mind; she then raised the issue with Darlington's board of directors, which ratified the president's decision.

Will Loomis be *subject to discipline* if she resigns as house counsel and reports the matter to the appropriate State A law enforcement authorities?

(A) Yes, because she is required to preserve the corporation's confidential information even after she resigns.

(B) Yes, because there is no adequate reason for permissive withdrawal on these facts.

(C) No, because she is entitled to reveal this type of confidential information.

(D) No, because her duty to preserve confidential information ceases with her resignation as house counsel.

GO ON TO THE NEXT PAGE

Question 23

Attorney Ashe is a partner in a four-partner law firm. Client Corbett entrusted $40,000 to Ashe, instructing Ashe to hold it in safekeeping for a few days and then to use it as the down payment on a piece of lakefront property. Ashe promptly deposited the money in his law firm's Law Office Account, a special bank account that the firm uses to pay the office rent, to pay staff salaries, to advance litigation expenses on behalf of clients, and the like. A few days later, when it was time to make the down payment, Ashe discovered that one of his law partners had made two large withdrawals from the Law Office Account, reducing the account balance far below the $40,000 needed for Corbett's down payment. Ashe was unable to come up with other money to make up the difference, and Corbett thus lost the chance to buy the lakefront property.

Is Ashe *subject to civil liability* to Corbett for mishandling the money?

(A) No, because it was Ashe's law partner, not Ashe, who made the two large withdrawals that made it impossible to come up with the down payment.

(B) Yes, because Ashe mishandled the money and is therefore civilly liable to Corbett for breach of his fiduciary duty.

(C) No, because the legal ethics rule governing safekeeping of clients' funds is for professional disciplinary purposes only; it is not intended as a standard for civil liability purposes.

(D) Yes, because a lawyer is strictly liable to a client for harm incident to the disappearance of money that the client has entrusted to the lawyer.

Question 24

The M & S law firm represented United Oil Company in a merger transaction in which United acquired all the assets of Mogul Petroleum Inc. in exchange for a specified amount of capital stock of United. M & S's work for United was limited to the antitrust and securities law issues raised by the merger, and the M & S lawyers who worked on the matter did not become privy to any confidential information concerning the routine operations of United's business. The merger work was completed two years ago, and M & S has not subsequently represented United in any other matter.

Recently, M & S took in a new partner, lawyer Lurner, who had previously practiced as a solo practitioner. One of the cases that Lurner brought to M & S from his solo practice was *Droan v. United Oil Co.*, an employment discrimination case in which Lurner's client, Droan, claims that United fired him solely because of his age. When Lurner became an M & S partner, United promptly made a motion in the trial court to disqualify Lurner and M & S as counsel for Droan due to M & S's earlier representation of United in the Mogul merger matter.

Are Lurner and M & S *subject to disqualification*?

(A) No, because the merger matter and the discrimination case are unrelated matters and because M & S did not gain confidential information from United that would be material in the discrimination case.

(B) No, because whatever material confidential information M & S might have picked up in the merger matter is not imputed to Lurner.

(C) Yes, because M & S owes continuing duties of loyalty and confidentiality to its former client, United.

(D) Yes, even though the merger matter and the discrimination case are unrelated and even though M & S did not gain confidential information from United that would be material in the discrimination case.

GO ON TO THE NEXT PAGE

Question 25

Lawyers Abner, Baker, and Clark formed a law partnership; each contributed $100,000 in capital to get the firm started. Their partnership agreement provided that when a partner dies, the firm will make certain payments to the dead partner's named beneficiary. Sometime later, Clark died, leaving his daughter Clara, a doctor, as his sole beneficiary.

Under the partnership agreement, the firm plans to make the following payments to Clara: $100,000, which represents Clark's share of the firm's assets, as measured by his capital contribution; $45,000, which represents Clark's share of fees that had been earned but not collected from clients at Clark's death; and a $125,000 death benefit, representing a percentage of Clark's earnings the year prior to his death, and payable in 12 monthly installments.

Which of the following payments *may* the firm make to Clara?

(A) $100,000 for Clark's share of the firm's assets.

(B) $270,000, which includes Clark's share of the firm's assets, Clark's share of uncollected fees, and the death benefit.

(C) $170,000, which represents the death benefit and Clark's share of uncollected fees.

(D) $145,000 for Clark's share of the firm's assets and Clark's share of uncollected fees.

Question 26

Client Chandler, a concerned environmentalist, hired lawyer Lipscomb to obtain preliminary and permanent injunctions against a highway construction project that would require draining and filling certain wetlands inhabited by migratory waterfowl. Lipscomb is the nation's leading expert in wetland preservation law, and he charges $400 per hour for his services. Chandler agreed to pay him at that rate. She gave him a $40,000 advance on attorneys' fees and a $5,000 advance to cover future litigation expenses. Lipscomb deposited the entire $45,000 in his client trust account.

Lipscomb then spent 80 hours preparing and filing a complaint and preparing and arguing a motion for a preliminary injunction. He paid a court filing fee of $50, plus $1,950 in witness fees to wetlands experts who testified at the hearing on the preliminary injunction motion. The judge denied the preliminary injunction motion. Lipscomb sent Chandler a bill for $32,000 in attorneys' fees and $2,000 in litigation expenses, and he told her he would deduct those sums from the advances she had given him unless he heard from her to the contrary within 15 days. In light of the loss of the preliminary injunction motion, Chandler was outraged at the size of Lipscomb's fee; she immediately fired him and demanded the prompt refund of her entire $45,000.

Which of the following amounts *must* Lipscomb promptly refund to Chandler?

(A) $0

(B) $43,000

(C) $11,000

(D) $13,000

GO ON TO THE NEXT PAGE

Question 27

Attorney Ambrose is admitted to practice only in State A, where he specializes in securities and real estate finance law. In that role, Ambrose advised his client, Corbuster, that the law of State B did not require Corbuster to include information about certain mineral rights in a disclosure statement that Corbuster had to file in State B in order to sell some real estate limited partnership interests to State B citizens. Acting on Ambrose's advice, Corbuster did not disclose the information and did sell partnership interests to State B citizens.

Later, Ambrose became a full-time trial court judge in State A. Later still, State B brought a criminal action against Corbuster for failing to disclose the mineral rights information in his State B disclosure statement. One of Corbuster's defenses is that he lacked the necessary criminal intent because he was acting in good faith based on the advice of his counsel, Ambrose. Corbuster needs Ambrose's testimony to prove that Ambrose did indeed advise him that he was not required to disclose the mineral rights information. Ambrose, in State A, is beyond the subpoena power of the State B court.

May Ambrose voluntarily testify on behalf of Corbuster?

(A) No, because judges are disqualified from serving as witnesses in criminal cases.

(B) No, because he is not admitted to practice in State B, and his testimony about State B law would be inadmissible.

(C) Yes, because a judge may testify as a witness, except in his own court or one under its appellate jurisdiction.

(D) Yes, because his testimony would concern the giving of the advice, not his client's character.

Question 28

Client Cristin sought the advice of lawyer Leona on a difficult and sensitive family problem. Cristin suspected that her husband had been molesting Daisy, Cristin's 12-year-old daughter by a prior marriage. Cristin asked Leona what she should do. Leona advised Cristin that all three members of the family should consult Frances, a licensed family counselor who specializes in precisely this sort of problem. Fearing that if Cristin were aware of the law she would not seek counseling, Leona purposely failed to tell Cristin that a new state statute requires family counselors to report to the district attorney all instances of suspected child abuse.

Cristin and her family consulted Frances, and Frances reported the matter to the district attorney, as she was required to do by law. The district attorney commenced criminal proceedings against Cristin's husband, much against the wishes of both Cristin and Daisy.

Were Leona's actions *proper*?

(A) Yes, if Leona believed in good faith that Cristin would not seek counseling if she knew about the statute.

(B) Yes, because it is the policy of the state that all instances of child abuse be reported to the appropriate authorities.

(C) No, because a lawyer should fully advise a client of relevant information.

(D) No, unless Leona believed in good faith that the daughter had actually been molested.

GO ON TO THE NEXT PAGE

Question 29

When lawyer Locke was an associate in the firm of Bliss & Buford, she did the legal work for one of the firm's clients, Cannon, on a land sale transaction that earned Cannon millions of dollars. In gratitude, Cannon asked Locke whether she had any unfulfilled wishes. Locke told him that she wished she had enough money to start her own solo law practice. Cannon then told her that he would lend her $100,000 to set up her new practice. In return, she would there-after do all of his legal work at a 5% discount from her normal hourly fee, and she would pay off the $100,000 loan by monthly payments equal to 10% of her net income for the prior month. Locke was delighted. She drafted a complete, detailed agreement between herself and Cannon, and she advised Cannon in writing to obtain outside legal advice before signing the agreement. Cannon obtained the outside advice and signed the agreement, and Locke set up her solo practice accordingly.

Is Locke *subject to discipline*?

(A) No, unless she allows Cannon to interfere with her professional judgment in handling work for other clients.

(B) No, unless Locke fails to give Bliss & Buford timely notice of the transaction.

(C) Yes, unless Bliss & Buford consented to the loss of Cannon as a firm client.

(D) Yes, unless Cannon is a lawyer.

Question 30

Lawyer Li represented Weaver in a court proceeding to raise the alimony and child support payments set in the decree that divorced Weaver from her ex-husband, Hyde. Hyde stubbornly refused to get a lawyer in the matter. The evening before the court hearing, Hyde telephoned Li at home and asked Li to explain the legal standard the judge would apply to Weaver's request for increased payments. Li responded:

> Mr. Hyde, I am not your lawyer, and I cannot give you legal advice. I think that you ought to get a lawyer in this matter, and if you need time to do that, I will ask the judge to postpone the hearing for a couple of weeks.

Hyde said he did not want a lawyer, and then asked Li whether Weaver and the children really needed more money to live on. Li responded:

> Mr. Hyde, I have no personal interest to serve here—I am simply trying to do what is best for you, and your ex-wife, and your kids. Now if you really want my opinion, I'd say yes, you should pay the extra money because they do need it to live on.

Hyde thanked Li and hung up.

Was Li's handling of the matter *proper*?

(A) No, because as Weaver's lawyer, Li should not have communicated directly with Hyde at all.

(B) No, because Li pretended to be disinterest-ed and advised Hyde to pay the extra money.

(C) Yes, because Li advised Hyde that Li was not his lawyer, that Hyde should retain one, and that Li could not give him legal advice.

(D) Yes, because Li only stated his opinion and did not purport to give Hyde advice.

GO ON TO THE NEXT PAGE

Question 31

Lawyer Lockwood represents defendant Downs in a drug smuggling case. Downs is in pretrial custody in a distant city and cannot be reached by telephone. One key issue in Downs's case is on the cutting edge of search and seizure law, and Lockwood believes that he needs help to deal with the issue competently. Lockwood's former law professor is a nationally known expert on search and seizure law. Lockwood calls his professor to ask for his help, and also asks that the professor keep this information confidential. To frame the issue accurately, Lockwood tells the law professor some information that Downs revealed to Lockwood in confidence. Lockwood does not tell the professor the name of his client.

Is Lockwood *subject to discipline* for disclosing Downs's confidential information to the professor?

(A) Yes, if the professor was not licensed to practice in that jurisdiction.

(B) Yes, unless Downs had specifically authorized Lockwood to make such a disclosure.

(C) No, because the disclosure was necessary to effectively carry out the representation.

(D) No, because Lockwood did not reveal his client's name.

Question 32

For many years, tax attorney Aguero has handled all of the tax work for client Carrara, a famous post-modern sculptor. Carrara's large sculptures cost hundreds of thousands of dollars each and are sold mostly to wealthy collectors and museums. Carrara also, however, produces the occasional small, modestly priced work. Aguero greatly admires Carrara's talent and yearns for one of the small sculptures to display in his office. One evening, Carrara invited Aguero to his studio to discuss some tax returns that had to be filed the next day. In the studio, Aguero saw a small sculpture that would be perfect for his office. At the close of their tax discussion, Aguero told Carrara how much he admired the small sculpture and offered to buy it for $10,000, its approximate fair market value. Carrara told Aguero that it was not for sale. In due course, Aguero sent Carrara a $750 fee bill for the tax work. A few days later, the small sculpture was delivered to Aguero's office with the following note from Carrara:

> My dear Aguero: I hope this small piece of my work will satisfy your recent fee bill. I want you to have it as a token of my gratitude for the excellent tax advice you have given me all these years. I hope you will enjoy having it in your office. Your friend, Carrara.

Would Aguero *be subject to discipline* for accepting the small sculpture from Carrara?

(A) Yes, because the gift is of significant monetary value.

(B) Yes, because the value of the sculpture is far out of proportion to the $750 worth of work Aguero did for Carrara.

(C) No, because Aguero did not solicit the gift.

(D) No, unless $10,000 would be an unreasonably high legal fee for the work Aguero did for Carrara.

GO ON TO THE NEXT PAGE

Question 33

Public defender Purdum was assigned to represent defendant Dewitt at Dewitt's preliminary hearing on a charge of kidnapping for ransom. Against Purdum's advice, Dewitt testified on his own behalf at the preliminary hearing. Dewitt was bound over for trial. At that point, Dewitt's elder brother provided money to hire a private lawyer to defend Dewitt, and public defender Purdum was discharged. Dewitt testified on his own behalf at the trial, and the jury acquitted him. Later, in connection with his work on another matter, Purdum read the transcript of Dewitt's trial. Based on information Purdum learned while representing Dewitt, Purdum concluded that Dewitt had committed perjury, both at the preliminary hearing and at the trial.

May Purdum reveal Dewitt's perjury?

(A) Yes, but only with respect to the perjury at Dewitt's preliminary hearing.

(B) Yes, Purdum may reveal both instances of perjury if Dewitt refuses to recant.

(C) No, unless Purdum believes Dewitt is dangerous.

(D) No, because disclosure would violate Purdum's duty of confidentiality.

Question 34

United Consumers Bank operates a "Professional Referral Hotline" for its depositors. Any United depositor who needs to find a physician, lawyer, accountant, dentist, or the like can telephone the hotline and obtain a free referral from lists of professionals compiled by United. The lists are limited to professionals who maintain an average balance of at least $10,000 in a time deposit account at United, but the professional does not pay a fee to United for receiving a particular referral. Lawyer Lomax keeps $10,000 on deposit with United for the express purpose of being included on its lawyer referral list.

Is this arrangement *proper*?

(A) Yes, because United is functioning in the role of a lawyer referral service.

(B) Yes, because neither United's depositors nor the professionals pay a fee for referrals.

(C) No, because Lomax is required to keep $10,000 on deposit to be included on the list.

(D) No, because this arrangement constitutes an association with a nonlawyer for the practice of law.

Question 35

Inventor Inovacio asked patent lawyer Patton to represent him in obtaining a United States patent on a new computer technique for predicting the growth patterns of tumors in the human body. Patton informed Inovacio that he had never worked on that kind of patent application before, and that he would have to do extensive background research on the patentability of computer techniques. Patton will be able to use the knowledge that he gains through the research to serve other clients who wish to obtain patents for all manner of other computer techniques. Patton offered to do the work for Inovacio for his standard hourly rate, but Inovacio proposed instead to assign Patton a 10% interest in the patent, if and when it was issued. Patton agreed to do the work on that basis, and he and Inovacio entered into an appropriate written fee agreement.

Patton did the work; the patent was ultimately issued and proved so valuable that Patton was able to sell his 10% interest for $9.7 million.

Is Patton *subject to discipline*?

(A) Yes, because he acquired a proprietary interest in the subject of the representation.

(B) Yes, because it is unreasonable to charge one client for background research that will be used to earn fees from other clients.

(C) No, because Inovacio agreed to the fee arrangement.

(D) No, unless $9.7 million is an unreasonably high fee for the work that Patton did.

Question 36

Lawyer LeBrille is admitted to practice in State A. One of her regular clients is Chatsworth Inc., which is incorporated in and has its principal place of business in State A. The president of Chatsworth went to France to negotiate a business contract for Chatsworth that would be governed, in part, by the law of the European Union ("EU"). The president telephoned LeBrille to ask whether a particular provision of the proposed contract would be lawful under EU law. The president needed a quick answer because he had to resume the contract negotiation a few minutes later. LeBrille had studied EU law, but she was not admitted to practice in any nation that is a member of the EU. LeBrille warned the president about the danger of relying on off-the-cuff, unresearched legal advice, but he asked her to do the best she could. She then advised him that the contract provision would be lawful under EU law. The president thanked her, continued the contract negotiation, and signed a contract for Chatsworth that included the questioned provision. As it turned out, LeBrille's advice was mistaken: the provision violated EU law and rendered the contract unenforceable.

Is LeBrille *subject to discipline*?

(A) No, because she did the best she could in an emergency situation.

(B) No, because a State A lawyer is not expected to be competent in EU law.

(C) Yes, because she is not licensed to practice EU law.

(D) Yes, because she gave legal advice without adequate research.

GO ON TO THE NEXT PAGE

Question 37

Entertainment lawyer Labrie has for many years represented country music star Spangles Truhart. One evening, Labrie and Truhart were having a quiet business dinner together at a well-known restaurant. A brutish drunk, Duke Sirosis, lurched up to their table and in a loud voice began a vulgar and defamatory tirade against Truhart. Everyone in the restaurant heard the vile names Sirosis called Truhart. While all of the defamatory comments about Truhart involved her personal life, about which Labrie had no real knowledge, he felt that they could not possibly be true. At Truhart's request, Labrie commenced a slander suit against Sirosis. In his answer to the complaint, Sirosis admitted making the allegedly slanderous statements, and as an affirmative defense, he alleged that the statements were entirely truthful.

When the case comes to trial, would it be *proper* for Labrie to act as Truhart's trial counsel?

(A) Yes, but only if Truhart gives informed, written consent.

(B) Yes, because Labrie is not a necessary witness.

(C) No, because there is a possibility that Labrie may be called as a witness.

(D) No, unless he associates and prepares co-counsel to take over in the event he is called as a witness.

Question 38

Lawyer Lacey is on the in-house legal staff of Transcorp, Inc. In that capacity, she works daily with Transcorp's top executive officers. She was assigned to defend Transcorp in a lawsuit brought by West America Bank to collect a $750,000 promissory note. The note was signed on behalf of Transcorp by Willard Westerman, Transcorp's treasurer and chief financial officer. Transcorp's defense is that Westerman had no authority to sign the note and that the bank knew it. Transcorp has advised Westerman that it may seek indemnification from him if it is held liable to the bank. Westerman is not represented by counsel. Shortly before Westerman was to have his deposition taken by the bank, Westerman called Lacey and asked her what to expect at the deposition and how to respond to the bank's questions.

What *should* Lacey do?

(A) Not discuss the matter with Westerman, and, if appropriate, advise him to hire a lawyer to represent him at the deposition.

(B) Tell Westerman that she cannot discuss the matter with him unless he wants her to represent him at the deposition.

(C) Advise Westerman to tell the truth, to answer fully all questions that are asked, and to pause before each answer to give her time to object to the bank's questions.

(D) Advise Westerman that his own interests will be best served by answering truthfully and demonstrating, if he can, that he had authority to sign the note.

Question 39

Attorney Anderson is licensed to practice law in State Red, but he is not engaged in the active practice of law. Anderson and Benson, a non-attorney partner, operate a temporary placement service for legal secretaries in State Green, which borders State Red. Anderson is not licensed to practice law in State Green, nor does he hold himself out to be so licensed. An investigation by State Green authorities results in the discovery that Anderson and his partner have intentionally filed improper state business tax returns.

Is Anderson *subject to discipline* in State Red?

(A) Yes, because his actions in State Green constitute fraud.

(B) Yes, if he supervises the temporary service business from State Red.

(C) No, because Anderson is not licensed to practice law in State Green.

(D) No, because this situation does not involve the practice of law.

Question 40

Client Carson, a self-employed furnace repairman with no assets, was run over in a pedestrian crosswalk by a moving van driven by an employee of Deluxe Transport and Storage Corporation. Carson's injuries were so severe that he could not work, or even seek work, for a period of 18 months after the accident. Carson asked lawyer Lucas to represent him in a personal injury action against Deluxe. At Carson's request, Lucas agreed to represent Carson on a contingent fee basis. Carson requested that Lucas provide him with certain financial assistance during the pendency of the lawsuit.

Which of the following *may* Lucas do?

I. Lend Carson $5,000, pursuant to an agreement reviewed by independent counsel, to be used to support Carson's family during the pendency of the suit.

II. Lend Carson $10,500, pursuant to an agreement reviewed by independent counsel, to pay for Carson's medical treatment.

III. Advance Carson $1,250 for court-filing fees and deposition-reporter fees, subject to repayment by Carson when the case is concluded.

IV. Advance Carson $2,000 to pay the expert witness fee of Dr. Stromberg, a medical expert consulted solely for testimony and not for treatment. Carson promises to repay the money when the case is concluded.

(A) I., II., and III. only.

(B) II. and III. only.

(C) II., III., and IV. only.

(D) III. and IV. only.

GO ON TO THE NEXT PAGE

Question 41

In an effort to prevent homosexual persons from moving to Elmville, the Elmville City Council passed a zoning ordinance that prohibits the use of any dwelling house as a residence for two or more adults of the same sex unless they are related to each other. Violation of the ordinance is a misdemeanor and carries a fine of $10,000. Carlo owns several rental houses in Elmville, and he was outraged when the City Council passed the ordinance. He sought the legal advice of attorney Ahmad. Ahmad advised him that the ordinance could probably be overturned as a violation of rights guaranteed by the state constitution, but that one would have to obtain legal standing to challenge the ordinance. Ahmad advised that one way to obtain legal standing would be for a landlord to bring an appropriate action for declaratory judgment, and another way would be to simply violate the ordinance and raise the constitutional challenge as a defense to its enforcement.

After receiving this advice, Carlo promptly rented one of his houses to two gay men. Carlo was cited for violation of the ordinance.

Was Ahmad's conduct *proper*?

(A) Yes, because violating the ordinance was one of the few ways to gain legal standing to challenge the constitutionality of the law.

(B) Yes, if the ordinance is ultimately held unconstitutional.

(C) No, because Ahmad counseled and assisted Carlo in conduct Ahmad knew was illegal.

(D) No, because Ahmad did not advise against renting houses to unrelated adults of the same sex.

Question 42

Attorney Aronson has just opened an office in a town where he does not know many people and has few contacts. Aronson is attempting to build up a clientele for his general civil and criminal law practice.

Aronson has just heard on the radio that a group of several hundred townspeople have been arrested and are being held at the county jail for conducting a noisy demonstration outside the local high school to protest an impending strike by the teachers. The radio reports that the townspeople are charged with unlawful assembly, resisting arrest, and disorderly conduct. Aronson believes that the arrest of these demonstrators is a politically motivated trick, and that the demonstrators have been deprived of their freedom of expression in violation of the First Amendment.

Aronson goes down to the county jail and offers his legal services, free of charge, to any of the arrested demonstrators who want legal assistance.

Are Aronson's actions *proper*?

(A) Yes, unless he is motivated in any way by a desire to obtain publicity for his law practice.

(B) Yes, because Aronson was offering his services free of charge.

(C) No, because to do so would involve in-person solicitation of legal business.

(D) No, unless he has previously represented some of the arrested demonstrators on other legal matters.

Question 43

Judge Jardon is a full-time trial judge in State A. State A has a statute that prohibits employment discrimination against gays and lesbians. In addition to her judicial work, Judge Jardon is the chief executive officer of a corporation that is closely held by Judge Jardon and her three brothers. The corporation owns and operates a nursing home in State A. Because of strong anti-homosexual religious beliefs on the part of residents, the nursing home does not employ gays and lesbians.

Is it *proper* for Judge Jardon to continue as chief executive officer of the corporation?

(A) Yes, because a judge is prohibited from association with an organization that practices invidious discrimination on the basis of race, sex, religion, or national origin only.

(B) Yes, unless the management of the family-owned business takes so much time that it interferes with the judge's judicial duties.

(C) No, because a judge is not allowed to serve as an officer, director, manager, general partner, advisor, or employee of a business entity.

(D) No, because the nursing home practices employment discrimination against gays and lesbians.

Question 44

Attorney Angstrom was appointed by the court to defend client Cheever at Cheever's criminal trial for second degree murder. Angstrom started interviewing potential witnesses. When she interviewed Cheever's landlord, the landlord said that on the night of the murder, Cheever came home very late and was wearing a shirt covered with blood. The landlord died before trial without speaking to state authorities.

Which of the following best states what Angstrom *should* do with respect to the information she has learned from the landlord?

(A) Angstrom should voluntarily reveal the information to the prosecutor prior to trial because the death of the landlord has made it impossible for the prosecutor to obtain the information in any other way.

(B) Angstrom should urge Cheever to allow her to reveal the information to the prosecutor, and if Cheever refuses, Angstrom should withdraw.

(C) Angstrom should keep the information in confidence unless Cheever authorizes her to reveal it, even though the death of the landlord has made it impossible for the prosecutor to obtain the information other than from Angstrom.

(D) Angstrom should use her own best judgment about how to treat the information; it is neither privileged nor confidential because it was not given to her by her client or by an agent of her client.

GO ON TO THE NEXT PAGE

Question 45

Judge Jackson is a trial court judge who hears primarily civil tort and contract cases. Judge Jackson's mother, Martha, owns a small business. Martha wishes to sell the business and retire to Florida. Martha and a prospective buyer come to terms on the sale, and the buyer has her lawyer draw up a sales contract. When Martha receives her copy of the contract, she is shocked to see that it is 20 pages long and full of what she considers to be legal gobbledygook. Martha realizes that she needs a lawyer to review the document. Martha does not see any reason why she should have to pay a lawyer when her own son, a judge no less, could review the document for free. Martha asks Judge Jackson to review the contract. Judge Jackson agrees. Judge Jackson marks up the contract, drafts an important rider to be attached, and returns it to Martha to present to the buyer's attorney.

Were Judge Jackson's actions *proper*?

(A) Yes, unless the buyer is likely to appear in Judge Jackson's court in the future.

(B) Yes, because he did not charge Martha a fee.

(C) No, because a full-time judge is not permitted to practice law.

(D) No, unless his identity was not disclosed to the buyer or the buyer's attorney.

Question 46

Stork, Inc. is a large private adoption agency that handles over 65% of all private adoptions in State Blue. Stork provides each set of adoptive parents with a list entitled "Approved List of Lawyers Handling Private Adoptions." Stork's representatives tell prospective adoptive parents that it is in their best interest to obtain counsel who has experience in adoptions. Stork has checked out every lawyer on its list to make sure that the lawyer had experience in private adoptions as well as a reputation for honesty and ethical behavior.

Because of Stork's volume of business, State Blue lawyers recognize the advantages of being placed on the "Approved List." After a lawyer desiring placement on the list has been screened by Stork, the lawyer is required by Stork to sign a form agreement before the lawyer's name is placed on the list. To assure the adoptive parents that any lawyer on the list would follow through with the adoption to its conclusion, the required form agreement contains the statement, "I agree that under no circumstances will I withdraw from any case where I have been retained by parents adopting through Stork."

Lawyer Lenny has handled many private adoptions and is highly regarded as an honest and competent lawyer. He would like to be placed on Stork's list.

Would it be *proper* for Lenny to have himself included in the list?

(A) Yes, because the Approved List is a valuable service, and people often do not know where to find a lawyer qualified to handle a matter such as a private adoption.

(B) Yes, provided Lenny does not give anything of value to Stork in exchange for being placed on the list.

(C) No, because Stork is acting as Lenny's agent, and a lawyer may not use an agent to contact prospective clients in a manner that would be unethical solicitation if done by the lawyer.

(D) No, because the form agreement allows a third party to exercise influence over the lawyer-client relationship.

Question 47

Attorneys Agnes and Barnaby have been law partners for six years. They share a suite of offices in a large downtown office building and use the same secretarial staff. Unfortunately, Barnaby had difficulties with the Internal Revenue Service and was found guilty of intentionally understating his income for one tax year. Barnaby paid the taxes due, plus interest, penalties, and a $5,000 fine. He did not receive a prison sentence. The Disciplinary Committee of the State Bar Association suspended Barnaby from the practice of law for one year.

Agnes took over Barnaby's clients when his suspension went into effect. Shortly before his suspension, Barnaby had negotiated a $30,000 personal injury settlement on behalf of his client, Charlotte. Two weeks after the settlement was reached, the defendant's insurer sent a $30,000 check to the law offices. By this time Barnaby's suspension had gone into effect. Agnes placed the check in the proper account and confirmed the amount of the fee with Charlotte. Agnes then promptly forwarded a $20,000 check to Charlotte and a $10,000 check to Barnaby, the latter check representing Barnaby's one-third contingent fee.

Is Agnes *subject to discipline*?

(A) Yes, because she should have held the $10,000 in the client trust account until Barnaby's suspension had ended.

(B) Yes, because a lawyer is prohibited from sharing legal fees with a nonlawyer.

(C) No, because Barnaby earned the fee prior to his suspension.

(D) No, because the $10,000 belonged to Agnes's firm, and she could do anything she wished with it, including sending it to Barnaby as a gift.

Question 48

Judge Jones is a loyal member of the alumni association of Heathmoor, the women's college from which she was graduated. The 25th reunion of her graduating class is coming up next June, and she has been asked to participate in some activities designed to raise money for a gift from the class to the college scholarship fund.

Which of the following activities would be *proper* for Judge Jones to do?

I.   Make a substantial personal donation to the class gift fund.

II. Telephone other members of her graduating class and urge them to make a donation to the class gift fund.

III. Serve on the scholarship fund committee, which devises the various fund-raising strategies.

IV. Be the guest of honor at a dinner to raise funds for the class gift.

V.   Attend a fund-raising dinner for the class gift.

(A) I. and V. only.

(B) I., III., and V. only.

(C) I., IV., and V. only.

(D) I., II., IV., and V. only.

GO ON TO THE NEXT PAGE

Question 49

Defendant Dennis asked lawyer Liston to defend him in a criminal case in which Dennis was charged with running a gambling operation. Dennis was known in the community as a wealthy person, but one who seldom kept his word and seldom paid his bills. Liston agreed to do the necessary work for a flat fee of $5,000, which was reasonable in light of the difficulty of the case and the number of hours required. However, Liston required that Dennis pay $3,000 in advance. When Dennis protested that he did not have that amount available in ready cash, Liston accepted Dennis's full-length fur coat in lieu of the cash advance. The fair market value of the coat is $3,000, and Liston agreed to return it upon payment of his fee. Their agreement was reduced to writing and signed by both parties.

After Liston had put in considerable time in preparing the case for trial, Dennis fired Liston for no good reason and refused to pay him anything for the work already done. Assuming the reasonable value of Liston's services to date is $4,000, which of the following statements is correct?

I. Liston is *subject to discipline* for demanding that Dennis pay $3,000 in advance, before any legal services had been rendered.

II. Liston is *subject to discipline* for taking the coat in lieu of cash as an advance on legal fees.

III. Liston *must* promptly return the coat to Dennis upon termination of their relationship, and submit a bill for his services.

IV. If Liston returns the coat and sues Dennis to collect his fee, Liston will be entitled to recover the full contract price ($5,000) because Dennis terminated the contract without good cause.

(A) None of the above.

(B) I., II., and III. only.

(C) IV. only.

(D) I., III., and IV. only.

GO ON TO THE NEXT PAGE

Question 50

Lawyer Leroy is interested in obtaining legal business from the United Smelter and Mining Employees Union ("USMEU"), which has many organized workers in the state. As a result of a recent mine fire and explosion in which several miners were killed, the USMEU has succeeded in persuading the appropriate state agency to bring an administrative action against the mining company for failing to install smoke detectors, which might have saved some lives in the mine disaster.

Although Leroy is in no way involved in the case, he sees this as an opportunity to obtain future business from the union by showing the USMEU that he is strongly on their side in the mine disaster case. Leroy telephones a popular call-in radio show, and makes the following statement:

> My name is Leroy and I am an attorney. I'd just like to say that I am shocked and appalled at the callousness of the mining company that caused the recent disaster in which so many miners were killed. From what I have read, it appears to me that the mining company was willful and wanton in its failure to install smoke detectors. I am behind the union 100%; I hope the company will not be allowed to escape the consequences of this despicable conduct.

Without Leroy's knowledge or consent, his statement was later printed in several newspapers in the state.

Is Leroy *subject to discipline* for his conduct?

(A) Yes, because he was substantially motivated by his desire to attract fee-paying business.

(B) Yes, because lawyers must not make public comments concerning pending litigation.

(C) No, because he did not make any false or misleading claims about himself or his services.

(D) No, because the statement was printed in the newspapers without his knowledge or consent.

GO ON TO THE NEXT PAGE

Question 51

Attorney Ayers limits her practice to family law. Married couple Hector and Wanda came to her, hoping to save their marriage. After hearing their story, Ayers explained that she could act as a third-party neutral between them—not representing either one of them, but facilitating their efforts to work through their difficulties. Ayers explained that neither of them would have the protections afforded by an ordinary attorney-client relationship, such as the attorney-client privilege, and both said that they understood. Ayers held a series of meetings with the couple (sometimes with both, and other times with just one). Ayers began each meeting with a reminder that, in the event of later litigation between Hector and Wanda, the attorney-client privilege would not protect what was said at the meeting. At one of Ayers's individual meetings with Hector, he disclosed that he "occasionally" uses cocaine and that he "sometimes" uses the family's savings to buy the drug. Ultimately, Hector and Wanda were unable to resolve their differences, and Wanda sued Hector for a divorce and for custody of their three children. At the custody hearing, Wanda's lawyer called Ayers to the witness stand and asked: "What, if anything, did Hector tell you about his use of cocaine?" Ayers refused to answer, citing the attorney-client privilege.

Which of the following is most nearly correct?

(A) The privilege claim should be overruled; if Ayers refuses to answer, she would be **subject to litigation sanction**.

(B) The privilege claim should be sustained; if Ayers reveals what Hector said, she would be **subject to discipline**.

(C) Ayers is **subject to discipline** for attempting to serve as a third-party neutral in a family law matter.

(D) Ayers is **subject to civil liability** for attempting to serve as a third-party neutral in a family law matter.

Question 52

Intron, Inc. makes computer chips. It is incorporated in State One; its headquarters and principal place of business are in State Two, and it has chip manufacturing plants in States Three and Four. Lawyer Linz is admitted to practice in State Two. He is a domiciliary and resident of State Two, and he is employed full-time as an employment discrimination lawyer in Intron's in-house law department in State Two. Intron is his only client. Intron's General Counsel—Linz's supervisor in the in-house law department—instructed him to move temporarily to State Four, where the Intron manufacturing plant was afflicted with a rash of employment discrimination claims. The General Counsel told Linz to settle all existing meritorious claims, to prepare all nonmeritorious claims for trial, and to train the managers of the State Four plant to comply with federal and state employment discrimination laws. The General Counsel knows that Linz is not admitted to practice in State Four.

May Linz do as the General Counsel has instructed?

(A) Yes, because Linz's right to practice temporarily in State Four is a debatable issue of legal ethics, and it is appropriate for such an issue to be decided by a lawyer's supervisor.

(B) Yes, but if State Four requires out-of-state lawyers to be admitted pro hac vice in order to engage in pretrial preparations, Linz must seek such admission.

(C) No, unless Linz takes and passes State Four's short-form bar exam for out-of-state lawyers within six months of his arrival in State Four.

(D) No, unless Linz associates a State Four lawyer who will actively participate with Linz in settling the meritorious claims and preparing the nonmeritorious claims for trial.

Question 53

The State One Bar certifies specialists in nine fields of law, one of which is tax law. Attorney Ataris has not yet earned her certificate of specialization in tax law, but she is working toward that goal. Ataris's ad in the Yellow Pages phonebook states:

Alma Ataris
Specialist in tax law,
a field in which the State One Bar grants
Certificates of Specialization
Call Today (209)795-6875

Ataris limits her practice to tax matters; she refers all other kinds of legal matters to lawyer Leacox, a solo practitioner in general practice. Leacox, in turn, refers all tax matters to Ataris. Without exception, Leacox and Ataris have followed that pattern of referrals for five or six years; they have no formal reciprocal referral agreement, but each invariably follows the pattern, expecting the other to reciprocate.

Which of the following most correctly describes Ataris's situation?

(A) Ataris is *subject to discipline* for her Yellow Pages ad, but not for maintaining the referral relationship with Leacox.

(B) Ataris's Yellow Pages ad is *proper*, and so is her referral relationship with Leacox.

(C) Ataris is *subject to discipline* for her Yellow Pages ad, and her referral relationship with Leacox is *improper* because it would need to be nonexclusive, and the two lawyers would need to disclose it to referred clients.

(D) Ataris's Yellow Pages ad is *proper*, but she is *subject to discipline* for maintaining the referral relationship with Leacox.

Question 54

Lawyer Lubovich is one of only nine lawyers who practice probate law in Chihachepi County. In that county, all probate matters go before a single judge, not surprisingly called the Probate Judge of Chihachepi County. The probate judge's duties include appointing counsel for the administrators of intestate estates—serving as an administrator's counsel can be very lucrative if the estate is large and complicated. The incumbent probate judge recently retired. Her custom was to appoint out-of-county lawyers to serve as administrators' counsel; she believed that such lawyers are less subject to local political and social pressures than Chihachepi lawyers. The probate judgeship will be filled in six months in a partisan, contested election, and lawyer Lubovich is one of the candidates.

Lubovich met jointly with Chihachepi County's eight other probate lawyers and said: "My friends, I welcome your support and assistance in my quest for the probate judgeship. I will be making some important changes, such as appointing only local lawyers as counsel for administrators of intestate estates; I see no reason to send that work out of the county. To win, I need your financial support and your public support, walking precincts, handing out brochures, talking up my qualifications to the voters—whatever you can do to help. If you'd like to contribute money or time, please get in touch with my campaign committee at www.lubovich4judge.org." Five of the eight lawyers sent generous monetary donations to the Lubovich campaign committee for the self-confessed purpose of securing legal appointments if Lubovich wins. The other three lawyers volunteered generous amounts of their time in the Lubovich campaign, but their motives for doing so were unexpressed and unclear.

Which of the following is most nearly correct?

(A) Lubovich is *subject to discipline* for personally soliciting money and publicly stated support from the eight lawyers. The

GO ON TO THE NEXT PAGE

five lawyers who contributed money will be *subject to discipline* if Lubovich wins and if they accept appointments from him.

(B) Lubovich's conduct was *proper* because he was a candidate for a judicial office in a contested election. All eight lawyers, however, are *subject to discipline* because a practicing lawyer must not contribute either money or time to the political campaign of a judge before whom the lawyer expects to appear.

(C) Lubovich is *subject to discipline* for promising to appoint only local lawyers as counsel for administrators, in the hope of securing the publicly stated support of the eight lawyers. The conduct of all eight lawyers, however, was *proper* because lawyers are permitted to support or oppose candidates in contested elections for judgeships.

(D) Lubovich's conduct was *proper* because he was a lawyer-candidate, not a judge, at the time he met with the eight lawyers. The conduct of the five lawyers who contributed money was *proper* because a person's motive for making a political contribution is a private matter that is protected by the penumbra of the First and Fourteenth Amendments.

Question 55

Lawyer Liu volunteers her legal services every Tuesday night on the Lake County Free Legal Advice Hotline. The hotline is run under the auspices of the Lake County Superior Court, and it supplies free legal advice by telephone to callers who could not otherwise obtain legal services. Every caller assents to a "Statement of Understanding" at the outset of the call, consenting to the limited nature of the legal services the hotline provides. Eighty-five lawyers volunteer their services as Liu does. They come to the hotline office at various times on various days, and the volunteers hardly ever see or talk with each other, except at the hotline's annual chicken and beans barbeque. The nature of the hotline's work makes it impossible for the lawyers to conduct the kind of conflict-of-interest checks that an ordinary law firm would conduct before taking on a new client. One Tuesday night, Liu counseled a distraught mother about her husband's physical and mental abuse of their school-age children. Liu told the mother how to seek help from the Lake County Child Protective Services and the local law school's Domestic Violence Clinic. On the following Friday evening, a different hotline volunteer, attorney Ashcraft, counseled the mother's husband about how to prevent the Lake County Child Protective Services from scooping up his children and putting them in a foster home. Because the hotline does not do conflict-of-interest checks, Ashcraft had no way to know that Liu had counseled the mother a few nights before.

Which of the following is most nearly correct?

(A) The judges of the Lake County Superior Court are *subject to discipline* for permitting the hotline to operate under their auspice without making a conflict-of-interest check before dispensing legal advice to a new client.

(B) Liu, Ashcraft, and the judges of the Lake County Superior Court all acted *properly* because the hotline cannot do the kind of conflict-of-interest checking that a private law firm would do.

(C) Liu acted *properly* in advising the mother, but Ashcraft is *subject to discipline* for giving legal advice to the father on the same subject as Liu's advice to the mother.

(D) Neither the mother nor the father was a "client" of the respective lawyers who advised them. Therefore, there was no conflict of interest, and both Liu and Ashcraft acted *properly*.

Question 56

Attorney Aghai practices sports law. Her legal specialty is the representation of women professional basketball players who play for teams in the Women's National Basketball Association. When wearing her lawyer hat, Aghai represents her clients in various types of contract negotiations and in all other kinds of civil matters. Aghai also serves as sports agent for several women professional basketball players. When wearing her sports agent hat, Aghai's job is to advance her clients' careers in every way possible, such as team placement, public relations, product sponsorship, favorable media coverage, coach and teammate relations, healthy lifestyle, and the like. Aghai uses a single office for her law work and her sports agent work, but she charges her clients separately for the two types of work. For her sports agent work, she charges a flat annual fee that she negotiates with the client once a year. For her law work, she charges the client by the hour at a reasonable hourly rate. Aghai is lawyer and sports agent for two players on the Topeka Tigers, Daphne Dobbs and Edith Elgin. Both women are excellent players, and both are well-educated, well-spoken, pleasantly photogenic, and popular with fans in the Midwest. The First Continental Bank of Topeka approached Aghai, expressing interest in signing up Daphne Dobbs to serve as the bank's spokeswoman in a new ad campaign. The bank said it would pay Dobbs "a high six-figure fee" if she would work for them, and not for any other financial institution, during the 18-month ad campaign. Aghai responded that Dobbs would fit the bank's needs very well, but that Edith Elgin would be an equally good fit and would do the work "for substantially less money." In due course, Aghai served as Elgin's lawyer in negotiating an 18-month exclusive sponsorship contract with the bank.

Is Aghai *subject to discipline*?

(A) No, because when Aghai acts on behalf of a client as sports agent, she need not follow the lawyer conflict of interest rules.

(B) Yes, because Aghai was in essence charging twice for the same work when she attempted to serve as sports agent for both Dobbs and Elgin.

(C) Yes, because Aghai does not keep her sports agent work clearly distinct from her lawyer work, and therefore she must follow the lawyer conflict of interest rules in both kinds of work.

(D) No, because Aghai charged her clients separately for her sports agent work and her law work, and therefore she need not follow the legal ethics rules when doing sports agent work.

GO ON TO THE NEXT PAGE

Question 57

Solo practitioner Sololei limits her law practice to two kinds of cases. First, she represents plaintiffs who have been physically injured by medical malpractice. Second, she represents plaintiffs who have been physically injured by household products that have turned out to be harmful to health. When Sololei turned 67, she began looking for someone to buy her law practice. Ultimately, she sold the medical malpractice part of her practice to lawyer Lang for $400,000, and she sold the household products part of her practice to attorney Abel for $250,000. Sololei invested the sale proceeds in high-yield stocks and bonds, and she moved to Fiji to sit on the beach, sip refreshing fruit drinks, and enjoy her retirement. Unfortunately for Lang and Abel, within 30 days after the sales, approximately 40% of the clients they received from Sololei decided to collect their case files and take their business to different lawyers.

Were the sale from Sololei to Lang and the sale from Sololei to Abel *proper*?

(A) Yes, even though Sololei sold pieces of her practice to two different buyers, and even though 40% of Sololei's clients left the buyers within 30 days.

(B) Yes, but Sololei is *subject to civil liability* to the two buyers for unjust enrichment because 40% of Sololei's clients left the buyers within 30 days.

(C) No, because Sololei sold pieces of her practice to two different buyers.

(D) No, because 40% of Sololei's clients left the buyers within 30 days.

Question 58

Gerard Goop is a pimp; he makes a handsome living by arranging tricks for a group of prostitutes and protecting them from harm. As a sideline, he also distributes high-quality heroin to his prostitutes and to a few carefully selected cash customers. When one of Goop's prostitutes was arrested for prostitution, Goop asked young solo practitioner Prentice to defend her at her trial. Goop explained the nature of his business to Prentice so that Prentice would understand why it was important to defend the young woman vigorously and successfully. Goop offered Prentice a "down payment" on the legal fee, consisting of a shoebox full of crisp, new $100 bills. Prentice was uncertain about getting involved with Goop, and especially about accepting a large sum in cash from Goop. Prentice told Goop that he would think about Goop's request and would let him know later that day. When Goop left the office, Prentice telephoned his friend and mentor, retired judge Judson. Prentice told Judson the entire story, including Goop's name, and asked Judson whether it would be ethical to defend the prostitute and accept Goop's cash.

Is Prentice *subject to discipline* for telling Judson the whole story?

(A) Yes, because the attorney-client privilege forbids Prentice from revealing what Goop told Prentice in confidence.

(B) No, because Prentice's prospective client was the accused prostitute, not Goop.

(C) Yes, but it would have been *proper* if Prentice had not used Goop's name.

(D) No, because the ethical duty of confidentiality has an exception that allows a lawyer to reveal confidential information to obtain legal ethics advice.

GO ON TO THE NEXT PAGE

Question 59

Robbins & Hood Chemical Corp. ("R&H") is a family owned corporation, the shares of which have never been offered to the public. It is not subject to the jurisdiction of the Securities and Exchange Commission ("SEC"). It sells a variety of chemicals throughout the United States. The United States antitrust laws prohibit competitors from agreeing among themselves about the prices they will charge their customers (a practice called horizontal price fixing). The board of directors of R&H long ago adopted a rule that all employees must obey the antitrust laws, and that anyone who does not will be fired and will lose all company benefits. R&H's in-house General Counsel got wind of a rumor that some R&H sales people on the West Coast had met with their counterparts from competing companies and had reached an agreement that, without too much of a stretch, could be called horizontal price fixing. After consulting with R&H's chief executive officer ("CEO"), the General Counsel hired an outside antitrust lawyer, Leona Leopard, to investigate the situation, advise the company on what to do, and defend the company if it is sued for antitrust violations. Leopard and her young associate, Arthur Athol, investigated and found that R&H's West Coast sales employees had indeed met with competitors about prices, thus exposing R&H to possible criminal liability, not to mention millions of dollars worth of civil treble-damage suits. Leopard reported these findings and her antitrust advice in a confidential letter addressed jointly to the General Counsel and the CEO. The General Counsel wrote back, thanking Leopard for her work and asking her to stand by to defend the company if needed. Months went by, and Leopard heard nothing more. Athol, the young associate, grew restless; without telling Leopard, he told a friend in the United States Justice Department what R&H's sales people had done. The Justice Department began a price fixing investigation of R&H and its competitors.

Which of the following is most nearly correct?

(A) Leopard is *subject to discipline* for failing to report R&H's situation to the antitrust enforcement authorities in the Justice Department, but Athol's conduct was *proper*.

(B) The conduct of both Leopard and Athol was *proper*, and neither of them will be *subject to civil liability* if R&H sues them for legal malpractice.

(C) Athol is *subject to discipline* for tipping off the Justice Department, but Leopard's conduct was *proper* unless she knew what Athol was about to do or ratified it later, failed to rectify it when she could have, or failed to train and supervise Athol properly.

(D) Neither Leopard nor Athol is *subject to discipline*, but both of them may be *subject to civil liability* if R&H sues them for legal malpractice.

GO ON TO THE NEXT PAGE

Question 60

BioTek, Inc. is a small, modestly financed company that develops methods to use a medical patient's own stem cells to repair nerve damage caused by disease. BioTek obtained a very valuable United States patent on one of these methods. BioTek's wealthy competitors trembled when the patent was issued, and they joined as plaintiffs in a federal court declaratory judgment suit to have the patent declared invalid on the ground that BioTek had publicly used the patented method more than one year before the date of the patent application. If proven, that is enough to invalidate the patent under United States law. Attorney Adler represents BioTek in the litigation. Adler knows, because of a privileged conversation with BioTek's Director of Research, that only one person in the world knows for sure when the patented method was first publicly used. That one person is Elmo Wintz, Ph.D., a bright but reclusive research biochemist who spends every waking hour in his lab at BioTek.

Which of the following would be **proper** for Adler to do to prevent the plaintiffs from learning what Dr. Wintz knows?

I.   Fail to tell counsel for the plaintiffs that they should take Dr. Wintz's deposition.

II.   Advise BioTek to grant Dr. Wintz a two-year sabbatical leave, at full pay, on a remote tropical island in the South Pacific.

III. When the plaintiffs pose an interrogatory asking for the identity of witnesses who know when the patented method was first publicly used, advise BioTek to answer, "We lack certain knowledge of any such witness."

IV.   At Dr. Wintz's deposition, object to any question touching on the date the patented method was first publicly used, and instruct Dr. Wintz not to answer the question.

(A) All of the above.

(B) None of the above.

(C) I. only.

(D) I., III., and IV. only.

STOP

ANSWER SHEET

1 (A) (B) (C) (D)		31 (A) (B) (C) (D)
2 (A) (B) (C) (D)		32 (A) (B) (C) (D)
3 (A) (B) (C) (D)		33 (A) (B) (C) (D)
4 (A) (B) (C) (D)		34 (A) (B) (C) (D)
5 (A) (B) (C) (D)		35 (A) (B) (C) (D)
6 (A) (B) (C) (D)		36 (A) (B) (C) (D)
7 (A) (B) (C) (D)		37 (A) (B) (C) (D)
8 (A) (B) (C) (D)		38 (A) (B) (C) (D)
9 (A) (B) (C) (D)		39 (A) (B) (C) (D)
10 (A) (B) (C) (D)		40 (A) (B) (C) (D)
11 (A) (B) (C) (D)		41 (A) (B) (C) (D)
12 (A) (B) (C) (D)		42 (A) (B) (C) (D)
13 (A) (B) (C) (D)		43 (A) (B) (C) (D)
14 (A) (B) (C) (D)		44 (A) (B) (C) (D)
15 (A) (B) (C) (D)		45 (A) (B) (C) (D)
16 (A) (B) (C) (D)		46 (A) (B) (C) (D)
17 (A) (B) (C) (D)		47 (A) (B) (C) (D)
18 (A) (B) (C) (D)		48 (A) (B) (C) (D)
19 (A) (B) (C) (D)		49 (A) (B) (C) (D)
20 (A) (B) (C) (D)		50 (A) (B) (C) (D)
21 (A) (B) (C) (D)		51 (A) (B) (C) (D)
22 (A) (B) (C) (D)		52 (A) (B) (C) (D)
23 (A) (B) (C) (D)		53 (A) (B) (C) (D)
24 (A) (B) (C) (D)		54 (A) (B) (C) (D)
25 (A) (B) (C) (D)		55 (A) (B) (C) (D)
26 (A) (B) (C) (D)		56 (A) (B) (C) (D)
27 (A) (B) (C) (D)		57 (A) (B) (C) (D)
28 (A) (B) (C) (D)		58 (A) (B) (C) (D)
29 (A) (B) (C) (D)		59 (A) (B) (C) (D)
30 (A) (B) (C) (D)		60 (A) (B) (C) (D)

Answer to Question 1

(D) Febell and Spryte are subject to discipline for entering into the partnership agreement because of the restriction on Spryte's right to practice. A lawyer must neither make nor offer a partnership agreement that restricts a lawyer's right to practice after termination of the relationship, except for an agreement concerning benefits upon retirement. [ABA Model Rule 5.6(a)] Under this agreement, if Spryte leaves the partnership within the first three years, he must pay Febell 75% of the fees he earns thereafter from municipal bond work he does in State A. This provision unduly restricts Spryte's right to practice. (A) is wrong because it overlooks the improper restriction on Spryte's right to practice. (B) is wrong because it overlooks the restriction on Spryte. Furthermore, it implies that the sale of assets in exchange for the restriction on Febell is necessary to restrict Febell's right to practice; it is not. (C) is wrong because the restriction on Febell's right to practice is properly incident to the retirement benefits he will receive from Spryte.

Answer to Question 2

(B) Jacobs may not represent Dillon in the habeas proceeding because, while serving as a supreme court justice, Jacobs granted Dillon a stay of execution. A lawyer must not represent a client in a "matter" in which the lawyer earlier participated "personally and substantially" as a judge. [ABA Model Rule 1.12(a)] The habeas corpus proceeding and the earlier appeal should be regarded as the same matter because the habeas corpus proceeding will doubtless raise many of the same issues that were decided on the earlier appeal. (The effective assistance of counsel issue is one example.) The stay of execution should be regarded as personal, substantial participation. (A) is wrong because it confuses the roles of judge and lawyer; a

judge is expected to be impartial, but a lawyer is expected to be a partisan. (C) is wrong because one of the proper reasons for turning down a court appointment is that it would require the lawyer to violate a disciplinary rule. [ABA Model Rule 6.2(a)] (D) is wrong because it elevates form over substance; the similarity of legal issues, not the case caption, should be determinative here.

Answer to Question 3

(B) Anderson is subject to discipline because she did not consult Farner about associating Ling. A lawyer may split her fee with a lawyer outside her firm if the total fee is reasonable, the split is either in proportion to the work done (or in some other proportion if the splitting lawyers assume joint responsibility), and the client agrees to the split in a writing that discloses the share that each lawyer will receive. [ABA Model Rule 1.5(e)] Because Anderson did not tell Farner about the arrangement, she is subject to discipline. (A) is wrong because a lawyer may take on a case she knows she is not competent to handle if she does the study needed to become competent, or if she associates a lawyer who is competent to handle it. [Comment 1 to ABA Model Rule 1.1] (C) and (D) are wrong because they ignore the need to inform Farner.

Answer to Question 4

(C) Aoki's advice to Counter was proper because Counter acted as Childs's agent in rendering accounting advice. An attorney may request that someone other than a client refrain from voluntarily giving relevant information to another party if the person is a relative or agent of the client and the attorney reasonably believes that the person's interests will not be adversely affected by refraining from giving the information. [ABA Model Rule 3.4(f)] Here, Aoki reasonably believed that refusing to talk informally with the plaintiff's counsel would not harm Counter, and Counter was Childs's agent in rendering the accounting advice. (A) is wrong because it is Counter's agency, not privilege, that affects the propriety of Aoki's advice. The lack of an evidentiary privilege does not give the plaintiff's counsel a right to talk to Counter informally if Counter chooses not to. (B) is wrong because Aoki did not interfere with the plaintiff's access to evidence; if the plaintiff wants to know what Counter has to say, he can simply take Counter's deposition. (D) is wrong because it was not improper for the plaintiff's counsel to attempt to talk informally with a third-party witness such as Counter.

Answer to Question 5

(C) Armer may not take the case even if Arias and Armer believe that they can effectively represent their respective clients, and even if all parties give informed, written consent. The key issue is whether Arias and Armer are considered a "firm" for purposes of the imputed disqualification rule with respect to conflicts of interest. Because lawyers in a firm are usually treated as a single unit for conflict of interest purposes, different lawyers in the same firm must not represent opposing parties in a civil case. [ABA Model Rule 1.10(a)] Relevant factors in determining whether lawyers who share office space are deemed a firm include whether they: hold themselves out to the public as a single unit, frequently consult and assist each other, refer cases to each other, work jointly on cases, and have access to each other's files. All of these factors are present in this case. Thus, Armer and Arias are deemed a firm, and Armer is disqualified from accepting the employment because Arias's disqualification is imputed to her. (A) is wrong because a client must not be asked to consent if a disinterested lawyer would conclude that the client should not agree to the representation.

Representing both sides in litigation is such a circumstance. [ABA Model Rule 1.7, Comment 23] Moreover, ABA Model Rule 1.7(b)(3) does not permit client consent to solve a conflict of interest when one client sues another client represented by the lawyer in the same proceeding. (B) is wrong because, as discussed above, the rule of imputed disqualification does apply to Arias and Armer even though they are not partners. (D) is wrong because, as discussed above, representation is improper here even if the lawyers believe that they can effectively represent the clients and even if the clients consent.

Answer to Question 6

(A) A lawyer must not state or imply that he has the ability to improperly influence a government official or that he can achieve results by means that violate the Rules of Professional Conduct or other law. [ABA Model Rule 8.4(e)] Thus, Lear is subject to discipline for saying that he knows how to get a favorable ruling from Judge Johnson, which implies that he can influence the judge. Advising Crowell to make the campaign contribution can be viewed in two ways, both of which subject Lear to discipline. If the $2,000 is viewed harshly as a bald bribe, then Lear is subject to discipline for counseling a client to commit a crime. [ABA Model Rule 1.2(d)] If the $2,000 is viewed benignly as a campaign contribution, Lear is subject to discipline for assisting a judge to violate a judicial ethics rule. [ABA Model Rule 8.4(f)] The Code of Judicial Conduct prohibits Judge Johnson from personally accepting campaign contributions, and it prohibits his campaign committee from accepting contributions more than a year before the election. [CJC 5C(2)] Thus, item II. subjects Lear to discipline. Lear is subject to discipline for item III. because Lear apparently believes that Wampler is an "honest fellow," yet his editorial implies that

Wampler is a crook. A lawyer is prohibited from making a statement about a judicial candidate, either knowing that the statement is false or with reckless disregard as to its truth or falsity. [ABA Model Rule 8.2(a)] Lear is not subject to discipline for item IV. because he was not offering **unsolicited** free legal advice, then accepting employment arising from it. [*See* ABA Model Rule 7.3] Crowell initiated the contact, asked for the advice, and was in the midst of negotiating Lear's employment when the advice was given.

Answer to Question 7

(C)   Axelrod is subject to discipline because she should have known that the statement was likely to prejudice the trial. A lawyer who is connected with a case must not make a public statement outside the courtroom that the lawyer reasonably should know would have a substantial likelihood of materially prejudicing the case. [ABA Model Rule 3.6(a)] Axelrod's comment to the reporter falls in that category because it revealed very damaging material that had not been, and probably would not be, admitted into evidence. A defendant's prior convictions generally are inadmissible as evidence of his conduct on the occasion in question. [*See* Fed. R. Evid. 404] Even if Diablo elected to waive his privilege against self-incrimination and testified on his own behalf, the prior convictions would probably not be admissible to impeach him. [*See* Fed. R. Evid. 609(a)—mugging does not involve dishonesty or false statement, and a judge would probably exclude felony mugging convictions because of the high risk of prejudice] Note that there is an additional constraint on the prosecutor in a criminal case. A prosecutor must not make extrajudicial comments that have a substantial likelihood of heightening public condemnation of the accused. [ABA Model Rule 3.8(f)] Axelrod's statement also runs afoul of this rule by revealing prior crimes that would heighten public condemnation of Diablo. (A) is wrong because even if the prior convictions are a matter of public record, that does not absolve Axelrod for making a statement she knew would substantially prejudice the case. Furthermore, while in a technical sense Diablo's prior convictions in other states are matters of public record (if one knew where to go and what to look for, one could dredge them out of the court records of the other states), the prior convictions were doubtless not part of the public record in Diablo's present prosecution. (B) is wrong because it is too broad; lawyers do have First Amendment rights to express themselves about pending cases, but those rights are limited by the due process rights of litigants to fair court proceedings. (D) is wrong because it is also too broad; a prosecutor may make some kinds of public comment about pending cases, but not comments that are likely to cause prejudice.

Answer to Question 8

(C)   Lederlee is not subject to discipline unless 30% of the book royalties is unreasonably high for the contract negotiation work. Here, the lawyer has, in essence, agreed to negotiate the publication contract in return for a contingent fee. Like all other fees, a contingent fee is subject to the general requirement of reasonableness. [ABA Model Rule 1.5] (A) is wrong because this is not the kind of literary rights contract that is prohibited. A lawyer must not acquire literary or media rights to a story concerning the lawyer's representation of a client until after the legal matter is entirely concluded. [ABA Model Rule 1.8(d)] Here, the client is the author, and the book is about her life in prison, not about her case or her lawyer's representation of her. A lawyer may represent a client in a transaction concerning literary property in which the lawyer's fee consists of a share of the ownership of the property, provided that the arrangement complies with the general rules about attorneys' fees and does not give the lawyer a proprietary interest in the subject of litigation. [Comment 9 to ABA Model Rule 1.8] (B) is wrong because a lawyer may advance litigation expenses for a client, even though he is aware that she probably cannot pay him back. ABA Model Rule 1.8(e)(2) permits the lawyer simply to pay the litigation expenses for an indigent client, even without the pretense of calling it an advance. (D) is wrong because all lawyer fees are subject to the general requirement of reasonableness.

Answer to Question 9

(A) Adamson is subject to discipline because he did not put the coins in a safe place. When a lawyer comes into possession of property to be held on a client's behalf, the lawyer must identify it as belonging to the client and must put it in a safe place. [ABA Model Rule 1.15(a)] Although the Rules do not define "safe," common sense suggests that allowing a valuable coin collection to be viewed by employees, placing it into an unlocked desk file, and then leaving the office is not safe. A lawyer should use the same level of care required of professional fiduciaries. Adamson's actions fall well short of that. (B) is wrong. Adamson may be liable to the estate in civil damages for his secretary's dishonest act, but the question here is professional discipline, not civil liability. Adamson could be disciplined if he did not take reasonable steps to train his secretary properly [ABA Model Rule 5.3], but if he took such steps, he should not be disciplined for her criminal act. (C) is wrong. The issue here is Adamson's failure to safeguard the coins; the proximate cause of the loss is beside the point. Technically, Adamson could be subject to discipline for failure to safeguard the property even if no loss occurred. (D) is wrong. Placing the coins in an unlocked desk file and leaving the office was not a reasonable way to safeguard them.

Answer to Question 10

(A) Dahlers is subject to discipline for failing to warn Sentz not to take the case. If Platten were a lawyer, her conduct would violate ABA Model Rule 7.3(a), which prohibits in-person solicitation. The partners in a firm are responsible for educating their nonlawyer employees about ethics issues and making reasonable efforts to assure that those employees comply with ethics rules. [ABA Model Rule 5.3(a)] Moreover, a partner is subject to discipline if he learns about the violation of an ethics rule by a nonlawyer employee "when its consequences can be avoided or mitigated," but the partner "fails to take reasonable remedial action." In this case, the consequences of Platten's solicitation could have been avoided by warning Sentz not to take the pedestrian's case. Because he failed to warn Sentz, Dahlers is subject to discipline. (B) is wrong because it is too broad. A lawyer's responsibility for a nonlawyer employee's ethics violation is limited to situations in which the lawyer orders it, ratifies it, or learns about it in time to remedy it and does not do so. [ABA Model Rule 5.3(c)] (C) is wrong because even though people are generally free to recommend a lawyer to someone else, that does not allow paralegal Platten to solicit business for the firm that employs her. [ABA Model Rule 8.4(a)] (D) is wrong because Dahlers and the other partners in the firm had a duty to educate Platten about ethics rules. [ABA Model Rule 5.3(a)] Furthermore, even if Platten acted innocently, that does not excuse Dahlers's failure to warn Sentz not to take the case.

Answer to Question 11

(C) Aston is not subject to discipline for taking the case because the relevant information he obtained while working as a government attorney is not confidential. The general rule is that a government lawyer who receives confidential government information about a person must not later represent a private client whose interests are adverse to that person, if the information could be used to the material disadvantage of that person. [ABA Model Rule 1.11(c)] The rule covers only "confidential" information, which means information that the government is prohibited from revealing or has a privilege not to reveal, and which is not otherwise available to the public. Here, because the information is available under the Freedom of Information Act, it is not confidential. In fact, any attorney representing Charles could obtain the information; thus, Aston is free to use it. (A) is wrong because an attorney is not barred from ever working on a case where he gained any relevant information while working for the government. To bar representation, the information must be confidential. (B) is wrong because this type of consent is required when the attorney takes on a representation in private practice in a matter in which the lawyer participated personally and substantially while in government service. A "matter" is a set of specific facts involving specific parties. Here, Aston was not involved in any matter while in government service that concerned Charles's claim against Chemco. (D) is wrong because the information is not confidential and thus can be used against Chemco. Furthermore, even if the information were confidential, mere nonuse would not be sufficient; Aston would not be permitted to represent Charles.

Answer to Question 12

(C) Alexander is subject to discipline because she did not advise Cardone to seek outside counsel. A lawyer may not settle a legal malpractice claim or potential claim with an unrepresented client or former client without first advising that person in writing to seek outside legal advice about the settlement and giving the person a reasonable chance to obtain such advice. [ABA Model Rule 1.8(h)(2)] Although Cardone has apparently not made a formal claim of malpractice here, he has asserted that Alexander's services were "defective," and that is regarded as sufficient to bring Rule 1.8(h)(2) into play. The settlement agreement in this question also gives the client an incentive not to report a lawyer's misconduct to the bar. Some state bars have found similar settlement agreements improper because they frustrated the bar's efforts at self-regulation and could be prejudicial to the administration of justice. [See Arizona State Bar Op. 91-23 (1991)] (A) is wrong because although lawyers are urged to settle fee disputes amicably [Comment 9 to ABA Model Rule 1.5], this particular settlement agreement involves both a fee dispute and a malpractice claim. (B) is wrong because the dispute about the quality of Alexander's services is what causes the problem here, as explained above. (D) is wrong because it is too broad. A lawyer may settle a malpractice claim if the claimant is independently represented or if the lawyer advises the claimant in writing that he should seek independent legal advice before entering into the settlement. [ABA Model Rule 1.8(h)(2)]

Answer to Question 13

(D) Lenhart is subject to discipline because he lied about having movies. When dealing on behalf of a client with a third person, a lawyer must not knowingly make a false statement of law or material fact. [ABA Model Rule 4.1(a)] Lenhart knew that he had no movies; his statement to Workman's lawyer was a bald lie. (A) is wrong because Lenhart's statement was a knowing misrepresentation of material fact, not the kind of puffery that is tolerated in settlement negotiations. [See Comment 2 to ABA

Model Rule 4.1] (B) is wrong because the ends do not justify the means. (C) is wrong because Drexel consented to the $400 settlement. Given Drexel's risk of going to trial in a case where the plaintiff is claiming total and permanent disability due to a back injury, the small settlement was not unreasonable.

Answer to Question 14

(C) Item I. would not be proper because a bar applicant must not make untrue statements on a bar application. [ABA Model Rule 8.1(a)] Item II. would be proper, because it is truthful; it may, of course, provoke a further inquiry by the bar. Item III. would be proper because it openly challenges the validity of the question on legally tenable grounds. [*See* ABA Model Rule 3.4(c)] Item IV. would not be proper because the self-incrimination privilege is inapplicable here. Even if the privilege against self-incrimination applies to questions on bar applications (a debatable proposition), it does not apply when criminal punishment is barred by the statute of limitations. [*See* Hazard & Hodes, §62.6]

Answer to Question 15

(D) Item I. is proper; the judge's campaign committee may begin soliciting contributions one year before the election [CJC 5C(2)], and her retention election is nine months away. Item II. is proper; the judge may allow her name to be listed on a party ticket or other election materials along with the names of other party candidates. [CJC 5C(3)] Item III. is improper; a judge may not publicly endorse a candidate for a public office, and the Code contains no exception to that prohibition. [CJC 5A(1)(b)] Item IV. is improper; the judge may attend a political gathering in the company of her husband, and she may speak on her own behalf, but she must not speak on his behalf. [CJC 5A(1)(b), 5C(1)(b)(i)] Item V. is improper; a judge is

prohibited from personally soliciting contributions for her own campaign. [CJC 5C(2)] Item VI. is improper; a judge is also prohibited from personally soliciting contributions for her spouse's campaign. [CJC 5A(1)(e)]

Answer to Question 16

(C) The firm may continue to use the name Hardwicke & Chandler if it is not misleading. ABA Model Rule 7.5(a) permits a firm to practice under a trade name, provided that the trade name is not misleading in violation of ABA Model Rule 7.1. (A) is wrong because a firm may continue using the name of a deceased partner. [Comment 1 to ABA Model Rule 7.5] (B) is wrong because Hanna Hardwicke is not a name partner. Generally, when a name partner enters public service and is not in private practice for a substantial period, the firm must cease using that person's name. [ABA Model Rule 7.5(c)] Hanna Hardwicke's elevation to the State A Supreme Court does not by itself require the firm to cease using the name Hardwicke because that surname refers to her great-great-grandfather. If, however, the use of the Hardwicke name in the firm name would mislead potential clients (*e.g.*, by making them think they could gain an advantage in the State A Supreme Court by hiring that firm), then continued use of the name would violate the ethics rules. [*See* ABA Model Rule 7.1] (D) is wrong because the rules on firm names are subject to the more general provisions on misleading communications.

Answer to Question 17

(B) It would be proper for Able to represent Carlton because neither Able nor any other lawyer in Able & Aman gained access to Cobb's confidential information. Even though Cobb's bank loan is not substantially related to Carlton's personal injury suit, the confidential information that Arnett got from Cobb may well become important in

Carlton's suit. Knowing the extent and nature of Cobb's assets could be of great value to counsel for Carlton in advising Carlton whether to settle or in collecting on a judgment against Cobb. Here, however, Arnett was the only lawyer who gained access to Cobb's financial information, and Arnett is now dead. Under ABA Model Rule 1.10(b), Able may represent Carlton, because neither he nor any other lawyer remaining in the Able & Aman firm had access to Cobb's confidential information. (A) is wrong because it ignores the issue presented by the confidential information. (C) is wrong because ABA Model Rule 1.10(b) creates an exception to the ordinary rule that confidential information gained by one lawyer in a firm is deemed to be known by all lawyers in the firm. (D) is wrong because ABA Model Rule 1.10(b) allows Able to serve even without the consent of Cobb.

Answer to Question 18

(D)   Aster should abide by Parker's resolution of the matter. A subordinate lawyer does not violate the Rules of Professional Conduct by acting in accordance with a supervisor's reasonable resolution of an ***arguable question*** of professional duty. [ABA Model Rule 5.2(b)] Here, it seems clear that the question was arguable because the third attorney called in to determine the relevance of the case also felt it was not on point. (A) is wrong because Aster only has a duty to call the case to the court's attention if the case is directly on point. That is a debatable question, and Aster's supervisors have determined the case is not directly on point. Thus, Aster need not reveal the case. (B) is wrong because this is not the situation intended to be addressed by the rule against allowing a third party to influence the lawyer's judgment, which usually arises when a third party pays the lawyer's fees to represent another. Of course, a subordinate lawyer

should be influenced by his supervisor. That is not an excuse for clearly unethical conduct, but on a debatable issue, such as the one presented here, the subordinate lawyer is free to defer to the supervisor's judgment. (C) is wrong because in most jurisdictions a lawyer may communicate in writing with the court about the merits of a pending case if he sends a copy to opposing counsel. This communication is not considered ex parte. [*See* Restatement §113, comment c]

Answer to Question 19

(A)   Londrell is not subject to discipline because admission to practice in State A is not required to negotiate a licensing agreement there. A lawyer must not practice law in a state where she is not admitted to practice. [ABA Model Rule 5.5(a)] No state, however, would regard Londrell's conduct as unauthorized practice. Londrell was admitted in State B, she was representing a State B client, and the trademark license has an important nexus to State B because DonnaDell's manufacturing operations will take place in State B. [*See* Hazard & Hodes, §46.6] Moreover, ABA Model Rule 5.5(c)(4) permits a lawyer to temporarily practice out of state if that practice is reasonably related to the lawyer's home-state practice. Here, Londrell's going to State A to negotiate the licensing agreement was reasonably related to her State B practice of representing DonnaDell. (B) is wrong because where the agreement is actually drafted or executed is not relevant. Londrell would not be engaging in unauthorized practice in any event. (C) is wrong because Londrell need not be admitted in State A to negotiate with a company located there. (D) is wrong because a lawyer need not be admitted to practice before the United States Patent and Trademark Office in order to negotiate a trademark license. One must be admitted to practice before that agency to prosecute an application for a United States patent, but Londrell is obviously not doing that here.

Answer to Question 20

(C) A lawyer can be disciplined for trying to avoid a court appointment without good cause. [ABA Model Rule 6.2] Item I. is a legitimate reason for declining an appointment. A lawyer is permitted to turn down a court appointment if it "is likely to result in an unreasonable financial burden." [ABA Model Rule 6.2(b)] Item II. is also a legitimate basis for declining appointment because a lawyer may turn down a court appointment if it is likely to cause the lawyer to violate a rule of professional conduct. [ABA Model Rule 6.2(a)] If Denton and Drews are to be tried jointly, and if Denton did coerce Drews into helping with the kidnapping and killing, there is a sharp conflict of interest between Denton and Drews. [*See* ABA Model Rule 1.7(a)] It would be an ethical violation to represent co-defendants with conflicting interests (consent will not solve the conflict); thus, Abrahamson can decline the appointment on this ground. The reason stated in item III. is not an acceptable reason for declining the appointment; a lawyer has a duty to represent his fair share of indigent or unpopular clients. [Comment 1 to ABA Model Rule 6.2] Item IV. raises another conflict of interest that would justify Abrahamson in declining the appointment. Had he not gained confidential information from the prosecution's witness, he might have discovered that information independently and been able to use it to impeach the witness. As it stands, however, his ability to impeach is constrained by his duty not to use the confidential information to the disadvantage of the witness, his former client. [ABA Model Rule 1.9(c)(1)]

Answer to Question 21

(C) Fedman is subject to criminal liability because his evidence-gathering technique amounted to extortion, an interstate threat against Bucks for the purpose of extracting information to use against Phatseaux. Under modern statutory law, the crime of extortion covers obtaining anything of value, tangible or intangible, by making various kinds of threats, including a threat to accuse a person of a crime. [*See, e.g.,* 18 U.S.C. §875(d)—felony to obtain something of value by transmitting in interstate commerce a threat to accuse a person of a crime; *see also* Perkins & Boyce, 442-52] The information that Fedman wanted from Bucks was something of value in the Phatseaux investigation, and Fedman clearly threatened to accuse Bucks of a crime if Bucks did not cooperate. Furthermore, the threat was transmitted interstate between Maryland and Florida, thus bringing it within the scope of the federal statute cited above. (A) is incorrect because Fedman did have a legal right to tell the Florida prosecutors about Bucks and the savings and loan, but Fedman did not have a right to threaten to do so (*i.e.*, to commit extortion) in order to coerce Bucks to cooperate. (B) is incorrect because it ignores the law of extortion. Just as it would have been illegal for Fedman to extract the information by physical torture, it was illegal to extract it by extortion. (D) is not as good as (C) because it is vague and because the right to be free from extortion, though important, is not a federally protected civil right.

Answer to Question 22

(C) Lawyer Loomis will not be subject to discipline for reporting the matter to the appropriate authorities because she is entitled to reveal this type of confidential information. Loomis may resign her in-house counsel position because Darlington's board insists on following a course of action that is both repugnant and criminal. [ABA Model Rule 1.16(b)(2), (4)] The children's sleepwear is likely to cause substantial bodily harm or even death. Because an attorney is entitled to reveal confidential information to the extent she reasonably believes necessary to prevent reasonably certain death or substantial bodily harm, Loomis may report this matter to the appropriate authorities. [ABA Model Rule 1.6(b)(1)] In addition, if the highest authority for an organization fails to take appropriate action regarding a violation of law, then a lawyer for the organization may report the relevant information to an appropriate person outside of the organization, if the lawyer reasonably believes that reporting is necessary to prevent substantial injury to the organization. This is true even if the information would otherwise be protected by the duty of confidentiality (which is not the case here because the sale of the fabric is likely to cause substantial bodily harm). [ABA Model Rule 1.13(c)] Here, the sale of the fabric is a violation of law, and selling the fabric could result in substantial injury to the organization if the fabric catches fire. (A) is wrong because Loomis is entitled to reveal confidential information to prevent reasonably certain death or substantial bodily harm or to prevent substantial injury to the organization. (B) is wrong because the repugnance and criminality of the proposed conduct are both sufficient grounds for permissive withdrawal. [ABA Model Rule 1.16(2), (4)] (D) is wrong because the duty of confidentiality continues even after the termination of the attorney-client relationship. [*See* Comment 18 to ABA Model Rule 1.6]

Answer to Question 23

(B) Ashe is subject to civil liability for mishandling Corbett's money because he breached his fiduciary duty to Corbett. When Ashe received the $40,000 from Corbett, he should have deposited it in a client trust account, not in the account that the law firm uses for office expenses. Ashe's failure to put the money in the correct account was a breach of fiduciary duty that can result in both professional discipline under ABA Model Rule 1.15(a) and in civil liability under the principles expressed in the Restatement. [*See* Restatement §49; *see also* Lurz v. Panek, 527 N.E.2d 663 (Ill. 1988)—lawyer civilly liable for loss client suffers from lawyer's delay in paying money over to client] (A) is incorrect because Ashe remains liable even though it was Ashe's law partner who withdrew the money from the law firm account. [*See, e.g.,* Blackmon v. Hale, 1 Cal. 3d 548 (1970)—lawyer civilly liable when former law partner converted client's funds] (C) is incorrect because a lawyer's breach of fiduciary duty can result in both professional discipline and civil liability to a client who suffered loss as a result. (D) is incorrect because the legal standard is breach of fiduciary duty, not strict liability.

Answer to Question 24

(A) Lurner and M & S are not subject to disqualification because from the facts given in the question, it appears that the merger matter and the age discrimination case are not substantially related to one another, and that the M & S lawyers did not gain confidential information in the merger matter that would be material to the discrimination case. [*See* ABA Model Rule 1.9] Therefore (C) and (D) are incorrect. (B) is incorrect because if the M & S lawyers who worked on the merger matter had obtained confidential information that would be material in the discrimination case, their knowledge would be imputed to Lurner, even though he was not a member of M & S when the knowledge was obtained. [*See* ABA Model Rules 1.9, 1.10]

Answer to Question 25

(B) The firm may pay all of the money as planned. Even though Clara is a nonlawyer, the firm may make certain kinds of payments to her from moneys that were originally earned as legal fees. [ABA Model Rule 5.4(a)(1)] The $100,000 is a proper payment because it reflects Clark's share of the capital assets of the firm. The $45,000 is a proper payment because the fees it represents had been earned, albeit not collected, at the time Clark died. The $125,000 is a proper payment because it is a reasonably computed death benefit payable over a reasonable period of time.

Answer to Question 26

(C) Lipscomb must promptly refund $11,000 because that amount is not in dispute. Lipscomb claimed $32,000 in fees (80 hours at $400 per hour) from the $40,000 fee advance (leaving an excess of $8,000). Lipscomb further claimed $2,000 from the $5,000 advance for expenses (leaving an excess of $3,000). Adding $8,000 + $3,000 produces an $11,000 refund due immediately from Lipscomb to Chandler. [ABA Model Rule 1.16(d)] Chandler apparently disputes Lipscomb's right to $32,000 in fees; thus, that disputed amount must remain in Lipscomb's client trust account until the fee dispute is settled. [ABA Model Rule 1.15(c)] (A) is wrong because when a lawyer is fired or withdraws, he must immediately refund the unspent portion of the expense advance and the portion of the fee advance that he does not claim to have earned. [ABA Model Rule 1.16(d)] (B) is wrong because Lipscomb is entitled to retain the disputed $32,000 in his client trust account until the fee dispute is settled. (D) is wrong because Lipscomb may retain the disputed portion of the expense advance, as explained above.

Answer to Question 27

(D) Judge Ambrose may testify because he is testifying to facts, not the defendant's character. CJC 2B prohibits a judge from testifying voluntarily as a character witness, but it says nothing about serving as an ordinary fact witness. (A) is wrong because there is no such rule. Judges are not disqualified from testifying in criminal cases. (B) is wrong because Ambrose did not need to be admitted to practice in State B in order to advise Corbuster about State B law. Even if that were untrue, Ambrose's testimony would still be admissible as evidence of Corbuster's lack of criminal intent. (C) is wrong because it states a nonexistent rule. While a judge is not competent to be a witness at a trial over which he himself is presiding [*see* Fed. R. Evid. 605], no rule forbids a judge from serving as an ordinary fact witness in a case that is pending before a different judge on his own court or a court that is under his court's appellate jurisdiction.

Answer to Question 28

(C) Leona's actions were not proper because a lawyer should fully advise a client of all relevant information, particularly when the lawyer has reason to believe that the information would be regarded as important by the client. The lawyer should furnish the client with all the information that is necessary to allow the client to participate intelligently in making decisions about the matter. [ABA Model Rule 1.4] Here, the existence of the statute was a fact necessary for Cristin to make an intelligent decision about how to proceed. (A) is wrong because it is not Leona's place to withhold information because she believes she knows what is best for Cristin. Cristin is entitled to all relevant information. (B) is wrong because the state policy does not absolve Leona from her ethical duty to keep her client informed. (D) is wrong because, again, withholding information is not an option regardless of whether Leona thought she was doing the right thing.

Answer to Question 29

(A) Locke is not subject to discipline unless she allows Cannon to interfere with her judgment in handling other clients' matters. [*See* ABA Model Rule 5.4] (B) is wrong because there is no law or disciplinary rule that requires Locke to notify Bliss & Buford regarding the transaction. (C) is wrong because no law or disciplinary rule requires Bliss & Buford's consent to Cannon's leaving the firm and giving his business to Locke as a solo practitioner. (D) is wrong because the loan payback clause does not violate the rule against splitting a legal fee with a nonlawyer. [ABA Model Rule 5.4(a)] True, the clause does measure the monthly payments as a percentage of Locke's net income in the prior month and most of her net income will probably come from legal fees. However, it makes sense to tailor her loan payments to her income, and the arrangement does not invite the evil that the no splitting rule was designed to prevent—interference with the lawyer's professional judgment.

Answer to Question 30

(B) Li's conduct was not proper because Li pretended to be disinterested and advised Hyde to pay the extra money. When dealing on behalf of a client with a person who is not represented by counsel, a lawyer must not state or imply that the lawyer is disinterested, and the lawyer must not give that person advice (other than advice to secure counsel) if the lawyer knows that the person's interests may conflict with those of the client. Clearly, Hyde's interests do conflict with Weaver's interests. [ABA Model Rule 4.3] Here, Li advised Hyde that he ought to pay increased alimony and child support. He compounded the problem by pretending to be disinterested, a direct violation of Rule 4.3. (A) is wrong because it is overbroad; it was proper, for example, for Li to advise Hyde to get a lawyer and to offer to postpone the hearing. Moreover, if an adversary refuses to retain counsel, a lawyer must communicate directly with that person. (C) is wrong because making those statements does not exempt Li from those provisions that prohibit implying disinterest and giving advice. (D) is wrong because Li did give advice to Hyde—the advice to pay the extra money that Weaver was asking for.

Answer to Question 31

(C) Lockwood is not subject to discipline for disclosing Downs's confidential information to the professor because the disclosure was necessary to effectively carry out the representation. Unless a client has specifically instructed the lawyer to the contrary, that lawyer can reasonably assume that he has implied authority from the client to disclose confidential information when necessary to carry out the representation. That is particularly true in cases such as this one where the lawyer cannot easily communicate with his client. [ABA Model Rule 1.6(a)] (A) is wrong because a lawyer may seek advice from an expert without the expert being licensed in the jurisdiction; and in any case, it does not affect the confidentiality rules. (B) is wrong because specific authorization is not required; it can be implied. (D) is wrong because refraining from revealing the client's name is not sufficient to permit revelation of confidential information. There must be an exception to the confidentiality rules or authorization by the client.

Answer to Question 32

(C) Aguero would not be subject to discipline for accepting the sculpture because he did not solicit the gift. Although ABA Model Rule 1.8(c) prohibits a lawyer from soliciting a substantial gift from a client when the lawyer is not related to the client, it does not prohibit a lawyer from *accepting an unsolicited gift* from a client, even if the gift is substantial (although the gift may be voidable for undue influence). Moreover, Comment 6 to ABA Model Rule 1.8 states that a lawyer may accept a gift from a client if the transaction meets general standards of fairness. Here, Aguero did not solicit the gift, and there are no facts to suggest undue influence or unfairness. Thus, the gift is proper. (A) is wrong because it is too broad. A lawyer may accept a gift of substantial value from a client if the conditions stated above are satisfied. (B) and (D) are wrong because the value of Aguero's recent work for Carrara is irrelevant. Aguero did not charge more than the $750. In addition to discharging the $750 fee bill, Carrara obviously intended to make a gift to Aguero in gratitude for years of work in the past.

Answer to Question 33

(D)   Purdum may not reveal Dewitt's perjury because to do so would violate Purdum's duty of confidentiality. No exceptions to the confidentiality requirement apply to these facts. There is no indication that revealing the perjury is necessary to prevent reasonably certain death or substantial bodily harm. Also, there is no indication that Dewitt's perjury is a crime that is reasonably certain to result in substantial injury to the financial interests of another, in furtherance of which Dewitt has used Purdum's services. The obligation to reveal perjury under the Model Rules does not apply because that obligation ceases at the end of the proceedings, and both proceedings here have concluded. (A) is wrong because the proceeding has ended and, therefore, Purdum is obligated to keep the information in confidence. (B) is wrong for the same reason. The prerequisite of urging the client to recant is relevant while the proceeding is in progress, but not after. Furthermore, even if the trial was ongoing, Purdum would not be obligated to reveal the perjury because he was not representing Dewitt at trial. Purdum represented Dewitt in the preliminary hearing, which has concluded, ending his

obligation to disclose. (C) is wrong because what Purdum believes about Dewitt's dangerousness is not relevant. There is no exception to the duty of confidentiality based on the client's violent propensities.

Answer to Question 34

(C)   The arrangement is not proper because Lomax is required to keep $10,000 on deposit to be included on the list. A lawyer may not give "anything of value" to a person for recommending the lawyer's services. [ABA Model Rule 7.2(b)] The bank benefits in many ways by increasing the amount of its deposits; for example, its deposits determine how much it can lend to borrowers. Thus, obtaining deposits from lawyers is of value to the bank, and that is one reason it has devised the referral scheme. (A) is wrong because although a lawyer may pay the usual charges of a *not-for-profit* or qualified lawyer referral service [ABA Model Rule 7.2(b)], banks operate for profit, and there is no indication that the bank has been approved by the appropriate regulatory authority as a qualified lawyer referral service. (B) is wrong because Lomax is giving something of value for the referrals, as explained above, even though there is no fee for individual referrals. (D) is wrong because this arrangement does not constitute an improper partnership or association with a nonlawyer for the purpose of practicing law. A lawyer's professional association with a nonlawyer is improper if the nonlawyer: (i) owns an interest in the practice; (ii) is an officer or director of a business involving law practice; or (iii) has the right to control the lawyer's professional judgment. [ABA Model Rule 5.4(d)] None of these is the case here; United is acting solely as a referral agent, and has nothing to do with the operation of the lawyer's practice.

Answer to Question 35

(D)   If $9.7 million is within the bounds of

reason as a fee for the work Patton did, he is not subject to discipline. [*See* ABA Model Rule 1.5(a)] Among the various factors that point to the reasonableness of Patton's fee are: the novelty and difficulty of the patentability issue, the fact that Inovacio was the one who suggested the fee arrangement after having been offered a standard hourly fee, the value of the result that Patton obtained for Inovacio, and the contingent nature of the arrangement which imposed a high risk on Patton. (A) is wrong because a lawyer is prohibited from acquiring a proprietary interest in the subject of *litigation* he is conducting [ABA Model Rule 1.8(i)], and obtaining a United States patent is not litigation. Even if this were a litigation case, the contingent fee exception to the rule would apply. [ABA Model Rule 1.8(i)(2)] (B) is wrong because a fee that is otherwise reasonable does not become unreasonable simply because the lawyer can use the knowledge gained to earn fees from other clients. (C) is wrong because the mere fact that the client agreed to the fee arrangement does not by itself make the fee reasonable. Many factors, including the time, labor, and skill required to do the job, are considered in determining whether the fee is reasonable. [ABA Model Rule 1.5(a)]

Answer to Question 36

(A) LeBrille is not subject to discipline because she did the best she could in an emergency situation. In an emergency situation, a lawyer may give legal advice on a matter that she would not be competent to handle in an ordinary situation. [Comment 3 to ABA Model Rule 1.1] Here, LeBrille's advice was limited to the narrow question the client posed. She is not subject to discipline because she did the best she could in the heat of the moment, and she warned the client about the dangers of relying on unresearched legal advice. (B) is wrong because a State A lawyer who renders advice about the law of another jurisdiction in an ordinary, nonemergency situation is expected to be competent to render such advice. [ABA Model Rule 1.1] (C) is wrong because LeBrille is not engaged in unauthorized practice when she advises a State A client about EU law. She need not be admitted in an EU member nation in order to advise her State A client about EU law. (D) is wrong because LeBrille is not subject to discipline for rendering legal advice that turns out to be mistaken if she acted competently in light of the time-constrained circumstances in which she found herself.

Answer to Question 37

(B) Labrie may act as Truhart's trial counsel because he is not a *necessary* witness. [ABA Model Rule 3.7(a)] A roomful of witnesses heard Sirosis's comments and could testify to them. Moreover, Sirosis has made a judicial admission that he made the statements; thus, no testimony is required on that point. Labrie has no knowledge as to the truth of the statements, as he knows nothing of Truhart's personal life; thus, he would have no relevant testimony on that issue. Therefore, Labrie is neither a "necessary" witness, nor a witness that "ought" to be called. (A) is wrong because there is no need for informed, written consent in this situation. (C) is wrong because even if there is a remote possibility that Labrie might be called, he is not a necessary witness, and it is unlikely that he would be called by Sirosis's lawyer because he could not have anything favorable or relevant to add. A mere remote possibility that the lawyer will be called as a witness is not sufficient to disqualify the lawyer from representing a client. (D) is wrong because associating and preparing co-counsel is not a prerequisite for an attorney taking a case when he is not a necessary witness and merely witnessed an event that is the subject of litigation.

Answer to Question 38

(A) Lacey should not discuss the matter with Westerman, and should advise him to hire his own attorney. When an organization is the lawyer's client, the lawyer owes the duty of loyalty to the organization—not to the people who are its constituents. If there is a conflict between the interests of the organization and the interests of one of its constituents, the lawyer should advise the constituent to obtain independent legal counsel. [Comment 10 to ABA Model Rule 1.13] Lacey's client is Transcorp, and Transcorp's interests are in conflict with the interests of Westerman. If Transcorp proves that Westerman had no authority to sign the note, the bank may sue Westerman himself. If Transcorp is held liable to the bank, Transcorp may sue Westerman for indemnification. In these circumstances, Westerman needs his own lawyer, and Lacey must not try to represent both him and Transcorp. Furthermore, because Westerman is presently unrepresented in the matter and his interests conflict with those of Transcorp, Lacey must not try to give him legal advice, except to get a lawyer. [See ABA Model Rule 4.3] (B) is wrong because Lacey must not try to represent Westerman at the deposition due to the conflict of interest explained above. (C) is wrong because Lacey must not try to give Westerman legal advice, except to get a lawyer. (D) is wrong for the reason just stated. Furthermore, as Transcorp's lawyer, Lacey must not give legal advice to a person with conflicting interests (particularly advice to testify in such a way as to damage her client's position).

Answer to Question 39

(A) Anderson is subject to discipline because his actions in State Green constitute fraud. A lawyer is subject to discipline not only for violating a disciplinary rule, but also for committing a criminal act that reflects adversely on his honesty, trustworthiness, or fitness as a lawyer in other respects, or for engaging in conduct involving dishonesty, fraud, deceit, or misrepresentation. [ABA Model Rule 8.4] The type of fraud described clearly falls within this rule. (B) is wrong because a lawyer is subject to discipline in a state where he is licensed to practice even if the misconduct occurred in another jurisdiction. [ABA Model Rule 8.5(a)] (C) is wrong because the fact that Anderson was not licensed in State Green is irrelevant. He was not practicing law in State Green, so he is not subject to discipline on the ground of unauthorized practice. He is subject to discipline, however, for filing improper tax returns. As discussed above, Anderson cannot escape discipline for his fraudulent conduct because it occurred in another jurisdiction. (D) is wrong because, as discussed above, a lawyer may be disciplined for dishonest conduct regardless of whether it is related to the practice of law.

Answer to Question 40

(D) A lawyer may advance court costs and litigation expenses on the client's behalf. A lawyer is subject to discipline, however, for rendering any other kind of financial assistance to a client in the context of contemplated or pending litigation. [ABA Model Rule 1.8(e)] Items III. and IV. represent court costs and litigation expenses, which are permissible. Family support is not an expense of litigation; thus item I. is improper. Similarly, treatment of Carson's injuries is not an expense of litigation, therefore item II. is also improper.

Answer to Question 41

(A) Ahmad's conduct was proper because violating the ordinance was one of the ways to gain legal standing to challenge the constitutionality of the ordinance. A lawyer must not counsel or assist a client in conduct that the lawyer knows is criminal or fraudulent. However, a lawyer may counsel or assist a client to make a good faith effort to determine the validity, scope, meaning, or application of a law even if it requires the client to disobey the law. [ABA Model Rule 1.2(d)] This usually arises when a lawyer is asked how a particular law may be challenged, and the lawyer advises the client on ways to obtain legal standing, which includes disobedience of the law. Here, Ahmad was merely advising Carlo on methods of obtaining legal standing, including renting houses in violation of the ordinance. (B) is wrong because the ultimate outcome of the challenge is irrelevant. It is important that Ahmad believed there was a good faith basis for challenging the validity of the ordinance, but whether the challenge succeeds does not determine the propriety of his conduct. (C) is wrong because, as discussed above, there is an exception to this rule for a good faith effort to determine the validity of a law. (D) is wrong because there is no affirmative duty to counsel the client in this way. In fact, as discussed above, there is an exception for a good faith challenge to the law that would permit Ahmad to do just the opposite.

Answer to Question 42

(B) Aronson's actions are proper because he offered his services free of charge. Generally, a lawyer is prohibited from seeking employment by initiating personal contact with a prospective client. However, this prohibition applies only when "a significant motive" for the solicitation is the lawyer's pecuniary gain. [ABA Model Rule 7.3(a)] Thus, a lawyer who volunteers to represent someone free of charge is not subject to discipline for solicitation. (A) is incorrect because Aronson's actions are proper even if he is motivated by a desire to obtain publicity, provided that this is not a *substantial* motive in his offer. (C) is incorrect because, as discussed above, this situation falls within an exception to the ban on in-person solicitation. (D) is incorrect because, as discussed above, it is not

necessary for Aronson to have previously represented the demonstrators in order for his actions to have been proper.

Answer to Question 43

(D) It is not proper for Judge Jardon to continue as chief executive officer of the corporation because the nursing home practices employment discrimination in violation of state law. [CJC 2C] While CJC 2C concerns only organizations that discriminate based on race, sex, religion, or national origin, the Commentary to that rule states that a judge's membership in an organization that discriminates on *other* grounds in violation of local law would violate CJC 2 and 2A, which relates to the appearance of impropriety and the judge's duty to comply with the law. (A) is incorrect because the nursing home's discrimination violates state law and is thus improper. (B) is incorrect because, as discussed above, the judge's remaining an officer in the corporation would be improper even if the time it took did not interfere with her judicial duties. (C) is incorrect because it is too broad; CJC 4D(3)(a) allows a judge to be involved with a business that is closely held by the judge or her family.

Answer to Question 44

(C) Angstrom should keep the information in confidence unless Cheever authorizes her to reveal it, even though the death of the landlord has made it impossible for the prosecutor to obtain the information other than from Angstrom. Angstrom obtained this information from the landlord in the course of representing her client; therefore, it is subject to the attorney's duty of confidentiality. Absent the consent of the client, an attorney must not reveal *any* information relating to the representation of the client. [ABA Model Rule 1.6] (A) is incorrect because an attorney has no ethical obligation to reveal harmful facts, and in fact, may be disciplined for doing so. (B) is incorrect because, as noted above, there is no duty to reveal this information; thus, there is no obligation to urge the client to reveal the information or withdraw. (D) is incorrect because this information is confidential. The ethical duty of confidentiality covers more kinds of information than the attorney-client privilege, which covers only confidential communications between the attorney and client. The ethical duty of confidentiality covers any information the attorney obtains relating to the representation of the client, no matter what the source of the information.

Answer to Question 45

(B) Judge Jackson's actions were proper because he did not charge Martha a fee. Although a full-time judge may not practice law, there is an exception for this type of transaction. A judge may, without compensation, give legal advice to, and draft and review documents for, a member of the judge's family. [CJC 4G] (A) is wrong because whether the buyer might appear in Judge Jackson's court does not affect Judge Jackson's ability to prepare documents for his mother. If the buyer does appear in his court, Judge Jackson's participation in that proceeding will be evaluated at that time in light of the facts. (C) is wrong because, as stated above, there is an exception for reviewing documents for relatives without compensation. (D) is wrong because, although Judge Jackson cannot act as a negotiator, there is no requirement that his identity as the person who made the revisions be kept a secret.

Answer to Question 46

(D) It would not be proper for Lenny to have his name included on Stork's list because the form agreement he is required to sign allows a third party to exercise influence over the lawyer-client relationship. A lawyer must not allow a person who recommends, employs, or pays her for serving a client to direct or regulate the lawyer's professional judgment. [ABA Model Rule 5.4(c)] Stork is, in effect, recommending the lawyer, and the restriction on withdrawal in the form agreement clearly interferes with the lawyer's professional judgment. (A) is wrong because the good intentions behind the list do not remove the interference with the lawyer's professional judgment. Likewise, (B) is wrong because, even if Lenny does not give Stork anything of value, the arrangement is still improper because of the restriction on withdrawal. (C) is wrong because the list does not amount to improper solicitation.

Answer to Question 47

(C) Agnes is not subject to discipline because Barnaby earned the fee prior to his suspension. Despite his suspension, Barnaby is entitled to the fees he earned while he was still lawfully practicing law. It is true that a lawyer is prohibited from aiding a non-lawyer in the unauthorized practice of law, but here Barnaby is not practicing law, and Agnes is merely forwarding his previously earned fee. (A) is wrong because Barnaby need not wait until he is reinstated to collect a fee he earned prior to his suspension. (B) is wrong because Barnaby is not a non-lawyer, and Agnes is not splitting legal fees with him in any case. Agnes is merely transmitting Barnaby's own money to him. (D) is wrong because the money does not belong to Agnes, and even if it did, she cannot do anything she wishes with it. For example, there are rules prohibiting the sharing of legal fees with nonlawyers.

Answer to Question 48

(B) Item I. is proper because Judge Jones, like anyone else, may contribute to any cause she likes. Item II. is not proper because a judge may not personally participate in the solicitation of funds or other fund-raising activities. [CJC 4C(3)(b)] Item III. is proper because a judge may assist an organization in planning fund-raising, although the judge may not actually participate in the fund-raising activity. [CJC 4C(3)(b)(i)] A judge must not be a speaker or guest of honor at an organization's fund-raising event, but mere attendance at such an event is permissible. [CJC 4C(3)(b), Commentary] Thus, item IV. is improper and item V. is proper.

Answer to Question 49

(A) Item I. is wrong because a lawyer may require his fee to be paid in advance. [Comment 4 to ABA Model Rule 1.5] Item II. is wrong because a lawyer may accept property in return for services, provided it does not involve a proprietary interest in the subject of litigation. [Comment 4 to ABA Model Rule 1.5] Here the coat is not the subject of litigation; thus, accepting the coat as payment was proper. Item III. is wrong because (i) as noted above, it is acceptable to take property in payment for services, and (ii) Liston has earned the fee represented by the coat. When a lawyer-client relationship is prematurely terminated, the lawyer is required to return to the client any unearned advance on attorneys' fees. [ABA Model Rule 1.16(d)] In this case, at the time he was fired, Liston had earned $4,000 in fees. Because the coat is worth only $3,000, not only may Liston keep the coat, he may sue Dennis for the $1,000 difference. Item IV. is wrong because in the event the relationship is prematurely terminated, the lawyer is generally entitled only to fees actually earned under a quantum meruit theory of recovery. Thus, in this case, Liston could recover $4,000.

Answer to Question 50

(C) Leroy is not subject to discipline because he did not make any false or misleading claims about himself or his services. Lawyers, like other citizens, have the right to express their views in the media on newsworthy issues. Even if a lawyer's sole purpose in seeking media publicity is to lure clients, the state may not impose professional discipline on the lawyer absent a compelling state interest. A lawyer who uses the media to lure clients may, however, be disciplined for making statements or claims that are false or misleading about the lawyer or his services. [ABA Model Rule 7.1] Here, Leroy made no statements about himself or his services other than the fact that he is a lawyer and his opinion about the incident. There is nothing false or misleading in his communication. (A) is wrong because, as discussed above, the fact that Leroy was motivated by the desire to attract fee-paying business is irrelevant. This is not a case of in-person or live electronic solicitation, which is the only circumstance in which this consideration is relevant. (B) is wrong because it is overbroad. Lawyers can and do make public statements about pending litigation all the time. Lawyers who are involved in a proceeding cannot make statements that they know will have a substantial likelihood of materially prejudicing an adjudicative proceeding. [ABA Model Rule 3.6(a)] That is not the case here; Leroy has no reason to believe his opinion will materially prejudice the state agency bringing the action. (D) is wrong because the fact that the statement was printed in the newspapers is of absolutely no consequence; it does not affect the propriety of Leroy's behavior regardless of whether he gave consent.

Answer to Question 51

(A) (C) is incorrect because there is no disciplinary rule against a lawyer acting as a third-party neutral in a family law matter, and it was proper for Ayers to undertake the neutral's role in helping Hector and Wanda try to resolve their marital problems. [*See* Restatement §130, comment d] (D) is incorrect because the facts contain nothing to support a civil claim against Ayers for the work she did as a third-party neutral. (B) is incorrect because when two parties jointly consult an attorney on a matter of common interest, neither of them can claim the attorney-client privilege in subsequent civil litigation between them. [*See* Restatement §75] (A) is correct because Hector cannot claim the privilege for the reason stated above. If the judge overrules the privilege claim and Ayers nevertheless refuses to answer the question, she can be sanctioned for contempt of court.

Answer to Question 52

(B) ABA Model Rule 5.5(c) concerns temporary practice in a state where the lawyer is not admitted. ABA Model Rule 5.5(c)(4) permits Linz to practice temporarily in State Four to the extent that his work in that state is reasonably related to the work he does for Intron in State Two. If State Four requires out-of-state lawyers to seek pro hac vice admission before engaging in pretrial preparation, then ABA Model Rule 5.5(c)(2) and (3) would require Linz to seek such admission. (A) is wrong because the application of ABA Model Rule 5.5(c) to Linz's situation is clear, not debatable. (C) is wrong because ABA Model Rule 5.5(c) allows Linz to perform the assigned tasks without taking a bar exam in State Four. (D) is wrong because associating a local lawyer is only one of four different ways to satisfy ABA Model Rule 5.5(c).

Answer to Question 53

(C) ABA Model Rule 7.4(d) prohibits a lawyer from stating or implying that she is a certified specialist unless she has been certified by an appropriate organization that is clearly identified in the lawyer's communication. Ataris's Yellow Pages ad appears to have been artfully crafted to make unsophisticated readers think that Ataris has been certified by the State One Bar. Thus, the ad violates both ABA Model Rule 7.4(d) and ABA Model Rule 7.1, which prohibits misleading advertising. As for Ataris's reciprocal referral relationship with Leacox, the applicable rule is ABA Model Rule 7.2(b)(4), which permits a reciprocal referral agreement between lawyers, provided that the agreement is nonexclusive and the referred clients are told about the existence and nature of the agreement. ABA Model Rule 7.2(b)(4) has not yet been prominently interpreted, leaving one to wonder whether the relationship between Ataris and Leacox should be regarded as an "agreement." On the one hand, the question states that they have no "formal reciprocal referral agreement." On the other hand, in some legal contexts, a consciously reciprocal course of dealing can be the equivalent of an agreement. [*See, e.g.,* United States v. Container Corp. of America, 393 U.S. 333 (1969)—competitors' reciprocal exchange of price data was held to be an agreement under section 1 of the Sherman Antitrust Act] However, for purposes of this question, the relationship between Ataris and Leacox will be deemed an agreement under ABA Model Rule 7.2(b)(4) because it is bound to influence their judgment about referrals to some degree. Here, the relationship violates the nonexclusive requirement because the two lawyers follow the pattern "without exception." Furthermore, the relationship would be proper only if Ataris tells referred clients about the relationship so that they can decide for themselves how to value the referral. One can reach the same conclusion by applying ABA Model Rule 1.7(a)(2)— Ataris's reciprocal relationship with Leacox gives Ataris a personal interest (obtaining future referrals) that is in conflict with the interest of her client (obtaining an unbiased referral). The conflict could be solved only by full disclosure and written consent of the affected client. [ABA Model Rule 1.7(b)]

Answer to Question 54

(A) Lubovich is subject to discipline under CJC 5(C)(2), which prohibits a judicial candidate from personally soliciting campaign contributions or publicly stated support. The five lawyers who contributed money will be subject to discipline if Lubovich wins and if they accept appointments from him. [*See* ABA Model Rule 7.6] (B) is wrong because Lubovich is subject to discipline under CJC 5(C)(2), as noted above. The second sentence of (B) is wrong because it overstates the constraints on a lawyer's participation in a judicial campaign. (C) is wrong because the five lawyers who contributed money violated ABA Model Rule 7.6, as noted above. The first sentence of (C) is a misapplication of CJC 5(A)(3)(d)(i), which prohibits a judge from making pledges or promises that are inconsistent with the impartial performance of the judge's adjudicative duties "*with respect to cases, controversies, or issues that are likely to come before the court.*" Here, the policy on whom the Attorney General will appoint as administrators' counsel is not the kind of litigation issue to which the highlighted language of CJC 5(A)(3)(d)(i), above, refers. The second sentence of (C) is wrong because the motive of the five money contributors was to obtain appointments if Lubovich won. [*See* ABA Model Rule 7.6] (D) is wrong because a lawyer who runs for a judicial post must follow the CJC. [*See* CJC 5(A)(3)(a) - (c)] The second sentence of (D) is wrong because ABA Model Rule 7.6 trumps whatever privacy rights one can find in the peripheral glow of the First and Fourteenth Amendments.

Answer to Question 55

(B) The Lake County Free Legal Advice Hotline is the kind of operation envisioned in ABA Model Rule 6.5. Under ABA Model Rule 6.5, walk-in legal clinics, advice-only clinics, legal advice hotlines, and the like, are not held to the high conflict-of-interest standards that govern ordinary law offices. Legal hotlines, walk-in clinics, and similar providers of quick legal service typically operate under conditions that make it difficult or impossible to conduct ordinary conflict-of-interest checks. Under ABA Model Rule 6.5(b), Ashcraft would be subject to discipline only if he **actually knew** that Liu had previously counseled the mother of the abused children. A lawyer's actual knowledge can be inferred from the circumstances [ABA Model Rule 1.0(f)], but the question does not mention any circumstances from which an inference could be made that Ashcraft had actual knowledge. (A) is wrong because it fails to account for ABA Model Rule 6.5. (C) is wrong because, absent **actual knowledge** of a conflict, the rule of imputed disqualification does not apply between two lawyers in a quick-legal-service program. [*See* Comment 4 to ABA Model Rule 6.5] (D) is wrong because both the mother and father were "clients" of the respective lawyers who advised them. [Comment 1 to ABA Model Rule 6.5] This is important because ABA Model Rule 6.5 loosens only the conflict-of-interest rules, not other aspects of the lawyer-client relationship such as the duty of competence, the duty of diligence, and the duty of confidentiality.

Answer to Question 56

(C) ABA Model Rule 5.7 provides that when a lawyer offers another kind of service ancillary to her practice of law, and the ancillary service is provided "in circumstances that are not distinct from the lawyer's provision of legal services," the lawyer must follow the legal ethics rules in the ancillary service as well as the legal service. Here, Aghai does bill separately for her two kinds of service, but she offers both out of the same office, and the tasks she does as sports agent shade imperceptibly into the tasks she does as lawyer, as is illustrated by the exclusive sponsorship contract with the bank. Thus, Aghai must follow the lawyer conflict of interest rules when she acts as sports agent. [*See* Comment 10 to ABA Model Rule 5.7] When Aghai diverted the bank ad campaign from Dobbs to Elgin, she violated ABA Model Rule 1.7(a)(1) (concurrent conflict when the representation of one client will be directly adverse to another client), or at least ABA Model Rule 1.7(a)(2) (significant risk that the representation of one client will be limited by the lawyer's responsibility to another client). Incidentally, Aghai may also be **subject to civil liability** in a suit by Dobbs for breaching the duty of loyalty an agent owes to a principal. [*See* Restatement of the Law of Agency 2d §§391, 394] (A) is wrong for the reasons stated above. (B) is wrong because Aghai is not doing the "same work" when she acts as sports agent for two different players. (D) is wrong because the separate charging arrangement is not sufficient by itself to clearly segregate Aghai's sports agent work from her lawyer work.

Answer to Question 57

(A) ABA Model Rule 1.17 permits a lawyer to sell her entire law practice, or an area of her law practice, to one or more lawyers or law firms. Here, Sololei sold her entire law practice to two different lawyers, and ABA Model Rule 1.17 permits that. The departure of 40% of Sololei's clients does not cause the sales to violate ABA Model Rule 1.17. Indeed ABA Model Rule 1.17(c)(2) requires the selling lawyer to notify her clients that they have a right to pick up their files from the buyer and take them to a different lawyer. [*See also* Comment 2 to ABA Model Rule 1.17] (B) and (D) are wrong because clients are not like sheep that can be bought and sold, willy-nilly. To hold Sololei either subject to discipline or civilly liable in unjust enrichment would be inconsistent with the clients' right to pick up their files and take them to a different lawyer. Sololei, Lang, and Abel made their sales contracts in the context of ABA Model Rule 1.17 so Lang and Abel cannot claim that they were surprised when clients departed. (C) is wrong because ABA Model Rule 1.17(b) permits a lawyer to sell her entire practice to **one or more** lawyers or law firms. One might also argue that Sololei's medical malpractice cases are in a different "area of practice" (professional malpractice) from her household products cases (products liability). But that argument is not necessary here because Sololei sold her entire law practice.

Answer to Question 58

(D) ABA Model Rule 1.6(b)(4) and Comment 9 explain that a lawyer may reveal information that would otherwise be confidential if the lawyer's purpose is to obtain legal advice about complying with the legal ethics rules. (A) is wrong because the applicable doctrine here is the ethical duty of confidentiality, not the attorney-client privilege, and the ethical duty contains the exception described above. (B) is wrong because the exception to the ethical duty would apply in this situation no matter whether Goop is regarded as the client, or the prostitute as the client, or both of them as joint clients. (C) is wrong because the exception to the ethical duty would apply in this situation, whether or not Prentice identified Goop by name. As a practical matter, however, a lawyer who discloses confidential information to obtain legal ethics advice may wish to couch the information hypothetically, in order to minimize the chance of harm to the client. [*See* Comment 4 to ABA Model Rule 1.6]

Answer to Question 59

(C) This question is governed by ABA Model Rule 1.13, not by the SEC's regulations under the Sarbanes-Oxley Act, because R&H is not publicly owned and is not subject to the jurisdiction of the SEC. Athol is *subject to discipline* for tipping off the Justice Department because he violated the duty of confidentiality imposed by ABA Model Rule 1.6(a). When Leopard and Athol investigated the price fixing rumor at the request of R&H's General Counsel, they were operating under ABA Model Rule 1.13(d), which applies to lawyers who are hired "to investigate an alleged violation of law" or to "defend an organization" or its people against a claim arising out of an alleged violation of law. That means that ABA Model Rule 1.13(c) does *not* apply, and they *must not* report to outsiders about what they find. The passage in (C) about Leopard's conduct correctly states the standard expressed in ABA Model Rule 5.1(c) about the duties of a supervising lawyer. Both parts of (A) are wrong—Leopard acted properly, and Athol is subject to discipline, as explained above. (B) is wrong because Athol's conduct was not proper. Moreover, Athol probably committed legal malpractice when he tipped off the Justice Department, and Leopard might be vicariously liable for his malpractice because she was his supervisor. (D) is wrong because Athol is subject to discipline for violating ABA Model Rule 1.6(a).

Answer to Question 60

(C) Item I. is correct. The adversary system assumes that the parties will gather the relevant evidence competitively. [Comment 1 to ABA Model Rule 3.4] Adler does not have a duty to voluntarily tell opposing counsel where the golden egg is located. On the other hand, if opposing counsel asks in a proper discovery request, "Where is the golden egg?" then counsel must provide an honest response. [ABA Model Rules 3.3(a)(1), 3.4 (a) - (c)] Item II. is false. Adler must not unlawfully obstruct the opposition's access to evidence [ABA Model Rule 3.4(a)], and if he knowingly violates the rules of discovery, he will be subject to both professional discipline and litigation sanction. [ABA Model Rule 3.4(c); Fed. R. Civ. P. 37] Item III. is false. Because the term "certain" has at least eight meanings, the quoted answer to the interrogatory is either incomplete or affirmatively misleading. When advising his client on how to respond to an interrogatory, Adler must not recommend a misleading, incomplete, or evasive response; doing that is treated the same as failing to respond. [Fed. R. Civ. P. 37(a)(2)(B)(3); ABA Model Rule 3.4(c)—knowing disregard of an obligation under the rules of a tribunal] Item IV. is false. At Dr. Wintz's deposition, the only time Adler may advise Dr. Wintz not to answer a question is (i) to preserve a privilege, (ii) to enforce a court-ordered limit on discovery, or (iii) to give Adler a chance to move for a protective order. [*See* Fed. R. Civ. P. 30(d)(1)] The question does not mention anything to indicate that Dr. Wintz's knowledge is privileged, that the court has previously imposed a limit on discovery, or that a protective order would be appropriate. Therefore, Adler will be subject to both discipline and litigation sanction if he instructs Dr. Wintz not to answer questions about the date of first public use. [*Id.*; ABA Model Rule 3.4(c)]

PRACTICE EXAM 3

Question 1

Attorney Dave is defending Datatec Corporation in an employment discrimination suit in which the plaintiffs are represented by attorney Perello. Wallner is a Datatec employee, but he is not an officer or shareholder in Datatec, and he is not a party to the lawsuit. Wallner is in charge of Datatec's Personnel Department, and he is responsible for insuring that Datatec's hiring practices comply with the laws against employment discrimination. Wallner is in poor health, so Dave scheduled the taking of Wallner's deposition as a precaution in case Wallner should die before trial. Without seeking Dave's consent, or even telling him, Perello had lunch with Wallner several days before the deposition, and on that occasion Perello pumped Wallner for information relevant to the lawsuit. When Dave learned what had happened, he telephoned Perello and called him a slimy, mud-sucking shyster.

Which of the following is most nearly correct?

(A) Dave's conduct was *proper*.

(B) Perello's conduct was *proper*.

(C) Perello is *subject to discipline* because he should not have talked with Wallner about the case without Dave's consent.

(D) Perello is *subject to discipline* because he talked with a deposition witness about the subject of the litigation before the deposition was taken.

Questions 2 and 3 are based on the following facts:

Diplock, a juvenile, has been charged with auto theft, a felony, and has hired Lucinda to represent him. Before the case comes to trial, Lucinda confers with Patrick, who has been assigned by the district attorney's office to prosecute the case. Patrick knows that Lucinda plans to run for public office and is always interested in getting as much publicity as possible. She is often referred to in the press as a "hotshot" criminal defense attorney, and almost all of her victories over the state are publicized. Patrick suggests to Lucinda that, because Diplock is a juvenile, the charge might be reduced to "joyriding," a misdemeanor. Lucinda refuses, telling Patrick, "I win by *trying* cases. You must not have read the newspapers lately—there's going to be a lot of coverage of this case because Diplock's father is socially prominent, so I'm not about to cop a joyriding plea for the kid."

2. The *proper* conduct for Patrick is to:

   I. Ask the court to dismiss the auto theft charge and prosecute Diplock for joyriding.

   II. Prosecute the auto theft charge.

   III. Send an investigator to talk to Diplock about the offer to lower charges.

   (A) I. only.

   (B) II. only.

   (C) I. or II., but not III.

   (D) III. only.

3. If Diplock is convicted of auto theft, would it be *proper* for Patrick to report Lucinda to the disciplinary authorities?

   (A) Yes, but only if he is certain that Lucinda's motive was to gain publicity.

   (B) Yes, if he knows that Lucinda never conveyed the offer of a lesser charge to Diplock.

   (C) No, if Lucinda defended Diplock competently at trial.

   (D) No, unless Lucinda got publicity from the trial.

Question 4

During his second year in law school, Peter's wife divorced him, as a result of which he suffered serious emotional imbalance. Ultimately, he managed to graduate, and the state bar sent a routine form letter to Professor Schultze, asking her to comment on Peter's fitness to practice law. Professor Schultze is a member of the bar of that state. In response, she gave her candid opinion—that Peter was prone to extreme and irrational tirades against women, and that he was not yet recovered from his emotional trauma. Based partly on this information, the state bar denied Peter's petition for admission. Now, three years later, Peter has asked Professor Schultze to support his re-petition for admission. After carefully checking the facts, Professor Schultze concludes that Peter has regained his emotional balance.

Which of the following is most nearly correct?

(A) Three years ago, it would have been **proper** for Professor Schultze to keep her opinion to herself because emotional imbalance is not a valid ground for denying admission to the bar.

(B) Three years ago, it would have been **proper** for Professor Schultze to keep her opinion to herself because she is untrained in psychology or the science of emotional illness.

(C) Now, Professor Schultze **may** support Peter's re-petition because she believes that he has regained his emotional balance.

(D) Now, Professor Schultze **may** remain neutral because she is untrained in psychology or the science of emotional illness.

Question 5

Attorney Alex has a high-profile divorce law practice in Centerville. Because of his heavy case load, Alex often appears before the four chancery judges of the county court. One of the chancery judges, Jamal, is getting married, and he sends a wedding invitation to Alex. Alex wishes to send Judge Jamal, as a wedding gift, an imported Italian machine that makes espresso and cappuccino coffee because Alex knows that Judge Jamal loves fine coffee. The coffee machine sells for $200 at Centerville's best cooking equipment store.

Would it be **proper** for Alex to send the coffee machine to Judge Jamal?

(A) Yes, unless Judge Jamal believes that he would be unduly influenced by the gift.

(B) Yes, but only if Alex and Judge Jamal are friends and only if the gift is not excessive for the occasion and the relationship.

(C) No, because the gift is not a campaign contribution, and lawyers should not give other types of gifts to judges.

(D) No, because the value of the gift exceeds $150.

GO ON TO THE NEXT PAGE

Question 6

The state in which attorney Lawrence practices levies an annual tax on trusts for the benefit of minors. Tax returns must be filed, and the taxes must be paid, by March 15; late filing results in an automatic penalty of 15%. In mid-January, trustee Morris retained attorney Lawrence to prepare and file a tax return. Morris heard nothing from Lawrence during February, and he became seriously alarmed when the first week of March passed with no apparent action from Lawrence. He called Lawrence repeatedly during late February and early March, but the secretary always said that Lawrence was "in conference," "in court," or "in deposition." Lawrence never returned any of Morris's phone calls. On March 10, Morris fired Lawrence and hired Donita to do the necessary work. She was able to complete the tax return and get it filed on time.

Is Lawrence *subject to discipline*?

(A) Yes, even if he would have been able to complete the necessary work between March 10 and March 15.

(B) Yes, provided that the excuses given by his secretary were not in fact true.

(C) No, provided that he would have been able to complete the necessary work between March 10 and March 15.

(D) No, because neither Morris nor the trust suffered any loss.

Question 7

Judge Johnnie heard through the "courthouse grapevine" that the District Attorney was investigating corrupt practices in the courts and that the investigation focused on some as yet unascertained time in the past. The "rumor mill" also indicated that several judges and former judges were likely to be indicted for taking bribes to "fix" cases and to generate business for certain attorneys. Judge Johnnie was alarmed at this news, and he telephoned Abe, a retired attorney, arranging to meet Abe for cocktails and dinner. At the restaurant, Judge Johnnie slipped the maitre d' a 10-dollar bill to secure seating at a secluded corner booth. Over dinner, Judge Johnnie told Abe that he had accepted bribes in the past and that he did not know what he should do in light of the District Attorney's investigation. Abe advised Judge Johnnie to do nothing. Judge Johnnie picked up the $120 dinner tab, and Abe thanked him for the fine meal.

A month later, indictments were handed down against two sitting judges and three former judges. Judge Johnnie was not among them, and it turned out that the period covered by the District Attorney's investigation was prior to Judge Johnnie's election to the bench. Six months after the indictments were announced, a member of the state appellate court died, and the Governor announced that he was appointing Judge Johnnie to serve the remaining three years of the justice's unexpired term.

Must Abe report his knowledge of corruption in office by Judge Johnnie?

(A) Yes, because Abe never entered into an attorney-client relationship with Judge Johnnie.

(B) Yes, because Abe's knowledge bears upon maintaining the integrity of the courts, which takes precedence over other ethical considerations.

(C) No, because Abe is retired from practice.

(D) No, because Judge Johnnie's disclosures to Abe dealt with past crimes.

GO ON TO THE NEXT PAGE

Question 8

In a trade secret action against defendant Devere Corp., pending in a United States district court, plaintiff's lawyer Latimer gave timely notice that on July 22 at 9 a.m., he would take the deposition of Devere's Vice President for Manufacturing and Marketing, Sigmoid Fletcher, Ph.D. From earlier discovery in the case, Latimer had good reason to believe that Dr. Fletcher's testimony would prove that Devere had stolen and was using the plaintiff's trade secrets. On the appointed day, defense lawyer Lakk showed up with no witness; she explained that Dr. Fletcher was a very busy man and had been "unavoidably detained" on a trip to one of Devere's factories in Asia. Latimer rescheduled the deposition for August 3, and Lakk promised to have Dr. Fletcher available that day.

On August 3, Lakk again showed up with no witness, explaining that Dr. Fletcher had to take his aged mother to the doctor that day. Latimer rescheduled the deposition for August 14, and Lakk promised: "If I don't have Sigmoid Fletcher with me on August 14, I will eat your socks on the courthouse steps at noon." On August 14, Lakk showed up for the deposition in the company of a nine-year-old boy, whom she introduced as Sigmoid Fletcher. Upon questioning by Latimer, Lakk laughingly explained that young Sigmoid was Dr. Fletcher's son, that the boy knew nothing about the case, and that Dr. Fletcher was "unable to attend." At that point, Latimer invited Lakk to accompany him to see Judge Jackson to whom the case was assigned.

After hearing the story, Judge Jackson asked Lakk what day and time the witness would assuredly be available, and Lakk said that August 16 would be good. Judge Jackson then entered a formal order that Dr. Fletcher's deposition would be taken that day; Judge Jackson also warned Lakk that she would be sanctioned if she did not present Dr. Fletcher on August 16, and that the issues of trade secret misappropriation and use would be deemed proven in plaintiff's favor. Alas, on August 16, Lakk again showed up alone, explaining that Dr. Fletcher "had to make an unexpected trip out of state." After appropriate notice and hearing, Judge Jackson ordered that the issues of trade secret misappropriation and use would be deemed proven in plaintiff's favor. She also ordered Dr. Fletcher to pay 60% of the plaintiff's expenses and attorneys' fees incurred because of the failed deposition attempts, and she ordered Lakk to pay the other 40% of plaintiff's expenses and attorneys' fees.

Was Judge Jackson correct in holding Lakk *subject to litigation sanction*?

(A) Yes, because Lakk violated the court's discovery order by showing up on August 16 without the witness.

(B) No, because the facts show that Lakk could not control Dr. Fletcher, and that she was therefore not at fault when he failed to show up on August 16.

(C) Yes, because the facts show that Lakk acted obstinately and disrespectfully in defiance of Judge Jackson's direct order.

(D) No, because when a party or a managing agent of a party violates a discovery order, the sanction must be imposed on the party or managing agent, not on the lawyer.

GO ON TO THE NEXT PAGE

Question 9

While she was attending law school at night, Adela served as a clerk for Judge Jones of the county court. During the course of her employment by Judge Jones, the case of *Lyndon v. Baines* came before Judge Jones. The case was very complicated, and Adela did a lot of research on the case for Judge Jones, submitting a number of memoranda on issues in the case. Judge Jones always carefully supervised his clerks, and this case was no exception. He was exceptionally pleased with the care and high quality of Adela's work. Shortly after Judge Jones handed down his final judgment on *Lyndon v. Baines*, Adela was admitted to the bar and she accepted employment with Nixon, Dixon & Yates, a prominent local law firm. A few days later, Baines, who was the loser in the *Lyndon v. Baines* case, appeared at the offices of Nixon, Dixon & Yates. He told the interviewing attorney, "My lawyer at the trial was terrible. I hired him because he was cheap, and I guess I got what I paid for. I'd like your firm to handle the appeal."

If Nixon, Dixon & Yates accepts Baines as a client, and Adela's supervising attorney asks Adela to handle the appeal, would it be *proper* for Adela to do so?

(A) Yes, if no confidential information was revealed to Adela during her work on the case for the judge.

(B) Yes, because Adela was not licensed to practice law when she worked on the case for the judge.

(C) No, unless Judge Jones consents.

(D) No, because Adela was previously personally and substantially involved in work on the case.

Question 10

The State Bar and the State University are joint sponsors of the State Continuing Legal Education Foundation. The purpose of the Foundation is to provide continuing legal education to lawyers and judges in the state. Its board of directors is composed one-half of members of the legal profession and one-half of university personnel. Judge Anistopolous has been invited to serve on the board of directors.

Which of the following are correct?

I.   She *may* serve on the board of directors if it does not interfere with her judicial duties.

II. It would not be *proper* for her to serve on the board of directors because to do so would involve her in the teaching of law.

III. If she serves on the board of directors, it would not be *proper* for her to accept the modest salary that is paid to other directors.

IV. If she serves on the board of directors, she *may* accept the modest salary that is paid to other directors.

(A) II. only.

(B) I. and III. only.

(C) I. and IV. only.

(D) None of the above.

GO ON TO THE NEXT PAGE

Question 11

Assistant District Attorney Krytzer has been assigned to prosecute Abdala for petty theft and attempted sale of stolen property. Abdala's arrest was the result of information provided by O'Leary, a local pawnbroker. O'Leary has himself been in trouble with the law on prior occasions, but he is not suspected of any present crime. Abdala is represented by Public Defender Fuchinello. Krytzer wants to interview O'Leary for possible use as a prosecution witness.

Which of the following is most nearly correct?

(A) Krytzer *may* interview O'Leary without Fuchinello's consent.

(B) Krytzer *may* interview O'Leary without Fuchinello's consent, but he would be *subject to discipline* for inquiring about O'Leary's prior criminal record.

(C) Krytzer would be *subject to discipline* if he interviewed O'Leary without Fuchinello's consent.

(D) Krytzer *may* interview O'Leary, but only with Fuchinello's consent, and Krytzer would be *subject to discipline* for inquiring about O'Leary's prior criminal record.

Question 12

The city of Auburn is located in State A. The city of Burnett is located right across the river in State B. Many people who live in Burnett work and shop in Auburn and vice versa. Lawyer Alford is admitted to practice in State A, but not State B, and Alford has his law office in Auburn. When he is asked to represent a criminal defendant in the Burnett Superior Court, he usually (but not always) refers the case to lawyer Bemis. Bemis has his law office in Burnett. He is admitted to practice in State B, but not State A. Likewise, when Bemis is asked to represent a client in the Auburn Municipal Court, he usually (but not always) refers the case to Alford. Bemis and Alford have evolved their mutual arrangement in order to provide better service to their respective clients, and they always tell referred clients about the arrangement.

Is the arrangement *proper*?

(A) Yes, because Alford is not licensed in State B, and Bemis is not licensed in State A.

(B) No, because, on the facts given, the referral fee could not be proportionate to the services rendered by the referring lawyer, and there is no indication of joint representation.

(C) Yes, because the arrangement between Bemis and Alford is nonexclusive and is always disclosed to referred clients.

(D) No, because a lawyer is not allowed to participate in a reciprocal referral arrangement with another lawyer.

Question 13

Attorney Bob was engaged in a partnership law practice with his sister, Sarah, for almost 10 years. Sarah then decided to run for judge. She was successful in her efforts and was duly sworn in as one of the 15 sitting judges on the district court. According to state venue rules, at least 90% of the cases that Bob usually handles must be filed with the district court.

Would it be *proper* for Bob to continue to handle such cases and appear before the district court?

(A) Yes, unless an opposing party objects.

(B) Yes, unless Bob implies that his clients will receive unfair advantages because his sister is a judge.

(C) No, because it creates an appearance of impropriety.

(D) No, because an attorney should not appear in a district court where a close relative serves as one of the judges.

GO ON TO THE NEXT PAGE

Question 14

Capra hired lawyer Laslo to represent him in a personal injury action against Giant Co. As Capra and Laslo discussed the case, Capra stated, "Of course, I can't predict what the future will hold, but I am ready to go all the way on this. If we have to go to trial to see justice done, so be it. I probably wouldn't agree to a settlement under $500,000, no matter what." Laslo agreed that the claim was worth at least that, but felt they would receive a much higher award if the case went to a jury. Shortly before the trial started, the lawyer for Giant Co. contacted Laslo with a settlement offer of $150,000. Laslo tried to call Capra, but couldn't reach him. After two hours of trying to reach Capra, Laslo called Giant Co. back and rejected the offer. At trial, the jury awarded Capra $1 million.

Is Laslo *subject to malpractice liability* for his actions?

(A) Yes, because a lawyer has a duty to keep his client informed of all settlement offers.

(B) Yes, because decisions to accept or reject settlement offers are to be made by the client.

(C) No, because Capra impliedly authorized Laslo to reject any offer under $500,000.

(D) No, because the jury award was much greater than the settlement offer.

Question 15

During the course of researching a reply brief, attorney Amy discovered a case in the controlling jurisdiction that seemed to be right on one of the key issues involved in Amy's case. Although much of the dicta in the case seemed to favor Amy's client, one critical sentence in the holding clearly put the court behind the position asserted by Amy's opponent, Bertram. However, Bertram had done a slipshod job of researching the issues and had failed to find the case and to cite it in his brief. Amy decided to cite the case in her reply brief, but she cited the case as favoring her client by quoting much of the dicta and deliberately omitting the key sentence in the holding. Amy filed the reply brief with the court and sent a copy to Bertram, who she knew often bragged, "I haven't actually *read* a case since my first year of law school." Amy was also aware that this judge's clerks tended to be overworked and so did not always read all the cases cited by attorneys in their briefs. Therefore, she hoped that the negative aspects of the case might slip by unnoticed by the judge and opposing counsel.

Is Amy *subject to discipline*?

(A) Yes, because an attorney has a duty to cite all opposing cases accurately and objectively.

(B) Yes, because Amy is attempting to mislead the tribunal.

(C) No, because an attorney has a duty to present cases in the light most favorable to her client.

(D) No, because an attorney has no duty to educate, and Amy fulfilled her duties to the court and opposing party by citing the case.

GO ON TO THE NEXT PAGE

Question 16

Attorney Almas was fully licensed to practice in State Green. Her office was located in Endogreen, a small town located on the extreme western border of State Green. Almas received a retainer from client Chum, with the agreement that Almas would use funds from the retainer for such things as filing fees when they came due. There was no federally insured bank or savings institution in Endogreen. The nearest such institution in State Green was located in the county seat, which was over 60 miles away from Almas's office and where Almas and Chum resided. Therefore, Almas decided to put Chum's money in his client trust account in a bank in Bluestart, a medium-sized city located just across the state line in neighboring State Blue. The account was fully insured by the federal government, but was not an interest-bearing account. Almas is not licensed to practice law in State Blue.

Was it **proper** for Almas to place Chum's money in an account in State Blue?

(A) Yes, because retainer fees belong to the attorney and not to the client.

(B) Yes, but only if Chum consented to the deposit in State Blue.

(C) No, because Almas is not licensed to practice in State Blue.

(D) No, because the funds were not placed in an interest-bearing account.

Question 17

Defendant Devereaux was charged with first degree murder. It is claimed that Devereaux captured his victim, dragged her into dense woods, and stabbed her with a knife. Devereaux has pleaded not guilty. Pamela is the prosecutor, and Denise is Devereaux's defense attorney. During the prosecution's case-in-chief, one of Pamela's witnesses testified that he had seen Devereaux's car near the scene of the crime shortly before the murder. This courthouse has no private room set aside for conferences between defendants and their counsel. Thus, at the next recess, Denise and Devereaux held a hurried, whispered conference in the hallway, as follows:

> Denise: "Were you driving around that area at the time?"
>
> Devereaux: "Yes."
>
> Denise: "Why didn't you tell me that before?"
>
> Devereaux: "I didn't realize that anybody saw me."

Unbeknownst to Denise and Devereaux, Pamela was standing nearby and overheard their whispers.

Which of the following are correct?

I. Pamela **must** seek the court's permission to withdraw as trial counsel and testify to what she heard.

II. Pamela **must** ignore what she heard and proceed with the case in the normal manner.

III. Denise **must** seek the court's permission to withdraw as trial counsel and inform the trial judge in chambers what Devereaux said.

IV. Denise **must** proceed with the case in the normal manner, even though Devereaux's statement may cause her to doubt his innocence.

(A) Only II. and IV.

(B) Only I. and III.

(C) Only II. and III.

(D) Only I. and IV.

GO ON TO THE NEXT PAGE

Question 18

Attorney April represents Chuck, plaintiff in a personal injury suit arising out of an automobile collision. Chuck asserts that he had the right-of-way to enter the intersection where the accident occurred. The defendant claims otherwise, but Chuck tells April that there was a witness present who would be able to verify Chuck's version of the accident. April obtains a copy of the police report on the accident, but the name of the witness is not contained in the report. April contemplates running an ad in the newspaper or hiring an investigator to find the witness, but April concludes that Chuck's testimony ought to be strong enough to win the case. The case comes to trial, and the jury finds for the defendant.

Is April *subject to discipline* for failure to try to find the witness?

(A) Yes, because she failed to properly prepare the case.

(B) Yes, because her client lost.

(C) No, if she reasonably believed that Chuck's testimony would be sufficient.

(D) No, because the name of the witness was not in the police report.

Question 19

Newspaper reporter Dabba Ratchet writes a semi-humorous gossip column in which she reports on the vices and victories in the private lives of prominent citizens. Among her favorite targets are judges and lawyers. Over the years, Ms. Ratchet and lawyer Lubner have worked out a tacit arrangement. Every now and then in her column, Ms. Ratchet gives glowing praise to Lubner's legal talents and recommends him to her readers. In return, Lubner calls Ms. Ratchet whenever he learns a juicy tidbit about another lawyer or judge.

Is Lubner's conduct *proper*?

(A) Yes, unless the information that Lubner gives her is untrue.

(B) Yes, unless the information that Lubner gives her is the subject of a privilege or a confidential relationship.

(C) No, because a lawyer is subject to discipline for demeaning members of the legal profession.

(D) No, because a lawyer should not give something of value in return for a recommendation.

Question 20

After a major airplane crash in the vicinity of Biggston, in which 122 passengers and crew were killed, Biggston's attorneys swarmed like locusts to get a "piece of the action" and the potentially huge contingent fees that were likely to arise from the case. Interested in fees himself, but also rather disgusted at the performance of some of his colleagues of the bar, attorney Axel placed an ad in the *Biggston Law Journal*, a weekly newspaper whose readership was almost entirely lawyers. The ad suggested that any attorneys representing plaintiffs in the airline crash matter contact him in order to consolidate lawsuits against the airline. The ad ended with a statement, "This should materially benefit everyone in that it should reduce court costs and encourage prompt settlements for our clients." The ad was signed by Axel and indicated his office address and telephone number.

Was it *proper* for Axel to place such an advertisement?

(A) Yes, provided the ad was not misleading.

(B) Yes, if the lawyers will split the fees in proportion to work done.

(C) No, because Axel is soliciting business.

(D) No, because the ad is in bad taste.

Question 21

Sales manager Morton testified before a federal grand jury that was investigating price-fixing in the automobile tire industry. Ultimately, the grand jury indicted Morton for price-fixing, a felony under the Sherman Act. After his indictment, Morton sought to hire attorney Agnes to represent him at his criminal trial. Morton is a middle class business executive with enough savings to pay for private counsel. He told Agnes in confidence that he had lied to the grand jury about several meetings he had had with competitors. Furthermore, he told her that he wanted to plead not guilty to the criminal charge and that he intended to testify at trial as he did before the grand jury.

Which of the following would be *proper* for Agnes to do in this situation?

I.   Decline to represent Morton.

II. Agree to represent Morton but warn him what will happen if he insists on testifying falsely at the trial.

III. Inform Morton that unless he pleads guilty to the criminal charge, she will tell the prosecutor about his false testimony before the grand jury.

IV. Decline to represent Morton and inform the prosecutor about his false testimony before the grand jury.

(A) IV. only.

(B) I. or II. only.

(C) I. or III. only.

(D) I. only.

Question 22

Attorney Patricia limits her law practice to the representation of plaintiffs in actions for medical malpractice. She has developed a standard employment contract to use with all clients who desire a contingent fee arrangement. The contract requires the client to pay in advance the first $500 of litigation expenses, and states that Patricia's fee shall be 20% of any amount recovered without going to trial, 30% of any amount recovered if the case goes to trial, and 35% of any amount recovered if the case is appealed. Client Nesbitt signed Patricia's standard form contract. After putting in only 10 hours' work on Nesbitt's case, Patricia was able to work out a settlement agreement in which Nesbitt received $10,000 from the defendant's malpractice insurance carrier. Nesbitt was delighted with the settlement, but he is unhappy with having to pay 20% of it ($2,000) to Patricia for so few hours' work.

With respect to the clause of Patricia's standard form contract that requires the client to pay in advance the first $500 of litigation expenses, which of the following is most nearly correct?

(A) The clause is *proper*, unless $500 is a clearly excessive estimate of the amount of litigation expenses that will be incurred in the ordinary medical malpractice case.

(B) Patricia *must* delete the clause because it is an effort to impose a uniform provision on all clients, irrespective of their particular needs and situations.

(C) Patricia is *subject to discipline* for using the clause because an attorney is required to advance reasonable litigation expenses to contingent fee clients.

(D) Patricia is *subject to discipline* for using the clause because clients are required to pay litigation expenses as they are incurred.

Question 23

Charlene was involved in an aviation mishap. The airline company has admitted liability and has settled with 10 other persons involved in the mishap for amounts ranging between $120,000 and $150,000. Charlene's injuries are very similar to those suffered by the persons with whom the airline has settled. Charlene received a settlement offer of $135,000 from the airline company. Upon receiving the offer, Charlene decided to employ counsel to determine if the offer was a fair amount, and generally to read over the settlement papers and the release that the airline asked Charlene to sign to get the $135,000. Charlene went to the offices of attorney Alp, bringing the settlement papers and release with her. She asked Alp what his hourly fee for reading the papers would be. Alp responded that Charlene had a personal injury case and that Alp's standard fee for personal injury cases was 30% of any settlement or judgment received by the plaintiff.

Is Alp *subject to discipline*?

(A) Yes, because Alp's fee bears no rational relationship to the time and effort required to perform the work requested by the client.

(B) Yes, if 30% exceeded the usual contingent fee percentage in Alp's geographical area of practice.

(C) No, because contingent fees are appropriate in personal injury cases.

(D) No, because Charlene was free to obtain counsel other than Alp.

Question 24

Before Judge Jerkins was elected to the bench, she and her law partner, Perkins, purchased a piece of property to be held in co-tenancy by Perkins and Jerkins. After Judge Jerkins was elected to the bench, Judge Jerkins agreed to pay Perkins an annual fee to manage the property because Judge Jerkins's time would be severely limited by her judicial duties. Judge Jerkins and Perkins meet every three months to discuss the status of the property. Perkins sometimes appears as an attorney in Judge Jerkins's courtroom.

Was it *proper* for Judge Jerkins to make this arrangement with Perkins?

(A) Yes, because Judge Jerkins acquired the property before she became a judge.

(B) Yes, if dealings concerning the property do not take up so much of Judge Jerkins's time that her judicial duties will suffer.

(C) No, because judges should not engage in remunerative outside enterprises.

(D) No, because Perkins appears in cases before Judge Jerkins's court.

GO ON TO THE NEXT PAGE

Question 25

Lawyer Lewellen represented defendant Devonshire in a felony case that charged him with intentional evasion of over $9 million in state income tax. Devonshire allegedly earned the unreported income from selling child pornography. The state's criminal procedure law requires a unanimous jury verdict to convict in a felony case. Midway through the prosecutor's case-in-chief, Lewellen instructed one of Devonshire's employees, Snagg, to attend the trial daily, to sit in the spectator section as close as possible to the defense counsel table, and to "put the evil-eye on Juror No. 4, the little guy with the pink nose." Snagg, a wicked-looking man with a jagged scar down the side of his face, attended every court session and stared constantly with cold, squinting eyes at Juror No. 4. One day, when no one but Juror No. 4 was looking, Snagg pointed his hand like a pistol directly at Juror No. 4's head and pretended to shoot by moving his thumb downward. Then Snagg smiled an evil smile and continued to stare. Juror No. 4 was too frightened to tell anyone, but he endured the torment day after day. Finally, the case was submitted to the jury, and Juror No. 4 joined the rest of the jurors in returning a prompt, unanimous verdict of guilty.

Is Lewellen *subject to criminal liability* for what Snagg did?

(A) No, Lewellen may be subject to sanction by the court or discipline by the bar, but not criminal liability.

(B) No, because Juror No. 4 was not intimidated; he voted to convict along with the rest of the jury.

(C) Yes, but only if it is proven that Lewellen gave Snagg money, or something else of value, to stare and gesture at Juror No. 4.

(D) Yes, but only if it is proven that Lewellen induced Snagg to intimidate Juror No. 4 for the purpose of influencing the jury verdict.

Question 26

Attorney Arla placed an advertisement in the *Clarion*, a newspaper of general circulation published in Old Salem, the city in which Arla practiced. The ad contained Arla's name, office address, telephone number, and the following additional information: (i) "Attorney Arla is a graduate of State University Law School"; (ii) "Attorney Arla has an M.B.A. from the Graduate School of Business of Laffercurve University"; and (iii) "Attorney Arla is the only lawyer in town who speaks fluent Spanish."

Is Arla's advertisement *proper*?

(A) Yes, if all statements contained therein are true.

(B) Yes, provided the *Clarion's* distribution area is limited to Old Salem.

(C) No, because the ad is self-laudatory.

(D) No, because an M.B.A. is not law-related.

GO ON TO THE NEXT PAGE

Question 27

Lawyer Munoz was employed to represent Claus Schnauffler at his trial for treason. Schnauffler was charged with smuggling top secret military information to a foreign government. Munoz had reason to suspect that some of the prosecution's witnesses were paid liars. Therefore, with Schnauffler's consent, Munoz hired Dr. Clara Belle to assist him in the defense. Dr. Belle is a psychologist whose specialty is the behavior of liars. Munoz agreed with Schnauffler that Munoz would advance Dr. Belle's fee as a part of the expenses of litigation. At the trial, Dr. Belle sat with Munoz at the counsel table. She watched the witnesses testify, and she advised Munoz when she believed that a witness was lying and ought to be pursued on cross-examination. Most of the time, Munoz followed Dr. Belle's advice, but sometimes he did not. Ultimately, Schnauffler was convicted and sent to prison for 20 years.

Which of the following propositions are correct?

I. Munoz is **subject to discipline** for allowing a third party to interject herself into the relationship between him and his client.

II. Munoz is **subject to discipline** for advancing Dr. Belle's fee as a part of the expenses of litigation.

III. Munoz is **subject to discipline** for allowing a nonlawyer to sit at the counsel table and to participate in his legal representation of a criminal defendant.

(A) None of the above is correct.

(B) Only I. and III. are correct.

(C) I., II., and III. are all correct.

(D) Only III. is correct.

Question 28

Hal and Wilma, a married couple, experienced continuing marital difficulties and, being unable to resolve their problems, decided to divorce. Wilma retained attorney Ambrose, and Ambrose filed papers on Hal. Shortly after he was served, Hal telephoned Ambrose and suggested that "all this can be resolved amicably." Ambrose asked Hal if he was represented by counsel. Hal replied that he was not, to which Ambrose said, "I strongly advise you to retain an attorney to represent you and safeguard your interests." Hal insisted, "I don't need a lawyer." A few weeks later, after ascertaining that Hal still had not retained counsel, Ambrose sent Hal a proposed "Division of Marital Property." There were spaces at the bottom for both Hal and Wilma to sign, but the copy sent to Hal was unsigned by Wilma. In his cover letter to Hal, Ambrose indicated that Hal could sign the settlement agreement, which Ambrose characterized as "fair and equitable." However, Ambrose also stated in the letter that, "I am not your attorney and therefore cannot advise you whether you should sign this, and I strongly urge that you obtain independent counsel to review these papers before you sign them. However, Hal, the choice remains yours, and I cannot compel you to hire an attorney to protect your interests."

Were Ambrose's actions in handling Hal and Wilma's divorce **proper**?

(A) Yes, because Ambrose did not give Hal legal advice.

(B) Yes, because Ambrose urged Hal to obtain representation.

(C) No, because Ambrose did not have Wilma sign the settlement papers before sending them to Hal.

(D) No, because Ambrose should have required that Hal have the papers reviewed by an attorney.

Question 29

Walters is insured under an auto liability policy issued by Farmers Insurance Company. The policy requires Farmers to provide a lawyer to defend Walters, and it requires Walters to cooperate in the defense. Walters had an accident and was sued. In a sworn statement to Farmers' insurance investigator, Walters told a story that showed he was clearly not at fault. Based on that story, Farmers rejected plaintiff's offer to settle the case for a modest sum. Farmers hired attorney Chen to represent Walters at the trial of the case. Shortly before trial, Walters told Chen in confidence that he had lied to the investigator, and he recounted facts that showed he was clearly at fault in the accident. Chen realized that under the applicable state law, Walters's falsehood was a breach of the "cooperate in the defense" clause, and that it relieved Farmers of any further duties to Walters.

At this juncture, what *must* Chen do?

(A) Promptly advise Farmers of the situation and carry out Farmers's instructions as to how to dispose of the matter.

(B) Promptly advise Walters that his best interests will be served by reverting to the story he told originally to the insurance investigator.

(C) Promptly seek the court's permission to withdraw from the matter, without revealing Walters's confidential statement to anyone.

(D) Promptly advise Walters of the legal consequences of his false statement, and continue representing Walters and Farmers in the matter as best he is able in the circumstances.

Question 30

Three months from now, Judge Torpor will be up for reelection. His opponent is Vernon Vigoroso, a bright and ambitious young attorney in the prosecutor's office. Due to the press of his judicial duties, Judge Torpor has not paid much attention to the upcoming election. One afternoon an old law school friend, Getta Movin, visits him in his chambers. She convinces him that he must get busy if he hopes to defeat Vigoroso. Getta frequently represents clients in Judge Torpor's court, and he trusts her judgment and ability; thus, he agrees to have her serve as chairperson of his reelection campaign committee.

Which of the following would be *proper* in the context of Judge Torpor's campaign for reelection?

I. Getta contributes $200 of her own money to the campaign fund.

II. Getta urges other lawyers who appear in Judge Torpor's court to make contributions to his campaign fund.

III. Getta urges other lawyers who appear in Judge Torpor's court to allow their names to be listed in a half-page newspaper advertisement in favor of Judge Torpor's reelection.

IV. Getta urges the local newspaper that will run the half-page advertisement to give her a discount from the regular commercial advertising rate because her advertisement concerns a campaign for public office.

(A) All of the above.

(B) I. only.

(C) I. and II. only.

(D) I., II., and III. only.

GO ON TO THE NEXT PAGE

Question 31

Attorney Astrid represented Charles and Wanda, a married couple, for many years, handling such matters as wills, real estate closings, and the occasional lawsuit. Wanda died suddenly, and shortly after her funeral Astrid paid a visit to Charles, wishing to pay her respects as a friend as well as Charles's attorney. Astrid found Charles in an obviously drunken state. He told Astrid that he just "couldn't go on" without his wife and that he planned to commit suicide that evening. He told Astrid directly, "I know you're a friend and you mean well, but I don't want you to do anything to try to stop me." Using a ruse to distract the intoxicated Charles, Astrid called the police, who promptly took Charles to the psychological emergency receiving area of University Hospital.

Was Astrid's conduct *proper*?

(A) Yes, because her client was drunk.

(B) Yes, because her client proposed to commit suicide, which act would result in his death or substantial bodily harm.

(C) No, because she revealed a client's confidences to the police.

(D) No, because she disobeyed a clear directive of her client.

Question 32

Attorney Alice and attorney Baxter were brother and sister. They were licensed to practice in the Province of Manitoba, Canada. For five years they practiced together in a partnership in Winnipeg, Manitoba. Alice then moved to International Falls, Minnesota, where she passed the Minnesota Bar Examination and was duly licensed to practice law in the state of Minnesota. She opened up a law office in International Falls and had letterhead stationery printed which read: "Alice and Baxter, Partners, Attorneys at Law."

Is it *proper* for Alice to use such letterhead?

(A) Yes, because American courts have no jurisdiction over Canadian attorneys.

(B) Yes, because both Alice and Baxter are licensed to practice law.

(C) No, because the letterhead indicates Alice is aiding the unauthorized practice of law.

(D) No, because Canadian lawyers must swear an unconstitutional oath of loyalty to a foreign monarch.

GO ON TO THE NEXT PAGE

Question 33

Lewis, an attorney, was formerly employed by the Environmental Protection Agency ("EPA") as government counsel in the New York office. In this capacity, Lewis acted as chief counsel in several suits brought by the EPA involving chemical dumping into public waterways. Two years after leaving the employ of the EPA, Lewis was retained to represent Acme Chemical Corporation in a suit brought by the EPA alleging violations of certain EPA regulations regarding the dumping of chemical wastes. While with the EPA, Lewis was never directly involved in a case concerning Acme Chemical Corporation. The EPA Washington office had exclusive responsibility for the drafting, promulgation, and enforcement of the regulations in question.

Which of the following statements is correct?

(A) Lewis *may* represent Acme, but only with the consent of the EPA.

(B) Lewis *may* represent Acme, whether or not the EPA consents.

(C) If Lewis represents Acme without the consent of the EPA, he will be *subject to discipline*.

(D) If Lewis represents Acme, he will be *subject to discipline*, even if the EPA consents to the representation.

Question 34

Criminal defendant Daggs is facing trial for the unlawful possession of a large quantity of a controlled substance—specifically, 400 kilograms of cocaine. Daggs originally asserted that he could not afford to pay a lawyer, and the court arranged for him to be represented by a public defender. Later, Daggs was visited in jail by one Wiggens, who identified himself as a skilled criminal defense lawyer who had been hired by Daggs's "friends" to defend him. Wiggens said that Daggs would not have to pay anything for the legal defense if Daggs "played the game straight" and did not implicate the "friends" in the cocaine caper. Daggs orally consented to the conditions and gave written consent as to the third party payment of his legal fees. In due course, Wiggens was substituted in as defense counsel. Shortly before trial, the prosecutor offered Daggs an attractive plea bargain—a mere six months in jail in exchange for a guilty plea, an identification of the persons for whom Daggs was transporting the cocaine, and testimony against those persons. Wiggens solemnly advised Daggs to reject the plea bargain, saying: "Not only would you owe me a big fee, but your friends would dismember you." Daggs did reject the plea bargain. Thereupon the prosecutor moved to disqualify Wiggens as defense counsel on the ground that he was being paid by an unidentified third party and that the third party was unduly interfering with Daggs's constitutional right to effective assistance of counsel.

Is Wiggens *subject to disqualification*?

(A) Yes, because in a criminal case it is unlawful for a private criminal defense lawyer to accept compensation from an outsider for his legal services.

(B) Yes, because both the prosecutor and the judge have a duty to protect the defendant's constitutional right to the effective assistance of legal counsel.

(C) No, because Daggs consented to the fee arrangement after having been informed of the conditions on which it was offered.

(D) No, because the prosecutor has no right to interfere with a criminal defendant's choice of counsel.

GO ON TO THE NEXT PAGE

Question 35

Cesar comes to attorney Abigail with an invention he wants to patent. Cesar explains that he and a competitor have been racing one another to come up with the ideal cleaning solution. If Cesar's competitor were to find out that Cesar was at the patent stage, and worse, if he found out Cesar's formula, Cesar would be ruined. Abigail, a trained and certified patent attorney, agrees to represent Cesar in the patent process. The invention involves complex chemical formulae, and Abigail's particular area of expertise is electronic devices. However, having worked with inventions of all types, she has no doubt that she can properly shepherd the solution through the patent process. In putting together the necessary paperwork, Abigail asks Barbara and David, who are associates in her firm and hold chemistry degrees, to help her out on the project. In due time, Cesar's product receives a patent. Cesar's total bill for legal fees was $60,000, which was reasonable for the work done. When Abigail received Cesar's final payment, she decided to give Barbara and David each a $10,000 bonus from the fee.

Are Abigail's actions *proper*?

(A) Yes, because with the aid of her associates, she was competent to handle the matter.

(B) Yes, unless the division of the fee is not in proportion to the work performed by Barbara and David.

(C) No, unless Cesar gave informed consent to the disclosure of information to Barbara and David.

(D) No, unless Cesar consented to the splitting of the fee with Barbara and David.

Question 36

Attorneys A and B are law partners. They are, however, contemplating incorporation of their law practice.

With respect to the proposed incorporation, which of the following statements best describes what A and B may *properly* do?

I.   A and B may incorporate their law practice and convey an interest in the corporation to their children.

II. A and B may incorporate their law practice and thus avoid liability to clients for malpractice.

III. A and B may incorporate their law practice and when they die, a fiduciary representative of their estates may hold the stock in the corporation for a reasonable time during administration.

IV. A and B may incorporate their law practice and make their accountant treasurer of the corporation as long as the accountant does not own any interest in the corporation.

(A) I., II., and IV. only.

(B) III. and IV. only.

(C) III. only.

(D) None of the above.

GO ON TO THE NEXT PAGE

Question 37

Jones, the driver of a car, and Smith, his passenger, were injured as the result of a collision with a bus. Jones and Smith believe the bus driver was entirely at fault, and they want to bring a negligence action against the bus company. Jones and Smith seek to hire attorney Adams to represent them.

Which of the following would be **proper** conduct by Adams?

I. Accept the proffered employment only after informing Smith that he may have a cause of action against Jones and obtaining Jones's and Smith's written consent to represent them both against the bus company.

II. Withdraw from the common representation if discovery shows that Smith has a claim against Jones.

III. Represent Jones and Smith, and also represent the bus company in a solely unrelated matter before the Transportation Board.

(A) I. only.

(B) II. and III. only.

(C) I. and II. only.

(D) None of the above.

Question 38

Attorney A wants to advertise his legal services in a local newspaper.

Which of the following true statements would be **proper** for A to make in the advertisement?

I. That he graduated Phi Beta Kappa from Lewis College and now teaches a course in Law and Economics.

II. That he is a licensed real estate broker and a member of the National Broker's Association.

III. That he speaks Polish and accepts credit cards.

IV. That he is a major with the National Guard and a former State Senator.

(A) All of the above.

(B) I., III., and IV. only.

(C) II. and IV. only.

(D) I. and III. only.

Question 39

The Department of Children's Services ("DCS"), a state agency, has removed Clara's children from her home and is attempting to terminate her parental rights. Clara retains lawyer Laura to fight DCS's actions. Prior to the first hearing on the matter, a lawyer from DCS contacted Ben, Clara's brother, to set up an interview. The lawyer told Ben that he wanted to talk to him about Clara, and that the interview would last for about one hour. Ben, who is childless, had never had any contact with DCS before, and did not know what his duties were. He told the lawyer he would get back to him. Ben then called Laura. He told Laura that he does not want to talk to DCS because he is afraid he might inadvertently say something that will hurt Clara's case. Ben asked Laura how he should proceed. Laura replied, "My advice to you is to simply refuse the interview. You do not have to talk to them, and your sister will be better off if you don't. If they really want to talk to you, they can get a subpoena."

Is Laura *subject to discipline*?

(A) Yes, because she is attempting to secure the noncooperation of a witness.

(B) Yes, because she gave advice to an unrepresented party.

(C) No, but only if she also advised Ben to seek the advice of independent counsel.

(D) No, because Ben is Clara's brother and he did not want to hurt her case.

Question 40

Attorney Avery is representing Client Cassidy. Judgment at the trial court is against Cassidy. Cassidy wants to appeal the case. The appellate court rules provide a 60-day deadline for the filing of appeals, and no exception is ever granted. During the first 30 days of the period, Avery was frantically busy in his office on other matters, and he had no chance to file the appeal. Then, during the second 30 days, he went on vacation and simply forgot to file the appeal. The trial court's error was so obvious that the appellate court would undoubtedly have reversed the case and entered judgment in Cassidy's favor.

Which of the following is most nearly correct?

(A) Avery is both *subject to discipline* and *liable for malpractice*.

(B) Avery is neither *subject to discipline* nor *liable for malpractice*.

(C) Avery is *subject to discipline*, but he is not *liable for malpractice*.

(D) Avery is *liable for malpractice*, but he is not *subject to discipline*.

GO ON TO THE NEXT PAGE

Question 41

A basic tenet of the professional responsibility of lawyers is that every person in our society should have ready access to the independent professional services of a lawyer of integrity and competence.

In this regard, which of the following statements are correct?

I. A lawyer *may* charge a reasonable fee because this allows the lawyer to serve his client effectively and preserves the integrity and independence of the legal profession.

II. A lawyer *may* decline representation because a client or a cause is unpopular or community reaction is adverse.

III. A lawyer *may* decline employment if the intensity of his personal feelings will impair his effective representation of a prospective client.

(A) All of the above.

(B) I. and II. only.

(C) I. and III. only.

(D) II. and III. only.

Question 42

Attorney Acheson represents Dell, who has pleaded guilty to a burglary charge. Dell told Acheson during one of their confidential conversations that this is the fourth time he has been busted for burglary—one other time in this state and two times in the neighboring state. Dell could be facing a mandatory 5-10 years in prison as a repeat offender, but he and Acheson are hoping that his pleading guilty will result in a shorter sentence. Unknown to Acheson or Dell, a glitch in the state computer files resulted in a presentencing report that did not pick up either Dell's in-state or out-of-state prior convictions. At sentencing, Judge Johnson states, "Normally, I throw the book at young men like you who have no respect for the property of others. However, because I see you have no prior criminal record, I think you deserve another chance. I sentence you to two years probation and 300 hours community service." Both Acheson and Dell remain silent.

Is Acheson *subject to discipline*?

(A) Yes, because failure to speak out when one knows that the court is operating on false information is the equivalent of affirmative misrepresentation.

(B) Yes, because this is a sentencing hearing rather than a trial.

(C) No, because the mistake did not originate with Acheson or Dell.

(D) No, because Acheson could not reveal the confidential information even if he had been asked directly.

Question 43

Lawyer Lucy represents client Charlie, who is a writer and producer of Broadway stage plays. This morning Charlie telephoned Lucy and said: "Great news, Lucy! Anthony Hopper, the famous actor, has agreed to star in my new stage play, Guardian Angel. With Anthony Hopper in the lead, the play is certain to be a long-running blockbuster. Don't tell a soul because it's not public information yet. Please draft up the necessary legal papers and meet Hopper and me for dinner at 6 p.m. at the Franklin Club." After drafting the legal papers as Charlie requested, Lucy telephoned her friend Mitchell, who owns one of the best theaters on Broadway. Lucy said: "Mitch darling, I have a tip for you, but it will cost you $5,000. Are you buying?" Mitchell agreed to pay Lucy $5,000 for the tip, at which point she said: "Make a deal with Charlie to run his new play, Guardian Angel, in your theater. Set the rent so low Charlie can't refuse—even at a low rent you will make millions because Guardian Angel is going to be a long-running blockbuster. I can't tell you how I know that, but trust me." Mitchell promptly made the deal with Charlie, and he paid Lucy the $5,000.

Is Lucy *subject to civil liability* to Charlie for selling the tip to Mitchell?

(A) No, because Lucy did not reveal Charlie's confidential information to Mitchell; indeed, Lucy told Mitchell that she could not disclose how she knew that Charlie's play would be a long-running blockbuster.

(B) No, because Charlie was not harmed by what Lucy told Mitchell; in fact, Charlie benefited by getting one of the best theaters at a low rent.

(C) Yes, because Lucy profited by $5,000 from trading on Charlie's confidential information. She can be ordered to disgorge her profit to Charlie.

(D) Yes, but only if Charlie was harmed by Lucy's unauthorized disclosure to Mitchell.

Question 44

In which of the following situations is the attorney-client privilege applicable?

I. Client Carmen telephones her accountant and has him deliver tax returns and work papers to attorney Alexis, who has been engaged to represent Carmen in a tax case.

II. Client Carmen hires attorney Alexis to represent her in a relatively simple tax case. Alexis employs her son Andy, a newly certified accountant, to help her with the case. At Alexis's request, Carmen discusses certain tax accounting facets of the case with Andy.

III. Client Carmen discloses confidential information to attorney Alexis with the intention of hiring Alexis to represent her. Alexis, however, decides not to take the case.

(A) All of the above.

(B) II. and III. only.

(C) I. only.

(D) None of the above.

Question 45

Attorney Allison, a member of the state bar, and Judge Jack, who sits on the district court, set up "The Profitable Probate School" ("PPS"). The announced purpose of the school was to educate laypersons as to probate procedures, to enable them to file their own papers and avoid the expenses of obtaining counsel for the probate process. The tuition was a modest $50 per student, which barely covered the expenses of books and forms handed out to the students. Despite the "Profitable" in PPS's name, Allison and Judge Jack donated their time and received no remuneration from the school. However, each student was required to sign a paper that stated, "The $50 tuition fee establishes an attorney-client relationship between an attorney teaching at PPS and all students. PPS and attorneys teaching therein are not liable for any damages that might be incurred by students as a result of pro se filings made in accordance with or at variance from instructions given by PPS." The statement was signed by Allison and Judge Jack as "officers of the school."

Is Allison *subject to discipline*?

(A) Yes, because she has participated in the forcing of an attorney-client relationship upon the students.

(B) Yes, because an attorney may not limit her malpractice liability by contract.

(C) No, because Allison is helping the public to avoid excessive legal fees through her participation in the school.

(D) No, because the clients agreed to the contract as a precondition for obtaining the benefits offered by PPS.

GO ON TO THE NEXT PAGE

Question 46

Attorney Anita is a fully licensed member of the state bar, but she is a rather junior associate with the prominent firm of Alpha, Beta, and Gamma, which handles many securities law matters. Anita interviewed Curry, a client who brought an exceedingly complex securities matter to the firm. Although Anita was highly competent, a couple of points in Curry's complex case were beyond her range of experience. Therefore, she consulted Gamma, one of the firm's senior partners, regarding these complicated issues. Gamma gave her excellent advice on how to handle the matters based upon his 30 years of experience in securities law. Anita continued to handle Curry's case and brought it to a successful conclusion.

Was Anita's conduct **proper**?

(A) Yes, if she kept the identity of her client secret when she consulted Gamma.

(B) Yes, because she consulted with a lawyer in her own firm who had no reason to be screened from the case.

(C) No, unless her client consented first.

(D) No, if she revealed any of her client's confidences to Gamma.

Question 47

Paul is a title insurance agent. In serving his customers, he routinely fills in the blanks in standard form documents that are prepared by lawyers. These documents include warranty deeds, quitclaim deeds, mortgages, releases of mortgages, affidavits as to debts and liens, lien waivers, and the like. On occasion, when his customers specifically ask, he advises them about the meaning and legal effect of the technical language used in the forms.

Which of the following constitutes the unauthorized practice of law by Paul?

I.   Filling in the blanks on warranty deeds, quitclaim deeds, and mortgages.

II. Filling in the blanks on affidavits as to debts and liens and lien waivers.

III. Advising customers, at their request, about the meaning and legal effect of the technical language used in the forms.

(A) None of the above.

(B) All of the above.

(C) III. only.

(D) I. only.

Question 48

Linda, Phil's attorney, knows that the statute of limitations on Phil's claim against Debbie has run. However, the statute of limitations is an affirmative defense that Debbie would waive if she failed to plead it.

What **may** Linda do?

(A) File the suit if Phil is willing to incur the legal fees and court costs.

(B) File the suit but inform the court that the statute of limitations has run.

(C) Not file the suit unless Phil consents to disclose the fact that the statute of limitations has run.

(D) Not file the suit as it is now a frivolous claim.

Question 49

Attorney Arnold is a friend of Shelby, a real estate broker. Shelby is of the opinion that Arnold is one of the best real estate lawyers in the community, and Shelby recommends him to those persons seeking an attorney to close real estate transactions.

Which of the following statements most correctly describes what Arnold *may* do?

I. Arnold may represent clients referred by Shelby if Arnold does not pay Shelby a referral fee.

II. Arnold may give Shelby some of his professional cards to give to those persons seeking a real estate lawyer and accept employment resulting therefrom.

III. Arnold may take Shelby and her husband out to dinner as a way of expressing his appreciation for Shelby's referrals.

(A) All of the above.

(B) I. only.

(C) II. only.

(D) None of the above.

Question 50

According to the Code of Judicial Conduct, which of the following activities are *improper* for a judge?

I. Teaching a course in advanced trial practice at a seminar for practicing attorneys, for a fee.

II. Soliciting funds from the public to support the National Council on Penal Reform.

III. Writing an article for a national magazine on fishing in the Great Lakes region.

IV. Serving as the weekend manager at a local antique store.

(A) All of the above.

(B) I. and III. only.

(C) II. and IV. only.

(D) I., II., and IV. only.

GO ON TO THE NEXT PAGE

Question 51

John Naylor is a wealthy building contractor. For many years, lawyer Lawton has represented Naylor in a wide variety of legal matters, including disputes with Naylor's suppliers and customers. Naylor is a contentious man; indeed, he is Lawton's most lucrative client. Naylor built a single-family home for Jill and George Holmes. When Naylor finished, the Holmeses confronted him with a list of 289 items that they claimed were either construction defects or uncompleted tasks. The Holmeses refused to pay Naylor the final 25% installment under their construction contract until all 289 items were remedied. Naylor contested all 289 items and demanded immediate payment. The Holmeses refused to pay and refused to talk further with Naylor. At that point, Naylor called in Lawton. Lawton met with the Holmeses and offered to represent both them and Naylor in trying to find an amicable solution to their dispute. Lawton said that, if his efforts failed, he would charge no fee; if his efforts produced an amicable solution, then his total fee would be $2,500, half to be paid by the Holmeses and half by Naylor.

May Lawton represent both the Holmeses and Naylor on those terms?

(A) No, because Lawton has proposed a contingent fee arrangement, and there is no *res* from which the fee can be paid.

(B) Yes, because Lawton would, in essence, be serving as a third-party neutral between the Holmeses and Naylor.

(C) Yes, but only if both the Holmeses and Naylor give informed, written consent to the arrangement.

(D) No, because Lawton cannot reasonably believe that he can represent the Holmeses competently and diligently in light of his relationship with Naylor.

Question 52

Lawyer Lupine works full-time for the United States Department of Agriculture's Forest Service. She is assigned to the Forest Service's Pacific Northwest Region, which covers Oregon and Washington. Her office and home are in Oregon. She went to law school and is admitted to practice in South Carolina; she is not a member of the bar in any other state. Her work for the Forest Service does not require her to litigate, mediate, or arbitrate claims before any tribunal. She is strictly an office lawyer, and most of her workday is spent advising Forest Service managers on environmental law issues that arise under federal law or under Oregon or Washington law. To earn some extra money on the side, Lupine moonlights as an estate planner, drafting wills and trust agreements for other Forest Service employees who live and work in Oregon or Washington. She does not advertise her estate planning services, and she serves only Forest Service employees, not outsiders.

Is Lupine *subject to discipline* by the Oregon State Bar for unlicensed law practice?

(A) No, because the Oregon State Bar has no jurisdiction to discipline her, but she could be disciplined by the South Carolina Bar for practicing without a license in Oregon.

(B) No, because her work for the Forest Service is done under federal authority, and her moonlighting is done only for other federal employees, not members of the general public.

(C) Yes, with respect to her moonlighting as an estate planner, but not with respect to her environmental law work for the Forest Service.

(D) Yes, with respect to both her moonlighting as an estate planner and her environmental law work for the Forest Service.

Question 53

Lawyer Ladd limits his practice to the defense of people accused of felonies. Bondsman Boyd is licensed by the state to act as a surety on bail bonds, subject to extensive state regulations. When he acts as surety on a bail bond, Boyd pledges to pay the court a specified sum if a person who has been released on bail fails to show up for court proceedings on a given date. Often a family member or friend of an accused person comes to Boyd's office to arrange for a bail bond. On these occasions, the family member or friend sometimes asks Boyd to recommend a good criminal defense lawyer. Boyd always refers the person to Ladd, whom he believes to be the best criminal defense lawyer in the county. Boyd and Ladd have worked out a reciprocal referral agreement. In return for the referrals he gets from Boyd, Ladd always sends people to Boyd for bail bonds. Ladd would do that even without the reciprocal agreement because he regards Boyd as the most honest and dependable bondsman in the county. Ladd does not disclose the reciprocal referral agreement to the people he refers because they are invariably under great stress and not interested in arcane technicalities.

Is Ladd's participation in the reciprocal referral agreement *proper*?

(A) No, because Ladd does not disclose the agreement to the people he refers to Boyd.

(B) Yes, because the agreement simply reflects what Ladd would do even without the agreement.

(C) No, because lawyers must not encourage nonlawyers to refer legal work to them.

(D) Yes, because Ladd has a right of free speech under the First and Fourteenth Amendments to refer people to whomever he wishes.

Question 54

Attorney Adkins limits his practice to criminal defense. About 40% of his workload comes from court appointments. When a conflict of interest prevents the public defender from representing an indigent defendant, the presiding judge appoints defense counsel from a list of volunteer lawyers. The state pays appointed defense counsel at a modest hourly rate. Adkins observed with envy that his friend, lawyer Landry, was appointed about twice as often as Adkins. Adkins asked Landry how one goes about getting more appointments, and Landry responded: "The presiding judge supposedly picks lawyers randomly from the list of volunteers, but you will find that the P.J.'s finger lands on your name more often if you contribute to the political campaigns of local incumbent judges who are running for re-election." Adkins took this advice to heart and started making significant contributions to the campaign committees of incumbent judges running for re-election; he would not have made such contributions but for Landry's advice. As predicted, Adkins started getting significantly more appointments than before.

Are Adkins's political contributions *proper*?

(A) Yes, even though his motive in making the contributions is to obtain more appointments.

(B) No, because his motive in making the contributions is to obtain more appointments.

(C) Yes, because lawyers are permitted to participate freely in the political process.

(D) No, but only because his contributions constitute common law bribery.

Question 55

Attorney Allen is a partner in Bellicozi & Warlik, a 300-member law firm that serves as outside general counsel to Heedlock-Spartan, one of the world's largest manufacturers of tactical-guided missiles. Heedlock-Spartan employs many engineers, mechanics, and assembly-line workers who have immigrated to the United States from various parts of the world. The United States Department of Homeland Security "strongly advised" the company to fire 42 of these employees, whose names appear on the federal government's terrorist watch list. Heedlock-Spartan regards all 42 people as valuable, dependable employees, so it consulted Allen in the strictest of confidence, asking for legal advice about what to do. Other lawyers at Bellicozi & Warlik were not told about Heedlock-Spartan's request, nor about the advice Allen gave the company. The company ended up firing two engineers and one assembly-line worker, but it kept the other 39 people. The fired assembly-line worker went to the Belcher Street Advice-Only Legal Clinic to obtain some advice about his legal rights. The clinic is run by Saint Steven's Church, a non-profit religious organization; the clinic's mission is to offer free, fast legal advice to anyone who cannot afford to obtain it elsewhere. The clinic receptionist sent the worker to the desk of volunteer attorney Allgood. She is a brand new associate in the Bellicozi firm, and she did not know that Heedlock-Spartan is one of the firm's clients. She also knew nothing about the advice Allen gave Heedlock-Spartan. Allgood dutifully advised the worker of his rights under state and federal employment law and under the collective bargaining agreement between his union and Heedlock-Spartan.

Which of the following is most nearly correct?

(A) Both Allgood and Bellicozi & Warlik will be *subject to civil liability* in a legal malpractice action brought by Heedlock-Spartan if Allgood's advice causes the worker to sue Heedlock-Spartan for discriminatory termination.

(B) Allgood is *subject to discipline* for failing to do a conflict-of-interest check before giving legal advice to the fired worker.

(C) Allgood's conduct was *proper* because she did not know that Heedlock-Spartan was her firm's client or that Allen had advised Heedlock-Spartan on the issue at hand.

(D) If the worker sues Heedlock-Spartan for discriminatory termination, Allen would be *subject to discipline* for representing Heedlock-Spartan in the litigation because Allgood gave legal advice to the worker at the clinic.

Question 56

Lawyer Lombardi limits her practice to corporate securities law. A small start-up company wholly owned and operated by two brilliant young computer geeks has hired Lombardi to guide them through an initial public offering of shares in their company. One of Lombardi's first recommendations was to fire their current lazy, in-house accountant and hire a skilled outside accounting firm to keep the company's books and prepare the financial documents required for an initial public offering. Lombardi recommended a small, local accounting firm called Hammers & Naylor, but in doing so Lombardi orally cautioned the company owners as follows:

> I want you both to know that I am a certified public accountant as well as a lawyer, and I own one of the three partnership shares in Hammers & Naylor, so I have a significant financial interest in the firm. I no longer practice accounting; Ms. Hammers, Mr. Naylor, and their associates do all of the accounting, but I keep my partnership share as an investment. You need to understand something else—if you decide to hire Hammers & Naylor, your dealings with them will not be governed by the rules of legal ethics. For example, what you tell them in confidence will not be protected by the attorney-client privilege. Do you understand?

The company owners orally indicated that they understood, and they subsequently hired Hammers & Naylor.

Was Lombardi's conduct *proper*?

(A) Yes, because Lombardi was not offering the accounting service ancillary to her legal service; the accounting service was offered by Hammers & Naylor, an independent entity.

(B) No, because Lombardi was essentially entering into a business transaction with her client.

(C) Yes, because Lombardi fully disclosed the situation to the company's owners and obtained their informed consent.

(D) No, because Lombardi did not put her cautionary words in writing, she did not give the company owners a chance to consult an outside lawyer, and she did not obtain their consent in writing.

GO ON TO THE NEXT PAGE

Question 57

The law of State Alpha prohibits agreements not to compete, except for agreements that are ancillary to the sale of a business or professional practice and are reasonable in both duration and geographic scope. For 20 years, lawyer Lasalle practiced patent, copyright, and trademark law in the Silicon Hills area of State Alpha. Seeking a new challenge, Lasalle entered the political race for a trial court judgeship in Silicon Hills. He won a four-year term. Before taking the oath of judicial office, Lasalle sold his entire law practice to young lawyer Younger for $150,000. In the sale contract, Lasalle promised Younger not to re-enter the practice of patent, copyright, or trademark law in the Silicon Hills area for five years. At the end of his four-year term, Lasalle ran for re-election to his judgeship; to everyone's great surprise, Lasalle lost the election to a much less qualified opponent. Because he needed to earn a living, Lasalle immediately re-entered the practice of patent, copyright, and trademark law in Silicon Hills.

Is Lasalle *subject to discipline*?

(A) Yes, because Lasalle re-entered law practice in Silicon Hills after the sale to Younger.

(B) Yes, because Lasalle made an agreement that restricts his right to practice law and it was not incident to a retirement benefits plan.

(C) No, but Lasalle could be *subject to civil liability* to Younger in a suit to enforce the agreement not to compete, assuming that the agreement was reasonable in duration and geographic scope.

(D) No, because the sale of Lasalle's law practice was *proper*, but the agreement not to compete is void, even if it is reasonable in duration and geographic scope.

Question 58

Lawyer Lecter practices election law. In the most recent election, Lecter represented candidate Zechariah Zama. Several days before the election, Zama told Lecter in confidence that he had hired some gangs of thugs to frighten voters away from the polls in neighborhoods where most people would vote for Zama's opponent, Karl Krup. Lecter was shocked and immediately advised Zama to call off the thugs or withdraw from the race. Zama refused to do either, whereupon Lecter withdrew as Zama's lawyer. Lecter did not, however, tell anyone about Zama's evil plan. On election day, Zama's thugs did what Zama paid them to do, and Zama defeated Krup by a narrow margin. A few days later, Krup learned what the thugs had done. Krup was furious and called a press conference at which he accused Zama and Lecter of conspiring to intimidate Krup's supporters and keep them away from the polls. The local newspaper printed Krup's allegations in a front-page story, accompanied by a large photograph of Zama and Lecter smiling at each other.

Which of the following propositions are true?

I. It was **proper** for Lecter to withdraw after Zama refused to call off the thugs or drop out.

II. It was **proper** for Lecter not to tell anyone before the election about Zama's evil plan.

III. After Krup's press conference and the newspaper story, but before any kind of formal proceedings, it would be **proper** for Lecter to disclose what Zama told him in confidence about the thug plan and about Lecter's response.

IV. If Krup sues Zama and Lecter for conspiring to violate Krup's constitutional rights and for tortious interference with prospective advantage, then it would be **proper** for Lecter to disclose what Zama told him in

confidence about the thug plan and about Lecter's response.

(A) All of the above.

(B) I. only.

(C) II. only.

(D) I., II., and IV. only.

GO ON TO THE NEXT PAGE

Question 59

Lawyer Lysle practices in the state of East Carolina. East Carolina's rules of legal ethics depart from the ABA Model Rules in one significant respect: East Carolina has no "financial injury" exception to the lawyer's duty of confidentiality. Thus, when an East Carolina lawyer learns in confidence that her client is about to use her legal services to inflict serious financial injury on someone, the lawyer may withdraw, but she must not reveal what she learned in confidence. Lysle limits her practice to federal securities law, and she regularly appears before the Securities and Exchange Commission ("SEC"). One of Lysle's major clients is Carolina Mills, Inc., which makes and sells cotton textiles. Carolina Mills's shares are traded on the New York Stock Exchange and in securities matters the company is regulated by the SEC. While working on an SEC registration statement for Carolina Mills, Lysle learned in confidence that three of the company's top executives were cooperating in a scheme to loot the company of millions of dollars. If their scheme continues, it could drive the company into insolvency. Lysle alerted the chief legal officer ("CLO") of Carolina Mills to the situation, but he did nothing. She then alerted the chief executive officer ("CEO"), who also did nothing. Finally, she alerted the six outside members of the board of directors, but they too failed to act. In disgust, Lysle withdrew from the matter and vowed never again to represent Carolina Mills.

Must Lysle now tell the SEC about the scheme?

(A) Yes, the SEC's regulations under the Sarbanes-Oxley Act require her to alert the SEC if her other efforts have proven fruitless.

(B) No, the SEC's regulations give her discretion to either reveal or not reveal the matter to the SEC.

(C) Yes, because the shareholders could be seriously financially injured if the scheme continues.

(D) No, because East Carolina's legal ethics rules do not allow her to reveal confidential information in this situation.

GO ON TO THE NEXT PAGE

Question 60

When great-grandfather Grant sold the family farm back in 1927, he told his lawyer that he wanted to reserve all of the subsurface rights— *i.e.*, the rights to mine or drill for oil, gas, minerals, geothermal energy, and the like. The lawyer drafted a deed that was supposed to accomplish that goal. When great-grandfather Grant died, the subsurface rights passed by his will to his beloved great-granddaughter, Dahlia. Thirty years later, Dahlia received a letter from ExplorCo, a petroleum exploration and drilling company. ExplorCo offered to lease the subsurface drilling rights from Dahlia in return for $10,000 plus 15% of the wellhead selling price of all gas and oil obtained from the property. All Dahlia had to do was sign the lease and supply ExplorCo with a letter from a qualified oil and gas lawyer, certifying that Dahlia was indeed the owner of the subsurface rights. Dahlia hired Prudence, an oil and gas lawyer, to research her title, write the letter, and send it to ExplorCo. After doing a little research, Prudence concluded that great-grandfather Grant's lawyer had bungled the deed. Instead of reserving the subsurface rights, Grant had inadvertently sold them to the man who bought the farm. With a heavy heart, Prudence put her findings in an opinion letter and mailed duplicate originals to ExplorCo and Dahlia.

Was it **proper** to do so?

(A) No, because Prudence should have obtained Dahlia's informed consent before sending the letter to ExplorCo.

(B) No, because the interests of ExplorCo and Dahlia were concurrently conflicting.

(C) Yes, because Dahlia had previously authorized Prudence to send the letter to ExplorCo.

(D) Yes, because to withhold the information from ExplorCo would amount to a misrepresentation of a material fact.

STOP

ANSWER SHEET

1 Ⓐ Ⓑ Ⓒ Ⓓ		31 Ⓐ Ⓑ Ⓒ Ⓓ	
2 Ⓐ Ⓑ Ⓒ Ⓓ		32 Ⓐ Ⓑ Ⓒ Ⓓ	
3 Ⓐ Ⓑ Ⓒ Ⓓ		33 Ⓐ Ⓑ Ⓒ Ⓓ	
4 Ⓐ Ⓑ Ⓒ Ⓓ		34 Ⓐ Ⓑ Ⓒ Ⓓ	
5 Ⓐ Ⓑ Ⓒ Ⓓ		35 Ⓐ Ⓑ Ⓒ Ⓓ	
6 Ⓐ Ⓑ Ⓒ Ⓓ		36 Ⓐ Ⓑ Ⓒ Ⓓ	
7 Ⓐ Ⓑ Ⓒ Ⓓ		37 Ⓐ Ⓑ Ⓒ Ⓓ	
8 Ⓐ Ⓑ Ⓒ Ⓓ		38 Ⓐ Ⓑ Ⓒ Ⓓ	
9 Ⓐ Ⓑ Ⓒ Ⓓ		39 Ⓐ Ⓑ Ⓒ Ⓓ	
10 Ⓐ Ⓑ Ⓒ Ⓓ		40 Ⓐ Ⓑ Ⓒ Ⓓ	
11 Ⓐ Ⓑ Ⓒ Ⓓ		41 Ⓐ Ⓑ Ⓒ Ⓓ	
12 Ⓐ Ⓑ Ⓒ Ⓓ		42 Ⓐ Ⓑ Ⓒ Ⓓ	
13 Ⓐ Ⓑ Ⓒ Ⓓ		43 Ⓐ Ⓑ Ⓒ Ⓓ	
14 Ⓐ Ⓑ Ⓒ Ⓓ		44 Ⓐ Ⓑ Ⓒ Ⓓ	
15 Ⓐ Ⓑ Ⓒ Ⓓ		45 Ⓐ Ⓑ Ⓒ Ⓓ	
16 Ⓐ Ⓑ Ⓒ Ⓓ		46 Ⓐ Ⓑ Ⓒ Ⓓ	
17 Ⓐ Ⓑ Ⓒ Ⓓ		47 Ⓐ Ⓑ Ⓒ Ⓓ	
18 Ⓐ Ⓑ Ⓒ Ⓓ		48 Ⓐ Ⓑ Ⓒ Ⓓ	
19 Ⓐ Ⓑ Ⓒ Ⓓ		49 Ⓐ Ⓑ Ⓒ Ⓓ	
20 Ⓐ Ⓑ Ⓒ Ⓓ		50 Ⓐ Ⓑ Ⓒ Ⓓ	
21 Ⓐ Ⓑ Ⓒ Ⓓ		51 Ⓐ Ⓑ Ⓒ Ⓓ	
22 Ⓐ Ⓑ Ⓒ Ⓓ		52 Ⓐ Ⓑ Ⓒ Ⓓ	
23 Ⓐ Ⓑ Ⓒ Ⓓ		53 Ⓐ Ⓑ Ⓒ Ⓓ	
24 Ⓐ Ⓑ Ⓒ Ⓓ		54 Ⓐ Ⓑ Ⓒ Ⓓ	
25 Ⓐ Ⓑ Ⓒ Ⓓ		55 Ⓐ Ⓑ Ⓒ Ⓓ	
26 Ⓐ Ⓑ Ⓒ Ⓓ		56 Ⓐ Ⓑ Ⓒ Ⓓ	
27 Ⓐ Ⓑ Ⓒ Ⓓ		57 Ⓐ Ⓑ Ⓒ Ⓓ	
28 Ⓐ Ⓑ Ⓒ Ⓓ		58 Ⓐ Ⓑ Ⓒ Ⓓ	
29 Ⓐ Ⓑ Ⓒ Ⓓ		59 Ⓐ Ⓑ Ⓒ Ⓓ	
30 Ⓐ Ⓑ Ⓒ Ⓓ		60 Ⓐ Ⓑ Ⓒ Ⓓ	

Answer to Question 1

(C) (A) is incorrect because lawyers should treat all participants in a proceeding with courtesy, respect, and cooperation. [*See* Restatement §106] (D) is incorrect because there is nothing that prohibits a lawyer from talking with a deposition witness about the case before a deposition. However, a lawyer must not communicate about a case with a person he knows to be represented by a lawyer, without first getting the lawyer's consent. [ABA Model Rule 4.2] Also, Comment 7 to that Rule states that, in the case of an organization, a lawyer for one party may not communicate concerning the matter with persons whose acts or omissions in connection with the matter may be imputed to the organization for purposes of civil or criminal liability. Wallner fits the description of such a person. Thus, (C) is correct, and (B) is incorrect.

Answer to Question 2

(C) III. is clearly improper, as a lawyer must not communicate about a matter with a person the lawyer knows is represented by counsel, unless that person's counsel consents or the law authorizes the communication. [ABA Model Rule 4.2] It is within a prosecutor's discretion to request that the court prosecute on a lesser offense; so I. is proper. II. is proper because there is no indication that Diplock could not legitimately have been prosecuted for auto theft.

Answer to Question 3

(B) In a criminal case, it is for the client to decide what plea to enter. [ABA Model Rule 1.2(a)] Also, Lucinda's apparent lack of concern for Diplock's interests raises a serious question about her fitness to practice law. [*See* ABA Model Rule 1.3] Therefore, Patrick must report the incident to the disciplinary authorities. [ABA Model Rule 8.3(a)] Thus, (B) is the correct answer. (A) is incorrect because as long as Lucinda properly represented her client and did not violate the Rules, her desire to gain publicity is irrelevant. (D) is also irrelevant. (C) is incorrect because even if Lucinda competently defended Diplock at trial, she would still have violated attorney ethics if she failed to convey the offer to Diplock.

Answer to Question 4

(C) An applicant for admission to the bar may be unqualified for mental or emotional instability. Professor Schultze had an obligation three years ago to report her candid opinion to the state bar, even though she lacks training in the field of mental health. Likewise, she is now obliged to support Peter's re-petition for admission to practice. ABA Model Rule 8.1 prohibits a lawyer in connection with a bar admission application from knowingly making a false statement of material fact. Thus, the professor must now disclose her current feelings regarding Peter's fitness to practice law. Thus, (C) is correct, and (A), (B), and (D) are incorrect.

Answer to Question 5

(B) ABA Model Rule 3.5(a) forbids a lawyer from seeking to influence a judge by means prohibited by law. CJC 4D(5)(d) permits a judge to accept a wedding gift from a friend if the gift is "fairly commensurate with the occasion and the relationship." (A) is wrong because some gifts are prohibited even if the judge does not believe they would create undue influence. (C) is wrong because campaign contributions are not the only types of gifts lawyers may make to judges. (D) is wrong because the $150 reporting requirement of CJC 4D(5)(h) is irrelevant to this situation.

Answer to Question 6

(A) A lawyer must not neglect a legal matter that has been entrusted to him; *i.e.,* a lawyer must act with reasonable diligence and promptness in representing a client. [ABA Model Rule 1.3] Furthermore, a lawyer has a duty to keep the client reasonably informed about the status of a matter and to promptly comply with reasonable requests for information. [ABA Model Rule 1.4(a)(3), (4)] Lawrence's failure to begin the work before March 10, coupled with his failure to return Morris's telephone calls or otherwise assure Morris that the work would be completed on time, constitutes client neglect and is grounds for discipline. Thus, (A) is correct, and (B) and (C) are incorrect. (D) is incorrect because, as stated above, Lawrence neglected his client and is subject to discipline even though Morris and the trust ultimately suffered no loss.

Answer to Question 7

(D) Although Abe has retired from active practice, it is clear from the facts that Judge Johnnie consulted Abe ***as an attorney***, rather than as a friend; thus, Abe may not reveal Judge Johnnie's disclosures of past crimes. [*See* ABA Model Rule 1.6] Therefore, (D) is correct and (C) is incorrect. (A) is incorrect because an ongoing lawyer-client relationship need not be established for the rules of confidentiality to apply. (B) is an incorrect statement of a lawyer's ethical obligations, as no present fraud upon the tribunal or system of justice is contemplated, and ABA Model Rule 8.3 specifically states that matters considered confidential under Rule 1.6 are not included in the obligation to reveal judicial misconduct.

Answer to Question 8

(A) There are several legal theories on which sanctions could be imposed here, but the most obvious is Rule 37 of the Federal Rules of Civil Procedure, which is specifically designed for discovery abuse. When a party's managing agent fails to show up for a properly scheduled deposition, Rule 37 gives the judge a wide choice of sanctions, including such things as: an order that the issues in question be deemed proven in favor of the innocent party; an order forbidding the offender from offering proof on the issues in question; an order striking the offender's pleadings; an order finding the offender guilty of contempt of court; and an order that the offending party, its lawyer, or both must pay the innocent party's expenses and attorney fees incurred because of the violation. (A) is better than (C) because (C) implies an incorrect legal standard; a lawyer can be sanctioned under Rule 37 even if she did not act obstinately or disrespectfully. (B) and (D) are not as good as (A) because they imply that a lawyer cannot be sanctioned for discovery abuses by her client or her client's managing agent. That is not correct. A lawyer has to walk a thin line between bullying her client and being bullied by her client. Lakk was not blame-free here. She was on notice that Dr. Fletcher was an uncooperative witness. He had failed to show up three times previously, and Judge Jackson had specifically warned Lakk that she would be sanctioned if she showed up without Dr. Fletcher on August 16. Lakk could have informed Dr. Fletcher's corporate superior about the situation, seeking to have the superior force Dr. Fletcher to behave. Lakk could also have reminded her client that she ***may*** withdraw as counsel if Dr. Fletcher does not cooperate [ABA Model Rule 1.16(b)], and that she ***must*** withdraw if Dr. Fletcher's mulishness forces Lakk to violate a court order [ABA Model Rule 1.16(a)]. Lakk's failure to take these or similar steps to assure Dr. Fletcher's presence makes the sanctions order appropriate.

Answer to Question 9

(D) Under ABA Model Rule 1.12(a), Adela should be barred from representing Baines because she was personally and substantially involved in his case while a law clerk. (Note that ABA Model Rule 1.12(a) would permit the representation if both parties gave informed, written consent to the representation, but there is no mention of both parties giving informed, written consent in these facts.) (A) is incorrect because Adela's previous personal and substantial involvement in the case will prohibit her from representing Baines regardless of whether Adela learned any confidential information. (B) is incorrect because Adela is presently licensed, and Model Rule 1.12 clearly applies to former law clerks. (C) is incorrect because Model Rule 1.12 allows such representation only if *all parties* consent after full disclosure.

Answer to Question 10

(C)   Under CJC 4B and 4C(3), it would be proper for the judge to serve on the board of this foundation that provides legal education for lawyers and judges. CJC 4H(1) would permit her to accept the modest salary that is paid to other directors. Accordingly, the other choices are not correct.

Answer to Question 11

(A)   A lawyer does not need the consent of adversary counsel to interview a nonparty witness. Furthermore, nothing in the Rules would prevent Krytzer from asking O'Leary about his prior criminal record, and he would have good reason for doing so because O'Leary's criminal record can be used to impeach his testimony. Thus, (A) is correct, and (B), (C), and (D) are incorrect.

Answer to Question 12

(C)   ABA Model Rule 7.2(b)(4) permits reciprocal referral arrangements among lawyers if the arrangement is nonexclusive and disclosed to referred clients. (A) is wrong because the parties to a reciprocal referral arrangement need not be licensed in different states. (B) is wrong because the facts do

not involve the division of a legal fee. (D) is wrong because it ignores ABA Model Rule 7.2(b)(4).

Answer to Question 13

(B)   A lawyer must not imply that he can improperly influence a government official. [ABA Model Rule 8.4] Bob is not actually appearing before his sister, and so (C) and (D) are incorrect. Without more, the mere objection of an opposing party should not keep Bob from appearing in district court; thus, (A) is incorrect. (B) is therefore the best answer.

Answer to Question 14

(D)   Laslo is not subject to *malpractice* liability because Capra has no damages. Damages are part of the cause of action for legal malpractice. Laslo may be subject to discipline, but not malpractice liability. (A) is incorrect because, although it correctly states Laslo's duty, there is no malpractice claim because of the lack of damages. (B) is incorrect for the same reason. (C) is incorrect because Capra's statement that Capra "probably" would not accept an offer under $500,000 does not constitute authorization of Laslo to accept or reject offers without consulting Capra. Furthermore, to avoid problems such as this, authorization to accept or reject settlement offers without consulting the client should be in writing.

Answer to Question 15

(B)   An attorney is subject to discipline for making a false statement of law to the court. [ABA Model Rule 3.3(a)(1)] (A) is overbroad because an attorney need not cite opposing cases from noncontrolling jurisdictions, and an attorney may argue the case from an advocate's viewpoint, which may not necessarily be "objective." (C) and (D) are incorrect because they do not take into account the stricture against making a false statement of law. Amy has gone beyond the bounds of zealous representation.

Answer to Question 16

(B) Client's funds are ordinarily deposited in an account where the lawyer's office is located, but they can be deposited elsewhere with the client's consent. [ABA Model Rule 1.15(a)] (A) is wrong because Chum's funds appear to be an expense advance, not a "true retainer fee." (C) and (D) are wrong because there are no such requirements.

Answer to Question 17

(A) The old common law of attorney-client privilege allowed an eavesdropper to testify to an otherwise privileged communication, but the modern law is to the contrary. [*See, e.g.*, Cal. Evid. Code §§952, 954] Because Pamela can reasonably anticipate that Devereaux will claim the attorney-client privilege, she has no obligation to try to testify to what she heard. In addition, ABA Model Rule 3.8(b) mandates the prosecutor to protect the defendant's right to counsel. Accordingly, item I. is incorrect, and item II. is correct. As to Denise's obligations, the facts given in the question do not justify an assumption that Devereaux has asked Denise to present false evidence on his behalf, or that Devereaux is planning to take the witness stand and perjure himself. Accordingly, we are not faced with any questions under ABA Model Rule 3.3. Thus, Denise should preserve what Devereaux said in confidence and proceed with the case in the normal manner. [*See* ABA Model Rule 1.6(a)] This makes item III. incorrect and item IV. correct.

Answer to Question 18

(C) A lawyer must provide competent representation to a client. [ABA Model Rule 1.1] This includes use of methods and procedures meeting the standards of competent practitioners. It also includes adequate preparation. In the case at bar, April's decision on whether to further search for the unknown witness was a matter of judgment. If she was reasonable in believing that Chuck's testimony would be sufficient, then her preparation will not be deemed inadequate. Thus, (C) is the correct answer, and (A) is incorrect. (B) is incorrect because even though Chuck lost, April may have provided him with competent representation. (D) is irrelevant.

Answer to Question 19

(D) ABA Model Rule 7.2(b) prohibits a lawyer from giving anything of value to a person in return for a recommendation of the lawyer's services. (A) and (B) are incorrect because the truth of the information or lack of confidentiality is beside the point. (C) is incorrect because there is no prohibition, as such, against demeaning members of the profession.

Answer to Question 20

(A) This is the best answer here because nothing in this advertisement violates the ABA Model Rules. The fact that the ad is not misleading is important because neither the ABA Model Rules nor the First Amendment protects misleading or deceptive advertising. (B) is incorrect because fee splitting is a separate issue; it does not affect the propriety of the ad. (C) is incorrect because Axel is *not* soliciting business, and also because the traditional ban on all solicitation is no longer constitutional. (D) is incorrect in that the ad is *not* patently in bad taste, and even if it were, it would probably be protected by the First Amendment unless it was misleading or overreaching.

Answer to Question 21

(B) Item I. is proper because Agnes has no duty to represent Morton. Item II. is proper because Agnes may represent Morton if he does not insist on testifying falsely. [*See* ABA Model Rule 3.3(a)(3)] Item III. is improper because it is a form of extortion. Item IV. is improper because Morton's confession to past perjury is protected by the duty of confidentiality. [*See* ABA Model Rule 1.6]

Answer to Question 22

(A)   There is nothing in the ABA Model Rules that prohibits a lawyer from requiring a client to pay in advance the first $500 of litigation expenses, so long as the $500 payment is reasonable. [ABA Model Rule 1.5(a)] (B) is incorrect because the ABA Model Rules do not suggest that every clause of a standard form employment contract must be individually tailored to each client. (C) is incorrect because ABA Model Rule 1.8(e) *permits* lawyers to advance litigation expenses, but does not *require* them to do so. (D) is incorrect because nothing in the Rules requires the client to pay litigation expenses as they are incurred.

Answer to Question 23

(A)   The usual rationale supporting relatively high contingent fees is that the lawyer is taking a gamble in handling the case. Here, no gamble is involved, and Alp is subject to discipline under ABA Model Rule 1.5(a) for attempting to exact an unreasonable fee. The criteria of (A) more clearly establish excessiveness than those in (B). (C) is incorrect because even though contingent fees may be thought generally appropriate for personal injury cases, an excessive fee, whether contingent or hourly, is never appropriate. (D) is incorrect because even though the client could have gone to another attorney, Alp tried to exact an unreasonable fee from her.

Answer to Question 24

(D)   A judge should refrain from financial and business dealings that might be perceived to exploit her judicial position or involve her in frequent transactions with lawyers or persons likely to come before the court on which she sits. [CJC 4D(1)] Here, Judge

Jerkins's close business relationship with a lawyer who appears in her courtroom violates CJC 4D(1). It makes no difference that Judge Jerkins acquired the property before she became a judge. Thus, (A) is incorrect. (B) is incorrect because even if Judge Jerkins's dealings with the property do not take up too much of her time, there will still be an adverse reflection on her impartiality. (C) is incorrect because CJC 4D(2) permits a judge to hold investments, including real estate, and to engage in other remunerative activity.

Answer to Question 25

(D)   All jurisdictions in the United States have obstruction of justice statutes that prohibit threatening jurors, witnesses, and judges and also prohibit similar misconduct. For example, 18 U.S.C. section 1503 makes it a felony to "endeavor . . . to influence, intimidate, or impede any . . . juror." The term "endeavor" is broader than "attempt," and one can be guilty of endeavoring to intimidate a juror even though the juror is not intimidated. [*See also* United States v. Atkin, 107 F.3d 1213 (6th Cir. 1997)— attorney violated section 1503 by obtaining money from defendant to bribe judge, even though attorney ultimately did not offer the bribe] (A) is incorrect because it overlooks obstruction of justice statutes such as section 1503. (B) is incorrect because the effort need not be successful, as in the *Atkin* case, above. (C) is incorrect because Lewellen can be punished as an accomplice, even if he did not give Snagg anything of value. Snagg did the intimidating, but it was Lewellen who instructed or induced him to do it.

Answer to Question 26

(A)   This is the best answer here because it complies with the ABA Model Rules' view that advertising must not be "false or misleading." [*See* ABA Model Rule 7.1] It also takes into account First Amendment freedoms. (B) is incorrect because the geographic scope of lawyer advertising is not limited to the city in which the lawyer practices. (C) is incorrect because there is no prohibition on "self-laudatory" advertising in the ABA Model Rules. Arla's statement regarding proficiency in Spanish compared with other local attorneys is factually verifiable and thus does not run afoul of ABA Model Rule 7.1. (D) is incorrect because the listing of academic degrees is clearly proper.

Answer to Question 27

(A) Proposition I. reflects a misconception of ABA Model Rule 1.8(f), which prohibits a lawyer from allowing the interests of a third party to interfere with the relationship between the lawyer and the client. That is not the case where an alleged expert like Dr. Belle is hired to assist the lawyer in representing the client. Proposition III. reflects a similar misconception. Attorneys frequently use a variety of experts to advise them during trial. Munoz did not give up his discretion to Dr. Belle, as evidenced by the fact that he sometimes did not follow her advice. Furthermore, such experts frequently sit at counsel table so they can be close to the lawyer during trial. Proposition II. is incorrect because a lawyer is allowed to advance litigation expenses. [*See* ABA Model Rule 1.8(e)(1)] Although some lawyers might question the wisdom of spending money on a purported expert on liars, that would seem to be a matter best left to the discretion of the individual lawyer, and the Model Rules do not suggest otherwise.

Answer to Question 28

(A) ABA Model Rule 4.3 forbids an attorney to give advice to an unrepresented person if the lawyer knows that the person's interests conflict with those of the client. Thus, (A)

is correct. The attorney is ***allowed*** to advise the unrepresented person to obtain a lawyer, but the critical issue is giving advice. Thus, (A) is a better answer than (B). (C) is irrelevant to any ethical issue. (D) is incorrect because there is no way a lawyer can compel a third party to obtain counsel.

Answer to Question 29

(C) Ordinarily, an attorney can act for both the insured and the insurance company because their interests are only potentially in conflict. But here they have come into present, actual conflict. Chen cannot adequately represent Walters without harming Farmers, and he cannot protect Farmers's interests without harming Walters. Therefore, he must seek the court's permission to withdraw from the case entirely, and he must not reveal Walters's confidential statement. [*See* ABA Model Rules 1.6, 1.7, 1.16(a)(1)] In a case very much like this one, the Seventh Circuit held that the attorney "should have refused to participate further in view of the conflict of interest" between the insured person and the insurance company. [State Farm Mutual Automobile Insurance Co. v. Walker, 382 F.2d 548 (7th Cir. 1967); *and see* ABA Informal Op. 1476 (1981)] Thus, (C) is correct, and (A) and (D) are incorrect. (B) is incorrect because of the conflict of interest and because Chen may be advocating perjury.

Answer to Question 30

(A) CJC 5C(2) allows a candidate for an elected judicial office to have a campaign committee to solicit campaign funds and publicly stated support for the candidate. No provision of either the CJC or the ABA Model Rules prohibits a lawyer who frequently appears before a judge from contributing to or publicly endorsing the campaign. Finally, the CJC and the Model Rules are silent about asking for a discount on advertising.

Answer to Question 31

(B)   ABA Model Rule 1.6(b)(1) allows a lawyer to disclose a client's confidential information to prevent reasonably certain death or substantial bodily harm. Charles planned to commit suicide, which clearly falls within this rubric. Thus, (B) is correct, and it logically follows that (C) and (D) are incorrect. (A) does not go directly to the ethical question involved.

Answer to Question 32

(C)   A lawyer who is licensed to practice in one state (or in a foreign country or province) is not, without more, entitled to practice in any other state. A lawyer is subject to discipline for practicing in a jurisdiction without being licensed to do so. Because there is no indication on the letterhead regarding limitation of Baxter's practice to Manitoba, Alice is abetting the unauthorized practice of law. [*See* ABA Model Rule 5.5(a)] It logically follows that (C) is correct and (B) is incorrect. (A) is irrelevant. (D) is silly.

Answer to Question 33

(B)   ABA Model Rule 1.11(a) prohibits a lawyer from representing a private client in a matter in which the lawyer participated personally and substantially as a public employee, unless the government agency in question gives its informed, written consent. Because Lewis was neither personally nor substantially involved with any matter concerning Acme, he may now represent Acme without obtaining the EPA's consent. Thus, (B) is correct, and (A), (C), and (D) are incorrect.

Answer to Question 34

(B)   ABA Model Rule 1.8(f) prohibits a lawyer from accepting compensation for representing a client from anyone other than that client, unless two conditions are satisfied:

(i) the client gives informed, written consent, and (ii) the person who pays the compensation does not interfere with the representation of the client or with the lawyer's independence. [*See also* Restatement §134, comment d] In this case, the "friends" are interfering with the lawyer's representation of the client and with his independence by conditioning their financial aid on Daggs's not implicating them in the cocaine caper. The results of their interference become obvious when Daggs is coerced into turning down the attractive plea bargain. [*See* Quintero v. United States, 33 F.3d 1133 (9th Cir. 1994)— similar facts] (A) and (C) are both incorrect because they misstate the principles expressed in ABA Model Rule 1.8(f)—(A) is too broad, and (C) is too narrow. (D) is incorrect because the prosecutor has an ethical obligation to help assure a criminal defendant's right to counsel. [*See* ABA Model Rule 3.8(b)]

Answer to Question 35

(A)   Abigail's actions are proper. With the aid of her associates, Abigail, an experienced patent lawyer, was clearly competent to handle the case. (B) is wrong because it states one of the limitations on fee splitting between lawyers in different firms. It does not apply to lawyers in the same firm. (C) is wrong because this is the type of disclosure that is impliedly authorized to carry out the representation. It does not abrogate the protections of privilege or confidentiality, and no formal consent by the client is required. [*See* ABA Model Rule 1.6(a)] (D) is wrong because it too states a limitation concerning fee splits between lawyers in different firms. No client consent is required to split a fee in any manner among lawyers in the same firm. [ABA Model Rule 1.5]

Answer to Question 36

(C)   Item I. is incorrect because under ABA Model Rule 5.4(d)(1), a nonlawyer may not own an interest in a professional legal corporation. Item II. is incorrect because incorporation will limit the malpractice liability of the lawyers only to the extent permitted by the law of the state in question. [Restatement §58, comment c] Item III. is correct because ABA Model Rule 5.4(d)(1) permits this exception to the general rule that a nonlawyer may not hold stock in a professional legal corporation. Item IV. is incorrect because under ABA Model Rule 5.4(d)(2), a nonlawyer must not serve as a director or officer of a professional legal corporation.

Answer to Question 37

(C) Adams may represent both Smith and Jones even though there is a *potential* conflict of interest between them if: (i) Adams reasonably believes that he can represent both clients effectively; and (ii) Smith and Jones give informed, written consent. Thus, item I. is correct. Adams must withdraw from the joint representation, however, if later discovery shows that Smith has an actual claim against Jones. Thus, item II. is correct. [*See* ABA Model Rules 1.7, 1.9(a)] Item III. is incorrect because a lawyer must not represent a client if the representation of that client will be directly adverse to the representation of another client, unless both clients give informed, written consent. [*See* ABA Model Rule 1.7] There is no indication that Jones, Smith, and the bus company gave informed, written consent.

Answer to Question 38

(A) ABA Model Rules 7.1 and 7.2 provide that communications about legal services must not be false or misleading; thus, these rules are not likely to stand as an obstacle to any of the statements in the ad if true.

Answer to Question 39

(D) Laura is not subject to discipline because Ben is Clara's brother. A lawyer may advise a person not to voluntarily give information to an opponent or other party if the person is a relative of the client and that person's interests will not be harmed by not volunteering the information. [ABA Model Rule 3.4(f)] Here, Ben is Clara's brother, and there is nothing in the facts to suggest his interests would be harmed by not volunteering the information. (A) is wrong because of the exception stated above. (B) is wrong because this type of advice is not prohibited. If the facts indicated that Ben's interests might be harmed by not granting the interview (*e.g.,* if he had a matter pending with DCS that might be negatively influenced by his noncooperation), Laura could not have advised him as she did and should then have advised him to seek independent counsel. (C) is wrong for the reason just stated.

Answer to Question 40

(A) A lawyer must act with reasonable diligence and promptness in representing a client. [ABA Model Rule 1.3] Thus, a lawyer must not neglect a matter entrusted to him. An example of neglect is failure to file necessary papers, as in this case. It seems clear that Avery has violated this standard. He is, of course, also liable to Cassidy for Cassidy's loss due to Avery's neglect. Thus, Avery is guilty of malpractice and violating an ethics rule. Therefore, (A) is correct, and (B), (C), and (D) are incorrect.

Answer to Question 41

(C) Item I. is correct. There is nothing in the ABA Model Rules to the contrary. Item II. is incorrect because regardless of his personal feelings, a lawyer may not decline representation because a client or a cause is unpopular or community reaction is adverse. [*See* Comment 1 to ABA Model Rule 6.2] Item III. is correct according to ABA Model Rule 6.2(c), which states that a lawyer may decline employment if the intensity of his personal feelings, as distinguished from a community attitude, will impair his effective representation of a prospective client.

Answer to Question 42

(C)   Acheson is not subject to discipline for failure to correct the court's mistake because the mistake did not originate with Acheson or Dell. In this setting, Acheson would have a duty to speak out if something he or his client had done had given the court a false impression, but otherwise, he cannot breach his duty of confidentiality to the disadvantage of his client. [*See* ABA Model Rules 1.6(a), 3.3] Thus, (A) is incorrect. The fact that this is a sentencing hearing does not affect Acheson's duties in any way. This is not an ex parte proceeding (which would be a much thornier issue). Thus (B) is incorrect. (D) is incorrect because had the judge asked Acheson directly whether this was Dell's first offense, Acheson would have had to respond truthfully or have asked to withdraw (which would also have given the judge his answer). To answer otherwise would be perpetrating a fraud on the court.

Answer to Question 43

(C)   Restatement section 60(2) states that a lawyer who self-deals in a client's confidential information can be forced to disgorge any profit she makes, even if the client is not harmed by the self-dealing. Lucy was self-dealing here, even though she did not tell Mitchell the precise reason why she was certain Charlie's play would be a hit. For that reason, (A) is incorrect. (B) and (D) are incorrect because harm to the client is not required.

Answer to Question 44

(B)   Item I. is incorrect because Carmen would have no Fifth Amendment right to withhold the papers even if they were in her personal possession, and delivery of the papers to Alexis does not cloak them with the attorney-client privilege. [Fisher v. United States, 425 U.S. 391 (1976)] Item II. is correct because the attorney-client relationship covers communications to an authorized representative of the attorney. [City & County of San Francisco v. Superior Court, 37 Cal. 2d 227 (1951)] Item III. is also correct because the information was acquired in Alexis's role as an attorney. It is irrelevant that Alexis subsequently refused to handle the case. [*See* Restatement §§70, 72]

Answer to Question 45

(B)   ABA Model Rule 1.8(h) makes it clear that an attorney is subject to discipline for attempting to prospectively limit malpractice liability by contract with a client. The ABA Model Rules provide an exception if the client secures independent counsel in making the agreement. That exception does not apply here, so (B) is correct. (A) is incorrect because the "clients" are free to go elsewhere for representation and no relationship is "forced" on them. (C) is incorrect because high-sounding rhetoric and purpose do not change the impropriety of attempts to limit malpractice liability by contract. (D) is incorrect because the clients were not independently represented in making agreements to the contract.

Answer to Question 46

(B)   An attorney has implied authority to consult other members of her firm regarding a case unless there is a specific instruction from the client to the contrary or some other compelling reason. [*See* ABA Model Rule 1.6(a) and Comment 5] It logically follows that (A), (C), and (D) are incorrect.

Answer to Question 47

(C)   Generally, title insurance agents and others whose businesses border on the practice of law are allowed to fill in the blanks on standard form documents that have been prepared by lawyers. Therefore, items I. and II. do not constitute the unauthorized practice of law. But in *State Bar v. Guardian Abstract & Title Insurance Co.*, 587 P.2d 1338 (N.M. 1978), it was held that a title insurance company could not advise its customers about "the legal effect of the language contained in" such standard form documents. Thus, item III. is an example of unauthorized practice. (C) is therefore correct, and (A), (B), and (D) are incorrect.

Answer to Question 48

(A) (D) is incorrect; Phil's claim is not frivolous under ABA Model Rule 3.1. The statute of limitations merely destroys the remedy and not the right. Unless Debbie pleads the statute of limitations, Phil's claim is valid. (B) and (C) are incorrect; there is no duty to inform the court that the statute of limitations has run.

Answer to Question 49

(B) Item II. is incorrect. A lawyer must not initiate an in-person contact with a non-client, personally or through a representative, for the purpose of being retained to represent him for compensation. [ABA Model Rule 7.3] Item III. is also incorrect. ABA Model Rule 7.2(b) provides that a lawyer must not give anything of value to a person for recommending the lawyer's services. Thus, (B) is correct and (A), (C), and (D) are incorrect.

Answer to Question 50

(C) Item I. is proper under CJC 4B, which permits a judge to teach law. Item II. is improper under CJC 4C(3)(b)(i), which prohibits a judge from personally soliciting funds for a law-related organization. Item III. is proper; the CJC does not forbid

avocational activities that do not interfere with a judge's official duties. [*See* CJC 4A] Item IV. is improper under CJC 4D(3), which states that a judge must not serve as a manager or employee of a business. Thus, (C) is correct and the other answers are incorrect.

Answer to Question 51

(D) (A) is wrong because a contingent fee can be proper even if there is no *res*—no pool of money—from which the fee can be paid. [*See* ABA Model Rule 1.5(c), (d)] (B) is wrong because Lawton is not neutral; he was called into the matter by Naylor, his most lucrative client. ABA Model Rule 2.4(a) says that a lawyer can serve as a third-party neutral when he "assists two or more persons **who are not clients** of the lawyer to reach a resolution of a dispute or other matter that has arisen between them." (C) and (D) draw upon Comments 26 - 33 to ABA Model Rule 1.7(b), concerning concurrent conflicts of interest between two clients in a non-litigation matter. Here, Lawton cannot **reasonably believe** that he can represent the Holmeses competently and diligently in negotiating with Naylor, his longtime and most lucrative client. [*See* ABA Model Rule 1.7(b)(1)] Moreover, the interests of Naylor and the Holmeses are so "fundamentally antagonistic" that the conflict is "unconsentable." [Comment 28 to ABA Model Rule 1.7]

Answer to Question 52

(C) (A) is wrong because ABA Model Rule 8.5(a) permits Oregon to discipline an out-of-state lawyer "if the lawyer provides or offers to provide any legal services" in Oregon. Lupine's work for the Forest Service is authorized by federal law, so Oregon could not discipline her for that, but it could discipline her for her moonlighting work. [*See* ABA Model Rule 5.5(d)(2)] (B) is wrong because federal law does not authorize Lupine to draft wills and trust agreements in Oregon, even though that work is done only for other federal employees. [*See* Comments 16 and 18 to ABA Model Rule 5.5] (D) is wrong because Lupine's work for the Forest Service is authorized by federal law, so Oregon cannot discipline her on that score. [*See* ABA Model Rule 5.5(d)(2) and Comment 18]

Answer to Question 53

(A) The general rule is that a lawyer must not give anything of value to a person for recommending the lawyer's services. [ABA Model Rule 7.2(b)] Referral of business is certainly something of value, so Ladd's agreement with Boyd would violate the general rule unless one of four exceptions applies. Ladd might try to invoke the exception stated in ABA Model Rule 7.2(b)(4), which permits a lawyer to have a reciprocal referral agreement with another lawyer, or with a nonlawyer professional, if two conditions are satisfied. Before examining the two conditions, one must first decide whether a bail bondsman is a "professional." Black's Law Dictionary defines "profession" as a vocation that requires advanced education and training, such as the three traditional professions: law, medicine, and the ministry. [Black's Law Dictionary 1246 (8th ed. 2004)] Black's notes, however, that common parlance has expanded the term, and for purposes of this question, ABA Model Rule 7.2(b) would be served by including a state-licensed and regulated bail bondsman as a "professional." That brings us to the two conditions. First, a reciprocal referral agreement must be nonexclusive—*i.e.*, each party must be free to refer a person to a competitor of the other party. Second, the referral agreement must be disclosed to the person who is referred. The agreement between Ladd and Boyd fails to satisfy the second condition, and perhaps the first as well. (B)

is wrong because the agreement must be disclosed, whether or not it changes what the lawyer would do absent the agreement. (C) is wrong because it overstates the general rule expressed in ABA Model Rule 7.2(b). (D) is wrong because Ladd's free speech rights are trumped by the legal ethics rule, and the same is true for many other legal ethics rules.

Answer to Question 54

(B) ABA Model Rule 7.6 says that a lawyer must not accept an appointment made by a judge if the lawyer makes a political contribution "for the purpose of obtaining or being considered for" that type of appointment. The question states that Adkins would not have made the contributions but for the advice he obtained from Landry; that is sufficient proof of his improper motive. [*See* Comment 5 to ABA Model Rule 7.6] (A) is wrong for the reason stated above. (C) is wrong because ABA Model Rule 7.6 limits one specific kind of participation in the political process—so-called pay to play political contributions. (D) is wrong. Common law bribery is the giving of money, or something else of value, in return for a specified act by a judge or other public official; the person on the receiving end also commits common law bribery. Adkins's contributions are improper under ABA Model Rule 7.6, whether or not they rise to the level of common law bribery. [*See* Comment 6 to ABA Model Rule 7.6]

Answer to Question 55

(C) This question is governed by ABA Model Rule 6.5, which relaxes the ordinary conflict of interest rules for legal service programs that offer quick legal advice to a client without expectation that the lawyer will continue representing the client. ABA Model Rule 6.5(a)(2) states that the ordinary rule of imputed disqualification will apply only if the lawyer who offers the quick legal advice **knows** that a different lawyer in her firm would be disqualified by a conflict, and "knows" means **actually** knows. Here, Allgood did not know that Allen had advised Heedlock-Spartan on the matter; indeed, she was a new associate and did not even realize that Heedlock-Spartan was one of the firm's clients. Therefore, Allgood acted properly in advising the fired worker. (A) is wrong because the question does not supply any facts that would support a valid legal malpractice claim or other civil claim against either Allgood or the law firm. (B) is wrong because ABA Model Rule 6.5 recognizes that quick-service providers cannot realistically perform the thorough conflicts checks that private firms perform. (D) is wrong because Allgood's legal advice to the fired worker will not disqualify Allen from representing Heedlock-Spartan in later litigation. [*See* Comment 4 to ABA Model Rule 6.5]

Answer to Question 56

(D) Comment 5 to ABA Model Rule 5.7, states: "When a client-lawyer relationship exists with a person who is referred by a lawyer to a separate law-related service entity controlled by the lawyer, individually or with others, the lawyer must comply with Rule 1.8(a)." ABA Model Rule 1.8(a), in turn, says that when a lawyer enters into a business transaction with her own client, she must (i) disclose the terms to the client **in an understandable writing,** (ii) give the client a chance to **consult independent counsel,** and (iii) obtain the client's **consent in writing**. Lombardi did not do those things, so her conduct was not proper. (C) is wrong for the same reason. (B) is not as good as (D) because (B) overlooks the circumstances that would make it proper to enter into a business transaction with one's

own client. (A) is wrong because it misses the point. Accounting service is a "law-related" service, and Lombardi and the other two partnership owners control Hammers & Naylor. Thus, if Lombardi recommends their accounting service, she must take the precautionary steps outlined in ABA Model Rule 1.8(a).

Answer to Question 57

(C) ABA Model Rule 1.17 permits a practicing lawyer to sell his entire law practice or an area of his law practice to one or more lawyers or law firms. That is what Lasalle did here shortly before becoming a judge. One of the conditions specified in ABA Model Rule 1.17 is that the seller must cease "to engage in the private practice of law . . . in the [jurisdiction or geographic area] in which the practice has been conducted." [ABA Model Rule 1.17(a)] Lasalle satisfied that condition by becoming a judge—engaging in judicial duties does not constitute the private practice of law, nor does working as a government lawyer, lawyer for the poor, or an in-house lawyer for a business. [*See* Comments 2 and 3 to ABA Model Rule 1.17] Lasalle's re-entry into private practice does not violate ABA Model Rule 1.17 because it was caused by an "unanticipated change in circumstances"—*i.e.*, his failure to win re-election. [*See* Comment 2 to ABA Model Rule 1.17, which uses re-election defeat as an example of "unanticipated change"] (A) is wrong for the reason just stated. (B) is wrong because ABA Model Rule 5.6 (the rule that prohibits agreements that restrict a lawyer's right to practice) does not apply to agreements that are ancillary to the sale of a law practice. [Comment 3 to ABA Model Rule 5.6] (D) is wrong because the law of State Alpha makes Lasalle's agreement not to compete **valid** if it is reasonable in duration and geographic scope.

Answer to Question 58

(A) Item I. is true. ABA Model Rule 1.16(b)(4) permits a lawyer to withdraw if the client insists upon taking action that the lawyer considers repugnant or with which the lawyer has a fundamental disagreement. Item II. is true. The applicable doctrine here is the lawyer's ethical duty of confidentiality. The duty has some exceptions, but none of them quite fits this situation. One might argue that ABA Model Rule 1.6(b)(2) fits because Lecter could reveal Zama's evil plan in order to prevent "substantial injury to the financial interests or property of another." Perhaps Krup has a financial interest in being elected to the post. However, there is nothing to suggest that Zama used Lecter's services to form or carry out the evil plan, and that is an important requirement of ABA Model Rule 1.6(b)(2). Even if ABA Model Rule 1.6(b)(2) would *permit* Lecter to reveal the confidential information, it does not *require* him to do so—it gives Lecter discretion as to whether to reveal. [*See* Comment 15 to ABA Model Rule 1.6] Item III. is true. ABA Model Rule 1.6(b)(5) allows a lawyer to reveal confidential information "to establish a defense to a criminal charge or civil claim against the lawyer based upon conduct in which the client was involved, or to respond to allegations in any proceeding concerning the lawyer's representation of the client." The lawyer's right to disclose in self-protection does not require that a criminal charge, civil complaint, disciplinary case, or other formal proceeding has already started. "The lawyer's right to respond arises when an assertion of complicity has been made." [Comment 10 to ABA Model Rule 1.6] Krup's press conference and the newspaper story amply satisfy that requirement. If item III. is true, then item IV. is *a fortiori* true because here Krup has started a formal proceeding. Lecter can protect himself against Krup's tort and constitutional claims by revealing what really happened between him and Zama.

Answer to Question 59

(B) The SEC's regulations under the Sarbanes-Oxley Act *permit,* but do not require, a securities lawyer to reveal a client's confidential information to the SEC when the lawyer reasonably thinks that doing so is necessary to prevent or rectify a securities act violation (or similar law violation) that is likely to cause substantial financial injury to the client or its shareholders. [*See* 17 C.F.R. §205.3(b)(2)(i), (iii)] (A) and (C) are wrong because the regulation permits, but does not require, the lawyer to alert the SEC. (D) is wrong because the SEC regulations purport to preempt any inconsistent state ethics rules. [*See* 17 C.F.R. §§205.1, 205.6(c)] (It remains to be seen whether courts will uphold the SEC's effort to preempt the field and override inconsistent state ethics rules.)

Answer to Question 60

(A) Dahlia hired Prudence to evaluate her title for the use of a third party, ExplorCo. ABA Model Rule 2.3 governs this kind of representation. ABA Model Rule 2.3(b) states that when the lawyer knows (or should know) that the representation will harm the client, the lawyer should not provide the evaluation without first obtaining the client's informed consent. Dahlia apparently told Prudence at the outset to send the evaluation to ExplorCo, but Dahlia did not know at that point what the evaluation would show. One purpose for Prudence to obtain Dahlia's informed consent before sending the letter to ExplorCo is to give Dahlia a chance to obtain a second opinion from a better oil and gas lawyer; perhaps it is Prudence who fouled up rather than great-grandfather Grant's lawyer. (B) is wrong because ABA Model Rule 2.3 permits a lawyer to undertake an evaluation for a third party, and the third party's interests are quite commonly in concurrent conflict with those of the client. (C) is wrong because Dahlia's prior authorization is not enough; Prudence should have obtained informed consent after she discovered that the letter would harm Dahlia. [*See* ABA Model Rule 2.3(b) and Comment 5] (D) is wrong because, if Prudence never sent the opinion letter to ExplorCo, she would have no duty to disclose anything to ExplorCo.

PRACTICE EXAM 4

Question 1

Attorney Aggie is prosecuting a complex tax case. After two government witnesses testified, the defendant, Daft, took the stand in his own defense. Daft asserted that he always complied with all tax rules and regulations. He also testified that the two government witnesses had deliberately falsified Daft's Internal Revenue Service records because the witnesses belonged to a Satanic cult which bore a long-standing grudge against Daft. In Aggie's closing argument, she made the following statements relative to the defendant's testimony:

I.   "Defendant's testimony is clearly in conflict with the testimony of two government witnesses."

II.   "Of the persons who have given testimony, who has the better reason to lie, the defendant or the government's witnesses?"

III. "If you believe the testimony of the defendant, you will also believe that the Moon is made of green cheese!"

For which, if any, of these statements would Aggie be **subject to discipline**?

(A) III. only.

(B) II. and III. only.

(C) I., II., and III.

(D) Neither I., II., nor III.

Question 2

Judge Josephine ruled in favor of Plaintiff in a civil action where Defendant was ordered to pay Plaintiff $50,000 in damages. Josephine has since resigned from the bench. Defendant has refused to pay the $50,000, asserting that the verdict was obtained through improper means. Defendant asks Josephine, now in private practice, if she will represent him.

Would Josephine be **subject to discipline** if she represents Defendant?

(A) No, because Josephine is no longer on the bench.

(B) No, unless Josephine was a party to fraud when the original verdict was handed down.

(C) Yes, because Josephine ruled on this case when she was a judge.

(D) Yes, because former judges may not engage in private practice.

GO ON TO THE NEXT PAGE

Question 3

Attorney Arlo has hired Clarissa, a third-year student at a local law school, to assist him as his clerk. Clarissa is not licensed under any state law or court rule that allows third-year law students to engage in practice under the supervision of a licensed attorney. Arlo has Clarissa perform the following tasks:

I.   Draft a release form for personal injury plaintiffs to sign after their cases have been settled. (Arlo himself has the plaintiffs sign the forms.)

II.   Interview witnesses to accidents, and have them sign Clarissa's written version of the interview.

III.   Reach settlement agreements with insurance company representatives before suit has been filed.

For which of the above is Arlo *subject to discipline*?

(A)   I. only.

(B)   III. only.

(C)   I. and II., but not III.

(D)   II. and III., but not I.

Question 4

Alfonso is the mayor of the city of Dustbowl. Alfonso is also a licensed attorney who has a law partnership with Bella. Under the city charter of Dustbowl, the mayor has the authority to determine what issues are to be placed upon the agenda of the city council. Several council members have told Alfonso that they would like to see a particular zoning measure placed upon the agenda. This proposed ordinance would ban commercial development of a certain area within the city limits.

Bella has been retained as attorney for Octopus Development Corp. Octopus has acquired land in the proposed noncommercial zoning area and has plans to construct a large shopping center there.

May Bella represent Octopus in this matter?

(A)   Yes, because Octopus is not a client of Alfonso.

(B)   Yes, if Alfonso is not present at any city council meetings at which the matter is discussed.

(C)   No, because of Alfonso's position as mayor.

(D)   No, unless Alfonso has no direct role in the representation and does not share in any fees from the case.

GO ON TO THE NEXT PAGE

Question 5

Attorney Arlette represented Ted Tingus in a wrongful discharge action against Apex Petroleum Corporation. Apex had fired Tingus from his job as a "service station field representative." Such representatives are responsible for visiting and inspecting Apex service stations to ensure that the station operators are obeying the terms of their leases; following Apex's rules about retail gasoline pricing; keeping full stocks of Apex brand tires, batteries, and accessories; not carrying competitors' tires, batteries, and accessories; and maintaining the stations in a clean and attractive condition. Apex claimed that it fired Tingus for poor job performance, but Tingus claimed that he was fired because he refused to enforce certain Apex policies that he believed were violations of federal and state antitrust laws. In the course of preparing the case for trial, Arlette and Tingus talked in confidence at great length about how Apex expects its field representatives to enforce its allegedly anticompetitive rules against service station operators. Shortly before trial, Apex settled with Tingus for a generous sum. Tingus did not, however, return to his job at Apex, nor has he communicated with Arlette since the case ended.

Now, three years later, a former Apex service station operator named Operman has hired Arlette to represent him in a federal antitrust action to collect treble damages from Apex for subjecting him to the very same anticompetitive policies that cost Tingus his job. Arlette is handling Operman's case on a contingent fee basis. In preparing Operman's case for trial, Arlette was able to save many hundreds of hours of discovery and research work because of the information she learned in confidence from Tingus about the way Apex treats its service station operators. Thanks to what Tingus taught her about Apex's business practices, Arlette was ready for the Operman trial in record time—which panicked the lawyers for Apex and ultimately resulted in an extraordinarily generous settlement for Operman. Arlette, of course, took her share of the settlement under the contingent fee arrangement and thus profited personally from Tingus's information.

Is Arlette *subject to civil liability* to Tingus for using his confidential information for her own monetary benefit?

(A) No, because Arlette's recycling of Tingus's information did not harm Tingus; she simply took advantage in her law practice of her earlier experience and accumulated knowledge.

(B) No, because Tingus ceased being Arlette's client at the time he settled his case with Apex, and Arlette's duty of confidentiality ended when the lawyer-client relationship ended.

(C) Yes, because Arlette did not obtain informed, written consent from Tingus before using his information to hasten her preparation of the Operman case.

(D) Yes, because the contingent fee arrangement allowed Arlette to profit personally from material disclosed to her in confidence by Tingus.

Question 6

Attorney Archer is representing Davis in the civil case of *Preston v. Davis*, which arose out of a business deal gone sour. One evening after court was out of session, but with the trial set to resume the next day, Archer attended a $5,000 per person charity fund-raising dinner. When he found his assigned seat, he was shocked to find that he was seated next to Preston, the plaintiff in the suit. Archer asked the hostess if she could change his seat, but she said it would be impossible. Determined to make the best of it, Archer and Preston did not discuss the case but made small talk about the charity, the weather, etc. They soon found that they had much in common, including a love of sports. After a long, enjoyable evening of discussing their favorite teams, Preston gets up to leave. Preston turns to Archer and says, "You're not a bad fellow after all. It has been a real pleasure talking to you this evening. First thing in the morning, I'm going to talk to my lawyer about reaching an agreeable settlement in this case. I'll have her call you." The next day, Preston calls lawyer Layton and tells her, "After talking to Archer last night at the fund-raiser, I have decided to settle the case for the amount proposed in our last negotiating session. If Davis agrees to it, please notify the court and draw up the appropriate papers." Furious, Layton does as Preston asks, but reports Archer to the proper disciplinary authorities.

Is Archer *subject to discipline*?

(A) Yes, because he communicated with a represented party without his attorney's consent.

(B) Yes, because this is an improper ex parte communication while the matter is still pending.

(C) No, because they discussed the charity, the weather, and sports.

(D) No, because Archer did not know he would be seated next to Preston and asked to have the seating assignment changed as soon as he discovered it.

Question 7

Hemoglobin, a licensed attorney, represents the plaintiff, Portia, in a personal injury case. Portia has authorized Hemoglobin to settle the case for $2,000. She further tells Hemoglobin that if he receives $2,000 from the defendant, he may keep $750 of it as his fee, and that he should pay Dr. Arzt, the physician who examined Portia, $250 for his examination and treatment of her injuries. Hemoglobin reaches a $2,000 settlement with the defendant. Upon receipt of a $2,000 check from the defendant, he immediately places $750 in his personal account, sends Dr. Arzt a check for $250, and places $1,000 in his clients' trust account at Beelzebub National Bank. Sixty days after Hemoglobin received the $2,000 check, Portia calls him to inquire about any progress made on a settlement of her case. Hemoglobin tells her that he has settled the case and paid Dr. Arzt. Immediately after he hangs up the phone, he writes out a check to Portia in the amount of $1,000 and mails the check on his lunch hour.

Is Hemoglobin *subject to discipline*?

(A) Yes, because he paid himself his fee without informing his client.

(B) Yes, because he did not promptly pay his client the money due her.

(C) No, because he placed the funds due Portia in his clients' trust account.

(D) No, because Hemoglobin was negligent but did not violate a disciplinary rule.

GO ON TO THE NEXT PAGE

Question 8

Attorney Aoki represents client Carson, the plaintiff in a personal injury suit arising out of a tour bus accident in Hawaii. Nearly all of the eyewitnesses were tourists who have now returned home to the mainland. Without notifying the defense attorney, Aoki has interviewed most of the witnesses by phone. By far the most compelling witness, and the one most favorable to Carson, is Willa. Willa is a librarian who lives in North Dakota and had spent the bulk of her life savings on a vacation to Hawaii. It was on this vacation that Willa witnessed the tour bus accident. Willa is a very appealing witness, and Aoki is confident that if a jury saw her testify personally, Carson would win his suit. Aoki tells Willa that if she is willing to come to Hawaii for one week to testify, he will pay for her plane tickets, an oceanfront hotel room at a first class hotel, all meals, and one week's salary for her lost time. This is the same offer Aoki makes to all witnesses traveling to testify in any of his cases. Willa, who cannot believe her good fortune, readily agrees.

Is Aoki *subject to discipline*?

(A) Yes, because a lawyer may not offer an inducement to a witness to testify.

(B) Yes, because he interviewed the witnesses without notifying the defense attorney.

(C) No, because a lawyer may pay a witness's reasonable expenses and lost wages.

(D) No, unless the trip and accommodations are substantially more expensive than Willa could afford.

Question 9

Charlene went to the law office of Leopard and told Leopard that she wished to divorce her hard-drinking, abusive husband Buster. However, because she did not work outside the home, she told Leopard that she could not afford to pay a big lawyer's fee. Leopard was sure that Charlene had adequate grounds for divorce in that Buster was adulterous, an alcoholic, and frequently beat Charlene. Therefore, Leopard told Charlene, "The filing fees for a divorce in this county amount to $200. If you can put up that much money, I'll do all the work for 10% of whatever I get you for alimony and child support." Charlene was elated and replied, "Thank you! Thank you! I'm sure I can find or borrow $200. So many lawyers want a big fee up front, and you've just told me you'll get me out of this living hell for $200 up front! God bless you, Leopard, you're a wonderful man!" Leopard left his office that night with a warm feeling that he had helped a fellow human being, secure in the knowledge that at least one person in the community would have something nice to say about lawyers.

However, personal satisfaction aside, was Leopard's conduct *proper*?

(A) Yes, unless the fee that Leopard eventually earns proves to be excessive.

(B) Yes, because he is providing legal services to persons who might not otherwise be able to afford them.

(C) No, because a contingent fee arrangement is prohibited when the fee is based on the amount of alimony or a division of marital property.

(D) No, if Charlene was indigent and Leopard did not advance her the filing fees.

GO ON TO THE NEXT PAGE

Question 10

Bellatrix, a local attorney, has recently defended David Defendant in a civil action tried before a jury. Defendant lost the case, and Paul Plaintiff was awarded a substantial amount of damages. Bellatrix receives an anonymous, handwritten letter that states: "Joan Juror, who sat on the jury when Paul Plaintiff got that big damages award, was bribed to influence other members of the jury to side with Paul and to award a large sum in damages." Bellatrix hires Seamus Sleuth, a local private investigator, to investigate Joan Juror, and to determine if the anonymous charges are true.

Is it *proper* for Bellatrix to hire the private investigator?

(A) Yes, provided the investigator notifies Joan Juror of his investigation and obtains her consent.

(B) Yes, because the investigation may disclose evidence sufficient for the granting of a new trial.

(C) No, because such an investigation is likely to affect the willingness of the jurors to serve on juries in the future.

(D) No, if the investigation is to be conducted in such a manner as to harass the jurors.

Question 11

Castor and Pollux are law partners. Castor represents Scurvy, and Pollux represents Smythe. Both are criminal defendants whose cases are seemingly unrelated. During the course of an interview with Castor, Scurvy tells him that he was involved in the crime with which Smythe is charged and that he is willing to testify against Smythe if he can be granted immunity from prosecution on that charge and plea bargain the crime with which he is presently charged down to a lesser offense.

Which of the following courses of action is *proper* for Castor?

(A) Inform Pollux of what Scurvy has told him and continue to represent Scurvy.

(B) Inform Pollux of what Scurvy has told him and withdraw from representing Scurvy.

(C) Not inform Pollux and continue representation.

(D) Not inform Pollux and withdraw from representation.

Question 12

Attorney Quarles is embittered because he has recently had to expend a great deal of time and money defending himself against a frivolous malpractice suit brought by a disgruntled former client. To forestall such suits in the future, Quarles decides to take extra precautions. As a result, he enters into the following arrangements with clients:

I.   Tapes a "closing interview," during the course of which Quarles explains to the client each aspect of his handling of the case and asks the client if she understands fully the explanation, or if she has any further questions about the case. Quarles tells the client that he is taping the interview.

II. Agrees to represent a client for no fee or for a low fee, but only if the client promises not to sue him for malpractice.

III. Refuses to return a client's papers until the client signs a release of liability for malpractice.

For which of the above is Quarles *subject to discipline*?

(A) I. only.

(B) III. only.

(C) I. and II., but not III.

(D) II. and III., but not I.

Question 13

Attorney Ariadne has an arrangement whereby a local radio station broadcasts four times each day a prerecorded tape advertising her services. Ariadne pays the station its standard rate for "spot advertising." The advertising tape is as follows:

> Ariadne Attorney, 355 Main St., is a fully licensed member of the State Bar engaged in general practice. She will handle bankruptcies for $150 and uncontested divorces where there are no custody or property problems for $250 plus the filing fee. She will take personal injury cases on a contingency fee basis, her fee being 30% of the amount recovered after deduction for costs. Ariadne Attorney offers a free consultation regarding your case. You may call 922-2739 for an appointment.

Is Ariadne's advertising *proper*?

(A) No, because an attorney may not advertise contingent fees.

(B) No, unless Ariadne is a certified specialist in personal injury law.

(C) No, because Ariadne advertises free consultations.

(D) Yes; there is nothing wrong with Ariadne's advertising.

Question 14

The law firm of Rice & O'Malley represents P.J. Kilmer, a successful businessperson who has given the firm almost all of his substantial legal business. Kilmer is presently involved in complex civil litigation in which Kilmer stands to receive a large damages award if the suit is successful. Harmon, the attorney for the defendant in the case, has filed a motion that, if granted, would result in dismissal of the suit. The named partners of Rice & O'Malley have studied the motion and feel that there is some merit in the motion, and at least a 50% chance that Judge Jensen, who is trying the case, will rule in favor of the defendant. During the course of explaining the defendant's motion to Kilmer, Rice and O'Malley call in Costello, who is a recently hired associate. Costello is Judge Jensen's former law clerk, and he wrote several speeches for her when she was running in a contested reelection campaign. Rice and O'Malley tell Kilmer that it would be to his advantage for Costello to argue against the motion. Costello, during the course of the meeting with the client, tells Kilmer, "I think we'll get a break on this because Judge Jensen owes me a favor."

Is Costello *subject to discipline*?

(A) Yes, because his statement implies that Judge Jensen will give him preferential treatment due to their past association.

(B) Yes, if Costello plans to use his knowledge of Judge Jensen's character to his advantage.

(C) No, if Costello honestly believes that he will do the best job of arguing the motion on its merits.

(D) No, unless Costello plans to use improper influence on the judge.

GO ON TO THE NEXT PAGE

Question 15

In April 2003, plaintiff ProTex, Inc. sued defendant Datasafe Corp. in United States District Court for infringement of ProTex's copyright on a computer software program that protects computer data from being destroyed by so-called computer viruses. ProTex's complaint alleges that Datasafe infringed the copyright by copying ProTex's anti-virus program in January 2003. In August 2003, ProTex filed a document discovery request that asked Datasafe to hand over a copy of the "source code" of Datasafe's anti-virus program as it existed in January 2003. The source code is the precise material written in computer language by the programmer. Only by comparing source codes could a person be sure whether one software program had been copied from another program. Source codes are therefore vital evidence in software copyright infringement cases, and all competent lawyers who work in the field know that fact.

As is customary in the computer industry, Datasafe periodically creates improved versions of the computer software it sells. Whenever Datasafe creates an improved version, it routinely destroys the source code of the former version, keeping only the source code of the improved version. This routine destruction is the customary practice in the computer industry. In June 2003, and again in September 2003, Datasafe created improved versions of its anti-virus program. On both occasions, Datasafe asked its lawyer, Littleman, whether it would be all right to destroy the former source code. Without giving the matter much thought, Littleman responded on both occasions: "Sure you may. It's the routine practice in the industry, and I see no problem with it." In due course, ProTex moved for a court order to enforce its document discovery request for the January 2003 source code. In response, Littleman turned over the then-current version of the source code and explained why the January 2003 version was no longer available.

After a detailed factual hearing, Judge Juno concluded that Datasafe's two acts of destruction made it impossible for ProTex to prove that Datasafe had copied ProTex's copyrighted material in January 2003. As a sanction for destroying evidence, Judge Juno entered a partial summary judgment in favor of ProTex on the copying issue. Judge Juno also sanctioned Littleman by ordering him to pay all of the expenses and attorneys' fees ProTex had incurred due to Datasafe's two acts of destruction.

Was Judge Juno correct in holding Littleman *subject to litigation sanction*?

(A) Yes, as respects the destruction in September 2003 (after ProTex's document request), but no, as respects the June 2003 destruction because ProTex did not request the source code until August 2003.

(B) Yes, because in both June and September 2003, Littleman either knew or ought to have known that the January 2003 source code was vital evidence.

(C) No, unless there is clear and convincing evidence that Littleman intended to commit a fraud on the court by allowing his client to destroy the January 2003 source code.

(D) No, unless Littleman actively encouraged his client to destroy the January 2003 source code.

GO ON TO THE NEXT PAGE

Question 16

Attorney Alpheus worked for two years for the Veteran's Administration. While there, his main function was to investigate claims filed by veterans. During the course of his employment, he once investigated a claim filed by Charles, a Vietnam War veteran. After Alpheus left the Veteran's Administration, the agency denied Charles's claim. Charles comes to Alpheus, who is now engaged in private practice, and asks him to represent him in a suit against the Veteran's Administration for the benefits to which Charles believes he is entitled.

Is Alpheus *subject to discipline* if he accepts Charles's case?

(A) No, because Alpheus has left the Veteran's Administration.

(B) No, if Alpheus was not privy to confidential information regarding Charles, arising from his employment at the Veteran's Administration.

(C) Yes, because Alpheus had at least some knowledge of Charles's claim when Alpheus was employed by a government agency.

(D) Yes, if Alpheus had substantial and personal responsibility for Charles's Veteran's Administration claim.

Question 17

Client Celia comes to attorney Adnan seeking representation in bringing a breach of contract action. Celia tells Adnan that she originally retained lawyer Louis about a year ago, but that as far as she knew he had not even filed the papers. According to Celia, Louis never returned her calls, and when she went to his office to find out the status of her case, he was drunk and verbally abusive. Celia told her friends and family about Louis's treatment of her, and when her brother fared no better in getting information from him, he suggested that she contact Adnan.

Celia advised Adnan that because Louis did not return her calls, she had sent a certified letter to him notifying him that he was discharged. Adnan knew that there was only a one-year statute of limitations on this type of action, so he quickly checked the dates and discovered that he had only a few days to file the action. Adnan called Louis to get the information from Celia's file. Louis did not recall the letter of discharge and was surprised to get Adnan's call. He was, however, very cooperative and agreed to send a messenger to Adnan's office with Celia's file. Louis tells Adnan, "I feel terrible about this. My wife has been very ill this year, and I haven't been myself. Tell Celia I am sorry. And I would appreciate it if you would keep this between the two of us. I would hate for this incident to scare away any more clients. I could sure use the money with my wife's illness and all."

Adnan filed the papers in Celia's suit on time, and did not report Louis to the disciplinary authorities. Were Adnan's actions *proper*?

(A) Yes, because Adnan is an attorney, and Louis asked him to keep the matter confidential.

(B) Yes, because it is Celia's decision whether to report Louis to the disciplinary authorities.

(C) No, because Louis's actions indicate that he is not currently fit to practice law.

(D) No, because he did not urge Celia to report Louis to the appropriate authorities.

GO ON TO THE NEXT PAGE

Question 18

Preacher is a law school graduate but is not a licensed member of the bar. After Preacher graduated from law school, he felt called to the ministry, received a degree in divinity, and was formally ordained as a minister of his faith. Preacher is now the pastor of a local church, where Alfred Attorney is a member of the congregation. Preacher has been very disturbed about the high rates of divorce and the breakdown in American family life. Therefore, he holds frequent "family counseling sessions" where, among other things, he explains to the parishioners who attend these sessions many of the legal ramifications of divorce, alimony, child support, and child custody. These sessions are usually followed by question-and-answer periods, during which Preacher gives legal advice to parishioners who cannot afford a lawyer. Preacher knows that the legislature has passed a new marriage dissolution law that changes the law substantially from what Preacher was taught in law school. Preacher asks Alfred if he will prepare an outline and a memorandum fully explaining the new law so that Preacher will be better informed for the sessions with his parishioners.

If Alfred agrees to do this, is he *subject to discipline*?

(A) Yes, because Preacher may bring Alfred before the State Bar Disciplinary Committee if Alfred makes any mistake of law in the memorandum.

(B) Yes, because Alfred is assisting in the unauthorized practice of law.

(C) No, because Alfred has a duty to help educate the public regarding the law.

(D) No, because marriage counseling is an important part of Preacher's duties as pastor.

Question 19

Windy was a named partner in the law firm of Blowhard, Windy & Crooke. After being approached by officials of his political party, Windy decided to run for Governor of State North. Windy won both the primary and the general election and was recently sworn in as the state's new Governor. Although Windy has made it clear to his law partners and the public that he will not practice law during his tenure as Governor, senior partner Blowhard has decided to leave Windy's name on the firm's stationery and on the door of the firm's plush offices.

Is Blowhard's decision *proper*?

(A) Yes, if Windy still has fees coming due from prior cases.

(B) Yes, if Windy has been a member of the firm for a period of at least five years prior to his election as Governor.

(C) No, because Windy is not actually practicing with the firm.

(D) No, because it may create the appearance that the firm has special influence with the state government.

GO ON TO THE NEXT PAGE

Question 20

Pilate, a local assistant district attorney, has just finished prosecuting a case against Dudley Defendant, who was accused of committing a serious felony. Pilate believed he had a strong case, but Justinian, the judge trying the case, ruled to acquit the defendant. Judge Justinian is running for reelection in a contested campaign. The judicial election will occur in two months. Immediately after Dudley's trial is over, Pilate makes the following statement to reporters assembled on the courthouse steps:

> Dudley Defendant is walking away from this courthouse a free man only because of the erroneous rulings of Judge Justinian. In the many years that I have tried cases for the state in this courthouse, I have become aware that in every case heard by Judge Justinian where I have appeared before him as prosecutor, there have always been clearly erroneous rulings in favor of the defendant. I am going to do everything in my power to see that Judge Justinian is not reelected, and I am going to work very hard for the election of Genseric, his opponent in the forthcoming judicial election.

Pilate has personally tried four cases in front of Judge Justinian.

Is Pilate's statement *proper*?

(A) No, because Pilate is a public official and he should not have criticized another public official.

(B) No, because Pilate has brought the administration of justice into disrepute.

(C) Yes, because Pilate spoke out after the verdict had been rendered.

(D) Yes, because the public needs to be informed about incompetent judges.

Question 21

Cato Client brings an extremely complicated case to Art Attorney. This case is so complex that it will require the undivided attention of a qualified attorney for three months to do the necessary research, draw up the proper papers, and take the case to trial. Cato, realizing the complexity of the case, makes the following offer to Art. Cato promises to pay Art $30,000 in advance for three months if Art agrees not to work on other cases during that period of time, it being determined that Art's usual income from fees for a three-month period was $30,000. Art agreed to this arrangement and proceeded to work on Cato's case only. During the first month that he was preparing Cato's case, Art was approached by more than the usual number of prospective clients. Had he accepted employment from those who asked him to represent them during this period, he would have received $30,000 in fees from them. Art, however, in compliance with his agreement with Cato, refused to take on any of these prospective clients. At the end of the first month, Art and Cato had a conference to discuss the case. A number of points of disagreement arose between them; Cato became angry, and summarily fired Art as his counsel. Cato demands the return of the $30,000 fee advance.

Which of the following best describes *proper* conduct for Art?

(A) Retain nothing because the work was not completed to the client's satisfaction.

(B) Retain an amount that represents fair compensation for work actually performed on the case.

(C) Retain the entire $30,000 because Art turned away business worth $30,000 to devote his full attention to Cato's case.

(D) Retain the entire $30,000 because Cato, not Art, breached the agreement.

GO ON TO THE NEXT PAGE

Question 22

Judge Jonathan, considered a great personal injury litigator when he was in private practice, is trying a very complicated commercial law case. He has carefully listened to the opposing attorneys' arguments and has read the briefs several times. He has found neither the oral arguments nor the briefs to be very enlightening. Sheba, a former law partner of Judge Jonathan, is considered to be one of the leading experts on commercial law in the state. Judge Jonathan wishes to lend the briefs to Sheba, and have her write an advisory memorandum on the issues of the case. Judge Jonathan sincerely feels that this will enable him to render a proper judgment in a difficult case.

Is it *proper* for Judge Jonathan to seek such help from Sheba?

(A) Yes, if Judge Jonathan sincerely believes such advice is needed.

(B) Yes, because a judge may seek outside advice on any case.

(C) No, unless he gives notice to the parties and allows them time to respond to Sheba's memorandum.

(D) No, unless he receives written permission from the parties prior to the consultation.

Question 23

Attorney Alondra and client Cyprian agree that Alondra will represent Cyprian for a contingent fee of 25% of any eventual settlement or judgment in Cyprian's personal injury action. The case comes to trial, and the judgment awarded is $20,000. The day after the trial, Cyprian calls Alondra and tells her, "I just talked to my brother-in-law's cousin; he's a file clerk for an insurance company, and he says that any good attorney would've gotten $40,000 for the kind of injury I had. You shouldn't get any fee for getting me a measly $20,000." That afternoon, a check for $20,000, payable to Alondra from the defendant, arrives in Alondra's office.

It would be *proper* for Alondra to:

I. Send $20,000 to Cyprian.

II. Send $15,000 to Cyprian and deposit $5,000 in her client trust account.

III. Send $15,000 to Cyprian and deposit $5,000 in her personal account.

(A) I. only.

(B) III. only.

(C) I. or II., but not III.

(D) II. or III., but not I.

Question 24

Attorney Alex has been retained by Cal Carbon, a wealthy and socially prominent resident of Salt City, where Alex maintains his offices. Cal has held a number of local political offices and is presently engaged in a hotly contested primary election contest for the seat in the United States Congress for Salt City and environs. Cal tells Alex that he is being black-mailed by Sarah Sadstory, who is threatening him with a paternity suit. Cal admits to a brief dalliance with Sarah, but denies being the father of her child. Cal tells Alex that he is willing to settle with Sarah for $10,000 to prevent the bad publicity that would result from the filing of a paternity suit against him and which would probably ruin his chances for election to Congress.

Alex approaches Sarah and tells her that he is willing to negotiate a settlement with her on Cal's behalf. He strongly urges Sarah to retain counsel, as there will be legal documents to be signed should the negotiations succeed, and she should be fully informed of her rights. Sarah tells Alex that she is presently unemployed and lacks the funds to employ an attorney. She further tells him that she thinks she can ade-quately represent her interests herself.

Sarah meets with Alex in a private area of his law offices. During the course of their discus-sions, Alex tells Sarah, "Blood tests will establish that Cal is not the father of your child. Be that as it may, we are willing to offer you $10,000 in settlement of this matter only to avoid unfavor-able publicity."

The next day, Sarah calls Alex and tells him that she will agree to the settlement. Alex tells her to be in his office at 3 p.m., to sign the settlement papers and receive a $10,000 settle-ment check. Alex shows Sarah the settlement papers and explains them to her. Sarah signs the papers and receives a $10,000 check from Alex.

Is Alex *subject to discipline* for negotiating with Sarah?

(A) Yes, because she is a potential adverse party.

(B) Yes, because she is too poor to afford a lawyer.

(C) No, because he advised her to retain coun-sel.

(D) No, because this is not a criminal matter.

Question 25

Lawyer Linda placed an advertisement in *The Clarion*, a newspaper of general circulation published daily in the community in which Linda practiced. The ad was to run every Tues-day and Thursday for a six-month period. The ad listed Linda's office address and office telephone number and properly identified her as an attorney. The ad also included the statement "after 5 p.m., call 932-4585," which was Linda's home telephone number. The ad further included Linda's fax number, which was identified as such.

Was Linda's ad *proper*?

(A) Yes, because all restrictions on lawyer advertising are unconstitutional.

(B) Yes, because the information supplied will make it easier to contact her and make her services more accessible to more people.

(C) No, because it lists her home telephone number.

(D) No, because it is inappropriate to include a fax number in an ad.

Question 26

Alexandra is a recent law school graduate who has just been admitted to the State Bar. She returns to her hometown, Sodville, a town of 20,000 in population in the center of the state. Gastrix, who has practiced out of a one-person office in Sodville for many years, asks Alexandra to associate with him. He produces an employment contract that he asks Alexandra to sign. Gastrix is the only attorney in Sodville who regularly handles bankruptcy cases. The following provisions in the employment contract would bar Alexandra, for one year after leaving Gastrix's employ, from:

I. Practicing law within a 50-mile radius of Sodville.

II. Accepting any cases dealing with bankruptcy.

III. Accepting business from clients who had been represented by Gastrix's law firm during the period of Alexandra's employment.

For agreeing to which of the above provisions would Alexandra be *subject to discipline*?

(A) I. only.

(B) III. only.

(C) I. and II., but not III.

(D) I., II., and III.

Question 27

Shortly after the county grand jury handed down an indictment for armed robbery against fugitive Drooles, District Attorney Daly met with the working press outside the door to the grand jury room. Daly told the press, "You all know that I'm limited as to what I can say about pending cases, so I only have three statements to make to you. You can save your time and mine by not asking any other questions because 'no comment' is the only way I'll be able to answer them." Daly made the following three statements to the press:

I. "Drooles has been indicted by the grand jury for armed robbery, but like all other American citizens he should be considered innocent until proven guilty."

II. "Drooles was indicted after grand jury testimony by two credible witnesses."

III. "The public should be warned that Drooles is a fugitive and is considered to be armed and dangerous."

Which of the above numbered statements was *proper* for the District Attorney to make?

(A) I. only.

(B) I. and II. only.

(C) I. and III. only.

(D) I., II., and III.

GO ON TO THE NEXT PAGE

Question 28

Athos and Porthos are law partners. For many years their firm has represented Cardinal Industries, a local manufacturing firm. Cardinal gives the bulk of its legal business to the firm. Such business is handled by Athos. Porthos has never done any work for Cardinal, but he knows that Cardinal is a major client of the firm. Along with other work for Cardinal, Athos is doing some collection work for Cardinal. A number of Cardinal's customers have not paid their bills, and Athos is in the process of obtaining judgments against them. These particular judgments are all default judgments, as none of the customers have filed answers to the complaints within the time limit stated. Thus, the judgments will be handled in a routine manner by the court with virtually automatic rulings in favor of Cardinal. In the meantime, Porthos has been retained by Dartagnan Products, Inc. Porthos has been asked by Dartagnan to draw up a number of contracts.

Athos files the papers for default judgments against Cardinal's delinquent customers. Among these customers is The Aramis Company. After the papers have been filed, Athos discovers that Aramis is an unincorporated division of Dartagnan Products. Athos tells Porthos. Porthos in turn tells the appropriate officer of Dartagnan that he will have to withdraw from representing Dartagnan because of a conflict of interest. After explaining the problem fully to the Dartagnan officer, they part on very cordial terms with Porthos being given permission to withdraw. Athos proceeds with his cases against Cardinal's delinquent customers.

Is Athos *subject to discipline*?

(A) Yes, because his firm has a conflict of interest.

(B) Yes, unless his client gives informed, written consent.

(C) No, because the default judgments are routine and uncontested.

(D) No, because Porthos no longer represents Dartagnan.

Question 29

Attorney Axelson has been retained by Sludge Corporation. Axelson has done legal work for Sludge for many years and is on very friendly terms with its officers and directors. Axelson is also Chair of the State Bar Association's Committee on Corporate Law. A bill has been introduced into the state legislature that would allow corporate boards of directors to vote by telephone, thus eliminating the necessity for the directors to be physically present at meetings. The State Bar Committee on Corporate Law has been studying the bill and is about to have a meeting where a vote will be taken on whether to recommend to the legislature that the bill be passed. The committee's recommendation will probably carry a great deal of weight with the legislators, and in fact may well be determinative of whether the bill is enacted into law. Axelson meets the president and the treasurer of Sludge after work for cocktails at the Snob Club, a private club to which Axelson and the officers of Sludge belong. Although the occasion is primarily social, the president of Sludge tells Axelson that he is very interested in the work of the State Bar Committee on Corporate Law. The president tells Axelson that he and the other officers of Sludge strongly favor the bill pending in the legislature, as telephone voting would be much more efficient for Sludge and would save all the time and trouble of gathering the directors together for meetings. He urges Axelson to argue in favor of the bill in the committee meeting and to vote in favor of recommending that the bill pass.

Is it *proper* for Axelson to support the corporation bill in the State Bar Committee?

(A) Yes, because he will be acting to further the interests of a client.

(B) Yes, if he conscientiously believes the bill is in the public interest and if he discloses to the committee that one of his corporate clients will benefit if the bill passes.

(C) No, because he has a conflict of interest.

(D) No, if his vote will be decisive in determining the State Bar Committee's recommendation.

Question 30

Wanda is greatly distraught because her late husband Harry provided only a $1,000 bequest for her in his will. Under the terms of his will, the rest of his substantial estate (over $1 million) will go to a fraternal lodge of which Harry was a lifelong member. Wanda consults Anita Attorney. Anita studies the will and determines that there has been an important flaw in its execution. Anita successfully challenges the will's validity, and the probate court rules that Harry's estate will descend by the laws of intestate succession, which means, in this jurisdiction, that Wanda will take all of Harry's estate. Anita charges Wanda a reasonable fee, which Wanda pays promptly. Wanda, however, is so pleased with Anita's work that she wants to give Anita a gift as a token of her gratitude. Wanda goes to an antique shop and purchases a $500 vase. She smilingly presents the vase to Anita.

Will Anita be *subject to discipline* if she accepts the vase?

(A) No, because there is nothing wrong with an attorney accepting a gift from a client.

(B) No, but only if Anita tells Wanda that she should discuss the gift with an informed outside party.

(C) Yes, because Anita has been adequately compensated for her work on Wanda's case and acceptance of the gift constitutes an excessive fee.

(D) Yes, because Anita would be overreaching if she accepted the gift.

Question 31

Newshound regularly wrote the "Courts and the Law" column that appeared twice each week in the *Daily Bugle*, a newspaper of general circulation in the Bricktown area. Newshound approached Arlington, an attorney with offices in Bricktown. Newshound told Arlington that Arlington's name would appear frequently in Newshound's column in a favorable light if Arlington would supply Newshound with "behind the scenes" items about local judges, lawyers, and important or otherwise interesting cases. Arlington readily agreed to Newshound's proposal, and Arlington began supplying information to Newshound. Arlington's name did appear often in Newshound's column, and Arlington was characterized as a "top legal eagle," an "outstanding trial tactician," and otherwise touted in the newspaper.

Is Arlington *subject to discipline*?

(A) Yes, because Arlington has given consideration for favorable publicity.

(B) Yes, because it is unethical to spy on fellow attorneys and judges.

(C) No, because Arlington received nothing of pecuniary value from Newshound.

(D) No, because Arlington's activities are protected by the First Amendment to the United States Constitution.

Question 32

Claude walked into the law offices of lawyer Leda. As Leda was not busy at the time, she agreed to talk to Claude right away. Claude told Leda that he had "a criminal problem," and was concerned that he might be indicted soon. He explained the details of his predicament at length to Leda, but after he finished, Leda told Claude, "You certainly do need a lawyer, but I only handle civil matters. I suggest you consult with my friend Swann; he has a large criminal practice and he's pretty good." Claude went on to retain Swann. A few days after her interview with Claude, Leda read a news item announcing Claude's indictment. It quoted the district attorney at some length. After reading the article, Leda became convinced that something Claude had told her during their interview would probably exonerate Claude or, at the very least, lead to a reduction in the charges against him if the district attorney became aware of the information in Leda's possession.

May Leda reveal the information to the district attorney?

(A) Yes, because Claude did not retain Leda as his counsel.

(B) Yes, because the information will help Claude.

(C) No, because Leda learned the information during the course of an attorney-client relationship.

(D) No, unless Claude consents to the disclosure.

Questions 33 and 34 are based on the following fact pattern:

Booker is employed as an accountant for Hyrax Corporation. Several months ago, Hyrax's president, Potsdam, noticed that there were some discrepancies in the company's books, and that some funds seemed to be missing. Unbeknownst to Booker, Potsdam has been checking Booker's work after hours and he is convinced that Booker has been embezzling funds from Hyrax. Potsdam, on behalf of Hyrax, retains the services of Arnold Attorney to determine if Hyrax has a case against Booker. Arnold agrees with Potsdam that there is a strong indication that Booker has been embezzling funds. In fact, Arnold has already determined that tomorrow he will file a civil suit against Booker to recover Hyrax's money and go to the prosecutor's office to sign an embezzlement complaint against Booker. Arnold, however, tells Potsdam that the more evidence they can obtain against Booker, the stronger their case will be. Potsdam suggests that Arnold interview Booker before he presses charges, as Booker may make some remarks that would implicate him in the embezzlement. Arnold readily agrees to this. Potsdam tells Booker that Arnold is investigating some problems in account recordkeeping to make sure Hyrax's procedures comply with all applicable laws and regulations. He asks Booker to explain how his operation works. Arnold and Booker go to a private office, where Arnold interrogates Booker for approximately two hours. During the course of the interrogation, Booker becomes suspicious of the line of questioning and asks if he is in any trouble. Arnold tells him not to worry, as the amount of money involved is so small that the action may not be worth pursuing.

33. Is Arnold *subject to discipline* for questioning Booker?

   (A) Yes, because of his statements urging Booker not to worry.

   (B) Yes, because all communications with parties who are not represented by counsel are prohibited.

   (C) No, because Arnold was trying in good faith to further the interests of his client.

   (D) No, because Arnold has not yet filed suit on behalf of his client.

34. Assume that during the questioning, Booker not only admitted to embezzling funds, but also described company-wide accounting practices that could subject Hyrax to civil and criminal liability. In an effort to avoid publicity and liability, Hyrax fired Booker but agreed not to turn the matter over to the police. Hyrax has since rectified its accounting problems. Some time later, Hyrax was sued by Cable Corp., one of its creditors, for fraud based on the above accounting practices. During the trial, Cable's attorney calls Arnold to the stand to testify about his conversation with Booker. Hyrax's attorney objects, claiming attorney-client privilege.

   The objection should be:

   (A) Sustained, because Booker talked to Arnold at Potsdam's request and his statements concern accounting.

   (B) Sustained, because Hyrax can claim the privilege on behalf of Booker, its employee.

   (C) Overruled, because Booker was not seeking legal services from Arnold.

   (D) Overruled, because Booker is no longer an employee of Hyrax.

Question 35

Lawyer Lydia represents defendant Dave, who is being prosecuted in a jury trial for an armed robbery and attempted murder that occurred on June 15. Dave has pleaded not guilty to the charges, but Lydia knows that Dave is the perpetrator and that the crime occurred at approximately 10 p.m. Vivian, the victim, testifies that she is certain that the crime occurred at midnight. Dave has an airtight alibi for midnight. At 11:40 p.m. he was arrested on a drunk driving charge, and he was in police custody until 6 a.m. on June 16. On cross-examination, Lydia does nothing to challenge Vivian's recollection of the time of the attack. Also, as the trial unfolds, Lydia does not introduce any evidence at her disposal that would help establish the time of the attack as 10 p.m. Lydia calls as a witness Officer Tatum, who testifies that Dave was in fact in custody at midnight on the night in question. Dave does not testify and is acquitted.

Are Lydia's actions *proper*?

(A) Yes, because Lydia's client is a criminal defendant and constitutional protections take precedence over ethical rules.

(B) Yes, because Lydia did not present false evidence.

(C) No, because she knew that Vivian's testimony was wrong and would mislead the jury as to a crucial component of the case.

(D) No, unless she notified the judge of the true facts outside the presence of the jury, and he instructed her to proceed.

Question 36

Tom Tuttle is the trustee of a trust for the care and support of his deceased sister's minor children. Tuttle wishes to sell some of the trust property to pay for the schooling of one of the children who has special needs. Tuttle hires lawyer Lemke to file the appropriate papers to obtain court approval for the sale. In the course of the conversations between Lemke and Tuttle, Tuttle discloses that he has committed several breaches of trust in the past, including borrowing trust funds to pay for his home improvements and gambling trust funds at the race track. Most of the money has been repaid with reasonable interest, and Tuttle tells Lemke that he has learned a few things about being a trustee, and will be much more careful about his handling of trust funds in the future. Lemke urges Tuttle to tell the court of his wrongdoing and resign as trustee, but Tuttle refuses. Lemke proceeds to represent Tuttle in the proceeding seeking court approval for the sale of trust assets. Lemke fills out all of the court papers truthfully and does not in any way state anything false or misleading to the court. The court does not inquire about the management of the trust or any dissipation of trust assets, and neither Lemke nor Tuttle volunteer the information.

Is Lemke *subject to discipline*?

(A) Yes, because he could have prevented future fraud by Tuttle.

(B) Yes, because he owes a duty of candor to the tribunal.

(C) No, because the information was confidential.

(D) No, because it is the court's duty to supervise a trustee.

GO ON TO THE NEXT PAGE

Question 37

Lawyer Lou LaCosta represented Carter Corp. in some business negotiations with Alconn Construction Inc. Only four persons were present during the negotiations: (i) Carter Corp.'s president, Cora Carter; (ii) Carter Corp.'s business lawyer, Lou LaCosta; (iii) Alconn's chief executive officer, Al Conn; and (iv) Alconn's attorney, Arlo Askew. During the negotiations, Cora Carter and LaCosta clearly heard Al Conn make a certain representation that was vital to the success of the negotiation. Based on Al Conn's representation, the parties reached an oral, handshake agreement to pursue a certain business opportunity as a joint venture. Six months later, after Carter Corp. had invested $11 million in the joint venture, Carter Corp. discovered that Al Conn's representation was false and that Al Conn undoubtedly knew it was false when he made it. Due to the false representation, the joint venture failed, and Carter Corp. lost its $11 million. Carter Corp. sued Alconn Construction Inc. and Al Conn in federal court for intentional misrepresentation. Carter Corp. selected one of LaCosta's law partners, Liddy Gator, as its trial counsel. The defendants denied making the representation. Carter Corp.'s final pretrial statement listed Cora Carter and LaCosta as witnesses for Carter Corp., stating that they would testify that they heard Al Conn make the representation. Counsel for the defendants then moved to disqualify Liddy Gator as trial counsel due to LaCosta's role as a witness for Carter Corp.

Is Liddy Gator *subject to disqualification*?

(A) Yes, because LaCosta is a necessary witness for Carter Corp.; he is the only nonadversary witness who can corroborate Cora Carter's testimony about the representation Al Conn made at the meeting.

(B) Yes, because LaCosta's testimony does not relate to a minor, uncontested matter or to the nature and value of the legal services rendered in the case; nor is this a situation in which disqualification of Liddy Gator would work a substantial hardship on Carter Corp.

(C) No, because there is no conflict of interest presented by LaCosta's role as a witness for Carter Corp., and because a lawyer is ordinarily allowed to serve as trial counsel in a case where her law partner will testify on behalf of her client.

(D) No, because LaCosta's testimony will be merely corroborative; he will simply confirm Cora Carter's testimony that Al Conn made the representation at the meeting.

GO ON TO THE NEXT PAGE

Question 38

Lawyer Larry happened upon an accident scene and stopped his car to see if there was anything he could do to help. Several police officers were on the scene, and Larry told one of them that he was a lawyer and asked if he could do anything to assist the accident victims. The police officer told Larry, "One of the victims is a physician and he claims that he knows that he's going to die from his injuries and he keeps moaning about wanting a will." Larry went over to talk to the physician, who lay on a stretcher. The physician, Peter, begged Larry to write a will for him on the spot. Larry at first demurred, explaining to Peter that he had only been sworn into the state bar two weeks before, he had never written a will for a client, and he had received a "D" in his only law school class covering the subject. Peter said, "I know the police officers will be glad to act as witnesses and I'll keep it simple; I just don't want those greedy worms in my mother's family to get their hands on my estate." After listening to five minutes more of Peter's pleading, Larry agreed to write the will for Peter. He wrote the will on the blank backside of an accident report. Peter signed the will and two police officers witnessed it. Larry told Peter, "Of course, there's no fee for this." Peter died two hours later.

Was Larry's conduct *proper*?

(A) Yes, because he acted in a humane manner appropriate to an emergency situation.

(B) Yes, because Larry was a licensed attorney when he wrote the will.

(C) No, because Larry lacked sufficient knowledge of the law of wills.

(D) No, unless Peter agreed to limit Larry's malpractice liability.

Question 39

Agnes and Bertram represent two corporations who oppose each other in a civil suit. Agnes has filed a petition with the court, seeking to have Bertram removed as opposing counsel. She claims he has a conflict of interest because he once did certain work for her present client. Bertram calls Agnes and tells her that he thinks the conflict of interest matter can be resolved if she listens to his explanation. Agnes and Bertram meet and begin to negotiate the conflict of interest issue, and during the same meeting discuss a settlement of the lawsuit. Agnes and Bertram agree to meet again and continue their discussions. Immediately after the first meeting, Agnes goes to her office and dictates a letter to Judge Jowly, who is trying the case. The letter tells Judge Jowly that Agnes and Bertram are attempting to resolve their differences on the conflict of interest matter and are also negotiating a settlement of the underlying lawsuit. Agnes mails the letter to Judge Jowly that afternoon.

Is Agnes *subject to discipline*?

(A) No, because it is courteous to inform the judge that a settlement is being negotiated.

(B) No, if there were no false or prejudicial statements in the letter.

(C) Yes, unless Agnes sends Bertram a copy of the letter.

(D) Yes, because Agnes failed to inform Bertram before she sent the letter.

GO ON TO THE NEXT PAGE

Question 40

Lawyer Lapin represented defendant Defiance Holding Corp. in a West Dakota civil case brought by three named plaintiffs suing on behalf of a class of similarly situated people. The plaintiffs allege that Defiance owns nearly 100 apartment houses throughout West Dakota and that it refuses to rent apartments to persons of color, in violation of the West Dakota discrimination law. The civil discovery rules of West Dakota do not require voluntary document production—*i.e.,* a litigant does not have to produce a document until the adversary asks for it in a timely, specific document request. Immediately after the complaint was filed, and before any discovery had started, Lapin made a quick but careful investigation of the types of records Defiance keeps concerning tenants and prospective tenants. She found that, starting more than 20 years ago, the manager of each Defiance apartment house filled out a paper "application form" for each person who wanted to rent an apartment. The application form called for information about the person's age, sex, marital status, race, religion, current and past employment, and approximate yearly income.

About eight years ago, Defiance started entering information from the application forms into a computer system, but the computer version omits information about the person's race and religion. The computer system makes it unnecessary to keep and store the paper application forms. Nonetheless, through inertia and corporate ineptitude, Defiance has carefully preserved all of the paper application forms for the past eight years. Lapin advised her client as follows: "I suggest that you get rid of those old paper application forms before the plaintiffs get around to requesting document production. The paper forms are of no use to you, and they could prove embarrassing if the plaintiffs get hold of them." Defiance did as Lapin suggested.

Is Lapin *subject to criminal liability* for suggesting the destruction of the paper application forms?

(A) Yes, because Lapin knew that the paper application forms were relevant and would probably be requested by the plaintiffs.

(B) No, because the class action is a civil case, and there is no criminal liability for discovery misconduct in a civil case.

(C) Yes, because a litigant's destruction of any documents whatsoever while a civil case is pending can be punished as a fraud on the court.

(D) No, because the plaintiffs had not yet requested the production of documents.

Question 41

Jillian has just been elected a judge of the circuit court. She has been assigned to the probate division. Prior to Jillian's elevation to the bench, Jillian was a partner in the law firm of Judkins & Jarvis. During her last week with the firm, Jillian filed a number of very routine, uncontested probate motions. At the time, Jillian had no idea that she would be assigned to the probate division. These routine probate motions have been assigned to her courtroom by a lottery system of random assignment that the circuit court regularly employs to assign cases.

Is it *proper* for Judge Jillian to rule on these motions?

(A) Yes, because they are routine and uncontested.

(B) Yes, if reassignment would cause unreasonable delay.

(C) No, because Judge Jillian has a conflict of interest.

(D) No, because judges may never rule on issues when their former law firm is involved.

GO ON TO THE NEXT PAGE

Question 42

Mr. Smith and Ms. Jones wish to trade parcels of real estate. Smith presently owns Puceacre and Jones owns Limeacre. Jones retains Alan Attorney as counsel. Jones wishes to complete the deal as cheaply as possible. She asks Alan to draw up papers for the transfer of property and asks him to order a title search and survey of Puceacre. Alan recommended a similar search and survey for Limeacre as well, but Jones replied that she wished to save money and did not need a search and survey for Limeacre. Jones and Smith exchange warranty deeds. Smith takes possession of Limeacre, and Jones takes possession of Puceacre.

A year later, Smith contracts to sell Limeacre. The prospective purchaser of Limeacre orders a title search and survey. He then discovers that there are defects that will substantially reduce the value of the property. Smith eventually sells Limeacre, but at a price much lower than he could have commanded had the defects not been present. Smith sues Jones for damages and receives an award of $10,000. Jones feels that Alan is responsible for this and sues him to recover the $10,000.

Is Alan *subject to liability for malpractice?*

(A) Yes, because a competent attorney would have insisted upon a title search and survey for Limeacre.

(B) Yes, because Jones was a foreseeable plaintiff in a malpractice case.

(C) No, because he was following his client's instructions.

(D) No, because Smith did not insist on Jones presenting a title search and survey.

Question 43

Lawyer LePage represents Prudence, the plaintiff in a sexual harassment case against defendant Dartmore Industries, Inc. Dartmore is represented by its regular corporate counsel, Clem. Prudence, who works on an assembly line, alleges that she was repeatedly harassed by the foreman on her work shift, Frank Farmer. Furthermore, she alleges that the plant manager, Marianne Martin, was aware of Farmer's misconduct and did nothing to stop it. Prudence tells LePage that two of her co-workers on the assembly line, Will Whorley and Wendy Winston, each witnessed harassment incidents, but neither Whorley nor Winston reported the incidents to supervisory personnel. Whorley quit working for Dartmore at about the time Prudence filed her lawsuit.

LePage wants to do some fact investigation before he starts discovery in the case. Which of the following best states *proper* conduct for LePage in interviewing the potential witnesses?

(A) LePage may freely interview Martin, Whorley, and Winston because they are simply third-party witnesses, but he must obtain Clem's consent to interview Farmer.

(B) LePage may freely interview Whorley and Winston, but he must obtain Clem's consent to interview Farmer and Martin.

(C) LePage may freely interview Whorley, but he must obtain Clem's consent to interview Farmer, Martin, and Winston.

(D) It would be improper for LePage to interview any of these people without Clem's consent.

GO ON TO THE NEXT PAGE

Question 44

Arlington is an attorney engaged in private practice in the city of New Novgorod. Arlington has many friends who belong to the Ancient Society of Sultans, a fraternal and charitable organization with chapters throughout the state. Arlington is not a member of the Society, but knows a number of its officers socially and has performed legal work for them on matters unrelated to the Society. The officers of the Society are sometimes consulted by members who have legal problems. The officers, being very pleased with the quality of Arlington's work, often refer such members to Arlington. Arlington has never asked the officers for such referrals, but is, of course, very pleased because he has earned substantial fees from these referrals.

The Society is presently organized as an unincorporated association, but the leaders are interested in incorporating the Society under the State Nonprofit Corporation Act. One of the officers asks Arlington what his fee would be for incorporating the Society. Arlington tells the officer that he is very grateful for the client referrals from the Society and, as a token of his appreciation, he will not charge a fee for the incorporation work.

Is Arlington *subject to discipline*?

(A) Yes, because an attorney must not give something of value in return for client referrals.

(B) Yes, because only clients unable to pay should be given free legal services.

(C) No, because an attorney always has the option of waiving a fee.

(D) No, because Arlington did not solicit the referrals.

Question 45

Attorney Ace placed an advertisement that ran daily in the classified section of the *Pikeville News Journal*, a newspaper of general circulation, widely read in the Pikeville area where Ace practiced. Besides stating Ace's office address and telephone number, and identifying Ace as a licensed attorney, the advertisement included the following statement:

DIVORCES - LOW RATES!!!
Just $300, plus costs for uncontested divorces

According to bar association surveys, the "low average" fee in the Pikeville area for an uncontested divorce is $325, plus costs.

Is Ace's advertising *proper*?

(A) Yes, because the legal profession imposes no substantive limitations on comparative advertising.

(B) Yes, because Ace's rates really are low.

(C) No, because Ace fails to state his range of fees for contested divorces.

(D) No, because the advertisement is in bad taste and constitutes a self-serving attempt to solicit business at the expense of fellow attorneys.

Question 46

Attorney Augusta decided to run against incumbent Judge Isadore in the forthcoming election. Judge Isadore was widely regarded by members of the local bar as a "party hack," who had no business being on the bench. The opposition party was very pleased to be able to slate Augusta because she had a high reputation for intelligence, honesty, and overall competence as an attorney. Augusta realizes that she will have to fight an uphill battle to unseat Judge Isadore because her political party is a minority party in the county and most voters know very little about judges and candidates for the judiciary and therefore, voters are likely to vote a straight ticket for judges of their own political party. Augusta wants the public to know that Isadore has been a poor judge, but she also wishes to comply with all ethical rules governing judicial campaigns. Attorney Eve, Augusta's best friend and chief advisor, suggests that Augusta should make the following statements during her campaign:

I.   "Judge Isadore has had the highest percentage of cases reversed on appeal of any judge in the state over the past two years."

II. "Eighteen months ago, Judge Isadore was publicly disciplined by the State Judicial Conduct Board."

III. "A recent poll taken by the local bar association indicates that a majority of bar association members feel that Judge Isadore lacks the proper judicial temperament."

IV. "A recent newspaper article comparing judges of the county states that Judge Isadore has handed out an average sentence of only two and a half years to persons convicted of serious felonies. I won't be soft on crime!"

Assume that all the facts cited in the numbered statements are accurate.

Which, if any, of the numbered statements would it be *proper* for Augusta to make in her judicial campaign?

(A) I. and II., but not III. and IV.

(B) II. and III., but not I. and IV.

(C) III. and IV., but not I. and II.

(D) I., II., and III., but not IV.

Question 47

Judge Jacques is often referred to behind his back as "Judge Continuance" by lawyers who practice in Bayou County. This soubriquet is well-deserved because Judge Jacques is known to grant continuances whenever requested by an attorney, regardless of the substantiality of the attorney's grounds. He has turned down a continuance request on occasion, but such occasions are so few and far between that local attorneys are shocked when they hear of them. When queried by his colleague Judge Jeanne about his policy on continuances, Judge Jacques told her, "This society has gotten to be litigation crazy. It's sue, sue, sue over every little thing. Most of this stuff can be settled between the parties if they really want to try. If I grant a continuance, it gives the parties that much more time to come to their senses and settle. If they settle, it saves them and the taxpayers the expense of a full-blown trial. This country and its court systems would be a lot saner if more judges tried to promote settlements like I do."

Is Judge Jacques's policy of granting continuances to promote settlements *proper*?

(A) Yes, because the granting of continuances is clearly within the bounds of judicial discretion.

(B) Yes, if Judge Jacques sincerely believes that his lenient continuance policy promotes settlements and that settlements promote a more rational and amicable system of justice.

(C) No, because judges have no duty to promote settlements.

(D) No, because judges have a duty to expedite litigation.

Question 48

The legislature of State A conducted open hearings concerning a bill pending in the state legislature that would make it much more difficult for corporations chartered in State A to be taken over by corporate raiders. By making unfriendly takeovers more difficult, the proponents of the bill hope to save jobs in State A and to encourage corporations not now chartered in State A to obtain State A charters, which would bring added revenue to the state. Attorney Armor, a senior partner in the prestigious firm of Armor, Baldwin & Chase, asked to testify at the hearings. Armor had been retained by Tentacle Corporation and was asked by Tentacle's president to testify against the pending legislation at the legislative hearings. Tentacle's president also told Armor that under no circumstances was he to tell the legislature that he was working for Tentacle or to mention the name of Tentacle in his testimony. Armor complied with Tentacle's strictures and never mentioned that he was being retained to give testimony against the pending legislation. Armor's testimony before the legislative committee was effective and hard-hitting. After his testimony, Armor was asked a few questions by committee members, but he was never asked if he was appearing on some other party's behalf.

Was Armor's conduct at the hearing *proper*?

(A) Yes, because his client specifically instructed him not to reveal the client's name.

(B) Yes, because no one asked Armor if he was appearing at the hearings on behalf of a client.

(C) No, because he did not disclose that he was appearing at the hearings in a representative capacity.

(D) No, because an attorney may not practice deception upon a legislative body.

GO ON TO THE NEXT PAGE

Question 49

Uncle, a wealthy landowner in Moocow County, has become very infirm in his old age, even though his mind is still very sharp. His doctor tells Uncle that although Uncle has survived open-heart surgery, he will never be really robust and healthy again. In fact, the doctor says that Uncle should either enter a nursing home or employ a nurse to care for him full-time at his ranch. Uncle, who has always prided himself on his independence, shudders at the thought of being put in a nursing home. He also finds the thought of bringing a stranger into his home to nurse him distasteful. Uncle contacts Niece, his youngest sister's daughter, who is a registered nurse employed as a head nurse at a major research hospital in a large city in another state. Uncle urges Niece to come and live with him at the ranch and take care of him. Uncle, always known in Moocow County for his generosity, tells Niece that he understands she would be making a major sacrifice and that "I aim to make this worth your while. The Doc tells me I don't have more than a year or two left anyway, but I know it's tough for a young, educated, city gal to be stuck out here in Moocow County with nothin' but old men, steers, and no-account cowboys. So if you stay and take care of me until I die, I'll leave you one-third of my ranch in my will." Niece agrees to care for Uncle.

Niece arrives in Obelisk, the county seat of Moocow County where Uncle is hospitalized. She is met at the train by Cowhand, one of Uncle's employees, who takes Niece to the hospital. Uncle is then released from the hospital, but before going home he stops by the law offices of Archon, his attorney, to pick up some tax documents Archon has completed for him. Uncle tells Archon, in the presence of both Niece and Cowhand, "The next time I come to town, I'm going to have you draw up a new will for me, leaving one-third of my ranch to Niece, who's come all the way out here to Obelisk to take care of her poor old uncle."

Uncle never has another opportunity to go into Obelisk. Niece feels he is too weak to travel very much after his operation, and she insists that he stay home where she can care for him. Two months later, Uncle has a massive heart attack, followed by a stroke. He goes into a lingering coma and dies after two weeks in the comatose state. Uncle's will is duly admitted to probate, and under its terms, Uncle left everything he had to Son, Uncle's only child, who is a highly successful businessman in another state.

Son arrives in Obelisk to attend Uncle's funeral and to settle the affairs of his father's estate. Naturally, he consults with Archon. Son mentions to Archon that he thinks that it was very good of Niece to come all the way to Obelisk to care for Uncle, and that he is sure that Uncle would have wanted to reward her in some special way, even though there is no mention of Niece in the will. Son tells Archon that he would like to do the "right thing," but has no idea what Uncle might have had in mind.

Which of the following states the *most* that Archon *may* do in attempting to carry out Uncle's wishes?

(A) Remain silent.

(B) Suggest that Son might want to talk to Cowhand about Uncle's intentions.

(C) Tell Son about Uncle's statement about leaving one-third of the ranch to Niece, but offer no further advice.

(D) Tell Son about Uncle's statement and counsel Son to deed one-third of the ranch to Niece.

GO ON TO THE NEXT PAGE

Question 50

Larry Litiger has been practicing law for two years. The following statements were broadcast in a recent radio ad:

I. "Larry Litiger specializes in personal injury and divorce cases."

II. "Larry Litiger comes from a long line of lawyers. In fact, his father and grandfather are both judges."

III. "Larry has never lost a jury trial, and 99% of his clients end up receiving some form of payment."

IV. "Litiger succeeds where others fail. Don't find out the hard way; call Litiger first."

Assuming that all of the above statements are true and that Litiger complied with all the procedural requirements for running a radio advertisement, which of the statements are *proper*?

(A) I. and II., but not III. or IV.

(B) I. only.

(C) II. and III., but not I. or IV.

(D) I. and IV., but not II. or III.

Question 51

State One is right across the river from State Two, and there is a constant flow of people and commerce from one state to the other. Many people work in one state and live in the other, and many people cross the river to shop, go to school, seek entertainment, attend religious services, and the like. Attorney Agnew, a solo practitioner, lives in State One but maintains his law office in State Two. He limits his practice to drunk driving defense. In 1967, Agnew became a member of the bar in States One and Two, but a few years ago, he stopped paying his bar dues in State One and stopped fulfilling State One's continuing legal education ("CLE") requirements. State One placed him on its inactive list, which means that he cannot practice law in State One until he pays the balance in his dues account and completes the CLE requirements. Nevertheless, Agnew advertises his law office in the State One Yellow Pages phone book and in various other media in State One. He regularly represents drunk driving clients who live in State One and who are charged with drunk driving in State One's courts. When a State One client finds it inconvenient to travel to Agnew's law office in State Two, Agnew meets the client at Agnew's home in State One. Recently, Agnew appeared on behalf of a drunk driving client before a young, newly appointed State One judge who asked him: "Counselor, are you admitted to practice here?" Agnew responded cheerfully: "Your Honor, I was admitted to practice here back in 1967, long before Your Honor was born." The judge replied: "Very well then, you may proceed."

Is Agnew *subject to discipline* by the bar of State One?

(A) No, because Agnew does not maintain a law office in State One, and because his response to the young judge was the literal truth.

(B) No, because State One has no jurisdiction to discipline a lawyer who is not actively engaged in law practice in State One.

(C) Yes, not because of unauthorized law practice in State One, but because he misled the judge by his half-true response to the judge's question.

(D) Yes, both because of his unauthorized law practice in State One, and because he misled the judge by his half-true response to the judge's question.

Question 52

State One has a so-called three strikes law that is designed to give life sentences to career felons. When a person is convicted of her third felony, the three strikes law forces the sentencing judge to give the person a life sentence, even if the third felony does not involve violence, and even if the maximum punishment for the third felony by itself would be as little as two years in state prison. Many State One judges believe that the three strikes law is unconscionably harsh and should be repealed. State One's legislature, however, has refused to act. A citizen group was successful in qualifying a voter initiative to abolish the three strikes law. Many activist judges have spoken out publicly in favor of the voter initiative. Lawyer Logan has both an accounting degree and a law degree. She earns most of her living by serving as a court-appointed master in complex cases where her dual skills are useful. The bulk of her service is in a court that is dominated by activist judges who favor the voter initiative. For the sole purpose of getting more court appointments from those judges, Logan has contributed 200 hours of her time to the campaign in favor of the voter initiative.

Which of the following statements are true?

I.   The activist judges acted **properly** in speaking out in public in favor of the voter initiative.

II. The activist judges are **subject to discipline** for speaking out in public in favor of the voter initiative.

III. Logan acted **properly** in contributing her time to the campaign in favor of the voter initiative.

IV. Logan is **subject to discipline** for contributing her time to the campaign for the purpose of getting more court appointments.

(A) II. and III. only.

(B) I. and IV. only.

(C) II. and IV. only.

(D) I. and III. only.

GO ON TO THE NEXT PAGE

Question 53

Attorney Aufhalter and lawyer Lebenhoff are law partners in the firm of Aufhalter & Lebenhoff. They practice in a rural community in mid-America; only three other law firms practice in that community. Aufhalter volunteers her time every Saturday morning to sit in a little room at the County Public Library where she provides quick answers to simple legal questions posed by community members who cannot afford to consult a lawyer in the ordinary manner. The program is sponsored by the County Bar Association, a nonprofit organization. Aufhalter makes clear to each person that she will answer the person's question as best she can, without doing legal research, and that she will not represent the person in any long-term sense. One Saturday morning, Aufhalter advised farmer Feeney about how to represent himself, *in propria persona,* as plaintiff in a lawsuit against a local company, Ralph's Roofing Corp., for putting a defective roof on Feeney's barn. A few weeks later, Feeney filed the suit, and Ralph's Roofing Corp. hired Lebenhoff to defend it against Feeney's suit. That was the first time Ralph's had consulted either Lebenhoff or his firm. When he agreed to defend Ralph's, Lebenhoff did not realize that Aufhalter had previously advised Feeney on how to bring the suit; indeed, Aufhalter purposely never tells Lebenhoff anything about her Saturday morning volunteer work.

Which of the following is most nearly correct?

(A) Lebenhoff *may* defend Ralph's, even though Aufhalter had previously advised Feeney on the matter.

(B) Lebenhoff *may* defend Ralph's, but only if both Feeney and Ralph's give informed, written consent.

(C) Lebenhoff *may* defend Ralph's, but only if Aufhalter is screened off from the case and is apportioned no part of the fee in the case, and only if Feeney gives informed, written consent.

(D) Lebenhoff *may* defend Ralph's, but only if Aufhalter promises in writing not to tell Lebenhoff anything that Feeney told her in confidence about the matter.

Question 54

Attorney Arquette recently graduated from law school and set up his own solo practice law office. He hopes to develop a prosperous clientele of business clients, but meanwhile, he drives a taxi four nights a week, from 6 p.m. to midnight. Sometimes when a taxi passenger appears to be a prosperous business person, Arquette mentions that he is looking for clients in his new business law practice; at that point, he usually hands the passenger one of his professional cards and says: "Please call me the next time you need a lawyer." When a taxi passenger is drunk, inexperienced, or not paying attention, Arquette sometimes does not start the taxi meter running. At the end of the ride, he charges the passenger as much as he thinks the passenger will pay without starting a fight. Because the ride is not recorded on the taxi meter, Arquette pockets the entire fare without having to divide it with the taxi company.

Is Arquette *subject to discipline* by the bar?

(A) Yes, because he must follow all of the legal ethics rules when he drives the taxi.

(B) No, because his solicitation of legal business is limited to people with whom he already has a relationship as a taxi driver.

(C) Yes, because he sometimes cheats by failing to start the taxi meter.

(D) No, because he is not providing legal services to his taxi passengers.

GO ON TO THE NEXT PAGE

Question 55

Attorney Arbuckle was in solo practice on the West Coast. His wife got a new job on the East Coast so he started looking for someone to buy his West Coast practice. Arbuckle's labor and employment law practice consisted entirely of representing plaintiffs in ongoing litigation and administrative proceedings to redress employment discrimination, dangerous or hostile conditions in the workplace, sexual harassment, race discrimination in the workplace, and the like. All of Arbuckle's clients had signed contingent fee agreements in which they promised to pay the litigation or administrative expenses, and Arbuckle promised to represent them in return for 20% of their net pretax winnings. This arrangement is more favorable to the clients than any other arrangement they could get from other lawyers in the community for similar work. Arbuckle quickly found seven different interested buyers for his practice. Because Arbuckle wanted to sell promptly, he did not investigate the training, experience, or disciplinary records of the seven. Rather, he sold the practice to the one who offered the highest price, and that was attorney Adder. If Arbuckle had investigated, he would have discovered that Adder had almost no experience in labor and employment law, and that the state bar had disciplined her twice for client neglect and client abandonment. Arbuckle gave the requisite notice of sale to his clients, and Adder took over the office, the case files, the books, the computers, the books of account, and the debts, duties, and assets of Arbuckle's practice. In due course, Adder worked her way through the case files, separating them into two piles—the likely winners and the likely losers. She then wrote letters to the likely losers, offering them a new contingent fee agreement that would give her 35% of their net pretax winnings. She explained that if they did not wish to sign the new agreement, she would seek permission from the tribunal to withdraw as their counsel.

Which of the following is most nearly correct?

(A) Arbuckle is *subject to discipline* for selling his practice to the highest bidder.

(B) Adder is *subject to discipline* for threatening to withdraw from representing clients who would not sign the new 35% contingent fee agreement.

(C) Adder's identification of likely winners and likely losers was *proper*, as was her offer of a new 35% contingent fee agreement to the likely losers.

(D) Arbuckle's decision not to investigate the backgrounds of the seven prospective buyers was *proper*, as was his decision to sell his law practice.

GO ON TO THE NEXT PAGE

Question 56

In the federal courts and the courts of some states, when a litigant claims that a document is protected by the attorney-client privilege, the trial judge can order the litigant to produce the document for in camera inspection (*i.e.*, private, confidential inspection by the judge) so that the judge can decide whether the document really is privileged. State Acadia is one of a few jurisdictions that follow the opposite rule: a trial judge must not force a litigant to produce a privileged document for in camera inspection; the trial judge must use the surrounding circumstances and whatever other evidence is available when deciding whether the privilege claim is valid. In a federal case where jurisdiction is based only on diversity of citizenship, the federal judge must apply the privilege law that would be applied by a state court in the state where the federal court sits. Federal District Judge Jenner was presiding in a diversity case in State Acadia. The defendant's lawyer refused to produce a particular letter from defendant's outside patent counsel to defendant's president. The defendant's lawyer asserted the attorney-client privilege on behalf of her client. Judge Jenner glowered down at the defendant's lawyer and ordered her to produce the letter for in camera inspection so that he could see whether the letter was about a legal matter or some nonprivileged subject. The defendant's lawyer would not allow the judge to see the letter, referring him to the clear law of State Acadia. Judge Jenner growled: "Listen here, young lady, I've been a federal judge longer than you've been alive, and I am ordering you to hand me that letter."

Which of the following is the *proper* response for the defendant's lawyer to make?

(A) Don't try to push me around, you old coot. You've got no right to see the letter, and if you want to take it from me, you'll have to wrestle me for it.

(B) I respectfully ask the court to stay the order to allow me time to consult with my client and to seek an interlocutory appeal or extraordinary writ if necessary.

(C) Very well, Your Honor, but I want the record to show that I am handing you the letter under protest and that my client does not waive its attorney-client privilege.

(D) Oh, stop it, Your Honor. I've cited you to the law of State Acadia, which is as clear as it could possibly be—you've got no right to see the letter. You're way out of line here.

GO ON TO THE NEXT PAGE

Question 57

Counsel Cloe is the chief in-house legal officer of VaxTec, a multibillion-dollar corporation that makes and sells a range of vaccines, serums, and pharmaceuticals in the United States, Canada, Mexico, and several nations of the European Union ("EU"). VaxTec's stock is publicly traded in interstate commerce, and the company is within the jurisdiction of the Securities and Exchange Commission ("SEC"). Cloe hired an outside lawyer, Lancelot, to supervise the preparation of VaxTec's Form 10-K annual report to the SEC. When Lancelot was eating lunch by himself in the company cafeteria one day, a low-echelon VaxTec employee named Skrannel passed Lancelot a note stating that she had heard from someone in a position to know that VaxTec had sold 144 units of snake anti-toxin in Germany without obtaining a proper EU sales clearance. Selling without a proper sales clearance violates EU law, for which the EU could theoretically fine VaxTec 1% of the sales price, which in this case would be $26. Assume that a contingent liability of $26 is too low to require disclosure in the Form 10-K. When he asked around the company about Skrannel, Lancelot learned that she is a malicious gossip who passes along all kinds of stories, some true, some false.

Which of the following reasons would excuse Lancelot from reporting Skrannel's information to Counsel Cloe pursuant to the SEC's Sarbanes-Oxley regulations?

I.   Lancelot was hired merely to supervise the preparation of the Form 10-K, not to appear before the SEC on behalf of VaxTec.

II. A reasonable lawyer would regard Skrannel's story as not credible.

III. A $26 violation of the EU's law on sales clearances is not the kind of law violation that a securities lawyer must report under the Sarbanes-Oxley regulations.

IV. What Skrannel told Lancelot is privileged, and Lancelot therefore must not reveal it to Cloe.

(A) I. and IV. only.

(B) II. only.

(C) IV. only.

(D) II. and III. only.

GO ON TO THE NEXT PAGE

Question 58

Two days after the jury convicted her client for second degree murder, lawyer Laura Loudin made an uninvited visit to the home of jury member Janice Jergins. Loudin is a physically imposing woman, just over six feet tall and close to 180 pounds. Jergins is seven inches shorter, 70 pounds lighter, and 45 years older than Loudin. The law of this jurisdiction is completely silent about lawyers talking with members of a discharged jury, and the trial judge did not make any orders or comments on that subject. Here is the opening of the conversation between Loudin and Jergins:

Loudin: Good afternoon, Miss Jergins. I wonder if I might come in to chat with you for a few moments about the *Hopkins* trial?

Jergins: Yes, I suppose so. Please come in.

Loudin: [Seating herself in the living room] No doubt you will understand my dismay when my client, Mr. Hopkins, was convicted the other day. I have heard that one of the jurors, Ms. Snupe, went to the scene of the incident by herself and made some measurements. Did that happen?

Jergins: Yes. No . . . well. I don't want to cause any trouble.

Loudin: Did Ms. Snupe tell the rest of you jurors about the measurements she made?

Jergins: I really don't want to cause any trouble. Do I have to talk to you about this?

Loudin: I am not your lawyer, so I am not allowed to discuss your legal duty with you, but I can say that I think you have a moral duty to tell me whether Ms. Snupe brought outside evidence into the jury deliberations.

Jergins: Oh dear, I don't know what to do. I'd like you to leave, please.

Loudin: I will if you answer just one question for me: Did Ms. Snupe tell the jury about the measurements she made at the scene?

What is the *earliest* point in this conversation at which Loudin becomes *subject to discipline*?

(A)   She is *subject to discipline* for going to Jergins's home in the first place because a lawyer who was involved in a case must not talk about the jury deliberations with a discharged juror.

(B)   She is *subject to discipline* for entering Jergins's home because the disparities in size and age between Loudin and Jergins make the conversation inherently coercive.

(C)   She is *subject to discipline* for asking the final question because at that point Jergins had clearly asked her to leave.

(D)   She is not *subject to discipline* at all because a lawyer has a right to communicate with a discharged juror to find out whether improper information found its way into the jury deliberations.

GO ON TO THE NEXT PAGE

Question 59

Attorney Aaron and lawyer Lotus represent the opposing parties in a hard-fought civil case. Each attorney knows that the opposing attorney is diligent, forthright, and careful. One morning, Aaron received an e-mail from Lotus's secretary. The e-mail read: "Ms. Lotus has come down with the flu, and we don't expect her back at the office for the rest of this week. She has asked me to send you this message, along with these four attachments, which are documents that the two of you have discussed in connection with the *Cryolite* litigation." The first three e-mail attachments were documents that Lotus had agreed to produce in response to Aaron's discovery request. The fourth attachment was a letter to Lotus from the in-house counsel of Lotus's client. Aaron could tell from reading the first few lines that the letter was a confidential communication between attorney and client, and that Lotus obviously did not intend for it to be sent to Aaron.

Which of the following best states the *proper* course of action for Aaron to take?

(A) Continue reading the fourth attachment and preserve a hard copy for possible further use on behalf of his client.

(B) Delete the fourth attachment from his computer's memory and not tell anyone about the mistake.

(C) Stop reading the fourth attachment and notify the judge about the mistake.

(D) Stop reading the fourth attachment and notify Lotus about the mistake.

Question 60

New World Theatricals Corporation ("NWTC") owns the copyrights to a large repertoire of plays, and it licenses the copyrights throughout the United States. NWTC's headquarters is in State One, and it uses Marlowe & Jonson, a large private law firm in State One, to do all of its legal work. NWTC licensed the movie rights from one of its copyrighted plays to Panther Productions, Inc., a major motion picture studio headquartered in State Two. All of Marlowe & Jonson's lawyers are admitted to practice in State One, but not a single one of them is admitted to practice in State Two. The license agreement between NWTC and Panther was drafted by counsel for Panther, and it specifies that any dispute about the license will be resolved by arbitration in State Two. Attorney Attaway, one of Marlowe & Jonson's copyright lawyers, represented NWTC in the license negotiations, which took place in State Two. When Panther finished making the movie, a dispute arose about how much royalty it owed NWTC under the license. Pursuant to the arbitration clause of the license, the parties arranged to arbitrate the dispute in State Two. NWTC asked lawyer Lunge, one of Marlowe & Jonson's best litigators, to represent it at the arbitration. State Two's arbitration act says nothing about pro hac vice admission of out-of-state lawyers in arbitration proceedings.

Which of the following is most nearly correct?

(A) Attaway is *subject to discipline* for negotiating the license in State Two, and Lunge will be *subject to discipline* if he represents NWTC in the arbitration in State Two.

(B) It was *proper* for Attaway to negotiate the license in State Two, and Lunge *may* represent NWTC at the arbitration in State Two.

(C) Attaway is *subject to discipline* for negotiating the license in State Two, but Lunge *may* represent NWTC at the arbitration in State Two.

(D) It was *proper* for Attaway to negotiate the license in State Two, but Lunge will be *subject to discipline* if he represents NWTC in the arbitration in State Two.

STOP

ANSWER SHEET

1 Ⓐ Ⓑ Ⓒ Ⓓ		31 Ⓐ Ⓑ Ⓒ Ⓓ	
2 Ⓐ Ⓑ Ⓒ Ⓓ		32 Ⓐ Ⓑ Ⓒ Ⓓ	
3 Ⓐ Ⓑ Ⓒ Ⓓ		33 Ⓐ Ⓑ Ⓒ Ⓓ	
4 Ⓐ Ⓑ Ⓒ Ⓓ		34 Ⓐ Ⓑ Ⓒ Ⓓ	
5 Ⓐ Ⓑ Ⓒ Ⓓ		35 Ⓐ Ⓑ Ⓒ Ⓓ	
6 Ⓐ Ⓑ Ⓒ Ⓓ		36 Ⓐ Ⓑ Ⓒ Ⓓ	
7 Ⓐ Ⓑ Ⓒ Ⓓ		37 Ⓐ Ⓑ Ⓒ Ⓓ	
8 Ⓐ Ⓑ Ⓒ Ⓓ		38 Ⓐ Ⓑ Ⓒ Ⓓ	
9 Ⓐ Ⓑ Ⓒ Ⓓ		39 Ⓐ Ⓑ Ⓒ Ⓓ	
10 Ⓐ Ⓑ Ⓒ Ⓓ		40 Ⓐ Ⓑ Ⓒ Ⓓ	
11 Ⓐ Ⓑ Ⓒ Ⓓ		41 Ⓐ Ⓑ Ⓒ Ⓓ	
12 Ⓐ Ⓑ Ⓒ Ⓓ		42 Ⓐ Ⓑ Ⓒ Ⓓ	
13 Ⓐ Ⓑ Ⓒ Ⓓ		43 Ⓐ Ⓑ Ⓒ Ⓓ	
14 Ⓐ Ⓑ Ⓒ Ⓓ		44 Ⓐ Ⓑ Ⓒ Ⓓ	
15 Ⓐ Ⓑ Ⓒ Ⓓ		45 Ⓐ Ⓑ Ⓒ Ⓓ	
16 Ⓐ Ⓑ Ⓒ Ⓓ		46 Ⓐ Ⓑ Ⓒ Ⓓ	
17 Ⓐ Ⓑ Ⓒ Ⓓ		47 Ⓐ Ⓑ Ⓒ Ⓓ	
18 Ⓐ Ⓑ Ⓒ Ⓓ		48 Ⓐ Ⓑ Ⓒ Ⓓ	
19 Ⓐ Ⓑ Ⓒ Ⓓ		49 Ⓐ Ⓑ Ⓒ Ⓓ	
20 Ⓐ Ⓑ Ⓒ Ⓓ		50 Ⓐ Ⓑ Ⓒ Ⓓ	
21 Ⓐ Ⓑ Ⓒ Ⓓ		51 Ⓐ Ⓑ Ⓒ Ⓓ	
22 Ⓐ Ⓑ Ⓒ Ⓓ		52 Ⓐ Ⓑ Ⓒ Ⓓ	
23 Ⓐ Ⓑ Ⓒ Ⓓ		53 Ⓐ Ⓑ Ⓒ Ⓓ	
24 Ⓐ Ⓑ Ⓒ Ⓓ		54 Ⓐ Ⓑ Ⓒ Ⓓ	
25 Ⓐ Ⓑ Ⓒ Ⓓ		55 Ⓐ Ⓑ Ⓒ Ⓓ	
26 Ⓐ Ⓑ Ⓒ Ⓓ		56 Ⓐ Ⓑ Ⓒ Ⓓ	
27 Ⓐ Ⓑ Ⓒ Ⓓ		57 Ⓐ Ⓑ Ⓒ Ⓓ	
28 Ⓐ Ⓑ Ⓒ Ⓓ		58 Ⓐ Ⓑ Ⓒ Ⓓ	
29 Ⓐ Ⓑ Ⓒ Ⓓ		59 Ⓐ Ⓑ Ⓒ Ⓓ	
30 Ⓐ Ⓑ Ⓒ Ⓓ		60 Ⓐ Ⓑ Ⓒ Ⓓ	

Answer to Question 1

(A)   A lawyer at trial must not state her own personal opinion about the credibility of witnesses. [ABA Model Rule 3.4(e)] Item III. reflects personal opinion on the credibility of a witness. The other comments are acceptable. Thus, (A) is correct, and (B), (C), and (D) are incorrect.

Answer to Question 2

(C)   ABA Model Rule 1.12(a) provides that a lawyer must not represent anyone in connection with a matter in which the lawyer participated personally and substantially as a judge, unless all parties to the proceedings give informed, written consent. Thus, (C) is correct, and (A) and (B) are incorrect. (D) is incorrect because a judge may subsequently engage in private practice, except she may not participate in cases where she was personally and substantially involved.

Answer to Question 3

(B)   Under ABA Model Rule 5.5(b), a lawyer must not aid a nonlawyer in the unauthorized practice of law. Although a lawyer may delegate certain tasks to laypersons, such delegation is professionally acceptable only if the lawyer: (i) supervises the delegated work, and (ii) remains professionally responsible for the work product. [Comment 2 to ABA Model Rule 5.5] The drafting of forms by a law student is permissible if the lawyer complies with the conditions stated above, which Arlo appears to have done from the facts. Thus, the facts in item I. do not subject Arlo to discipline. There is nothing impermissible about item II.—laypersons conducting interviews and obtaining the interviewees' signatures on written versions of the interviews. However, reaching a settlement on behalf of a client clearly constitutes the practice of law. Thus, Arlo is subject to discipline only on the facts of item III. Therefore, (B) is correct, and (A), (C), and (D) are incorrect.

Answer to Question 4

(C)   If one lawyer within a firm has a conflict of interest and cannot take on a matter, no other lawyer in the firm may take on the matter either. [ABA Model Rule 1.10(a)] One situation that would create a concurrent conflict would be if there is a significant risk that the representation of a client will be materially limited by the lawyer's own interest or his responsibilities to another client, a former client, or a third person. [ABA Model Rule 1.7(a)] Alfonso would be prohibited from representing Octopus in this matter because such representation would be materially limited by his responsibilities, as mayor, to the city. Thus, Alfonso's partner Bella is also prohibited from such representation. Therefore, (A) and (B) are incorrect. (D) is also incorrect; it makes no difference whether Alfonso has a direct role in the representation or shares any fees.

Answer to Question 5

(A)   In this case, Arlette has personally profited from her former client Tingus's confidential information; in essence, Tingus's information boosted the dollar value of Arlette's time. However, Arlette's use of the information did not harm Tingus. Furthermore, Arlette used the information *in connection with her law practice*. Therefore, she does not have to account to Tingus for the profits she earned from the information. [*See* Restatement §60(2)] A lawyer may use one client's confidential information for the benefit of another client, even if doing so might benefit the lawyer, if the original client would not be harmed. [ABA Model Rule 1.9(c)] (B) is incorrect because a lawyer's duty of confidentiality does not end when the lawyer-client relationship ends. (C) is incorrect because Arlette did not need Tingus's consent to use his confidential information in her later practice of law. (D) is incorrect for the same reason—Arlette used Tingus's confidential information in her later practice of law, not in some side venture.

Answer to Question 6

(C) Archer is not subject to discipline because he did not discuss the case with Preston. It is permissible for a lawyer to talk to a represented party without his lawyer's consent if they do not discuss the subject of the representation. [ABA Model Rule 4.2 and Comment 4] Because Archer and Preston discussed the charity, the weather, and sports, Archer did not act improperly. Thus, (A) is wrong. (B) is wrong because this is not an ex parte communication. Ex parte means (roughly) by one party only and usually refers to contact with the trier of fact, and here both parties are present and neither is communicating with the trier of fact. The only limitation on opposing parties communicating with one another is the one stated above concerning a lawyer talking to a represented party. (D) is wrong because Archer's knowledge of the seating assignment and his attempt to change it are not dispositive; the dispositive fact is that Archer and Preston did not discuss the case.

Answer to Question 7

(B) Under ABA Model Rule 1.15, a lawyer must promptly notify a client when a third party turns over money or property to the lawyer to hold on the client's behalf, and the lawyer must promptly pay or deliver to the client money or property that the client is entitled to receive. Because Hemoglobin failed to fulfill these obligations, he is subject to discipline. Thus, (B) is correct, and (D) is incorrect. (A) is incorrect be-

cause Hemoglobin received the $2,000 settlement and thus was entitled to the agreed-upon fee. (C) is incorrect not because Hemoglobin placed the funds in the trust account, but because he failed to notify Portia of the settlement.

Answer to Question 8

(C) Aoki is not subject to discipline because a lawyer may pay a witness's reasonable expenses, including travel expenses, hotel, and meals. [Comment 3 to ABA Model Rule 3.4; Restatement §117, comment b] (A) is wrong because the payment of expenses is not an improper inducement. It is simply Aoki's good fortune that the trial is in such a desirable tourist spot. (B) is wrong because it is not improper for lawyers to interview third-party witnesses without notifying the opposing side. (D) is wrong because there is no limitation on expenses other than reasonableness.

Answer to Question 9

(C) ABA Model Rule 1.5(d)(1) subjects a lawyer to discipline if the fee in a domestic relations matter is contingent upon the securing of a divorce, the amount of alimony or support, or the amount of the property settlement. (A) is incorrect because the size of the fee is irrelevant because the ABA Model Rules forbid a contingency fee in this situation no matter what the amount of the fee. Although (B) states a rationale behind contingency fees, this rationale will not support a contingency fee in this case. (D) is incorrect because a lawyer may, but is **not required** to, pay or advance costs to an indigent client.

Answer to Question 10

(D) ABA Model Rule 3.5 prohibits a lawyer from communicating with a discharged juror if the communication involves misrepresentation, coercion, duress, or harassment.

[ABA Model Rule 3.5(c)(3)] Thus, Bellatrix can hire a private investigator only if the investigation is not conducted in a harassing manner. (A) is incorrect because the investigator does not need to notify Joan Juror of his investigation or obtain her consent. (B) is incorrect because new evidence will not justify the investigation if it is conducted in an improper manner. (C) is incorrect because if properly conducted, there is no reason to believe the investigation will affect future jury service.

Answer to Question 11

(D) A lawyer must not represent a client whose interests are directly adverse to those of another client. [ABA Model Rule 1.7(a)] This conflict of interest is imputed to other lawyers in the lawyer's firm. [ABA Model Rule 1.10(a)] Because Castor's law firm is now representing two clients whose interests are directly adverse, it would be proper for Castor to withdraw from representation. Thus, (A) and (C) are wrong. Also, Castor must maintain his client's confidence by not informing Pollux. [ABA Model Rule 1.6] Thus, (B) is wrong.

Answer to Question 12

(D) Generally, lawyers are subject to discipline for attempting to exonerate themselves from or limit their liability to their clients for personal malpractice. ABA Model Rule 1.8(h) prohibits a lawyer from making an agreement to limit such liability unless the client is independently represented in making the agreement. Clearly, these rules encompass the situations presented in items II. and III. However, careful lawyers often preserve documents that will serve as evidence that they did not commit malpractice. For example, lawyers may keep copies of court papers and memoranda, or write their clients letters to record the fact that a particular decision was made by the client

contrary to the lawyer's advice. It appears that the tape recording mentioned in item I. falls under the category of preserving evidence that Quarles did not commit malpractice, because it documents Quarles's handling of the case, as well as the client's understanding of the case. Thus, Quarles is not subject to discipline for the conduct in item I. (D) is therefore correct, and (A), (B), and (C) are incorrect.

Answer to Question 13

(D) Ariadne's advertising complies with ABA Model Rules 7.1 and 7.2. As long as her ad is not false or misleading, she may properly advertise fee arrangements, fields of practice such as personal injury, and free consultations. Thus, (D) is correct, and (A), (B), and (C) are incorrect.

Answer to Question 14

(A) A lawyer must not state or imply that he is able to influence improperly or upon irrelevant grounds any tribunal. [ABA Model Rule 8.4(e)] (B), (C), and (D) are incorrect because regardless of Costello's honest belief or his plans to use improper influence on the judge, the *statement* itself subjects him to discipline.

Answer to Question 15

(B) ProTex filed its complaint in April 2003. Datasafe had 20 days after the filing date to study the complaint and respond to it by answer or otherwise. Starting with day 20, Datasafe had a duty not to destroy evidence that it either knew or should have known would be relevant to the case. [*See* Computer Associates International, Inc. v. American Fundware, Inc., 133 F.R.D. 166 (D. Colo. 1990); Wm. T. Thompson Co. v. General Nutrition Corp., 593 F. Supp. 1443 (C.D. Cal. 1984)] Datasafe was alert enough to ask Littleman whether it would be all right to follow the usual custom of destroying the former source codes when creating improved versions of the anti-virus program. The question states that competent lawyers in the field know about the importance of source codes in copyright cases involving software. Littleman's nonchalant approval of Datasafe's two acts of destruction made it impossible for ProTex to prove Datasafe's copying. Judge Juno was correct in sanctioning Datasafe by entering partial summary judgment for ProTex on the copying issue, even though that is a drastic sanction. Judge Juno was likewise correct in sanctioning Littleman; if Littleman had been doing his job, the destruction would never have occurred. (A) is incorrect because the duty not to destroy relevant evidence does not depend on the adversary's formal request for the evidence. The duty arises when the litigant either knows or should know that the evidence is relevant to the case. (C) and (D) are incorrect because both of them state overly lenient legal standards for imposing sanctions on a lawyer who approves the client's destruction of relevant evidence.

Answer to Question 16

(D) ABA Model Rule 1.11(a) states that a lawyer must not represent a private client in connection with a matter in which the lawyer participated personally and substantially as a public employee, unless the appropriate government agency gives informed, written consent. Thus, (A) is incorrect. (B) is incorrect because even if Alpheus did not have confidential information, he substantially participated in the investigation of Charles's claim. (C) is incorrect because the disciplinary rule requires responsibility in the matter and not mere public employment in an agency where the case is pending or casual contact with the case.

Answer to Question 17

(C) Adnan's actions were improper because a lawyer is subject to discipline for failing to

report a disciplinary violation committed by another lawyer that raises a substantial question as to the other lawyer's honesty, trustworthiness, or fitness as a lawyer. [ABA Model Rule 8.3(a)] Here, Louis committed numerous disciplinary violations, including neglecting a matter and failing to communicate with a client. His drunk and abusive behavior also indicates an unfitness to practice. (A) is incorrect because Louis was not seeking legal services from Adnan and thus is not protected by the duty of confidentiality. (B) is incorrect because a lawyer has a duty to report a disciplinary violation by another lawyer. It is not up to the client, unless the lawyer's only knowledge of the violation is through a confidential client communication and the client refuses to allow disclosure. (D) is incorrect because Adnan's duty is not to encourage Celia to report Louis, but for Adnan to report Louis himself.

Answer to Question 18

(B) Under ABA Model Rule 5.5(b), a lawyer must not aid a nonlawyer in the unauthorized practice of law. Under these facts, Alfred would improperly be assisting Preacher, who has not in fact been authorized to practice law despite his law school degree. (A) makes no sense; Preacher's potential remedy for Alfred's mistakes does not subject Alfred to discipline. (C) is incorrect because any duty a lawyer may have to educate the public does not justify a lawyer's assisting in the unauthorized practice of law. (D) is irrelevant.

Answer to Question 19

(C) A private law firm must not use the name of a lawyer who holds public office during any substantial period in which the lawyer is not regularly and actively practicing with the firm. [*See* ABA Model Rule 7.5(c)] It logically follows that (A) and (B) are incorrect. (D) is incorrect because it states but one underlying justification for the general rule.

Answer to Question 20

(B) Under ABA Model Rule 8.2(a), a lawyer must not make a statement that the lawyer knows to be false or with reckless disregard as to its truth or falsity concerning the qualifications or integrity of a judge. In the case at bar, Pilate's sweeping statement to the news media regarding Judge Justinian appears to be just such an unrestrained and intemperate action as to lessen public confidence in the legal system. Also, it appears to have been made with reckless disregard as to its truth or falsity. Thus, (B) is correct, and (D) is incorrect. (A) is incorrect because Pilate's status as a public official is not the key here; it is his status as a lawyer that brings the ethics rules into play. (C) is incorrect because the timing of the statement does not make it proper.

Answer to Question 21

(B) When an attorney-client relationship is prematurely terminated (either by the attorney or by the client), the attorney must return to the client any advanced fees that have not yet been earned. [ABA Model Rule 1.16(d)] The fee here was an advance, not a "true retainer." Thus, (B) is correct, and (D) is incorrect. (A) is incorrect; under the ABA Model Rules, Art may keep the fees he earned. (C) is incorrect; Art is limited to the portion of the $30,000 he earned no matter how much money he could otherwise have made.

Answer to Question 22

(C) It is not improper for a judge to seek an outside expert's advice on legal issues if the judge informs the parties as to who was

consulted, tells them the substance of the advice received, and permits them to respond. [CJC 3B(7)(b)] (A) is incorrect because to seek such help, more is needed than just the judge's sincere belief that such help would be beneficial or even necessary; the judge must meet the above requirements. (B) is incorrect because it does not take into account these requirements for such help. (D) is incorrect because written permission alone is insufficient.

Answer to Question 23

(C) If a client disputes the amount that is due to the lawyer, then the disputed portion must be kept in a client trust account until the dispute is resolved. [ABA Model Rule 1.15(e)] Clearly, item III. is improper. Item II. describes precisely what the lawyer should do. While a lawyer is not required to send the entire amount to the client (as in item I.), she may do so if she so desires. Thus, (C) is correct, and (A), (B), and (D) are incorrect.

Answer to Question 24

(C) During the course of a lawyer's representation of a client, the lawyer should not give advice to an unrepresented person, other than the advice to obtain counsel, if the client's interests conflict with those of the unrepresented person. [ABA Model Rule 4.3] In this case, Alex urged Sarah to retain counsel. He gave her no other advice. Thus, he is not prohibited from negotiating with her. (A) and (B) are irrelevant. (D) is incorrect as, even if this were a criminal matter, Alex is a private lawyer—not one employed as a prosecutor.

Answer to Question 25

(B) This is correct because it presents a sound reason for the inclusion of a home telephone number and a fax number in the ad. (A) is incorrect because *some* limitations on lawyer advertising (*e.g.*, the ban on false or misleading ads) are constitutional. (C) and (D) are incorrect because nothing in the ABA Model Rules can constitutionally bar use of a home telephone number or a fax number in lawyer advertising.

Answer to Question 26

(D) A lawyer must not be a party to, or participate in a partnership or employment agreement with, another lawyer that restricts the right of a lawyer to practice law after the termination of a relationship created by the agreement, except as a condition to the payment of retirement benefits. [ABA Model Rule 5.6(a)] Items I., II., and III. restrict in some way Alexandra's right to practice law after terminating the relationship with Gastrix. Thus, (D) is correct, and (A), (B), and (C) are incorrect.

Answer to Question 27

(C) Statement I. is proper because an attorney may announce that a party has been charged with a crime, provided there is an accompanying statement that the charge is only an accusation and the party is deemed innocent until proven guilty. [ABA Model Rule 3.6(b) and Comment 5] Statement II. is improper because it includes an extrajudicial statement regarding the credibility of witnesses. [ABA Model Rule 3.6(a) and Comment 5] Furthermore, a prosecutor in a criminal case must refrain from making statements that have a substantial likelihood of heightening public condemnation of the accused unless the statements are necessary to inform the public and serve a legitimate law enforcement purpose. [ABA Model Rule 3.8(f)] Statement III. is proper because the public may be warned about the behavior of a person likely to result in harm to the public. [ABA Model Rule

3.6(b)(6)] Thus, (C) is correct, and (A), (B), and (D) are incorrect.

Answer to Question 28

(B) Here, there is a potential conflict because Athos's actions against The Aramis Company could be affected by the firm's past and possibly future representation of Dartagnan. It would be proper that disclosure of the conflict of interest be made to Cardinal. [ABA Model Rule 1.7(b)] Thus, (B) is correct and (D) is incorrect. (A) is incorrect because disclosure to and consent by Cardinal will allow Athos to continue to represent Cardinal without being subject to discipline. (C) is incorrect because Athos must obtain Cardinal's consent even if the matters are routine.

Answer to Question 29

(B) When a lawyer seeks to influence legislation and is purporting to act in the public interest (rather than as an advocate for a client), the lawyer should espouse only those positions he believes to be in the public interest. ABA Model Rule 6.4 imposes an additional requirement: "When the lawyer knows that the interests of a client may be materially benefited by a [law reform] decision in which the lawyer participates, the lawyer shall disclose that fact but need not identify the client." Thus, (B) is correct, and (C) is incorrect. (A) is incorrect because the lawyer in this situation also has a duty to the public. (D) is incorrect because if he complies with the ethical obligations above, he may properly vote on the matter.

Answer to Question 30

(A) If a client voluntarily offers to make a gift to his lawyer, the lawyer may accept the gift without being subject to discipline. [Comment 6 to ABA Model Rule 1.8] (B) is incorrect because ABA Model Rule 1.8

does not require a lawyer to instruct the client to discuss a gift such as the one in this case with an outside party. (C) is incorrect because the vase is not a payment of a fee—it is a gift; an unexpected, un-requested gratuity. (D) is incorrect because, as stated above, a lawyer may accept a gift.

Answer to Question 31

(A) This is the best answer here because ABA Model Rule 7.2(b) prohibits a lawyer from giving anything of value in return for a recommendation of the lawyer's services. Therefore, (A) is correct, and (C) is incor-rect because "value" does not necessarily mean that cash has changed hands. (B) is incorrect because there is no such restric-tion in the ABA Model Rules. (D) is incorrect because Supreme Court decisions broadening the range of advertising and solicitation have not extended into the area of referral fees, and in fact allow the bar to ban misleading advertising.

Answer to Question 32

(D) An attorney may reveal or use confidential information if the client gives informed consent. [*See* ABA Model Rules 1.6, 1.18] (C) is incorrect because it does not take into account exceptions to the general rule of confidentiality. (A) is incorrect because Claude consulted Leda as an attorney, and it is irrelevant that he did not retain her. (B) is incorrect because the attorney may not reveal information, even if it will help the client, unless the client consents or the information falls into recognized excep-tions to the confidentiality rule, which are not present here.

Answer to Question 33

(A) When dealing on behalf of a client with an unrepresented person, a lawyer must not give advice to the unrepresented person, other than the advice to obtain counsel, if the interests of the client conflict with those of the unrepresented person. [ABA Model Rule 4.3] Because Arnold was representing the corporation, and the corporation's interests conflict with those of Booker, Arnold should not have given Booker advice (told Booker not to worry), other than to secure counsel. (B) is incorrect because it is too broad. (C) is incorrect because furthering a client's interest does not excuse violation of the ethics rules. (D) is incorrect because the ethics rules apply regardless of whether a lawsuit has been filed.

Answer to Question 34

(A) The objection should be sustained because the communication falls under the attor-ney-client privilege. When the client is a corporation, the privilege covers communi-cations between the lawyer and an employee of the corporation if: (i) the employee communicates with the lawyer at the ***direc-tion of his superior***; (ii) the employee knows the purpose of the communication is to obtain legal advice for the corporation; and (iii) the communication ***concerns a subject within the scope*** of the employee's duties. Here, Booker was directed to speak with Arnold about accounting practices, and he believed the reason was to procure advice for Hyrax. (B) is wrong because Hyrax is the client and is claiming the privilege on its own behalf, not Booker's. (C) is wrong because Hyrax, the client, was seeking Arnold's legal services, and Hyrax is claiming the privilege. Likewise, (D) is wrong because the privilege is not abro-gated by Booker's dismissal.

Answer to Question 35

(B) Lydia's actions were proper because she did not offer false evidence, and she is under no duty to volunteer harmful facts. [*See* ABA Model Rule 3.3; Comment 14 to

ABA Model Rule 3.4] In fact, to do so would probably be a breach of ethics. (A) is incorrect because her actions were proper regardless of the constitutional protections afforded criminal defendants. (C) is incorrect because an attorney is under no obligation to volunteer harmful facts in an adversarial proceeding even if the jury will be misled by the testimony of a witness. It is up to the state to establish the time of the crime; if it cannot do so, it has not met its burden of proof. (D) is incorrect because Lydia should not disclose the facts to anyone, not even the judge. These facts are information related to the case and cannot be disclosed or used to the client's disadvantage absent some recognized exception to the duty of confidentiality. None applies here. Had Lydia presented a witness (other than Dave) who testified that the time was midnight when Lydia knew it was 10 p.m., Lydia would have had to rectify the false testimony. Here, however, the testimony came from the opponent, and Lydia is under no obligation to rectify it.

Answer to Question 36

(C) Lemke is not subject to discipline because the information concerning the misuse of trust funds was confidential and not subject to any exception. The ABA Model Rules contain an exception to the duty of confidentiality when the lawyer reasonably believes it necessary to prevent an act that is reasonably certain to cause death or substantial bodily harm. [ABA Model Rule 1.6(b)(1)] Here, the information concerned past, not future acts, and did not concern any future action that could lead to death or substantial bodily harm. The ABA Model Rules also contain an exception to the duty of confidentiality when the client intends on committing a *crime or fraud* that is reasonably certain to cause *substantial financial harm* to someone, if the client is using or has used the lawyer's services in

the matter. [ABA Model Rule 1.6(b)(2)] Here, Tuttle has not expressed an intent to commit a future crime or fraud that would result in substantial financial injury to his deceased sister's children. Thus, (A) is incorrect. (B) is incorrect because the duty of candor to the tribunal does not entail revealing confidential information unless necessary to prevent a fraud on the tribunal. Here, Lemke did not offer false evidence of any kind or make, or allow anyone to make, any misleading statements. (D) is incorrect because had the information not been confidential, Lemke would have a duty to bring it to the court's attention, regardless of whose duty it is to supervise a trustee.

Answer to Question 37

(C) The rule that conflicts of interest are imputed to all lawyers who work in the same office does not ordinarily apply to the advocate-witness rule. [*See* ABA Model Rule 3.7(b)] Thus, (A) and (B) are incorrect; the advocate-witness rule would prevent LaCosta himself from serving as Carter Corp.'s trial counsel, but it does not prevent LaCosta's law partner Liddy Gator from serving as such. The imputation rule does apply, however, if there is some other kind of conflict of interest caused by a lawyer's role as witness. [*Id.*] Suppose, for example, that LaCosta's testimony would contradict Cora Carter's testimony rather than corroborate it. If that were true, it would create a conflict under ABA Model Rule 1.7(a) between LaCosta's own interest (telling the truth) and Carter Corp.'s interest (proving the representation was made). That conflict could well be so serious that even Carter Corp.'s informed consent could not overcome it. No such situation is presented here, and Liddy Gator may therefore serve as Carter Corp.'s trial counsel. (C) is better than (D) because (C) correctly invokes the principles of ABA Model Rule 3.7(b), while (D) invents a bogus "merely corroborative" exception to the advocate-witness rule.

Answer to Question 38

(A) In an emergency, a lawyer may assist a client, even if the lawyer does not have the skill ordinarily required in the field in question. However, the assistance should not exceed what is reasonably necessary to meet the emergency. [*See* Comment 3 to ABA Model Rule 1.1] (B) is incorrect because ordinarily a lawyer should be competent to handle a particular issue before accepting a case. [ABA Model Rule 1.1] (C) is incorrect because an emergency is involved. (D) is incorrect because an attempt to limit malpractice liability makes a lawyer subject to discipline.

Answer to Question 39

(C) ABA Model Rule 3.5(b) prohibits ex parte communications by a lawyer with a judge except as permitted by law. Lawyers may generally communicate with a judge in writing if the lawyer sends a copy to the adversary. [Restatement §113, comment c] Thus Agnes's letter could be proper only if a copy was sent to Bertram. Thus, (C) is correct, and (A) and (B) are incorrect. (D) is incorrect; the lawyer need not inform opposing counsel *before* writing to the judge.

Answer to Question 40

(A) When a civil case is pending, a litigant must not destroy or conceal documents that the litigant knows are either relevant or likely to be requested by the adversary. [*See* United States v. Lundwall, 1 F. Supp. 2d 249 (S.D.N.Y. 1998)] Lapin would, of course, be subject to litigation sanctions in the civil case itself, and she could also be disciplined by the bar, but criminal liability for obstruction of justice is also appropriate in a blatant case such as this. [*Id.*; *see also* Perkins & Boyce, 558-59—destruction or suppression of evidence as criminal obstruction of justice] (B) is wrong for the reason just stated. (C) is wrong because it is too broad; when a civil case is pending, a litigant may destroy documents that the litigant does not believe are either relevant or likely to be requested by the adversary. (D) is wrong because it is not necessary that the documents have already been requested by the adversary.

Answer to Question 41

(C) A judge should disqualify herself in a proceeding in which her impartiality might reasonably be questioned, including but not limited to instances where she served as lawyer in the matter in controversy. [CJC 3E(1)(b)] The fact that these matters are routine or uncontested does not excuse her from this rule; thus (A) is incorrect. (B) is incorrect because avoiding delay does not allow a judge to ignore CJC 3E(1)(b). (D) is incorrect because it is too broad.

Answer to Question 42

(C) Alan suggested a title search for Limeacre. Upon learning that Jones did not want to spend money for it, he was not required to order the search and pay for it himself, or to try to force Jones to pay for it. All he can do is give advice. If his client unwisely decides to accept only part of that advice, and suffers because of it, the client cannot successfully sue him for malpractice. The client's injury cannot be said to have been proximately caused by any negligence on the part of the lawyer. Thus, (C) is correct, and (A) and (B) are incorrect. (D) is irrelevant.

Answer to Question 43

(B) It would be proper for LePage to interview Whorley and Winston, but for all of the other witnesses, he must first obtain Clem's consent. A lawyer must obtain the consent of the organization's counsel before communicating with: (i) a person who supervises, directs, or consults with the organization's lawyers about the matter (here, Farmer and Martin); (ii) a person whose conduct may be imputed to the organization for purposes of criminal or civil liability (Farmer and Martin again); or (iii) a person whose statements may constitute an admission by the organization (again, Farmer and Martin). [Comment 7 to ABA Model Rule 4.2] Consent is not needed, however, before talking with a *former* employee. Thus, LePage can speak to Whorley without Clem's consent. Likewise, consent of the corporation's counsel is not necessary to interview an employee who is merely a witness to the incident in question and is neither a management employee nor involved in the incident. Thus, LePage may interview Winston without Clem's consent.

Answer to Question 44

(A) An attorney must not give anything of value to a person (or organization) for recommending his services. [ABA Model Rule 7.2(b)] Thus, (A) is correct, and (D) is incorrect. While an attorney has the option of waiving a fee, under these facts, Arlington is in fact rewarding the Society for past referrals, and so (C) is incorrect. (B) is incorrect; an attorney may give free legal services to wealthy people if he chooses and if he does not violate the ethics rules.

Answer to Question 45

(B) (A) is incorrect because unverifiable statements of comparison are improper. [*See* Comment 3 to ABA Model Rule 7.1] Conversely, (D) is incorrect because the federal Constitution protects many ads that are in bad taste, self-serving, and designed to attract business. The difficult choice is between (B) and (C). Although statements

that fail to state material information are considered misleading and therefore improper [ABA Model Rule 7.1], Ace has clearly stated that the low rate applies only to uncontested divorces and does not imply in any way that contested divorces can be obtained for the same rate. Therefore, (B) is a better answer than (C).

Answer to Question 46

(D) ABA Model Rule 8.2(a) bars attorneys from making false statements about candidates for the judiciary. Furthermore, CJC 5A(3)(d)(ii) prohibits a judicial candidate from knowingly misrepresenting the identity, qualifications, present position, or other facts concerning herself or her adversary. We are told that all the facts in the numbered statements are accurate. Thus statements I., II., and III. are proper. However, in statement IV., the assertion "I won't be soft on crime" violates CJC 5A(3)(d)(i), which prohibits a judicial candidate from making pledges, promises, or commitments with respect to cases, controversies, or issues that are likely to come before the court that are inconsistent with the impartial performance of the adjudicative duties of the office.

Answer to Question 47

(D) CJC 3B(8) requires a judge to dispose of all judicial matters promptly, efficiently, and fairly. The Comment to that rule explains that a judge should insist that court officials, litigants, and their lawyers cooperate with the judge in disposing of matters promptly, efficiently, and fairly. Thus, (D) is correct, and (A) and (B) are incorrect. (C) is incorrect because a judge may choose to promote settlements provided that such policy does not conflict with other requirements for proper judicial conduct.

Answer to Question 48

(C)   ABA Model Rule 3.9 requires that a lawyer reveal the fact that he is appearing before the legislative body in a representative capacity. (A) is incorrect because a client's specific instructions do not vitiate the ethical rules. (B) is incorrect because a lawyer must volunteer the fact that he is appearing in a representative capacity. (D) is incorrect because it is an overbroad statement that does not deal with the specific ethical issue at hand with the exactitude of (C).

Answer to Question 49

(C)   In the exercise of his professional judgment on those decisions that are for his determination in the handling of a legal matter, a lawyer should always act in a manner consistent with the best interests of the client. If the disability of a client and the lack of a legal representative compel the lawyer to make decisions for his client, the lawyer should consider all circumstances then prevailing and act with care to safeguard and advance the interests of his client. [ABA Model Rule 1.14] (C) is the best answer because Archon is acting in a manner consistent with the best interests of his client, and because his client is unable to make any decisions or express his wishes, Archon is advancing the interests of his client as stated by the client prior to his death. [*See also* Restatement §80— exception to attorney-client privilege in dispute between two claimants through a deceased client] Thus, (C) is correct, and (A) and (B) are incorrect. (D) is incorrect because Son should exercise complete discretion without outside influence in deciding whether to carry out Uncle's wishes.

Answer to Question 50

(B)   Statement I. is proper because a lawyer may state his area of concentration. [ABA Model Rule 7.4(a)] Note that Larry must not state or imply that he has been *certified* as a specialist unless he satisfies ABA Model Rule 7.4(d). Statement II. is improper because it implies that Litiger can obtain results by improper means; *i.e.*, it implies that Litiger receives favorable treatment because his father and grandfather are judges. [ABA Model Rule 8.4(e)] Statement III. is improper because it creates unjustified expectations. Lawyers are generally not permitted to advertise their track record. [Comment 3 to ABA Model Rule 7.1] In two years, Litiger may have only tried one or two jury cases, and the people who received some form of payment may have received very small settlements. Statement IV. is improper because it makes an unverifiable comparison between Litiger and other lawyers. [*Id.*]

Answer to Question 51

(D)   Agnew advertises his practice in State One, he meets with clients in his home in State One, and he regularly represents drunk driving clients in State One courts. Thus, he maintains "a systematic and continuous presence for the practice of law" in State One. [*See* ABA Model Rule 5.5(b) and Comment 4] That makes him subject to discipline for the unauthorized practice of law, and it gives State One jurisdiction to discipline him. [*See* ABA Model Rule 8.5(a)] Furthermore, Agnew's response to the judge's question, though literally true, was artfully misleading and that makes him subject to discipline. [*See* ABA Model Rule 3.3(a)(1) and Comment 2; ABA Model Rule 8.4(c)] (A) is wrong because Agnew maintains a systematic and continuous presence for the practice of law in State One, and because Agnew's response to the judge was misleading. (B) is wrong because ABA Model Rule 8.5(a) permits the State One Bar to discipline Agnew for unauthorized practice in State One. (C) is wrong for the same reason—the State One Bar can discipline Agnew for the unauthorized practice of law in State One.

Answer to Question 52

(D) Item I. is correct. CJC 4(B) allows judges to speak out publicly concerning the law, the legal system, and the administration of justice. Comment 1 to CJC 4(B) *encourages* judges to speak out publicly on such issues because judges are in a unique position to help improve the law, especially criminal and juvenile justice. Item II. is incorrect for the above reason. Item III. is correct. Lawyers are permitted to participate in the political process, except when the law or a legal ethics rule prohibits it. The legal ethics rule nearest to the point is ABA Model Rule 7.6, which prohibits a lawyer from making a political contribution for the purpose of securing judicially appointed legal work. That rule does not apply here for two reasons. First, the rule does not apply to voter initiatives and referendums, and second, the rule does not apply to contributions of uncompensated services. [Comment 2 to ABA Model Rule 7.6] Item IV. is incorrect for the above reason.

Answer to Question 53

(A) ABA Model Rule 6.5 loosens the ordinary conflict-of-interest rules for legal service programs that are sponsored by a nonprofit organization or a court and that provide quick, short-term legal advice without any expectation that the lawyer-advisor will continue to represent the client-advisee in the matter. When a lawyer dispenses advice in such a program, ABA Model Rule 6.5(b) modifies the ordinary rule of imputed disqualification, thus making it possible for someone else in the lawyer's firm to represent a client whose interests are adverse to the advisee. [*See* Comment 4 to ABA Model Rule 6.5] (B) is wrong because ABA Model Rule 6.5 does not require consent of the affected clients. (C) is wrong because ABA Model Rule 6.5 does not require any of the three things listed in that answer choice. (D) is wrong because ABA Model Rule 6.5 does not require such a promise, nor would such a promise solve any other kind of conflict problem.

Answer to Question 54

(C) ABA Model Rule 8.4(c) makes a lawyer subject to discipline by the bar for engaging in "conduct involving dishonesty, fraud, deceit, or misrepresentation." Arquette's dishonesty toward passengers and the taxi company makes him subject to discipline by the bar, even though the dishonesty did not occur in connection with his law practice. [*See* Comment 2 to ABA Model Rule 8.4] (A) is wrong because Arquette's taxi driving is not a "law-related service" within the meaning of ABA Model Rule 5.7(b). Therefore, Arquette need not follow all of the legal ethics rules when he drives the taxi. He must, however, refrain from conduct that violates ABA Model Rule 8.4, which applies to everything a lawyer does. [*See* Comment 2 to ABA Model Rule 5.7] (B) is wrong because Arquette's solicitation of legal business from taxi passengers violates the solicitation ban. [*See* ABA Model Rule 7.3.] ABA Model Rule 7.3 does contain an exception that allows a lawyer to solicit legal business from a person with whom he has a "family, close personal, or prior professional relationship." [ABA Model Rule 7.3(a)(2)] Here, however, neither "close personal" nor "professional relationship" would include a taxi passenger-driver relationship. (D) is wrong because Arquette's dishonesty toward passengers and the taxi company make him subject to discipline by the bar even though the dishonesty did not occur in connection with his law practice.

Answer to Question 55

(B)   A lawyer is expected to "carry through to conclusion all matters undertaken for a client" [Comment 4 to ABA Model Rule 1.3], unless the client fires the lawyer or the lawyer terminates the relationship by a mandatory or permissive withdrawal in accordance with ABA Model Rule 1.16. Furthermore, in the sale of a law practice, "existing agreements between the seller and the client as to fees and the scope of the work must be honored by the purchaser." [Comment 10 to ABA Model Rule 1.17] When a lawyer buys a law practice, she is "required to undertake all client matters in the practice . . . subject to client consent," except when she cannot do so because of a conflict of interest. [Comment 6 to ABA Model Rule 1.17] The reason ABA Model Rule 1.17 requires the sale of an *entire* practice, or area of practice, is to protect "those clients whose matters are less lucrative and who might find it diffi-cult to secure other counsel if a sale could be limited to substantial fee-generating matters." [Comment 6 to ABA Model Rule 1.17] In short, ABA Model Rule 1.17 seeks to protect the very clients that Adder put into her "likely loser" pile. Adder should be disciplined for her empty, but coercive, threat to withdraw if the "likely loser" will not agree to a higher fee because ABA Model Rule 1.16 would not permit Adder to withdraw in these circumstances. (C) is wrong for the same reasons discussed above. (A) is wrong because there is no disciplinary rule against selling a law practice to the highest bidder. Note, how-ever, that Comment 11 to ABA Model Rule 1.17 imposes an ethical obligation on the seller "to exercise competence in identifying a purchaser qualified to under-take the representation competently." (D) is wrong because Arbuckle did not fulfill the ethical obligation just quoted; if he had done so, he would have discovered that Adder was inexperienced in the field and had twice been disciplined for client neglect and client abandonment.

Answer to Question 56

(B)   Comment 13 to ABA Model Rule 1.6 explains what a lawyer should do when push comes to shove with a judge about a privilege issue: A lawyer may be ordered to reveal information relating to the represen-tation of a client by a court or another tribunal or government entity claiming authority pursuant to other law to compel disclosure. Absent informed consent of the client to do otherwise, the lawyer should assert on behalf of the client all nonfrivolous claims that the order is not authorized by other law or that the information sought is protected against disclosure by the attor-ney-client privilege or other applicable law. In the event of an adverse ruling, the lawyer *must consult with the client about the possibility of appeal* . . . . Unless review is sought, however . . . [the lawyer may] comply with the court's order. (A) is wrong. Judge Jenner spoke condescend-ingly to the defense lawyer, in violation of CJC 3(B)(4), which requires a judge to be "patient, dignified and courteous to liti-gants, jurors, witnesses, lawyers and others with whom the judge deals in an official capacity." However, that does not license the defense lawyer to be disrespectful in response. Comment 4 to ABA Model Rule 3.5 explains that "refraining from abusive or obstreperous conduct is a corollary of the advocate's right to speak on behalf of litigants. A lawyer may stand firm against abuse by a judge but should avoid repro-cation; the judge's default is no justifica-tion for similar dereliction by an advocate." (D) is wrong for the same reason, although it is milder than (A). The first and third sentences of (D) are flippant, and they challenge Judge Jenner to demonstrate who is in charge, which he is likely to do by sanctioning the defense lawyer for direct contempt of court. (C) is wrong because giving Judge Jenner a free and unauthorized look at the patent counsel's letter could seriously prejudice the defendant, especially if Judge Jenner will be presiding over further proceedings in the case. The attorney-client privilege belongs to the defendant, not to the defense lawyer, and the defense lawyer should not waive it without talking over the options with her client. [*See* Comments 12 and 13 to ABA Model Rule 1.6]

Answer to Question 57

(D) Item I. is false. Lancelot must obey the SEC's Sarbanes-Oxley regulations because he is advising a securities issuer about a document that will be filed with the SEC. [*See* 17 CFR §205.2(a)] Item II. is true. The SEC regulations require a lawyer to report up the corporate ladder if the lawyer comes across "evidence of a material violation" of the securities laws or similar laws. The regulations use a tricky double negative to define "evidence." "Evidence" means "credible evidence, based upon which it would be unreasonable, under the circumstances, for a prudent and competent attorney not to conclude that it is reasonably likely that a material violation has occurred . . . ." [17 CFR §205.2(e)] The SEC's comment on that definition says that an attorney is "not required (or expected) to report 'gossip, hearsay, or innuendo.'" [*Id.*] If a reasonable lawyer would doubt the credibility of Skrannel's scrap of anonymous hearsay, that is more than enough to satisfy the double negative and thus to excuse Lancelot from reporting the story to Counsel Cloe. Item III. is true. A lawyer is not required to report violations of foreign law—only violations of federal or state securities law, a breach of a fiduciary duty imposed by federal or state law, or a similar violation of federal or state law. [*See* 17 CFR §205.2(i) and comments thereto] Furthermore, $26 is doubtless too small to have a material effect on the company's financial health. Item IV. is false for two reasons. First, Skrannel herself is not in a privileged relationship with Lancelot, and Skrannel's volunteered gossip probably would not be protected by the corporation's attorney-client privilege. [*See* Upjohn Co. v. United States, 449 U.S. 383 (1981); *but see* Restatement §73, comments d, f, and h] Second, even if Skrannel's statement were protected by the corporation's attorney-client privilege, a disclosure by Lancelot to Counsel Cloe would not waive or destroy the privilege.

Answer to Question 58

(C) None of the four answers is perfect, but (C) is the best. ABA Model Rule 3.5(c) and Comment 3 teach us that a lawyer may sometimes want to communicate with a discharged juror. The lawyer may do this unless it is prohibited by law or a court order, the juror has indicated that she does not want to talk to the lawyer, or the communication involves misrepresentation, coercion, duress, or harassment. (C) is not perfect because one may well conclude that Loudin started harassing and misleading Jergins earlier in the conversation when she gave the contorted answer to Jergins's simple question, "Do I have to talk to you about this?" (A) is wrong because lawyers are allowed to talk to discharged jurors except in the situations listed above. (B) is wrong because there is no law or ethics rule that makes size and age disparities inherently coercive. (D) is wrong because a lawyer's communication with a discharged juror is subject to the restrictions stated above.

Answer to Question 59

(D) ABA Model Rule 4.4(b) says that if a lawyer receives a document relating to the lawyer's representation of a client, and if the lawyer "knows or reasonably should know that the document was inadvertently sent, [the lawyer] shall promptly notify the sender." ABA Model Rule 4.4 does not touch on several related questions on which state law is presently split. These include whether the receiving lawyer must return the errant document to its sender and whether a lawyer's transmission error can waive a privilege. (A) and (B) are wrong because they do not require Aaron to notify the sender about the mistake. (C) is wrong for two reasons. First, it does not require Aaron to notify the sender. Second, it needlessly shames Lotus and involves the judge in a matter that does not need a judge's attention.

Answer to Question 60

(B)   The governing rule here is ABA Model Rule 5.5(c), which concerns temporary law practice in one state by a lawyer who is licensed in a different state only. Lunge may represent NWTC in the arbitration in State Two because the arbitration arises from Marlowe & Jonson's representation of NWTC in State One. [*See* ABA Model Rule 5.5(c)(3)] Furthermore, it was proper for Attaway to negotiate the copyright license in State Two because the negotiation is reasonably related to Marlowe & Jonson's representation of NWTC in State One. [*See* ABA Model Rule 5.5(c)(4)] (A) is wrong with respect to both Attaway and Lunge. (C) is wrong with respect to Attaway. (D) is wrong with respect to Lunge.

TABLE OF CITATIONS TO
ABA MODEL RULES OF PROFESSIONAL CONDUCT

TABLE OF CITATIONS TO
ABA CODE OF JUDICIAL CONDUCT

INDEX